KING COTTON DIPLOMACY

KING COTTON DIPLOMACY

Foreign Relations of the Confederate States of America

By

FRANK LAWRENCE OWSLEY

SECOND EDITION, REVISED BY
HARRIET CHAPPELL OWSLEY

THE UNIVERSITY OF CHICAGO PRESS

CHICAGO & LONDON

Library of Congress Catalog Card Number: 58-11952

THE UNIVERSITY OF CHICAGO PRESS, CHICAGO 60637
The University of Chicago Press, Ltd., London W.C. 1

*Copyright 1931, 1959, by The University of Chicago. All rights
reserved. Published 1931. Second Edition 1959. Third Impression
1969. Printed in the United States of America*

TO
LARRY AND HARRIET
AND TO
THE MEMORY OF MY MOTHER
THIS BOOK IS LOVINGLY DEDICATED

FRANK LAWRENCE OWSLEY, 1890–1956

A MEMORIAL FOREWORD

The republication of *King Cotton Diplomacy* at this time serves to emphasize the loss suffered by the cause of historical scholarship in and concerning the South through the untimely death of Frank Lawrence Owsley in Winchester, England, on October 21, 1956. The original publication of this book in 1931 brought from one reviewer the statement that because it told for the first time the full story of the foreign relations of the Confederate States of America it constituted "the most important contribution that has so far been made to the diplomatic history of the United States during this period [1861–65]." But to Owsley himself, the fact that the book covered only the Confederate side of the story presented a standing challenge to make a similar study of Union diplomacy for the same period and thus to prepare the ground for a more adequate synthesis of the whole range of American relations with other parts of the world during the Civil War. Although much of his time and energy for the next twenty-five years was divided between the completion of another significant project and the responsibilities of academic and graduate teaching, he never abandoned the idea of completing the diplomatic study. During those years he took advantage of every opportunity for further research in the field, and the broad outline of the proposed work had been sketched and some preliminary writing had been done. Thus, when he went to England in the late summer of 1956 on a Fulbright Fellowship, he had planned to spend the year in completing the research in British and French archives and in preparing at least a tentative draft of the entire study. This, of course, he did not live to do.

Without the completion of this work, however, Frank Owsley's character, his career, and his contributions to scholarship had already established for him a place as one of the leading figures in the annals of twentieth-century southern historiography. Born on a farm near Montgomery, Alabama, on January 20, 1890, and reared

in a rural environment, he retained throughout his life a strong attachment to the soil and an abiding interest in and understanding
of the problems of an agricultural community. No less abiding were
his pride in his background, his devotion to the South as a region,
and his firm belief in certain concepts of its role in the nation. "To
him," one of his professional contemporaries has said, "the South
was an intimate part of his spiritual being which he was ever ready
to defend"; and while his defense was sometimes vigorous and colorful, it was always sincere and honest and closely related to reality.
Convinced that the region was misunderstood and misinterpreted
because of incomplete or incorrect knowledge of its past, he dedicated
himself to the work of enlarging the historical perspective through
the discovery and presentation of new facts which would provide a
more adequate view of some of the basic elements in southern life
and institutions.

Any interest in history that he may have derived from his early
environment was sure to be stimulated when, following the Alabama
farm-boy tradition, he went to the Alabama Polytechnic Institute
at Auburn for his college education. There George Petrie, as professor of history, had already established a reputation for his "laboratory" in historical study through which potential farmers who possessed superior intellectual ability were transformed into embryo
historians. Owsley became one of that group, and following his grad-
uation in 1911 he returned to earn a master's degree under Petrie's
supervision in 1912. After a year of public school teaching and two
years as instructor in history and Latin at Auburn, he began advanced graduate study at the University of Chicago, where the in-
spirational teaching and guidance of William E. Dodd completed
what Petrie had begun in preparing him for a scholarly career in the
field of southern history. He received a second master's degree at
Chicago in 1917, and following military service in World War I he
divided his time between teaching and graduate study until he received the Ph.D. degree in history at Chicago in 1924. In 1918 he
returned to Auburn as instructor in history and a year later became
professor of history at Birmingham-Southern College, where he
served for only one year before going to Vanderbilt University in

1920. After twenty-nine years of distinguished service at Vanderbilt, he went back to his native Alabama in 1949 to spend the remainder of his life as the first incumbent of the Hugo Friedman Chair in Southern History at the University of Alabama.

His move to Vanderbilt marked the beginning of a professional career in which he gained an enviable reputation as a stimulating teacher and an inspiring guide for graduate students and in which his research and writing established him as one of the outstanding scholars in the field of southern history. But in 1920 this future could be only dimly foreseen. He had not yet completed the requirements for the doctorate, and while the superiority of his intellectual ability and the sincerity of his desire to devote his talent and energy to historical research and writing were recognized, his qualities as a university teacher and as a scholar were still to be demonstrated. Success in the early years would probably depend upon the influence and inspiration brought over from his training under Petrie and Dodd, but the nature and direction of his progress were more likely to be determined by factors and conditions in the new environment. For Owsley, two important new influences made significant contributions toward the development of his career from the time he began his work at Vanderbilt.

The first of these was the fact that his move to Vanderbilt brought him into close association with Dean Walter Lynwood Fleming—himself an earlier product of Petrie's "laboratory" at Auburn—whose plans for strengthening the program of graduate work at Vanderbilt were taking shape during the 1920's. On the recommendations of Dodd and Petrie, Fleming had chosen Owsley as the key man in building a department of history capable of offering advanced graduate work; and, because he recognized the importance of productive scholarship in the development of such a program, the dean provided unfailingly the spiritual and material encouragement that made research possible.

Equally important for the progress of Owsley's professional career was the fact that while at Birmingham-Southern he had met and married Harriet Chappell. From the beginning of their life at Vanderbilt her gracious hospitality made their home a favorite gathering place for colleagues, students, and a growing circle of friends, while her genuine interest in his work provided not only sympathetic understanding and encouragement but also active co-operation. As each of his projects developed she assisted in the necessary research, gave discerning advice in matters of style and organization, relieved him of much of the routine involved in handling details, and in several instances served as collaborator or as co-author. In dedicating his first book to her in 1925, he included in the inscription, "without whose help this work would not have been possible"; and in the Preface of his last major work, in 1949, he said: "As in former publications, my wife is essentially the joint author of this book." And now, in preparing this new edition of *King Cotton Diplomacy* for publication, she has carried to completion one of the unfinished projects on which the two of them had begun work together.

By 1930 any doubts that may have existed at the time of Owsley's appointment at Vanderbilt had long since been removed. Within that ten-year period he had completed the requirements for the doctorate with distinction; had proved his ability as a stimulating teacher; had successfully supervised the work of more than a score of master's candidates; had published one book and completed the research and much of the writing on another; and had become one of the central figures in the original thinking which produced the "Agrarian Group," whose vigorous essays in defense of the South created the best-known southern intellectual movement of the late 1920's and the 1930's. The publication of *State Rights in the Confederacy* in 1925 had not only demonstrated his capacity for thorough research but had also presented a convincing new interpretation of the fundamental weakness of the Confederacy. No longer was it possible for historians to ignore the conflicts between the states and the general government as factors in the failure of the South to establish its independence. Work on the second book, which had been begun before the first was published, was nearing completion and its publication as *King Cotton Diplomacy* in 1931 again marked him as a scholar who was not satisfied to follow the beaten paths of historical interpretation. With the aid of a Guggenheim Foundation grant he had explored hitherto unused records in European archives and through them had given new meaning to a relatively unknown phase of Civil War history. On the basis of both experience and achievement, therefore, he was ready to assume responsibility for directing the work of doctoral candidates in his field when Fleming's plans for the development of the advanced graduate program were put into operation in a few carefully selected departments near the close of the decade.

With the designation of the history department as one of those qualified to grant the Ph.D. degree at Vanderbilt, a new dimension was added to Owsley's professional activities. Thus far his major attention over and above his teaching duties had been concentrated upon his own research and writing; but the appearance of doctoral candidates brought the responsibility of training others to become historians. Although this new work was sure to consume time and energy that would otherwise have been devoted to his own research, he entered into it with enthusiasm, and through it he probably made his most substantial and enduring contribution to the promotion of historical scholarship in the South. Under his direct guidance some thirty capable men and women completed the work for the doctorate at Vanderbilt during the next twenty years, and half that many more who were working under other members of the department received the benefit of his advice and collateral supervision; and following his move to Alabama in 1949 he was responsible for the work of at least another dozen successful candidates. To each of these he gave generously of his time for personal conferences, advice in the selection of dissertation subjects and in research procedures, and critical appraisal of findings and conclusions. That most of them absorbed from him the passion for exploration and the thrill of presenting new discoveries is perhaps indicated in the fact that within the past twenty-five years his former students at Vanderbilt have published thirty-nine scholarly monographs and more than three hundred articles in historical journals.

Most of the dissertation projects represented topics in which Owsley himself was keenly interested but which he would probably never have found time to undertake. In some instances they were closely connected with questions growing out of his own earlier research on state rights or Confederate diplomacy; in others, they reflected his desire to probe more deeply into the background and causes of the sectional conflict; and several dealt with military figures or events of the Civil War itself. Whatever the subject, however, they were always genuine searches for new information rather than exercises in the application of historical method, and the published product greatly exceeded the amount of new historical knowledge that could have been discovered and made available through the work of Owsley alone during the same period. For him, the satisfaction of seeing these students develop into productive scholars, together with his pride in their contributions toward the advancement of knowledge, constituted ample reward for the time and effort spent in guiding them through the period of preparation.

Meanwhile, he was hard at work on a new project of his own which took the form of a re-examination of the social and economic structure of the Old South and culminated in the publication in 1949 of his third major book. While he entered into the research with the same zeal and enthusiasm that had characterized his work of the earlier years, the progress was inevitably at a slower pace, partly because of the time now being devoted to the Ph.D. candidates. Perhaps more important, however, was the fact that here, more definitely than in his first two books, he was blazing new trails in historical research and methods. The story of his reaction against the stereotyped picture of a sharply stratified three-class society—slaveholders, "poor whites," and Negroes—in the ante-bellum South, of his discovery of the vast store of detailed personal information in the manuscript census schedules—hitherto practically unknown to historians—and in county records, and of his adaptation of statistical methods and procedures to the uses of historical research is now so well known to serious students of southern history that it requires no elaboration here. The vastness of the project threatened to become overwhelming until the adoption of the sampling methods of the statistician and the public opinion polls made it possible to reduce the wealth of materials and the intricate processing required for interpreting them to manageable proportions. The development of this project with the collaboration of his wife and a selected group of his graduate students led first to the publication by the students of two books and several articles on segments of the study, and resulted in the rediscovery of the large and respectable middle class of the ante-bellum South. And with the publication of his own synthesis and interpretation in *Plain Folk of the Old South* in 1949, he had for the third time produced a book which made a significant contribution toward the restudy and rewriting of some important aspect of southern history.

But these major research projects and his work with graduate students represent only a part of Owsley's interests and activities. Although they naturally occupied a large share of his time and thought, he never permitted them to become his sole scholarly or professional concern. His participation in the activities of the Agrarian Group, for example, led to the writing of such interpretative essays as "The Irrepressible Conflict" for *I'll Take My Stand*, or "The Foundations of Democracy" for *Who Owns America?* He could take the time to prepare a scholarly study on "America and the Freedom of the Seas, 1861–1865" for the volume of *Essays in Honor of William E. Dodd*, published by Dodd's former students on the occasion of his presidency of the American Historical Association in 1934. He could also contribute more than a score of articles and some fifty trenchant book reviews and review articles to historical and literary journals, one of which, begun as a review of Freeman's *Robert E. Lee* and expanded into a two-part essay entitled "The Soldier Who Walked with God," has been accorded a place among the South's best literature. In addition to service on the executive committee of the Mississippi Valley Historical Association and on the Southern Regional Committee of the Social Science Research Council, he was an active participant in the work of the Southern Historical Association from its beginning and served on its executive council, on the editorial board of the *Journal of Southern History*, and, in 1940, as president of the Association. In academic circles he consistently sought to remain free from administrative responsibilities; though he served briefly and efficiently as chairman of the history department at Alabama in 1951–54, he relinquished the post at the first opportunity. He held summer appointments as visiting lecturer in several American universities, delivered the Walter Lyn-wood Fleming Lectures in Southern History at Louisiana State University in 1948, and at the time of his death was Fulbright lecturer at Cambridge University.

In spite of all these scholarly and professional activities, Frank Owsley never ceased to be a very human individual. In addition to greatness of mind, he had greatness of spirit, kindness, and conviviality not always found among very productive scholars. A colorful personality and a lover of vigorous discussion, he was a stimulating influence in any company, and his personal qualities endeared him to a wide circle of friends outside as well as within the realm of scholarship. Possessed of a keen sense of humor, he was a gifted raconteur, with a special fondness for telling tall tales, which had an intriguing way of growing taller with each retelling. He had a deep and abiding interest in his students, and they held him in such high esteem and affection that they may be expected to become one of the principal agencies through which the influence of his work as a productive scholar and a great teacher will continue to be felt and appreciated.

WILLIAM C. BINKLEY

TULANE UNIVERSITY

PREFACE TO THE FIRST EDITION

Of late much interest has been shown in the public opinion and diplomacy of the period of the war of southern independence. C. F. Adams, Jr., Henry Adams, E. D. Adams, J. F. Rhodes, J. M. Callahan, West, Jordan and Pratt, Bancroft, and others have contributed to the literature of this subject. But with the exception of Callahan's pioneer work, the *Diplomatic History of the Confederacy*, written before any of the European archives for this period were opened, these writers have dealt only incidentally with Confederate diplomacy. None except C. F. and E. D. Adams has had access to the British Foreign Office papers, and none has had access to the French Foreign Office since it was only opened in the fall and winter of 1927–28. In view of these several facts, it seemed to the present writer that a diplomatic history of the Confederacy was not only desirable but essential to a clearer understanding of the history of this period. (It might be further added that a diplomatic history of the United States for this same period is yet to be written! And what a history it might be if some scholar is willing to spend ten years or more in its preparation.) These are the justifications for beginning this book; but further justification for completing it is that the present writer has been forced by new material and new combinations of old material to abandon many well-accepted interpretations and draw new conclusions.

In assembling the data for this book the writer was amazed and pleased to find fundamental order underlying chaos and to discover purpose in confusion. That which gives order and purpose to Confederate diplomacy is the rôle which cotton played. Hence the title, *King Cotton Diplomacy*.

The diplomatic efforts of the Confederacy were directed primarily toward obtaining European intervention in the war. The form of intervention sought differed with the exigencies of the situation. At times the Confederate agents sought European repudiation of the blockade; at other times they sought friendly mediation. Always they sought the recognition of the independence of the Confederacy. Any form of intervention—whether the repudiation of the blockade, mediation, or recognition—would, they believed, end in independence.

In dispatching diplomatic agents abroad the Confederate government approached England, France, Belgium, Spain, the Holy See in Europe, and Mexico in America. Quasi-diplomatic agents were sent to Canada, Cuba, Bermuda, and the Bahamas; but with these we are only incidentally concerned. Lamar, who was to go to Russia, was recalled before he had done so. Belgium, Spain, and the Holy See were minor objectives. It was primarily England and France with whom Confederate diplomacy and propaganda were concerned, for these two maritime powers held the fate of the Confederacy in their hands—and the Confederacy for over a year, because of its monopoly of the cotton supply upon which these two nations depended, believed that it held the fate of those two countries in its hands.

The writer wishes to express his gratitude to the John Simon Guggenheim Memorial Foundation in its support of this project, especially in their grant of a European traveling fellowship in 1927–28; and to the Social Science Research Council for its several grants-in-aid. He is under deep obligations to Dr. Thomas Staples, of Hendrix College, for reading the manuscript and offering vital criticisms; and to Dr. J. Fred Rippy, of Duke University, and to Mr. William Robinson, of Augusta, Georgia, for reading the galley proof of this book.

His wife's rôle in the preparation of this book has been virtually that of joint author. She aided in the research, typed the manuscript, read both galley and page proof, and prepared the Index and Bibliography.

He wishes to express his appreciation to the staff of the American Embassy in Paris in helping to obtain permission to do research in the French Foreign Office archives for the period 1861–65 and to M. Briand for granting this favor.

Acknowledgment is due to the British Foreign Office for the courtesy shown the writer while engaged in the research on this book. Full access was given to all archives relating to the American war of secession.

He wishes to express deep obligations to Mr. Tyler Dennett and Mrs. Summers, of the United States Department of State, for the aid given him while engaged in research upon the diplomatic papers of the period 1861–65.

He wishes to thank the staffs of Vanderbilt University Library, Library of Congress, the British Museum, and the Bibliothèque Nationale for the valuable aid given in the preparation of this book.

FRANK LAWRENCE OWSLEY

PREFACE TO THE SECOND EDITION

In the Preface to the first edition of *King Cotton Diplomacy* the author stated, "It might be further added that a diplomatic history of the United States for this same period is yet to be written! And what a history it might be if some scholar is willing to spend ten years or more in its preparation." When *King Cotton Diplomacy* went out of print in 1954 and the copyright was returned to the author, he determined to carry out this larger project rather than republish the book as it stood. The ten years of which he spoke had been spent in gathering the material, and the Fulbright grant to England in the fall of 1956 was partly for the purpose of finishing the research and the writing of this larger book. My one consuming idea when my husband could no longer carry out the plan was to finish the work which he and I had begun together. With the aid of a Fulbright award and a grant from the University of Alabama Research Committee, I spent nine months in England and France and six months in Washington completing the research. In January, 1958, I accepted the interesting and stimulating position of Senior Archivist in charge of Manuscripts with the Tennessee State Library and Archives. But with the ever growing demand for a new edition of *King Cotton Diplomacy* constantly before me and the realization that with my new duties it would take years to complete the larger work as planned, the decision was made to republish this book. Some revisions have been made and some new material added but the most gratifying result of my work has been the discovery that the ideas presented in *King Cotton Diplomacy*, many of them new and revolutionary at the time, were completely sustained by later research.

My acknowledgments are necessarily numerous for this second edition. First of all, I am most grateful to the University of Alabama Research Committee for their support of the research and the preparation of the manuscript for this second edition and for the larger project by grants both to my husband and to me. They have been most generous, considerate, and understanding of all of the many problems involved in this undertaking. Mrs. W. K. E. James, executive secretary of the committee, has been most helpful.

Second, I am deeply indebted to the United States Educational Commission in the United Kingdom (Fulbright Commission) for their support of the project by grants both to my husband and to me. Dr. William Gaines, the executive secretary of the commission, and the members of the staff of the American Embassy in London, could not have done more to make my work and continued stay in England possible. Sir Sydney Roberts, Master of Pembroke College, Cambridge University, and an influential member of the commission, encouraged and supported my application for a grant. I also wish to express my appreciation to Dr. O. C. Carmichael, former president of the University of Alabama, and Dean A. B. Moore, graduate dean of the same institution, for their untiring efforts in behalf of my appointment. The unanimous approval of both the English commission and the Fulbright committee in the United States gave me the courage and confidence needed to carry on the work.

My daughter-in-law, Dorothy Sellers Owsley, typed the manuscript for the second edition and offered valuable suggestions. My son, Dr. Frank L. Owsley, Jr., a member of the teaching staff of the United States Naval Academy, Annapolis, Maryland; my brother, Dr. Gordon Chappell, Huntingdon College, Montgomery, Alabama; and my daughter, Margaret Owsley, a student at Vanderbilt University, gave me much needed counsel.

Dr. Thomas B. Alexander and Miss Elizabeth Coleman, members of the faculty of the University of Alabama read the manuscript of the second edition and offered many excellent suggestions for which I am deeply indebted.

To the staff of the Foreign Affairs Section of the National Archives, especially Dr. Carl Lokke and Mrs. Judy Carroll, I am greatly obligated for their genuine personal interest and for assistance far beyond the call of duty. During the many years in which my husband and I worked in this division of the Archives their courtesy and co-operation made our work most pleasant and rewarding.

Acknowledgment is made to Mr. E. K. Timings of the British Public Record Office and other members of the staff for co-operation and aid during my several months' work in that office. I wish also to thank Dr. Taylor Milne, secretary of the Institute of Historical Research of the University of London for accepting me as a Fulbright scholar for membership in the institute and for the hospitality shown me.

I wish to thank M. Jean Ballou, le Ministre Plénipotentiaire Directeur des Archives, Paris, France, and other members of his staff for assistance in obtaining the microfilms of many valuable documents necessary for my research.

I am indebted to the staffs of the Manuscripts Division of the Library of Congress; the Library of the University of Rochester; the War Department of the National Archives; the Massachusetts Historical Society, especially Mr. L. H. Butterfield, editor-in-chief of the Adams Papers; the Library and Archives of Alabama; the Library of the University of Alabama, especially Dr. W. Stanley Hoole; the Joint University Library, especially Miss Clara Brown; and Dr. Dan Robison, Mr. Robert Quarles, and Miss Isabel Howell of the Tennessee State Library and Archives, who have rendered valuable aid. Miss Howell has helped with the Bibliography and has been ready with advice and encouragement when needed. Many other friends, too numerous to mention, have offered encouragement and I wish to thank them.

My good friend and colleague in former research projects, Dr. Blanche Henry Clark Weaver, has been my competent aid in proofreading this second edition and I am indebted to her. I wish also to thank Miss Alice Hoy for her very efficient work in typing the index.

Last, but not least, I wish to express my appreciation to Dr. William C. Binkley for the very fine Foreword and for reading the manuscript and offering discerning advice and suggestions.

I am grateful for the memory of my husband, Dr. Frank L. Owsley, who allowed me to share in his lifework and thus gave me in his unfinished tasks a purpose for living.

HARRIET CHAPPELL OWSLEY

CONTENTS

CHAPTER I

THE FOUNDATION OF CONFEDERATE DIPLOMACY

THE DEVELOPMENT OF KING COTTON PHILOSOPHY

If slavery was the corner stone of the Confederacy cotton was its foundation. At home its social and economic institutions rested upon cotton; abroad its diplomacy centered around the well-known dependence of Europe, especially England and France, upon an uninterrupted supply of cotton from the southern states. Until well into the third year of the war the Confederate government and its people relied primarily upon this power of cotton to coerce rather than persuade England and France to interfere in some way with the struggle in America. This interference might take the form of a denunciation and breaking of the blockade on the grounds that it was a paper blockade contrary to international law and especially to the provisions of the Declaration of Paris; it might be in the form of a peaceful mediation or of an outright recognition of the independence of the South; or, finally, it might be armed intervention. The result of such interference would be the ending of the war, the opening of the source of the cotton supply, and the independence of the Confederacy.

The "King Cotton theory," as this was called, has been spoken of since its failure as the "King Cotton delusion." Considerable scorn has been heaped upon the intelligence of the political and intellectual leadership which foisted such a false philosophy upon credulous and uninformed people. A close scrutiny of the origin and development of this King Cotton philosophy, however, especially when strict account is taken of slowness and inaccuracy in the transmission of information or "news," will convince one of the logic of the doctrine. The southern people in 1860 were very susceptible to logic and philosophical matter generally. While the rest of America and Western Europe had long since turned away from rationalism to science and romanticism, the people of the South were still clinging to the rationalism of the seventeenth and eighteenth centuries. To them a "state of nature," the "compact theory," and other such ideas were realities and not philosophical theories. They believed with sublime faith in "logic" and "reason," and without mental reservations accepted conclusions if they were drawn from a well-established premise. This attitude and state of mind was fertile ground for the King Cotton philosophy.

The King Cotton idea grew out of the transfer of the British and Continental cotton industries from the use of Indian to American cotton after the invention of the cotton gin. American cotton was superior to and cheaper than the Indian cotton. Starting with practically no exportations in 1790, the American planters by 1796 saw their cotton surpass Indian cotton in the European industries and practically supersede it by the end of the War of 1812. Year by year the Industrial Revolution in England and on the Continent progressed, and the cotton industry which formed the groundwork of the new industrial system grew mightily and leaned more heavily upon the American staple. The Board of Trade reports, census statistics, and the reports of parliamentary committees and cotton-supply associations, especially during the last two decades before the Civil War, were read in the South with growing interest and consciousness of the important rôle the South was playing in the industrial primacy of Great Britain.

Table I,[1] based upon the census and trade reports, will graphically illustrate the dependence of Great Britain upon the South, during the period 1840–58 when so much interest was being displayed in the South touching England's dependence.

Southern planters found deep satisfaction in such figures, which showed the greatest industrial nation on earth, whose largest industry was cotton, depending upon the South for three-fourths to five-sixths of her cotton supply. The same proportions held for France and other Continental countries, though the industry on the

[1] *Cotton Is King and Pro-slavery Arguments* (comprising the writings of Hammond, Harper, Christy, Stringfellow, Hodge, Bledsoe, and Cartwright on this important subject; ed. E. N. Elliott, president of Planter's College, Miss., with an essay on slavery, etc., by the editor; Augusta, Ga., 1860), Tables 250–67. (Cited hereafter as *Cotton Is King.*)

Continent was small as compared to that of England during these years. The South was fully conscious from the very beginning that all of the cotton used in the northern industry came from Dixie, and that the cotton industry of the North was its largest and most lucrative business.

The dependence of the world upon the South for its cotton received irrefutable demonstration after 1840, for the British especially made a prolonged but futile series of attempts to get back to East

TABLE I

	Total Imports into Great Britain (£)	Imports from South U.S. (£)
1840.........	592,488,010	487,856,504
1841.........	487,992,355	358,240,964
1842.........	531,750,086	414,030,779
1843.........	673,193,116	574,738,520
1844.........	646,111,304	517,218,662
1845.........	721,979,953	626,650,412
1846.........	467,856,274	401,949,393
1847.........	474,707,615	364,599,291
1848.........	713,020,161	600,247,488
1849.........	755,469,012	634,504,050
1850.........	663,576,861	493,153,112
1851.........	757,379,749	596,638,962
1852.........	929,782,448	765,630,544
1853.........	895,278,749	658,451,796
1854.........	887,333,149	722,151,346
1855.........	891,751,952	681,629,424
1856.........	1,023,886,304	780,040,016
1857.........	969,318,896	654,758,048
1858.........	931,847,056	732,403,840

Indian cotton. The Manchester Chamber of Commerce, made up of England's most important cotton manufacturers, sent agents to India to study the situation and report back home. Public-spirited men both in and out of Parliament set out for India to study the possibilities of freeing England from the American shackles. Emancipation societies made strenuous efforts at finding a substitute for the product produced by slave labor. Parliament appointed a standing committee on Indian cotton and conducted long hearings on the prospects of using cotton from India instead of American cotton. A cotton-supply association went into the field and studied the question. Book after book was published; the trade and news journals took up the hue and cry to drive King Cotton out of the Empire.[1] These reports and hearings all lamented the "dangers of our continued reliance upon the United States for so large a proportion of our cotton."[2] They insisted that "the very singleness of that source" constituted "an element of danger; while the peculiar circumstances which affect that single source (danger of civil war and slave insurrection) greatly aggravate that danger." "Lancashire may any year be laid prostrate by causes from whose action she has no escape and over which she has no control."[3] If the American supply were never interrupted by internal troubles, these reports urged, it could not under the slave system keep pace with the English demand and the world-demand.[4] They sometimes urged, also, that by establishing a rival cotton source in India, American cotton would finally be put off the market, and not only would England hold the whip hand, but slavery would inevitably disappear.[5]

The southern planters read of these efforts of Great Britain with some forebodings at first, but as the years went by and the demand for cotton expanded with tremendous rapidity and the Indian supply remained practically stationary, complete confidence in the dependence of the world upon the cotton of the South came upon them. The Board of Trade reports of 1859 were profoundly satisfying to the southern people, for they showed that, in spite of twenty years or more of great effort, England could obtain only about 60,000,000 pounds from India, whereas, in 1800, nearly sixty years earlier, she was drawing around 50,000,000 pounds from that source.[6] In the

---

[1] *De Bow's Review and Industrial Resources* (statistics, etc., devoted to commerce, agriculture, internal improvements, education, political economy, general literature, etc.; ed. J. D. B. De Bow; New Orleans and Charleston, 1861), XXXIV (July, 1866), 509–26 (cited hereafter as *De Bow's Review*); *London Index*, July 10, 1862.

[2] Henry Ashworth, *Cotton: Its Cultivation, Manufacture and Use* (a paper read before the Society of Arts, London, March 10, 1858; Manchester, 1858), *passim*. (Cited hereafter as Ashworth.)

[3] John Chapman, *The Cotton and Commerce of India Considered in Relation to the Interests of Great Britain, etc.* (London, 1851), pp. 1–3. (Cited hereafter as John Chapman.) Chapman was founder and late manager of the Great Indian Peninsula Railway.

[4] Cf. *ibid.*, Preface, p. iv; *De Bow's Review*, O.S., XXXIV (July, 1866), 509–26.

[5] An article by David Christy, author of *Cotton Is King*, entitled "Emancipation and Cotton—the Triumph of British Policy," *De Bow's Review*, O.S. XXXIV, 509–26.

[6] *Ibid.*

face of a demand which had increased 1,000 per cent since 1800, England was able to obtain after many years of earnest effort less than a 20 per cent increase from India.

The *London Economist*[1] conceded defeat. Indian cotton could never compete with its American rival. It "yields," said that organ, "more waste, that is, loses more in the process of spinning" due to the dust and trash collected with the lint; "the Surat [Indian cotton] when cleaned, though of a richer color than the bulk of the American, is always much shorter in staple or fibre; the result of which is that in order to make it into equally strong yarn it requires to be harder twisted. . . . . The consequence is that the same machinery will give out from 10 to 20% more American yarn than Surat yarn." "The working people prefer the American as it spins better, does not break so easily and cause delay in work." "The cloth made from Surat does not take the finish so well, and is apt, after washing, to look poor and thin. . . . . In all respects (except color) the Indian cotton is an inferior article. . . . ." Henry Ashworth[2] pointed out in 1858 that even if Indian cotton were as good as American, it could not compete because of inadequate transportation and precarious land tenure. There were no railroads, nor did the navigable streams penetrate into the cotton areas to any extent, with the result that the peasants had to pack their cotton across the desert and jungle upon the backs of donkeys and oxen for hundreds of miles, taking sometimes as long as a month to complete the transaction. As for the land tenure, it was not unlike the peonage system of some of the South American countries. The peasants were always bound down by obligations which they could never meet, with the result that they took slight interest in increasing the output of a product which the money-lender and landlords would seize upon eventually. A prominent Englishman, J. W. B. Maney, residing at Calcutta, reported that even when the tenure of land was comparatively unrestricted the peasant could not sell in the open market because the local money-lender who had advanced on his crop forced him to sell to the lender at the latter's price.[3] Furthermore, because of the inferiority of soil and climate

[1] *London Economist*, April 13, 1861.

[2] Ashworth, *passim*. Cf. *London Times*, June 20, 1861; *London Economist*, July 19, 1862.

[3] *London Economist*, Sept. 27, 1862.

and more especially because of ignorance in the cultivation of the crop, it took five times as much acreage in India to produce the same amount of cotton as in America.[1] After a great deal of futile effort by the government and interested individuals, the *London Times*[2] declared in disgust that it seemed utterly impossible to introduce an improved system of cotton culture among the Indian peasants. Government agents had tried and failed completely; they had gone into the peasant village and demonstrated the iron plow of the improved English type. The populace had been amazed and overawed by the marvelous execution of this beautiful new implement and its superiority over their crude wooden tools—in fact, so overawed that when "the agent's back was turned, they took it, painted it red, set it up on end, and worshipped it."

After years of struggle to free themselves from the single, precarious southern source of raw cotton and the futility of their efforts was seen, the people realized that the danger of England's position was alarming. For the industry which depended so completely upon a threatened source of supply was the industry which appeared to underlie the whole industrial and economic system of Great Britain. The enormous importance of the cotton industry to the very existence of the island kingdom was fully canvassed in England during the ten or twelve years preceding the Civil War in America. In 1851 John Chapman in his book[3] lamented the fact that so large a portion of England's income was derived from the cotton industry. He reminded the English people that out of a total export of £54,000,000 nearly £29,000,000 was cotton fabric, about five-ninths of the total British exports. This did not include about £3,500,000 worth of raw cotton re-exported out of which the British merchants and shipowners took a substantial profit. Then about £20,000,000 worth of manufactured cotton material was retained in Great Britain for home consumption, thus making the volume of the sale of cotton goods and raw cotton mount up to about £52,000,000 in 1851, almost

[1] See *London Index*, Sept. 25, 1862, for address of Mr. Laing, former minister of finance from India.

[2] Cited in *De Bow's Review*, O.S., XXXIV, 510.

[3] John Chapman, *op. cit.*, pp. 1-3.

the equivalent of England's entire export trade. Henry Ashworth[1] pointed out that the trade statistics for 1853 showed that the export of manufactured cotton goods had increased to £32,712,902 and that England retained £21,224,494 worth of cotton goods for home consumption. Adding about £2,000,000 worth of raw cotton re-exported, the sale of cotton goods for that year amounted to £55,937,396. In 1856 the volume had grown larger; £38,284,000 worth of cotton goods had been exported, £23,200,000 retained at home, making the total manufacture of cotton goods in England amount to £61,484,-000; and £2,000,000 worth of raw cotton re-exported[2] brought the British cotton sales up to about £63,000,000 for 1856. The *London Economist*, England's most conservative commercial and trade journal, reported for 1859 an export of £48,209,000 worth of manufactured cotton goods out of a total export of £130,440,005, or about two-fifths of the entire export.[3] Not less than £25,000,000 was retained for home use, making the cotton industry thus turn out about £73,000,000 worth of manufactured goods. During the same period £4,000,000 worth of raw cotton re-exported[4] swelled the sale of cotton and goods for the United Kingdom in 1859 to the enormous amount of £77,000,000. The *Economist's* figures for 1860—based upon the Board of Trade reports—showed that something over £50,000,000 worth of cotton goods had been exported, and £5,100,-000 worth of raw cotton re-exported,[5] out of a total export trade of £164,500,000.[6] The goods retained for home use were worth about £24,000,000,[7] making the entire cotton business total around £80,-000,000.[8]

The English political and industrial leaders thus estimated the ex-

[1] Ashworth, p. 6.

[2] *London Economist, Commercial History and Review Supplement for 1864*, March 11, 1865.

[3] *Economist*, Jan. 19, 1861.

[4] *Ibid., Com. Hist. and Rev. Suppl. for 1864*, March 11, 1865.

[5] *Ibid.*   [6] *Ibid.*

[7] R. Arthur Arnold, *History of the Cotton Famine, etc.* (London, 1864), pp. 36–38. (Cited hereafter as Arnold.)

[8] M. E. Potter, M.P. from Carlisle, estimated that the annual returns from the cotton trade about 1860 were £80,000,000. John Watts, *The Facts of the Cotton Famine* (London and Manchester, 1866), p. 284. (Cited hereafter as Watts.)

portation of cotton goods as making up about two-fifths to five-ninths of the total exports of the country from 1850 to 1860, and constituting a large part of their domestic trade. The profits from the trade ranged from 150 to 300 per cent.

Their chief anxiety was not the mere size of the industry but the fact that such a large percentage of the British population had come to depend completely upon this single industry which in turn depended almost completely upon the single American cotton crop. John Chapman[1] estimated that in 1851, 500,000 operatives were employed in the cotton mills; and Henry Ashworth[2] estimated that in the subsidiary cotton industry, including the hosiery, cotton-lace, and sewed-muslin establishments, around 400,000 more were employed, thus making in the neighborhood of 900,000 operatives directly employed in the elaboration of raw cotton in the early fifties. Then there were the laborers in the industries and trades which were of a parasitical nature, whose entire subsistence depended upon the steady turning of the cotton-mill wheels. Among these may be classed the warehousemen, stevedores, mechanics, bakers, and small tradespeople of the cotton districts of Lancashire, Derbyshire, and Lanarkshire, etc., adding perhaps another 150,000. It is estimated that there were three dependents to every employee, thus making about 4,000,000 people dependent upon the cotton industry out of a total population of about 21,000,000 for England, Scotland, Ireland, and Wales.[3] Alarmed at the rapidly expanding cotton industry, the *London Economist*[4] said, "The cotton manufacture, from the first manipulation of the raw material to the last finish bestowed upon it, constitutes the employment and furnishes the sustenance of the largest portion of the population of Lancashire, North Cheshire and Lanarkshire, of a considerable number in Derbyshire, Leicestershire, Nottinghamshire and Yorkshire, and of scattered individuals in several other parts of England, Scotland and Ireland . . . . and if we

---

[1] John Chapman, pp. 1–3.   [2] Ashworth, pp. 6–7.

[3] Cf. figures in 14th annual report of the Poor Law Board (1861–62), House of Commons, *Sessional Papers*, Vol. XXIV, No. 3037 (1862). Annual reports of the Poor Law Board for 1863–66 are to be found in the *Sessional Papers*, Vol. XXII, No. 3197 (1863), Vol. XXV, No. 3379 (1864), Vol. XXII, No. 3549 (1865), Vol. XXXV, No. 3700 (1866).

[4] *London Economist*, Jan. 19, 1861.

take into account the subsidiary trades and occupations and add the dependent members of their families we may safely assume that nearer four than three millions are dependent for their daily bread on this branch of our industry." Other estimates of the number in the British Isles dependent upon the cotton industry about 1860 ranged from 4,000,000 to 5,000,000.[1]

Lancashire and West Derbyshire owed their existence to the cotton industry. In 1801 the whole population of Lancashire had been only 674,486, whereas in 1861 the population was 2,429,440, an increase of 258 per cent in sixty years, compared with an increase of only 87 per cent for the whole of England and Wales.[2] In 1815 the taxable property of England and Wales had an annual value of £51,790,878, while that of Lancashire was £3,087,744, or 6 per cent of the whole; in 1861 the annual tax value of the property of England and Wales was £112,802,749 and that of Lancashire £11,289,575, or 10 per cent of the whole.[3] The growth of Manchester and Liverpool in Lancashire and West Derby, respectively, one the seat of the cotton manufacture and the other the cotton port, further illustrated the importance of the cotton industry in this region. In 1801 Manchester had 94,000 inhabitants; in 1841, 311,000; and in 1861, 460,000. In 1801 Liverpool had a population of about 77,000; in 1841, 286,000; and in 1861, 437,740. In 1801 the latter city had a merchant fleet of only 459,719 tons, but in 1861 this fleet measured 4,977,272 tons, an increase of about 1,000 per cent. All this development was fundamentally due to the growth of the cotton industry.[4]

The relative importance of the British cotton industry with reference to the other cotton-manufacturing countries in 1860 may be seen, in Table II, from the amount of cotton used and the number of spindles in the leading countries of Europe and America.[5] England, it would appear, had 30,000,000 spindles as against less than 20,000,000 for the rest of Europe and the United States combined, and she consumed in her factories, in 1860, 2,633,000 bales as compared to

[1] Watts, p. 284; *De Bow's Review*, XXX, No. 1 (Jan., 1861), 93.

[2] Watts, p. 34.   [3] *Ibid.*, p. 35.   [4] *Ibid.*, p. 97.

[5] Figures compiled from M. B. Hammond, *The Cotton Industry* (New York, 1897), pp. 257–58; *London Economist, Com. Hist. and Rev. Suppl.*, March 11, 1865; Watts, pp. 40, 53, 59. Some of the figures for the minor countries are estimates.

2,268,000 for the United States and Continental Europe combined.[1] Great Britain was the cotton factory for the world. Another significant fact, not conveyed by the statistics, was that, with the exception of France and the small state of Belgium, Continental Europe carried on most of its cotton manufacture in the homes of the peasants and in small factories. To a large extent it was merely a supplementary occupation for the spinners and weavers, their main time being taken up in farming and rural pursuits. Further, the bulk of the cotton goods was not only woven in the peasant cottages but made

TABLE II

	No. of Spindles	Bales of Cotton
Great Britain......	30,000,000	2,633,000 or 50,633 per week
United States......	4,300,000	650,000 or 12,000 per week
France...........	4,000,000	621,000 or 11,942 per week
Germany..........	2,000,000	307,000 or 5,904 per week
Russia...........	2,000,000	324,000 or 6,211 per week
Italy............	500,000	140,000 or 2,800 per week
Spain............	300,000	106,000 or 2,039 per week
Belgium..........	500,000	64,000 or 1,231 per week
Austria..........	1,500,000	100,000 or 1,900 per week
Switzerland.......	1,300,000	100,000 or 1,900 per week

for family use. Hence, cotton was not primarily a source of wealth for them, and the possible failure of the American source would work no great hardship upon them as compared to workers in England and France. The peasantry and people generally would simply shift back to linen and woolen materials when cotton became too dear and scarce to be used with economy.

So England, whose cotton industry was larger than that of the rest of the Caucasian race combined, a seventh of whose population —that is, between 4,000,000 and 5,000,000—depended upon this industry, contemplated in deep anxiety the almost complete dependence of this gigantic industry upon American slaveholders. *Blackwood's Magazine*[2] in 1853 protested that the dependence of England upon the South for its cotton placed the subsistence "of millions in

[1] *London Economist, Com. Hist. and Rev. Suppl.*, March 11, 1865.

[2] *Blackwood's Magazine*, Jan., 1853.

every manufacturing country in Europe within the power of an oligarchy of planters." The *London Economist* of the same year[1] was depressed over the possibilities of an interruption of the American crop. "Let any great social or physical convulsion visit the United States," it prophesied, "and England would feel the shock from Land's End to John O'Groat's. The lives of nearly two million of our countrymen are dependent upon the cotton crops of America; their destiny may be said, without any kind of hyperbole, to hang upon a thread. Should any dire calamity befall the land of cotton, a thousand of our merchant ships would rot idly in dock, two thousand mills must stop their busy looms; two thousand thousand mouths would starve for lack of food." The *London Times* was greatly alarmed during this period.[2] Henry Ashworth[3] reminded England in 1858 that the dependence of her most important industry upon the single American crop "constitutes the structural weakness, the 'feet of clay' of our otherwise gigantic commercial power. . . . . The entire failure of a cotton crop," he continued, "should it ever occur, would utterly destroy, and perhaps for ever, all the manufacturing prosperity we possess. Or, should the growth in any one year be only one million instead of three millions of bales, the manufacturing and trading classes would find themselves involved in losses, which, in many cases, would amount to irretrievable ruin—millions of our countrymen would become deprived of employment and food—and, as a consequence, the misfortune would involve this country in a series of calamities, politically, socially, and commercially, such as cannot be contemplated without anxiety and dismay."

The *London Times*[4] concluded that "so nearly are our interests intertwined with America that civil war in the States means destitution in Lancashire." And again[5] it exclaimed, "the destiny of the world hangs on a thread—never did so much depend on a mere flock of down!"

[1] Quoted in *Cotton Is King*, p. 62. The seeming discrepancy in the figures given here and those previously cited is due to the addition of those workmen employed in subsidiary industries.

[2] *London Times*, Oct. 7, 1858.   [4] *London Times*, April 29, 1861.

[3] *Ashworth*, pp. 27–29.   [5] *Ibid.*, June 1, 1861.

In fact, after Great Britain had experimented in establishing a rival source of raw cotton in India and, in her failure, came to realize fully the almost complete dependence of her greatest industry and over four millions of her people upon the more and more precarious southern crop, many leaders in commerce and industry and Parliament and most newspapers and journals became apprehensive and filled with fear, which they discussed frequently and at great length. Operatives, manufacturers, merchants, government agents, prime ministers, all, believed alike, according to their expressed opinion during the few years before the war, that the cutting-off of the cotton supply in the South would destroy England's chief industry, starve the operatives, and bring ruin and revolution upon the land. Major W. H. Chase, of Florida, writing in *De Bow's Review*,[1] January, 1861, insisted that all England was convinced of the ruin of that country if the South's cotton failed to reach England. "This is the language of English statesmen, manufacturers and merchants in Parliament and at Cotton Association's debates and it discloses the truth."

This assertion of W. H. Chase is significant. It was the English leaders themselves who contributed most to convincing the southern people that England's very existence seemed to depend upon the cotton of the South. As has already been suggested, the South had been watching the efforts in England and even in France to establish a rival source for raw cotton, and had realized for a long time that the South had no real rival. But there is not much evidence that the South attached any great political significance to this situation before 1850. In fact, in the controversies which ended temporarily in the Compromise of 1850, there is little to indicate that the South was depending upon the power of cotton to win it independence in case of withdrawal from the Union. The reliance of the South was chiefly upon its strength, which was not far inferior to that of the North before 1850. But after 1850, following the widespread alarm in England and France over the dependence of their chief industry upon the South, the King Cotton idea came to its logical culmination. These countries would surely be bankrupted and perhaps precipitated into a revolution if their American cotton were cut off or badly threatened. This the English themselves freely

[1] *De Bow's Review*, XXX, No. 1 (Jan. 1861), 93.

confessed. The conclusion of the South was that England and perhaps France would interfere in behalf of the South, in case of secession and a threatened interruption of the cotton supply. It was necessary to obtain the precious white staple for the hungry cotton mills, and thereby save the country from bankruptcy and political and social revolution.

Before committing themselves too openly to the program involved in the King Cotton theory, southern leaders had considered carefully the importance of their cotton both to France and to the United States, as well as to England. It was certain that cotton played a major rôle in American international trade which was carried on by and for the North. It was southern rice, tobacco, cotton, and naval stores that furnished the great bulk of American export. Without this, the North would dry up, according to southern belief, for it would lose the middleman's profits which it derived from purchasing and exporting these southern staples. More than that, there would be nothing with which to pay for the goods imported from Europe and sold to the South at a large profit.[1] Figures were at hand in the census and trade reports for the southern leaders. These figures showed that the South furnished the most of the export. In 1851 the South had exported $112,815,317 worth of cotton, $9,219,251 worth of tobacco, $2,170,997 worth of rice. The income from its three major staples made a total of $124,205,565 while the total exports for the whole country were only $178,620,138. Thus only $54,414,573 was exported by the rest of the country, and a great part of this was of southern origin.[2] In 1853 the South exported in cotton, rice, and tobacco $120,000,000 out of $153,809,000, leaving $33,809,000 for the rest of the United States.[3] In 1858 out of a total export of $279,-000,000 the South sent abroad about $185,000,000.[4] In 1859 the

[1] Lynn M. Case (comp. and ed.), *French Opinion on the United States and Mexico, 1860–1867: Extracts from the Reports of the Procureurs Généraux* (New York, 1936), pp. 6–8. Mr. Case elaborates this statement and in addition claims that not enough attention has been "given to the effect of that struggle [Civil War] on French industries other than cotton."

[2] *Index*, Jan. 15, 1863.

[3] *Cotton Is King*, Tables 250–67.

[4] Hammond, *Speech on Admission of Kansas, March 4, 1858* (pamphlet; Washington, 1858).

South exported in cotton, tobacco, rice, etc., $198,389,351 out of a total for the whole country of $278,392,080.[1]

If the North was dependent upon the South for cotton as the medium of international trade, it was just as dependent upon cotton to carry on its own cotton industry which ranked—though far below—second to that of England. The northern mills had consumed from 200,000,000 pounds a year in 1849 to 364,000,000 pounds in 1860,[2] roughly one-fourth the consumption of the British industry.

As to France, while the volume of her consumption of cotton was only one-fifth that of Great Britain, the South knew that the cotton industry was one of her largest. Because of its fineness and the tediousness of the work, it employed a much larger number of operatives in proportion to the raw material utilized than did England or the United States. They also knew that it was one of the most profitable industries of France, and constituted a chief item of her export. But to find out the exact situation, the Federal government—under southern control—sent John Claiborne over to study the whole situation and report back to Congress. His report in 1858 was very illuminating.[3] He reported that there were 2,606 factories in France (many of them very small, of course, compared to the large American and English mills) and 275,930 operatives engaged in the various branches of the cotton trade. The cotton consumed in 1855, 1856, and 1857 was 167,752,521; 187,851,768; and 180,634,521 pounds, respectively. He pointed out that the profits from start to finish were 400 per cent. For example, one year the raw cotton cost $17,519,756, but the spinners raised it by their labor to $38,395,372, and then the weavers of the finer textiles increased its value to $61,111,167, netting a profit of $43,792,411. Compared to the Eng-

[1] De Bow, *The Interest in Slavery of the Non-slaveholder* (1860), Tract 5, p. 11; cf. Scherer, *Cotton as a World Power* (New York, 1916) (cited hereafter as Scherer), pp. 235–43; *Cotton Is King*, Tables 250–67; *London Index*, June 12, 1862; *ibid.*, Jan. 15, 1863; census of 1860. Later studies such as Johnson's *History of Domestic and Foreign Commerce of the United States* give larger figures for American export trade, but it was not these studies to which the South had access.

[2] *Cotton Is King*, Tables 250–67; Arnold, p. 257.

[3] Report of the secretary of the interior communicating the report of John Claiborne, Esq., special agent appointed to collect statistics on the consumption of cotton, *Executive Document* (35th Congress, 1st sess., Senate), *passim*. (Cited hereafter as Claiborne, *Cotton Consumption in Europe*.)

lish cotton industry, the output of which sold out in 1860 for $400,-000,000, the French cotton trade seemed small. But what made it have such great significance to the South at this time was the fact that around 700,000 workers depended upon the industry for their bread, and the further fact that these people were restless and rebellious and easily persuaded to revolution.

Satisfied that the three great nations England, France, and the United States could not live without the southern cotton, the southern statesmen at length came out boldly and proclaimed the fact to the world.

It was a writer living in Cincinnati, Ohio, whose words caught the attention and captured the imagination of the South. In 1855 David Christy published his famous *Cotton Is King: or Slavery in the Light of Political Economy*. He proposed to save the Union on southern terms, or if not, to assure the peaceful secession of the South. His book summed up all that had been said in England and elsewhere as to the dependence of the world upon the cotton crop of the South. He summed up all the most important data and figures in support of this point; he summed up what the southern leaders were already thinking and had been endeavoring to express. And to the South he gave as a shibboleth, "Cotton is king." The phrase was soon on every tongue, carrying conviction among the masses. Reiteration was the sole argument necessary, and the slogan soon became shortened to "King Cotton." Stump orators, Fourth of July speakers, economists, governors, congressmen, and senators seized upon the phrase, "Cotton is king." Presently Christy brought out another edition of his book, and at last in 1860 incorporated it in a large volume together with essays by Senator Hammond and by other southern writers and slavery champions. This time the book was given the title of *Cotton Is King and Pro-Slavery Arguments*, and was published under the editorship of Professor E. N. Elliott of Planter's College, Mississippi.

The next two men of importance to seize upon and spread the new gospel were Senator Hammond from South Carolina, planter, writer upon scientific farming and political economy, and De Bow, editor of the well-known *Review* and prolific writer upon economic and social problems of the South. Senator Hammond was widely known as a champion of slavery through his letters to Clarkson and other abolitionists of England. During the debates and bitter quarrels in the Senate over the Kansas question, especially the Lecompton Constitution, on March 4, 1858, Hammond caught up the watchword originated by Christy and sent a ringing challenge to the North and to the world. He had been told by Seward that soon the country was to take control of the government from the unworthy hands of the slaveholders and give it into more trustworthy hands. On every side secession was talked openly, and there were threats of civil war. Hammond, cool, sarcastic, scornful, taunting, answered that the North dare not drive the South to secession, or if the South seceded, the Federal government dare not lay unfriendly hands upon it, for no sane nation would make war on cotton. "Without firing a gun, without drawing a sword, should they make war on us we could bring the whole world to our feet. The South is perfectly competent to go on, one, two, or even three years without planting a seed of cotton. I believe that if she were to plant but half her cotton, for three years to come it would be an immense advantage to her. I am not sure but that after three years' total abstinence she would come out stronger than ever she was before, and better prepared to enter afresh upon her great career of enterprise. What would happen if no cotton was furnished for three years? I will not stop to depict what every one can imagine, but this is certain: England would topple headlong and carry the whole civilized world with her, save the South. No, you dare not make war on cotton. No power on earth dares to make war upon it. Cotton is king!"[1] Always in the capacity of champion of southern economic independence and of the divine rights of slavery, he was widely known, admired, and trusted. With the Kansas struggle as a background, his speech gave the King Cotton philosophy great impetus.

De Bow had caught up the cry and passed it on in his *Review and Industrial Resources.* "To the slave-holding states," he wrote, "it

[1] Hammond, *Speech on Admission of Kansas, March 4, 1858* (pamphlet); cf. Scherer, pp. 257 ff.; M. B. Hammond, *The Cotton Industry,* p. 64.

[cotton] is the great source of their power and their wealth, and the main security for their peculiar institution. Let us teach our children to hold the cotton plant in one hand and a sword in the other, ever ready to defend it as the source of commercial power abroad and through that, of independence at home."[1] In the late fifties *De Bow's Review* became the vehicle of the idea of King Cotton, which reached a climax about the time of secession in an article by Major W. H. Chase, "The Secession of the Southern States."[2] "The secession of these states must necessarily be a peaceful one," Chase argued, "because England, France and the rest of commercial Europe, and the Western and Northern States of the Union require that it should be." The world must have the South's cotton at any price. "The first demonstration of blockade of the Southern ports would be swept away by the English fleet of observation hovering on the Southern coast to protect English commerce and especially the free flow of cotton to English and French factories. The flow of cotton must not cease; because the enormous sum of £150,000,000 is annually due to the elaboration of raw cotton and because 5,000,000 people derive their daily and immediate support therefrom in England alone and every interest throughout the kingdom is connected therewith. The stoppage of the raw material from the cotton states of the South, either by failure of crop or civil war and its consequences, would produce the most disastrous political results—if not a revolution in England." Not only would England and France not permit a blockade of the South; they would not even permit the North to disturb the South and threaten the precious cotton supply by invasion. King Cotton protected the South both by land and by sea.

Perhaps there was an element of argument in Chase's article; but, after this, persuasion was no longer resorted to. Henceforth, the theory of King Cotton became a cardinal principle upon which all the men who were to lead the South out of the Union and to guide its destiny through the Civil War were almost unanimously agreed. It seems to have been classed along with Newton's laws of motion and

[1] De Bow, *Commercial Resources*, I, 178.
[2] *De Bow's Review*, O.S., XXX, No. 1 (Jan., 1861).

other natural laws, and during the secession period, the southerners, on every hand, mouthed the words "King Cotton" with relish. Hammond was still proclaiming it in his writings and speeches.[1] Senator Iverson from Georgia in his parting speech in the United States Senate warned his former friends of the North to tread lightly and beware of war, for the world needed southern cotton. "We can live, if need be, without commerce," he told them, "but when you shut out our cotton from the looms of Europe, we shall see whether other nations will not have something to do on that subject. Cotton is king and will find some means to raise your blockade and disperse your ships."[2]

Governors, legislators, factors, merchants, planters, and newspaper editors of the southern states all held practically the same views regarding the power of cotton to push England into the fray as soon as cotton was needed, and all urged the doctrine of embargo upon the people of the South. Some of these leaders continued to support the doctrine long after its efficacy had been disproved. Governors Milton[3] of Florida; A. B. Moore[4] and his successor, Gil Shorter,[5] of Alabama; Thomas Moore[6] of Louisiana; Joseph E. Brown[7] of Georgia; as well as Confederate Senator Benjamin Hill[8] and state legis-

---

[1] See E. D. Adams, *Great Britain and the American Civil War* (2 vols.; London, 1925), II, 2–3. (Cited hereafter as E. D. Adams.)

[2] Quoted in Callahan, *The Diplomatic History of the Confederacy* (Baltimore, 1898), pp. 79–80. (Cited hereafter as Callahan.)

[3] See, e.g., John Milton to the Hon. Senators and Representatives of the state of Florida, etc., Aug. 18, 1862, *The War of the Rebellion* (a compilation of the *Official Records of the Confederate Armies* [Washington, 1880–1901]), Ser. 4, Vol. II, pp. 56–59 (cited hereafter as *O.R.*); Milton to President Davis, April 16, 1863, *ibid.*, pp. 488–89.

[4] Moore to President Davis, Feb. 3, 1862, *ibid.*, p. 905.

[5] Shorter to Seddon, March 28, 1863, *ibid.*, pp. 461–63.

[6] Moore to Benjamin, Jan., 1862, *ibid.*, Vol. I, pp. 836–37.

[7] See British Foreign Office, America, Despatches, Vol. 849, Consul Molyneux to Russell, No. 24, Nov. 11, 1862. (These consular and diplomatic papers in the British Public Record Office will be cited hereafter as F.O. Amer., etc. In later years these records have been designated as F.O. 5. However, it has been decided to retain the earlier form in this edition.); also speech, Nov. 6, 1862, before legislature, *Confederate Records of Georgia*, Vol. II; *O.R.*, Ser. 4, Vol. II, p. 376, Davis to Brown, Jan. 27, 1863.

[8] E.g., see speech on proposed cotton loan in the *Savannah Republican*, July 4, 1861.

lator J. E. Ward,[1] both of Georgia; and Duncan Kenner[2] of Louisiana and Mississippi were convinced of the power of cotton to coerce England into breaking the blockade or recognizing the South. S. R. Cockerill, planter, soldier, and politician from the Arkansas River bottoms where cotton grew tall, writing General Walker about the state of crops, characterized cotton as "the king who can shake the jewels in the crown of Queen Victoria."[3]

Jefferson Davis followed the widespread discussion in Great Britain among the industrial, financial, and political leaders, of England's dependence upon southern cotton, and the publication of Christy's *Cotton Is King*. He became a firm believer in the power of cotton to bring British and European intervention in behalf of the South in case of an attack by the North. Davis, however, was too discreet to blurt out such an arrogant confession of faith as had Senators Iverson and Hammond, or to express the naïve trustfulness in the power of cotton which Major Chase had expressed in his essay in *De Bow's Review*. Mrs. Davis in her *Memoirs*[4] asserted that President Davis and his advisers thought the power of cotton so great "that foreign recognition was looked forward to as an assumed fact." "The president and his advisers," she wrote,[5] "looked to the stringency of the English cotton market, and the suspension of the manufactories to send up a ground swell from the English operatives, that would compel recognition." Charles Francis Adams, the younger, said[6] that Davis was dominated "by an undue and indeed an over-weening faith in the practical world mastery enjoyed by that section—the South—through its exclusive control of cotton . . . . that cotton was king and would in the end so be found, was his unwavering convic-

[1] *Ibid.*, Aug. 27, 1861.

[2] *Journal of the Congress of the Confederate States of America*, I, 290, 308-9. (Cited hereafter as *Jour. Confed. Cong.*)

[3] *O.R.*, Ser. 1, Vol. LII, Part II, Suppl. (June 2, 1861).

[4] Quoted in *Charles Francis Adams* by his son Charles Francis Adams, American Statesmen Series (Boston, 1900), p. 163. (Cited hereafter as Adams, *Charles Francis Adams*.)

[5] *Jefferson Davis: A Memoir by His Wife* (New York, 1890), II, 160.

[6] Adams, *Charles Francis Adams*, pp. 161-64.

tion." If England could not get cotton she "would in less than six months be starved into subjection. She must raise the blockade to preserve her internal peace if not prevent revolution."

One of the most reliable and widely informed witnesses of southern opinion at the outbreak of the war was William Howard Russell of the *London Times*, who visited the chief cities and points of interest in Virginia, North Carolina, South Carolina, Georgia, Alabama, Louisiana, and other southern states. Wherever he went he found opinion apparently unanimous as to the power of cotton to force England to intervene. Judah P. Benjamin, Confederate Secretary of State, was quite frank in the expression of this doctrine, telling Russell that when England needed cotton badly enough "all this coyness about acknowledging a slave power will come right at last."[1] Edmund Rhett of South Carolina, relative of Robert Barnwell Rhett, told the *Times* correspondent during the spring of secession that because of England's need of cotton "you British must recognize us before the end of October."[2] Russell was irritated by the frankly expressed low opinion of England's integrity, for southerners were constantly telling him that when England needed the cotton she would not scruple to intervene to get it. "We know John Bull," they told him at an exclusive Charleston club, "he will make a great fuss about non-intervention at first, but when he begins to want cotton he will come down off his perch."[3] At the home of the British consul, Bunch, where Russell was entertained, one of the guests exclaimed, "Why, sir, we have only to shut off your supply of cotton for a few weeks and we can create a revolution in Great Britain. There are four millions of your people depending on us for their bread, not to speak of the many millions of dollars. No sir, we know that England must recognize us."[4]

Russell called upon most of the leading merchants in Charleston,

[1] William Howard Russell, *My Diary North and South* (London, 1863), p. 70. (Cited hereafter as Russell, *My Diary*.)

[2] *Ibid.*, p. 61.

[3] *Ibid.*, p. 43; John B. Atkins, *The Life of Sir William Howard Russell* (2 vols.; London, 1911), II, 25.

[4] Russell, *My Diary*, p. 51.

including Trenholm of the house of Fraser, Trenholm /
of Liverpool, New York, and Charleston (later Secr
Treasury for the Confederate States), Muir, Rose, and others,
found the mercantile element as strong in the belief of the power of
cotton as the planters and politicians. One of these gentlemen told
him that if the United States attempted to blockade the South and
keep England from southern cotton, he believed that country would
send the blockading ships to the bottom and recognize the South
before autumn. "Look out there," he told Russell, pointing to the
wharf where great piles of cotton lay, "there's the key that will open
all our ports and put us into John Bull's strong box as well."[1] In
Georgia, Russell found the same sentiment.[2] When he went to Montgomery, the Convention and all the people gathered there were thoroughly convinced that cotton would prove the deciding factor in the
crisis. Russell wrote the *Times* that the southern people "firmly believe that the war will not last a year. . . . . They believe in the irre-
sistible power of Cotton" to force England to intervene.[3] In Louisiana, after having become acquainted with leading men of the state—
including Governor Moore, Slidell, former Governor Hèbert, Duncan Kenner, Norton, General Lewis, Major Ranney, Claiborne,
Hunt, and Fellows—Russell came to the conclusion that the whole
South was unanimous in the bold and arrogant boast that they were
"masters of the destiny of the world. Cotton is king—not alone
king, but czar."[4]

The British consuls stationed at the chief southern ports reported
the widespread belief of the South in the power of cotton to bring
foreign aid. Consul Bunch wrote Lord John Russell, British Secretary of State for Foreign Affairs, that the belief in the power of cotton was universal. The southerners thought, he concluded, "that to

[1] *Ibid.*, p. 52.   [2] *Ibid.*, p. 64.

[3] Quoted in Rhodes, *History of the United States*, III, 416; cf. J. C. Schwab, *The Confederate States of America, 1861–5: A Financial and Industrial History of the South during
the Civil War* (New York, 1901), p. 250 (cited hereafter as Schwab); Scherer, p. 258;
Adams, *Charles Francis Adams*, p. 160; Du Bose, *Life and Times of William Lowndes
Yancey* (Birmingham, Ala., 1892), p. 586. (Cited hereafter as Du Bose, *Yancey*.)

[4] Russell, *My Diary*, pp. 96–97.

withhold cotton one year would be to plunge England into a Revolution. . . . . The exultation which they feel at having placed us in the position of dependence on their pleasure, cannot be concealed in their conversations with me, whilst those with whom I am familiar openly tell me that we cannot live without them. . . . . I shall be much mistaken if your Lordship does not discover the existence of this feeling, should the commissioners be honored by personal intercourse with you."[1] In June, two or three months afterward, Bunch reported as universal the "conviction entertained by the South that Great Britain will make any sacrifice, even of principle or of honor to prevent the stoppage of the supply of cotton."[2] Again and again, during the secession and early war days, Bunch referred with growing exasperation to the widespread belief in the South that cotton would presently force England to recognize the South and to break the blockade.[3]

Consuls Magee at Mobile,[4] Lynn at Galveston,[5] Coppell and Mure at New Orleans,[6] Molyneux at Savannah,[7] and other consular agents scattered throughout the South informed the Foreign Office of Great Britain that the South expected cotton to win the struggle by coercing Great Britain into intervening in behalf of that section.[8]

The London Times, summing up the situation in the spring of 1862, declared,[9] "It is clear from the language used by the seceders in and out of Congress that they thought they could extort our cooperation by the agency of king cotton."[10]

[1] F.O. Amer., Vol. 780, Part I, Bunch to Russell, No. 37, March 21, 1861; ibid., Vol. 843, Bunch to Russell, March 19, 1862.

[2] Ibid., Vol. 780, Part I, Bunch to Russell, No. 9, June 5, 1861.

[3] Cf. ibid.; also ibid., Vol. 781, Part II, Bunch to Russell, passim.

[4] Ibid., Vol. 786, Magee to Russell, Aug. 21, 1861, and passim.

[5] Ibid., Vol. 788, Lynn to Russell, No. 25, Aug. 7, 1861, and passim.

[6] Ibid., Vol. 908, passim.   [7] Ibid., Vol. 849, Molyneux to Russell, passim.

[8] See further, ibid., Vols. 746, 843, 846, 971, passim, for reports from consuls during this period.

[9] London Times, May 22, 1862.

[10] Cf. F. W. Sargeant, England, the United States and the Confederacy (2d ed.; London, 1864), p. 38.

The South had begun to realize by 1840 that Europe, especially England and France, obtained the bulk of raw cotton from America; between 1840 and 1860 it witnessed the futile efforts of Great Britain to restore India to her former place as a principal source of supply for cotton. Especially did the southern leaders read the reports, books, papers, and speeches of the British leaders who, after twenty years of effort, conceded the impossibility of obtaining cotton in sufficient quantities outside the South. The dependence of the English and French cotton industries upon southern cotton, and the seeming dependence upon the cotton industries of England and France for their existence, caused the southern people, led by Christy, Hammond, and De Bow, to conclude that the need for southern cotton would force England and France to interfere on behalf of the South in case of secession and war. This belief was epitomized in the expression "Cotton is king," shortened to "King Cotton." By 1860 the belief in the power of cotton to force European intervention was almost universal.

THE ATTEMPT AT ECONOMIC COERCION

With the King Cotton theory so universally accepted in the southern states by 1860, the South naturally and as a matter of course based its diplomacy upon Europe's need of its cotton when the Confederacy was set up. Neither the southern governments nor the people were willing to let nature take its course. Instead they undertook heroic measures to assist nature in aid of the Confederate diplomats. What they did affords an irrefutable proof—if proof is needed—of the unfaltering faith of the southern people in an idea, for they staked their existence upon the infallibility of the power of cotton. It is also just another illustration of that grim unanimity with which the people supported the Confederacy in the beginning. The southern people did not propose to wait for the Federal blockade proclaimed by Lincoln to become slowly effective, and by the same slow stages reduce the supply of southern cotton going to the British and French factories, pinching these industries more and more until finally the cotton famine should arrive and intervention follow. They proposed to meet the blockade at the threshold with restrictive measures which would produce an immediate cotton famine: England and France should have no cotton with which to stave off the cotton famine and postpone intervention.

THE EMBARGO, 1861–62

The first step in this direction was to meet the Federal blockade with a cotton embargo. Let us follow out, then, the complex of public opinion and legislative action by which the embargo was produced. "The cards are in our hands!" the *Charleston Mercury* gloated,[1] "and we intend to play them out to the bankruptcy of every cotton factory in Great Britain and France or the acknowledgment of our independence." An embargo would kill more people and do more injury in England and France than in the Confederacy and impress Europe with the power of the South, for the people "of these countries do not seem yet to realize that the Confederate States are a power on earth—and the most important power to them the sun shines on."

For practically the first year of the war this sentiment, so confidently and arrogantly expressed by the *Charleston Mercury*, was that of the other leading southern newspapers. The screws were to be put on the North to convince it of the necessity of peace with the South, and on England and France whom the South considered as very low, selfish nations, mercenary and materialistic to the highest degree, to induce these nations to break the blockade and intervene in behalf of the South. "Let the blockade be effectual," was the cry, "the stricter the better; the sooner will it be over; the sooner will rescue from Europe reach us; the sooner will the strong hand of the 'old country' remove our difficulties."[2] The *Charleston Courier*[3] urged that if England did not have the manhood to disregard a sham blockade but preferred rather to support five millions of the factory population by charity funds "we at least of the South ought not to complain. . . . . The course, therefore, in relation to this staple is a very plain one—no foreigner can get any of our cotton during the con-

[1] *Charleston Mercury*, June 4, 1861.

[2] Quoted in the *London Economist*, June 22, 1861.

[3] *Charleston Courier*, July 23, 1861.

tinuance of this blockade." Again a few days later[1] the *Courier* urged the non-exportation of cotton as the sure means of raising the blockade and gaining independence by foreign intervention. The *Memphis Argus* advised: "Keep every bale of cotton on the plantation. Don't send a thread to Orleans or Memphis till England and France have recognized the Confederacy—not one thread." Allowing even a partial supply to dribble through Lincoln's ramshackle blockade to England would "enable that Government to defer an active interference in our favor; and that interference, though not needed to secure our independence, is the speediest road to peace. . . . . Keep the cotton from the cities."[2] On hearing it rumored that Lincoln might bribe England and France from interfering to break the blockade or aid the South by opening one port long enough to allow these countries to get out cotton enough to tide them over, the *Charleston Courier*[3] exclaimed in indignation: "Let us give England and France and other nations notice at once that we have business of much more weighty importance to attend to at present than that of selling cotton—that we shall suspend all commercial operations for a year or two, at least, until we have driven the armies of Abraham from our borders—that until the blockading fleet shall cease to cast a shadow on our waters we will sell no cotton, at any price, to friend or foe, nor will we entertain any proposition in relation to exporting any part of our crop—and that we will not allow a bale of our cotton to leave our plantations upon any pretext whatever." A few weeks later the *Courier* asked:[4] "Shall we let our cotton go out now, under the connivance of Lincoln?" in order "that England may stand aloof till we are conquered, or shall we burn every pod of it before we allow it to be carried from our ports while this war lasts?" Again and again during the summer and fall of 1861 the *Courier* reiterated the common determination that no cotton should be allowed to leave southern ports until the blockade was raised or until the South had gained the recognition

[1] *Ibid.*, July 26, 1861.

[2] *Memphis Argus.* Quoted in the *Charleston Courier*, July 26, 1861.

[3] *Charleston Courier*, Aug. 5, 1861.

[4] *Ibid.*, Sept. 25, 1861.

of France and England.[1] This it firmly believed would happen
as soon as the new crop was gathered and it was found impossible
for those countries to obtain sufficient cotton elsewhere for their
mills.[2]

The *Savannah Republican*'s position was similar to those of the
Mercury, *Courier*, and *Argus*. It constantly urged that no cotton
should be sent to the seaports because it would fall into Federal
hands if allowed to run the blockade, but more important, because
it would relieve the distress in England and France upon which
the South was relying to force intervention.[3] This paper, like
the *Courier*, maintained that the scarcity of cotton would force
England and France to intervene by the end of the year 1861.
"We are," said the *Savannah Republican*,[4] "of the opinion that the
close of the year 1861 will also terminate the present conflict
between North and South, if not by the breakdown of the North,
it will be closed by European intervention."[5] The cantankerous
Richmond Enquirer[6] approved of the withholding of cotton as
a means of coercing Europe. The *Memphis Appeal*,[7] the *Mobile
Register and Advertiser*,[8] and the *New Orleans Crescent*[9] agreed
upon the wisdom of coercion by an embargo. The *Richmond Examiner*[10] took the optimistic attitude assumed by the *Courier* and
Savannah Republican that only a few months' pressure would
be necessary to put England into action on the side of the Confederacy. If cotton were withheld from Europe until the end of the
summer, she would be precipitated into revolution and social
upheaval. "It is therefore a matter of compulsion that they should
break through the blockade and obtain our crop. . . . . ."

[1] See *ibid.*, Aug. 12; Sept. 21, 24, 26, 30; Oct. 2, 4, 7; and Nov. 5, 1861.

[2] See *ibid.*, July 16, 18, 27, 1861.

[3] See the *Savannah Republican*, July 4; Aug. 5; Sept. 17, 27; Oct. 2, 7, 8, 16; Nov. 22;
and Dec. 4, 27, 1861.

[4] *Ibid.*, Oct. 16, 1861.   [5] Cf. *ibid.*, Aug. 20, 22, 27, 1861.

[6] See, e.g., *Richmond Enquirer*, Aug. 20, 1861; April 10, 1862.

[7] *Memphis Appeal* quoted in the *Savannah Republican*, Dec. 4, 1861.

[8] *Mobile Register and Advertiser* cited in the *Charleston Courier*, Jan. 15, 1862.

[9] *New Orleans Crescent*, March 21, 1862.   [10] *Richmond Examiner*, July 2, 1861.

Indeed, the economic coercion of Europe by means of an embargo was supported widely the first year of the war. There was almost complete unanimity in the public press, and among the whole articulate southern population. Indeed, so unanimous was the approval of an embargo that a writer in the *Charleston Courier* exclaimed with pained surprise in September[1] that "for the first time yesterday, I heard questioned the policy of withholding the cotton of the Confederate States from export as long as our ports were closed to imports from abroad."

More important, even, than the newspaper advocacy of an embargo—though unquestionably greatly influenced by the newspapers—was the attitude of the cotton-planters, the men who would be more affected by the failure to dispose of the cotton crop. These men, though heavily in debt, agreed, practically without a dissenting voice, that no cotton be allowed to leave the plantations until the blockade had been lifted and southern independence recognized. Consul Bunch, at Charleston, reported to Lord Russell[2] that while the crop of 1861 would be around 4,000,000 bales, "a strong feeling exists as to the expediency of keeping the cotton in the interior. . . . . It is quite certain that the planters and their government are resolved to part with none of their produce until the blockade is raised. Their pride is involved in the question and they will suffer loss and inconvenience themselves rather than yield the point." A few days later he wrote Russell: "I am sure that the planters of the South will retain upon their plantations every bale of cotton they may grow until the end of the blockade."[3] At the end of September, Bunch reported that the planters were still unchanged in their purpose.[4] Consul Lynn reported from Galveston that the farmers and planters of Texas and the West were going to hold every bale of their cotton on the plantations;[5] and Consul Molyneux, of Savannah, reported to the British Foreign Office that the farmers and planters of Georgia and the seaboard showed

[1] *Charleston Courier*, Sept. 21, 1861.

[2] F.O. Amer., Vol. 781, Part II, Bunch to Russell, No. 87, July 23, 1861.

[3] *Ibid.*, No. 93, Aug. 3, 1861.   [4] *Ibid.*, Sept. 28, 1861.

[5] *Ibid.*, Vol. 788, Lynn to Russell, No. 25, Aug. 25, 1861.

not the slightest disposition to relax their determination to hold their cotton back from the seaports as late as December. They were determined to go on with the embargo, and force Europe to intervene or suffer a terrible cotton famine.[1] Consul Magee, writing from Mobile, asserted that the cotton-planters of the South would stand behind the cotton embargo almost to a man.[2] The newspapers of the South all pretty much agreed with the *New Orleans Price Current*,[3] which reported that "the planters of the country appear to be firm in their determination to withhold their crops until the blockade shall be removed."[4]

Intimately related, both in sentiment and in business with the planters, were the cotton factors or exporters of the southern seaports and inland cotton markets. The most important port in the South was New Orleans, and because of the great volume of business done in cotton export, whatever the cotton merchants and the warehouse and insurance men decided to do there would be decisive in Mobile, Savannah, Charleston, and the smaller southern ports. Feeling the responsibility resting upon them in helping to decide such a vital policy as the cotton embargo, the cotton factors and insurance and warehouse men issued a circular to the planters about the first of August, 1861, urging them not to ship a bale of cotton to New Orleans. So earnest were these men about the matter that they declared that if anyone attempted to ship cotton to that port, the cotton-buyers and other members of the cotton-exporting trade would absolutely refuse to receive a bale. They urged upon the planters the wisdom of aiding the Confederate government in bringing pressure upon England and France.[5] Mobile quickly followed suit in urging that no cotton

[1] *Ibid.*, Vol. 786, Molyneux to Russell, No. 35, Dec. 4, 1861.

[2] *Ibid.*, Magee to Russell, Aug. 21, 1861.

[3] *New Orleans Price Current*, Sept. 14, 1861.

[4] See files of *Savannah Republican, Mobile Register*, etc.; *Montgomery Advertiser, Charleston Mercury, Charleston Courier, Memphis Argus, Memphis Appeal, New Orleans True Delta, New Orleans Price Current, Richmond Enquirer, Richmond Examiner, passim*, during summer and fall of 1861 for the attitude of the planter class.

[5] See F.O. Amer., Vol. 781, Part II, Bunch to Russell, No. 93, Aug. 3, 1861; *London Economist*, Sept. 7 and Oct. 26, 1861.

be brought to that city until the blockade should be raised.[1] The cotton factors in the city of Savannah at about the same time issued a circular in which they urged the planters "not to ship any portion of their crop of cotton to this city, or not to remove it from their plantations until the blockade is fully and entirely abandoned."[2] A few days later the factors and merchants of Charleston recommended that the planters "send none of their cotton to market until the blockade is expressly removed from all ports of the Confederate States."[3] By August 21 Consul Magee was able to write Lord Russell that all the cotton men in every southern seaport—exporters, merchants, insurance and storage men—had advised the planters against bringing any cotton to the seaports until the southern Confederacy had been acknowledged and the blockade raised.[4] This urging by the cotton merchants and cotton men generally was probably like carrying coals to Newcastle, for it was among the planters such as Hammond and Duncan Kenner that the King Cotton philosophy found its "bitter ender" disciples more than among the cotton factors and merchants.

Thus were the newspapers, the planters, and the cotton factors and merchants firmly convinced of the wisdom of putting an embargo upon the shipment of cotton through the blockade to Europe as a means of gaining recognition and aid from England and France. With these powerful groups advocating a cotton embargo, one would naturally expect the state and Confederate lawmaking bodies and executive officers to respond by putting a legal sanction upon the King Cotton doctrine by laws and regulations to prevent cotton leaving the ports.

Sentiment was just as strong in Congress as out of it in regard to the wisdom of putting an embargo upon cotton to meet the paper blockade of the North which had been so quickly accepted by England and France. But, while much restrictive legislation was

[1] F.O. Amer., Vol. 781, Part II, Bunch to Russell, No. 93, Aug. 3, 1861.

[2] *Charleston Courier*, Aug. 7, 1861.

[3] *Ibid.*, Aug. 12, 1861; F.O. Amer., Vol. 781, Part II, Bunch to Russell, No. 111, Aug. 12, 1861.

[4] *Ibid.*, Vol. 786, Magee to Russell, Aug. 21, 1861.

enacted, this sentiment was never translated into an outright embargo. Act after act was passed which bore some faint traces of the embargo sentiment, and a perusal of the journals of the Confederate Congress and of the published fragments of the debates discloses a constant succession of bills, which provided for the complete embargo of all cotton, but which always died in committee or before the final vote, or which lost all but a faint trace of their original intent before final enactment. There seemed to be some hidden, mysterious force that always stopped Congress short of the prohibitory legislation during the time when the sentiment was so strong in favor of an embargo. This mysterious hand was that of Davis, who had a well-considered scheme of strategy amid all this apparent fumbling with an idea. This was to allow and—perhaps, through Benjamin and friends of the administration in Congress—encourage the discussion of bills and the actual passage of resolutions as indicative of sentiment so that a threat of an embargo might be constantly held over Europe. But it was plain to the Confederate President that it would not be good diplomacy to allow the enactment of a law placing an embargo upon cotton. Such a law, especially if sanctioned by the administration, instead of bringing England and France to the aid of the Confederacy would drive those countries into the arms of the enemy. But to assume the position of champion of unrestricted intercourse with all friendly powers, in the face of a Congress straining over-eagerly at the leash in its desire to pass an embargo, would be good diplomacy—provided, of course, that it could be assured through other means, as was actually the case, that no cotton should be sent through the blockade, and relieve Europe.[1]

Let us, now, observe the attitude of Congress both as giving a further insight into the opinion of the South and as actually

[1] See, e.g., Pickett Papers, which are the Confederate state papers and diplomatic correspondence, Manuscripts Division, Library of Congress. The most important of the diplomatic correspondence has been published in the *Official Records of the Navy* (cited hereafter as *O.R.N.*). See Pickett Papers, Instructions, Benjamin to Mason, No. 2, April 8, 1862; *O.R.N.*, Ser. 2, Vol. III, pp. 378–84, Benjamin to Mason, April 8, 1862; Pickett Papers, Slidell to Hunter, No. 2 with inclosures, Feb. 26, 1862; *O.R.N.*, Ser. 2, Vol. III, pp. 350–51.

placing obstacles in the way of exportation of cotton without even enacting an embargo, and as stimulating the extra-legal restrictions upon cotton export.

On May 10, 1861, a bill passed the provisional Congress prohibiting trade with the United States.[1] The interdiction of trade with the enemy was in accordance with universal practice, and should have caused no comment if there had not been disclosed in the debates during the passage of the bill the embargo idea. Not only was the North to be reduced by cutting off the supply of cotton, but Europe was to be struck down by this indirect method, for it was through the North that Europe had largely obtained southern cotton. Bunch wrote Lord John Russell that the law was aimed as much at Europe as at the North, in order to coerce England and France into taking sides with the South.[2] On May 20 a bill was passed prohibiting the exportation of cotton and other produce except through southern seaports (Mexico excepted).[3] On July 27 Congress instructed the "Committee on Foreign Affairs to inquire into the expediency of reporting a bill to prevent the exportation of cotton, tobacco, and naval stores."[4] The discussion of this proposition disclosed almost a unanimous sentiment in favor of an embargo on cotton and other southern staples, yet the proposed bill was sunk in the Committee on Foreign Affairs almost without a trace. Word had probably been passed out that the administration, while approving the purpose of the bill, and the discussion of the subject, believed its enactment into law would be inexpedient. Two days later Duncan Kenner of Louisiana —to be heard more of later in connection with the mysterious "Kenner mission" to Europe—reported resolutions from the Ways and Means Committee which carried in milder language the embargo idea. It insisted that cotton be prevented from accumulating in the seaports, under cover of the fear that such accumulation, if allowed, would draw an attack from the United States, but in reality for the purpose of preventing, indirectly, the shipment

[1] *Jour. Confed. Cong.*, I, 205–6.

[2] F.O. Amer., Vol. 780, Part I, Bunch to Russell, No. 69, June 5, 1861.

[3] *Jour. Confed. Cong.*, I, 251, 264. [4] *Ibid.*, p. 288.

of cotton to Europe.[1] After discussion it was decided to drop the resolutions.[2]

During the time this resolution was under discussion the law prohibiting the export of cotton except through the seaports was brought up for amendments and extensions. Duncan Kenner took the position that this law should be changed into a general embargo to last until the blockade was raised.[3] He did not carry his proposal—in fact, it is doubtful, in view of his close relations with the administration, whether his suggestions were at best more than a gesture for the benefit of Europe and for the purpose of stimulating the continuance of the extra-legal embargo which was rendering any kind of congressional enactment totally unnecessary. Benjamin, at least, if not Davis, was probably in consultation with Kenner. Again, as late as March, 1862, Kenner reported a bill from the Ways and Means Committee to place an embargo on cotton.[4] The bill was to be in operation until the blockade ceased. This proposal also must be taken as a gesture to accompany the pressure being brought upon England and France at this time, by the Mason-Slidell mission, to declare the blockade ineffective and illegal, as in violation of the terms of the Treaty of Paris.[5]

During the period in which Congress was recurring constantly to the proposition of enacting a straight-out embargo, it was considering also another less direct, but as effective, way of preventing the exportation of cotton abroad: the purchase and control of all cotton in the South. Farmers' conventions at Richmond,[6] Macon,[7] and other places,[8] as well as newspapers, public men, and state legislatures,[9] urged that the Confederate government take over all cotton in the South.

[1] *Ibid.*, p. 290.   [3] *Ibid.*, pp. 308-9.

[2] *Ibid.*, p. 312.   [4] *Ibid.*, V, 117.

[5] For further discussion of the embargo idea in Congress see *ibid.*, pp. 150-52, 162-65, 185, 256-58.

[6] *Charleston Courier*, March 3, 1862.

[7] *De Bow's Review*, Oct. and Nov., 1861.

[8] *Richmond Examiner*, No. 4, 1861; *Charleston Mercury*, Jan. 16, 1862; Schwab, p. 15.

[9] Cf. Schwab, pp. 16-17, for Mississippi legislature.

Congress assumed about the same attitude toward the purchase of the cotton crop as it had with reference to the enactment of an embargo. It passed several acts embodying the idea of purchasing the entire cotton crop, and showed strong sentiment in favor of the project, but was always checked beyond a certain limit by the administration, especially Memminger, who thought the war would be over by foreign intervention before such an act could be carried out and who, besides, lacked the largeness of vision to undertake such a gigantic project.[1] On July 23 Perkins of Louisiana offered resolutions in the House to the effect that the Confederate government take over the control of all cotton and tobacco so long as the blockade should continue, through means of a produce loan or by outright purchase by government notes.[2] A few days later Chilton brought up a bill with a similar provision,[3] but after reference to the Committee on Finance it was considered inexpedient at the time to undertake such a measure.[4] On September 24, 1862, Sparrow of Louisiana proposed in the Senate that the Confederacy take control of all cotton throughout the South.[5] On January 23, 1863, Phelan introduced a bill into the Senate calling for the condemnation of all cotton and tobacco for the use of the Confederacy.[6] As late as June, 1864, the question was still being discussed in Congress, but at this stage of the war the idea of preventing the exportation of cotton had grown very feeble, the dominant idea then being to provide the Confederate government through the sale of cotton with a means of purchasing materials of war in Europe.

The only material results from the agitation in Congress, aside from adding stimulus to the extra-legal and voluntary embargo, were the produce-loans by which a portion of the surplus cotton was turned over to the Confederate government in return for Confederate bonds. Congress had incorporated the produce-loan features in the acts of May 16, August 19, and December 24, 1861, by which fifty, one hundred, and one hundred and fifty million dollars' worth of bonds were issued, part of which were for the

---

[1] *Ibid.*

[2] *Jour. Confed. Cong.*, I, 276–77.

[3] *Ibid.*, p. 367.

[4] *Ibid.*, p. 429.

[5] *Ibid.*, II (1862), 325.

[6] *Ibid.*, III, 37.

purchase of cotton.[1] The produce-loan features were continued in the acts of April 21, 1862, and February 20 and April 30, 1863.[2] In placing these loans before the country the idea of the Confederacy's coercing England and France by a cotton famine into intervention and recognition was played upon strongly. It was urged by Ben Hill of Georgia that if the planters would subscribe a million bales of cotton in the fall of 1861, England would speedily break the blockade and recognize the independence of the South.[3] J. E. Ward assured a Georgia audience, some time later, that three million bales in the hands of the Confederacy would be a powerful means of coercing Europe, especially England, into intervention. England, he explained to his audience, was utterly selfish, utterly destitute of chivalry, but keenly alive to her own material interests and fearless in asserting those interests. When her mills should need the cotton, and the cotton was controlled by a determined government, she would have no scruples in interfering in behalf of the government which possessed the desired staple.[4] The cotton loan was a big success while the embargo idea was at its height. Under it 400,000 bales were subscribed by the first of December, 1861, and had the Confederacy offered notes instead of bonds that could not be negotiated, the entire supply of cotton would have been gladly turned over to the Confederacy. After 1861, however, when the idea of preventing cotton from going abroad had declined, only about 30,000 more bales were subscribed.[5]

Most of the state legislatures and executives assumed an attitude of opposition to the exportation of cotton, and placed many impediments both legal and extra-legal in the way of shipping cotton out. Governor Thomas Moore of Louisiana early in the fall of 1861 issued a proclamation that no cotton—not one bale—should be brought into New Orleans after October 10 of that year. Any

[1] Schwab, p. 12.   [2] *Ibid.*, pp. 24–25.

[3] Speech in *Savannah Republican*, July 4, 1861.

[4] *Ibid.*, Aug. 27, 1861.

[5] For discussion of cotton loans as a financial expedient see Schwab, pp. 1–44 and *passim.*

boat or other vehicle of transportation which should attempt to bring cotton into the city or within the proscribed territory was to be "forthwith indicted." The Governor explained in this proclamation that he was acting in concurrence with the expressed desire of the factors and merchants who had in August and several times since urged that no cotton be allowed to be brought into New Orleans or the surrounding districts;[1] and that, above all, he was acting in accord with public opinion. On this point he wrote Judah P. Benjamin, Confederate Attorney-General and acting Secretary of War, who had questioned on diplomatic grounds the legality of Moore's prohibition of the export of cotton: "I never supposed that I had any legal authority to obstruct the shipment of cotton from this state. The power that I exercised was in deference to and thoroughly supported by the well-matured opinion of the people of this city and state. Like other assumptions of power by me, it was sustained by public opinion, without which it would not have been undertaken and would have certainly been disregarded."[2]

In the spring of 1862 the Governor and Council of South Carolina passed a resolution forbidding the exportation of cotton from Charleston and other ports in the state.[3]

Governor Milton of Florida was the most ardent disciple of the King Cotton philosophy, and he did all in his power, whether legal, extra-legal, or actually illegal, to stop what he termed the "villainous traffic" of cotton through the blockade. For months he refused to allow a single bale of cotton to go to sea, and would have continued this refusal until the end of the Civil War had not Benjamin, as in the case of Moore of Louisiana, intervened for reasons of state.[4] But he continued to keep a jealous eye on the cotton trade and urged the Florida legislature to prohibit cotton export.[5] And later when realizing the inadequacy of the legislature

---

[1] *Charleston Courier*, Oct. 18, 1861; *London Economist*, Oct. 26, 1861; *Richmond Enquirer*, Oct. 15, 1861.

[2] *O.R.*, Ser. 4, Vol. I, pp. 836–37, Thomas O. Moore to Benjamin, Jan. 9, 1862.

[3] *Charleston Courier*, April 23, 1862; Schwab, pp. 250–51.

[4] *O.R.*, Ser. 4, Vol. II, pp. 58–59.   [5] *Ibid.*, p. 489.

to deal with the problem, he wrote the Florida members of the Confederate Congress to use their influence to pass a law "prohibiting under severe penalties shipments of cotton or other products from our ports, and under like penalties prohibiting the introduction of merchandise, not only from the United States, but all foreign countries which refuse to recognize the independence of the Confederate States of America." "Foreign subjects thus deprived of the cotton of the South," he urged, "will have a direct and powerful interest in the removal of the blockade." "Foreign nations will not recognize the independence of the Confederate States until Commerce with the Confederate States will become not only desirable, but necessary to their own prosperity."[1] Failing to obtain the cotton embargo, Milton appealed to Davis to bring about a law prohibiting the exportation of cotton, even going so far as to urge a complete non-intercourse act to force foreign intervention. "I know of no reason why, if England and France were willing to engage in war with China to secure commerce in opium with the Chinese people against their will and the decree of their government, England and France would not raise a blockade for commerce in cotton, tobacco, etc., with the Southern States, while their people desire and their Government proposed the commercial intercourse."[2]

Governor A. B. Moore of Alabama and his successor, Gil. Shorter, were for a long time actively opposed to the exportation of cotton from Mobile. Moore urged that the Confederate government come out with a regular embargo. "I would ask," he wrote Davis, February 3, 1862, "that the attention of Congress of the Confederate States be called to the interdiction of the export of cotton from all the Confederate ports until the close of the war or the negotiation of treaties of amity and commerce with the nations of Europe that may want cotton from us for their consumption. This leaky blockade system should be deprecated as one that parties to it are either dupes or knaves, and not in the least calculated to demon-

[1] *Ibid.*, pp. 56–59, Milton to Hon. James M. Baker, Hon. A. E. Maxwell, Hon. J. B. Dawkins, and Hon. A. B. Hilton, Aug. 18, 1862.

[2] *Ibid.*, pp. 488–89, Milton to Davis, April 18, 1863.

strate the fact that our cotton crops are a necessity to the commerce of the world."[1] Governor Shorter, who succeeded Moore, was backed by one of the ubiquitous committees of public safety so much complained of by the British consuls (see below). Its chairman, Peter Hamilton of Mobile, opposed the traffic and urged Confederate authorities to back him up in preventing it.[2]

Governor Clark of North Carolina voiced the same objection to the exportation of cotton and declined to interfere when the Committee of Public Safety in Wilmington refused to allow six English vessels to clear with their cargo.[3]

The Mississippi legislature and the Louisiana legislature both took steps to purchase cotton: in part to relieve the planters, but in part to prevent the cotton from being exported to Europe.[4]

Thus, newspapers, planters, factors, merchants, Congress, and state legislatures and executives all offered opposition to the export of cotton in the form of either advice or sterner means; but, backed by such strong sentiment in favor of an embargo, it was the citizens' organizations, usually taking the title of Committee of Public Safety, who said the final word in the matter of shipping cotton through the blockade. It was these local organizations, backed by public sentiment, which made it unnecessary, even superfluous, for Congress and the state legislatures to pass embargo acts. They saw that no cotton went through the blockade at the principal ports for many months—as long as the embargo policy was thought effective. It was these committees, so effectively preventing the British ships which ran the blockade from carrying out cotton, that caused the British consuls to warn the British government that the South was speaking one language through its diplomatic and administrative organs, but quite another through its more popular and informal mouthpieces. Consul Magee at Mobile had been worried lest the Confederate government place a legal embargo upon cotton, and had, during the spring and summer of 1861,

---

[1] *Ibid.*, Vol. I, p. 905, A. B. Moore to Davis, Feb. 3, 1862.

[2] *Ibid.*, Vol. II, pp. 461–63, 472–73.

[3] F.O. Amer., Vol. 781, Bunch to Russell, No. 115, Sept. 28, 1861.

[4] See Schwab, pp. 16–17, for details of acts of these legislatures.

so expressed his fears to the British Foreign Office.[1] Later[2] he wrote in disgust that he had been watching the wrong crowd, that though Congress might pass such a law, it would be unnecessary legislation as the local committees of planters, merchants, and exporters, and other citizens' groups had taken the situation into their own hands and were enforcing an embargo, without legal warrant. Consul Bunch, who had been worried, too, lest the Confederate government pass an embargo act,[3] wrote Lord Russell on September 13, 1861,[4] that the Confederate Congress had gone home without passing the dreaded embargo act; but a few days later he explained to Russell[5] indignantly what Magee had just said, that an act of Congress was unnecessary to prevent cotton from leaving the Confederate ports. "So far as the legislation of the South goes, there is no obstacle in the way of a foreign vessel which may run the blockade. But I regret to say that a very serious and probably insuperable impediment is to be found in that which has been the bane of this Republic since the introduction of universal suffrage,—I mean the uncontrollable will of an irresponsible community, which sets itself up above all law and supersedes constituted authority wherever it thinks fit to assume the management of office. The foreign commerce of both North Carolina and South Carolina is at this moment under their rule." He complained that in Charleston a leading mercantile firm "is prevented by outside pressure from sending to England a cargo of cotton in a vessel which had run the blockade bringing a valuable supply of articles of prime necessity." In Wilmington six British vessels were lying in port because a self-constituted Committee of Public Safety opposed their clearance. And these committees were all basing their action in preventing cotton from getting out of the South "upon the supposed vital necessity to England of southern cotton upon which very unstable basis it appears that

[1] F.O. Amer., Vol. 786, *passim*, Magee to Russell, July 18, 1861.

[2] *Ibid.*, Magee to Russell, Aug. 21, 1861.

[3] *Ibid.*, Vol. 781, Part II, *passim*.

[4] *Ibid.*, No. 107, Bunch to Russell, Sept., 13, 1861.

[5] *Ibid.*, No. 115, Sept. 28, 1861.

the southern people are content to found their empire." No appeal to the governors of the states had been effectual in removing these extra-legal impediments. They would pay the consul no heed!

The *Charleston Mercury* boasted that for a long time the Committee of Public Safety, in conjunction with the local authorities, had prevented the exportation of cotton from Charleston and that it was only when the influential house of John Fraser & Company had been given a special permit by the Confederate government to ship on government account that any cotton at all had gone out of the port. The *Mercury* lamented that this permission was the entering wedge which broke up the embargo at that port.[1] The *Richmond Enquirer*, quoting the *New Orleans Delta*,[2] summed up the situation, saying that in every southern state where the state authorities had not prevented the exportation of cotton it had been stopped by "the action of local committees and authorities."

There was then a real embargo for the greater part of the first year of the war, partly legal, but for the most part extra-legal or actually illegal. Congress had, as we have observed, passed numerous acts carrying certain restrictions upon the exportation of cotton. These acts included the law forbidding trade with the enemy; the act restricting the export of cotton to the Confederate seaports—which cut out the traffic in small boats along hundreds of miles of shallow seacoast; and the acts providing for produce loans. The first of these produce loans obtained control of practically all the residue of the 1860 cotton crop and prevented any exportation of this cotton during the summer and fall of 1861. Congress passed a joint resolution approving of the stand taken by the factors and cotton men generally in the seaports against the exportation of cotton until after the raising of the blockade. It was constantly discussing, during the first year, the proposal to forbid by law the exportation of cotton until the blockade had ceased and independence had been gained, creating the impression that Congress was thoroughly opposed to cotton leaving the South during the

[1] *Charleston Mercury* cited in *New York Herald*, Jan. 12, 1863.
[2] *Richmond Enquirer*, Oct. 15, 1861.

blockade. The governors of most of the states had been actively opposed to the exportation of cotton, favoring an embargo as a means of coercing Europe, and especially had public safety committees in all seaports, backed by public opinion, been actively engaged in seeing that no vessel loaded with cotton should start through the blockade. The newspapers had cried down without ceasing any idea of shipping cotton out. This complex of obstacles thrown in the path of cotton exportation created the impression in the South that the Confederate government objected to the shipment of cotton abroad, and the people, including many of the newspaper editors, had the idea that it was "against the law."[1]

The impression created abroad was that there was during 1861 an air-tight embargo on cotton, and that it would be useless to attempt to come into the blockaded ports to obtain it. (This impression, it might be stated here as an aside, was actively encouraged by the United States government through its consuls and ministers and special agents as it would serve to throw the blame of the cotton famine upon the Confederate government as well as to act as a restraint upon the blockade running business.) The *London Economist*,[2] whose judgment was entitled to weighty consideration and was trusted by the cautious commercial classes, including the cotton and shipping interests, expressed the opinion that the exportation of cotton was forbidden in the Confederacy during 1861, that the North and the South presented the strange spectacle of conspiring to prevent cotton from reaching Europe. The *London Times*[3] said that the running into Savannah of the ship "Bermuda" with the cargo of rifles and munition in the fall of 1861 proved to the world that the blockade was merely nominal and that the embargo was "the work of the South as much as the North." In addition, continued this paper, "If ships can get in they can also get out, and if the South desires to send us cotton it has not lacked the opportunity. But it seems to be quite true

[1] See, e.g., *O.R.*, Ser. 4, Vol. I, p. 633, Fraser & Co. to Benjamin, Sept. 30, 1861; *New Orleans True Delta*, Oct. 2, 1861; *Charleston Courier*, Sept. 24 and Oct. 12, 1861.

[2] *Economist*, June 22 and Sept. 21, 1861.

[3] *London Times* quoted in the *Savannah Republican*, Nov. 22, 1861.

that all cotton exportation has been forbidden by the Confederate Government in order that foreign nations may be forced to take a side in the quarrel." The *London Post*, Palmerston's official mouthpiece, was of the opinion that Congress had prohibited the exportation of cotton "to coerce England and France into the recognition of their national independence and sovereignty."[1] The *London Illustrated News*[2] asked what was the use for vessels to run the blockade if they were not permitted to bring out cotton. Even the British consul, Molyneux, residing at Savannah, wrote Lord Russell as late as December 4, 1861, that the Confederacy had passed an act making it a penal offense to ship cotton abroad.[3]

John Slidell on reaching Europe immediately wrote Benjamin, February 26, 1862, that the impression was universal that cotton could not be obtained from the South. He said the United States agents had been quite active in spreading this impression.[4] Some time later Benjamin wrote Mason, Confederate diplomatic agent residing in England, that he had learned that the impression was widespread that the Confederacy had placed an embargo upon cotton "with a view to extort from the necessities of neutral powers, that acknowledgement of our independence which they would otherwise decline to accord."[5] (It is probable that this was just the impression that the Confederate cabinet, especially Benjamin, who was well known as a champion of the King Cotton doctrine, had desired. But the results had been to cause resentment against the Confederacy and at the same time help create the impression that the blockade was really effective.)

The effectiveness of the embargo, during the year 1861 and far into the winter of 1862, was complete. It was, as the English had supposed, just as near air-tight as human effort could make

[1] *London Post* quoted in the *Charleston Courier*, Oct. 2, 1861.

[2] *London Illustrated News* quoted in the *Charleston Courier*, Sept. 30, 1861.

[3] F.O. Amer., Vol. 786, Molyneux to Russell, No. 35, Dec. 4, 1861.

[4] Pickett Papers, Slidell to Benjamin, No. 2 with inclosures, Feb. 26, 1862; also reprinted in *O.R.N.*, Ser. 2, Vol. III, pp. 350–51.

[5] Pickett Papers, Benjamin to Mason, instructions No. 2, April 8, 1862; *O.R.N.*, Ser. 2, Vol. III, pp. 379–84.

it. No embargo in history has been any more strict. The usual amount of cotton arriving at the ports of Memphis, New Orleans, Savannah, Mobile, and Charleston, taking the five most important ports, from September to January was around 1,500,000 bales. From September, 1860, to January, 1861, for instance, 1,488,004 bales had reached those ports. But from September, 1861, to January, 1862, the time covered by the embargo, only 9,863 bales had arrived at those ports.[1] Not only were less than 10,000 bales sent to the five principal cotton ports where the year before 1,500,000 bales had been sent during the same period, but quantities of cotton remaining in port from the previous year were removed back to the plantations.[2] Though the South had raised 4,490,586 bales of cotton during the first year of the war,[3] it was, as far as England and France were concerned, as though the South had not cultivated an acre or produced a bale of cotton. The power of cotton in diplomacy had been put to the test, and, as we know, failed to move England and France to intervene.

After the spring of 1862 the cotton embargo was slowly relaxed until it completely ceased. Some confidence had been lost in the power of cotton, but this was not so much the cause of the letting-up of the embargo as the absolute and immediate necessity the South labored under of obtaining supplies from abroad; and cotton was by the spring of 1862 the only medium of exchange left in the South which was acceptable abroad. Besides, it was realized now by the southern leaders that enough cotton could not get through the tightening blockade to stave off the cotton famine looming up like a black cloud over England and France.[4]

[1] *Charleston Courier*, Jan. 16, 1862; *London Times*, Jan. 10, 1862, cited in Scherer, p. 266.

[2] *Ibid.*

[3] *Department of Commerce Bull. 131* (Washington, D.C., 1915); cited in Scherer, p. 420 (Appendix F).

[4] See *New Orleans True Delta*, Oct. 7, 1861, which at that date held that the amount of cotton it was possible to ship abroad would have no effect upon the cotton famine, but might procure enough war material to assure the South its independence; a correspondent in the *Savannah Republican* thought it absurd to say that any amount of cotton it was possible to ship abroad under blockade conditions could relieve England so

REDUCING THE COTTON SUPPLY

The raising of the embargo did not mean that King Cotton had been dethroned, spat upon, and reduced to ranks as one observer remarked. The embargo always dealt with the supply of cotton on hand, and Europe might be little troubled by an embargo as long as it was known that there was an enormous quantity of cotton behind that embargo, only awaiting the favorable opportunity to be brought out. The South, far from giving up the King Cotton idea with the failure of the embargo, actually resorted to more spectacular and seemingly desperate expedients to coerce Europe into intervention. It undertook to put fear into the hearts of the English and French nations, not by withholding the cotton already produced, but by destroying the supply on hand with the torch and refusing to produce another crop. The burning of cotton and the drastic reduction of the crop after 1861 is more or less a familiar story to most students of the Civil War.

In the early months of the war nothing was said about burning cotton or the restriction of the cotton crop. The assumption was that war would not last any longer than the beginning of the year 1862, when England and France would be forced to intervene by the scarcity of cotton, thus making it unnecessary to plan any further ahead. But in the late fall of 1861 it began to appear that England and France were still not sufficiently reduced by the cotton shortage to intervene in the near future; and there commenced agitation to burn the present stock and not produce any further supply until recognition and the raising of the blockade should come. The *Memphis Appeal* sounded the call for the planters to rally for the new onslaught under the banner of King Cotton. The *Appeal* urged that little, if any, cotton should be planted in

---

she would bear her trials and not break the blockade. "Of one thing we may be sure, the distress of Europe from the want of cotton, whether more or less, whether from no supply or from a half supply, is more than she will consent to bear" (*ibid.*, Oct. 2, 1861). This point was more and more widely agitated as time passed. See, e.g., *Charleston Courier*, Sept. 24, 25, and Oct. 11, 25, 1861; *Savannah Republican*, Oct. 16, 1861; *New Orleans True Delta*, Aug. 11, 1861; *O.R.*, Ser. 4, Vol. I, p. 633, Fraser & Co. to Benjamin, Sept. 30, 1861.

1862. The less cotton planted, it argued, "the more forcibly we can impress upon the North and upon the powers of Europe, who countenance a sham blockade, their dependence upon our soil for the material that has hitherto kept their millions from want, and the scarcity of which has already caused the cry of bread and threatened revolution if not supplied."[1] The *Charleston Courier*, some weeks later,[2] was even more urgent and dramatic than the *Memphis Appeal* in its insistence that the planters refrain from producing cotton more than sufficient for home use. The *Courier* contended that not over a fifth of a crop should be planted in 1862, and urged that the curtailment of the crop should be heralded abroad as a powerful means of coercing England and France. The belief was prevalent that England could endure for a longer time the detention of cotton if supported by the knowledge that it was growing and would be obtainable for a few pence per pound when trade opened. "If we mistake not," remarked the *Courier*, "she is laboring under some such delusion as this. But this delusion must be exploded, and to do it effectually, it is necessary only to curtail the culture of cotton throughout every state in the Southern Confederacy. Let it be known to England .... it will strike terror throughout her entire domain, and she will be compelled by the first law of nature to strike through Lincoln's blockade and recognize the Confederacy as one of the independent sovereigns of the earth. This is an assertion which must come to pass if we adopt the only true policy—that of curtailing the culture of cotton." This sentiment was heartily indorsed by such papers as the *Charleston Mercury, Richmond Enquirer, Richmond Despatch, Mobile Register, Montgomery Advertiser*—in fact, by all the leading journals of the South. As the several southern-states legislatures assembled, they too urged that little cotton be planted, and a planters' convention was called to meet in Memphis in February representing every southern state, for the purpose of curtailing the 1862 cotton crop.[3]

[1] *Memphis Appeal* quoted in the *Savannah Republican*, Dec. 4, 1861.

[2] *Charleston Courier*, Jan. 18, 1862; cf. *ibid.*, Jan. 15, 1862.

[3] *Savannah Republican*, Dec. 27, 1861.

The country being well agreed as to the policy of curtailing the next cotton crop, the Confederate Congress went on record as approving the idea. Already Davis had foreshadowed the effects of restriction in his message on November 18, 1861.[1] On February 26, 1862, Holt of Georgia, one of the standing champions of the King Cotton doctrine, introduced a resolution in the Confederate House of Representatives asking that the Ways and Means Committee "be instructed to inquire into the expediency of restricting and limiting by law the production of cotton in the Confederacy during the continuance of the war and the blockade, etc."[2] After a couple of weeks of debate and discussion the House decided to take a more positive stand than Holt's resolution had called for. It passed a joint resolution that absolutely no cotton ought to be planted in 1862.[3] When this joint resolution was submitted to the Senate, it was at first rejected by a narrow majority.[4] On reconsideration it was passed.[5] Not only this but a measure for prohibiting the culture of cotton during the war and the continuance of the blockade was taken under serious consideration.[6] Thus Congress, in the spring of 1862, indorsed by joint resolution what had been determined to a certain extent already by public press, farmers' conventions, and state legislatures, namely, that the cotton crop of 1862 should be curtailed as a means of bringing pressure to bear upon England and France.

The idea of burning cotton went hand in hand with that of curtailing the crop. On February 25, 1862, immediately after the Federals began their advance into the Tennessee and Mississippi cotton belt, with all its hoard of wealth which would so quickly ease the strain on the Federal finances and relieve the distress of England and France if it were to fall into the clutches of the invading hosts, the Confederate Senate urged, in a resolution, that the Confederate government take charge of the cotton in this territory

---

[1] Richardson, *Messages and Papers of the Confederacy* (2 vols., Washington, D.C., and Nashville, Tenn., 1905), I, 136–44.

[2] *Jour. Confed. Cong.*, V, 29.

[3] *Ibid.*, p. 76.

[4] *Ibid.*, II, 57.

[5] *Ibid.*, pp. 59, 62, 67.

[6] *Ibid.*, pp. 67, 69, 72.

and all other threatened districts and burn it when there was danger of capture.[1] And on March 17, 1862, a few days after the joint resolution had passed urging the planters to refrain from the cultivation of cotton during that year, Congress enacted a law providing for the destruction of all cotton and tobacco, etc., when in the slightest danger of falling into the hands of the enemy.[2] During the debate, Brown of Mississippi, who was a firm believer in King Cotton until the bitter end, argued that the Confederacy should purchase all the cotton and then set fire to it and prohibit the further cultivation of cotton until England and France had come to the aid of the South.[3]

The cotton crop of 1862 certainly felt the weight of all this agitation in favor of curtailment. Only about a million and a half bales were produced as compared with four and a half million for 1861.[4] And hundreds of thousands of bales were put to the torch during the spring and summer of 1862. Every newspaper—southern, northern, and English—carried the story of the burning of cotton and the reduction of the crop. Lyons, the British minister at Washington, wrote dispatches about it; the French minister, Mercier, was even more worried in his letters to Thouvenel and De Lhuys;[5] and the French and British consuls in the South were in great agitation.

The Confederate government was keeping these agents of the French and English governments posted, of course, as the *Charleston Courier* had advocated in the early winter.[6] It was the business of the Confederate government to see that England and France were agitated by the sight of burning cotton and the report of short production. Henry Hotze, the secret agent of the Confederate

---

[1] *Ibid.*, p. 20.

[2] *Ibid.*, p. 69; see *O.R.*, Ser. 4, Vol. III, pp. 1066-67.

[3] See *London Times*, May 3, 1862, for report of debate; or *Jour. Confed. Cong.*, II, 30.

[4] *Dept. Com. Bull. 131* (Washington, D.C., 1915), p. 82; cited in Scherer.

[5] See, e.g., France F.O. Amer., Vol. 127, Mercier to Thouvenel, No. 97, April 28, 1862; U.S. Des., France, Vol. 51, Dayton to Seward, No. 129, March 25. 1862, "Confidential" describing interview with Napoleon, who feared burning of cotton.

[6] *Charleston Courier*, Jan. 18, 1862.

government and clever editor of the Confederate English journal, the *Index*, played up the news of crop curtailment and burning with great skill. On May 15, 1862, the *Index* carried the unpleasant announcement that very little cotton had been planted in the South. But more than that, thus far "the burning of cotton has . . . . lighted the footsteps of the enemy across our border, and henceforth they will get possession of none of that staple, whatever success may attend them."[1] On May 22 the *Index* quoted the *Louisville Despatch* as saying that "along the Mississippi from New Orleans to Memphis there is a general bonfire of prosperity, particularly cotton." Millions of dollars' worth of the white gold was going up in black smoke, so the reports indicated, and the English and French operatives were already on half-time and charity. Again and again this Confederate propagandist sheet, supplied with information by the Confederate government, recurred to the tale of frightful destruction painted in language such as to make the greedy eyes of the cotton manufacturers and speculators pop out on stems.[2] One time it was ten million dollars' worth of cotton destroyed on the fall of New Orleans, another time it was ten thousand bales destroyed near Franklin, Tennessee; fifty thousand bales ready for destruction on the approach of the enemy at Montgomery, Alabama; one hundred thousand bales burnt about Memphis. Another carried the distressing tale of between half and a million bales burned on the Mississippi.

Benjamin informed Consul Cridland some time in May that even at that date the Confederate government had already burned one million bales in the Mississippi Valley alone, and Cridland immediately wrote to Sir John Russell about this dreadful conflagration.[3] Russell allowed the newspapers to broadcast the consular reports touching these matters. Cridland wrote frequently during the spring and summer that England's future supply of cotton was going up in flame.[4] On June 22, 1862, Consul Bunch, who had

[1] *Index*, May 15, 1862; cf. issue of May 22, 1862.

[2] See, e.g., issues of June 5, 26, and July 17, 31, 1862.

[3] F.O. Amer., Vol. 846, Cridland to Russell, No. 13, June 9, 1862.

[4] *Ibid., passim.*

been informed through the Confederate government, reported to Russell that over a million bales had been burned.[1] Consul Molyneux reported the constant burning of cotton everywhere.[2] Consul Coppell at New Orleans reported a similar tale.[3] In short, the Confederate government did burn cotton ruthlessly—and even needlessly—and it was seen that both the British government and the British people should know about it, and a perusal of Mercier's correspondence with his government shows that the French consuls too were being well posted as to the burning and curtailment of the cotton crop.

And the stories that carried the news of the burning of the hundreds of thousands and eventually millions of bales usually bore the tidings of the less spectacular but just as effective expedient of coercion—the curtailment of the crop of 1862. The *Index* kept before the British the fact that there would be little cotton produced in 1862.[4] The British consuls reported to the Foreign Office, which in turn gave out the distressing news that not only was the crop of 1861 fast being destroyed, but that there would be practically no crop in 1862. Bunch, as early as April 5, informed Russell that there would be little cotton planted,[5] and in June he could assure Russell that little had been planted.[6] Cridland reported[7] that the South had made good its threats to plant but little cotton in 1862.

When the crop question of 1862 had been settled and it was seen that England and France were still not ready to interfere, there was agitation for further curtailment for 1863. The irascible Joseph E. Brown of Georgia urged the legislature of that state to tax every bale of cotton one hundred dollars in excess of a certain amount per hand. "Why raise cotton," he asked, "and keep it for the benefit of commercial nations after we have achieved our

[1] *Ibid.*, Vol. 843, Bunch to Russell, No. 85, June 25, 1862.

[2] *Ibid.*, Vol. 849, Molyneux to Russell, Nov. 11, 1862.

[3] *Ibid.*, Vol. 908, Coppell to Russell, No. 11, April 1, 1862.

[4] See, e.g., issues of May 22 and July 22, 1862.

[5] F.O. Amer., Vol. 843, Bunch to Russell, No. 60, April 5, 1862.

[6] *Ibid.*, No. 83, June 25, 1862, and *passim*.

[7] *Ibid.*, Vol. 846, Cridland to Russell, No. 13, June 9, 1862, and *passim*.

independence? They have left us at a critical period to take care of ourselves. Why then should we not leave them to feed their own operatives till such a time as it is compatible with our public interest to produce the supply of cotton without which they must number their paupers by millions and support them by taxation?"[1] The newspapers and leaders, including most of the governors, the President himself, and Congress, urged that the cultivation of cotton be practically dropped. Every state legislature advised or enacted laws prohibiting the culture of cotton beyond certain very low limits. Georgia, under the urging of Brown, prohibited the cultivation of over three acres of cotton to the laborer.[2] South Carolina limited the culture to one acre to the laborer.[3] Congress recommended as in 1862 that the cotton crop be restricted,[4] and the President urged that the advice of Congress be followed.[5] The cotton crop of 1863 was barely enough for home use, being only 449,059 bales.[6]

In 1864 the cotton crop was reduced again by half, being only 299,372 bales. As for the burning of cotton, though there developed strong private sentiment against it, there was no slacking-up. The Confederate government continued ruthlessly to burn wherever its armies were compelled to withdraw from a region. At least 2,500,000 bales must have been destroyed in this way by 1865.

Thus, we see, in retrospect, that the South believed so firmly in the power of cotton to break the blockade and gain recognition that when the war broke out, an air-tight embargo was placed upon the export of cotton, not by the Confederate Congress, but by state and local officials and public safety committees backed by an almost unanimous public opinion. When it was realized that not enough cotton could be shipped through the Federal blockade

[1] *Ibid.*, Vol. 849, Molyneux to Russell, No. 24, Nov. 11, 1862.

[2] See *O.R.*, Ser. 4, Vol. II, p. 376, Davis to Brown, Jan. 27, 1863.

[3] F.O. Amer., Vol. 906, Walker to Russell, No. 63, May 1, 1863; cf. *ibid.*, No. 50, April 6, 1863.

[4] *O.R.*, Ser. 4, Vol. II, p. 468, Joint Resolution, April 4, 1863.

[5] *Ibid.*, pp. 475–77, Proclamation of the President.

[6] Cited in Scherer; *Dept. Com. Bull. 131* (Washington, D.C., 1915), p. 82.

to stave off the cotton famine in England and France and when at the same time the Confederate government had no other means with which to purchase materials of war abroad, the embargo was gradually relaxed. It finally disappeared some time in 1862. After that, while the belief in King Cotton was weakening, the restriction of the cotton crop and the burning of the stock on hand were adopted as substitutes for the embargo in bringing pressure to bear upon England and France. After 1863 the King Cotton idea practically disappeared, as far as coercing Europe was concerned —though it was still hoped to bankrupt the United States—and the limitation of cotton crops after this was chiefly in the interest of a food supply.

CHAPTER II

THE FIRST ENVOYS OF THE COTTON KINGDOM

THE YANCEY-ROST-MANN MISSION

On March 16, 1861, Robert Toombs, Confederate Secretary of State, instructed three commissioners, William Lowndes Yancey, Pierre A. Rost, and Ambrose Dudley Mann, to proceed to Europe and seek recognition and treaties of commerce and amity from England, France, Spain, Belgium, and Russia.[1]

The three men selected to go to Europe were about the poorest choices possible. In the first place, William L. Yancey, of Alabama, who was to head the mission, was internationally known as a champion of slavery. He was known to have urged for years the reopening of the slave trade so that enough slaves might be spread over the South and made sufficiently cheap for every adult person to acquire at least one slave. Believing slavery not only to be right but a positive blessing to humanity, the Confederate leaders could naturally ill afford to assume an apologetic attitude toward the institution which was the corner stone of their new state. On the other hand, to dispatch as chief of the diplomatic mission a man who advocated a militant attitude on the slave trade was extremely naïve or extremely arrogant and, whether the one or the other, very disregardful of the strong antislavery sentiment of both England and France. As to the actual abilities of W. L. Yancey, that is another question. If he had not been so identified with the institution which both England and France hated, he might have been fairly well qualified to send to Europe to obtain recognition. Yancey was a very able man and perhaps the greatest orator of his day in America either North or South. Despite his reputation as a "fire-eater" he was possessed of poise and dignity. He could win and hold spellbound by his magnetism, self-command, and coolness the most hostile audiences. In private intercourse he was straightforward and pleasant mannered. He was

[1] Pickett Papers, Toombs to Yancey, Mann, and Rost, March 16, 1861; *O.R.N.*, Ser. 2, Vol. III, pp. 191–95.

known as a man of deep convictions. In a land of dreamers he was a rather clear-sighted realist in most matters, though he shared the "King Cotton delusion" along with the rest of the southerners.[1]

Pierre A. Rost was a former judge, born in France but reared in Louisiana. His qualifications as a diplomat are doubtful, though Henry S. Sanford, United States minister to Belgium, was convinced that his thorough knowledge of the French language and his acquaintance with the principal men abroad were beneficial to the secessionists.[2]

As for A. Dudley Mann, it is difficult to see just what Davis could have had in mind in sending him abroad; surely it was not to get him safely out of the country so as to render him harmless as is sometimes said about the sending abroad of William L. Yancey. Mann was harmless either at home or abroad. Never in the four years he was in Europe did he do any serious damage to the Confederacy. He seemed to have stepped out of the pages of a book. He spoke like a Polonius, full of words and wind; ever deducing wisdom from events and usually wrong; never using simple, direct language when it was possible to roll out some well-rounded period; ever waxing eloquent over the most trivial and unimportant thing; always calling upon Almighty God to whom he gave part credit for his trivial successes greatly magnified, retaining the remainder of the doubtful credit to himself. Lacking in penetration, and rather credulous, he believed the first man who got to him with a story and afterward believed no one else who gave a different version. Mann possessed great vanity and ego, but had social charm. He was able to penetrate inner circles and had friends in high places.

Under the old government he had served as a kind of ubiquitous

[1] There is no adequate life of Yancey, but see Du Bose, *Yancey*, and Joseph Hodgson, *The Cradle of the Confederacy, or the Times of Troup, Quitman, and Yancey* (Mobile, 1876), *passim*.

[2] Paul Du Bellet, "The Diplomacy of the Confederate Cabinet" (typed copy in the Pickett Papers, Manuscripts Division, Library of Congress), pp. 13–16. Du Bellet was the disgruntled Confederate citizen from New Orleans who stayed in Paris during the Civil War, trying to instruct Confederate agents how to run their jobs and, because he was singularly unsuccessful, disliked everything that was done. In this manuscript he gives sketches of the various Confederate agents. His opinion of Judge Rost is not flattering. Also see U.S. Des., Belgium, Vol. 5, Sanford to Seward, Private, Aug. 6, 1861.

peripatetic diplomat seeking out the petty German courts and drawing up some rather good treaties. Once during the Kossuth régime he had been appointed minister to the revolted Hungarian state, but had not been able to find the government to which he had been accredited.[1]

Toombs instructed Yancey, Rost, and Mann to proceed to Europe. They were to approach the English first. When that country had recognized the independence of the Confederacy, they were to go at once to the court of Napoleon, gain his recognition, and from there proceed to Russia and Belgium in the order named.[2] The commission was instructed to explain, in the first place, that the act of secession was not revolution, but that the seceding states had merely "reassumed the powers which they delegated to the Federal Government for certain specified purposes under the compact known as the Constitution of the United States, and have formed an independent government, perfect in all its branches, and endowed with every attribute of sovereignty and power necessary to entitle them to assume a place among the nations of the world." "In withdrawing from the United States," the commission was to hold, "the Confederate States have not violated any obligation of allegiance. They have merely exercised the sovereignty which they have possessed since their separation from Great Britain, and jealously guarded, by revoking the authority which, for defined purposes and within defined limits, they had voluntarily delegated to the General Government, and by reassuming themselves the exercise of the authority delegated." This would appeal to such reactionary governments as Russia, who might be offended at the idea of revolution, but deceived by clothing the act with legality. More than an assurance to reactionary governments, this was an appeal to the chief European powers to decide the whole issue of state rights which had been the subject of bitter controversy since the foundation of the republic. What Hamilton and Jefferson, Webster and Calhoun,

[1] Mann has left memoirs, but the opinion and estimate here expressed are based upon his letters and dispatches written while he was Confederate commissioner to Europe.

[2] Pickett Papers, Toombs to Yancey, Mann, and Rost, March 16, 1861; *O.R.N.*, Ser. 2, Vol. III, pp. 191–95.

could not settle, Europe was to be asked to decide in favor of the South. Strange as it may seem to this age of realism with its scorn of ideas and "principles," the state-rights argument impressed the Europeans, who were not so far removed from the political philosophy of John Locke and the Revolutionary philosophers as not to understand the significance of the terms "compact," "reserved rights," and other southern political phraseology.

Although secession was to be established as legal, it was to be shown that this legal right had been asserted as a last resort for self-preservation. It was to be shown in support of this assertion that by means of a protective tariff levied by force of numbers the North had forced the South to pay tribute to that section. "You can point with force to the efforts which have been persistently made by the manufacturing States of the North to compel the agricultural interests of the South, out of the proceeds of their industry, to pay bounties to Northern manufacturers in the shape of high-protective duties on foreign imports. Since the year 1828, whenever they had the power, the manufacturing Northern States, disregarding the obligations of our compact, in violation of the principles of justice and fair dealing, and in contempt of all remonstrance and entreaty, have carried this policy to great extremes, to the serious detriment of the industry and enterprise of the South." The recently enacted Morrill tariff was pointed out as a striking illustration of the self-seeking attitude of the North, which took advantage of a supposed temporary absence of the southern members of Congress to enact the highest tariff since the "tariff of abominations." Not only was the North overstepping the bounds of the compact by passing sectional tariff laws, but it was committing a general trespass upon the reserved rights of the states. Toombs instructed the commissioners to state that in addition to the tariff "by which millions were annually extorted from our people to foster Northern monopolies, the attempt was made to overthrow the constitutional barriers by which our property, our social system and our right to control our own institutions were protected," and that "separation from associates who recognize no law but self-interests and the power of numerical superiority became a necessity dictated by the instincts of self-preservation." Secession being thus justified upon legal and moral grounds, the commissioners were to show that the *sine qua non* of recognition had been fulfilled by the Confederacy in the premises; that is, that the South had set up an orderly government and was well prepared to maintain that government in the face of any opposition that the United States might offer. In support of the contention that the South could maintain itself, it was to be shown that it possessed about half the Atlantic Coast and the entire Mexican Gulf states, and including the border states which would join the Confederacy in case coercion were attempted, had a population of around eleven million people. But more than the resources for defense, it was to be shown that opinion in the North was largely opposed to coercion.

But the matters thus far noted offered no material inducements for Europe to grant recognition. Unless unmentioned political benefits of a divided America be considered, the Confederacy would be the sole gainer. However, the South did offer one positive inducement: It was to the effect that the duties levied upon imports would be for revenue only, in fact "so moderate as to closely approximate free trade," and "render this market peculiarly accessible to the manufactories of Europe"; and that the liberal navigation system of the Confederacy "will present valuable attractions to countries largely engaged" in trade and manufacture. The greatest inducement, in fact, as we have already seen in the previous chapter, almost the sole immediate inducement—and the basis of the hopes of the commissioners and the people who sent them—was the negative one that Europe could not get cotton unless it came after it; that is, unless it could break any attempted blockade. On this point Robert Toombs instructed the commission with reference to Great Britain from whom most was expected on this King Cotton theory. "There is," he asserted, "no extravagance in the assertion that the gross amount of the annual yield of the manufactories of Great Britain from the cotton of the Confederate States reaches $600,000,000. The British ministry will comprehend fully the condition to which the British realm would be reduced if the supply of our staple should suddenly fail or even be considerably diminished.

A delicate allusion to the probability of such an occurrence might not be unkindly received by the minister of foreign affairs, an occurrence, I will add, that is inevitable if this country shall be involved in protracted hostilities with the North."[1] This was high ground for a revolutionary state to assume. It might well be said that the commissioners went abroad armed with a dissertation on state sovereignty in their right pockets and a sample of New Orleans middling upland cotton in their left. Perhaps this was symbolical of the incongruous combination of hard materialism and lofty idealism which animated the South.

Having received their instructions and credentials the three commissioners set out for Europe the following day. Mann reached London on April 15; Yancey and Rost, on April 29.[2] Already there were active champions of the South at hand ready to aid the commissioners, and one of the most ardent of these, W. H. Gregory, M.P., arranged an informal interview with Russell for May 3, four days after the arrival of Rost and Yancey.

In the absence of new instructions they presented, unofficially, the substance of their original instructions of March 16, despite the fact that news of the outbreak of the war had reached England. Russell, they wrote to Toombs, warned the commissioners before they presented their case that though "it would give pleasure to hear what we had to communicate—he should, under present circumstances, have little to say." With this noncommittal opening and with the clear-spoken, intensely earnest, and convincing Yancey as chief spokesman, the interview proceeded. It was pointed out according to instructions that secession was legal, and that it was justified by the steady encroachment of the Federal government upon the reserved rights of the states—in fact, that the Federal government had become an instrument of oppression in the hands of the northern majority to squeeze tribute from the South and threaten the very destruction of southern society. They pled the peaceful nature

---

[1] *Ibid.*

[2] Pickett Papers, Yancey and Mann to Toombs, No. 1, May 21, 1861; *O.R.N.*, Ser. 2, Vol. III, p. 214.

of the secession of the South and its desire to remain at peace with the world. Above all, they attempted to prove to Russell the ability of the South to maintain its independence in case war should come. Russell seemed much interested in this question and roused himself out of his habitually cold and reserved manner to ask many searching and pertinent questions as to the strength of the South in the sinews of war and its determination to establish a separate state. The commissioners supplied him promptly with much convincing information, and if there were any doubts in his mind before the meeting as to the ultimate success of the South, there were few doubts when Yancey and the others had finished speaking. Saving their strongest weapon for the last, they dragged forth the lever which was calculated to topple England from her neutral perch: They followed Toombs's instructions by making a "delicate allusion" to the consequences to England of cutting off the supply of cotton from the South. "We concluded the conversation," wrote the commissioners to Toombs, "upon our part by expressing a hope that the government of Great Britain would find it to be not only for the benefit of industrial interests generally, but as tending to subserve the interest of peace, civilization . . . . that it should recognize the independence of the Confederate states of America at an early date." Russell asked about the rumor of the reopening of the slave trade, which Yancey promptly denied.[1] Finally, the Secretary assured the commissioners that though he could not express an opinion immediately, he would make the matter the subject of a cabinet discussion as soon as possible.[2] Yancey and Mann reported to Toombs in connection with this interview that although England was profoundly hostile to the Confederacy on the slavery question, the prevailing opinion of the public men in that country was that recognition would not be long withheld despite that hostility. In fact, they felt that England and France would grant recognition as soon as the Confederate States had gained a

[1] F.O. Amer., Vol. 755, Russell to Lyons, No. 128, May 11, 1861.

[2] For an account of this interview see Pickett Papers, W. L. Yancey and A. Dudley Mann to Hon. Robert Toombs, No. 1, May 21, 1861; W. L. Yancey, P. A. Rost, and A. Dudley Mann to Toombs, etc., No. 2, June 1, 1861. These dispatches are also printed in O.R.N., Ser. 2, Vol. III, pp. 214–16 and 219–21, respectively.

decisive victory in an important battle, for England at least "is not averse to a disintegration of the United States."[1]

In the meanwhile, Russell had been quietly laying the grounds for the recognition of the belligerency of the South by an agreement with France to act jointly upon this and other matters pertaining to America. He had on May 1 apprised the retiring American minister, Dallas, that France and England would act together, though he had not committed himself as to what their action would be.[2] On May 3, the day on which he had the first interview with the Confederate commissioners, Russell received a memorandum from the attorney-general advocating the necessity of recognizing the South as a belligerent;[3] and Russell wrote Lyons unofficially on May 4 that the South must be recognized as a belligerent.[4] On May 6 he notified Lyons officially of this contemplated action of Great Britain.[5] The same day Russell announced in Parliament that England would recognize the belligerent rights of the South and instructed Lord Cowley, British ambassador at the Tuileries, to request France to join in the recognition.[6] On May 7 Cowley wrote Russell that Thouvenel would act in harmony with Russell in issuing a proclamation of neutrality which would carry the recognition of belligerency.[7] On May 13 the proclamation was authorized by the Foreign Office, and on May 14 it was published in the *London Gazette*.[8] This was a tremendous step in favor of the Confederacy, and the whole thing was carried out without the aid and to a great extent without the knowledge of the Confederate diplomatic agents. It would seem that it were quite superfluous to have diplomatic representatives in England or France. Not only was this a great concession to the South, but it was a blow to the United States—one never forgotten during the war and for a long time afterward, for it continued for years to be the subject

[1] Pickett Papers, W. L. Yancey and A. Dudley Mann to Toombs, No. 1, May 21, 1861; *O.R.N.*, Ser. 2, Vol. III, p. 216.

[2] *U.S. Messages and Documents* (1861–62), pp. 83–84.

[3] E. D. Adams, I, 86.   [4] *Ibid.*

[5] F.O. Amer., Vol. 755, Russell to Lyons, No. 121, May 6, 1861.

[6] E. D. Adams, I, 88.

[7] F.O. France, Vol. 1390, Cowley to Russell, No. 677, May 7, 1861.

[8] E. D. Adams, I, 92 n.

of serious and threatening diplomatic controversies between the United States and England. In fact, because of the proclamation of neutrality, the South almost realized its ambitions of drawing England in upon its side. It was issued before the new American minister, C. F. Adams, had taken up his official duties at London; and Adams, May 18, in an interview with Russell, protested that the action was taken in unseemly haste, showing a bias in favor of the Confederacy, inasmuch as it pronounced the insurgents to be a belligerent state "before they had ever showed their capacity to maintain any kind of warfare whatever, except within one of their own harbors and under every possible advantage. . . . . It considered them a marine power before they had ever exhibited a single privateer upon the ocean."[1]

While this business of the neutrality proclamation was being worked out by the British and French Foreign Office, the Confederate commissioners were granted another interview on May 9 in order to present their recent instructions and information, received since their first interview with Russell, with reference to the outbreak of war. Russell assured them in this as in the first interview that he would take up the matter of recognition with the cabinet as soon as convenient. The commissioners, in summing up their opinions as a result of this conversation with Lord Russell, wrote Toombs that the English government would postpone the "recognition of the independence of those States [Confederate] as long as possible, at least until some decided advantage is obtained by them or the necessity for having cotton becomes pressing."[2]

After the interviews with Lord Russell, Judge Rost hastened to Paris to see whether anything could be gained there in the immediate future. He had an interview with Count de Morny, the half-brother and intimate friend and adviser of the Emperor. Rost urged recognition upon the Count, presenting the case as it had been presented to Russell. De Morny seemed very friendly; he assured Rost that

[1] *U.S. Messages and Documents* (1861–62), pp. 90–96, Adams to Seward, May 21, 1861.

[2] Pickett Papers, W. L. Yancey, P. A. Rost, and A. Dudley Mann to Toombs, No. 2, June 1, 1861; *O.R.N.*, Ser. 2, Vol. III, pp. 219–21.

the South should be treated with perfect neutrality for the present. He told Rost that neither France nor England desired the United States to be restored as before—it was not to their interests. But at the present nothing could be done beyond the recognition of belligerency. He advised Rost against trying to obtain recognition at this juncture, as it would only result in injury to the South. However, the recognition of the South "was, in his opinion, a mere question of time." While France would be unable to receive the commissioners officially, De Morny assured Rost that the "French Government would always be ready to receive unofficially and to give due consideration to any suggestions" offered by the Confederate agents "provided strict secrecy were maintained." One of the most hopeful promises was with reference to the blockade; De Morny virtually pledged Rost that France would not recognize the blockade. He assured Rost, according to the latter's report, that "so long as we produced cotton for sale, France and England would see that their vessels reached the ports where it was to be had." This looked very much as if the theory of King Cotton would work perfectly.[1]

Three weeks after this favorable conversation, Rost and Yancey, who had now joined the former in Paris, wrote Toombs again that both France and England were only lying on their oars waiting for a decisive southern victory. But, once they were satisfied that the North and South were irreconcilable, cotton would move these two powers to intervention. "They will be easily satisfied as to our ability to maintain our position, and . . . . when the cotton crop is ready for market, their necessities will force them to conclusions favorable to the South."[2]

After coming back to London for consultation around the first of June, Rost again returned to France to be followed soon by Yancey. Rost obtained an interview with Thouvenel, who assured him as De Morny had done that neutrality would be maintained and that

[1] Interview described in Pickett Papers, W. L. Yancey and A. Dudley Mann to Toombs, No. 1, May 21, 1861; also *O.R.N.*, Ser. 2, Vol. III, pp. 214–16. The interview is further described in Pickett Papers, Yancey, Rost, and Mann to Toombs, No. 2, June 1, 1861; *O.R.N.*, Ser. 2, Vol. III, pp. 219–21.

[2] Pickett Papers, Yancey and Rost to Toombs, June 10, 1861; *O.R.N.*, Ser. 2, Vol. III, p. 221.

it would be unwise at the moment to press for recognition. Rost and Yancey were impressed with the apparent lack of interest in American affairs on the part of the Emperor. Yancey was of the opinion that Napoleon was far more concerned with European affairs and would, therefore, let England make the decision. This is an interesting commentary upon the man who had already had his minister at Washington proposing joint intervention with England and who a few months later left no stone unturned to effect a separation of the North and South without himself becoming involved in a war, in order that he might get a supply of cotton and carry out his plans for a French empire in Mexico. The commission wrote again that if the South did not gain a decisive military victory which would cause England and France to act immediately, the question of recognition must be determined by the cotton situation. Recognition would come in the fall, it was thought, after cotton had been gathered "and the supply of that article here is exhausted and no other means of replenishing it can be found than through treaties with the Confederate States."

The commissioners reported that the sympathy of the English people seemed to be overwhelmingly in favor of the Confederacy by this time.[1] The French were becoming more favorable also, with the exception of the Republicans and Orleanists who were interested in maintaining America as a counter weight to England's maritime power.[2]

For several weeks following the interviews with Lord Russell on May 3 and 9 and with De Morny and Thouvenel, the French minister of foreign affairs, the commissioners contented themselves with spreading southern propaganda and spiking the guns of the Federal agents and diplomats by means of personal contacts with the political leaders, newspaper reporters, and editors. They wrote Toombs that the northern agents were ruining the Federal cause in Europe by too much obstreperousness, both in public speeches and in news-

[1] Pickett Papers, Yancey and Mann to Toombs, No. 3, July 15, 1861; *O.R.N.*, Ser. 2, Vol. III, pp. 221–25.

[2] Pickett Papers, Yancey, Rost, and Mann to Toombs, No. 2, June 1, 1861; *O.R.N.*, Ser. 2, Vol. III, pp. 219–21.

62   KING COTTON DIPLOMACY

paper correspondence. They, on the other hand, were pursuing just the opposite line of conduct so as to throw the representatives and people of the two belligerents into strong relief.[1] "Our own course here," the commission wrote Toombs later, "has been dictated by the most anxious desire to allow the blunders of our enemies to have full effect on the public mind. . . . . We are fully satisfied that this course has met with eminent success, and is duly appreciated in quarters where we desire to make a favorable impression."[2] They reported that even the antislavery sentiment seemed much less active than earlier in the summer. This state of things they held was true in both England and France.[3]

Mann was able to make considerable use, in this quiet counter campaign against Federal attempt at manipulating public opinion, of the Reuter Telegraph and News Agency of London. He reported to his secretary of state on August 3 that he had had two interviews with Reuter during the week and that the latter would use all the Confederate news supplied him and broadcast it throughout Europe.[4] The commission was in daily contact with Mr. Gregory, who had great influence with the government and in Parliament, and who was beginning to write letters in the *London Times* favoring the South and advocating recognition.[5] Also, Montagu, Beresford-Hope, Spence, Campbell, Hugo Reid, James Paul Scott, Thomas Colley Gratton, and other southern friends (whose activities in behalf of the South will be noted elsewhere) were writing letters to the newspapers, delivering harangues, and publishing books and pamphlets calculated to influence public opinion in favor of the South. Yancey, like his successor Mason, received constant aid and advice from the powerful William S. Lindsay, radical member of Par-

[1] *Ibid.*

[2] Pickett Papers, Yancey and Mann to Toombs, No. 3, July 15, 1861; *O.R.N.*, Ser. 2, Vol. III, pp. 221-25.

[3] Pickett Papers, Yancey and Mann to Toombs, No. 4, Aug. 1, 1861; *O.R.N.*, Ser. 2, Vol. III, pp. 229-30.

[4] Pickett Papers, Mann to Toombs, Aug. 3, 1861; *O.R.N.*, Ser. 2, Vol. III, pp. 232-33.

[5] See, e.g., Gregory's letter in the *Times* of June 12, 1861. Cf. *Savannah Republican*, July 3, 1861.

liament, intimately acquainted with Palmerston, Russell, and most of the leaders of the government and Parliament and the largest shipowner in England.[1]

This effort by the Confederate agents, including the commissioners and the agents of the War Department and Navy Department, Caleb Huse, James Bulloch, and Captain North, as well as other less important persons, must have been producing very visible fruits, for the secret agent and spy William M. Walker, U.S.N., reported to his chief, William H. Seward,[2] on October 20 that the situation with reference to public opinion in Europe was becoming serious. There were a swarm of "*southern gentlemen*," he complained, who had entrée to English and French society, and were rapidly bringing the upper classes and the educated under their influence. Some of these agents of the Confederacy were "occupied in conducting its purchases and making its shipments—others through the press either furnishing articles for publication or employing skillful writers to prepare them—others highly gifted in their social qualities and mingling in the various grades of society, adroitly enforced their views and opinions in the different circles in which they moved; all collecting and distributing such intelligence as might best advance the interest of the cause they represented." Walker urged that some northern "gentlemen" with good manners should be sent over at once to counteract these smooth-mannered southerners. The United States minister in France, Dayton, also wrote Seward in alarm[3] that Paris was swarming with Confederate agents who were fast getting control of the venal French press. At first the majority of the press had been for the United States, he thought, but now one by one the newspapers were falling away and going over to the Confederacy.

During these weeks when the commissioners and Confederate agents were busy building up a favorable opinion of the South in the press and among the leaders in the government and society, they were waiting for a southern victory important enough to justify a

[1] See Pickett Papers, Yancey to Hunter, Nov. 3, 1861; *O.R.N.*, Ser. 2, Vol. III, p. 291.

[2] State Department, miscellaneous letters, Oct., 1861.

[3] U.S. Des., France, Vol. 50, Dayton to Seward, No. 40, Sept. 2, 1861.

formal demand that England and France recognize the Confederacy. On June 10 they had written Toombs that as soon as this hoped-for event should occur they would demand an official recognition.[1] This victory, they wrote, was the *sine qua non* of English and French recognition at the present and until the need for southern cotton grew serious.[2] Two days before this communication was received, R. M. T. Hunter, the new secretary of state who had just taken over the office of the disgruntled Robert Toombs, wrote the commissioners that the South had won a great victory on July 21 at Bull Run, Virginia.[3] Before this dispatch could reach the commissioners, the New York papers and the *London Times* had announced the startling news to the world and produced a profound sensation in England and on the Continent, confirming what had already become a universal opinion, that the South was invincible. Without waiting for official dispatches from Richmond announcing the news, Yancey and Mann held a hasty consultation and then wired for Rost, who was in Paris, to join them at once with a view to presenting a demand for recognition. The result of the conference was that the commission dispatched a note to Lord John Russell asking for an informal interview as a preliminary to more formal action.

The commission had been thoroughly snubbed by the British ministry both socially and officially, and Yancey especially resented this attitude in view of the ready access which they enjoyed to the inner official society in Paris. But now that there was a great Confederate victory to discuss with Lord John, there seemed to be no reason to suppose that he would refuse to receive them unofficially. So they must have been somewhat puzzled when in reply to their request for an informal interview he sidestepped and asked for their communication in writing.[4]

[1] Pickett Papers, Yancey and Mann to Toombs, June 10, 1861; *O.R.N.*, Ser. 2, Vol. III, pp. 221–25.

[2] Pickett Papers, Yancey and Mann to Toombs, Aug. 1, 1861; *O.R.N.*, Ser. 2, Vol. III, pp. 229–30.

[3] Pickett Papers, Hunter to Yancey, Rost, and Mann, July 29, 1861; *O.R.N.*, Ser. 2, Vol. III, pp. 227–29.

[4] Pickett Papers, Yancey, Rost, and Mann to Toombs, Aug. 7, 1861; *O.R.N.*, Ser. 2, Vol. III, pp. 235–37.

As quickly as the proposed conversation which the commissioners had planned to have with Russell, could be reduced to writing, it was presented to Lord Russell. This was on August 14, a week after Russell had urged them to write their communications to him. In this letter to Russell the commissioners reviewed the arguments in favor of recognition which they had presented Russell on May 3 and 9. That is, they urged the legality of secession as a natural corollary of state sovereignty. They recalled again for Russell the wrongs which the South had suffered at the hands of the northern majority. One thing in particular they elaborated upon—the power of the Confederacy. They pointed out that the Confederacy now had four more states added—Tennessee, Arkansas, North Carolina, and Virginia—since the conversation of the past May. They showed the great wealth of the South by citing the census tables of 1850. They dwelt upon its vast territory and the impregnable military position it occupied. More particularly, they urged the complete failure thus far of all efforts at the conquest of the South. Not only had the North been unable to retake a single one of its great fortresses, but it had not been able to penetrate any distance into Confederate territory in the unfortified interior wherever there had been any attempt to oppose them. And above all, the North had been overwhelmed in the one great battle fought.

Finally, the commission, seizing upon the moment as opportune to combat the antislavery sentiment of the British government, urged that slavery was no issue in the struggle raging in America. Public opinion, it will be observed later, had already come to this conclusion, and even Lord John, who hated slavery, now held this opinion, pronouncing the war one of conquest on the part of the North and one for independence on the part of the South. "It was from no fear that the slaves would be liberated that secession took place," they wrote the foreign secretary. "The very party in power has proposed to guarantee slavery forever in the States if the South would but remain in the Union. Mr. Lincoln's message proposes no freedom to the slave, but announces subjection of his owner to the will of the Union; in other words to the will of the North. Even after the battle of Bull Run, both branches of Congress at Washington passed resolutions that the war is only waged in order to uphold" the Constitution, which recognized slavery and upheld the laws, many of which guaranteed slavery. "The great object of the war, therefore, as now officially announced, is not to free the slave, but to keep him in subjection to his owner, and to control his labor through the legislative channels which the Lincoln Government designs to force upon the master. The undersigned therefore submit with confidence, that as far as the antislavery sentiment of England is concerned, it can have no sympathy with the North; nay, it will probably become disgusted with the canting hypocrisy which would enlist those sympathies on false pretenses."

The commission called attention to the possibilities of the North's inciting a servile revolt if the war continued to be waged without success. This would forever destroy the production of the cotton and raw material upon which so many millions of Europeans depended for their existence. In connection with the cotton question the commission wrote Lord Russell that the cotton-picking season had commenced and that cotton could be obtained only if the countries who wanted it should go through the illegal blockade and get it. "It will be for the neutral powers whose commerce has been so seriously damaged to determine how long such a blockade shall be permitted to interfere with that commerce [cotton]." This invitation to raise the blockade to obtain cotton was the real point to this state paper as it was to all the other requests for recognition during this period. It mattered not how verbiage might obscure or embellish their arguments, always there was at the basis of the appeal the lure of southern cotton lying just behind the blockaded shores.[1]

The commissioners, however, did not hope to obtain British recognition at this time. They realized that the victory at Bull Run was not sufficiently crushing, and that as yet there was not sufficient distress in the cotton-manufacturing districts to force action upon the British cabinet. Their letter asking for an interview and the letter stating their case[2] were looked upon as merely paving the way for

---

[1] For copy of the letter to Lord Russell see Pickett Papers, Walker Fern to Robert Toombs, No. 6, Aug. 14, 1861, inclosing note of Yancey, Rost, and Mann to Russell, Aug. 14, 1861; O.R.N., Ser. 2, Vol. III, pp. 238–47.

[2] See Pickett Papers, Yancey, Rost, and Mann to Toombs, No. 5, Aug. 7, 1861; also O.R.N., Ser. 2, Vol. III, p. 235, for opinion of commission as to the prospects of immediate recognition.

action when the auspicious moment should arrive. But this moment was not regarded as far distant.

On August 24 Russell replied to this request. England, he said, could not pass judgment upon the issue between the North and South; it must maintain its neutrality and wait until "the fortune of arms or the more peaceful mode of negotiation shall have more clearly determined the respective positions of the two belligerents." In the meantime, he hoped that some kind of adjustment could be made which would satisfy both sections.[1] The commissioners were not disheartened by Russell's letter, but were of the opinion that the attitude of the English government would change presently. Rumors of growing distress in both the English and French industrial districts told them that the hour of the Confederacy might be at hand. It was reported that the stock of cotton in France was quite low and signs of growing distress were seen on all sides. England was reported as not having enough cotton to last until Christmas.[2] On October 5 the commission wrote Hunter[3] that the prospects of recognition were better "than we have had at any time before since our arrival in Europe." Cotton had already risen in England to twenty-two cents, and there was not enough to last, if the usual amount was consumed, until the middle of December. Mills were working little more than half-time, and wages were being reduced in the face of the approaching cotton famine. In France it was much worse, for that country had not stored up a surplus supply of cotton as had England. To add further pressure upon both the English and the French governments a great shortage in the wheat and grain crops had developed. Already, they wrote, there were signs, especially in France, of insurrection.

[1] Pickett Papers, Russell to Yancey, Rost, and Mann, Aug. 24, 1861; *O.R.N.*, Ser. 2, Vol. III, pp. 247–48; also James M. Mason Papers, Aug. 24, 1861. These papers are in eight folio volumes in the Manuscript Division of the Library of Congress. Russell's original letter is, perhaps, the one bound with the Mason Papers. Other letters of Russell to the Yancey-Rost-Mann mission are in these papers also, and were probably turned over to Mason on his arrival in Paris.

[2] See *Charleston Courier*, Sept. 7, 1861, for report of Paris correspondent on conditions; *ibid.*, Sept. 11, 1861, for report of recent traveler to France.

[3] Pickett Papers, Yancey, Rost, and Mann to Hunter, No. 8, Oct. 5, 1861; *O.R.N.*, Ser. 2, Vol. III, pp. 278–80.

Along with the growing distress were rumors that England and France would recognize the Confederacy and break the blockade to obtain cotton. The *London Economist*[1] reported that letters from Lancashire and the distressed cotton districts had been pouring in, demanding recognition, which the *Economist* thought would be ill timed as far as England was concerned. As for France, the *Economist* was of the opinion that the question might be different. The Emperor was unscrupulous, and might not feel moral compunctions in violating public decency by thus interfering to obtain cotton for his distressed operatives. There was much suffering and discontent; the chambers of commerce at Lyons, Rouen, and Mulhausen and other cotton-manufacturing centers were presenting petitions to the government to act in some way so as to relieve their distress. "In all likelihood," the *Economist*[2] continued, "Louis Napoleon sees before him an ominous and uncomfortable winter. If the American war and blockade continue he will have whole districts of miserable and malcontent workmen out of employ, whom he will have to keep down with one hand and feed with the other. The one will cost popularity; the other will cost money, and the Emperor has many reasons for not wishing to risk the one or spend the other. He may not improbably nor altogether irrationally be of opinion that it be both safer and cheaper to disregard and force the blockade with Imperial high handedness, even though it should involve a war with the Federalists, than to face a winter of insurrection and distress at home." The *London Daily News* wrote that "the reports that the Emperor contemplates a recognition of the Southern Confederacy are from trustworthy sources, the want of cotton being severely felt."[3] A Liverpool paper was sure that both England and France were anxious for some arrangement to be made between North and South so as to stop the war which had cut off the cotton supply, and that they might undertake joint action in the matter.[4]

On October 5 Yancey and Rost wrote Hunter that they had been informed by men who were privy to the counsels of the British cabi-

[1] *London Economist*, Oct. 12, 1861.   [2] *Ibid.*, Oct. 19, 1861.

[3] *London Daily News*, quoted in the *Charleston Courier*, Oct. 31, 1861.

[4] Cited in the *Charleston Courier*, Oct. 21, 1861.

net that that body had been seriously considering the question of recognition since Russell's letter to the commission of October 24. They had been told that the British ministry was urging that France take the lead in recognition, and that Great Britain would follow; that the Emperor stood ready to recognize the South the moment that England should join him, though he would not take the lead. There might be some hesitancy, but the commissioners believed that should the Confederate Army gain a signal victory over the Federals near Washington, that event would at once "sway the balance of opinion in Europe and in the ministries of England and France in favor of immediate recognition." This information, they reported, had been obtained in an interview with the French minister of marines and colonies.[1]

These rumors of intervention for the purpose of obtaining cotton were based upon fact. There had been considerable discussion of the question in the cabinets of British and French governments from the very beginning. The French government, notwithstanding the Confederate commissioners' opinion in June that Napoleon was indifferent to the American question, had been seriously considering the cotton question since war had appeared certain. In April, 1861, M. Mercier, the French minister at Washington, urged upon Lord Lyons and Baron de Stoeckl, the British and Russian ministers at Washington, that they join him in securing instructions from their respective governments empowering them to recognize the independence of the Confederacy, so that the cotton supply would be kept open.[2] The question was not brought up by Mercier again until September 30. On that day he received a private note from Thouvenel expressing great alarm over the approaching cotton famine in France and asking Mercier's advice in light of his knowledge of the American situation. Mercier, armed with this note, at once approached Lyons, upon whom he again very earnestly urged that England and France join in recognizing the Confederacy and in breaking the blockade as soon as the military situation and public

[1] Pickett Papers, Yancey and Rost to Hunter, No. 8, Oct. 5, 1861; *O.R.N.*, Ser. 2, Vol. III, pp. 278–80.

[2] E. D. Adams, I, 196, n. 2.

opinion should warrant such a move. Mercier believed that the joint action of the two countries would prevent the United States from declaring war. Lyons replied that England was not prepared to take such radical steps. Mercier answered that France must have cotton.[1]

The situation in France was becoming alarming, and before Thouvenel had had time to receive a reply to his private note to Mercier, he dispatched official instructions to the latter to take up the cotton question with the United States government. Thouvenel depicted a very grave situation in the French cotton industry and urged that the American government should relieve it by permitting the French to obtain southern cotton. He insisted that the war in the United States hurt France more than it did any other country. The French operatives were already in distress, and soon the situation would be desperate and beyond control. In that case it would be impossible, he believed, for France longer to refrain from intervening in the American conflict. He urged that the United States modify its blockade so as to permit the exportation of cotton.[2] On receipt of this note Mercier, before going to Seward, once again consulted with Lyons, urging that England and France join in raising the blockade and recognizing the Confederacy. Lyons refused, and warned Mercier that the United States would resent any such proposal to the extent of insulting the minister who suggested it, and that intervention would mean war with the United States.[3] But Mercier, who was impelled by strong urgings from his government, hastened alone to lay Thouvenel's dispatch before Seward, who handled it rather roughly.[4]

The interview in which Mercier presented Thouvenel's menacing dispatch occurred the latter part of October. Seward's reply to Mercier, embodied in a written dispatch to Dayton a day or two later,

[1] *Ibid.*, I, 196–97.

[2] U.S. Inst. France, Vol. 16, Seward to Dayton, No. 75, "Confidential" (reports the substance of Thouvenel's dispatch and Seward's reply to it), Oct. 30, 1861.

[3] F.O. Amer., Vol. 772, Lyons to Russell, No. 585, Oct. 21, 1861; cf. E. D. Adams, I, 198.

[4] *Ibid.*; F.O. Amer., Vol. 773, Lyons to Russell, No. 606, "Confidential," Oct. 28, 1861.

was a bold defiance of the powers of darkness. As always, Seward showed a willingness for the United States to fight all the world at the very time it was having great difficulty in keeping the South at bay. He was an arrant ass or a consummate poker-player—perhaps a bit of both. Anyway, his reply to the French threat of intervention was the counter threat of a wheat famine and a war. What "France is likely to need most and soonest," he said, "is supplies not of material [cotton] but of provisions." France might need American cotton; she must have American wheat or suffer famine and revolution. But let her attempt intervention and the United States would lay an embargo on all breadstuffs and treat intervention as an act of war. Should France or all Europe contemplate such action let them calculate "not only the cost but the probabilities of success in an enterprise which the conscience of the civilized world would forever reprobate and condemn."[1] This threat of a wheat famine as a counter threat to European intervention appears here apparently for the first time. It was presently passed on to Adams at London, who spread the idea to Forster and Bright. It was very definitely propaganda. Its effects will be discussed in a later chapter.

About November 5, before Mercier's report of his interview with Seward reached Thouvenel and before Seward's reply to Thouvenel's note reached Dayton, Thouvenel had pushed Dayton into a corner and urged upon him France's dire distress because of the growing cotton shortage. France had to have cotton, he said threateningly; the cotton operatives at Rouen, Lyons, Mulhausen, Bordeaux, and other points were unemployed and growing restless. Petitions were pouring in from the cotton-manufacturing districts demanding that France intervene in the American struggle to secure cotton. Thouvenel said that "the pressure might become so great from these quarters that the government could not but heed it and look to its interests."[2]

Thouvenel's conversation with Dayton had the same tenor as his note to Mercier. At the same time and in a similar vein he was

[1] *Ibid.*

[2] U.S. Des., France, Vol. 51, Dayton to Seward, No. 74, Nov. 6, 1861; quotation, Dayton's words.

urging upon the British government, through the French minister, Flahault, the necessity of intervention.

Mercier's report of his interview with Seward, and the latter's dispatch to Dayton embodying the official reply to Thouvenel's demand that France must have cotton or she would intervene, arrived about the same time. Dayton, who was living in momentary dread lest Napoleon should break the Federal blockade, gave Thouvenel a copy of Seward's warlike note and Thouvenel carried the dispatch to Napoleon.

The Trent affair supervened at this moment, and occupied the front of the world-stage for a few weeks. Nothing more was said during the interval to either Dayton or Seward touching the cotton question; but Dayton, as isolated as he was in Paris, was sure that Napoleon was plotting stealthily, only awaiting a better time to interfere in America.[1] Should the Trent affair result in war, Dayton had no doubt that France would seize the occasion as her best opportunity.[2] Nor was Dayton wrong. Thouvenel, despite his personal sympathies with the North, was writing Mercier that he should leave no opportunity untried to bring England into harmony with the French position on intervention.[3]

During the fall of 1861 the British cabinet was also discussing the prospects of the cotton famine and the question of intervention and recognition. Very likely the strong representations of the southern commissioners through their written communication and through more indirect channels were making the British cabinet uneasy, especially when the embargo in the Confederacy had so effectively cut off the cotton supply which the British government had expected to get because of the inadequacy of the blockade. But Flahault's and Mercier's proposals that England join France in breaking the blockade made a decision necessary, so Lyons, Palmerston, Russell,

[1] *Ibid.*, No. 91, Dec. 6, 1861.

[2] *Ibid.*, Dayton to Seward, No. 96, Dec. 24, 1861.

[3] See, e.g., French F.O. Amer., Vol. 126, Thouvenel to Mercier, No. 3, Jan. 16, 1862; Mercier to Thouvenel, No. 80, Jan. 14, 1862; and *ibid., passim.* Also *ibid.*, Vol. 125, *passim,* for correspondence between Mercier and Thouvenel during 1861.

and other members of the government thrashed the thing out in October and November. Lyons, on being approached by Mercier with Thouvenel's private note of September 30 suggesting joint intervention, refused co-operation and wrote Russell the warning that any kind of interference now would mean war.[1] Before he received Lyons' note, Russell wrote Palmerston on October 7, 1861, "I agree with you that the cotton question may become serious by the end of the year"; but as he had been informed by Lindsay that southern cotton could not be carried to the ports in the winter time, he did not see that intervention would do any good at the present, even should England feel inclined to take such a step.[2] However, when Russell received Lyons' report of Mercier's interview with Seward, he seemed to have considered that intervention might not be beyond future possibilities. He was rather impressed with the strong way in which Mercier had presented the dire need of cotton in Europe. He wrote Palmerston: "There is much good sense in Mercier's observations. But we must wait. I am persuaded that if we do anything, it must be on a grand scale. It will not do for England and France to break a blockade for the sake of getting cotton. But, in Europe, powers have often said to belligerents, make up your quarrels. We propose to give terms of pacification which we think fair and equitable. If you accept them, well and good. But if your adversary accepts them and you refuse them, our mediation is at an end, and you may expect to see us your enemies. France would be quite ready to hold this language with us."

Russell thought, "If such a policy were to be adopted the time for it would be the end of the year, or immediately before the meeting of Parliament."[3] Palmerston replied on October 18 agreeing it would not do to intervene just to obtain cotton "unless indeed the distress . . . . was far more serious than it is likely to be." He thought some cotton would get through the blockade and that more cotton could be obtained elsewhere. Therefore, as the situation stood, unless things got much worse than he expected "the only thing to do seems

<hr/>

[1] E. D. Adams, I, 196–97.   [2] *Ibid.*, p. 197.

[3] Walpole, *Life of Lord John Russell* (2 vols.; London, 1891), II, 344; quoted in E. D. Adams, I, 199.

to be to lie on our oars. . . . ."[1] On October 30 Russell wrote Gladstone with increasing apprehension concerning the growing shortage of cotton in England, but felt some hope in the reopening of a southern port like New Orleans through its possible capture by the Federal Army.[2]

This brief excursion into British and French diplomacy serves to show that the rumors which reached the ears of the Confederate commissioners and gave them renewed hopes were based upon solid facts. The French cabinet had been attempting to obtain the joint aid of England in recognizing the Confederacy and in breaking the blockade; Napoleon had developed the position regarding the South which he maintained until the end of the war, namely, that he ever stood ready to recognize the Confederacy and break the blockade, provided England should aid him. It discloses England's position which she was to maintain throughout the war. That is, the cabinet would discuss the question in the light of future intervention when the distress in the cotton districts should become unbearable, but was always unwilling to take the slightest step in that direction for the present.

Under the influence of rumors of what was going on in the French and English cabinets the Confederate commissioners held a conference and decided to hurry across the channel and urge their case upon the French government, as they had the British government in their letter to Russell on August 14. They sought an interview with Napoleon,[3] but as the Emperor was evidently unable to grant this interview at the time because of his preparations to leave Paris, the commissioners decided to lay their case before M. Thouvenel. Accordingly on October 24, 1861, they requested an informal interview with the Foreign Affairs Minister, stating in their request their official position as Confederate commissioners.[4] Their request was

---

[1] Evelyn Ashley, M.P., *The Life and Correspondence of Henry John Temple, Viscount Palmerston* (2 vols.; London, 1879), II, 410–11. (Hereafter cited as Ashley, *Palmerston*.)

[2] Cited in E. D. Adams, I, 200, n. 1.

[3] Pickett Papers, Yancey and Rost to Hunter, No. 8, Oct. 5, 1861; *O.R.N.*, Ser. 2, Vol. III, pp. 278–80.

[4] Pickett Papers, commissioners to Hunter, with inclosure No. 9, Oct. 28, 1861; *O.R.N.*, Ser. 2, Vol. III, pp. 287–88.

promptly granted and two days later, October 26, they had an interview with him. Thouvenel admitted that an important military success might induce France to recognize the independence of the South. But he assured the commissioners that whenever recognition should come it would be only by the joint action of England and France—that, in fact, there was an agreement between the two governments always to act together on the American question. Thouvenel also told the commissioners that unless some radical change should be decided on, England and France would continue to recognize the effectiveness and legality of the blockade against which the commissioners had protested.

This position, of course, was not in itself very encouraging, as it was chiefly through the breaking of the blockade to obtain cotton that the Confederacy hoped to obtain European intervention, which would ultimately involve recognition and possibly war in behalf of the Confederacy. Actually, however, in spite of Thouvenel's statement about the blockade, the commissioners were very optimistic of gaining recognition in the near future. Thouvenel had not said in so many words, but he left the impression, they wrote Hunter, "that the French Government entertained profound sympathy for the cause of the South and expected that events would transpire within no distant period which would cause it to recognize the Confederate States." They had information, too, of an unofficial character, that the Emperor and his ministry would support England in any action which that government should take with regard to recognition.[1] This information came partly from rumor, but unquestionably most of it came from Napoleon's cabinet itself. Rost was in communication with De Morny, Persigny, Baroche, and the minister of marines and colonies—all members of Napoleon's government, friends, and strong southern sympathizers. Undoubtedly, these French gentlemen of intrigue told their southern companions in intrigue that France at that moment was carrying on a diplomatic conversation in regard to obtaining cotton for the distressed cotton districts with the United States, both in Paris through the American am-

[1] *Ibid.*

bassador and the Foreign Office and in America between Seward and Mercier.

Before proceeding with the remainder of the diplomatic efforts of the Yancey-Rost-Mann commission which culminated in the notes sent to Russell and Thouvenel with reference to the inefficiency of the blockade and the surrender of Mason and Slidell, it is necessary to call attention to the provision for the dissolution of this commission and the dispatching of single diplomatic agents to the courts of France, England, Spain, and Belgium. After the commission had failed collectively to obtain recognition in either England or France, Davis and Hunter probably felt that it was going to be a little more of a wait for recognition than they had anticipated and that it would be better to have a permanent representative at each of the courts of England, France, Belgium and Spain than to have the group visiting the courts of Europe at intervals like Methodist circuit-riders. There is some evidence, too, that Mann and Yancey were not always on the best terms. Mann was more of a sycophant and more willing to submit to the snubbing of the British ministry than Yancey, who was always conscious of the dignity and worthiness of his country. Perhaps the commission would have been separated soon anyway, but Yancey precipitated its dissolution by resigning his post.[1] It has been the generally accepted view that Yancey resigned because he had lost hope of European intervention or recognition. He resigned some time around the first of September, about a week after Russell's letter of August 24 refusing to recognize the South. But it was after his resignation that he joined Rost in Paris and held an interview with Thouvenel and expressed his opinion that Napoleon and all his cabinet were sympathetic with the South, and that there were many signs of speedy recognition. Moreover, it was after Yancey's resignation that he and Rost had written Hunter that the approaching cotton famine was a potent stimulant "to urge both England and France to an act of recognition," and they had brighter and better assured hopes of achieving it than

[1] Pickett Papers, Hunter to Yancey, No. 10, Sept. 23, 1861; O.R.N., Ser. 2, Vol. III, p. 273.

at any time before or since their arrival in Europe. It was also during this period that the rumor of intervention was flying, and the various members of the French cabinet were informing the Confederate commissioners just what the attitude of Napoleon was. So, while Yancey might have been discouraged at the moment of resignation, his despondency was only temporary and had little to do with his resignation. His decision to give up his post was due partly to resentment against the British cabinet, partly to disgust with Mann, partly to ill health, but more to a desire to be back in the land of cotton and sunshine and the political arena where he could speak out. The velvet gloves of diplomacy were not worn well by an outspoken agitator.

The day on which Hunter accepted the resignation of Yancey, he wrote a dispatch to Mann under the order of the President and Congress dissolving the commission. Mann was to proceed to Brussels.[1] Rost had already been assigned to Spain, even before the dissolution of the commission.[2] James M. Mason was assigned to the post of London, and John Slidell to the court of Napoleon.[3] The commissioners, of course, were expected to remain in Europe until properly relieved—Mann in London, Rost in Paris, and Yancey dividing his time between the two cities.

After the interview with Thouvenel in October and the letter to Russell in August the commissioners settled down to await the evolution of events, expecting the grip of the cotton famine to crack the shell of the *status quo*. Mann spent his time altogether in England awaiting the coming of Mason who would relieve him; Rost spent his time in Paris waiting Slidell's coming, while Yancey was first in Paris and then in London, also waiting to be relieved by the arrival of the Mason-Slidell mission.

The monotony of this wait was suddenly broken when on November 27 news arrived of the seizure of the Confederate commissioners

[1] Pickett Papers, Hunter to Mann, No. 11, Sept. 23, 1861; *O.R.N.*, Ser. 2, Vol. III, pp. 273–74.

[2] Pickett Papers, Hunter to Yancey, Rost, and Mann, No. 9, with inclosure of instructions, Aug. 24, 1861; *O.R.N.*, Ser. 2, Vol. III, pp. 249–52.

[3] Pickett Papers, Hunter to Mason, Sept. 23, and Hunter to Slidell, Sept. 23, instructing the two envoys; *O.R.N.*, Ser. 2, Vol. III, pp. 257–64, 265–73.

and their secretaries on board of the British mail-steamer "Trent."[1] England went wild, and France was greatly stirred by the bold act of the United States Captain Charles Wilkes. War between England and the United States seemed almost certain, and this would mean recognition. Rost hurried back from Paris and joined Yancey and Mann in London where they held a caucus. It was decided at once to send a note of protest to the British cabinet; and on that very day the note was forwarded to the Foreign Office. It demanded reparations for the seizure of their commissioners, Mason and Slidell, while on a neutral vessel bound for a neutral port.[2]

On the same ship which brought them the news of the seizure of Mason and Slidell came the official papers and dispatches which they had with them, but which had not been seized. The instructions of these two commissioners enjoined them to work both for recognition and for the repudiation of the legality of the blockade. The thing which was considered the most practical at the time and most likely to produce a situation resulting in intervention was the attack upon the blockade. Yancey, Rost, and Mann acted promptly upon this phase of Mason and Slidell's instructions, feeling that in England's present temper an attack on the blockade would be a surer way of approach than by a renewal of the request that the South be recognized. So on November 30, before their note of protest against the seizure of Mason and Slidell was answered, they sent a second note. They insisted that the blockade was nothing but a paper blockade. In proof of this they submitted to Russell a list of four hundred vessels which had successfully entered and cleared southern ports through the blockade from Lincoln's proclamation, April 29–August 20, a period of less than four months. Since the latter date, though they had no official report, it was common knowledge that blockade running, if a traffic as regular as mail packets could be called blockade running, had become more formidable. They called special attention to the successful trips without difficulty of the famous munition carrier, the "Bermuda," through

[1] Pickett Papers, Yancey, Rost, and Mann to Hunter, No. 10, Dec. 2, 1861; *O.R.N.*, Ser. 2, Vol. III, pp. 304–6.

[2] *Ibid.*

the blockade at Savannah and to the voyage of the "Theodora," "Helen," and "Nashville." According to the declaration of Paris and to the generally accepted rules of international law especially championed by the United States, a blockade to be binding must be effective, that is, maintained with a sufficient force to prevent access to the enemy's coast.

But, after all, the inefficiency of the blockade would be merely the justification for European interference, which the Confederate commission were furnishing gratuitously lest the prime minister should not think of it. The real motive for interference would be the desire for cotton, and the Confederate commissioners made a strong appeal to this motive once the legality of any prospective interference was established on the ground of the inefficiency of the blockade. The commissioners explained in their note that they were fortified in their expectation that England and France would refuse to recognize the blockade not by the reciprocal agreements with regard to the Declaration of Paris alone, but more especially by "the nature of the interests affected by the blockade. So far, at least, it has been proved that the only certain and sufficient source of cotton supply has been found in the Confederate States. It is probable that there are more people without than within the Confederate States who derive their means of living from the various uses which are made of this most important staple. A war, therefore, which shuts up this great source of supply from the general uses of mankind, is directed as much against those who transport and manufacture cotton as against those who produce the raw material. Innocent parties who are thus affected may well insist that a right whose exercise operates so unfavorably on them shall only be used within the strictest limits of public law."

So necessary, indeed, was cotton, said the commissioners, that even a legal blockade should not be allowed to interrupt the trade in that staple. It was urged that as some trade routes had been neutralized for the interest of mankind, the trade in cotton should likewise be neutralized and excepted from the rights of blockade and capture. "The cheapest and most abundant sources of cotton supply" should not be subjected to blockade. The facts showing the illegality and ineffectiveness of the blockade, concluded the commissioners, "and the great interests of the neutral commerce of the world imperatively demand that her Majesty's Government should take decisive action in declaring the blockade ineffective."[1] This was an appeal to King Cotton. The specter of famine, the illegality of the blockade, and the bitter feeling in England over the Trent affair furnished facts which should produce a final interference in behalf of the Confederacy in some shape or other. If war came between England and the United States as the Confederates hoped and prayed, the interference would take the part of active aid and recognition. If war did not grow out of the Trent affair, then intervention would take the form of refusing to recognize the blockade.[2]

The commissioners presented a similar note on the blockade to Thouvenel, who expressed great surprise. He promised to lay the matter before the cabinet in the near future. The commissioners became very hopeful. For the moment, A. Dudley Mann was exuding optimism and self-satisfaction. On December 2, before Russell had replied to their notes of November 27 and 30, Mann wrote from London (Rost and Yancey were evidently in Paris), "At present there is a probability that our recognition by her Britannic Majesty's Government will not be much longer delayed. I congratulate you with all my heart upon the indications which so strikingly manifest themselves for a speedy termination of the noble sacrifices of our country for the attainment of its independence." England would insist on an apology from America or there would be war.

Mann took due credit for his share in bringing recognition so near. "By never losing sight for a moment of the object for which I was appointed and not quitting here for a day since my arrival I have succeeded in opening up channels of communication with the most important personages of the realm." In an hour after the cabinet decided to demand an apology for the seizure of Mason and Slidell, wrote Mann, "I was furnished with full particulars. What a noble statesman Lord Palmerston! His heart is as young as it was

---

[1] Pickett Papers, note to Russell, Nov. 30, 1861; *O.R.N.*, Ser. 2, Vol. III, pp. 298–301; cf. *ibid.*, pp. 304–6, Yancey, Rost, and Mann to Hunter, No. 10, Dec. 2, 1861.

[2] Pickett Papers, Rost to Davis, Dec. 24, 1861, in *O.R.N.*, Ser. 2, Vol. III, pp. 311–12.

40 years ago." One would judge from this implication that Palmerston and Mann were on very intimate terms. However, it is extremely doubtful whether Mann and Palmerston met during Mann's
residence in England. But he at least had evidence on all sides that
England would take drastic action against the United States with
reference to the Trent affair, and that intervention would probably
grow out of this shortly.[1]

Rost wrote Hunter from Paris that it looked like war between
England and the United States, and that France would presently
come in and command peace between the North, on the one hand,
and England and the Confederacy, on the other. Things were certainly more hopeful; recognition and independence were in the air.
The French government, through the ministry of the interior, wrote
Rost, was publicly advocating recognition and even the right of
secession.[2]

Yancey, too, was hopeful of intervention. He was of the opinion
that if war were avoided by the surrender of Mason and Slidell,
England would assume for a while a frigid neutrality, refusing to interfere with the blockade or recognize the Confederacy. However,
this would be for only a short time, first, because France was eager
to move and "may drive England into favorable action"; second,
public opinion in England was for the South, "and when Parliament meets, I feel confident that the ministry will be compelled to
act favorably or resign."[3]

Then Russell's reply to the commissioners' notes of November 27
and 30, referred to above, arrived on December 7. It was a blow to
the pride of the commission. Russell simply refused "in the present
state of affairs . . . . to enter into official communication with
them."[4] Yancey was convinced that this haughty refusal couched
in such inconsiderate terms required some kind of reply for the sake

[1] For letter see Pickett Papers, Mann to Hunter, No. 10, Dec. 2, 1861; O.R.N., Ser. 2,
Vol. III, p. 307.

[2] Pickett Papers, Rost to Davis, Dec. 24, 1861; O.R.N., Ser. 2, Vol. III, pp. 311–12.

[3] Pickett Papers, Yancey to Hunter, Dec. 31, 1861; O.R.N., Ser. 2, Vol. III, pp.
312–13.

[4] Pickett Papers, Walker Fern to Hunter, inclosure with No. 11, Dec. 20, 1861;
O.R.N., Ser. 2, Vol. III, pp. 309–10; also Mason Papers, Dec. 7, 1861.

of the dignity of the Confederacy,[1] but he was constrained by the others to keep silent.

But just after the reply had been received, and it had been decided that there should be no rejoinder, some of the diplomatic correspondence between Russell and the American minister, Charles Francis Adams, was published in the United States. It cast a reflective light over the curt reply of Russell and all his former refusals to see the commissioners in person, and his insistence that they communicate with him in writing. It was made apparent that Russell had refused to receive them or to be civil to them under diplomatic pressure from the United States which practically amounted to a threat of war. Seward had instructed Adams in so many words that he might present Russell with the alternative of refusing to receive the Confederate commissioners or war with the United States,[2] and Russell, feeling that England had antagonized the United States more than had been intended by the neutrality proclamation, had replied to Adams that he had seen the Confederate commissioners only twice, and that he "had no expectation of seeing them any more."[3] Yancey, on reading this in the published account of this affair, was very resentful. He was more convinced than ever, now, that the commission should have replied to Russell's refusal to enter into communication with them. "What truckling," commented Yancey, "to the arrogant demand of Mr. Seward, that England should forego her international privilege of hearing the case of a belligerent power. What a violation, in fact, of that impartial neutrality proclaimed,—a neutrality indeed, which includes the equal hearing of both sides, although upon unequal terms,—official on one side, unofficial on the other." All communication with the British government, he thought, was thus cut off until the Trent affair was settled.

But, in spite of Russell's refusal to treat them civilly, the commission, at the termination of its existence, was very hopeful of recog-

[1] Pickett Papers, Yancey to Hunter, Dec. 31, 1861; *O.R.N.*, Ser. 2, Vol. III, pp. 312–13.

[2] E. D. Adams, I, 105–6.

[3] *Ibid.*, also Pickett Papers, Yancey to Hunter, Dec. 31, 1861; *O.R.N.*, Ser. 2, Vol. III, pp. 312–13.

nition. Mann wrote Davis on January 18, 1862,[1] that, although war had not resulted from the Trent affair because of the cowardly apologies of America, intervention in the form of raising the blockade was rapidly coming to a head in France. "Louis Napoleon sustained Lord Palmerston by his moral aid in the affair of the Trent. The latter in his turn will sustain the former in this matter of raising the blockade of our ports. . . . . I have the best reasons for assuring you that there is a contract understanding upon the subject, and that all the powers and states of Europe will cordially become parties to it."

On January 27, 1862, Yancey wrote Davis privately that the American question fully occupied the public mind and that "I have some reason to think that France and England will unite in an armed intervention." The blockade, he wrote, was generally regarded as a paper blockade, and had the Confederate Department of State sent official reports of the numbers of vessels running the blockade instead of the details of minor military engagements, "we should have had it in our power to have broken it here also."[2]

On the same day Mann and Yancey joined in their last dispatch to the State Department[3] to report that public opinion was greatly occupied with the question of the blockade and that the European governments, especially England and France, were taking strong grounds against the paper blockade and the sinking of the stone fleet (old ships loaded with stone) at Charleston. They were of the opinion that England and France would demand that the North and South resort to an armistice. There would certainly be some form of intervention. "What form, however, intervention will assume, we have no information of, but we believe that it will take place in a short time."

On January 29 Mason arrived in London and the Yancey-Rost-Mann mission was automatically disbanded. Yancey went home,

---

[1] Pickett Papers, Mann to Davis, Jan. 18, 1862; *O.R.N.*, Ser. 2, Vol. III, pp. 318–19.

[2] Pickett Papers, Yancey to Hunter, Jan. 27, 1862; *O.R.N.*, Ser. 2, Vol. III, pp. 321–22.

[3] Pickett Papers, Yancey and Mann to Hunter, No. 14, Jan. 27, 1862; *O.R.N.*, Ser. 2, Vol. III, pp. 319–21.

Mason remained in London, Mann went to Belgium, Slidell proceeded to France, and Rost, though he had been commissioned to go to Spain, dallied in Paris for a while because he had been informed by the Spanish ambassador that Spain could not move until England and France had recognized the Confederacy.

The Confederate diplomats had not obtained recognition, but they were hopeful of imminent intervention, though the British government had not even during the ill feeling over the Trent affair veered from its strict neutrality, and the French government, while ever ready to intervene in company with England, had not abandoned its neutral position. The public opinion as expressed in the newspapers of both France and England was in favor of continuing strict neutrality. In France toward the end of the Yancey-Rost sojourn there, the semiofficial papers, the *Pays*, *Patrie* and *Constitutionnel*, changed to an advocacy of recognition, but the papers and journals which reflected the public opinion of France, such as the *Journal de débats*, *Revue des deux mondes*, *Revue contemporaine*, *Opinion nationale*, *Presse*, etc., were in favor of neutrality and in sympathy with the North.

In England public sympathy was with the South, but opposed intervention. On October 30 the *Times* protested that nothing could induce England to abandon her neutral position and take sides. "We can well afford to wait and see this contest brought to a close." No cotton famine could induce England to interfere and bring the war to a close. A month later[1] the *Times* said that nothing but positive proof on the part of the South of its ability to maintain its position and independence could ever induce England to recognize the Confederacy. The *Economist* was in favor of strict neutrality, though it was in sympathy with the South. Secession it considered as bound to be successful. But it was up to the South to prove it, and until the South could show its power to maintain its independence England could and would take no unneutral step.[2] In reply to those who demanded that the South be recognized in order to obtain cot-

[1] *London Times*, Nov. 28, 1861.
[2] *London Economist*, Sept. 14, 1861.

ton, the *Economist*[1] pointed out that "the recognition of the South by all the powers in the world would not affect the blockade one iota." "In the next place, the recognition of the South at the present epoch of the conflict would be a distinct and indefensible act of hostility towards the North. It is far too soon to affirm that the latter cannot subdue or reannex or entice back the seceded states." The war had only just begun, though this paper affirmed that the South would ultimately win. As to the clamor of those who demanded that the blockade be broken in order to obtain cotton, the *Economist* remarked that "to insist upon the United States ceasing the blockade would be neither more nor less than to declare war against them." The *Spectator*[2] approved of strict neutrality as to belligerent rights, but went so far in its sympathy for the North as to demand that the government pledge itself never to recognize the South. The *Saturday Review* held the position occupied by the *Times* and *Economist*, asserting that while England must maintain strict neutrality, the time would inevitably arrive when the South would establish a *de facto* independence which England was bound to recognize.[3] Adams[4] said that with the exception of the *Spectator* and a few provincial papers which favored a neutrality friendly to the North, the English press favored complete neutrality at this period—as well as later.

So the Yancey-Rost-Mann diplomatic mission came to an end and, with the exception of the Trent affair, which for a few weeks threatened to involve England in a war with the United States and would have resulted in southern independence, there had never been any near approach to recognition. The cotton famine in England and France, helped on by the coercive cotton embargo of the South during this first year of the war, had failed to bring the two leading European powers to their knees in supplication to King Cotton. The English government had remained strictly neutral; the British people had come to sympathize with the South, but they opposed their government's taking any part in the quarrel. Public opinion

[1] *Ibid.*, Oct. 12, 1861.
[2] *Spectator*, May 18, 1861.
[3] *Saturday Review*, June 1, 1861; cited in E. D. Adams, I, 100-101.
[4] E. D. Adams, I, 101..

regardless of party or sympathy backed up the ministry in its position of neutrality. In France the government had remained neutral, but, because of the Mexican question and the need for cotton, had been from the beginning anxious to intervene, provided England would join her. Public opinion in France was almost solidly on the side of the United States, and Napoleon was afraid to risk playing a lone hand in the face of public opinion.

CHAPTER III

THE TROUBLED WATERS OF MEXICO

Mexico was in many respects the most vital foreign problem with which the Confederacy had to deal. It was the only neutral country from which the Confederacy could not be cut off by blockade and for this reason it could supply the Trans-Mississippi Department with large quantities of lead, copper, tin, saltpeter, sulphur, powder, blankets, tents, cloth, coffee, and sugar; and it would serve as a legal bridge over which contraband and other supplies from Europe and the West Indies could pass into the Confederacy. Of great importance, too, was the problem of restraining the plundering bands of Mexican and American Indians, refugee Unionists, and southern bushwhackers from harassing the borders of both countries. But Mexico in the role of a pawn in the game that the Confederate commissioners, John Slidell and James M. Mason, were to play in England and France was of still greater consequence to the Confederacy. When the power of King Cotton failed to move Napoleon to intervene, the Confederate leaders hoped at first and eventually expected that Mexico would prove to be the lever by which the French Emperor would be toppled from his neutral perch.

A brief résumé of the Mexican situation in 1861 is necessary to a clear understanding of the attitude and relations of the Confederacy to Mexico. In signing the Treaty of Guadalupe Hidalgo, Mexico lost over half her national domain, if Texas be included. The successive administrations at Washington had never ceased their efforts to obtain the transit rights across the Isthmus of Tehuantepec and northern Mexico; they wished to purchase Lower California and the northern Mexican states lying eastward. James Gadsden, John Forsyth, and Robert M. McLane each had tried his hand at obtaining these concessions; but each had been unsuccessful in the principal objectives. At the time it was customary, for political advantage, to attribute this imperialistic ambition to the South's desire to spread slavery; but the majority of Americans, North and South, were doubtless believers at heart in the doctrine of Manifest Destiny. Had there been no slavery question to keep alive the political issue of the sectional balance of power, it is probable that Mexico and perhaps Canada would not have long survived mid-century American imperialism.

When the United States began to fall apart in the winter of 1860–61, Mexico was just bringing to a close a three-year civil war, which in turn had been preceded by innumerable other civil wars. In December Pablo Benito Juárez, the liberal leader and constitutional President, routed the armies of General Miguel Miramon, president of the conservative faction which had held sway at Mexico City for a number of years. Mexico was in a desperate plight from its civil wars and its war with the United States. It owed between sixty and a hundred million dollars to France, Great Britain, Spain, and the United States, if one includes the Jecker and other fraudulent claims of the French. Perhaps sixty million dollars would have covered its legitimate debts to foreign bondholders and governments. Yet the Juárez government was unable to obtain sufficient revenue even to service its debts and support its own government. European powers had for years attempted to collect these debts and to gain some form of control to stabilize and exploit that unhappy country. But the knowledge that the United States would in all probability go to war to defeat European intervention in the internal affairs of Mexico had since 1839 prevented the European powers from taking any more drastic action than blockading Mexican ports to obtain a portion of the revenue. But there was a growing sentiment in Great Britain, France, and Spain to challenge the paramount position the United States claimed under the Monroe Doctrine in all Latin America. As the fateful year of 1861 approached, American leaders, North and South, were not left in doubt that European powers were only biding their time to intervene in Mexico and other Latin-American countries. Impending European intervention accelerated the American desire to annex more Mexican territory, and the American attempt to acquire this territory further stimulated the European ambition to do likewise.[1]

JOHN T. PICKETT, SWASHBUCKLER

Just why President Davis selected John T. Pickett to represent the Confederacy as diplomatic commissioner to the Mexican government is not at all clear. True, he was forceful, bold, and shrewd and was widely acquainted in Mexico, for he had been consul at Vera Cruz for a number of years and had had a rather intimate association with Juárez and the small group of Liberals who made up his advisers and principal officers. But, to offset these advantages, he was quick-tempered, sharp of tongue, and, when angry, somewhat of a trouble hunter. In other words, Pickett was no diplomat.

On May 17, 1861, Robert Toombs, Confederate Secretary of State, notified Pickett of his appointment and issued him formal instructions. He was to proceed to Mexico City and establish some form of diplomatic relations with the Juárez government as quickly as possible. He was to explain that the southern states had seceded from the Union for just cause and that the Confederacy desired to negotiate a treaty of friendship between the two governments. Pickett was, however, not to insist on formal recognition or a formal treaty unless the Mexican government was prepared for such an undertaking. He was to stress the fact that the Confederacy and Mexico had many things in common that should contribute much to a close friendship. "The people both of the Confederate States and Mexico are principally engaged in agriculture and mining pursuits, and their interests are therefore homogeneous. The institution of domestic slavery in one country, and that of peonage in the other, establish between them such a similarity in their system of labor as

---

[1] For general accounts of the Mexican civil wars and the situation in the country just before and during the American Civil War the following works are especially recommended: Ralph Roeder, *Juárez and His Mexico* (2 vols.; New York, 1947); Daniel Dawson, *Mexican Adventure* (1935); H. Montgomery Hyde, *Mexican Empire: The History of Maximilian and Charlotte of Mexico* (1946); Count Egon Caesar Corti, *Maximilian and Charlotte*, trans. Catherine Allison Phillips (London and New York, 1929); and J. Fred Rippy, *The United States and Mexico* (New York, 1931).

to prevent any tendency on either side to disregard the feelings of the other." Of paramount importance to both countries was the common border between them. Confederate friendship, it was to be stressed, was essential to Mexico because the Confederacy was the only country so situated as "to guarantee Mexico against foreign invasion"—meaning, of course, invasion by the United States. Special attention was to be given to the prevention of border raids from each side. This, of course, was an old and familiar problem, and it promised increased trouble during the turbulent era at hand.

In presenting the case in favor of Confederate-Mexican friendship, Toombs with unconscious irony instructed Pickett to explain to the Juárez government that the South rather than the North had always been the friend of Mexico. "It will be well in your relations with the Mexican Government," Toombs said, "to remind them that the Southern statesmen and diplomatists, from the days of Henry Clay to the present time, have always been the fast friends of Mexico, and that she may always rely on the good will and friendly intervention of the Confederate States to aid her in maintaining those principles of constitutional liberty which she has so successfully asserted." In thus attempting to gain the friendship of the Mexican government, Pickett would at the same time do all in his power to circumvent the plans of the United States to gain Mexican friendship and obtain special favors in that country. Plainly Toombs was as suspicious of northern intentions toward Mexico as the northern politicians were of southern. "The grant to the United States of commercial, political, or territorial advantages which are not accorded to the Confederate States, would be regarded by this government as evidence of an unfriendly disposition on the part of Mexico, which it would sincerely deplore, and protest against in the promptest and most decided manner."

While Toombs was preparing Pickett's instructions, the latter apparently tried his rough and bold hand at drawing up additional memoranda which the State Department sanctioned and inclosed as a part of his general instructions. In note 11 of his memoranda Pickett with no inconsiderable experience in intrigue suggested the means by which the wheels of diplomacy might be made to turn in

Mexico. "The agent should be furnished with means sufficient to maintain a creditable personal and diplomatic figure and to pay for important information when not to be had otherwise, and other secret service. A million or so of money, judiciously applied, would purchase our recognition by the Government. The Mexicans are not overscrupulous, and it is not our mission to mend their morals at this precise period." No man, especially a diplomat, could retain his prestige in Mexico, Pickett believed, unless he was free with his money and neat and polished in his bearing. "The niggardliness of the late ex-Governor Letcher, of Kentucky, his aversion to clean linen, and profuse squirting of tobacco juice rendered him positively odious, though otherwise a most excellent minister plenipotentiary." The Spanish-Mexican character might be corrupt and venal, in Pickett's opinion, but it was always fastidious. Pickett was frankly contemptuous of the Mexicans, and his openly expressed opinions of this contempt and his rough-handed methods did much to destroy whatever usefulness he might have had. He certainly underestimated the character, integrity, and amazing fortitude of Benito Juárez and such associates as José-Maria Mata, Don Melchor Ocampo, Juan Alvarez, Manuel Doblado, and Ponciano Arriaga.[1]

On his arrival at Vera Cruz, Pickett found many old American and Mexican friends of his consular days. One of the first friends with whom he communicated was Señor José-Maria Mata, now member of Congress and former Minister of Finance. Mata was one of the little band of Mexican exiles, including Juárez, who in 1854 engineered the overthrow of Santa Anna. He was very close to Juárez, and Pickett felt that his friendship with Mata offered a most favorable means of getting access to the Juárez government. He wrote Mata a cordial and informal letter in which he stressed the early friendship of southern statesmen for Mexico. He compared the Juárez government and the southern Confederacy in their devotion to constitutional government, and compared the Federals of the North with the Conservative-Church party as bent upon destroying

[1] For Pickett's instructions and enclosed memoranda, see Pickett Papers, Toombs to Pickett, May 17, 1861; O.R.N., Ser. 2, Vol. III, pp. 202–7.

the constitution.[1] Pickett delayed his departure to Mexico City while awaiting a response from Mata in order to obtain an interview with another old friend, Don Ignacio de la Llave, governor of Vera Cruz. La Llave's friendship for the Confederacy would, Pickett believed, be worth much to the South. Vera Cruz, though nominally under the Juárez government, was, like Coahuila and Nuevo León under Santiago Vidaurri, in actual practice virtually independent. At least this was Pickett's view. It was here that the Confederate agent hoped to launch privateers and obtain permission to export munitions and military supplies to the Confederacy.[2]

When Governor de la Llave granted Pickett the interview, the latter found him friendly enough and well disposed toward the Confederacy. He was in all probability in sympathy with the state-rights doctrine of the southern states, but skeptical of the ultimate intentions of the Confederacy concerning his own country. He assured Pickett that as governor of Vera Cruz he would accord the same treatment to both Federal and Confederate vessels entering the waters of his state. He hastened to explain, however, that maritime questions such as granting letters of marque and reprisal, and fitting out privateers were under national jurisdiction. By thus evading any responsibility for a possible future unneutral policy of the Juárez government, he would be able to retain the outward friendship of both belligerents.[3]

When Pickett arrived at Mexico City, he found public opinion quite different from that in Vera Cruz, where it was either neutral or divided. In the national capital the majority of the public openly favored the United States. Thomas Corwin's as yet informal negotiations (he had not yet received Seward's instructions) to lend Mexico ten or twelve million dollars and the propaganda that the Confederacy was plotting the seizure of Mexican territories had undermined whatever chances the Confederacy had of gaining the friendship or neutrality of the Mexican government. Pickett arrived at the conclusion very quickly that the Confederacy had few friends of im-

[1] Pickett Papers, Pickett to Don José-Maria Mata, June 12, 1861.

[2] *Ibid.*, Pickett to Toombs, No. 2, June 15, 1861.

[3] *Ibid.*

portance in the national capital, and at first made no effort to lessen the hostility of the public. Indeed, he lost his temper and became very indiscreet in his conversations and in his conduct. Soon after his arrival in Mexico City he related in a letter to the Confederate Secretary of State—which the latter did not receive until November 30 of that year—several illuminating examples of his undiplomatic conduct. He avoided discussions with the Mexicans as long as possible, he wrote, but when conversation was forced upon him, he retorted usually with a point. When asked whether it was his mission to gain recognition from Mexico, he replied: "To the contrary. My business is to recognize Mexico—provided I can find a government that will stand still long enough." When he heard that the United States had obtained permission to march troops across Mexican territory into Arizona, Pickett sarcastically remarked that, should the rumor be true, there would be at least thirty thousand Confederate diplomatic agents crossing the Mexican border in a very short time. Perhaps the most insulting retort that Pickett made referred to the rumor that some Mexican officers might enter the military service of the United States. "I have expressed the hope," said Pickett, "that they would all go and only regretted that the entire United States army is not officered by Mexico. I also added that they ought to be very careful not to be taken prisoners by the South, as they would in that event, probably soon find themselves for the first time in their lives, usefully employed in agricultural pursuits—i.e. hoeing corn and picking cotton."[1]

These and other such unfriendly and cutting remarks were, of course, reported to the Mexican government and to the United States minister and his associates. Corwin made the most of Pickett's indiscretions, and presently he was writing Seward about the proposed Confederate seizure—by the thirty thousand diplomats—of Mexican territory.[2]

After his first ill-tempered outbursts, Pickett became more cautious for a while and undertook to counteract the successful propaganda of the United States agents and minister. He had threatened

[1] *Ibid.*, No. 3, July 11, 1861.
[2] U.S. Des., Mexico, Vol. 28, Corwin to Seward, No. 4, Aug. 28, 1861.

the annexation of Mexican territory—the most dreadful menace that he could have uttered to a Mexican. He was made quickly aware of the dire effect of this type of bluster and set out to make such repairs as were possible. He began to assure those with whom he conversed that the Confederacy was land poor, that, indeed, his country had enough territory "for a century to come" and "would not accept an entire Mexican state (with its people) as a gift." The southern states, he would explain, now independent from the North, no longer faced the necessity of maintaining the sectional balance of power in order to protect its interests. The "necessity of extension no longer exists; it is the United States which covets its neighbor's lands." In his letter to Toombs—which the Confederate State Department did not receive until January, 1862—he assured him that such remarks meant for the Mexicans must not be taken too seriously at Richmond. "It must not be supposed from the expression in this capital, of the foregoing diplomatic language, that I am not fully impressed with the fact that 'manifest destiny' may falsify the foregoing declaration."[1]

Near the last of July Pickett obtained an interview with Manuel Zamacona, Mexican Minister of Foreign Relations, and he assured Pickett of the friendship and neutrality of the Juárez government.[2] As yet the Mexican government could assume no other attitude, since there was no assurance that the United States would complete the loan to Mexico and guarantee its territory against Confederate aggression. Juárez did not desire to commit any offense that would bring down upon the Mexican border states the invading hosts of the "30,000 Confederate diplomats" that Pickett had promised. Later Pickett inquired as to the authenticity of the rumor that Mexico had granted permission for United States troops to cross Mexican territory, and Zamacona replied with apparent frankness that the rumor was correct. In granting this permission, however, Mexico had not supposed that the Confederacy laid claim to Arizona. No offense was intended. Mexico wished to remain neutral and treat both belligerents alike. Zamacona went so far in his written reply to Pickett's

[1] Pickett Papers, Pickett to Toombs, No. 5, Aug. 1, 1861.
[2] *Ibid.*

question as not only to assure the latter of Mexico's friendship and neutrality but to inclose a letter to Toombs acknowledging the latter's letter of credence and introduction which Pickett had presented. This was very near to an official recognition of the Confederacy.[1]

During the month of September, Pickett had further correspondence with Zamacona in which he again protested against the passage of United States troops across Mexican territory and strove to gain the favorable opinion of the Mexican government and the important Liberal leaders. As he had previously done in conversation with private citizens, he now attempted officially to convey the idea that the South no longer desired expansion. The motive for further acquisition of territory, he explained to Zamacona, had been removed. The need to maintain the sectional balance of power in Congress (the Senate) in order to protect the South against measures harmful to southern interests no longer existed. He repeated what he had said privately on other occasions, that the Confederacy had more land than it would need in a hundred years. But he added what might have been considered a daring proposal, had the Mexican official not had information, secretly obtained, that the proposal was neither authorized nor honest. He wrote Zamacona that "so far from desiring to acquire any portion of the lands of its Mexican neighbors, the undersigned would be happy to receive and transmit to Richmond proposals for the retrocession to Mexico of a large portion of the territory hitherto acquired from her by the late United States."[2]

Pickett immediately wrote Toombs and inclosed his note to Zamacona. He explained that his offer concerning the recession of lands was a political maneuver. It would, he thought, circumvent the United States agents who had injured the Confederate cause so badly by convincing the Mexicans that the South was planning to seize part or all of Mexico. "My offer," he wrote, "to receive and transmit to Richmond proposals for the retrocession to Mexico of a large portion of the territory hitherto acquired from her by the late United States means precisely what it says—nothing more nor less.

[1] *Ibid.*, No. 8, Aug. 28, and No. 9, Aug. 29, 1861.

[2] *Ibid.*, No. 10, Sept. 28, 1861, inclosing Pickett's note to Zamacona.

I derive grim satisfaction in fancying what manner of reply may be made to so embarrassing an offer. That proposition will at least neutralize the effect of one of the most formidable weapons at the command of the United States minister and silence this government on the subject of aggression until equitable proposals shall have been made by them and rejected by us."[1] Pickett knew, of course, that the Confederate government would not entertain such a proposition. On the other hand, he realized that it would take several months to transmit the proposal and the reply. In the meantime, so he thought, Federal propaganda guns would be spiked. This proposal did not reach Richmond until Pickett delivered it in person the following spring. For reasons of which he was not aware, the Mexican government showed no signs of being interested in his proposal. On the contrary, despite the constant assurance of the Mexican government that it was friendly and neutral, Pickett sensed a growing hostility. He soon harbored no illusions as to the real attitude of the Juárez government and the public in Mexico City. On November 29, 1861, Pickett reported that at the bottom of this unfriendliness was the proposed Corwin loan treaty, the annexation of Texas—and other territories—and a "real or pretended fear that the South would, at some indefinite day, conquer the entire country and enslave all the dark-skinned population (say nine tenths of it)." These ideas have been worked on by the United States minister, and "it is easy to conceive that this enmity has reached a degree of intensity little short of positive hostility."[2]

Pickett had advised as early as October 29 that the Confederacy should have no further dealings with the Juárez government. In fact, he insisted, in his communications with Toombs, that the permit given the United States to transport a military force across Mexican territory was a violation of neutrality and that the Confederacy should take appropriate action. Indeed, it would furnish "a golden opportunity to the people of the Confederate States of fulfilling speedily a portion of that inevitable destiny which impels them Southward." If for no other reason, the Confederacy should seize

[1] *Ibid.*

[2] *Ibid.*, No. 13, Nov. 29, 1861.

Mexican territory to prevent it from falling into the hands of the United States under the Corwin treaty. He advised the immediate seizure of Monterrey, Nuevo León—Vidaurri's stronghold and a center of Confederate influence and Mexican sympathy for the Confederacy, as we shall see presently. Pickett was indeed out of touch with his government.[1]

Almost from the time he had arrived at Mexico City, Pickett had been on friendly terms with former supporters of the Miramon Conservative government. As the days passed and the hostility of the government and the people of Mexico City became more pronounced, he openly courted those known to favor the Conservative-Church party. He considered it the party of decency; and he was convinced that it would in some fashion come back into power under the auspices of the European allies who were preparing to intervene. He was, of course, correct, for under the French Emperor the Conservatives gained a new lease of power and Juárez retreated to the mountain fastnesses of San Luis Potosí and North Mexico. But Pickett was not timely. He plucked his fruit while it was still green. The Liberal government remained in Mexico City until May 31, 1863.

By thus courting the enemies of Juárez, he wrote Toombs, he expected to be expelled from Mexico as a dangerous intriguer; but he was run out as an ordinary lawbreaker and disturber of the peace. He not only resumed his sarcastic and indiscreet remarks and associated with those known to be unfriendly to the Liberal government, but conducted himself in the manner of a common bully. He sought out places where Unionists and Union sympathizers gathered and insulted those who looked hostile or made derogatory remarks about the Confederacy or its leaders. Finally, he came upon the right opportunity to display his verbal and fistic skill. Bennett, a rawboned Yankee with as big a mouth as Pickett's and a combative temper, sent word to Pickett that the Confederate government and its officials, including Pickett himself, were scoundrels, liars, and generally a sorry lot. Pickett claimed later, as we shall see, that the name of the wife of a Confederate cabinet member was mentioned in a scandalous

[1] *Ibid.*, No. 12, Oct. 29, 1861.

way and that this was the real basis of his difficulty with Bennett. At any rate, Pickett seized upon the message that Bennett had sent as the justification to accomplish two things: to give an enemy a good beating and get sent out of the country for being *persona non grata*. He called upon Bennett and demanded to know whether or not he had been reported correctly. Bennett seized a club or ax handle and prepared for action. Pickett slapped his face, and "waded into Bennett." In his words, "it became necessary, in self defense, to inflict upon him severe chastisement—which I accomplished with no other weapons than my hands and feet. Despatching that business, I withdrew immediately, and there I supposed the affair would have ended."

Instead of being expelled as a diplomat who had become *persona non grata*, he was arrested, in violation of his diplomatic character, and was thrown in jail as an ordinary criminal. He was certain this was done at the demand of the United States minister. He was kept in jail for thirty days and finally, after bribing the judge and other court officials, he obtained his release.[1]

After this disgraceful episode and his imprisonment as a common lawbreaker, Pickett advised his government to have no further traffic with the Juárez government. The South should, on the contrary, ally itself with Spain, which he, like Corwin and others at the time, believed incorrectly to be the power aiming at the subjugation and annexation of Mexico. "I little thought a few years ago ever to counsel a Spanish alliance, but revolutions bring us into strange company, and I am now prepared to advocate any alliance which may tend to check the expansion of the North." Pickett felt that the Civil War had destroyed the usefulness of the Monroe Doctrine. "The Spaniards are now become our natural allies, and jointly with them we may own the Gulf of Mexico and effect the partition of this magnificent country."[2] Again on December 31, 1861, after he had left Mexico City—not as a diplomat but as disturber of the peace who had barely escaped assassination by certain violent partisans of the

[1] *Ibid.*, No. 13, Nov. 29, and No. 17, Dec. 31, 1861.
[2] *Ibid.*, No. 13, Nov. 29, 1861.

Juárez government—Pickett wrote another dispatch in which he repeated his advice that the Confederacy seize Mexican territory before the European allies engrossed the entire country. The unneutral conduct of the Mexican government and the insult offered the Confederacy by arresting and imprisoning its diplomatic representative furnished excellent grounds on which to act. But beyond all this immediate justification was a more fundamental one—the Mexican people, according to Pickett, were utterly incapable of self-government.[1] His last dispatch was written February 10, 1862, at Vera Cruz, where he had found it pleasant to linger and where he probably would have remained had not the Richmond government recalled him. Pickett handed this dispatch—rather, a copy of it—to the State Department on May 6, 1862, which indicates the time he arrived in the Confederate capital.

Pickett was instructed to return to Richmond as a result of developments which had been observed from Richmond rather than because of his erratic conduct. Assistant Secretary of State Browne explained that in the absence of most of his dispatches it was difficult for the President to determine the causes which had induced Pickett to leave Mexico City; but that in any case it was not deemed necessary now to have a minister at the seat of the Mexican government.[2] The Confederate government had had no information as to Pickett's arrival in Mexico or his activities from the last of May until November 30, a period of six months. About November 30 and December 11, 1861, Pickett's dispatches Nos. 1 and 12, respectively, arrived. These were not very informative, though in the latter Pickett did show a growing hostility to the Mexican government. It was not until about January 28, 1862, that Pickett's dispatch No. 17 of December 31 reached Richmond. In this dispatch, Pickett only mentioned the fight with Bennett but dwelt at length on his trial and imprisonment and the danger of assassination by Juárez partisans. These were apparently the only communications the Confederate

[1] *Ibid.*, No. 17, Dec. 31, 1861.
[2] *Ibid.*, Browne to Pickett, No. 3, Jan. 28, 1862; *O.R.N.*, Ser. 2, Vol. III, p. 322.

State Department received from Pickett until his return in May, 1862, when he delivered duplicates of all his dispatches.[1]

When Pickett delivered in person a complete duplicate file of the dispatches which the State Department had failed to receive, President Davis and his cabinet were outraged, disgusted, and angry. The President's door was literally closed in his face. After vainly seeking an interview with Davis, Pickett entered military service. He could not, however, forget his own mistakes and the humiliation at the hands of the State Department and the President, and he sought vainly to obtain an interview with Davis. The President apparently ignored Pickett in his quietest and most eloquent manner. As late as 1864 the unhappy former diplomatic agent was still seeking to explain away his inexcusably crude and maladroit conduct in Mexico. Pickett, sojourning at the Spottswood Hotel in January, 1864, finally wrote Davis a personal letter. The recent appointment of John Preston to be representative at the seat of the Maximilian government gave Pickett an opportune opening. Since he had never been permitted to render an account of his mission in Mexico, he would now do so in a private letter and memorandum. The fight, he said, had put him under a "cloud." He remarked facetiously that Preston should, on going to Mexico, refrain from "slapping" or "kicking" his opponents. Pickett now realized, if he had not at an earlier time, that his advice as to the annexation of Mexican territory was both foolish in terms of military possibility and contrary to Confederate diplomatic policy. He explained bitterly that his advice as to the policy which the Confederacy should follow had been based upon the belief in the great strength of the Confederacy and in the statesmanship of the Confederate leaders. Had he known that there was so much pettiness and bad temper in high places he would not have been so confident. He then attempted to give the true explanation of his fight with Bennett. The real cause, he wrote Davis, had not been Bennett's insults and slanders of southerners and their government, but a far more delicate matter which he had refrained from alluding to until this day: Bennett, he said, had put out a rumor, instigated by Edward Lee Plumb of the American embassy at Mexico City, "that

[1] See Pickett Papers, Browne to Pickett, No. 1, Nov. 30, No. 2, Dec. 11, 1861, and No. 3, Jan. 28, 1862; *O.R.N.*, Ser. 2, Vol. III, pp. 302–3, 308–9, and 322.

a criminal intimacy had existed for many years, between M. de Saligny, the French plenipotentiary in Mexico, and the wife of a distinguished member of your government." He had challenged Bennett to a duel, and on his refusal to engage in such an affair, had given Bennett a thrashing; and he had written a note to Plumb to stay "out of the reach of the toe of my boots which he ever afterwards did with great adroitness."

Aside from the brawl he had with Bennett and the successful diplomacy and propaganda of Thomas Corwin, Pickett had another and more important explanation for his failure to win even the neutrality of the Juárez government. This, which he inclosed in a separate memorandum, was also an explanation of the failure of the Confederate State Department to receive the dispatches he had written while in Mexico City. The Juárez government had seized all his dispatches and was aware of his real opinion of the Mexicans and their government and of the advice that he was giving the Confederate government to annex Mexican territory. The lost dispatches must have caused the gods to laugh. Pickett mailed duplicates and triplicates of his dispatches at times, and they were sent out of Mexico by way of Matamoras, as that offered the only unbroken route by which they could be sent. Perhaps the two or three letters he received from Richmond after he arrived at Vera Cruz, with their complaints of failure to receive his dispatches, aroused his suspicion. On his return to the Confederacy he passed through Matamoras and interviewed the acting governor of Tamaulipas concerning letters sent through the Mexican post-office at Matamoras. The Governor told him frankly and with relish that all Confederate dispatches and private letters passing in and out of the Confederacy through the Matamoras post-office were detained there indefinitely. Every piece of mail that bore the slightest appearance of an official document was listed and the list forwarded to Juárez, who frequently had the documents and letters themselves sent to his government. But this was not the end of the disaster. Some or all of these Confederate communications were delivered to Corwin or sent directly to Washington after Juárez had finished with them. The Governor further informed Pickett that Juárez had Confederate letters and dispatches thus held up or seized in accordance with the advice of Minister

Corwin. In brief, Zamacona, Juárez, and Corwin read Pickett's letters in which he indicated his low opinion of the Mexicans and their government and urged his government to seize Mexican territory. Indeed, the two sophisticated Mexican statesmen were probably reading the dispatches at the very time that Zamacona and Pickett were declaring the mutual friendship of their governments. Dispatch No. 10 of September 28 was probably lying on Zamacona's desk during Pickett's interview with him. This note, it may be recalled, contained a copy of a note to Zamacona in which Pickett offered to transmit a proposal to the Confederate government that a large portion of the territory acquired from Mexico by the United States should be returned. Pickett's dispatch to the State Department, in which this letter to Zamacona was inclosed, was a gleeful comment on the disappointment and chagrin in store for those who should make the proposal that former Mexican territory be returned to the mother country. Pickett must have indeed felt embarrassed even in 1864 when he thought of this dispatch in particular, which coincided with one of his interviews with Zamacona; and he must have blushed at the intelligence from the governor of Tamaulipas that his dispatches had probably all been turned over to Juárez and Corwin.

But the end of Pickett's trouble had not yet been reached, so he informed Davis in his memorandum of January 11, 1864. Aware that the Confederacy had not received his dispatches, he very carefully made entirely new copies of all of them from his letter book. It probably required several days to accomplish this arduous task. When done with this, he went on to New Orleans and held a conference with Dr. Riddle, the postmaster, in which he explained the need of haste in transmitting the copies of his dispatches to Richmond. Riddle assured him of his full co-operation, whereupon Pickett placed all his dispatches in the postmaster's care. When Pickett reached Richmond, these dispatches had not shown up and they never did. Riddle was a Unionist and a spy and of course these documents went to Washington and not to Richmond.[1]

---

[1] Pickett Papers, Pickett to Davis, Jan. 11, 1864, with memorandum. The memorandum gives an account of the seizure of the dispatches at Matamoras and the delivery of duplicates to Riddle.

Later, during the Presidential campaign of 1868, Pickett obtained possession of a large portion of the Confederate State Department Papers, transported them to Canada on the same train with federal agents, who bought them from him for about seventy thousand dollars after crossing the border. These papers contained, among other matters, accounts of the activities of the various diplomatic commissioners and secret service agents. The Republicans hoped—in vain—to find evidence of northern Democratic intrigue with the Confederacy, which would embarrass and help defeat the Democrats. Pickett probably had very little knowledge of what these papers contained, and it is a safe guess that he had little concern whom the documents might injure. The collection today bears the name of the man who thus disposed of it.

Although Pickett created much ill will at Mexico City, and in the Mexican government, he apparently did very little damage elsewhere to the Confederacy. Apparently there was pro-Confederate sympathy at Vera Cruz, Tampico, Lower California, and in the states of Sonora and Coahuila. In the other northern border states, under the control or influence of Santiago Vidaurri, relations with the Confederacy were friendly and profitable to the Mexicans and the southerners. Even Juárez, after his flight to San Luis Potosí in 1863 and during his residence in Nuevo León, was on good terms with the Confederates. The Corwin loan treaty had failed to materialize and so had military aid from the United States. Not that Juárez ever became unfriendly with the United States, but trade and good relations with the Confederacy were profitable and vitally necessary and Juárez became neutral—a state of mind not characteristic of him while in Mexico City.

THOMAS CORWIN, THE FRIEND OF MEXICO

Let us turn for a brief survey of the diplomacy and propaganda of the American diplomatic agents in Mexico which helped defeat Pickett. In April, 1861, Seward dispatched Thomas Corwin as minister to the Juárez government. This was a very clever and tactful move against the Confederate interests in Mexico, for Thomas Corwin had become widely known as a champion of Mexican rights as against southern aggression. It was he who had exclaimed at the outbreak of the Mexican War that he hoped the Mexicans would receive the invading American army with bloody hand and hospitable graves. Pickett could not mention his name and remain calm. The South regarded Corwin as a traitor to his country because of these remarks and his general attitude toward the Mexican War. His appointment would not only be a fine counter irritant for the southern diplomatic agents but an excellent antidote for the generally bad impression held in Mexico of the Secretary of State, William H. Seward, whose expansionist proclivities were even greater than those of Pickett or Davis or any Confederate, for he included not only Mexico and Central America but also Canada in his wild dreams of "Greater America."

Seward instructed Corwin on April 6 to proceed to Mexico. His chief duty at the time was to lay the ax to the roots of every Confederate scheme in Mexico, including Mexican recognition, neutrality, or annexation of Mexican territory, or any move whatsoever that would benefit the Confederate States. Seward wrote that there were good reasons to believe that the Confederacy had designs "to effect either a partial dismemberment or a complete overthrow of the Mexican Government with a view to extend over it the authority of the newly projected Confederacy. . . . . You may possibly meet agents of this projected new Confederacy busy in preparing some further revolution in Mexico. You will not fail to assure the Government of Mexico that the President neither has nor can ever have any sympathy with such designs in whatever quarter they may arise or whatever character they may take on." This was not only a warning to the Mexican government against southern aggression, but a self-denying ordinance on the part of the new United States Secretary of State both for himself and his government. Having convinced Mexico of the essential unselfishness of the North and its friendship for Mexico, and of southern enmity and greed, Corwin was to proceed then to convince the Mexican government that the safety and existence of Mexico depended upon the restoration of the Union, for the success of the Confederacy would be followed by the conquest of

Mexico. If Mexico could be convinced of the danger lying in Confederate success, then it would be easy to convince the government of the necessity of doing nothing which would aid the Confederacy. The work of Corwin, then, would consist primarily in proving American friendship and Confederate enmity.[1]

Corwin, on his arrival, found many rumors afloat concerning Confederate designs in Mexico. He, of course, proceeded to alarm the Mexican government and ingratiate himself and the United States with the Juárez régime. But if Juárez had only read his dispatches as he probably did those of the ill-starred Pickett, he must have indeed drawn his cloak about his head and resigned himself and his government to death. It turned out that Corwin was just as greedy for Mexican territory as any southerner had been in 1846. His whole solicitude for Mexico had been that it should not fall into southern hands. The real guardians of liberty were the North. Mexico would be free and happy under their control. But this anticipates the story. The rumor of southern aggression in Mexico which first upset Corwin was that the South was preparing to seize Lower California. Thomas Sprague, former United States commercial agent in that state, notified Corwin of the alleged schemes of the Confederacy. Corwin immediately urged upon Seward the necessity of circumventing these plans. "A glance at the map will satisfy any one that it is not to be permitted by the United States that any power but that of Mexico should possess the Peninsula of Lower California. If a power hostile to the United States were established there it could work incalculable mischief to our Pacific trade, and in many ways embarrass our states and territories on that coast." Corwin was ready to take vigorous action—ready to seize Lower California upon the basis of this rumor. "Should the Government at Washington deem it proper that I should take any steps to prevent the occupation of Lower California by any power hostile to us, I hope to receive instructions promptly pointing out the course to be pursued." Corwin forwarded the letter Sprague had written him indorsing the latter's opinion that "the possession of Lower California

[1] U.S. Inst. Mexico, Vol. 17, Seward to Corwin, No. 2, April 6, 1861; Roeder, *Juárez and His Mexico*, pp. 350–52.

is abolutely and indispensably necessary to the proper advancement
and protection of the Pacific interests of the United States . . . . rather
than the filibustering secessionists should get possession of the Peninsula of Lower California I think our Government quite warranted (in
case no arrangement could be made for its purchase) in taking possession of it for our own protection. At least to hold it against the designs of the secessionists."[1] This letter to Seward was about simultaneous with Corwin's official interview with the Mexican government
in which Seward's instructions proclaiming America's friendship for
Mexico had been presented, and in which the evil designs of the Confederacy had been urged as reasons why Mexico should cleave to the
United States and abhor the Confederacy as one would a viper.

Four days after Corwin's dispatch had been written Seward wrote
him that he had just received a message from Lower California disclosing the designs of the Confederates to seize that state from
Mexico. Though he was not to receive until later Corwin's letter
making the same disclosures and urging the purchase or seizure of
Lower California by the United States, Seward anticipated the
matter by instructing Corwin almost as Corwin had requested.
Seward urged that he hasten to lay the danger of Confederate designs before Juárez. This would checkmate the Confederate agents
by convincing the Mexican government of the friendship of the
United States and of Confederate hostility, and it might frighten
Juárez into selling Lower California to the United States. "The
United States do not desire to acquire any part of Mexico," wrote
Seward blandly. "They would, however, purchase Lower California
or any part of it in preference to seeing it inevitably fall into the
hands of the insurrectionary party of this Country by purchase or by
conquest." This was an excellent basis upon which to make the appeal to the Mexican government, namely, that the United States,
the friend of Mexico, would purchase Lower California to prevent
the Confederacy, Mexico's enemy, from getting it.[2] Seward instructed Corwin that the land and naval forces of the United States

[1] U.S. Des., Mexico, Vol. 28, Corwin to Seward, No. 1 with inclosure G, May 29,
1861.

[2] U.S. Inst. Mexico, Vol. 17, Seward to Corwin, No. 8, June 3, 1861.

would aid the Mexican government in preventing the seizure of Lower California by the Confederates.

By the time Pickett had arrived in Mexico City, Corwin and Seward, as has been observed, seem to have been successful in convincing the Juárez government of the good will of the United States and the evil designs of the Confederacy. Corwin wrote Seward on June 29, 1861, that Juárez now regarded the United States as Mexico's only friend,[1] and in his next letter[2] Seward was assured that "well informed Mexicans in and out of the Government seem to be well aware that the independence of a Southern Confederacy would be the signal for a war of conquest with a view to establish slavery in each of the twenty-two states of this Republic." This tallies with the very first report of public opinion in Mexico made by Pickett. It is an ironic commentary upon this dispatch to Seward, reporting the basis of Mexican friendship toward the United States as fear of Confederate aggression, to point out that in this very dispatch Corwin urged a loan to Mexico based upon Mexican land as a security, which "would end in the cession of the sovereignty to us."

Having convinced Mexico of the unfriendly designs of the Confederacy and to that extent checkmated Confederate diplomacy, Corwin and Seward reaped their first material fruits by obtaining the privilege of marching American troops across Sonora from California into Arizona. So well had the diplomacy and propaganda of the United States worked that when the question of allowing this passage of troops was considered in the Mexican Congress, it passed by unanimous vote. The members even took the ground that they must not only grant this privilege, but must take sides with the United States, and enter a treaty with that country which would guarantee them against further aggression from the South.[3]

Perhaps the most effective work done by Corwin in heading off southern diplomacy and intrigue in Mexico was the effort he made to induce the United States to lend Mexico first nine, and later eleven, million dollars. Pickett had very cynically urged upon the Confederate Secretary of State that a million dollars would purchase

---

[1] U.S. Des., Mexico, Vol. 28, Corwin to Seward, No. 2 with inclosures, June 29, 1861.

[2] *Ibid.*, No. 3 with inclosures, July 29, 1861.   [3] *Ibid.*, No. 2, June 29, 1861.

recognition from the Mexican government. Corwin determined to risk eleven million dollars partly for the purpose of defeating Confederate designs in Mexico and preventing Confederate recognition, and partly to defeat European intervention in Mexico. Corwin suggested that this loan be made to Juárez to put him in a proper state of mind as well as of defense before Pickett arrived in Mexico City. Perhaps Corwin's eagerness to lend Juárez so large a sum was greatly stimulated by discovery through one of Pickett's intercepted dispatches that Juárez was holding semiofficial intercourse with that gentleman.[1]

While Pickett was holding his interviews, Corwin urged the Mexican loan treaty, to make sure that no favors should be shown the Confederacy. His first recommendation to Seward was in his second dispatch of June 29. In that communication he urged that a loan of several millions be made to put Mexico in a state of defense against her Confederate and European enemies and to pay off the interest on the debts owed Spain, France, and England. The basis of this loan was to be the public lands of East Mexico. He also urged that Lower California might be bought and money supplied the needy Mexican government. This territory was of "no value to Mexico," he urged, and was indispensable to the United States.[2] On July 29, not having received instructions from Seward, Corwin renewed his urging that the United States must lend Mexico money to put its house in order and prevent the Confederates and the European powers from dividing up that unhappy land. He urged upon Seward the need of haste. Pickett had been in communication with the Juárez government, though that government maintained, said Corwin, that it would not "entertain any proposition coming from that quarter which may seem to recognize these States in any other light than as part of the United States." Corwin was sure this assertion as to the attitude of the Mexican government—made by Juárez himself— was honest, but nevertheless the loan should be granted soon to head off not so much Confederate diplomacy as Confederate and European conquest. "Mexico," he said, "would be willing to pledge all

---

[1] *Ibid.*, No. 8 with inclosures of correspondence with Mexican Foreign Minister, Nov. 29, 1861.

[2] *Ibid.*, No. 2 with inclosures, June 29, 1861.

her public lands and mineral rights in Lower California, Chihuahua, Sonora, and Sinaloa, as well as her national faith for the payment of this guarantee. This would probably end in the cession of the sovereignty to us. It would be certain to end there if the money were not promptly paid as agreed on." He would not advise such a step if Mexico were able to save herself from the despoiling hands of the Confederates and Europeans. But that seemed impossible. Besides, it would be only the good fortune of Mexico if that unhappy nation fell into the protecting arms of the United States, for "the United States are the only safe guardians of the independence and true civilization of this continent. It is their mission and they should fulfil it."

Besides, the annexation of these Mexican states would make up for the loss of the southern states. "England and Spain are now in possession of the best of the West Indies . . . . and Mexico, a colony of England with British power on the North of our possessions, would leave on the map of this continent a very unimportant part for the United States—especially should the present unnatural rebellion end in the final severance from us of the eight or nine or all of the slave states." Mexico must not be allowed to go to England; rather than that, the United States must have her, and the best way to prevent England or the Confederacy from getting her and to obtain a good portion for the United States was the proposed treaty which Corwin urged upon Seward.[1]

On August 29 Corwin again urged that Seward instruct him to draw up this treaty.[2] Especially urgent was this dispatch. Pickett's threat, that thirty thousand diplomatic agents would cross the border into Mexico if Juárez allowed American troops to cross the Mexican territory into Arizona, had recently reached him. Juárez might not have been so enthusiastic about a loan whose immediate purpose was to head off Confederate and European aggression if he had known that its ultimate design was aimed at the acquisition of Mexico by the United States.

Seward was just as anxious to circumvent Confederate or Euro-

[1] *Ibid.*, No. 3 with inclosure, July 29, 1861.

[2] *Ibid.*, No. 4 with inclosures, Aug. 29, 1861.

pean aggression as was Corwin. His expansionist tendencies, though somewhat subdued for the moment by the Battle of Bull Run and other minor defeats, responded to Corwin's proposed treaty. On August 24 he instructed Corwin to proceed with the negotiation. This was in dispatch No. 15. But Seward was by this time becoming a circumspect statesman. He did not send the dispatch to Corwin; he sent copies to Adams in England and Dayton in France. Before Corwin was to be allowed to make a loan treaty with Mexico, Dayton and Adams must sound out the French and English cabinets to find out whether those governments would approve of this loan and to find out whether they would refrain from intervention if the United States should thus guarantee the payment of the interest upon the Mexican debts. The Mexican question was ceasing to be merely one between the Confederacy and the United States and was involving Europe, and Seward did not intend to waste money on Mexico if Europe intended to intervene regardless of the loan. Nor did he intend to play into the hands of the Confederates by offending the English and French in an attempt to aid Mexico against them. He would ask their consent.[1]

A few days later, however, he instructed Corwin[2] to proceed to negotiate the proposed treaty, having Mexico pledge as security all her public lands in "the several Mexican states of Lower California, Chihuahua, Sonora and Sinaloa" with the condition that "the property so pledged to become absolute in the United States at the expiration of the term of six years. . . . ." But he informed Corwin that this treaty was to be ratified solely upon condition that England and France should promise not to intervene while it was pending ratification or while the interest was being paid upon the Mexican debts after ratification.

Dayton interviewed Thouvenel immediately on the proposed loan to Mexico. Thouvenel told him Lord Lyons had already sent dispatches which covered Seward's proposition. The upshot of the interview was that France did not agree to refrain from intervention on condition of America's paying the interest on the Mexican debt

[1] U.S. Inst., France, Vol. 16, Seward to Dayton, No. 49, Sept. 2, 1861.

[2] U.S. Inst. Mexico, Vol. 17, Seward to Corwin, No. 17, Sept. 2, 1861.

by such a loan. Thouvenel insisted that France wanted the principal and not the interest. Dayton protested that America could not see Mexico subjected. Thouvenel replied that thus far the only country which had subjugated and despoiled Mexico was the United States. But he assured Dayton that it was only to collect the debts that France was intervening. Dayton wrote Seward, however, that he could not help but feel that the European powers were taking an advantage of the "present distracted conditions of the United States" to commit an act they would not dare in peace times.[1] After sounding out the British, French, and Spanish governments[2] Dayton reported that no treaty such as that which Corwin proposed would be acceptable to the three intervening powers as a sufficient guaranty. France, Dayton reported, was especially hostile to any American interference. The other two, England and Spain, were at least willing for America to join in the intervention. On November 6, 1861, Dayton notified Seward that the question was closed. The allies had just drawn up their convention agreeing to intervene jointly in Mexico. America, he said, had been asked to join—after everything had been agreed upon. Dayton had rather pointedly told Thouvenel that it was a little late for such an invitation.[3]

In the meanwhile acting upon Seward's tentative instructions contained in No. 17, Corwin entered negotiations with the Mexican government for a loan of a million dollars.[4] On November 29, 1861, Corwin wrote Seward that he had completed the draft of such a treaty based upon the mortgage of the public lands in Lower California, Chihuahua, Sonora, and Sinaloa; but because of Mexican refusal to meet certain very moderate proposals of the British government, he would not ask the ratification of the treaty by the Mexican Congress until further instructions from Seward.[5]

On December 5 Seward had received a reply to his query sent to France, England, and Spain as to whether the proposed treaty would

[1] U.S. Des., France, Vol. 50, Dayton to Seward, No. 51, Sept. 27, 1861. See below.

[2] Ibid., No. 62, Oct. 16, 1861.

[3] Ibid., Vol. 51, Dayton to Seward, No. 74, Nov. 6, 1861.

[4] U.S. Des., Mexico, Vol. 28, No. 7, Corwin to Seward, Oct. 29, 1861.

[5] Ibid., No. 8, Nov. 29, 1861.

be acceptable and as to whether the powers would refrain from intervention in Mexico. Thereupon he wrote Corwin of the negative result obtained by his inquiry through Adams, Dayton, and Schurz. However, he directed Corwin to complete his treaty and forward it.[1] He thought the United States Senate might act favorably. But the Senate, after two or three months' intermittent deliberation, rejected the proposed treaty,[2] and Seward instructed Corwin that nothing else could be done.[3] Corwin, however, continued for some time to urge the ratification of the pact. It was the only way Mexico could be saved from Europe[4] and the Confederacy.

It is not the purpose, at this point, to give a full history of the Corwin treaty with all its ramifications. It is merely given in its main outlines as an aid in understanding one of the chief means of winning Mexican friendship for the United States and of defeating the diplomacy of the Confederates—especially that of Pickett. It was very effective. Though aimed at Europe, more and more as intervention menaced, it had the results of aiding very greatly in turning the Juárez government against the South, while there was any prospect of Juárez obtaining the eleven-million-dollar loan—in other words, until the late summer of 1862, when the Juárez government was no longer able to do the Federal government much good or harm. The prospect of the eleven-million-dollar loan and accompanying Federal protection enabled Corwin to have Pickett practically drummed out of Mexico, for there can be no doubt that many of Pickett's difficulties with the Mexican authorities, including his long term in jail and the threat of assassination, can be laid at Corwin's feet;[5] and Corwin induced Juárez to issue an order to Vidaurri and other border governors to cease intercourse with the

[1] U.S. Inst., Mexico, Vol. 17, Seward to Corwin, No. 32, Dec. 5, 1861.

[2] *Ibid.*, No. 36, Jan. 24, 1862; *ibid.*, No. 37, Feb. 15, 1862.

[3] *Ibid.*, No. 43, April 3, 1862; *ibid.*, No. 48, May 28, 1862.

[4] See, e.g., U.S. Des., Mexico, Vol. 29, Corwin to Seward, No. 21, April 16; No. 23, May 4; No. 24, May 20, 1862.

[5] See U.S. Inst. Mexico, Vol. 17, Seward to Corwin, No. 27, Oct. 14, 1861, and U.S. Des., Mexico, Vol. 28, Corwin to Seward, No. 8, with inclosures, Nov. 29, 1861. This latter dispatch gives an account of how Corwin protested against Pickett's claim to diplomatic immunity, and how he demanded that no kind of recognition be given the Confederacy. Just after this Pickett was thrown into jail again, undoubtedly to please Corwin.

Confederacy—though Vidaurri's greed for Confederate trade and desire for Confederate friendship caused him to ignore the order.[1]

After a year and a half of propaganda against the Confederacy and Europe, after a year of negotiation upon the eleven-million-dollar loan to Mexico—though Corwin showed as much anxiety and greediness for the acquisition of Mexican soil as Napoleon III or Pickett—he was able to write Seward: "Mexico, or rather the thinking men of Mexico, look upon our struggle with as deep and absorbing interest as that which they feel in regard to their own impending conflict. They seem to entertain a sad and profound conviction that our failure will be the doom of free government everywhere on earth."[2]

JUAN A. QUINTERO'S MISSION TO THE BORDER STATES

While Pickett's mission to the Mexican government was a complete failure, the Confederate diplomatic ventures in the border states, especially Nuevo León, Coahuila, and Tamaulipas (for a season), were successful beyond any earlier hopes. Even in the states of Sonora and Chihuahua, rather inaccessible, there was some success. It was wise on the part of the Mexican border states not to invite Confederate invasion by unfriendly acts. Furthermore, the states would be able to sell to the Confederacy many of their products— heretofore unsalable—and at exorbitant prices. As previously suggested, these same states—especially Nuevo León, Coahuila, and Tamaulipas—supplied a route over which European goods and materials of war could be carried into the Confederacy and cotton carried out. Furthermore, these states could levy high tariffs on goods going and coming and in addition act as middleman for the same articles.

Finally, there was a strong political reason for Mexican border-state friendship with the Confederacy. Several of these states had exercised almost complete independence for a number of years and opposed vigorously all serious attempts of the central government to assert its authority over them. The most powerful of the border-state rulers was Santiago Vidaurri, governor of Nuevo León and Coahuila.

[1] Pickett Papers, Quintero to Benjamin, July 5 and Sept. 24, 1862.

[2] U.S. Des., Mexico, Vol. 29, Corwin to Seward, No. 33, Sept. 28, 1862.

At times Vidaurri controlled Tamaulipas and exercised great influence in Chihuahua and other provinces. His government was stable and effective, despite the turmoil in the interior states. He became a nominal supporter of Juárez and so remained for some time after the American Civil War began. But because of his fear of Juárez he became more and more identified with the Conservatives. They were the weaker party—until the French intervention—and therefore seemed to offer less danger to his independent position than the Liberals. It seems that Vidaurri designed ultimately, if possible, to consolidate into an independent government all the border states lying along the northeast border. It was natural for Vidaurri to seek a strong connection with the Confederacy, but, as we shall see, the connection that he proposed seems astounding in view of the attitude toward the Confederacy of the populace of Mexico City and the members of the Mexican Liberal government.

President Davis sent a number of agents to the border states of Mexico. The most important and the most effective of these was Juan A. Quintero, a Cuban by birth, a former resident of Mexico, and a citizen of the Confederacy. He was a clever and resourceful diplomat who handled many delicate and involved situations with skill and success. On May 22, 1861, Quintero was given his instructions to undertake a mission to the Vidaurri government of about six weeks' duration. The chief purpose of the mission was to reach an agreement with Vidaurri—with whom Quintero was already acquainted—concerning border security. Rumors were already circulating that renegade Americans and Mexican outlaws were assembling across the Rio Grande with the intention of making incursions into Texas. Quintero was to stress the danger to both the Confederate and the Mexican border states of such raids, and at the same time to assure Vidaurri that the Confederacy would employ every effort to prevent raids by renegade Mexicans and others into Vidaurri's territory.[1]

Vidaurri welcomed Quintero most heartily on his arrival at Monterrey. He informed Quintero that the states of Nuevo León and Coahuila, over which he ruled, as well as the border states to the

[1] Pickett Papers, Toombs to Quintero, May 22, 1861; *O.R.N.*, Ser. 2, Vol. III, p. 217.

north and Tamaulipas to the south, were favorably disposed toward the Confederacy and that the Confederacy need have no fear that raids into Texas would be tolerated from any portion of his territory. Not only did Vidaurri meet the Confederacy over half way concerning border security, but he plunged headlong into a far more serious matter. He frankly told Quintero that he would like to ally his states with the Confederacy and, if necessary to secure these states against the subordination to the central government, he would join them to the Confederacy.[1]

Quintero, having received these unmistakable assurances of Vidaurri's friendship, set about to determine the extent of the material resources of Nuevo León and Coahuila, which could be placed at the disposal of the Confederacy. He soon found that Vidaurri's domain was very rich in natural resources. Lead, saltpeter, powder, copper, coarse cloth, and other products could be obtained in great quantities at reasonable prices.[2]

On his return to Richmond with the cordial greetings of the border governor, indeed the offer of an alliance and tentative application for membership in the Confederacy, and a report on the governor's ample resources to be made available at a reasonable price, Quintero's stock rose high in the Confederate State Department. It is easy to understand in the light of Quintero's report how the center of interest now shifted from Mexico City to Monterrey, Nuevo León. Pickett had not been heard of, or from, when Quintero made his reports on August 19 and 22, nor would any news of him arrive for months to come. The State Department promptly dispatched Quintero back to Monterrey as resident diplomatic and commercial agent accredited to Governor Vidaurri. He was far more important than Pickett could have been even had the latter been a first-class diplomat. The Vidaurri government to which Quintero was accredited was in a much better position to aid or injure the Confederacy than was the Juárez government, whose actual power was primarily in southern and western Mexico—far from the Confederate border. The Confederate State Department soon realized this, and as we

[1] Pickett Papers, Quintero to Toombs, Aug. 19 and 22, 1861, with inclosures.
[2] *Ibid.*

have seen, appointed no one to court the friendship or even the neutrality of Juárez after Pickett's failure.

Quintero was instructed to cultivate good relations with the border states, make convenient commercial arrangements, and seek to induce Vidaurri to prevent, if possible, the transportation of troops and munitions across Mexican territory. But the matter of an alliance with the Mexican border states or their admission into the Confederacy must be courteously rejected, for "the president is of the opinion," wrote Assistant Secretary of State William M. Browne, "that it would be imprudent and impolitic in the interest of both parties to take any steps at present in regard to the proposition made by Governor Vidaurri in his confidential communication with you in reference to the future political relations of the Confederate States and the Northern Provinces of Mexico. He may be assured, however, that the Government of the Confederate States feels a deep sympathy with all the people struggling to secure for themselves the blessings of self government and is, therefore, much interested in the cause and progress of these Provinces."[1]

Davis in refusing the possible accession of the Mexican border states was following the probable line of development that the Confederacy would have taken had it won its independence. There was no longer the balance of power between the sections to be considered as in former days when new territory was wanted for slave states to match the free states. Nor was pride in power and size as yet very strong. But even had he and his cabinet desired to add the border states to the Confederacy, Davis certainly had the good sense not to attempt it. It would have no doubt frightened and antagonized the border states not under Vidaurri's control and certainly would have brought the Confederacy into a state of war with the Juárez government. Furthermore, Davis and his cabinet were acutely aware of the European aspect of the Mexican question. It was understood in Confederate circles, earlier perhaps than at Washington, that Great Britain, France, and Spain would intervene, and that Napoleon would ultimately attempt to establish a puppet empire in Mexico.

[1] *Ibid.*, Browne to Quintero, Sept. 3, 1861, with inclosure; *O.R.N.*, Ser. 2, Vol. III, pp. 253–55; Rippy, p. 235.

It was also believed that the United States would oppose such intervention, which might lead to war with the European powers. This, of course, would result in the independence of the Confederacy. On the other hand, should the South attempt to acquire territory in Mexico at this time, it would incur the displeasure of the intervening powers, especially France.

Quintero, on his return to Monterrey, was cordially received as the official agent of the Confederate government. Had Vidaurri laid technical claims to the complete sovereignty of his states of Nuevo León and Coahuila, his official acceptance of Quintero would have been a recognition of the independence of the Confederacy. He warned Quintero that Juárez had granted permission to the United States to transport troops and munitions through Sonora and other Mexican territory into Arizona and New Mexico. But he assured him that he would oppose the passage of these troops across his own states of Nuevo León and Coahuila, and that he would use his influence with the other states of the North to prevent this violation of neutrality.[1] Quintero was greatly impressed with the two states under Vidaurri's rule and the general evidence of power and a well-ordered society. "Governor Vidaurri," he wrote Secretary of State R. M. T. Hunter, "is much feared not only by President Juárez but also by the people of the interior states. For years he has ruled supreme and the states of New León and Coahuila have under his administration been prosperous and happy. Hence his popularity on the frontier. He is our faithful friend and ally."[2]

Governor Vidaurri's blessings soon brought merchants and manufacturers to Quintero's office pressing for contracts to furnish supplies for the Confederacy. Confederate contractors and purchasing agents swarmed across the border to do business with those who had military supplies to sell or who would import supplies from abroad and exchange them for cotton. For example, the firm of Oliver and Brothers of Monterrey contracted to deliver all the powder and saltpeter that could be purchased in the state of Zacatecas, and stated that they would deliver everything in the way of military supplies,

[1] Pickett Papers, Quintero to Browne, Nov. 4, 1861.
[2] *Ibid.*, Quintero to R. M. T. Hunter, Nov. 10, 1861.

except small arms, that the Confederates desired.[1] A. Urbahan of San Antonio, operating with Milmo and Company of Monterrey, contracted to deliver a million pounds of flour in exchange for 850,000 pounds of cotton. Attrill and Lacoste; Dredge, Oetling and Company; and Marks and Company were other large firms of the Mexican border states, most of whom had their headquarters in Matamoras and Monterrey. But the largest and most powerful business firm was that of Milmo and Company, which operated its own large business and helped to finance other companies. Patricio Milmo, head of this company, was Governor Vidaurri's son-in-law, and it appears that Vidaurri had his own financial stake in the company. Vidaurri became so interested in the Confederate cause—and in making money—that in a burst of Latin enthusiasm he proposed in a personal letter to President Davis to supply as much ammunition as the Confederacy would be able to use.[2]

In the spring of 1862 Vidaurri gained control of Tamaulipas, whose principal seaports were Matamoras, at the mouth of the Rio Grande, and Tampico, about three hundred miles to the south. These ports had, of course, been of great importance to the Confederacy even when under the control of the Juárez officials; but sometimes excessive duties were levied. Vidaurri kept the ports open and was far less exacting in the tariffs on imports and exports than his predecessors had been. With Vidaurri in control of Tamaulipas, there were now over five hundred miles of the Rio Grande open to Confederate trade without any but physical obstacles. In a few months Quintero could report that Texas was well supplied with ammunition, principally from and through Nuevo León and Coahuila. He described in some detail the thriving trade between Texas and Northeast Mexico. "There are hundreds of Mexican teamsters and wagons engaged in the trade. Powder, of excellent quality, lead, copper, tin, blankets, coffee, sugar, hides, cloth, brown sheeting for Negro clothing, etc. are abundantly exported. The ports of entry in Texas are Roma, Laredo, and Eagle Pass (mostly from Monterrey). Should the proper arrangements be made I have no doubt that

[1] *Ibid.*, Quintero to Browne, Feb. 9 and March 8, 1862.

[2] *Ibid.*, March 8, 1862, inclosing Vidaurri's letter to Davis.

North Eastern Mexico will be able to fully supply the C.S. with many valuable articles." Quintero added that in the state of Nuevo León "there are eight cotton factories. They have 14,000 spindles and 451 looms. They use over a million and a half lbs. of cotton annually from which are turned out 131,000 pieces of brown sheeting, valued at $5 per piece. . . . . These factories are now furnishing all the necessary clothing for the slaves in Texas and could, if necessary, supply the balance of the C.S."[1]

Quintero soon after this wrote Secretary of State Judah P. Benjamin that he would be able to obtain in Monterrey and adjoining territory five hundred wagons to haul cotton out of Texas in exchange for supplies and specie.[2] This cotton, of course, was intended chiefly for export. The frontier was now quiet and the customhouse at Matamoras was charging only one-fourth of the regular duties on foreign goods imported into Texas, and no duty was charged on Mexican goods thus sold across the Rio Grande.[3]

The Confederate trade with the Mexican border states and through these states with Europe began to have a strong resemblance to the gold rush of '49. Cotton was the magnet. The cotton famine in Europe and the near famine in the United States impelled speculators and buyers to the Mexican ports on the Rio Grande and especially to Matamoras and Monterrey. Matamoras was the one great leak in the Federal blockade—though by inner routes and coastwise vessels cotton was sometimes taken to Tampico before being committed to ocean-going ships. Fleets of ships, a hundred and twenty-five at a time, anchored beyond the sandbanks at the little town of Bagdad, off the port of Matamoras a few miles. These ships brought in munitions and supplies for the Confederacy to be exchanged at exorbitant rates for the cotton painfully hauled by ox and mule teams across the scorching semi-deserts of West Texas.

To purchase the cotton required for this trade, the Confederate government appointed Major Simeon Hart, a well-known frontiersman, merchant, manufacturer, and friend of the businessmen of

[1] *Ibid.*, Quintero to Benjamin, Aug. 14, 1862.
[2] *Ibid.*, Oct. 19, 1862.   [3] *Ibid.*, Sept. 24, 1862.

Monterrey and Matamoras.[1] The state of Texas also had agents in the same territory buying cotton and exchanging it for supplies across the Rio Grande.[2] The several commanders of the military districts and subdistricts—Magruder, McCulloch, Bee, and Slaughter —of the Trans-Mississippi Department had cotton-buyers in the field; and E. Kirby Smith, commander of the Trans-Mississippi Department, established the Cotton Bureau under Lieutenant Colonel W. A. Broadwell for the purpose of obtaining cotton for the Mexican trade.[3] Finally, private speculators in large numbers obtained special permits from the military to enter the field. This latter group at one time managed to obtain the use of five thousand conscript teamsters from the governor of Texas by an agreement—which they did not carefully observe—to devote their importations to military and other necessary supplies.

This multiplicity of agents and the ensuing competition and confusion drove up the price of cotton and sometimes prevented the accumulation of an adequate supply in the hands of Simeon Hart and other agents who had legal priority in the business. This in turn occasionally caused delay in the payment for supplies purchased from the Mexican importers and local merchants. Perhaps the most serious occurrence resulting from such delay was Milmo and Company's seizure for debt of a sixteen-million-dollar fund of the Confederate Treasury in transit through the border states of Mexico to Texas.

But there were other difficulties and obstacles that occasionally impeded the free exchange of cotton and supplies between the Mexican border states and the Confederacy. Beginning in 1862 there occurred a series of border raids that brought into full use all of Quintero's diplomatic talent. As we shall presently see, he dealt with marked success with these border incidents. But two other difficulties which did not yield to diplomacy confronted the cotton trade. A great drought which had blanketed the Mexican border states and Texas for a time reached a blazing climax in 1863. It destroyed the grass and the already scarce water supply and rendered transporta-

[1] *O.R.*, Ser. 1, Vol. XV, p. 866.

[2] *Ibid.*, Vol. LIII, pp. 1008–10.   [3] *Ibid.*, Vol. XXII, Part II, p. 953.

tion of cotton and supplies extremely difficult and dangerous. During the same year, General Nathaniel Banks captured Brownsville across the Rio Grande from Matamoras and held it for several months. The supply of cotton and military equipment passing through Brownsville was thus checked at this point and was diverted at the cost of long delay and great expense through Eagle Pass, Roma, and Laredo from one to two hundred miles up the Rio Grande.

The first serious disturber of the peace on the border was José-María Carvajal. He was a well-educated, polished, and affable filibuster who had numerous and important Texas friends. Among these friends was Colonel John S. Ford, commanding at Brownsville in 1862. In the spring of this year Carvajal established headquarters at Brownsville, with Ford's tacit approval, and began his old habit of assembling a band of nondescript Mexicans and Texans and raiding across the Rio Grande against Tamaulipas, which Vidaurri controlled at the time. Carvajal and Vidaurri were both old supporters of the scheme to form the North Mexican states into a separate nation to be called the Sierra Madras Republic. But the two men were bitter personal enemies, for Carvajal, unlike Vidaurri, had been unsuccessful in gaining power and attracting a real following. In the light of Vidaurri's friendship for the Confederacy and his material aid, he naturally expected the Confederate officials to show Carvajal no favors. Then, too, he and the Confederate government had a mutual agreement to the effect that no such raids would be for one moment sanctioned or permitted to occur through carelessness. Naturally he was outraged at the Confederacy for harboring his enemy and allowing him to violate its neutrality.

Quintero shared Vidaurri's resentment against Ford—though he was certain that the higher authorities of the Confederate government did not sanction the harboring of Carvajal. After protesting vainly to Colonel Ford and his military superior, McCulloch, and to Governor Lubbock, he took the drastic step of offering his resignation in a letter to Assistant Secretary of State Browne. In his communication he minced no words. Ford was actually aiding Carvajal, he said, and friendly relations on the Mexican frontier were fast disappearing. He reminded Browne that he had already expressed his fears to the department and he now apprehended serious difficulties. "The General Government of Mexico as you are well aware sympathizes with the Black Republicans. We have, however, succeeded in securing the friendship of the Governors of the frontier states and now are on the eve of incurring their enmity, on account of the band of robbers who are permitted to abuse the hospitality of Texas." He wrote that he had exerted his efforts to avoid difficulty and "have on all occasions recommended the necessity of cultivating friendly relations with the Mexican frontier, in as much as the Governor of New León, Coahuila, and Tamaulipas sympathizes with us, controls the ports of Tampico, Sola La Morna, and Matamoras, and has heretofore allowed us to introduce all kinds of goods into Texas . . . . but I fear that new aggressions will change him or compel his troops on the right bank of the Rio Grande to retaliate."[1]

In a few days, Vidaurri began to fulfil Quintero's prophecy. He began to retaliate. He levied a duty of two cents a pound upon all cotton exports and he raised the import, transportation, and harbor duties to almost prohibitive levels. But Quintero, though he had not as yet heard from the Confederate State Department or from Generals Magruder and Smith, felt reasonably sure that the Confederate authorities did not sanction Carvajal's violation of Texas neutrality or of Colonel Ford's tolerance, if not support, of the filibuster's raids. Feeling thus, he sharply challenged the justice and expediency of Vidaurri's retaliatory measures. But Vidaurri blandly assured Quintero that the heavy duties were not retaliatory measures. They were, he insisted, levied solely for the purpose of increasing the revenue of which his government stood in great need. Quintero was not at all impressed by Vidaurri's explanation. A Latin himself, he understood the Latin characteristics of Vidaurri's conduct and he called his hand. He insisted in a strong but courteous note of protest that the new duties were levied for no other purpose than retaliation, and he affirmed that Vidaurri was pursuing such a course against a friendly government which did not approve of the harboring of the governor's enemy. It "looks too much (permit me to say it in all candor) like

---

[1] Pickett Papers, Quintero to Browne, March 28, 1862.

misuse of power to require duty to be paid upon goods passing through the country as if they were intended for consumption." He warned Vidaurri that he was killing the goose that laid the golden egg. Trade was already seeking an outlet through the blockade to avoid paying such duties. Quintero's forthright letter brought Vidaurri to a sense of reality. His position and influence as a political and military leader depended now almost entirely on the customs and profits received on the Rio Grande from the Confederate trade. Though still angry at the failure of the Confederate military authorities to dislodge Carvajal, he nevertheless repealed most of the duties.[1]

Before Vidaurri had devised other and less expensive ways of showing his displeasure at the Confederate military officials in West Texas, his grievance was suddenly removed. General McCulloch, who had received orders from higher up and who had had time to obtain more information about Carvajal, ordered Ford to arrest and deliver him to Vidaurri if he persisted in his lawless activities against Tamaulipas. This order put an end to Carvajal's activities on Texas soil, and Vidaurri's friendship was salvaged.

Quintero, always following up his successes, was not content to allow the matter to rest here; he insisted that the customs be reduced still further.[2] In a few months he had induced Vidaurri to abolish all export duties on Mexican goods shipped into the Confederacy.[3] At this time, too, Juárez, who was still laboring under the delusion that the Corwin loan treaty would be ratified and who wished to put the United States under obligation to him, ordered Vidaurri to cease all trade and intercourse with the Confederacy. Juárez was in Mexico City over six hundred miles by mountain trails from Monterrey, and already the French were preparing to march against him. Vidaurri, and even the officials in Matamoras who owed their appointment to Juárez, paid no heed to the order. The Confederate trade continued to increase in volume and in importance to the border states.[4]

The next raid to disturb the good relations between the Mexican border states and the Confederacy came from the Mexican side.

[1] *Ibid.*, April 17, 1862.   [3] *Ibid.*, July 5, 1862.
[2] *Ibid.*, April 28, 1862.   [4] *Ibid.*

A. J. Hamilton, Judge J. E. Davis, and William Montgomery, Confederate renegades, had "holed up" in Matamoras, where they received cordial treatment from General Traconis, another patriot bandit, who had succeeded Vidaurri as ruler of the city, though scarcely of the state of Tamaulipas. The new governor, egged on by the United States consul, L. Pierce, encouraged the Texan refugees and Mexican bandits who consorted with them to raid the Confederate border in retaliation for the harboring of Carvajal.[1] Thus encouraged, the bandit Zapata at the head of a gang of mixed Mexican outlaws and Texan Unionists and deserters, styling themselves the First Regiment of Union Troops, made a murderous and destructive raid on the Texas border.[2]

Retaliation from the Confederate side came swiftly and without consideration of diplomatic consequences. Confederates slipped into Matamoras and "spirited" to the left bank of the Rio Grande, Judge Davis, Montgomery, and several others who had been openly recruiting raiders in the streets of Matamoras. Several were promptly executed. Although Quintero was afraid that the raid would result in the alienation of the Mexican border states, he nevertheless felt a certain grim satisfaction. Doubtless he wished that the Confederate net had swept in the obnoxious Hamilton; but Davis and Montgomery, after all, were a good catch. They, at least, would give no more trouble. "I have reason," he wrote Benjamin, "to believe [that they] will not commit treason again in this world. They are permanently located in the soil of the Country."[3] General Lopez, who succeeded Traconis at Matamoras, demanded that the Confederate authorities return Davis and the others and he advised Juárez to close the entire frontier until this was done.[4] General Hamilton Bee, now in command of West Texas and well acquainted with the Mexican border, realized the gravity of the situation. Matamoras, he

---

[1] *Ibid.*, Quintero to Benjamin, Aug. 30, 1862.

[2] *Ibid.*, Jan. 30 and Feb. 26, 1863; for other examples of the incitement and planning of such raids by the U.S. consul, see U.S. Consular Des., Matamoras, Vol. 7, L. Pierce to Seward, April 30, 1862, and June 6, 1863.

[3] Pickett Papers, Quintero to Benjamin, March 21, 1863.

[4] *Ibid.*, April 20, 1863.

wrote Quintero, was becoming hostile to the Confederacy, and the friendship of Nuevo León and Coahuila was jeopardized. In view of this danger to Confederate relations with the border states General Bee returned all the prisoners except Montgomery, who, according to Quintero, had been permanently located in the soil of Texas.[1]

Other raids against Brownsville and the lower Rio Grande Valley of Texas occurred before the end of the war. The two most persistent filibusters were José-María Cobos and Juan Cortinas, both full-time bandits and occasional patriots. In the summer of 1863, when most of the Confederate forces had been pulled farther east, Cobos took possession of Brownsville and used it as a base of operation against Matamoras. With the help of Cortinas, he was able to get possession of Matamoras; but Cortinas turned upon him and had him executed for alleged disloyalty to Juárez. It is not unlikely that Cobos was actually working in the interest of the French, whom the Confederates were urging through the mission of A. Superviéle to occupy Matamoras.[2] The French did not occupy that city until 1863, after Banks had withdrawn from Brownsville, and Cortinas crossed from Matamoras and attacked Colonel Ford at that point at least once. General J. H. Walker, commanding that district, in complete exasperation advised General Slaughter that "should Cortinas fall into your hands he is not to be treated as a prisoner of war but as a robber and murderer, and executed immediately."[3] Apparently, however, such raids were not serious obstacles to the border trade as long as Vidaurri remained in control of Nuevo León, nor when Juárez briefly occupied Monterrey. When the French took over Matamoras and considerable stretches of the Rio Grande in 1864–65, trade was subjected to even less interruption.

Reference has been made to Patricio Milmo's seizure of Confederate funds. The superabundance of purchasing agents on the border, each competing with the others for cotton, often prevented the accumulation in the hands of the authorized agents of supplies of cot-

[1] U.S. Consular Des., Matamoras, Vol. 7, Pierce to Seward, March 26, 1863.

[2] Rippy, pp. 240–43, gives an excellent account of the extended mission of Superviéle to the French commanders and to France to induce the French to occupy Matamoras.

[3] O.R., Ser. 1, Vol. XII, Part III, pp. 972–73.

ton adequate to pay on time for the goods purchased from the contractors in Mexico. Major Hart was the principal victim of this chaotic situation. He had been sending cotton to the frontier to pay on his account only to have it seized by Major Russell, General Bee's quartermaster and agent for the Cotton Bureau, and applied on the debts Russell had made. Milmo and Company was the largest firm with which Hart had dealt and, according to the company's books at least, he owed them a large sum of money payable in cotton. Hart also owed about five hundred thousand pounds of cotton to A. Urbahan of San Antonio, whom Milmo had financed. Urbahan had contracted to deliver a million pounds of flour to the Quartermaster Department, and he had carried it out in good faith. But Hart, owing to Russell's diversion of his cotton, had not been able to meet his payments very promptly. Quite naturally Milmo and Company was concerned over the failure of the Confederate agent to pay Urbahan. But Milmo and Company suddenly became gravely concerned over the claims against the Confederacy of other companies. Indeed, Milmo became the assignee of several of these, most of whose claims were fraudulent or greatly inflated. Two of these companies were Attrill and Lacoste, and Dredge, Oetling and Company. Attrill and Lacoste of Matamoras had contracted to deliver a large quantity of supplies in exchange for cotton. They had attempted to force the Confederate officials to pay them on delivery of the goods prices far above those of the open market. Hart had refused to accept the goods, whereupon Russell, despite Hart's refusal, accepted them and agreed that they should be delivered at Brownsville—after that town had been captured by the Federals. Dredge, Oetling and Company claimed heavy damage against the Confederacy for breach of a contract which Russell had made with them. Russell, ignoring Hart and all other representatives of the Confederacy who had superior authority and prior obligations, agreed to ship to this firm all Confederate cotton that reached the border over a certain period. In addition to this monstrous favor, they were to receive an exceptionally large profit on their goods. There were numerous other sharks who claimed that they too were large-scale creditors of the Confederacy. They, also, were being gathered under the wings of Milmo and Company. The claims were so great, Major Hart said, that they would exhaust "not only what cotton the Government now has on hand in Mexico, but all it could get there within the next six months."[1] The reason for Milmo and Company's acting as agent and assignee of the contracts of these merchants and speculators lay in the fact that Patricio Milmo, head of the company, as before noted, was the son-in-law of Governor Vidaurri, who in turn had an interest in the company.

When Banks's capture of Brownsville severed the direct route to Matamoras, the supply of cotton en route had to be diverted by way of Eagle Pass, Piedras Negras, and Monterrey or other points up the Rio Grande into Nuevo León, Chihuahua, and Tamaulipas. This further delay in delivering cotton exasperated Hart's creditors still more, and Milmo and Company began making impatient and barely courteous demands on the Confederate agent. Then suddenly it must have seemed to Patricio Milmo and all the contractors whom he represented that Providence was indeed smiling upon them. Clarence C. Thayer, agent of the Confederate Treasury, after a long and harassing voyage through blockading squadrons during which his ship had been twice boarded, landed in Matamoras on November 6, 1863, on dangerous and important business. He had with him several boxes containing $16,000,000 for the Trans-Mississippi Military Department. Brownsville had just been captured by the Federals and Matamoras across the Rio Grande had been seized by the bandit patriot, Cortinas. Matamoras was not an ideal spot for a Confederate agent with seven boxes of money. Mexican bandits, Texas renegades, Federal agents, and hungry creditors who were also part-time bandits, were lying in wait for trouble—especially if one had money. Thayer was already badly shaken and when he discovered the situation in Matamoras and at Brownsville he must have been on the verge of panic. He learned that an important Confederate agent was in Matamoras—Major Russell—and he, after considerable difficulty, found Russell in hiding. (He did not want other Confederate agents to know of his presence in Matamoras.) Russell assured Thayer that he was the senior Confederate official in Matamoras and had the

[1] *Ibid.*, Vol. LIII, pp. 930–51.

authority to open all mail to Quintero, Latham (the collector who had been at Brownsville), and other Confederate officials on the border. He also told Thayer that he had authority to give him orders. Under Russell's instructions, Thayer intrusted the Confederate funds to Milmo and Company. Milmo with the strong guard that Vidaurri supplied would, Russell assured Thayer, transport the boxes of money in safety to Monterrey and across to Eagle Pass where the Confederate officials would receive them. But Russell, who was in the plot with Patricio Milmo, revealed the contents of the boxes.[1]

Thayer, relieved for the time of such a great responsibility, went on to Monterrey to await the arrival of the treasure chests. At Monterrey Milmo daily assured Thayer that the funds were safe and would be delivered intact. But while Milmo was making these assurances he wrote Hart on December 11, 1863, that he had seized the funds and would hold the money until the Confederate debts were settled. Furthermore he threatened to seize all cotton entering and leaving Mexico.[2]

Quintero and Thayer called upon Vidaurri as soon as they learned of the seizure. They were angry, but they kept their tempers and very courteously attempted to persuade the Governor to have the money released. He in turn was polite but refused to do anything about the matter. Quintero then wrote Vidaurri a firm but tactful letter in which he pointed out that his government, in failing to protect the property of a friendly neutral in its passage through his country, was violating international custom, amity, and indeed was committing an unfriendly act. He and Thayer followed up with another personal call on the Governor, but to no avail. General E. Kirby Smith, by this time, had heard of the seizure and was soon prepared to take drastic measures against Vidaurri. Thayer wrote the General that "every effort was made by arguments and persua-

---

[1] *Ibid.*, Thayer to Hart, Dec. 20, 1863; Thayer to Gen. E. Kirby Smith, Dec. 20, 1863. See also Pickett Papers, Reports of Confederate agent Fitzpatrick at Matamoras, No. 7, Nov. 17, 1863; No. 9, March 8, 1864.

[2] *O.R.*, Ser. 1, Vol. LIII, pp. 930–51, Milmo to Hart, Dec. 11, and Thayer to Smith, Dec. 20, 1863, in Smith to Davis, Jan. 20, 1864.

sion to obtain from the governor his interference in the matter, but all appeals met with a decided but respectful refusal. I can bear witness to the energy and indefatigable assiduity of Hon J. A. Quintero in this affair."[1] The bandit in Vidaurri and Milmo evidently rose to the top under the weight of such a tempting prize; but the Governor did suggest—with a smirk—that the case might be taken to court. Naturally the Confederate agents declined to sue. It is hardly to be doubted that Vidaurri, who was within a few months to take flight and join the French, was getting ready to build and feather his nest in a safe spot. He obviously assumed, too, that the Confederacy was hardly in a position to retaliate after its two great defeats at Gettysburg and Vicksburg. But the Governor was mistaken. Moreover, he was now dealing with some very angry and determined men.

Quintero reported his failure to obtain the release of the funds to Simeon Hart, Judah P. Benjamin, E. Kirby Smith, and other Confederate officials. He advised prompt and stern measures, the least of which was to seal the border to all trade—stop the exportation to Mexico of Confederate cotton, the importation of Mexican goods, and seize all Mexican goods in transit across Texas.[2] Major Hart was even more emphatic and specific. He advised Smith to close the border and seize all Mexican goods, just as had Vidaurri, and then to demand the release of the funds. "By the time that could be done the considerable force ordered by General Magruder to our Western border (said to be 2000 or 3000 cavalry) would be posted near the Rio Grande and would give significance to the demand. The stoppage of cotton and intercourse would at once array all the commercial influences of Monterrey, Matamoras, and the country generally in favor of the release of the funds." With this demand should go the assurance that the just claims of Milmo and all other Mexican citizens "should be adjusted and paid as soon as practicable."[3] Quintero

[1] *Ibid.*, Thayer to Smith, Dec. 20, 1863.

[2] *Ibid.*, Quintero to Hart, Dec. 20, 1863; Pickett Papers, Quintero to Benjamin, Dec. 23, 1863, and Jan. 25, 1864.

[3] *O.R.*, Ser. 1, Vol. LIII, pp. 930–51, Hart to Assistant Adjutant General of the Trans-Mississippi Department, Major George Williamson, Dec. 28, 1863. Williamson was on General E. Kirby Smith's staff.

did not wait to hear from Benjamin or General Smith, for the emergency was great and he felt that the Confederate authorities would support him. Nor did General Smith wait to hear from Richmond. Apparently he and Quintero prepared to go after Vidaurri about the same time. Quintero wrote Vidaurri that a continuation of the present situation would not hurt the Confederacy so much as it would the Governor, indeed, he flatly told the Governor that he was courting economic disaster, and in between the lines he barely hinted at a physical disaster. Cotton would be shipped through Laredo and other points on the Rio Grande into the state of Tamaulipas and into Matamoras, and much of it was already going through the bockade. Diverting this trade would, in Quintero's well-informed opinion, deprive the Governor of his principal sources of revenue as well as the profits to the Mexicans of the trade in cotton and supplies. The profits were great and the revenue from import and export was substantial. Vidaurri had been collecting fifty thousand dollars each month in duties at Piedras Negras alone.[1]

General Smith, whose position as commander of the Trans-Mississippi Department and trusted friend of Jefferson Davis gave him wide discretionary powers, issued an order closing the border to the cotton export trade and prohibiting the departure of all Mexican property in Texas. At the same time he appointed T. F. McKinney, Judge T. I. Divine, and Captain Ducayet of his staff, who with Quintero were to present stern but courteous demands upon Vidaurri for the release of the funds.[2] Quintero wrote Benjamin soon after the orders reached Monterrey that the matter would be amicably settled, since "Governor Vidaurri has no other resources at present but those derived from our trade. Besides he is surrounded by many difficulties and complications and will not endeavor to increase them by refusing an honorable and just settlement."[3]

Quintero and the commissioners soon reached an agreement with Vidaurri. The funds were released and the transportation across the

[1] Pickett Papers, Quintero to Benjamin, Jan. 25, 1864.

[2] O.R., Ser. 1, Vol. LIII, pp. 930–51, Smith to Davis, Jan. 20, 1864, inclosures No. 6 (Smith's letter of instructions, January, 1864), No. 7 (Smith to Vidaurri, Jan. 12, 1864), and No. 8 (special order closing the border).

[3] Pickett Papers, Quintero to Benjamin, Feb. 1, 1864.

border of Mexican cotton and other property detained in Texas was resumed. The Confederate agents pledged their government to pay the debts owed not only to Milmo and Company but to other bona fide creditors for whom Milmo was acting.[1] Once again Quintero, supported by General Smith and his commissioners, brought about good relations between Vidaurri and the Confederacy. Commerce resumed its usual course. Major Russell and some other agents who had participated in the Milmo seizure and other graft were relieved from duty by order of the President. It is doubtful that Russell, now known as a large-scale operator and a scoundrel, ever went back to Texas during the war.[2]

In the early spring of 1864 another cloud appeared upon the horizon. Benito Juárez, withdrawing before the forces of the French and the Imperialists, was approaching Monterrey. On more than one occasion Juárez had expressed unfriendly feelings toward the Confederacy. During the first two years of the war he had more than once ordered the closure of the border to the Confederate trade. The orders were, of course, ignored because of Vidaurri's friendship for the Confederacy and his dependence upon the revenue from this trade. Nor did the customs officials of Tamaulipas, particularly at Matamoras, even when appointees of the Juárez government, pay heed to the Juárez orders as long as the Liberal President was not near the border. But once Juárez occupied Monterrey—as he soon did—Quintero and his colleagues feared that the Liberal President would establish and enforce a non-intercourse policy with the Confederacy. It was feared, too, that Juárez, once in control of the border states, would deliver into the hands of the Federals all the Confederate agents in his reach. But Quintero, after Vidaurri fled from Monterrey to join the French, boldly approached General Manuel Negrete to discover what the Juárez policy would be concerning border commerce and Confederate agents in Mexican territory. General Negrete, speaking

[1] *Ibid.*, Feb. 28, 1864.

[2] The documents covering the Milmo affair with much of its background are inclosed in a report of General E. Kirby Smith to President Davis, Jan. 20, 1864, *O.R.*, Ser. I, Vol. LIII, pp. 930–51, and in the Pickett Papers, Reports of Quintero to R. Fitzpatrick, Confederate commercial agent at Matamoras, to Confederate State Department, December–March, 1863–64, *passim.*

for Juárez, assured Quintero that the channels of trade would remain open and that Confederate agents would not be molested. This meant, if true, that Matamoras would continue as a base of indirect blockade-running for supplies and cotton. It meant that the entire Rio Grande would be open to Confederate trade.[1]

Soon after these reassuring promises Quintero was again alarmed over the possibility of the Confederate agents being delivered up to the Federals on the lower Rio Grande. His fear had been aroused by the unhappy fate of Vidaurri's former secretary of state, Manuel Rejan, who had fled to Brownsville and had been seized by "General" Hamilton, and handed over to Juárez to be shot. It was reported that as a return favor for this benevolent act of handing over a political prisoner, Hamilton would demand the extradition of all Confederate agents, including Quintero, to face a firing squad of Federal bushwhackers. On hearing this rumor Quintero went to Juárez himself to learn the real intentions of the Mexican president. Juárez, a simple and straightforward man, assured Quintero that his government intended to observe perfect neutrality. No political offenders would be touched—Confederate agents and refugees were as safe upon Mexican soil as at home.[2] Not completely reassured by his own interview with Juárez—Quintero was more accustomed to dealing with the Spanish-Mexicans than the Indian-Mexicans—he sent former Governor Morehead of Kentucky to interview Juárez. The President earnestly assured Morehead that Mexico would maintain absolute neutrality between the two belligerents.[3]

Quintero and other Confederate officials on the border were at first somewhat surprised to find Juárez so well disposed toward the South, as well disposed for practical purposes as Vidaurri had been. On second thought, however, they realized it to be the practical and logical attitude for Juárez to take; for he would now have to depend, just as Vidaurri had, upon the revenue and the profits of the Confederate trade to maintain his armies and his government. He could not afford to risk retaliation from the Confederates by interfering with the border trade or by surrendering Confederate agents in

[1] *Ibid.*, Quintero to Benjamin, April 3, 1864.

[2] *Ibid.*, April 7, 1864.   [3] *Ibid.*, June 1, 1864.

Mexico to Hamilton and other Federals. Moreover, Juárez no longer felt either the hostility toward the Confederacy or the implicit confidence in the friendship and purity of motives of the United States that he had in 1861–62. During the three and a half years of war, though the Confederacy had cultivated friendly relations with Vidaurri and other border enemies of Juárez, it had never fulfilled Corwin's and Seward's incessant warnings and shown any desire to acquire Mexican territory. On the contrary Corwin and Seward had revealed a great urge to annex the northern Mexican border states through the loan treaty. The policy of permitting the Corwin treaty "to pend" long after the United States Senate had made it perfectly clear that it would not accept the treaty, despite its temporary advantages, left a residue of bitterness and distrust. Juárez and his ministers admired President Lincoln and felt that he was a friend of Mexico; but, as Romero said in 1862, they regarded Seward as the real power in all matters touching Mexico, and none of the "thinking Mexicans," to use Corwin's phrase of an earlier date, trusted Seward's disinterestedness. They knew his record as an apostle of Manifest Destiny. Ironically, too, Juárez never received a penny from the United States, and nothing from trade with the North at the ports on the Gulf after their seizure by the allies; but during his five months' occupation of Monterrey, he probably collected directly over a million dollars in revenue from the Confederate trade and a considerable amount indirectly through the taxation of Mexican merchants who carried on the trade.

At length, when Juárez was forced by the French and Imperialists to withdraw from Monterrey into the mountains of Chihuahua, Quintero and the military authorities acting closely with him entered the final stage of Confederate-Mexican border relations. The strings of the French puppet show now reached back to Paris and Richmond. Slidell and Napoleon III determined that relations upon the Rio Grande should be friendly. However, in dealing with everyday, practical questions rather than larger policy, Quintero proved as shrewd and successful in his relations with the Imperialists as he had been with Vidaurri and Juárez.[1]

[1] *Ibid.*, Nov. 5, 1864; *O.R.*, Ser. 1, Vol. XII, Part III, pp. 972–73, Major General J. G. Walker to Brig. General J. E. Slaughter, Oct. 1, 1864.

CHAPTER IV

THE COTTON FAMINE

As has been observed, both the first and second diplomatic missions of the Confederate government were predicated upon a cotton famine in Europe, which would by the aid of the cotton embargo occur in the summer and fall of 1861 or in the early winter of 1862. It had been universally predicted that England and France would be so reduced by the beginning of 1862 that they would intervene for the purpose of obtaining a supply of cotton. But, as we have noted, the Yancey-Rost-Mann mission had dissolved and, after the new year, 1862, each member had finally gone his own way with the cotton famine still unrealized; though many symptoms of distress were beginning to appear, and the commissioners were sure that it was only a matter of time until the expected famine would come.

When Mason and Slidell arrived in Europe in January, 1862, they knew that they would presently have the long-heralded opportunity of seeing the power of cotton put to the test.

While an ultimate cotton famine was a certainty, nevertheless, the fact that the famine did not occur at the time the South had calculated was a serious miscarriage of campaign plans. The matter of timing was as important in this economic coercion-diplomacy as it was in a military campaign. The South, of course, was compelled—if it were ever to do so—to secede from the Union on the first triumph of a hostile sectional party. This occurred in 1860 with the election of Lincoln. But 1860 was the wrong time for the South to secede if it must depend upon Europe's need of cotton to gain its independence, for it happened that the years 1859 and 1860 had been years of abnormally large cotton crops in America and elsewhere, and all this surplus, with a strange fatality for the South, had been taken by Europe, thereby making an immediate famine impossible. But the South did not realize this situation. The American crop for 1860 had been 3,656,086 bales and that of 1859 had been

4,666,770 bales.[1] Europe had taken 3,127,568 bales of the 1860 crop,[2] and 3,774,173 bales of the 1859 crop.[3] The total cotton purchases of Europe covering this period was 4,321,000 in 1860, mostly of the 1859 crop, and 3,936,000 in 1861, mostly of the 1860 crop,[4] showing that the southern crop made 85 per cent of the total used by Europe.[5]

Arnold in his history of the cotton famine[6] estimates that as a result of this series of huge American crops with corresponding production in Europe, England alone had manufactured and stored in her warehouses at home and in the East 300,000,000 pounds in excess of the normal productions, and that there was an enormous surplus of raw cotton in May, 1861. The Board of Trade returns showed that in June, 1861, there was a stock of 1,015,780 bales of cotton as against 636,960 for June, 1859, an excess of over 450,000 bales above the normal surplus.[7] Even on the last day of December, 1861, despite the fact that not a single American bale of the 1861 crop had come to England, there was a stock of 702,840 bales on hand, compared with 541,510 bales on hand December 31, 1860, and 441,710 for December, 1859, and 400,300 for December, 1857, still showing an excess stock of over 200,000 bales.[8] The stock on hand in France on December 31, 1861, was 143,345 bales as against 112,425 for the same date in 1860[9] and 46,750 in 1859. So France was well stocked as a result of the excessive crops of the South in 1859 and 1860.

By a strange irony of fate the South, by its overzealousness in producing cotton in the two years preceding the Civil War, destroyed the power of cotton to force an intervention in the fall and

[1] *London Economist*, Nov. 2, 1861.

[2] M. B. Hammond, *The Cotton Industry* (New York, 1897), p. 258; *Economist*, Nov. 2, 1861.

[3] *Economist*, Nov. 2, 1861.

[4] *Economist, Com. Hist. and Rev. Suppl.*, March 11, 1865.

[5] Watts, p. 59.   [6] Arnold, pp. 40–47, 79–83.

[7] *Economist*, June 7, 1865, giving statistics for 1859–63; based on compilation from Board of Trade reports.

[8] *Ibid.*, Dec. 31, 1864, gives stock on hand Dec. 31 from 1853 to 1864.

[9] *Ibid.*, Feb. 1, 1862.

winter of 1861–62, and rendered the embargo useless in the diplomacy of this period.

But the famine came in a few months after Mason and Slidell arrived in Europe. The deliveries of cotton in the calendar year 1861 were reduced by the elimination of the American crop of 1861. Even with the shipment of 1,650,000 bales of the 1860 crop from America and an excessive shipment from India,[1] the cotton supply of Europe was considerably decreased in 1861. England received about 2,253,000 bales as compared to 2,633,000 in 1860, France 578,000 compared with 621,000 in 1860, while all of Europe received 3,963,-000 in 1861 as compared with 4,321,000 in 1860.[2]

But the supply of cotton in Europe in 1862 experienced that shrinkage which the South had looked for in 1861. It was considerably less than half as much as the supply of 1861, and little more than a third as much as the 1860 supply. All Europe obtained only 1,910,000 bales as compared to 3,963,000 in 1861 and 4,321,000 bales in 1860. England obtained only 1,146,000 bales, which was about half that of 1861.[3] As we have noted, no American cotton had gone to Europe the first part of 1862, and not much over 70,000 bales finally reached there in the fall of 1862.[4] The year 1862 was the leanest of all the Civil War times as far as the European cotton supply was concerned, and it was the latter part of this year in which the much-hoped-for cotton famine, from the point of view of the South, and the much-dreaded famine, from the point of view of England, struck with all its force. Things began to collapse visibly immediately after December, 1861. The supply of cotton, as we have noticed, was above normal on December 31, 1861. But for the next three months —January, 1862, to March 31, 1862—only about 143,000 bales of cotton were imported into England,[5] while the stock of 702,840 bales had been reduced by 224,000 bales.[6] The *Economist*[7] exclaimed in

---

[1] Watts, pp. 250–67.

[2] *Economist, Com. Hist. and Rev. Suppl.*, March 11, 1865. Figures compiled from Board of Trade reports.

[3] *Ibid.*

[4] See below as to cotton running the blockade.   [6] *Index*, May 1, 1862.

[5] *Economist*, May 3, 1862.   [7] *Economist*, May 3, 1862.

alarm over the cotton situation: "No one can doubt now why we are suffering. More terrific figures have rarely been set before the world." The stock of American cotton had been reduced by April 25, 1862, to 124,000 bales as compared to over 1,000,000 of the year before.[1] By June 16, 1862, the total cotton stock was reduced to 260,000 bales compared with 1,334,610 bales on that date in 1860 and 1,105,780 bales in 1861. The supply was being used up in June, 1862, by export or consumption at the rate of 30,000 bales per week.[2]

By July the total stock in England was only 200,000 bales as compared with 1,200,000 in 1861; and only 70,000 bales were American as compared with 830,000 bales of American cotton in 1861.[3] The *Economist* feared that "the time when mills must stop and Lancashire must starve from an actual exhaustion of the whole supply of raw materials may be very near at hand."[4] By September the stock had been reduced to the frightful minimum of 100,000 bales with the weekly consumption and exportation averaging around 30,000 bales.[5] "These," exclaimed the *Economist*,[6] "are the figures of the cotton famine." This, as for the supply of cotton accumulated in Great Britain, was the climax of the famine. Never after that did the supply get so low. As we shall see below, the climax of unemployment and destitution among the workers came in December, 1862, three months later.

After 1862 the supply of cotton slowly grew in volume, owing to the increase of the American supply running the blockade and especially to the increase of supplies from India, China, Brazil, and Egypt. In 1863 Europe received 2,325,000 bales as compared with only 1,910,000 in 1862, England receiving 1,304,000 compared to 1,146,000 for 1862, and France 342,000 as compared with 311,000 in 1862.[7] In 1864 Europe received 2,683,000 bales as compared with 2,325,000 bales in 1863,[8] England receiving 1,606,000 and France

---

[1] *Index*, May 1, 1862; cf. *Economist*, March 15, 1862, Board of Trade figures.

[2] Cf. *Economist*, July 5, 1862, for rate of consumption, etc.

[3] *Ibid*.   [5] *Ibid*., Sept. 6, 1862; cf. *ibid*., Oct. 11, 1862.

[4] *Ibid*.   [6] *Ibid*., Aug. 2, 1862.

[7] *Ibid*., *Com. Hist. and Rev. Suppl.*, March 11, 1865.   [8] *Ibid*.

406,000. Had the war gone on through 1865 and the bulk of the American crop continued cut off, Europe would have received 3,000,-000 or more bales from other sources. This would have been more than three-fourths the normal supply of cotton. Because of the greater amount of work necessary to manufacture the cotton from India and China, the cotton operatives would have been employed full time and the cotton industry re-established on the basis of non-American cotton.

Such, then, in brief, was the situation of the cotton supply during the Civil War, in Europe, especially in England and France. The cotton supply might be described as a curve with an abrupt downward slant during the first eight months of 1862, when the lowest point was reached, after which it leisurely curved upward through 1863–64–65 until by the end of the war it had risen to three-fourths of the height of 1860.

The scarcity of cotton in England and France was not, however, the sole factor in producing the destitution and unemployment in the industrial districts. As we have just observed, there was an unusually large supply of cotton in these two countries in December, 1861, and had the scarcity of cotton alone been involved there would have been cotton enough to keep the mills turning for several months. Yet even at this date many mills were closing down and considerable distress was evident in Lancashire, Normandy, and Rouen. This first depression in the industry was the result of overproduction and overstocking of the markets during the years 1859 and 1860.[1] As we have already noted, England alone had manufactured an excess of 300,000,000 pounds of cotton goods. The markets of India and China were thus completely saturated. The warehouses were bursting and the natives had stopped buying.[2] The loss of the American markets was another factor in the situation. The American market was destroyed by the war itself and not by a lack of cotton. French exports had averaged for some years around $400,-000,000,[3] and nearly $100,000,000 worth had been exported to the

[1] See ibid., Jan. 31, 1863, for discussion of overproduction.

[2] See Arnold, pp. 40–47, 79–83; London Times, Feb. 11, 1862.

[3] Economist, Aug. 2, 1862, gives figures in francs for 1859, 1860, and 1861.

United States.[1] But the war in America, by practically destroying that market for the time being, reduced the total export trade to about $380,000,000, or $20,000,000 less than normal.[2] England lost greatly in the American market; her export trade fell from £164,-500,000 in 1860 to £159,500,000 in 1861, or £5,000,000—around $25,000,000.[3] As much of this loss in both England and France was in the export of cotton goods, it naturally added considerably to the necessity of cutting down production and contributed considerably to the unemployment and destitution in the cotton district.[4]

TABLE III

Year	Middling Fair (per lb.)	Mule Twist (per lb.)	39-in. Shirting (per lb.)
1860	$7\frac{1}{8}d.$	$11\frac{13}{8}d.$	$14d.$
1861	$9\frac{5}{8}d.$	$12d.$	$13\frac{5}{8}d.$
1862	$18\frac{1}{2}d.$	$17\frac{13}{16}d.$	$18\frac{1}{4}d.$
1863	$25\frac{1}{4}d.$	$27.62d$	$26.66d.$
1864	$28.33d.$	$28.88d$	$29.16d.$

The continuing low price of manufactured cotton goods which resulted from the loss of the American markets and the overproduction of 1859–61, and the high price of raw cotton resulting from the cutting-off of the American supply, also had a marked effect upon production in the mills, even when the mills could obtain a sufficient quantity of cotton to continue operation.

Table III will illustrate the narrow margin between the price of raw material and manufactured goods.[5] It will be seen from this table that two kinds of cotton goods were actually cheaper than the raw cotton during the year 1862, and usually just a fraction of a penny more a pound during the years 1863 and 1864. Naturally, with this narrow margin there would not be any great desire on the part of the manufacturers to pay their operatives to produce goods.

[1] Cf. John Claiborne, *Report, Cotton in Europe, etc., on France to 1856.*

[2] *Economist*, Aug. 2, 1862.   [3] *Ibid.*, Feb. 28, 1863.

[4] Cf. *ibid.*, April 26, 1862; *London Times*, March 11, 1862, for loss of markets.

[5] Watts, pp. 357, 364.

The only guaranty of profits in such a case was either to mix in cheaper grades of cotton or to manufacture for stock, that is, to manufacture and hold until prices rose. The larger, well-financed mills, of course, were able to manufacture goods in 1862 from cotton which cost $18\frac{1}{2}$ pence a pound at the time the goods were selling for $17\frac{13}{16}$ pence because these goods were not marketed until 1863–64 when the price had risen to nearly 30 pence the pound.[1] But the mills which had to manufacture and sell at once were forced to close down and wait until the price of manufactured material should have a safe margin above the cost of raw material.

Arnold[2] estimated that around 700 of the 2,270 cotton mills in Lancashire and neighboring counties were small mills which could not manufacture for stock, and therefore were forced to close down partly because of the actual loss involved in manufacturing goods for current sale. These mills, though a third of the whole number, did not employ anything like a third of the operatives in the cotton industry. Still, their closing-down in the fall of 1861 and winter of 1862, which was due to the dearness of cotton and the cheapness of goods rather than to the scarcity of cotton, accounted for a considerable amount of unemployment. In other words, it was these small mills and their operatives which paid the penalty of the overstocking of 1859–61 of manufactured goods.[3]

An element which added to this tendency to go slow in manufacturing goods was the constant dread that the American war might come to an end and dump four millions of bales of cheap American cotton upon the market. This was especially true after Europe had begun to stock up on cotton from India and the Orient at around two shillings, or nearly fifty cents a pound. Vast sums of money were involved in the stocks of cotton purchased after 1861, and the manufactured product involved even greater sums, so that there was always a fear lurking behind the production of goods, which at times checked manufacturing very greatly and added to the misery and destitution of the operatives.[4] England in 1860 paid about

[1] See Arnold, *passim*.   [2] *Ibid.*, pp. 48–49.

[3] See *Economist*, July 5 and 12; Sept. 6; Nov. 15, 1862, for effect of high price of raw cotton and cheap goods.

[4] See speech of Cobden in Parliament, July 4, 1862, in Parl. Deb. Commons, Vol. 168, pp. 746–55.

$129,805,000 for 1,083,600,000 pounds of cotton, but in 1864 she paid $269,040,000 for only 561,480,000 pounds, or twice as much for half the amount of cotton.[1]

The competition of linen and woolen goods with cotton goods as soon as the latter became dear also became a serious factor in retarding the production of cotton goods. Had the British and French factories been able to obtain a full supply of raw cotton outside of America, the price necessary to obtain it was so high that cotton would have been greatly displaced by wool, linen, and other materials which were more durable and better than cotton, but which had heretofore been unable to compete because of being more expensive than cotton goods.[2]

With all these factors—overproduction; the partial loss of the American markets; the cheapness of manufactured goods; the dearness of raw material; the competition of linen, wool, etc., with cotton goods; the fear of the markets being deluged with the great American surplus; and, finally, the scarcity of cotton resulting from the blockade and embargo—there developed in Europe, especially in England and France, a condition of destitution in the cotton districts among the operatives comparable in magnitude and severity only to the conditions which obtained in the Confederacy itself.

The cotton mills of Europe began to run short time in October, 1861.[3] The approach of winter brought distress with it. Many mills in Lancashire, England, and the district of the Lower Seine in France were closing down completely while many others were reducing their operating time to half. Only the larger mills could afford to run full time. The *London Times* and the *London Economist* soon began to express alarm. Early in 1862 the *Times*[4] spoke of the "paralysis of the cotton trade" with scores of mills closed, tens of thousands of operatives out of work, while distress and pauperism grew apace among heretofore thrifty and industrious people. The *Economist*[5] was alarmed at the rapid unfolding of what promised to

[1] Watts, pp. 356 ff. Watts's figures are in pounds sterling.

[2] See *ibid.*, p. 59, for comparison of cotton, linen, and woolen prices as illustrating their use.

[3] Arnold, *Cotton Famine*, pp. 40–47, 84–85; *Economist*, Aug. 10 and Nov. 16, 1861; *London Times*, Nov. 16, 1861.

[4] *Times*, Feb. 11, 1862.   [5] *Economist*, April 26, 1862.

be a most fearful catastrophe. This distress, thought the *Economist*, must become more and more serious until the American Civil War had come to an end and southern cotton could be obtained at a cheap price. By April, 1862, the vast industrial population in England was not averaging over half time. As a matter of fact, nearly half were entirely unemployed.[1] The *Manchester Examiner and Times* reported the latter part of April[2] that out of a total of 1,678 mills in the Manchester district alone only 497 were working full time, carrying 92,355 operatives; 278 mills which had employed 57,316 operatives were closed down, and the other 903 employing about 200,000 were operating two to five days a week. The average time for the whole number was three and a half days, or just a bit better than half time. If the remainder of the 2,887 mills in the United Kingdom were considered, the operatives were averaging only half time On July 4 it was reported in Parliament[3] that 80,000 operatives were completely idle, and 370,000 more were averaging only half time. In normal times, according to this report, the cotton operatives drew an average total wage of £250,000 a week, or nearly $1,250,000. By July, 1862, they were drawing only £110,000 a week and losing £140,000, or around $700,000 a week.

Steadily and rapidly the cotton industry seemed to collapse. The work of the blockade and the embargo, while late getting underway, was bearing out in 1862, apparently, the prophecies of the South which said that England and France would be plunged into destitution and perhaps revolution unless they could get the cotton of the South. The manufacture of cotton had been at the rate of 28,000 bales per week the first half of the year,[4] but by November England was manufacturing only 18,000 bales per week as compared to over 50,000 a week in 1860.[5] By the last of November and first of December only 121,129 of the 533,959 operatives were working full time, 165,600 were working part time, while 247,230 were entirely out of work with no prospect of employment. It was estimated that the average weekly loss of wages now stood at about £170,000, or

---

[1] See *Index*, May 1, 1862.

[2] Cited in *Economist*, May 3, 1862.

[3] Parl. Debates, Vol. 168, pp. 746–48.

[4] *Economist*, Sept. 6, 1862.

[5] See *ibid., Com. Hist. and Rev. Suppl.*, March 11, 1865, for tables of consumption for 1860–64.

about $850,000, as compared to £140,000, or $700,000, for July.[1] This dreary week of the latter part of November and the first of December was the climax of unemployment, and after that unemployment decreased slowly but steadily.

In April, 1863, 156,594 operatives were working full time, as compared with only 121,129 for the first week in December, 1862; 146,095 were partly employed compared to 165,600 in December— in other words, about 20,000 short-time employees had now gone on full time—234,946 were totally unemployed as compared with 247,230 in December.[2] This was only a slight improvement and times still looked gloomy and without much hope of relief. However, in less than two weeks a remarkable improvement transpired. The full-time workers were increased to 203,316, the part-time workers decreased to 124,564, and those totally unemployed decreased from 234,946 of April 28 to 186,193.[3] High prices, exhaustion of the surplus stock of manufactured goods, and an increased supply of cotton from India, Egypt, Brazil, and China were putting more mills to work. By July, 1863, the fully employed had increased to 234,642, the part-time workers now numbered only 125,000, and the totally unemployed had been reduced to 180,729.[4] The operatives were again working a great deal over half time as compared to just a little over fourth time in December, 1862. By September, 1863, 267,962 operatives were working full time, 104,198 short time, and 160,835 were unemployed.[5]

The average unemployment for 1863 in the cotton industry was

[1] Thomas Ellison, *The Cotton Trade, etc.*, p. 95; table printed in Hammond, p. 269; cf. *Seventeenth Ann. Rept. Poor Law Board, 1864-5*, XXII, 67–68, 74; especially H. B. Farnell, special commissioner for distressed district, to C. Pelham Villiers, president of the Poor Law Board, Feb. 1, 1865, p. 74, etc.; Watts, pp. 227–28, gives tables of unemployment, etc.

[2] See *Fifteenth Ann. Rept. Poor Law Board, 1863*, XXII, 65 ff., for H. B. Farnell, special commissioner's report; cf. Lord Derby's statement in Parliament, July 7, 1863, in Parl. Deb. Lords, Ser. 3, Vol. 172.

[3] *Fifteenth Ann. Rept. Poor Law Board, 1863*, XXII, 77–80.

[4] Lord Derby's statement, July 7, Parl. Deb. Lords, Ser. 3, Vol. 172.

[5] Report of Central Executive Committee in *Economist*, Oct. 24, 1863. Watts, pp. 227–28, gives 135,821 as the number unemployed. This is probably nearer correct as a great number of operatives had emigrated or had sought employment in the linen and woolen mills.

189,167 as compared with 247,230 for the first week in December, 1862, and the average short-time employees 129,219 as compared with 165,600 for 1862. The full-time employees for 1863 were 215,477 as compared with 121,129 for 1862, and the weekly average consumption of cotton about 23,000 bales as compared with 18,000 for the first week in December, 1862. The weekly loss in wages averaged £146,000 for 1863 as compared with £169,744 for the first week in December, 1862. In 1864 the full-time employees averaged 243,012; the short-time employees, 97,083; the totally unemployed, 133,847. The weekly average consumption of cotton was 27,000 bales, and the weekly average wage loss, £96,444. For the first five months of 1865 the full-time employees averaged 265,465; short-time employees, 68,572; and the totally unemployed, 106,916. The average weekly wage loss was £71,447, and the consumption of cotton, 32,000 bales per week. At the end of this period and before the news of the Civil War's having come to an end had reached England, 319,616 operatives were working full time as compared with 121,129 in December, 1862; 38,228 were working short time (though longer time) as compared with 165,600 in December, 1862, while there were only 86,001 unemployed as compared with 247,230 for December, 1862; and the weekly consumption of cotton was 34,000 bales as compared with 18,000 in December, 1862.[1]

As we noted in the study of the cotton supply above, the statistics of unemployment show that the cotton industry was becoming stabilized upon the basis of non-American, high-priced cotton. The foregoing figures also show that the cotton industry was being stabilized upon a smaller basis, for it shows that about 90,000 operatives had disappeared, probably into the linen and woolen industries and by emigration to America.[2] However it may be, regardless of the fact that Great Britain was readjusting her industry upon a different and somewhat narrower basis, there is no escaping from the

---

[1] These figures are given in Ellison, p. 95, and cited in Hammond, p. 269; cf. *Economist, Com. Hist. and Rev. Suppl.*, March 11, 1865. The consumption of cotton given here is some higher than that given by Ellison. Ellison doubtlessly did not include the small cotton-manufacturing districts in Lanarkshire, Scotland, and Ireland. The *Economist* figures are based upon the Board of Trade reports.

[2] Cf. *ibid.*, Oct. 24, 1863; Feb. 20, 1864; Jan. 28, 1865; also Watts, pp. 227 ff.

terrific figures which tell their own tale of agony. The shortage of cotton, the high percentage of unemployment—reaching practically three-fourths in December, 1862—the loss of wages which averaged more than half during the famine, indicate a great crisis in English life which the South had hoped would force the English government to take action in its behalf.

Nor do the foregoing statistics show the complete situation. They refer to the operatives in the cotton mills only. While these people were losing in 1862 £8,840,000 in wages,[1] there were thousands of subsidiary workers who were deprived of their means of livelihood just as completely as were the operatives. Mechanics, miners, stevedores, bakers, shopkeepers, the "small people" generally who sold to the operatives—all went down in ruin along with the workers in the mills. The operatives unemployed at the crisis in 1862 numbered 247,230, while 165,000 worked only part time, making thus 407,230 workers practically or completely unemployed. The thousands of auxiliary workers and laborers and small people dependent upon the patronage of the operatives would certainly have swelled the number thrown out of work by the famine another 50,000, making in round numbers about 450,000 unemployed workmen and tradesmen in the cotton districts. If we include the dependents of these workmen— it is estimated that there were three dependents, composed of the aged and the young and the disabled, to every workman—there must have been not far from 2,000,000 people with no means of support at the height of the cotton famine in December, 1862. Over half the population of the cotton districts were involved.

That about 2,000,000 were made destitute by prolonged unemployment is proved by a glance at the number who received aid from the Poor Law Guardians of the Parish and the relief committees. In 1861 there were, according to the Poor Law Board,[2] 48,000 people dependent upon charity, with an expenditure for the whole year of £208,728. But by midsummer 1862 the last savings had been spent, and nothing was left to sell among those who had lost their jobs in

[1] Cf. Parl. Deb. Commons, Vol. 169, p. 97, Nov. 2, 1862, for statement of Bains, who put the loss at £9,000,000 annually at the rate obtaining at that period.

[2] Farnell's report, *Fifteenth Ann. Rept. Poor Law Board, 1863*, XXII, 65 ff.

the fall of 1861, so that about 150,000 had to seek relief from the dreaded Guardians.[1] The number increased by great strides. In August 216,437 were on the list of paupers; in September, 277,198; in October, 371,496.[2] The Board reported that on December 6, 1862, when the unemployment had reached its climax, 508,293 destitute laborers were being relieved by charity,[3] at the rate of £42,677 a week, or about a fifth as much as had been expended the entire year of 1861. Then the number of paupers slowly and painfully decreased as the mills reopened. January 10, 1863, there was a decrease which corresponded to the decrease in unemployment: only 480,616 operatives were relieved; February 7, 460,312 received aid; February 28, 441,670 were on charity; April 28, 425,965; May 7, 370,063, a decrease of 135,000 or more in about five months.[4] The number relieved June 27, 1863, was 263,000; October 31, 1863, 177,882;[5] and May 28, 1864, 125,175 were being supported by charity as compared to 370,063 of May 7, 1863.[6] By May, 1865, only 75,784 were on charity as compared with the 48,000 who received charity in 1861 under normal conditions.[7]

Watts gives a table (see our Table IV based on Watts) of those relieved month by month from June, 1862, to May, 1865, which might be helpful in visualizing the destitution. In order to get the whole number destitute it will be necessary to multiply each person relieved by 4, since—as has been pointed out—there were three dependents to each laborer.

A better understanding of the cotton famine, the losses, the suffering, and the possible political reaction resulting therefrom in favor of intervention can be reached by a brief study of the process by which pauperism was reached, the total loss of wages, and the process of relief.

These people were thrifty and self-respecting. They had saved

---

[1] *Economist*, July 26, 1862, says one-third of the factory workers were on charity; Watts, pp. 227–28, gives 153,774 for July.

[2] Watts, pp. 227–28, table.

[3] *Sixteenth Ann. Rept. Poor Law Board, 1864*, XXV, 95 ff.

[4] H. B. Farnell's report, *Fifteenth Ann. Rept. Poor Law Board, 1863*, XXII, 65 ff.

[5] *Sixteenth Ann. Rept. Poor Law Board, 1864*, XXV, 78–79, 85.

[6] *Ibid.*, p 104.   [7] Watts, pp. 227–28.

their little pittance, some of them for a lifetime; they were members of co-operative aid societies, and looked with dread upon the work-

TABLE IV

	Relieved	Total Destitute Population
1862:		
June..............	129,774	519,096
July..............	153,774	615,096
August...........	216,437	865,748
September........	277,198	1,108,792
October..........	371,496	1,485,984
November........	458,441	1,833,764
December........	485,434	1,941,736
1863:		
January..........	451,343	1,805,372
February.........	432,477	1,729,908
March...........	420,243	1,680,972
April............	362,076	1,448,304
May.............	289,975	1,159,900
June.............	255,578	1,022,312
July.............	213,444	853,776
August...........	204,603	818,412
September........	184,136	736,544
October..........	167,678	670,712
November........	170,268	681,072
December........	180,298	721,192
1864:		
January..........	202,785	811,140
February.........	203,168	812,672
March...........	180,027	720,108
April............	147,280	589,120
May.............	116,088	464,352
June.............	100,671	402,684
July.............	85,910	343,640
August...........	83,063	332,252
September........	92,379	369,516
October..........	136,268	545,072
November........	149,923	599,692
December........	130,397	521,588
1865:		
January..........	119,544	478,176
February.........	125,885	503,540
March...........	111,008	444,032
April............	95,763	383,052
May.............	75,784 (as against 48,000 in normal times)*	303,136

* Cf. Watts, pp. 227–38, with Table in *Economist*, March 11, 1865.

house or public charity. When the mills began to stop in 1861 those who were thrown out of employment did not appeal to the Poor Law

Guardians of the Parish, but curtailed their expenses, wearing old clothes and eking out a bare existence. When their savings were gone, they pawned their treasured pieces of furniture, article by article—first the chest of drawers was replaced by a rude box, the chairs replaced by rough stools, and then the stools were used for firewood. The family pictures found their way to the pawnshop, the crockery and china followed, and then the cooking utensils down to a pot and pan. Day by day their homes became more and more barren. The bedsteads were sold, then the beds, then the blankets, until nothing but piles of old straw littered the desolated floor. Still, no appeal, in most cases, would yet be made to the dreaded Guardians of the Poor whose aid would forever brand them as paupers. The mothers and little children grew undernourished, many of them dying from slow starvation. The father and older members of the family wearily tramped the streets of Manchester or Ashton or Blackburn pathetically seeking a place to work during the winter and spring of 1862, only to meet others who had just been discharged. They returned to sunless homes, and frequently during these dark times dined upon musty corn meal and water. Many of the girls in despair resorted to prostitution, selling themselves for a pittance with which to feed the aged parents or the helpless children who often lay slowly dying from want upon the piles of dirty straw. Then the pride of the operatives gave way and heads of the family sought the Guardians of the Poor, who more appropriately might have been named the "Guardians of the Rich," and after being harshly and thoroughly humiliated and perhaps abused were at length put upon the list of those who were being supported by the rates. Frequently the family sought relief by singing upon the streets. Never in England's history, until the era of unemployment following World War I, did the drab streets of London, Manchester, Liverpool, and the towns of the industrial centers resound with the doleful wail of so many Methodist hymns. But sooner or later even these street musicians were forced to seek the poor-law support.[1]

[1] *Ibid.*, pp. 112–80, *passim*, for graphic account of the slow stages by which the operatives finally became public paupers; *Economist*, April 12 and 26, Sept. 13, 1862; *London Times* carried a section each day upon the distressed cotton districts; Lord Derby's speech at the meeting of the county of Lancashire on Dec. 2, 1862, described the process very graphically. This speech is published in Watts, pp. 18 ff.

Many public-spirited people soon saw the necessity of taking a more positive action than the tight-pursed, narrow-visioned Board of Guardians was taking in order to ferret out the tens of thousands who refused to the point of starvation to seek aid from the Guardians, or who were turned away. It was recognized that these people were not ordinary professional paupers though they were so treated by the Guardians. It was seen that private charity was the only possible means by which many people could be reached in time or at all. But even this move was very tardy as it hardly got under way before the summer of 1862, and it was fall before much aid was extended. Nor did the impetus to raise funds by private organization come from the scene of the suffering. In London the Mansion House Committee began raising funds which finally amounted to £528,904, or about $2,600,000.[1] These funds came from all over the world, even America making large contributions.

Public opinion turned scornfully upon the cotton barons who had not lifted their hands for a year to aid their destitute operatives.[2] Arnold wrote that "Manchester and Liverpool men made their millions and subscribed their thousands."[3] Charles Kingsley in a series of letters to the *Times* accused the manufacturers of desiring to pauperize the operatives by withholding aid and by closing down the mills and by opposing emigration. The manufacturers, supported by a few trade journals such as the *Economist*, insisted piously that they were doing their share by running their factories at a loss so as to furnish work.[4] The *London Times*[5] replied to this line of argument put up by the manufacturers to the effect that such cases were exceedingly rare. "All honor to such exceptions wherever they may be found! The great mass of examples, however, as the great facts unhappily prove, is largely on the other side."

Under fire of this kind the manufacturers bestirred themselves languidly and in August organized the Manchester Central Committee with Lord Derby as chairman.[6] But while money came pour-

---

[1] *Ibid.*, pp. 160–68.

[2] See, e.g., the *Times*, Sept. 12, 1862.

[3] Arnold, p. 164.   [4] *Economist*, Nov. 29, 1862; Arnold, pp. 173–75.

[5] *London Times*, Nov. 19, 1862.

[6] *Ibid.*, Aug. 27, 1862; Parl. Debates Commons, Ser. 3, Vol. 170, pp. 11–19, 27–30, debate on committee work, March 27, 1863.

ing in from other quarters it was a long time before the cotton lords showed interest in the pitiable spectacle around them. Not only did they not show much private benevolence, but they were accused of sidestepping the rates by which the Board of Guardians aided the indigent.[1] But by the height of the famine, December, 1862, the manufacturers began to support their own organizations to a certain extent.[2] So that finally about £500,000 were raised by the Central Committee of which Derby was president, making a total of about £2,000,000, or nearly $10,000,000, in the hands of the Central Committee and the Mansion House Committee together. This figure was reached by the summer of 1863, after which private subscriptions practically ceased.[3]

Finally, then, when 2,000,000 people had been practically reduced to starvation; when all their lifelong savings had been spent; their furniture, pictures, trinkets, clothing, kitchen utensils, and bedding were gone; when nothing but bare floors and walls and a roof were left; when the rent was months in arrears and they were afraid of ejection; when they were starving and their daughters in prostitution—then the leisurely philanthropy of comfortable wealth came to the partial aid of the stricken people. A fund of about £2,000,000 was being raised and disbursed by the time the unemployment had reached the greatest number in December, 1862. The Poor Law Guardians also finally raised and expended about £1,000,000 during the period 1862 to May, 1865,[4] so that eventually the distressed population was to receive about £3,000,000 for support from public and private sources. As we have seen, the weekly wage of the factory operatives, not including the laborers in subsidiary industries, etc.,

[1] See *Economist*, Nov. 22, 1862, in reply to Kingsley who had made this charge in the *London Times*.

[2] *Times*, Dec. 3, 1862; Parl. Debates, Ser. 3, Vol. 169, p. 271, debate on Feb. 12, 1863.

[3] See Arnold, p. 493; Watts, pp. 160–68, 233; Parl. Debates Commons, Ser. 3, Vol. 170, pp. 774–838, debates on April 27 and *post*, 1863, for statements of amounts raised by the several agencies including the Poor Law Guardians; *ibid.*, Ser. 3, Vol. 172, statement of Lord Derby, July 7, 1863; *Economist*, July 11, 1863.

[4] See *Economist, Com. Hist. and Rev. Suppl.*, March 11, 1865, for figures for 1863 and 1864; Ellison, *Cotton Trade of Great Britain*, p. 95; table printed in Hammond, p. 269, for figures for 1863, 1864, and 1865; Watts, p. 369, for expenditures through 1864.

was about £250,000, and for the three years 1862 to May, 1865, should have been £45,000,000. A calculation based upon the table printed in Ellison[1] shows that during this period the operatives received only about £22,000,000, or less than half their normal wage. Putting it the other way around, during this period the loss in wages by the cotton operatives amounted to about £23,000,000.

Watts[2] calculated the wage loss from the fall of 1861 to May, 1865, at £33,000,000. He adds to that £3,300,000 lost by shopkeepers, and does not include the auxiliary workers' loss which must have been about £5,000,000. According to his figures, we have, then, for the years 1861–65 a loss of £36,300,000 in wages with a possible addition of £5,000,000 for the workmen who were not directly employed in the mills, which would swell the total to £41,300,000. Watts was a member of the relief committee and a scientifically trained economist and statistician, and must have known quite well what the situation was. He insists that the figures put out by the Poor Law Board of Guardians presided over by Villiers were greatly understated.[3] His statistics are more correct than Ellison's, whose figures are based on the reports of the Board, whose interest it was to keep the figures down. To take the place of this enormous loss, which unfortunately was not evenly distributed among the 533,000 employees but which fell upon that part who were unemployed and drew no wages, there was only, at the outside, distributed by charity £3,000,000, or about one-tenth of the normal amount drawn by the operatives unemployed. The idea was to keep body and soul together and no more. Not enough should be given to make them comfortable, not enough to allow them to emigrate. The Central Committee, in fact, while dispensing charity looked after the interest of the manufacturers and did all possible to prevent emigration of the operatives.[4]

In France the situation was nearly as bad as in England. The foreign trade of France was badly crippled by the loss of the Ameri-

[1] Ellison, p. 95.

[2] Watts, pp. 369 ff.   [3] See *ibid.*, pp. 113–14.

[4] See *Times*, March 18 and 24, 1863; cf. *Economist* (esp. April 4, 1863), which opposed emigration.

can markets.[1] There were forty departments in the cotton industry[2] which consisted of 2,606 factories employing about 275,000 operatives with a yearly wage of about $20,000,000.[3] One-fourth of the industry was concentrated in the Seine-Inférieure.[4] Excerpts from the reports of the *procureurs généraux* show that there was much distress in France even after 1862 and it was not confined to the manufacture of cotton.[5]

In 1862 France, as we have noted, received only 311,000 bales of cotton in comparison with 578,000 in 1861 and 621,000 in 1860.[6] The weekly average consumption of cotton was only 5,981 bales in 1862 as compared with 11,114 bales consumed in 1861—about half.[7] The year 1862 was the *année terrible*—the year of the greatest unemployment and destitution. As in England the famine hit with full force in the fall of this year. The cotton areas of the Lower Seine suffered more than Picardy, Alsace, and Caux.[8] In Rouen, Dieppe, and Havre, the cotton mills came to a dead stop. By December, 1862, in this region 130,000 men were thrown out of work.[9] At Rouen 30,000 out of a possible 50,000 were unemployed in the fall of 1862,[10] and 300,000 to 390,000, including dependents, were thus destitute in the region of the Lower Seine.[11] There were many more in the other industrial areas which were dependent upon the American markets.[12]

[1] See W. Reed West, *Contemporary French Opinion on the American Civil War* (Johns Hopkins Press, 1924), pp. 56–61. (Cited hereafter as West.) Case, *French Opinion*, pp. 6–8.

[2] *Moniteur*, Dec. 8, 1862, in West, p. 59.

[3] John Claiborne, *op. cit., passim.* The yearly total of wages is calculated upon the basis of his figures.

[4] *Moniteur*, Dec. 8, in West, p. 59.   [5] Case, *French Opinion, passim.*

[6] See above.

[7] *Economist, Com. Hist. and Rev. Suppl.*, March 11, 1865.   [8] West, p. 61.

[9] *Ibid.*, p. 59; Adams, *Charles Francis Adams*, p. 271; Scherer, p. 271; *Index*, Dec. 11, 1862, and Jan. 8, 1863.

[10] Scherer, p. 271; Adams, *Charles Francis Adams*, p. 271.

[11] West, p. 59; *Index*, July 8, 1863; Scherer, p. 271; Adams, *Charles Francis Adams,* p. 271.

[12] Case, *French Opinion*, pp. 6–8.

In the distressed areas destitution was even more acute than in England, for a while. People lived upon bran, water, and herbs, while half-naked children infested the countryside begging food.[1] These people were losing at the rate of about 72,000,000 francs a year in wages by December, 1862, and private charity raised less than 1,000,000 at the time, and the government only 7,000,000.[2]

While only about 8,000,000 francs were raised to feed these destitute people during the entire famine, it was estimated that it would take 12,000,000 francs to feed them for three months at the rate of a franc a day for each unemployed.[3] But there is no calculating the length to which a Frenchman can stretch a franc, and the destitute population was tided over, though with much dissatisfaction and many threats. Conditions in the industrial districts, and the desire to annex Mexico, kept Napoleon willing to intervene in behalf of the South at any time England could be induced to join him.

As in England, the situation in France began to improve after 1862. In 1863 France consumed nearly 7,000 bales a week, and in 1864 nearly 8,000 a week, or about three-fourths of her regular amount. She received 342,000 bales in 1863 and 406,000 in 1864 as compared with 578,000 in 1861.[4] The French factories did more delicate work and made a greater profit from their raw material than did England.[5] They could afford to pay a higher price for raw material. Hence the famine in the Lower Seine abated sooner than that in England, though much distress continued throughout the country until 1865 owing to the loss of the American markets.[6]

It was this distress and destitution in France and England which the South had calculated upon to bring intervention. It came later than expected; but it was a terrible catastrophe involving several million people in the two countries and the bankruptcy of most of the small cotton mills.[7]

[1] West, p. 59.

[2] *Ibid.*, p. 60; Pickett Papers, De Leon to Benjamin, No. 5, Jan. 28, 1863; *Economist*, Jan. 31 and Feb. 14, 1863.

[3] *Index*, July 8, 1863.   [4] *Economist, Com. Hist. and Rev. Suppl.*, March 11, 1865.

[5] See Claiborne, *op. cit.*

[6] Case, *French Opinion*, pp. 6–8.   [7] Watts, p. 369.

CHAPTER V

CONFEDERATE PROPAGANDA AND
PUBLIC OPINION

HENRY HOTZE AND THE BRITISH PRESS

So much faith was placed in the coercive power of cotton that for the first few months the Confederate government made no special effort at conciliating the public opinion of Europe. But with the failure of cotton to force intervention in 1861 the Richmond government began to comprehend the necessity of winning public favor abroad. In England, as we shall see, public opinion had swung around from an initial hostility to the South to a position of sympathy and friendship. But this friendship was of a negative type and supported a continuance of neutrality. What the South had to have was positive sympathy, which would demand action and force the British government to take steps in favor of the Confederacy. In France public opinion had settled into a position of hostility toward the South because of the enmity of the French for slavery and the traditional friendship of the French nation for an undivided Union. This attitude had to be overcome and French sympathy won for the cause of the South.

Realizing the necessity of winning popular sympathy, the Confederacy and its friends in England and France launched a very energetic campaign to educate the public of those countries in the causes and purposes of the struggle in America. A study of this propaganda campaign is of interest both as part of the diplomatic history of the Confederacy and as an example of how in times of war the opinion of neutral countries is manipulated by secret agencies of the warring powers.

The campaign to control public opinion was directed by three groups which will be found common to most war-time efforts. The Confederate diplomatic commissioners, Mason, Slidell, and Mann, were the clearing house and center for the program. Then there were the regularly constituted propagandists agents, Henry Hotze and

Edwin de Leon, and their aides. Finally, there were the native pro-southern agitators who worked in co-operation with these other groups as well as independently. The whole formed a powerful "southern lobby" who constituted a board of strategy for all southern undertakings in Europe.

On November 14, 1861—not long after Mason and Slidell had been dispatched to Europe to succeed the Yancey-Rost-Mann mission, and before Wilkes had taken the prisoners from aboard the Trent—the Confederate government took the first step in establishing an organized system of propaganda in Europe by sending the twenty-seven-year-old journalist, Henry Hotze, to direct the "education" of public opinion in Europe, especially in England. Hotze was well equipped for this type of business. He was a native of Switzerland, and was well acquainted with the attitudes and politics of the Europeans. His training as a journalist—he was associated with John Forsyth on the editorial staff of the *Mobile Register* at the time of the outbreak of the war—would be of great service in winning *entrée* to the newspaper circles of Europe.[1] Above all, he was a very able man—as able as any agent who went abroad during the Civil War. He showed more insight into public opinion and tendencies than did either Mason or Slidell, and his fastidiousness, his deftness, and his lightness of touch in a delicate situation were remarkable. His resourcefulness had a masterly finesse that would have done honor to Cavour or Bismarck. Finally, he was intellectually honest and unafraid to face facts.

Secretary of State Hunter instructed Hotze to proceed to London, where after taking Mason into his confidence he was to begin a careful study of public opinion and keep the State Department informed. The chief object of his mission was to create a favorable attitude abroad and convince the public that the Confederacy had the strength and determination to maintain itself. As Hunter phrased it, he was to "impress upon the public mind abroad the ability of the Confederate States to maintain their independence," and he was to stress also "the universal sentiment of the people of the Confederate

[1] See *Mobile Register*, May 11, 1867, cited in Callahan, *Diplomatic History of the Confederacy*, p. 92, for sketch of Hotze's life.

States to prosecute the war until their independence shall no longer be assailed." In his good-will campaign Hotze was to attack the growing despotism of the Lincoln government, especially its policy of arbitrary arrests and imprisonments and its violations of the freedom of the press; he was to attack the prohibitive-tariff policy of the United States, and in contrast he was to show how the Confederacy respected personal liberty and invited virtually free trade.

In the light of Hotze's accomplishments and the failure of more pretentious efforts, the stipend and expense money tendered Hotze seem like a jest. His yearly salary was to be $1,500, an unimportant detail, perhaps, in view of the fact that his income seems to have fitted him for a "dollar-a-year" man, but he was given only $750 for his expenses—a rather absurd price to pay for the good will of a whole continent! Doubtless neither Benjamin nor Davis was greatly impressed by this boyish person, or else they had not at the time of his appointment seen the importance of winning public opinion.[1]

When Hotze arrived in London he joined the Confederate lobby and, whenever possible, listened while others talked. He found that, with the exception of the occasional efforts of Yancey and Mann and the group of native Englishmen like Spence and Beresford-Hope, to whom we shall return later, the Federal propaganda agents, whose head seemed to be Thurlow Weed, had a clear field. Hotze's sensibilities were finely attuned to the reaction of the public mind, and he discovered that Weed and his agitators were helping the Confederate cause by making the North and its people odious. The nasal twang, the strident tones, the aggressiveness of these Yankees, and their whole manner, Hotze discovered, were "most repulsive to English taste," and the example of these Federal agents warned him that he could not "be too cautious and circumspect" in his conduct. Let the Federals have enough rope to hang themselves. He would not write or speak until he felt sure of his words being well received, for he was convinced "that in this case more than any other 'whatever is not useful does harm.' "[2]

[1] For instructions to Hotze see Pickett Papers, Hunter to Hotze, Nov. 14, 1862; O.R.N., Ser. 2, Vol. III, pp. 293–94.

[2] Pickett Papers, Hotze to Hunter, No. 2, Feb. 1, 1862; O.R.N., Ser. 2, Vol. III, pp. 325–26.

For a month he kept out of print, studied the situation, and assiduously cultivated the acquaintance of public men, especially the newspaper fraternity. His first introductions were obtained through Mason and a few other southern "gentlemen" who were warmly received by the most exclusive social group in London at the time Henry Adams was bitterly complaining to his brother Charles Francis of the cold, snobbish English society.[1] After that, he seems to have needed no aid. He was a master-hand at dispensing good cigars and choice whiskey at the proper moment, and he became quite a favorite with all those whom he cultivated.[2] After Hotze had been in London nearly a month he found the opportunity to open up his "educational" campaign. And what an opportunity! No less an agency than the *London Post*, the official organ of Lord Palmerston himself, was placed at his disposal, and he wrote an editorial or "leader" in justification of the cause of the Confederacy and its right of recognition. His first coup almost created a sensation in the coffeehouses and clubs of London, for it was assumed that Palmerston had inspired the article and was coming out for recognition.[3] Immediately many other London papers opened their editorial columns to him, but he would not push the southern cause too hard. "I shall," he wrote, "use the privilege moderately, neglecting no opportunity nor seeking to create artificial ones." Nor would he write controversial matter; he would publish only matter which would interest the public. These British were fastidious people, and he would be fastidious in his approach to their sentiments and prejudices.[4]

By the last of April Hotze had gained a similar position with the Tory press and was contributing to the editorial columns of the *Standard* and the *London Herald*, the latter the organ of Lord Derby, opposition leader.[5]

[1] *A Cycle of Adams' Letters* (Boston, 1920), Vol. I, *passim*.

[2] See Pickett Papers, Hotze to Benjamin, No. 19, March 14, 1863; *O.R.N.*, Ser. 2, Vol. III, pp. 710–12, for use of little favors among his friends.

[3] Pickett Papers, Hotze to Hunter, No. 3, Feb. 23, 1862; *O.R.N.*, Ser. 2, Vol. III, pp. 346–47.

[4] *Ibid.*

[5] Pickett Papers, Hotze to Secretary of State, No. 7, April 25, 1862; *O.R.N.*, Ser. 2, Vol. III, pp. 399–401.

Soon Hotze felt himself cramped by his dependence upon the friendship of the London press, so he conceived and put into effect at once the idea of establishing an independent paper which would express his opinion and yet pass as a British organ. Thus came into existence the Confederate-British journal, the *Index*, the first number of which appeared on May 1, 1862.[1] Hotze was destined to please the British but displease many of his fellow-countrymen, whose ideal of a newspaper was more in line with that of Thurlow Weed's, whom Hotze adjudged a perfect example of what a propagandist should not be. His conception of the *Index* was high indeed even for a non-political, not to mention a non-propagandist publication. "To be cosmopolitan and yet to have a country, to be miscellaneous and yet to have an object, to be tolerant and yet not indifferent; to be moderate and yet have strong convictions; to be instructive and yet not dull; to be entertaining and yet not frivolous . . . ." were some of the specifications for the *Index* and its editors.[2] He desired the *Index* to comport itself with an "Olympic serenity" and consistently refused to publish articles by the most ardent Confederate sympathizers when these articles violated his exacting canons of taste. Thus he offended Percy Greg, a dyspeptic British author of an American history which reflected no credit upon the North,[3] and the hot-tempered and vitriolic Paul du Bellet,[4] and many others.

But Hotze had in mind very definite objectives for his newborn publication, and any deviation from his high standards would endanger the attainment of these objectives. He planned to reach the British cabinet through its columns and present to the several members the Confederate cause in such form that it would not be offensive even to Russell, the northern sympathizer. This proposed aim of the *Index* was well conceived in view of the fact that Russell refused to hold frequent intercourse with the Confederate diplomatic agents. The second objective was to create a source of information

---

[1] Pickett Papers, Hotze to Secretary of State, Nos. 7 and 8, April 23 and May 15, 1862; *O.R.N.*, Ser. 2, Vol. III, pp. 399–401, 423–24, respectively.

[2] Hotze's Letter Book, May 28, 1864—June 16, 1865, Hotze to John Witt, Sept. 10, 1864.

[3] *Ibid.*, Hotze to Greg, Oct. 8, 1864.

[4] See Du Bellet's *Confederate Cabinet, etc.*, p. 27 and *passim*.

for the British press concerning all things vital to the South. The third was to draw into the Confederate cause all the important journalists and editorial writers of London by employing them occasionally to write something for the *Index*, and thereby to induce them to study the Civil War carefully. As to making the *Index* a popular journal with a wide circulation Hotze apparently cared very little, as long as he could have the regular press echoing the sentiments and information promulgated in his own paper.

Hotze was very successful despite the displeasure of some ardent Confederates at his overmoderation. Some months after the establishment of the *Index* he wrote Benjamin that it was fulfilling all his hopes. It was constantly reaching the breakfast tables of the cabinet and the members of Parliament and carrying the necessary information. He thought, in fact, that "the value of an organ, not merely as a means of reaching public opinion but as a channel through which arguments and facts can be conveyed unofficially to the Government itself, appears to me difficult to overrate." He was employing, just as he planned, the most important editorial and special-feature writers of the London press, and each one of these writers had thus become "an ally in the column of some other paper." In fact, he said, "I frequently employ writers with no other object."[1] By employing these leader writers to make contributions to the *Index*, he wrote, he caused them to become interested in the cause of the Confederacy and to inform themselves concerning the war. Then, when they wrote for their own papers they became pro-southern propagandists without pay or any kind of material inducement, and as one writer usually contributed to several British papers "I have thus," wrote Hotze, "the opportunity of multiplying myself, so to speak, to an almost unlimited extent. . . . . It is my object and hope, by this means, to found a school of writers whose services in the moral battles we still have to fight will, from their positions, be more valuable than those of the ablest pens of our own country."[2]

Soon Hotze with his *Index* as a base of operation was either

[1] Pickett Papers, Hotze to Benjamin, No. 14, Nov. 7, 1862; *O.R.N.*, Ser. 2, Vol. III, pp. 601–2.

[2] Pickett Papers, Hotze to Benjamin, No. 11, Sept. 26, 1862; *O.R.N.*, Ser. 2, Vol. III, pp. 534–37.

furnishing editorials to leader writers on all the papers except the *London Star* and *News* (Federal organs) or the material and data out of which these writers produced their editorials.[1] Hotze carried as much information as could be obtained concerning the inefficiency of the blockade, hoping thereby to stimulate the British public and government into denouncing the Federal blockade as ineffective and illegal, and to encourage British merchants to enter the blockade-running business. He dwelt constantly upon the material resources of the Confederacy and gave surprisingly fair accounts of the military situation, thus gaining the confidence of the British press in the veracity of the *Index*. He constantly but moderately explained that the secession of the South was not for the purpose of perpetuating slavery but was rather an effort at establishing the independence of a section whose interests were in conflict with those of the North. He did much to soften the British hostility to slavery as it existed in America; and spoke subtly of the "mongrel" "non-British" character of the northern population, of the rivalry of northern industrialism, of the high tariff and the advantages to England of a divided union, of the heroism, military genius, and death of Jackson. The lofty character and brilliant powers of Lee were harped upon constantly but adroitly, and these matters were passed on to the journals of England either through the columns of the *Index* or through the leader writers whom Hotze had indoctrinated.[2]

Hotze in the meanwhile urged that his expense money be increased to $10,000 per annum,[3] and Benjamin and the President responded with a blanket approval of his work and the grant of $10,000 per annum—finally to be increased to $30,000 per annum. In fact, Benjamin and Davis had sent out De Leon with large funds and were so disappointed in him that Hotze pleased them immensely. On

[1] See Pickett Papers, De Leon to Benjamin, No. 2, Sept. 30, 1862.

[2] Pickett Papers, Hotze to Benjamin, No. 8, May 15, 1862; *O.R.N.*, Ser. 2, Vol. III, pp. 423–24; *Index*, May 28, 1863, through year, *passim*, was constantly dwelling upon Jackson; *London Times*, May 27, and *Evening Standard*, May 27, cited in *O.R.N.*, Ser. 2, Vol. III, pp. 779–80.

[3] See e.g., Pickett Papers, Hotze to Benjamin, No. 15, Nov. 22, 1862; *O.R.N.*, Ser. 2, Vol. III, pp. 610–12; Pickett Papers, Hotze to Benjamin, No. 16, Dec. 20, 1862; *O.R.N.*, Ser. 2, Vol. III, pp. 632–33.

January 16, 1863, Benjamin wrote Hotze: "Your despatches continue to afford interesting and gratifying proof of the intelligent zeal with which you are performing your duties, and it is desired by the Department that you continue. . . . . Your plan of engaging the services of writers employed in the leading daily papers and thereby securing not only their co-operation but educating them into such a knowledge of our affairs as will enable them to counteract effectually the misrepresentation of Northern agents appears to be judicious and effective."[1]

With his contingent funds raised from the measly $750 to $10,000 per annum, and the approval of Benjamin and the President, Hotze widened his activities. He printed circulars giving a digest of the needs of the southern markets and mailed them to the leading wholesale merchants of Great Britain;[2] he placarded London with designs of the newly adopted Confederate flag;[3] he subsidized the circulation of books and pamphlets dealing with the South;[4] and he aided Spence in drumming up the peace meetings in the north of England and in getting up the giant peace petition to be presented to Parliament;[5] and he organized and conducted campaigns against Federal recruiting in Europe.[6]

The cleverest and most successful "hearing" that Hotze obtained in behalf of the Confederacy was in France, where public opinion was, as we have observed, unfriendly to the Confederacy. But this phase of his work came later and after another Confederate agent, Edwin de Leon, had been rather unsuccessful with the French press.

---

[1] Pickett Papers, Benjamin to Hotze, No. 3, Jan. 16, 1863; *O.R.N.*, Ser. 2, Vol. III, pp. 659–60.

[2] Pickett Papers, Hotze to Benjamin, No. 22, May 14, 1863; *O.R.N.*, Ser. 2, Vol. III, pp. 767–69.

[3] Pickett Papers, Hotze to Benjamin, No. 23, June 6, 1863; *O.R.N.*, Ser. 2, Vol. III, pp. 783–86.

[4] Pickett Papers, Hotze to Benjamin, No. 49, Sept. 17, 1864; *O.R.N.*, Ser. 2, Vol. III, pp. 1207–12.

[5] *Ibid.*

[6] Pickett Papers, Hotze to Benjamin, No. 27, Aug. 27, 1863; *O.R.N.*, Ser. 2, Vol. III, pp. 875–81.

EDWIN DE LEON AND THE FRENCH PRESS

In France as in England the Confederate government made no special effort during the first year of the war to win the sympathy of the French people. Paul du Bellet and Edward Goulhac from New Orleans and Charles Girard, former secretary of the Smithsonian Institution, attempted as private citizens to combat the Federal propaganda in the press.[1] Despite the urgings of Du Bellet, it was not until a year later that Benjamin was willing to take time to think of something besides the repulse of the enemy around Richmond. At that time Benjamin and the President decided to send the distinguished journalist and former consul-general of Egypt, Edwin de Leon, to France to direct the dissemination of "truth" in both Great Britain and France. He was given a $25,000 slush fund—quite a contrast to Hotze's $750—which he was instructed to use for the "educational" campaign in Great Britain and even in France itself. As yet, few, if any, of Hotze's dispatches had reached the Confederacy, and Davis and Benjamin must have expected little of him and doubtless they had already forgotten him. One would hardly expect much out of a twenty-seven-year-old journalist whose working fund was only $750. But much was expected of De Leon. He was one of the big guns.[2] Mason and Slidell were instructed to give De Leon the "benefit of your counsels and impart to him all information you may deem it expedient to make public, so as to facilitate him in obtaining such position and influence amongst leading journalists and men of letters as will enable him most effectually to serve our cause in the special sphere assigned to him."[3]

The auspices seemed good as De Leon set sail for Europe. He had the advantage of Hotze, so it seemed, in his long and fairly intimate friendship with Davis. But his disadvantage seems to have been in

[1] See Du Bellet, pp. 11–12, 20–25, and *passim;* Pickett Papers, De Leon to Benjamin, No. 2, Sept. 30, 1862; *O.R.*, Ser. 4, Vol. II, pp. 99–100.

[2] See Pickett Papers, Benjamin to Mason, No. 3, April 12, 1862, and Benjamin to Slidell, No. 3, April 12, 1862; *O.R.N.*, Ser. 2, Vol. III, pp. 384–86, 386–90, for instructions to the Confederate commissioners concerning De Leon.

[3] *Ibid.*

his not being on intimate terms with Slidell and Benjamin, for it was on these two rocks that his ship was finally wrecked. He was, though a man of penetration and unusual common sense, unfortunately possessed with a too-keen desire to be part of the "inner circle" of Confederate statesmen in Europe. Perhaps his training as consul-general as well as his habits as a journalist had developed this hankering after "inside information" and a position of intimacy with those who sit in the seats of the mighty. No sooner had he got aboard ship than his mistaken conception of his function—or his ambition to be more than he was—led him into a serious blunder. He opened the dispatches which had been intrusted to him to carry over to the Confederate agents and whiled away his long and tedious journey reading and studying them. Doubtless, had he waited, he would have been permitted to read most of them, for the Confeder-ate agents frequently met in conclave and pooled their dispatches for the enlightenment and pleasure of all. However, there was one dispatch, at least, which was not intended for any but the eyes of Slidell—the proposal to bribe the Emperor of the French to break the blockade by the offer of an enormous amount of cotton.[1] But more of this later.

Continuing to play the rôle of personal representative of the President and diplomat at large, De Leon obtained an interview with Lord Palmerston and tried to wring from the foxy old premier some admission that the Confederacy would soon be received into the family of nations. Failing in this and finding that Hotze was taking care of the British press satisfactorily, he hastened to France,[2] where he sought an interview with the Emperor. Finding Napoleon preoccupied with Italian affairs and "that nothing could be effected for the moment in the field of diplomacy," De Leon turned his at-tention "to the manufacture and improvement of public opinion through the press." His first serious efforts were the writing of a brochure, *La vérité sur des Etats Confédérés*, with Davis' picture on it, in which he presented American slavery in its best light, argued

[1] See below for a discussion of this proposal.

[2] Pickett Papers, De Leon to Benjamin, No. 1, July 30, 1862; *O.R.*, Ser. 4, Vol. II, pp. 23–24.

the case of the Confederacy, and urged its right to recognition as shown by its military strength.[1]

His slush funds were poured upon the venal press—venal as long as his money lasted—and presently he reported that the press of the clergy, the industrialists at Lyons, Bordeaux, Havre, Rouen, etc., had become active in support of the Confederacy, whereas before they had been silent. Du Bellet, who was not quite so optimistic of De Leon's success as was De Leon himself, was of the opinion that outside of temporary alliances bought at "so much per," the French press was not much affected by De Leon.[2] The press of the clergy and the industrialists who supported Napoleon was merely falling in line with the policy of the semiofficial journals like the *Patrie* and *Constitutionnel*, etc., which always voiced Napoleon's attitudes.

It may be that the real mass opinion of France could not have been touched by any kind of propaganda hostile to the United States. But if it had been otherwise De Leon could not have been very successful with John Slidell against him at every turn. When De Leon handed Slidell the secret dispatch with its seal broken his career was blasted, for if there was anything which that old intriguer could not forgive it was the tampering with his secrets. He loved those who tampered with the secrets of his enemies—as when Napoleon had the wires tapped to catch United States dispatches to Dayton or Bigelow—but what De Leon had done was different. Slidell probably said nothing at the time, but after that he ignored his instructions and refused to give De Leon any kind of information. Nor did he introduce De Leon to any of the powerful friends who could have helped him gain access to the men of letters and journalists as Mason had done in the case of Hotze. All he ever did was to be as uncivil and as nasty as possible without evoking a personal difficulty.[3]

Because Slidell refused to share any of his inside information with De Leon and showed open contempt for him, De Leon developed a

[1] Pickett Papers, De Leon to Benjamin, No. 2, Sept. 30, 1862; *O.R.*, Ser. 4, Vol. II, pp. 99–105.

[2] Du Bellet, pp. 55–65.

[3] See Pickett Papers, Slidell to Benjamin, No. 50 *bis*, Dec. 6, 1863; Du Bellet, p. 60.

deep hostility and distrust of Slidell. He doubted Slidell's honesty and fitness, and his doubts had foundation, for the rumor went its rounds in Paris that the Confederate commissioner was an old reprobate, gambling and drinking, quarreling and speculating in Confederate bonds, and making money generally out of the misfortunes of his country. The rumors originated partly in his passionate display of temper at any criticism of Emile Erlanger—who milked the Confederacy of several millions of dollars, with the backing of Slidell, who seems never to have recognized that his government was being robbed. Moreover, Erlanger's son presently married Slidell's daughter Matilda. Slidell, in fact, was distrusted and hated by practically all the Confederate agents in Europe, for the same reasons as those which motivated De Leon. The only friends whom Slidell could count among these agents were Mason, Huse, McRae, and possibly Bulloch.[1] Embittered by Slidell's refusal of aid and by his failure to accomplish what had been expected of him, De Leon began to write in his private correspondence with Davis vague suggestions that all was not well. But this criticism of Slidell was confined to his private, unofficial correspondence with Davis, until the end of 1863, when he indicted the Confederate commissioner in an official dispatch. He delivered an unfavorable verdict upon the French in the same communication. They wanted money "literally and not figuratively" and were a "far more mercenary race than the English."[2] At the same time he wrote a private letter to the President in which he criticized Slidell. Unfortunately for De Leon his official and private dispatches both fell into the hands of the enemy, who published them in the *New York Daily Tribune*. When Benjamin's eye fell upon them, De Leon's career came to an end. As a propagandist his usefulness was over with the publication of his criticism of the French, and his criticism of Slidell made it impossible for the Confederate government to maintain them both in France.

[1] See the letters of W. B. Saunders, agent provocateur of Seward, who sat in on many of the Confederate conclaves and who was believed to be a Confederate agent by the Confederates residing in Europe (U.S. State Dept. Special Missions, Vol. 3 [Sept. 11, 1852—Aug. 31, 1866]). Saunders was in Europe in 1864; see Du Bellet, *passim*.

[2] West, p. 110; cf. Pickett Papers, Benjamin to De Leon, No. 5, Dec. 9, 1863.

So the ax fell upon his official head and it tumbled into the basket. Benjamin wrote him that he had perused his published dispatch and private letter "with painful surprise," and that they were "such as not only to destroy your own usefulness in the special service entrusted to you, but to render your continuance in your present position incompatible with the retention in the public service of our commissioner to Paris. . . . ." Benjamin assured De Leon that his criticisms and thrusts at Slidell were repudiated by the President, who had "the fullest confidence in the ability and patriotism of Mr. Slidell, whose services abroad have been very valuable and are highly appreciated by him." He added that the President could not "refrain under the circumstances from disclaiming any concurrence either in your estimate of that gentleman's conduct and character or in the opinions you express relative to the French government and people."[1]

Slidell had also read the published dispatches of De Leon and, just three days before Benjamin wrote his curt letter of dismissal to their author, had unburdened himself of his grievances against the Confederate propagandist. For nearly two years Slidell had maintained silence with regard to his hostility and distrust of De Leon, venting his feelings in snubs and insults, perhaps, but he had not been a tattler to his government. But when that individual's criticisms fell upon Slidell, all inhibitions were overcome and Slidell frankly told Benjamin that De Leon was worth less than nothing to the Confederacy. He had failed to gain access to any public man of importance; his time had been spent with the small fry; and now that his criticism of the French had been made public he was *persona non grata* to all.[2] Slidell then broke silence on the opening of the secret dispatch by De Leon and told Benjamin of the former's constant efforts at assuming the rôle of a special diplomatic representative of the President.[3]

[1] *Ibid.*; Papers of Henry Hotze, extract from Benjamin's letter to De Leon, Dec. 9, 1863.

[2] Pickett Papers, Slidell to Benjamin, No. 50 *bis*, Dec. 6, 1863; *ibid.*, Benjamin to Slidell, No. 29, Jan. 28, 1864, *O.R.N.*, Ser. 2, Vol. III, pp. 1013–14.

[3] *Ibid.*

When Benjamin received Slidell's letter concerning the sins of De Leon, he did not repent of having dismissed the propagandist chief from the service of the Confederate government, but rebuked Slidell for not having informed him earlier, especially about the opening of the dispatch. The opening of the dispatch, wrote Benjamin, with grave indignation, "without the slightest warrant of authority" was such an offense "that it alone would probably have sufficed to put an end to Mr. de Leon's agency."[1]

About the first of February, 1864, De Leon received Benjamin's dispatch No. 5 dismissing him. It was a bitter potion, and he felt that Benjamin had mixed the dose. He accepted his dismissal, but not the reasons for it as stated by Benjamin. It was not, he said, because of criticisms of Slidell. He denied that either his official dispatches or his private letters to the President, "with the latter of which you have no concern as a public man," contained matter which was injurious to Slidell. "My correspondence contains no allusion to any representative abroad, which could fairly be considered as disparaging either of his 'conduct' or 'character,' and you will search in vain for one to justify your assertion." A perusal of De Leon's official dispatches corroborates this assertion up until the published dispatch No. 10, and he denied in this letter to Benjamin that the published dispatch was authentic. Evidently, it was his private correspondence which had done the damage. "As the confidential personal friend and correspondent of President Davis," complained De Leon, "for many years past, it was my pleasure and duty to give him my frank opinions; and if there be any person who should not feel flattered by my 'estimate'—the 'galled jade' is not Mr. Slidell, but one of the 'men who surround the President at Home.' " He would accept his dismissal but he would appeal to the President in person to obtain justice.[2] But De Leon, like Pickett, had the door shut in his face. Unless Benjamin so desired, no man could get a hearing from the President, and Benjamin objected in this case. De Leon's private dispatches had contained innuendoes which Benjamin took to himself—correctly—as well as criticisms not

[1] *Ibid.*

[2] Pickett Papers, De Leon to Benjamin, No. 15, Feb. 3, 1864.

flattering to Slidell. He could not do anything but bide his time as long as De Leon confined such criticisms to private correspondence. His time came when the dispatches and letters were published. Besides, De Leon proved himself in Benjamin's estimation a complete failure in his rôle as propagandist agent in France, and he was *persona non grata* to Slidell.

De Leon had spent around thirty thousand dollars while in Europe, and if Slidell and Du Bellet are to be believed this money was wasted.

HOTZE AND THE FRENCH PRESS, 1864–65

No sooner had Hotze learned of De Leon's recall than he stepped into the breach and under his original instructions took up De Leon's work with the French press. His field of operation was already large and it absorbed all the funds he had in sight. He must find some method of reaching the French public which would not be costly. De Leon's lavish use of money could not be emulated. Hotze first undertook to draw to him as employees of the *Index* the journalists and editorial writers of France, as he had done with respect to the English, and thus to create a "school" of writers who would become on their own account zealous propagandist agents without pay. Their reward would be the satisfaction of their vanity and love of distinction.[1] He soon found, however, that the French writers were not to be approached through the same methods as the English. They were cynical, sophisticated, nonchalant, and apparently without deep convictions. They wrote to earn a fee as a lawyer champions a client.[2]

The first Napoleon's diagnosis of the French, that what they wanted was glory, did not prove correct in this case. Anyway, Dayton and Bigelow were counteracting at the moment any desire for glory by large expenditures of corruption funds. All unattached writers soon found themselves well supplied at a good rate with

[1] Pickett Papers, Hotze to Benjamin, No. 37, Feb. 13, 1864, *O.R.N.*, Ser. 2, Vol. III, pp. 1022–25.

[2] Pickett Papers, Hotze to Benjamin, No. 38, March 12, 1864; *O.R.N.*, Ser. 2, Vol. III, pp. 1060–63.

plenty to do. Even the political director of the French press, one of Napoleon's chief henchmen, was bought up at the time by American friends who took care of his gambling debts and I.O.U.'s.[1] Hotze ventured a further explanation of the preoccupation of French writers in the Union cause: that De Leon's "bought friends," now that the pap had been sucked dry, were seeking more profitable alliances elsewhere. Bought friendships do not outlast the money, he said,[2] nor is it to be overlooked, either, that the writers of France, despite their nonchalance and cool taking of fees from the Confederate agents, when there were fees to obtain, shared in the popular sympathy with the North.

Failing to reach the public by employing the newspaper writers for small fees, Hotze hit upon a clever and very inexpensive expedient. He would not attempt to have editorial or special features published in the French papers, but would approach the public through the news, the telegraphic dispatches, correspondence, and paragraphs. "I am satisfied," he wrote, "that if we can only induce or coax people to look across the Atlantic, the facts themselves will soon speak for themselves, and with more eloquence than rhetoric can give them," and such distribution of facts would cost little.[3]

Hotze managed to go to the fountain of "news" for Western Europe and particularly France in executing his new plan. He became acquainted with M. Havas of the Havas-Bullier Telegraphic and Correspondence Agency. Hotze convinced Havas that the news which he had to supply was far more reliable than anything which could be obtained through northern newspapers or agencies—which was probably correct as far as military matters were concerned—and Havas agreed to take all the news concerning the South and the Civil War that Hotze could furnish and to distribute it without pecuniary consideration. Hotze was so pleased at the agreement and so surprised at being able to obtain free publicity that he thought

[1] Pickett Papers, Slidell to Benjamin, No. 59, April 7, 1864; *O.R.N.*, Ser. 2, Vol. III, pp. 1077–79.

[2] Pickett Papers, Hotze to Benjamin, No. 41, April 16, 1864; *O.R.N.*, Ser. 2, Vol. III, pp. 1090–91.

[3] *Ibid.*

Havas "both a man of honor and a gentleman," especially since he entertained no partiality for the South. He felt that he had been able to "win his confidence to an extent which. . . . he seldom accords to political information from any quarter."[1]

In further establishing the confidence of Havas in the accuracy of his information Hotze used rather clever technique. He gave the news the stamp of authority by first publishing it in the British press, preferably the *Times* and *Post*. After that he used his scissors or put the matter on the wire with quotation marks securely guarding it, with the result that "Mr. Havas never has refused a single thing I have sent," wrote Hotze.[2]

As "the habit of lying is too inveterate in our enemies to be ever abandoned," and as this habit would create so much distrust that it would counterbalance the pecuniary advantages which the Federals had,[3] Hotze felt very optimistic over the prospects of reaching the French reading public with information concerning the Confederacy, and he believed that the North would not be able to compete with his plan. Hotze was more successful than he had expected, for he soon came to realize that Havas had a monopoly on supplying the French press with news. "All translations from papers in other languages, even English, are made for the whole French Press" by the Havas agency, wrote Hotze. This agency daily furnished "to each journal a copious selection ready to hand, from which each editor takes what suits him and comments upon it after his fashion," so that "whatever is not contained in the 'Blue Sheet' of Havas can only by the merest accident reach the columns of the French paper." Hence, with Hotze and his *Index* staff furnishing Havas with all his news concerning the South there was little opportunity that anything would get into the news sections of the papers which Hotze would not desire to have there.[4] By July 29 Hotze wrote that he had obtained results which exceeded his anticipations based upon the

[1] Pickett Papers, Hotze to Benjamin, No. 42, May 7, 1864; *O.R.N.*, Ser. 2, Vol. III, pp. 1115–17.

[2] *Ibid.*   [3] *Ibid.*

[4] Pickett Papers, Hotze to Benjamin, No. 43, June 3, 1864; *O.R.N.*, Ser. 2, Vol. III, pp. 1142–44.

connection with M. Havas. "The latest and most authentic news, either direct from New York and Richmond, or indirectly through the intermediation of the London Press, with the most important comments of the latter, are regularly laid by Telegraph and by a system of varied correspondence before the French Public." Three-fourths of the French press carried this news, which according to Hotze's idea served a double purpose. In the first place, it educated and stimulated French interest in the South; but, most important of all, he wrote that he was able almost completely to "fill up a vacuum in which northern rumors and falsehoods were previously rioting at will." "My work in this has been that of the husbandman who tills, manures, and sows and leaves bountiful nature and clement seasons to do the rest."[1]

To what extent Hotze influenced public opinion by such a campaign cannot be judged. Certainly the French showed more interest in the South than ever before, and it may be that much sympathy was aroused. Moreover, Hotze presented his cause widely and cheaply. If he did not sell his propaganda to Havas at least he succeeded in having Havas sell it to the French press as "news."

THE NATIVE PROPAGANDISTS

In France, with the possible exception of Thouvenel, Napoleon's cabinet formed a group of propagandists for the recognition of the Confederacy. The activity of this group is so identified with the diplomacy of the French court that no special treatment will be accorded them in this connection. In England the situation was different. There were powerful figures, members of Parliament, merchants, shipbuilders, and shipowners, who labored incessantly in behalf of intervention or recognition so as to establish the independence of the South. These men, though highly connected, were not members of the cabinet. Like Hotze and De Leon they directed their energies to develop a friendly public opinion for the Confederacy and to influence the government to act in some way to aid the Confederate government in establishing its independence. In the first

[1] Pickett Papers, Hotze to Benjamin, No. 47, July 29, 1864; *O.R.N.*, Ser. 2, Vol. III, pp. 1177–80.

ranks of this British group stood Beresford-Hope, Lord Montagu, Fitzgerald, the Marquis of Bath, William Lindsay, Eustace and Robert Cecil, the Marquis of Lothian, Lord Campbell, Colonel Greville, T. C. Halliburton, W. H. Gregory, Roebuck, Laird, Ferguson, Horsefall, and others, members of the House of Commons or Lords. Then there was James Spence, the most active, the most persistent, and the most effective of all the native group, who was not a member of Parliament. Hugo Reid and Colley Grattan were two outstanding propagandists among a host of other lesser ones who were also not members of Parliament. Spence, Lindsay, and Beresford-Hope formed the board of strategy, with Spence undoubtedly at the head of the board. This group of native propagandists undertook to win public opinion to their program by the publication of newspaper articles, pamphlets, and books; through petitions to Parliament; and by beating up mass meetings and organizing southern clubs—all for the purpose of influencing the government into favorable action.

From the very beginning of the war this native group had been exercising considerable influence upon public opinion through the press and the publication of pamphlets and books. Spence had written a steady stream of articles for the *Times*.[1] But the most effective propaganda of all by either native or Confederate agent was a book which Spence published in 1861, the *American Union*. By February, 1862, this book had been through four large editions and had been translated into German. On first arriving in England Hotze was amazed at the popularity of the book, which he compared with De Tocqueville's *Democracy*.[2] The *London Economist* was of the opinion at this time that Spence's book had done more "to mould into definite form the floating mass of public opinion on the right and wrong doing of the Southern States in the matter of secession" than any other work of its kind.[3] Charles E. Rawlins, who published a

[1] See, e.g., Mason Papers, Spence to Mason, March 18, April 11 and 28, May 3 and 18, 1862, and *London Times*, May 19, 1862.

[2] Pickett Papers, Hotze to Benjamin, No. 4, Feb. 28, 1862; *O.R.N.*, Ser. 2, Vol. III, pp. 352–55; Hotze's Letter Book, 1861–1865, Hotze to Hunter, No. 4, Feb. 28, 1862.

[3] *Economist*, June 21, 1862.

book in reply to Spence's work, pronounced the *American Union* "at once the most brilliant and the most mischievous which the present Civil War in America has produced."[1] In his book Spence had convincingly argued the sovereign nature of the American states and their constitutional right to secede. With even greater force he placed before the English the fundamental difference between the North and the South which made the secession of the South inescapable. The North was industrial, powerful, and constantly threatening the less powerful, rural and agricultural South. But the thing which created the deepest impression was not so much the economic differences between the two sections as the racial. The North, according to Spence, was composed of a conglomerate, unfused mass of nationalities—Irish, German, Swiss, Swedish, Danish, Italian, Hungarian, Polish, Russian, Jewish, Roumanian, and Turkish—an inferior, mongrel people, while the South was almost pure British. This idea stuck—and even today sticks in the British mind —and the majority of the British soon felt a racial sympathy with the South which they did not have for the North. It was easy, too, to shift all the qualities of rowdyism and ill-breeding from the South to the North. Henceforth the bragging, swaggering, dishonest American with the nasal twang came from north of the Mason and Dixon Line.

The others of the group wrote for the papers less frequently than Spence, but many of them published virulent pamphlets and books in behalf of the South. Alexander Jones Beresford-Hope published in 1862 *England, the North and the South,* scourging the North and praising the South. He advocated disunion and recognition for many reasons, but fear and hatred and jealousy were the dominant ones.[2] In 1861 in *A Mirror in America* Lord Montagu, who had been, like Beresford-Hope, lecturing public gatherings on the Civil War and the South, published a bitter attack on the Union and a strong argument in favor of southern independence. He argued the inevitability of separation, the justice of the cause of the South; but

[1] *Ibid.*

[2] See *A Popular View of the American Civil War* (3d ed.; London, 1861) and *England, the North and the South* (3d ed.; London, 1862), pamphlets by A. J. B. Beresford-Hope.

the crux of his appeal was that now was the opportunity to render powerless that gigantic and overweening American nation which had begun to be so menacing to England and to Europe in both a political and a commercial way.[1] Hugo Reid covered the same ground as that of Beresford-Hope and Montagu in his pamphlet, *The American Question in a Nut Shell, or Why We Should Recognize the Confederacy*, published in 1862. Thomas Colley Grattan published a bitter book in 1861, *England and the Disrupted States of America*, in which the American Union was savagely attacked and the independence of the South urged—largely on the grounds of selfish interest. He gnawed and shook and tore the supposedly dead carcass of the American nation. While he was supposed to be speaking in behalf of the South, his condemnation of all things American was so sweeping and so indiscriminate that even the southern agent in England must have had great difficulty in accepting the friendship of such an advocate.

In the spring of 1862, after the arrival of Hotze and Mason, the British propagandists undertook a more spectacular program of pro-southern agitation. Spence's *American Union* and the pamphlets of Beresford-Hope, Montagu, Reid, and others and the newspaper articles and editorials failed to stir the cotton operatives who had remained quiescent during 1861. The northern propagandists, especially Bright and Forster, had been active in urging non-intervention upon the factory population in mass meetings and by word of mouth, while the Confederate agitators had depended largely upon the force of the cotton famine and press articles to move them to ask intervention. But as the cotton famine approached and Bright and Forster multiplied their efforts in creating the impression that the freedom of the British workingman depended upon the preservation of the American Union, it was realized that the pro-southern agitators must go out upon the hustings and harangue the multitudes, draw up resolutions and petitions, and likewise create the impression of popular sympathy for the Confederate cause.

The shrewd and ubiquitous James Spence was well aware of the

[1] He summarized his arguments in his pamphlet, *A Mirror in America* (London, 1861).

attitudes of the populace in the cotton-manufacturing districts, and he was fully conscious of the plentiful use made of small coin by the pro-northern agitators to "pack" meetings with sodden, apathetic people whose chief desire at the moment was to earn a few pennies to tide their half-starved families over the period of distress. He knew that these people, with the exception of a few intelligent leaders, had little if any interest in the American conflict, and that it was a comparatively easy matter to drum up any kind of meeting or petition or carry a resolution for or against the southern cause according to what propagandist was most active. Spence seems to have been in fairly close touch with certain leaders in the cotton districts from the beginning of the Civil War, but it was not until the cotton famine began to approach that he felt the conditions of the operatives made a move opportune. The agitation in favor of intervention had to be timed so as to occur simultaneously with Confederate military success, thus differing from the agitation of Bright and Forster in favor of the North, which could always be carried on. In April, 1862, after the Battle of Shiloh and some of Jackson's successes in the valley, the time seemed ripe for the stirring-up of the Lancashire people in favor of intervention. Spence permitted some of the workingmen to call on him. He advised them to instigate mass meetings and he promised to help them draw up petitions to present to Parliament.[1] No sooner had he got his crowd into motion than news arrived that New Orleans had been taken by the Federals and Spence had to suspend his plans.[2]

The tide of battle swayed to and fro so uncertainly in the summer of 1862 that Spence was forced to repress any impulse toward agitation or mass protest in the cotton districts. He continued to perfect the organization of the southern clubs and to prepare the machinery for inciting the populace by mass meetings "for the purpose of pressing recognition when the day for action is considered to have arrived."[3] Again in September, 1862, the time seemed to be "nigh at hand." The first move made was at Staleybridge where William Boon organized a committee "to promote the recognition of

[1] Mason Papers, Spence to Mason, April 28, 1862.
[2] *Ibid.*, June 3, 1862.   [3] *Ibid.*, Sept. 15, 1862.

the Confederate States of North America as an Independent Nationality."[1] In connection with this early movement Spence experimented, with apparent success, in hiring idle workmen to pack the meetings and shout vociferously for the South and demand recognition and cotton.[2]

But Spence did not get far before news came that Lee had been turned back from Maryland and once again he felt compelled to call off the "popular agitation." Spence thought at this time that the cotton famine would speak with such eloquence that it, unaided, would move the cotton operatives to rise up and demand that the government stop the war. So the summer and early fall of 1862—when the British cabinet was most seriously considering intervention and when it feared an uprising of the operatives most[3]—was allowed to pass without great efforts being made to stir up mass meetings and draw up resolutions and petitions.

It was not until after the early failures in Grant's Vicksburg campaign, as well as the brilliant Confederate victory of Chancellorsville, that Spence got his agitation under way. This movement was definitely planned to come to a climax at the time when the Roebuck motion, to be discussed later, should be brought up in Parliament, June 30, 1863. It was a rather thoroughgoing campaign—except it was one year too late. Southern clubs were organized in every town in Lancashire, and most of the towns in Derbyshire, Cheshire, and Yorkshire during 1863.[4] Spence stumped all North England in behalf of the recognition of the Confederacy at his own expense and to the total neglect of his private affairs.[5] Beresford-Hope, Lindsay,[6] Roebuck, and others frequently aided in the agitation and organization. By this time Spence, had he ever been so

---

[1] *Ibid.*, Boon to Mason, Sept. 17, 1862; Mason to Boon, Sept. 19, 1862.

[2] See, e.g., *ibid.*, Spence to Mason, Oct. 3, 1862.

[3] See below.

[4] Mason Papers, Spence to Mason, June 16 and 19, Dec. 7 and 17, 1863, Jan. 22, 1864; Pickett Papers, Mason to Benjamin, No. 40, June 20, 1863; *O.R.N.*, Ser. 2, Vol. III, pp. 809–10; Pickett Papers, Hotze to Benjamin, No. 32, Nov. 21, 1863; *O.R.N.*, Ser. 2, Vol. III, pp. 960–63; *Index*, June 3, 1864.

[5] *Ibid.*; Mason Papers, Spence to Mason, 1863, *passim.*

[6] *Ibid.*, Aug. 3, 1863.

credulous and romantic, harbored no illusions as to the lofty ideals of the cotton-mill workers in time of distress. He was convinced that what they wanted and needed most were the bare necessities of life. So he made free use of coin both from his own purse and from that of Confederate sympathizers and profiteers such as Alexander Collie, of Glasgow, who "tithed" for the Confederate cause. He packed these meetings with "young men of energy with a taste for agitation but little money."[1]

With the collapse of the Roebuck motion in early July and the tidings of the Confederate losses at Vicksburg and Gettysburg, Spence and his colleagues abruptly abandoned their popular agitation. He told Mason that under the discouraging effects of the Confederate losses he "could not advocate recognition now." He was very much depressed because of the situation, "being liable to attacks of nervous depression."[2]

Spence, with Mason as his chief adviser, could not stay depressed long. Energy and hope were two characteristics of this Englishman. By the first of November, 1863, he and his fellow-British-Confederates had launched a really formidable movement to stir up British sympathies to the point of demanding that the government recognize the independence of the Confederacy. Three general committees or associations were organized: the Manchester Southern Independence Association, the London Southern Independence Association, and the London Society for Promoting the Cessation of Hostilities in America—all to head up and co-ordinate the southern clubs which had been formed in the summer and fall of 1863. The Manchester Association was especially designed to act as the dynamic head of all the southern clubs and it furnished the machinery for arousing the industrial population. The London associations were primarily intended as a parliamentary lobby and to impress the public with the importance of the recognition of the Confederacy or any other measure favorable to the South, by the mere weight of the names of the organization. Judged by the weight of names, the Committee of Organization of the Southern Inde-

[1] See, e.g., *ibid.*, June 16 and Dec. 17, 1863.
[2] *Ibid.*, Aug. 3, 1863.

pendence Association was indeed heavy. Most of the men were members of either Parliament or the House of Lords. Little came out of this Association in the way of agitation.[1]

By December Spence had resuscitated the southern clubs in many of the northern towns,[2] and he was enjoying himself thoroughly in beating the Forster and Bright gangs who, with their pockets stuffed with Federal slush funds, were rushed into southern meetings to break them up. It was a knock-down-drag-out game—this beating-up of northern or southern sympathy. Following a very successful meeting in Glasgow[3] in which the Forster-Bright northern sympathizers were greatly outnumbered, Spence laid his plans "to work from the secondary towns to the chief ones and take the latter, Liverpool, Manchester, and London as we come upon the assembling of Parliament."[4] The problem was not so much to arouse sympathy for the Confederacy as to induce those who entertained such sympathy to assume a positive attitude toward governmental action. In line with Spence's plans Manchester held a mass meeting and voted in favor of southern recognition, which was made easier by the use of funds obtained from Collie.[5] The *Index* was of the opinion that "between now and the opening of Parliament nothing will be left undone that may tend to give the Confederate movement in Lancashire all the co-operative power that can be produced by the unity of purpose, methodized action, and resources equal to the occasion."[6] By June the *Index* stated that "there is scarcely a town or populous village, whether in Lancashire or throughout the manufacturing districts of Cheshire or Derbyshire, where the American question has not been fully and warmly discussed."[7] Even in the fall of 1864 the Southern Independence Association was circulating

[1] For London Association see E. D. Adams, II, 186–218 *passim;* Mason Papers, Mason to Mann, Nov. 24, 1863, and Spence to Mason, Dec. 7 and 17, 1863; Pickett Papers, Mason to Benjamin, No. 1, Jan. 25, 1864; *O.R.N.*, Ser. 2, Vol. III, pp. 1007–9; *Index*, Jan. 14, 1864.

[2] Mason Papers, Spence to Mason, Dec. 7, 1863.

[3] *Ibid.*   [4] *Ibid.*

[5] See previously; Mason Papers, Spence to Mason, Dec. 17, 1863.

[6] *Index*, Jan. 14, 1864.   [7] *Ibid.*, June 2, 1864.

a petition in favor of recognition or mediation "in every town in Great Britain and Ireland, and it was being well supported."[1]

Before concluding this brief account of the native propagandists, it should be said in passing that there was no great difference between their attitude and that of the Bright group on the slavery question. Every southern friend was an enemy of slavery and openly proclaimed it in addressing the British people. Spence finally lost his position as Confederate financial agent for virtually promising the British public that if the South should win its independence it would free the slaves eventually—which was probably true.[2] The Southern Independence Association promised the freedom of the slave as one of its goals.[3] Likewise the Society for Promoting the Cessation of Hostilities in America promised ultimate emancipation in case the South should become independent.[4] Too much emphasis has been placed upon the antislavery feeling of the Lancashire population and of the radical group when as a matter of fact everybody was opposed to slavery and assumed that the end of slavery had come, regardless of the outcome of the war. This should be kept in mind in any attempt at understanding public opinion in England, which resulted from a complex of forces, one of which was the work of the propagandists.

FUNDAMENTAL TRENDS IN BRITISH AND FRENCH OPINION

Because there were so many forces at work upon public opinion at the same time, there is no way by which the effects of Confederate propaganda can be measured in either England or France. Self-interest, prejudices, constant friction between the United States and Great Britain, and many other factors, all combined to make propaganda against the United States effective in England, while

[1] *Ibid.*, Nov. 3, 1864.

[2] Pickett Papers, Hotze to Benjamin, No. 13, Oct. 24, 1862; *O.R.N.*, Ser. 2, Vol. III, p. 567; Pickett Papers, Domestic Letters, Benjamin to Spence, Jan. 11, 1864. Cf. Pickett Papers, Hotze to Benjamin, No. 31, Oct. 31, 1863; Benjamin to Hotze, No. 13, Jan. 9, 1864; *O.R.N.*, Ser. 2, Vol. III, pp. 944–48, and 993–96, respectively.

[3] *Index*, Jan. 14, 1864.

[4] Pickett Papers, Mason to Benjamin, No. 1, Jan. 25, 1864; *O.R.N.*, Ser. 2, Vol. III, pp. 1007–9; see chap. xvii for further discussion.

self-interest, prejudice, and tradition made Confederate propaganda in France less effective. It is comparatively easy, however, to arrive at a fairly accurate estimate of public opinion in the two countries which resulted from the many complex forces. In England opinion may be characterized as definitely hostile to the North and sympathetic with the South, while in France the reverse was true. No attempt is made here at a detailed study of public opinion; but certain fundamental trends are helpful to the full understanding of the diplomatic history of the period.

The election of Lincoln and the threatened secession of the South found the British press hostile both to the southern people and to their proposed withdrawal from the Union. This was primarily because of British hostility to slavery and because of the fact that for so many years the United States, with whom England had not been on good terms, had been ruled by southern men whom as representative Americans the British disliked. The *London Times* was delighted that Lincoln was elected because it meant "that the march of slavery and the domineering tone which its advocates were beginning to assume . . . . has been at length arrested and silenced." Secession, said the *Times*, was for no other purpose than to set up a slave empire.[1] The *Economist* shared in the opinion that the South had no excuse for secession other than the desire to set up an independent slave state. The South was the spoiled child who had suddenly been deprived of having its way.[2] The *Times*[3] insisted that there was a "right and wrong in this question and that the right belonged with all its advantages to the States of the North." The *Edinburgh Review*[4] insisted that public opinion in England should be with the North because its course was in behalf of freedom. The *Saturday Review*[5] denounced the South for its supposed schemes of setting up a new government devoted to spreading slavery over the entire North American continent: "A more ignoble basis for a great Confederacy it is impossible to conceive. . . . ." The *London Chronicle*,[6]

---

[1] *Times*, Nov. 21, 1860. [3] *Times*, Jan. 4, 1861.
[2] *Economist*, Jan. 12, 1861. [4] *Edinburgh Review*, April, 1861.
[5] *Saturday Review*, March 2, 1861, cited in Adams, I, 46.
[6] *London Chronicle*, March 14, 1861.

the *Dublin News*,[1] and the *London Review*[2] denounced the South for
its breaking up the Union to further the cause of slavery.[3] The old
anti-American feeling which was so strong in England concentrated
itself at this moment upon the southern people. The *Economist* reminded its readers that the South was a dreary land, dominated by
poor whites, perhaps "the most degraded, ignorant, brutal, drunken,
and violent class that ever swarmed in a civilized country," and
that "the slaves in most of the Southern States are equal to the
whites. . . . ."[4] The *Times* thought of the southern people as "a
proud, lazy, excitable and violent class, ever ready with the knife
and revolver."[5] The *Saturday Review*[6] believed the South was
dominated by the "most ignorant, most unscrupulous, and most
lawless race in the world." The *Times* at this moment professed a
very low opinion of the courage of the southern people. It believed
that "a few hundred thousand slave owners, trembling nightly with
visions of murder and pillage, backed by a dissolute population of
poor whites are no match for the hardy and resolute population of
the free states."[7]

By the last of January, 1861, however, British public opinion experienced a rapid change, and within a few months certain major
convictions and sympathies with regard to the Civil War had become well established and did not change except to become deeper
during the struggle. The first change began to be manifest on the
matter of secession. As soon as it was seen that it would cost a real
war to restore the Union, and that the war might bring distress upon
England's cotton industry, opinion began to hedge and to advocate
peaceable disunion. This advocacy of peaceable secession seemed to
confirm the southern belief in the power of cotton. The *Economist*[8]
admitted that "whatever view we may take of the political consequences of the movement there, whether we think of it favorably
or very unfavorably, we cannot but acknowledge that it must bring

---

[1] *Dublin News*, Jan. 26, 1861.

[2] *London Review*, April 20, 1861.

[3] Cf. Adams, I, 45–46.

[4] *Economist*, Jan. 26, 1861.

[5] *Times*, Jan. 12, 1861.

[6] *Saturday Review*, Jan. 12, 1861.

[7] *Times*, Nov. 26, 1860.

[8] *Economist*, Jan. 5, 1861.

pain and care to many large classes of comfortable people" in Great Britain. Three weeks later the *Economist*[1] urged that in view of the irreconcilable interests of the two sections, "efforts should be exerted not to prevent separation but to bring it about in a peaceable manner." In March the *Economist*[2] took the position that the South had established a well-organized government and was now in such a strong position that the North should agree to a "separation by acquiescence and negotiation," and thus save the border states who would secede at the first attempt of coercion. The *Times* followed a similar course. On January 19, 1861, it expressed great apprehension[3] that the North might resort to war to put down secession and thereby seriously injure British industry and commerce. Three days later[4] it suggested a recognition of the South as a possible means of averting a Civil War which would cut off the cotton trade. Before the middle of March,[5] the *Times* had become a confirmed advocate of peaceable disunion as a means of preventing the interruption of the British cotton trade with the South.

The British government in order that British cotton trade might flow uninterruptedly also began to favor peaceful disunion. Russell wrote Lyons privately: "I do not see how the United States can be cobbled together again by any compromise. . . . . I cannot see any mode of reconciling such parties as these. The best thing now would be that the right to secede should be acknowledged. . . . . But above all I hope no force will be used."[6] Lyons wrote Russell that though he felt sympathetic toward the United States he was afraid to express his sympathy for that would encourage the North in a war resulting in a suspension of southern cultivation "which would be calamitous to England even more than to the Northern States themselves."[7] There were attempts at trying to get the United States to forego war and its interruptions of trade. Lyons expressed to Seward a strong opposition to a northern attack on the South and the stop-

[1] *Ibid.*, Jan. 26, 1861.

[2] *Ibid.*, March 2, 1861.   [4] *Ibid.*, Jan. 22, 1861.

[3] *Times*, Jan. 19, 1861.   [5] *Ibid.*, March 12, 1861.

[6] Lyons Papers cited in E. D. Adams, I, 52–53.

[7] F.O. Amer., Vol. 763, Lyons to Russell, No. 197.

page of the cotton trade. "I said," he wrote to Russell, "if the United States is determined to stop by force so important a commerce as that of Great Britain with the cotton-growing states, I could not answer for what might happen." He told Seward that in case the United States resorted to war and thus interrupted the cotton supply, "an immense pressure would be put upon H.M.'s Government to use all the means in their power to open those Ports" which were blockaded.[1]

There was a far more important and permanent advantage to England of separation than the momentary relief in the cotton trade, and it was this advantage which really lay at the bottom of the attitude of the greater part of the British people. This was that a powerful and ill-mannered rival should be permanently weakened by disunion. England had, with the exception of a few radicals, always disliked the United States. This dislike was based upon maritime rivalry, commercial rivalry, colonial rivalry, and upon past bitter experiences with America. It could not be forgotten that America had once been an English possession which had successfully revolted and involved England in a series of humiliating defeats. Then there was the War of 1812 which rankled. After that were boundary and fishery disputes, the Oregon controversy, the Texas controversy, the clash in Central America, and, withal, the gigantic growth and the accompanying ill-concealed willingness of America to fight England on the most trivial pretext. This hostility we shall see becoming more and more manifest as the irritations of war rubbed the thin skin of the English raw. The *Economist*[2] suggested the advantages of disunion, for instead of one nation "showing an encroaching and somewhat bullying front to the rest of the world, we shall have two showing something of the same front to each other. Each will be more occupied with its immediate neighbor, and therefore less inclined to pick quarrels with more distant nations." Again in March[3] the *Economist* returned to the idea. "We do not see why three or four independent republics . . . . will not answer better than one ab-

---

[1] Newton, *Lord Lyons: A Record of British Diplomacy* (2 vols.; London, 1913), I, 31.

[2] *Economist*, Jan. 19, 1861.

[3] *Ibid.*, March 9, 1861.

sorbing and overwhelming dominion. We are certain that such an arrangement will be more conducive to the peace of Europe. We can feel little doubt that it will also be more conducive to the civilization of America. Limitation will produce modesty and caution. . . . . There may be jealousies and quarrels—as there are among contiguous European countries; but . . . . even if they occasionally proceed to bloodshed, will have a far less demoralizing influence on all concerned than the conviction of boundless power and unmatched grandeur which now inflates the bosom, disturbs the brain and damages the principles and sense of justice of nearly every American citizen. The several commonwealths will keep each other in order. . . . ."

The *Times*,[1] which had in the beginning expressed admiration and sympathy for the North, now exclaimed: "That the Americans should expect us to be swayed by any strong feeling of attachment to the United States Government argues an extraordinary forgetfulness of what the conduct of that government has been to us on all occasions. While our behavior to the people of the United States has been always conciliatory, it is no exaggeration to say that their government has been uniformly hostile and ungenerous beyond any European precedent, except perhaps that of the first French Empire. In our European disputes, our statesmen when called upon to face hostile despotisms have always been haunted by the fear of having the American government on their backs. . . . ." In the fall of 1861 the *Economist*[2] again reiterated the hostility toward America which every Englishman felt at heart: "Never did a nation not avowedly inimical labor so hard to alienate all friendly feeling. They have habitually treated England in a way which England would have borne from no other country." Even now the papers in America were advocating the seizure of Canada, which the present Secretary of State Seward had advocated during the campaign a year before, and even the accredited ambassadors to the chief European courts had recently in Paris used insulting and threatening language. Two weeks later,[3] this paper returned to the advocacy of the disruption

[1] *Times*, June 11, 1861.

[2] *Economist*, Sept. 14, 1861.   [3] *Ibid.*, Sept. 28, 1861.

of the Union. "We admit that we do regard the disruption of the Union as a matter for rejoicing rather than for regret. . . . . We avow the sentiment, and we are prepared to justify it as at once natural, statesmanlike, and righteous." The dissolution of the Union would confine slavery to a narrow region and ultimately result in its extinction; therefore, "we do not see why we should hesitate to declare our belief that the dissolution of the Union will prove a good to the world, to Great Britain and probably in the end to America herself." The Great Republic had grown in population, in prosperity, and in power at such a rate that it was not well either for her neighbors or herself. "Her course had been so triumphant, so un parallelled, so free from difficulties, so uncheckered by disaster or reverse, that the national sense and the national morality had both suffered in the process. A boundless territory, and exhaustless soil, a commerce almost unequalled, mineral wealth quite unfathomed and apparently untouched, a people rapidly increasing in numbers and endowed with most of the qualities which ensure empire and predominance to their possessors,—had fairly, and not unnaturally, turned the heads of the whole nation. They believed that no other nation could stand up against them. . . . . They were so rough, so encroaching, so overbearing, that all other governments felt as if some new associate, untrained to the amenities of civilized life and insensible alike to the demands of justice and courtesy, had forced its way into the areopagus of nations; yet at the same time they were so reckless and so indisputably powerful, that nearly every one was disposed to bear with them and defer to them rather than oppose a democracy so ready to quarrel and so capable of combat. The result was . . . . an increase of arrogance and a stretch of pretensions which made it clear that sooner or later all who did not wish to be habitually trampled on and insulted must prepare to fight." "This being so . . . . can we be charged with selfishness or want of generosity because we rejoice that an excess of power which was menacing to others and noxious to themselves has been curtailed and curbed?"

Truly fear, hatred, and jealousy—largely nationalistic, but partly economic—thus expressed by the conservative trade journal, usually so evenly keeled and calm, was that of the English nation with the exception of only a small group who saw in America either a haven of refuge or an example of successful democracy to be held up for the edification of political opponents.

This fear and jealousy of a powerful rival and the rejoicing over the downfall of that rival continued to be voiced by the public press during the war. In the late summer of 1862 the *Times*[1] remarked after the series of Federal defeats around Richmond: "Indeed, people are breathing more freely, and talking more lightly of the United States, than they have done any time these thirty years. . . . . We are no longer stunned every quarter of a year with the tremendous totals of American territory, population, and wealth, computed to come due, thirty, sixty, a hundred years hence: when of course the tallest empire of the old world will easily walk between the legs of the American Colossus." It was a "riddance of a nightmare." In March, 1863, the *Times* was of the opinion that "excepting a few gentlemen of Republican tendencies, we all expect, we nearly all wish, success to the Confederate cause."[2] The *Economist*, never changing its belief that the division of America into two or more independent states would be a benefit to the world at large, admitted in February, 1865,[3] that the British people, despite the neutrality of the government, did not wish the North success. "We cannot deny it: we cannot alter it, and it is this which irritates them."

Not just the press but members of Parliament and prominent leaders as we have already seen generally expressed the sentiment avowed by the *Times* and the *Economist*, the *London Herald*, and *Morning Post*, etc., as well as the reviews. Even Bulwer-Lytton thought that now was England's opportunity to make permanent the division of a rival that had grown too arrogant and strong.[4] Roebuck, Campbell, Lindsay, Horsefall, Fitzgerald, Gregory, and Ferguson in and out of Parliament frequently expressed such sentiments of hatred and fear of America with the fond hope that this was the end of her greatness. We shall hear them in other connections, and they are mentioned here merely to call attention at this juncture

[1] *Times*, Aug. 15, 1862.

[2] *Ibid.*, March 27, 1863.

[3] *Economist*, Feb. 11, 1865.

[4] *Spectator*, Sept. 28, 1861.

to the fact that the average member of Parliament, the average merchant, banker, shipper, and newspaperman, and the average man on the streets, hated America and wished her disruption. Baron Brunow, the Russian minister at the Court of St. James's, said that even the British government with its perfectly proper neutrality "at the bottom of their heart desire the separation of North America into two republics which will watch each other jealously and counterbalance one another. Then England on terms of peace and commerce with both would have nothing to fear from either: for she would dominate them, restraining them by their rival ambitions."[1] This fear and jealousy, then, was a fundamental and permanent factor in ranging British sympathies upon the southern side.

The initial sympathy of the British people for the North because of the belief that the South had seceded to set up a slave state and that the North stood for freedom of the slave was soon destroyed, and a strong conviction arose that the freedom of the slave was not an issue in the war. One can hardly escape the logic of events which forced this conclusion upon the English mind. During the winter of 1861, it will be recalled, numerous compromises of the American troubles were discussed, the most important of which was the Crittenden compromise conceding a permanent share in the territories to slavery. The *Economist*[2] upon hearing of such proposals spoke of the measures as iniquitous, and was not willing to believe that Lincoln would yield to them. But the final disillusionment came when in his inaugural address Lincoln said: "I have no purpose, directly or indirectly, to interfere with the institution of slavery in the states where it exists, ... I believe I have no lawful right to do so and I have no intention to do so." This was, in truth, the death knell of British sympathy based upon the moral righteousness of the northern cause. If freedom was not the cause, then what was it? The British press was not long in deciding, and its decision carried it at one stride to the championship of the righteousness of the southern cause. The *Economist*[3] late in the summer of 1861 pronounced a little stronger upon the issue of the war: It was not for

[1] E. D. Adams, I, 50–51.

[2] *Economist*, March 2, April 13, 1861.

[3] *Ibid.*, July 6, 1861.

freeing the slave on the part of the North or preserving slavery on the part of the South, but was for dominion and power on the part of the one and the right of self-government on the part of the other. After Lincoln's message to Congress, which was as tender of the rights of slavery as had been his inaugural, the *Economist*[1] was completely convinced, if there had been any doubts, that Lincoln and the North would be more than glad to continue or restore the old Federal union on the basis of slavery and all its abuses if the South would only consent to return. The inevitable conclusion was that the war was "a war of conquest and not of philanthropy." Returning again a few weeks later to the cause of the conflict in America, the *Economist*[2] was of the opinion that after all the South was only "fighting for that right to choose their government." All were now conscious that no really noble or soul-stirring cause was in any way at issue, since the abolition sentiment had "nothing to do with the quarrel and the protective tariff a great deal and the mere lust of dominion and empire more than either." The assumption that the quarrel between North and South was a quarrel between Negro freedom on the one side and Negro slavery on the other was untrue. Then if the freedom of the slave was not the issue, asked the *Economist*, "on what other ground can we be fairly called upon to sympathize so warmly with the Federal cause?"[3]

The *Times* likewise came to the definite conclusion that the North was not fighting for the freedom of the slave. According to the declarations of all the leaders of the Republican party and the government itself, remarked the *Times*,[4] "there was no question about slavery at all. Every politician throughout the states had over and over again declared that he has no wish to meddle with the 'peculiar institution' of the South; some have declared abolition unjust, some impossible, others have contented themselves with saying that it was illegal under the constitution by which the republic was bound. What then was the object of the war which President Lincoln proclaimed? It was simply to hold the South to

[1] *Ibid.*, July 20, 1861.   [3] *Ibid.*, Sept. 14, 1862.
[2] *Ibid.*, Aug. 17, 1861.   [4] *Times*, May 11, 1861.

its allegiance, to retain it with all its institutions, good or bad; in fact, to keep slavery as one of the social elements of the Union," and above all to retain the South because of its monopoly of the cotton supply and because of the large trade enjoyed with it by the North. The North then was fighting for dominion, the South for a principle "which is no other than the sacred right of self government."

In commenting upon Davis' recent message to Congress which touched upon the causes of the war, the *Times*[1] agreed that there was absolute truth in what Jefferson Davis contended, namely, that the war was not brought on by a single cause, but that it was the result of a long series of irritations between two sections with directly opposed economic and social systems. The industrial North had attempted to "render the common government subservient to their own purposes by imposing burdens on commerce as a protection to their manufacturing and shipping interests." It was now plain to the *London Times*, which had so upbraided the South at first for breaking up the Union in order to make slavery safe, that it had been mistaken, and that there were many other more important causes, and that the freedom of the slave had never been an issue. So plain was it to the *Times* that the South was fighting for the principle of self-government that it made frequent comparisons between the Civil War and the Revolution, the South occupying ground held by the colonies in 1776.[2] There was much relish in this comparison. The *Times* and the English generally felt that America was now getting some of the medicine she had so unkindly administered to Great Britain in 1776. "The real motives of the belligerents," remarked the *Times* a week later,[3] ". . . . appear to be exactly such motives as have caused wars in all times and countries. They are essentially selfish motives. . . . . Neither side can claim any superiority of principle. . . . . The question is simply whether the ten millions of the Southerners shall become independent according to their desires or the twenty millions of Northerners remain powerful according to their desires." Returning to the chief issues of the war in September, the *Times*[4] named as causes of war commercial and economic

[1] *Ibid.*, May 22, 1861.
[2] *Ibid.*, May 24, 1861.
[3] *Ibid.*, May 30, 1861.
[4] *Ibid.*, Sept. 9, 1861.

rivalry, different systems of society, constant quarrels, etc. But, it remarked: "It is easier to say what is not than what is the real issue at stake, and among the notions that we may thus dismiss is the notion that 'the liberty of the African race is the gage of battle.' . . . . Slavery is altogether thrust into the background."

The other papers, with the exception of John Bright's organ, the *Morning Star*, and the popular *Daily News*, the *Spectator*, and the *Westminster Review*, and a few obscure provincial journals, followed the *Economist* and the *Times* in changing the opinion that slavery was the cause of the war. *John Bull*, the country gentleman's paper, declared:[1] "Nothing can be clearer than this that black slavery has nothing whatever to do with this Civil War in America." Mrs. Stowe, then lecturing in England, indignantly accused England of taking the side of slavery. The *Saturday Review*[2] replied: "The North does not proclaim abolition and never pretended to fight for anti-slavery."

In 1863 the emancipation proclamation brought on another discourse on the issues of the war. The *Times* again failed to see that the freedom of the slaves was the objective. Neither the westerner who hated the Negro nor the "citizens of the Atlantic cities, who are warring in order to recover the profits of slave labour are honestly desirous to extinguish slavery." The English public did not believe that the President, who had over and over again declared that his object was to restore the Union, "with slavery if he can, without slavery if he must," desired emancipation for itself.[3] Even Russell, British foreign minister and Federal sympathizer, expressed the conviction that the issue was not slavery but that the North was fighting for dominion.[4] He wrote Lord Lyons that the emancipation proclamation was a vindictive war measure. It freed the slaves only in those states at war with the United States where it could not be carried out and not in those states still under Federal jurisdiction.[5]

[1] *John Bull*, Sept. 14, 1861.   [2] *Saturday Review*, Sept. 14, 1861.

[3] *Times*, Sept. 13, 1862; Jan. 19, 1863; April 9, 1863.

[4] *Times*, Oct. 17, 1861.

[5] F.O. Amer. Vol. 868, Russell to Lyons, No. 30, Jan. 17, 1863.

Englishmen were, therefore, absolved from all moral obligation of supporting the northern cause. They were free not to sympathize with a people whom they hated and a nation which they feared, and to sympathize with a people whom they had come to like. Charles Francis Adams summed up the British opinion as to the cause of the war in a letter to his son Charles Francis, Jr.: "People do not quite understand Americans or their politics. . . . . They do not comprehend the connection which slavery has with it, because we do not at once preach emancipation. Hence they go to the other extreme and argue that it is not an element of the struggle."[1]

The latter part of 1864 the *Times* was still convinced that the majority of the northern people would be perfectly willing to restore the Union with slavery unimpaired if the South would agree to the restoration.[2] This position that the freedom of the slave was not the issue was until the end of the war that of the *Times*, the *Economist*, the *Herald*, the *Post*, and practically all the important papers of the country as well as that of the reviews such as *Blackwood's Review* and the *Edinburgh Review*.

Closely allied with the jealousy, dislike, and fear of America was the British resentment against the high tariff levied by the overeager servants of the industrial interests of the East just at the moment when the southern states withdrew their representatives from Congress and left the Republican party in full control. In the first place, this tariff was pushed through at the very time when the British public was beginning to shift its sympathies to the South as described above, and it naturally found the British public critical and skeptical of northern motives. Again, it came at the time when the South was defending its action upon the basis that secession was undertaken by the minority agrarian section to prevent the northern industrial section from exploiting it by just such a tariff. In short, it justified the main contention of the leaders of the South. The *Economist* remarked in disgust at such short-sighted greediness in choosing this moment of secession to enact a legislative program so hostile to the interests of the seceding section that the North was "thus justi-

[1] *A Cycle of Adams' Letters*, I, 14–15, C. F. Adams to his son, June 21, 1861.

[2] *Times*, Sept. 19, 1864.

fying the slave states in their secession."[1] This paper not only agreed that the tariff made it quite clear that the North was interested more in exploiting the South than in freeing the Negro, but that it was reckless of the friendship of foreign countries with whom it carried on trade.[2] Many reasons were listed why England did not like America or wish her well, and concluded by asking, "Is the Morrill tariff a title to our gratitude and sympathy?"[3] In July, 1862,[4] the *Times* spoke indignantly of the rejoicing of the American public in the injuries done to British trade by the recently "revised tariff," and thought these "ecstasies only the aberrations of a mind and nature so thoroughly perverted that it can exclaim, 'Evil, be thou my God!'" America, said the *Times*,[5] was carrying on "two sets of hostilities;—a war of cannon and musketry, to be carried on against her kinsmen in the South, and a war of tariffs and prohibitions against her kinsmen" in England. So resentment against the tariff became merged with the general dislike of the American people.

Part of the turning-against the North was the changing conception of the southern people held by the British. From contempt they changed to unstinted admiration. The South ceased to be a land of poor whites and savage slave drivers; it became a highly cultural land controlled by gentlemen like the English aristocracy and inhabited by self-respecting, independent small farmers. The *Times* spoke of the southern aristocracy as "gentlemen . . . . well bred, courteous and hospitable," "a genuine aristocracy" who have "time to cultivate their minds, to apply themselves to politics and the guidance of public affairs," who "travel and read, love field sports, racing, shooting, hunting and fishing, are bold horsemen and good shots."[6] From being trembling cowards the southerners became heroic. "The people of the Confederate States," said the *Times* in the fall of 1862,[7] "have made themselves famous. If the renown of brilliant courage, stern devotion to a cause, and military achievement almost without a parallel can compensate men for the toil and

[1] *Economist*, Feb. 23, 1861.
[2] *Ibid.*, March 16, 1861.
[3] *Ibid.*, Sept. 14, 1861; cf. *ibid.*, Sept. 28, 1861.
[4] *Times*, July 11, 1862.
[5] *Ibid.*, July 17, 1862.
[6] *Ibid.*, May 28, 1861.
[7] *Ibid.*, Sept. 16, 1862.

privations of the hour, then the countrymen of Lee and Jackson may be consoled amid their sufferings. From all parts of Europe . . . . comes the tribute of admiration." "If the war has proved any thing," said the *Times* the following year,[1] "that was not known before, it has only made it more evident that, on the whole, the Southern temperament and the Social organization of the South produce the men best qualified to govern and command." The *Times* was typical of the British press in its attitude. The pamphleteers and lecturers, such as Beresford-Hope, Fitzgerald, Grattan, Reid, and Montagu, also took the position that the South was an aristocratic Anglo-Saxon people very much like the English country gentlemen. The most effective expression of this idea was Spence's *American Union*. This change in attitude of the English was evident to Henry Hotze, who wrote Benjamin late in December, 1863, that he was sending him two pamphlets written by Englishmen which "will show you what enormous progress we have made in English public opinion. The virus of antislavery prejudice was in the blood; no external application could cure it; but the antidote is now entered into the blood also, and follows it in its circulation through the body literary and politic."[2]

Perhaps as strong a conviction as any held by the British with regard to the Civil War was that the South could not be conquered and that its independence was inevitable. This faith in the success of the South helps explain England's impatience with the North in persisting in the war, also why England never seriously contemplated intervention, and many otherwise peculiar omissions or commissions.

This belief, though at first, perhaps, a justification for an about-face on the right of secession and therefore not a well-considered, honest conviction, soon became one of the most fundamental beliefs in the mind of the average Englishman. The best test of the sincerity of this conviction is the cotton-market report. Every northern victory until after the beginning of 1865 always sent the price of cotton up, because it was thought that as the South was

[1] *Ibid.*, July 9, 1863.
[2] Hotze's Letter Book, Hotze to Benjamin, No. 54, Dec. 26, 1863.

sure to win in the long run the victory of the North only prolonged the war. On the other hand, every southern victory sent the price of cotton down as it was thought each such victory brought the war nearer its end. The basis of this confidence in the South was to a large extent England's own experience with her revolting American colonies in 1776. Since that time it had become almost a political maxim that a determined, compact group of people occupying an extensive area could not be conquered. The English press had frequently assumed as successful the secession of the South during the winter of 1861, but this was largely based upon the belief that no serious effort would be made to win the South back. But when war began expressions of opinions as to the ability of the North to regain the lost states were all to the effect that conquest was impossible. The *London Economist*,[1] May 4, 1861, took the ground that though the North might after a long struggle overthrow the southern armies, it would be impossible to hold such a large area by military occupation, or in case this was not attempted, it would be impossible to gain any kind of co-operation from the South in the conduct of the government. A few days later[2] the *Economist* took more positive ground: "Every one knows and admits that the secession is an accomplished and irrevocable fact." Conquest of the South, it declared, was impossible. It[3] spoke of Seward's declared intention of saving the Union as "the most futile dream which ever passed over the excited brain of a rhetorical American." This paper[4] denied the claim that there was a large Union party in the South, but contended that there was really a population of six million desperate southerners standing as one man for separation. "Now the politician," exclaimed the *Economist*, "who believes that five or six millions of resolute and virulent Anglo Saxons can be forcibly retained as citizens of a republic from which they are determined to separate or that they would be desirable or comfortable fellow citizens if so retained must have some standard for estimating values and probabilities which is utterly unintelligible to us." In the latter part of June[5]

[1] *Economist*, May 4, 1861.
[2] *Ibid.*, May 15, 1861.
[3] *Ibid.*, May 25, 1861.
[4] *Ibid.*, June 3, 1861.
[5] *Ibid.*, June 29, 1861.

this opinion that the North could not win was again expressed: "They are fighting, not with savage Indians nor with feeble Mexicans but with Anglo Saxons as fierce, as obstinate and as untamable as themselves."

But suppose the North could forcibly reincorporate the South, "what has been gained thereby," queried the *Economist* a week later,[1] "and how much of what has been gained can be preserved? How is the conquest to be upheld? . . . . How are the captive millions to be retained in the forced allegiance? How can they be made to work a joint system of government of which they are thwarting members and unwilling constituents? How is the administration of ten distinct states, all recalcitrant and covering hundreds of thousands of miles to be carried on? Are Federal governors and Federal officers to be appointed to the work? And how amid a hostile people can they enforce their decrees? The slave states forced back into the Union must be governed either as conquered lands or as free and equally endowed portions of a Federal Republic."

The *London Times* agreed with the *Economist* on this point, and when the *Times* took snuff the rest of England sneezed. "The North," remarked the *Times*,[2] "has certainly undertaken a difficult task, that of conquering a vast territory inhabited by men of the same race as its own citizens, and even more accustomed to the use of arms. . . . . Unless the government contents itself with merely harassing the seacoast of the seceders, it must be ready to carry on a war which will be beyond the patience of even the most patriotic militia." A few weeks later the *Times* reaffirmed its opinion that the North could never succeed in restoring the Union.[3] "It is one thing," observed the *Times*, "to drive the rebels from the South bank of the Potomac, or even to occupy Richmond, but another to reduce and hold in permanent subjection a tract of country nearly as large as Russia in Europe and inhabited by Anglo Saxons." Several weeks later[4] the South was again compared with the revolting American colonies and the impossibility of the task of subjugation was repeated. "Experience shows that under ordinary circumstances a

[1] *Ibid.*, July 6, 1861.
[2] *Times*, May 15, 1861.
[3] *Ibid.*, July 18, 1861.
[4] *Ibid.*, Aug. 27, 1861.

comparatively small population, with little money and means of war is sufficient for a very good defence. . . . . Let the Northern States accept the situation as we did 80 years ago upon their own soil. . . . . Let them consider what they can do, and what neither they nor all the world can do." A week later[1] the *Times*, commenting upon the Battle of Bull Run, concluded that "enough has been learnt to show us that the subjugation of the South is next to impossible. . . . ." The *London Press*,[2] the *Spectator*,[3] the *Westminster Review*,[4] the *Saturday Review*[5]—in fact, practically all the British press—followed the *Economist* and the *Times* in 1861 in proclaiming the utter impossibility of the conquest of the South and for that reason advised the North to bow to the inevitable and save Europe from a cotton famine and the belligerents from a useless waste of blood and treasure. In 1862 the *London Times* on hearing the news of the fall of Fort Donelson did not think the Federal victories had brought the United States "any nearer than before to a reconstruction of the Union."[6] If the South was determined to resist—and no one doubted its determination—the capture of Fort Donelson "is but as the first milestone from London toward Exeter."[7] After the fall of New Orleans the *Economist* still thought there was no chance for the North to defeat the South.[8] Following the fall of Yorktown and McClellan's march upon Richmond, which was hourly expected to result in the capture of that city, the *Times* still expressed undimmed faith in the invincibility of the southern armies and people. "The very victories, indeed, of the Northerners have but brought to light the hopelessness of the case by revealing, in its true character and proportions, the spirit of the South."[9] When McClellan had been defeated on the peninsula and Pope in northern Virginia, the *Economist* and *Times* agreed that the further continuation of war on the part of the North was hopeless and unjustifiable.[10]

When Vicksburg and Gettysburg had been fought successfully by

[1] *Ibid.*, Sept. 4, 1861.   [6] *Times*, March 6, 1862.

[2] *London Press*, March 30, 1861.   [7] *Ibid.*, March 10, 1862.

[3] *Spectator*, April 27, 1861.   [8] *Economist*, May 17, 1862.

[4] *Westminster Review*, LXXVI (Oct., 1861), 487 ff.   [9] *Times*, May 21, 1862.

[5] *Saturday Review*, Jan., 1861.   [10] *Economist*, Sept. 6, 1862; *Times*, Aug. 29, 1862.

the Federals the *Times* and *Economist* still believed the South could not be subdued, and in 1864 when Grant had failed in Virginia the *Times* believed that the South was on the verge of independence.[1] Nor is there much sign of a decline in this belief until the beginning of 1865 when it became evident that the Union would be successfully reconstructed.[2]

French public opinion like the English was against the South during the secession movement and was almost universally in sympathy with the North. This may be explained in a few words: France hated slavery, and the old traditional friendship between America and France was grounded deeply in the minds of the French. Perhaps most important of all was the national policy going back to Revolutionary days and to the Napoleonic era of encouraging the development of a strong, maritime nation in North America as a counterpoise to Great Britain.

When the South began to withdraw from the Union the public press was as outspoken as the English in its condemnation of secession, of slavery, and of the character of the southern people. In fact, most of the information concerning America came through the Havas agency, as we have noted above, and that agency obtained its information from the British press and news agencies, so naturally the French press would reflect much of the British attitude as long as that attitude squared with the prejudices and interests of the French. Even the *Constitutionnel*, the semiofficial organ of Napoleon, controlled by Persigny, one of the chief councilors of Napoleon, showed no sympathy with secession at first and vented its wrath against the iniquitous institution of slavery and the idea of destroying a nation to secure it.[3] The *Moniteur* and *Patrie*, government organs, were of like opinion. The *Pays*, another semiofficial paper, thought that the North was right, that "abolition of slavery is a noble cause to defend and bring to a triumphant conclusion."[4] The *Revue germanique* considered the organization of the Confederacy

[1] *Economist*, Aug. 8, 1863; *Times*, July 5, 1864; Sept. 3, 1863; Sept. 8, 1864.
[2] See E. D. Adams, Vol. II, chap. xvi.
[3] *Constitutionnel*, Dec. 26, 1860; West, p. 10.
[4] *Pays*, Nov. 22, 1860; West, p. 10.

upon the basis of slavery "an outrage against human nature and divine justice."[1] The *Journal des débats* was an uncompromising enemy of the perpetuation of slavery by secession[2] as was the *Revue des deux mondes*,[3] the *Temps*, the *Opinion nationale*, the *Presse*, the *Siècle*—in fact, all the newspapers of Paris were from the beginning hostile to the South and its program and institutions. Du Bellet thought that Seward and Dayton had bought up the press or managed to excite the "sympathies of the editors for poor Sambo" by telling them that "the tale of Uncle Tom was the faithful picture of Southern slavery."[4]

By the early spring of 1861, however, the government organs, that is, the *Moniteur, Pays, Constitutionnel, Patrie,* and a few provincial satellites, parted company with the real representatives of French opinion and became ardent and unflagging advocates of intervention. They followed the change in British opinion and within a short while stood far in advance, in the matter of advocating a positive program. There were certain attitudes in common, however, between the Liberal French press and the government organs. One of these was the conviction that the North could not conquer the South. As early as December 7, 1860, when only South Carolina had seceded, the *Journal des débats* conceded that the South must succeed in establishing a separate state independent of the old Union, but it hoped and prophesied that the new Confederacy would be confined to the states east of the Mississippi River and would be too weak to stay the progress of the larger Union.[5] Presently that *Journal* gave up the idea of such limitations for the Confederacy and urged that the North accept the inevitable.[6] The *Revue des deux mondes* believed that separation was inevitable and felt that the North would have to accept a *fait accompli*.[7] The attitude of the Liberal press was

[1] West, p. 10.

[2] E.g., *Journal des débats*, April 22, Dec. 7 and 25, 1861; West, pp. 11, 12.

[3] E.g., *Revue des deux mondes*, Jan., 1861; West, p. 11.   [4] Du Bellet, pp. 10–12.

[5] West, p. 18; cf. *Journal des débats*, Jan. 7 and April 27, 1861.

[6] *Ibid.*, Sept. 28, 1861; West, pp. 19–20.

[7] E.g., *Revue des deux mondes*, April 1, 1861, p. 758; *ibid.*, June 15, 1861, pp. 1001–2; West, pp. 20 ff.

represented by these two publications, who with their unbelief in the power of the North to conquer the South combined admiration for the Union. The government press was more positive in its belief in southern success which it combined with great admiration for the South. These papers took the position of the British pro-southern group which contended, as in Spence's book, the *American Union*, that the social, economic, and racial antagonism made separation inevitable and right.[1] The *Constitutionnel* thought that the idea of subjugating ten or twelve million men and such a large territory was absurd.[2] At the end of 1861, says West,[3] "the papers of France, no matter where their sympathies lay, had given up the idea that the Union would be preserved in its entirety." The French minister at Washington, M. Mercier, epitomized the French attitude when he wrote Thouvenel in the winter of 1862 that "there is no other outcome of the crisis except a pacific arrangement based upon separation."[4]

As in England, the French press, both Liberal and Imperialist, assumed at first that secession and war were caused by the hostility of the North to slavery and the desire of the South to perpetuate that institution. The *Constitutionnel* attributed secession to the desire of the South to "safeguard that dear peculiar institution."[5] It might have a legal right to secede, but the real principles of the founders of the American republic were with the North.[6] The Liberal *Journal des débats* could see nothing in secession but the setting-up of a slave empire. The North to the *Journal*, which represented the attitude of the Liberal press, symbolized freedom and liberty struggling against slavery and oligarchy. The issue of slavery with the North on the side of freedom and the South on the side of slavery blinded the French *Journal*, as it did the British radical papers, to all other issues.[7] The Liberal *Revue des deux mondes* was uncompromis-

[1] E.g., *Pays*, May 29; *Patrie*, March 25, 1861; West, p. 21.

[2] *Constitutionnel*, July 7, 1861; West, p. 21.   [3] West, p. 21.

[4] French F.O., Amer., Vol. 126, No. 80, Jan. 14, 1862.

[5] *Constitutionnel*, Jan. 20, 1861; West, p. 27.

[6] *Constitutionnel*, Jan. 24, 1861; West, p. 28.

[7] See *Journal des débats*, Dec. 4 and 30, 1860; Jan. 10, Feb. 20, May 17, Oct. 19, Dec. 10 and 14, 1861; also West, pp. 22–25.

ing in its contention that the South was not fighting for state rights or against a protective tariff or to establish economic independence or because it was a separate race and had a different culture from the North; it fought to maintain slavery and the North to free it. "The war is . . . . a war against slavery, not in form but in essence, not in words but in action."[1]

The Imperialist organs, as we have said, changed in the beginning of 1861 to an attitude of sympathy for the South. The change merely reflected the change in the position of the government. Because of the need for cotton and the ambitions of Napoleon in Mexico, Napoleon had shifted his position to one of sympathy as soon as he saw that the South really meant to break up the Union and the opinion of the Imperialist press was an echo of his own opinion. The *Constitutionnel*, which at first had proclaimed the war as one for the preservation of the institution of slavery, in the spring of 1861 assumed the position of the British press and vigorously denounced its former attitude and contended that the war was one of conquest on the part of the North and for independence on the part of the South. The *Constitutionnel* challenged the North in the name of the principles upon which America was founded, those of self-government! By what right "does the North desire to impose its government upon the South who do not desire it?"[2] By late fall the *Constitutionnel* was occupying the position that Spence and the British Confederates were holding in regard to the cause of the war, namely, that it was the outgrowth of a conflict between two divergent social and cultural systems.[3] The *Pays* agreed in this and added that the conflict between these two systems was largely an aggression on the part of the North which had been in progress for years, and that not only did the South have a moral right but also a legal right of secession.[4] This legal and moral justification of separation was taken up vigorously by the other Imperialist organs, the *Moniteur* and *Patrie*, which reiterated the contention of the *Constitutionnel* that the war

[1] *Revue des deux mondes*, Nov. 1, 1861, pp. 152–57.

[2] *Constitutionnel*, May 16, 1861; West, pp. 29–30.

[3] *Constitutionnel*, Nov. 19, 1861; West, pp. 29–30.

[4] *Pays*, April 29, May 14 and 15, July 27, 1861; West, p. 30.

was a war of conquest and not for freedom for the Negro. So by the end of 1861 all the semiofficial or Imperialist papers, reflecting the position of the Emperor and of the British press, though they still condemned slavery, agreed that slavery was not the issue. So, like the British papers, they felt themselves freed from all obligations of sympathy with the North, while the belief that the war was one of nationalism on the part of the South and conquest on the part of the North justified their sympathy with the South.

Like the British press, the Imperialist organs, once they were committed to southern sympathy and absolved from their obligation to the Union, mustered up numerous reasons for desiring the division of America. The idea of a powerful, overbearing rival nation which threatened the interests of France and all other weaker nations was urged as earnestly as in the British press. The *Patrie* expressed this very frankly. Europe ought to "favor or at least not to hinder, a revolution which caused to disappear from European politics a great state whose rôle could have become embarrassing at any time," and whose interests clashed with those of France.[1] Free trade and the weakening of an industrial rival were mentioned as benefits, also, in the *Pays*.[2]

The Liberal press, which represented the opinion of the majority of the French nation who had an opinion, and certainly the prejudices of the majority, did not respond as did the British and Imperialist press to the shower of hatred and jealousy rained upon the American Union. From the standpoint of sentiment, far from feeling jealousy and hatred of a strong North America, they were in love with the idea. It was the bulwark of liberty and freedom to men who were longing for the time when they could rid themselves of the oppressive weight of the Napoleonic tyranny and return to the days of liberty, equality, and fraternity. From the cold-blooded standpoint of self-interest, too, they cherished the idea of an undivided America as a makeweight against the arrogant maritime British nation. The *Opinion nationale* could not endure the idea of doing anything to weaken America which had been such a strong opponent to the en-

[1] *Patrie*, July 26, 1861; West, p. 34.

[2] *Pays*, Feb. 28, 1861; West, p. 30; *Pays*, May 7, 1861; West, p. 33.

croachments of the British. "France has but one enemy in the world—that enemy is England." "Let us figure to ourselves France marching gaily to the aid of England in the destruction of the only marine in the world which can act as a counterpoise against the naval superiority of England. This would be a monstrous absurdity, a treason against traditional French policy." It was bad enough for America to become weakened by her own domestic struggle; then for "God's sake do not let us be asked to aid her [England] against our natural allies. All France would rouse at such a thought."[1] The *Revue des deux mondes*, while fearing that the war would end in the independence of the South, was also fearful lest France do something to forward the division of the Union, for France had "a great interest in the maintenance of a power for the foundation of which it had labored so generously, and which could contribute to the mainte- nance of the maritime equilibrium."[2] The *Journal des débats* agreed with the *Opinion nationale* and *Revue des deux mondes* that a strong, undivided Union should be one of the chief objectives of French policy, and a defense against the encroachments of Great Britain.[3]

The general attitude, then, of the French people favored an un- divided America while the interests of the Emperor favored a weakening of the Union by the establishing of an independent South. Despite Napoleon's despotic powers it can be readily seen that this situation made it very dangerous for him to take any steps which would lead to armed conflict with the United States.[4]

[1] *Opinion nationale*, Dec. 19, 1861, quoted in *New York Herald*, Jan. 4, 1862.

[2] *Revue des deux mondes*, Feb. 1, 1861, pp. 752–54; cf. *ibid.*, June 15, 1861, pp. 1001–2; West, p. 32.

[3] *Journal des débats*, Oct. 25, 1861; West, p. 32.

[4] See Du Bellet, pp. 20–25.

CHAPTER VI

MASON AND SLIDELL'S FIRST ATTACK ON THE LEGALITY OF THE BLOCKADE

Mason and Slidell arrived in London on January 29, 1862, and Slidell proceeded at once to Paris. After weeks of delay the two men whom the American public seem to have feared worse than the loss of an important campaign or the capture of Washington, and whom Henry Adams[1] called "the two unhung," had at last arrived at their destination and were ready to make a drive upon the European governments for some form of interference in behalf of the South. Just why these two men should have been considered such enemies of mankind or such dangerous antagonists of the Union is not clear to those who look at the thing from the present-day vantage point, realizing that unless powerful economic and social forces are at work no person or personalities can move a nation or a people in a direction contrary to its inclinations.

Mason, the grandson of George Mason of Revolutionary fame, was a man of great personal charm, despite the accusation of his enemies that he was shabby in appearance and chewed tobacco and spat upon the floor of Parliament. He was overwhelmed with courtesies and cordial comradeship by the British aristocracy. His social calendar was the English gentry.[2] Kindliness and moderation seem to have been his leading traits. Slidell was more subtle, more pugnacious, in fact, very daring, dignified, reserved, but withal possessed of chivalry and charm. His friends in Paris were the friends and court of Napoleon himself, as well as many others not included in that circle. Both men had been senators and had been identified for years with the extreme southern-rights party—Mason being credited with the Fugitive Slave Act of 1850. Unquestionably these

---

[1] *A Cycle of Adams' Letters*, I, 108.

[2] Mason Papers; Mason, Virginia, *The Public Life and Diplomatic Correspondence of James M. Mason with Some Personal History* (Roanoke, Va., 1903). (Cited as Mason, *Life of Mason*.) His official letters are in the Pickett Papers.

two men were much abler and stronger than either Rost or Mann, and they were more acceptable than Yancey, both socially and politically.

It will be recalled that the instructions of Mason and Slidell had preceded them after their removal from the Trent, and that these instructions had been in part acted upon by the Yancey-Rost-Mann mission just at the time of the commotion over the Trent. The tenor of the instructions did not differ from the earlier instructions to the Yancey-Rost-Mann mission. There were the same appeals to state sovereignty, the compact theory, Federal encroachment upon state rights, and the same appeal to the King Cotton theory and to the well-known desire in England, and of Napoleon, to see the powerful United States divided into two or more separate nations. The size and strength of the Confederacy were pointed out along with its military success as sufficient grounds for believing the South was able to maintain its independence, and worthy of recognition. Virtually free trade was held out as a prospect as against the prohibitive Morrill tariff of the United States, and the South was represented as being a great market for the manufactured goods of Europe and a great source for raw material other than cotton. Hunter's instructions, however, far excelled those of Toombs or perhaps any other contemporary in stating the cause for the South's withdrawal from the Union. He struck at the core of the problem of secession with convincing clearness. The Union, he said, had been formed of two different systems, and "when the Government of that Union instead of affording protection to their social system itself, threatened not merely to disturb the peace and the security of its people, but also to destroy their social system, the States thus menaced owed it to themselves and their posterity to withdraw immediately from a union whose very bonds prevented them from defending themselves against such dangers. Such were the causes which led the Confederate States to form a new Union to be composed of more homogeneous materials and interests." Experience had demonstrated to them that a union of two different and hostile social systems under a government in which one of them wielded nearly all the power was not only ill assorted but dangerous in the extreme to the weaker section whose scheme of society was thus unprotected." "It was because a revolution was sought to be made in the spirit and ends of the organic law of their first union by a dominant and sectional majority operating through the machinery of a government which was in their hands and placed there for different purposes, that the Confederate States withdrew themselves from the jurisdiction of such a government and established another for themselves."[1]

According to these instructions, Slidell and Mason were to ask for recognition and the termination of the blockade which they were to insist was ineffective, and, according to the Declaration of Paris and international law, not binding on neutrals.[2] It will be recalled that Yancey, Mann, and Rost acted upon these instructions just as the Trent affair came up, tendering figures to show how more than four hundred vessels had run the blockade up to August 20, 1861. They insisted that England and France should refuse to acquiesce longer in a paper blockade. It will be recalled likewise that the commission presented, especially to Russell, that part of the instructions which dealt with the dependence of Europe upon the Confederacy for its cotton as an argument in favor of breaking the blockade. It will be further remembered that just before the Trent affair there had been serious conversations and correspondence between England and France and the United States concerning the cotton supply and the blockade.

So the new commissioners came upon the stage after the blockade and cotton question had been under considerable discussion. With the cotton famine approaching, the signs of the times pointed to further developments on these subjects. True, there was a lull in the public discussion of the blockade and in the possibility of interfering in the struggle to obtain cotton, while the Trent affair was pending.

But after the Trent affair was ended, intervention began to loom again. On January 20, 1862, Dayton wrote Seward in alarm that the rumors were once more flying that France and England would

[1] See *Pickett Papers*, Hunter to Mason, Sept. 23, 1861; *O.R.N.*, Ser. 2, Vol. III, pp. 257–64, for full instructions.

[2] For instructions to Slidell see Pickett Papers, Hunter to Slidell, Sept. 23, 1861; *O.R.N.*, Ser. 2, Vol. III, pp. 265–73.

attack the blockade. The semiofficial press, he said, was putting out
the rumors, and he reminded Seward that it was the type of information which had been circulated in the fall preceding, just before the
Trent affair. He said that Thouvenel had said nothing to him about
it—had not referred to the blockade or cotton since his interview on
November 6. But since that time the cotton famine and trade conditions had grown acute "and the pressure upon the industrial interests
of France had increased until at last, in certain of their manufacturing districts and cities, the wants of their suffering population are so
great that neither the Government nor private subscription can
provide for them. All this destitution is attributed to the civil war
in America and the consequent closing of the Southern ports. They
seem to think that the removal of the blockade would relieve their
difficulties; that it would meet at once their two great wants—cotton
and markets." Under the circumstances Dayton felt that it would
be wise for the United States to allow trade with certain southern
ports, so as to allow Europe to obtain cotton. "Without this, if these
principal ports remain in Southern hands, I repeat what I have heretofore said, there is yet, in my judgment, danger of France and England, one or both, interfering with the blockade."[1]

Seward was fully conscious of the tendencies in Europe. Dayton's and Adam's dispatches written in November and December touching upon the impending cotton famine and the uneasiness
in the European chancelleries, along with Mercier's persistent nag-
ging on the subject during the same time, had put him fully on his
guard. So on January 2, 1862, as soon as he could report on the
settlement of the Trent affair, Seward wrote Dayton that the next
and perhaps most dangerous obstacle in the path of the United
States would be European interference with the blockade. He proposed to circumvent all interference until the impending military
successes which he anticipated should remove the danger of intervention. His procedure seems fantastic as did his proposed
"foreign war policy" of the year before, yet as in nearly all of
Seward's diplomacy it aimed at the most vulnerable points in the
European complex. He proposed, and he was partly successful, to

[1] U.S. Des., France, Vol. 51, Dayton to Seward, No. 104, Jan. 20, 1862.

drive a wedge between the English and the French. He bundled together the correspondence and papers relating to the Trent affair and sent them to Dayton. He did not condone the seizure of Mason and Slidell. On the contrary, he now assumed the rôle of champion of neutral rights, resuming, for the United States, the garb of former days. He proposed that Dayton should take up with Thouvenel the whole question of neutral ships and commerce and blockade with a view of defining the law. The United States, he urged, was willing to go the whole length, even abolishing all blockades. Dayton must urge that America and France ought to stand together in insisting that Great Britain accept as fixed the principles championed in the case of the Trent—principles which England had never conceded as international law. Unquestionably Seward realized that if France and the United States should approach England for all practical purposes as allies in the cause of maritime neutral rights, it would not fail to arouse suspicion and distrust of France on the part of England. This in itself might break up any joint intervention. Moreover, he would offer France something to keep her soothed. He instructed Dayton, who had been urging this very point, to inform Thouvenel that the present blockade might be terminated or relaxed almost any day—especially in view of the prospect of immediate military success. ". . . . Do not lose an opportunity," he urged, "for saying that with our past and present and coming successes we are quite sure that the need of the blockade will not continue very long. If necessary speak of it as a thing daily more and more fully within our power to modify, if not terminate altogether."[1] As we shall see, the promise that the blockade should be relaxed or withdrawn in case southern ports fell into Federal possession became a fixed policy with Seward for the next few months.

Dayton received the dispatch around January 25, 1862, and hastened to lay it before Thouvenel, who was apparently pleased both at the prospect of a relaxation of the blockade which would make it possible to secure cotton and with the championship of neutral rights by the United States. However, he refused to walk into Seward's

[1] For instructions to Dayton see U.S. Inst., France, Vol. 16, Seward to Dayton, No. 97, "Confidential," Jan. 2, 1862.

trap and join the United States in presenting the demand upon England that she consent to fix the position she had championed in the Trent case as a future policy.[1] But there seems considerable reason to conclude that despite the fact that Thouvenel saw Seward's trap —he was always setting them—and did not step into it, the wedge was driven into the *entente* by this move. As we shall see later, Napoleon in his interviews with Lindsay, and with Slidell and Roebuck, invariably harked back to the Trent affair, as the beginning of a coolness and attitude of suspicion of him on the part of England concerning the entire American question. Napoleon complained that England, instead of appreciating the stand France had taken as a champion of England's position in the Trent controversy, had seemed, as soon as the event was over, to have cooled off. Considering the conversations between Dayton and Thouvenel over Seward's proposals and the French note, upholding the neutral principles championed by England in the Trent affair, Palmerston and Russell saw that they themselves had walked into a *cul-de-sac* formed by Napoleon and abetted by Seward. It represented the very nation which had only a few weeks before apparently been on the verge of stretching belligerent rights of search and seizure to the limit.

But all this was not apparent, or if it was, it did not ease the cotton situation or assure the success of Napoleon's venture in Mexico —the two matters which made him willing to interfere in behalf of the South. The rumors which had given rise to Seward's dispatch and Dayton's warning of impending intervention were indeed kites which Napoleon was flying through the semiofficial press. An examination of the correspondence between Thouvenel and Mercier discloses a constant agitation of some form of intervention. On January 14, 1862, Mercier wrote that sooner or later the South would gain its independence. However, he apprehended desperate fighting before it would be safe for France to step in, so "I do not

[1] See U.S. Des., France, Vol. 51, Dayton to Seward, Jan. 27, 1862, for description of interview with Thouvenel.

see," he wrote, "anything better than to wish that the two armies should come to blows as soon as possible."[1] Two days later Thouvenel wrote Mercier that the situation in trade and manufacturing in France was becoming unbearable. He instructed Mercier that anything which he might do to relieve the situation would be approved—subject to the condition that he do nothing without England.[2]

The question of intervention was also stirring again in England now that the Trent affair was over. The newspapers, especially the *Economist*, the *Times*, and the *Star*, were discussing though not advocating the question of breaking the blockade. The *Times* reported the harangues of Massey over the blockade, which both he and the *Times* denounced as ineffective. The *Times* spoke piously of the long-suffering, law-abiding British people, but ventured the opinion that, as Massey had suggested, the patience of England was about exhausted with "a war in America which no man was able to understand—which had no beginning and no end." Massey had urged that the paper blockade be disregarded and the *Times* agreed that that sentiment was growing rapidly.[3] The *Economist*[4] denounced the blockade as "quite inefficient," and asked, "Is it in consequence illegal, and *ipso facto* invalid?—We believe there can be no doubt that it is," according to the Declaration of Paris, "and we are quite entitled to disregard it if we please." Cotton could thus be obtained, said the *Economist*. However, that paper was for good reasons not in favor of breaking the blockade despite the prospect of getting cotton. The latter part of January the *Times* came out stronger than the week previous. "We cannot help seeing," remarked the *Times*, "that from some quarter or other intervention will very soon arrive." The surplus goods stored in India and China and at home did not make it necessary or even profitable for England to intervene now, but France was not suffering from an overstuffed market. She had no surplus, and the *Times* prophesied with pleasure that France could not be expected to refrain much longer from breaking the blockade

[1] French F.O., Amer., Vol. 126, Mercier to Thouvenel, No. 80, Jan. 14, 1862.
[2] *Ibid.*, Thouvenel to Mercier, No. 3, Jan. 16, 1862.
[3] *Times*, Jan. 23, 1862.   [4] *Economist*, Jan. 25, 1862.

to get cotton.[1] Consul Dudley of Liverpool reported, January 24, 1862, that unless the United States won a great victory in the near future intervention would come soon, for the press, the shippers, the merchants, and the manufacturers who were in need of cotton were growing restless and were talking intervention.[2]

Henry Adams wrote his brother, Charles Francis, Jr., on January 22: "The truth is, we are now in a corner. There is but one way out of it and that is by a decisive victory. If there's not a great success, and a success *followed up*, within six weeks, we may better give up the game than blunder any more over it. These nations, France probably first, will raise the blockade. . . . . McClellan must do something within six weeks or we are done."[3]

Rumors were flying, then, in both the French and the English press that the blockade might be set aside soon as ineffective. It was into this atmosphere of renewed agitation that Mason and Slidell came at the end of January, 1862. Naturally, they believed that these rumors were the shadows of coming events and that England and France were contemplating an immediate move.

They fully realized that France and England would not interfere with the blockade unless it was doing sufficient injury. Being thoroughly steeped in the doctrine of King Cotton, and bearing eyewitness to the rapid approach of the cotton famine in both France and England, they were thoroughly convinced, as had been Yancey, Rost, and Mann, that these countries would soon break the blockade in order to get cotton, justifying the act by the mere illegality of the blockade. Their business, then, was to help supply the British and French governments with sufficient proof of the ineffectiveness of the blockade. The character of the rumors and of the information supplied by the former mission and British friends such as Gregory, Spence, and Lindsay in England, and by Persigny, Rouher, and Billault in France—members of the Emperor's cabinet—all indicated the attack upon the blockade as the proper line of strategy.

Perhaps the gullibility of Mann contributed to induce Mason

---

[1] *Times*, Jan. 27, 1862.

[2] U.S. Consular Despatches, Liverpool, Vol. 20, Dudley to Seward, No. 8, Jan. 24, 1862.

[3] *A Cycle of Adams' Letters*, I, 104.

and Slidell to begin their attack upon the legality of the blockade, in England and France, and upon the sinking of the stone fleet. Some few days before their arrival Mann had obtained what was supposed to be a copy of a memorandum sent out by England to the chief powers of Europe asking two vital questions: Is the sinking of the stone fleet a violation of public law and humanity; is the blockade effective, and is it binding if not? Mann's copy of the supposed memorandum credited Russia, Prussia, Austria, Sardinia, and France with denouncing the stone fleet[1] as barbarous and the blockade as ineffective.[2] It was evidently a gold brick which Mann had purchased, but at least for a few days it caused the hearts of the Confederate agents to beat faster.

Slidell determined at once to present to Thouvenel the protest of his government against France's recognition of the effectiveness of the Federal blockade. He was considerably influenced in his course by the counsel of Persigny, Billault, Baroche, and other members of Napoleon's government.[3] Slidell arranged an interview with the foreign minister, through Rost, for February 7, though Thouvenel let it be known that he was not willing to discuss recognition but was interested in the blockade.[4] Slidell found him courteous but extremely cold and reserved. In fact, he got the impression that Thouvenel was a friend of an undivided Union in America. Slidell went at considerable lengths into the inefficiency of the blockade, presenting figures which, unfortunately, were nearly six months old. His array of figures was formidable; but again, unfortunately, Thouvenel placed him in a *cul-de-sac* by asking him why, if the blockade were not effective, so little cotton had come to neutral ports. Slidell, if he had told the truth, could have answered: "Because the South will not permit cotton to leave the ports as long as Europe recognizes an ineffective blockade, and because, furthermore, the South believes that by holding back the cotton, a cotton famine will be produced and Europe will intervene to get cotton." Slidell, however, beat

[1] The "Stone Fleet" was the sinking of vessels by the Federals in Charleston harbor to stop up the entrance.

[2] Mason Papers, Jan., 1862.   [3] *Ibid.*, Feb. 5, 1862.

[4] *Ibid.*; Pickett Papers, Slidell to Hunter, No. 1, Feb. 11, 1862; *O.R.N.*, Ser. 2, Vol. III, pp. 336–42.

around the bush by explaining that it was more profitable for the small-type vessel which was then running the blockade to bring out turpentine than cotton. Thouvenel would not be satisfied with just this explanation, since it would not take a great number of ships to handle this trade, so Slidell gave another explanation, which was true as far as it went, namely, that the great bulk of trading vessels had been frightened away from the southern coasts by the mere knowledge that a blockade had been proclaimed.[1]

Had it not been for his interview with Persigny and Baroche, two of Napoleon's cronies and fellow-conspirators, Slidell would have been discouraged by Thouvenel's attitude. These two men assured him, however, that Thouvenel was not as much of an iceberg as he seemed, but that, even so, the rest of the cabinet was heart and soul with the South, and that the Emperor was eager to recognize the Confederacy and only waited for England to take the initiative.[2] Slidell was convinced of the sympathy of the Emperor and his court, but at the same time he was disappointed, too, in the discovery that Napoleon would not move without England. Part of the Emperor's timidity, he thought, was due to conditions in Europe. The international situation was precarious—Greece, Italy, Poland, Prussia, all of Napoleon's neighbors, were restless and some were on the point of war. But Slidell discovered that the real secret of Napoleon's timidity in the American question lay in the domestic French situation. "I am surprised," Slidell wrote Hunter,[3] "how little popular the Emperor is at Paris, and probably throughout France among the higher classes. . . . ." Slidell was convinced that Napoleon was hesitating in taking the lead in breaking the blockade because "he does not feel strong enough to take, in his foreign policy, any important step that may not meet with the assent of Great Britain."

Slidell set about combating this timidity. Napoleon must be induced to take the initiative; and the Confederate agent began urging upon the influential members of the government and others the necessity of repudiating the blockade. Just as Seward was attempting to prevent England and France from acting together in breaking the blockade, so Slidell attempted to drive a wedge between the British

[1] *Ibid.*   [2] *Ibid.* (inclosure).
[3] Pickett Papers, No. 2, Feb. 26, 1862; *O.R.N.*, Ser. 2, Vol. III, pp. 347–52.

and French *entente*, in order to get France to act alone in case England would not move with her. The interesting point about his method of approach was that it was identical with Seward's procedure.
He urged upon all with whom he came in contact that the interests
of France and England differed, and that they differed because England was a powerful maritime nation bent upon stretching belligerent rights upon the sea as far as possible. Seward had urged the
"search and seizure" practices of England as the chief point to win
France, while Slidell used the argument of a paper blockade. But
the argument of both was that weak maritime powers would suffer
as neutrals at the hands of Great Britain unless that nation could
be forced to recognize certain curtailments of maritime belligerent
rights. Slidell insisted that the South did not ask aid, but only impartial neutrality of France—and other nations—and neutrality impartially exercised would require a repudiation of what all the world
knew was a paper blockade. But the interests of England and France
were different as to the blockade. England might be temporarily
injured by it, but looking at the matter in the large it was to the
interest of England to recognize the paper blockade as legal. England was and would be for years to come the dominant sea-power.
"Peace between her and France will not be eternal; it may cease
to exist at a moment the least expected. She is now willing to
recognize the validity of the Federal blockade, that at some future
and perhaps not distant day she may by royal proclamation declare
the entire coast of France blockaded, prevent all neutral commerce
with her enemy, and appeal to the silence and submission of France
in 1862 to her tacit interpretation of the fourth article of the conference of Paris as a sufficient answer to any protest against her
action." Slidell was touching a very vital spot just as Seward
touched in presenting such arguments to the several members of the
French cabinet.[1] He was, however, always embarrassed by being
asked the question, "Why, if the blockade was a paper blockade, did
not cotton arrive in Europe?"

It will be recalled that it was due to just this situation that Slidell
urged the Confederacy to do all it could to remove the obstacles to
the export of cotton, and it was in part due to this urging that the

[1] *Ibid.*

embargo on cotton was removed or relaxed. Slidell, to impress the French with the inefficiency of the blockade, promised all the prominent French shippers and merchants whom he could interest that if they would send ships to the Confederacy with goods they could get cotton. ". . . . Two or three steamers," he wrote Hunter, "arriving at Havre with cotton on French account, after having run the blockade, would go further to convince people here of its inefficiency than all the certified lists from our customhouses."[1] It is an interesting and ironic commentary that the Confederate embargo aimed at creating a cotton famine and bringing about intervention, had only created the impression that the blockade was effective, thus making it difficult to present a convincing case against the blockade.

While Slidell held this line of argument with Count Walewsky (minister of state), Rouher (minister of finance),[2] Baroche, Fould,[3] and other high governmental officials, he staked most upon his conversations with Count de Persigny. After a conference with Persigny in which the latter probably urged him to put his arguments into writing, Slidell finally stated his case in a letter which he requested Persigny to give to the Emperor for his perusal and consideration. In this letter he reiterated his contention that England would recognize the American blockade as effective in order to use it as a precedent. Slidell went so far, in fact, as to contend that "no proof adduced of the insufficiency of this pretended blockade would be deemed by her strong enough to declare it invalid." He called up as proof of this contention the recent statement of Russell in the British Parliament and his letter to Lyons published in the parliamentary papers on the blockade, both of which contended that the blockade was effective and legal. This, if acquiesced in by France, would amount "to the complete resuscitation of the old exploded system of paper blockades."[4]

[1] *Ibid.*

[2] Pickett Papers, Slidell to Hunter, No. 3, March 10, 1862; *O.R.N.*, Ser. 2, Vol. III, pp. 356–58.

[3] Pickett Papers, Slidell to Hunter, No. 1, Feb. 11, 1862; *O.R.N.*, Ser. 2, Vol. III, pp. 336–42.

[4] Pickett Papers, Slidell to Hunter, No. 3 with inclosures, March 10, 1862; *O.R.N.*, Ser. 2, Vol. III, pp. 356–58.

Evidently, Slidell considered that he was making progress—certainly not slipping backward—in inducing the French government to move, separately if need be, in repudiating the blockade. But just about this time a serious setback came to his plans. On February 17 the *projet d'adresse* in the Senate was reported, and it precipitated a debate not favorable to Slidell's plans. The part of the address dealing with the American question stated that the government "has recognized that the amicable relations of France with the United States dictated to the French cabinet a policy of neutrality upon the basis of that distressing dispute, and that the struggle would be so much the shorter in that it was not complicated with foreign interferences."[1] Slidell, however, was not struck with the full significance of the *adresse* until on February 24 the portion dealing with America came up for debate, and Billault, minister *sans portfolio* and spokesman for the Emperor, urged continued non-intervention upon the country as the wisest policy. In truth, he urged, the "Emperor has a friendship for the United States, a sincere desire to see them pacified, a disposition to further as much as he can that reconciliation which is so desirable; but as for doing anything that could be in contradiction to those sentiments which are those of France, the Senate may be tranquil, the Emperor is not so disposed."[2] Moreover, the Emperor himself declared in his *adresse* to the Chambers that "so long as the rights of neutrals are respected, we must limit ourselves to prayers that those dissensions will soon end."[3] A few days later the *projet d'adresse* in the *corps legislatif* took a decided position in favor of non-intervention in America, and after several Liberals had attempted to amend the address in favor of a sympathetic expression for the North and condemnation of slavery, it was adopted as an expression of strict neutrality, with an avowed hope that the quarrel in America might soon reach an amicable settlement.[4] Once more Billault, as representative of the government, spoke in behalf of neutrality.[5]

Why did the Emperor and his minister choose to hold one language in public and another in private conversation and through the

---

[1] Quoted in West, p. 67.
[2] *Ibid.*, pp. 67–68.
[3] *Ibid.*, p. 68.
[4] *Ibid.*, pp. 68–71.
[5] *Ibid.*

official journals? It was always Napoleon's technique to do this to some degree; he frequently held one tone in a private interview and had his ministers deny what he had said, while the semiofficial journal would insist that he had said it, and he through his private secretary Mocquard would assure the injured party in whom he had confided that the Emperor had been wrongly interpreted by his minister who issued the denial. In this particular case Napoleon took a more positive official step in publicly scotching the rumors of his intention of repudiating the blockade. There were good causes for his sudden apparent backing-down. The news of the capture of Forts Donelson and Henry and the general offensive in the West warned him to be cautious lest he get into a war; and the failure of his underground diplomacy with England in an attempt to get that country to join him in breaking the blockade increased his caution.

Let us look briefly at the failure to get England to act with him. We have seen that Mercier had urged in 1861 that England join France in breaking the blockade or in recognizing the South, and that England had refused. This proposal had been renewed by Flahault, as we will recall. Now some time in February, 1862, Napoleon seems once more to have proposed that England join him. As we shall see later, this proposal was denied by Russell and Palmerston, and even by Thouvenel himself. But the Emperor always insisted that it was made, and not only made, but that Seward had been apprised of it. As Russell always refused to take official cognizance of any informal communication, his denial is comprehensible, and as Thouvenel followed the same practice of denying the existence of anything but formal communications, his position does not signify anything. The French Foreign Office fails to reveal any official correspondence on the blockade at this time, yet in view of Napoleon's former proposals of a similar nature, and his constant contention that he had approached England at the time, one could hardly doubt that he was telling the truth.[1] The failure to gain England's co-operation, followed by news of an American victory, made the French government cautious.

This caution was intended to allay the apprehension of America

[1] U.S. Des., France, Vol. 51, No. 120. Dayton wrote Seward, Feb. 27, 1862, that he had almost positive evidence that Napoleon was proposing joint intervention.

and disarm the belligerent Seward, now doing the war dance again. So Mercier, warned by Thouvenel of the sudden change in the French outlook, took particular pains to go to Seward and deny officially that France had any intention of intervening in America, and Thouvenel wrote Mercier a hearty approval of this step. Moreover, he informed Mercier that the recent speeches by Billault in the senate and *corps legislatif* were the official statements of the position of the government—that of benevolent neutrality; and he took the occasion to speak of the recent interview with Slidell in which he had destroyed all of that person's illusions as to French intervention in behalf of the Confederacy.[1]

A few days later, March 6, Thouvenel wrote Mercier cautioning him further against any appearance of taking the initiative in the American question. It was to the interest of France that the war should stop and the blockade cease, but owing to the success of the Federal armies the Washington cabinet alone could now take the initiative in bringing these about.[2] Dayton wrote Seward about this time, too, that the flare-up for interfering with the blockade had temporarily subsided. He said that there existed a feeling among the Confederate sympathizers that something had suddenly occurred and "the switch had been turned off." He further observed that the British press had followed the change in the French public attitude.[3] This change of the British press would seem to indicate the connection between Napoleon's sudden subsidence and the refusal of the British government to co-operate in Napoleon's proposal, for the British papers, especially the *Times* and the *Economist*, were seldom active in advocating a policy which the government opposed.

Slidell was acutely aware of the sudden shift in the official attitude of the French government. His hopes of detaching Napoleon from the British yoke were dashed for the moment. He wrote Mason, March 16, that Billault's speech, expressing the position of the government, destroyed all hopes of Napoleon's independent action in

[1] French F.O., Amer., Vol. 126, No. 6, Feb. 27, 1862.
[2] *Ibid.*, Thouvenel to Mercier, No. 7, March 6, 1862.
[3] U.S. Des., France, Vol. 51, Dayton to Seward, No. 120, Feb. 27, 1862.

breaking the blockade. He ventured the opinion that the northern victories in the West had made Napoleon cautious.[1] On March 26 he wrote Hunter that much to his surprise he had found that Napoleon would not and could not be induced to take the lead in American mediation. He said that in his interview with Thouvenel the latter had assured him that England and France were in accord on the American question, but that he (Slidell) had thought Napoleon's influence great enough to force England to act. He had found this an erroneous opinion, however, for he now believed that "in all that concerns us, the initiative must be taken by England, that the Emperor sets such value on her good will, that he will make any sacrifice of his own opinions and policy to retain it." The fact that France had publicly announced through Billault's speeches in the Senate and *corps legislatif* that she would adhere to the paper blockade in America was sufficient proof that France was the follower and not the leader in the American question.[2]

Two days later, March 28, Slidell wrote in a like manner to Mason in London: He believed that Napoleon had done all in his power to induce England to declare the blockade ineffective, but, having failed, he "is prepared to leave the whole matter in her keeping, when she is prepared to act he will cheerfully go with her. Until then, he will be silent if not indifferent."[3] Slidell, then, did not take the public declaration of Billault, that France would continue to adhere to neutrality, to mean that Napoleon had changed his desire or hopes to break the blockade. He took it merely to mean that Napoleon did not feel himself strong enough to move alone or to take the initiative and compel England to follow as he had at first supposed Napoleon might do. Nor was this a final opinion, for presently Napoleon was in the midst of plans which made Slidell feel that he might at any moment resume the initiative.

In the meanwhile, larger forces were set in motion in England to bring about a repudiation of the Federal blockade of the Confederate

[1] Mason Papers, March 16, 1862.

[2] Pickett Papers, Slidell to Hunter, No. 4, March 26, 1862; *O.R.N.*, Ser. 2, Vol. III, p. 372.

[3] Mason Papers, March 28, 1862.

coast. As we have noted, the cotton famine was rapidly approaching by the time Mason arrived. Thousands of operatives were thrown out of employment week by week and the cotton supply sank even as rapidly. As we have seen, too, it was at this time that Henry Hotze commenced his efforts to win the British press to the support of the Confederacy, especially in the contention that the blockade was illegal. Finally, Mason, advised by the Confederate lobby, especially by Spence, Lindsay, Gregory, Beresford-Hope, and Campbell, prepared to attack the blockade through the Confederate sympathizers in Parliament and in personal interview with Lord John Russell.[1]

Gregory guided Mason in his interview with Russell. He advised Mason not to attempt an official interview. "I should state that you are here as an envoy from the Southern Confederacy, but that as the Confederacy is not yet recognized, you apply for an unofficial interview—this is, I think, the most dignified course to pursue."[2] Following Gregory's advice, Mason wrote Russell a request for an interview at the latter's convenience, and Russell replied immediately, granting an unofficial interview for the tenth of February.[3] Mason repaired to Russell's residence on February 10 as arranged and was received courteously. He offered to read his credentials to Russell, but the latter felt it was unnecessary as their relations were unofficial. But he finally consented to Mason's reading them, not as instructions but as unofficial expressions of the opinion of his government. Mason was cautious in selecting the portions to read. He had been warned by the several English advisers not to mention the portion dealing with cotton and England's dependence upon the South, or the advantages which would grow out of having an independent source of cotton. That point had been stressed, so Mason was advised, "until England had become a little sensitive." Realizing that the approaching cotton famine could argue the case much

[1] Pickett Papers, Mason to Hunter, Feb. 7, 1862; *O.R.N.*, Ser. 2, Vol. III, pp. 330–32.

[2] Mason Papers, Gregory to Mason, Feb. 7, 1862.

[3] Pickett Papers, Mason to Hunter, No. 2 with inclosures, Feb. 7, 1862; *O.R.N.*, Ser. 2, Vol. III, pp. 330–32; Pickett Papers, Mason to Hunter, No. 4 with inclosure, Feb. 22, 1862. See the notes of Mason to Russell and Russell to Mason of Feb. 8, 1862, in *O.R.N.*, Ser. 2, Vol. III, pp. 343–46.

better than he, Mason omitted reference to those points and read those portions dealing with recognition and the blockade. However, he assured Russell that the Confederacy, while it thought recognition was its just right, would not insist upon that point now. What it did insist upon was the inefficiency of the blockade. He laid the case of the South against the blockade before Russell, but the statistics, unfortunately, went no farther than August and September for most of the ports, only those for Charleston and Savannah extending to about the first of November. Russell, of course, had already received most of this information from the Yancey-Rost-Mann mission.

When Mason left Russell he was convinced that Russell's sympathies were with the North and that his policy was to do nothing at all. Russell would not enter into any discussion as to what his government might do in the future. His only comment was that it would wait events.[1] Mason followed up his interview by sending Russell an official list of blockade violations. The statement[2] was practically the same as that which Mason and Slidell had possessed when they were taken from the Trent in 1861, and which had been presented to Russell in the interview. He did have a partial, unofficial list sent him by the Confederate agent at Havana, Cuba, giving further violations for November and December.[3] The total number contained in this list was about five hundred, and, as we shall see presently, if Mason had been able to submit a list of violations for the entire Confederate coast, the number would have been above seven hundred for the eight months from May to December inclusive. This information was at the time in the hands of the Confederate Treasury Department, and, as a matter of fact, it was already, to a great extent, in the hands of Russell himself through the admiralty and consular reports. But more of this later. When Rus-

[1] Ibid.

[2] Pickett Papers, Mason to Russell, Feb. 17, 1862, O.R.N., Ser. 2, Vol. III, pp. 342-43.

[3] Pickett Papers, Helm to Yancey, Rost, and Mann, Jan. 5, 1862; cf. ibid., Helm to Hunter, Jan. 7, 1862, and Havana Mercantile Weekly Report, Jan. 4, 1862 (extra); Havana Price Current, Jan. 6, 1862—all containing a list of blockade-runners coming to Cuba.

sell received this list he formally acknowledged Mason's courtesy but made no comments.[1]

Russell was receiving pressure from members of Parliament, too. Even before the interview between Mason and Russell it had been agreed that Lindsay, the biggest shipowner in England, should make the first move to force Russell to commit himself on the blockade. Lindsay, therefore, in conjunction with his friends, framed a letter which was calculated to draw Russell out on the legality of the blockade. "My Lord," he addressed Russell, "being desirous of despatching one of my vessels with an assorted cargo of British goods, not contraband of war, to the Southern States . . . . with which I have carried on commerce at various ports, I shall be greatly obliged by your lordship's informing me, before I undertake the enterprise, what port or ports of the coast are now in such a state of blockade as to render it imperative on one to avoid them in order to be protected against lawful capture? I trust your lordship will consider the importance of maintaining commerce, as far as it may be lawfully prosecuted (especially with ports where a return cargo of cotton or other produce of which the people of this country are much in want, can be obtained), a sufficient apology for making this request."[2] This request would demand a categorical answer, for the shipping interests of Great Britain were behind Lindsay and in sympathy with the South. Russell must say either that the blockade was entirely effective or that it was not, for it was a blockade of the entire Confederate coast line and not of any particular port. If he admitted that the coast of Florida was unguarded or that Charleston and Wilmington were inadequately blockaded, then the British acquiescence in the legality of the blockade would need explaining.

The Confederate lobby of Spence, Gregory, Lindsay, Roebuck, Campbell, Beresford-Hope, and others, and the Confederate agents Mason and Hotze, as we have already noted, were at the same time planning the interview between Russell and Mason[3] which took place five days after the date of Lindsay's letter to Russell. Three days

---

[1] Pickett Papers, Russell to Mason, Feb. 20; *O.R.N.*, Ser. 2, Vol. III, p. 343.

[2] Mason Papers, Lindsay to Russell, Feb. 5, 1862.

[3] *Ibid.*, Mason to Slidell, Feb. 7, 1862, and Gregory to Mason, Feb. 7, 1862.

after Mason's interview of February 10 Russell made his first move in reply to this agitation. He and Palmerston attempted to head it off and postpone any official commitment on the blockade at the moment. Spence was summoned from Liverpool to consult with the government. But Spence, along with the others of the group, was bent upon forcing Russell to commit himself and the government. Their plans were laid and delay was not on the program.[1] Mason, however, must have realized by this time that there was hard sledding ahead. His interview with Russell on February 10 disclosed a policy of delay on the part of the government, and just about two days later—perhaps, on the very day Spence was summoned to London by Russell—Mason received word from Slidell that his interview of February 7 with Thouvenel had been very discouraging.[2] Mason felt that the *entente cordiale* was in full operation between the two governments. Slidell had said the French government was waiting for England to take the first step, and Mason was of the opinion now after his interview that the British government would await events. "The English mind seems averse to so strong a step as breaking the blockade and I doubt very much from what I can learn whether the House of Commons will take the initiative." But Mason had high hopes that Parliament would press the government for full information on the blockade, and create a strong impression on the public mind in favor of the rights and duty of breaking the blockade.[3] The next step, in fact, was to bring the question up in Parliament. Lindsay's letter, Mason's interview with Russell, Spence's summons to London, together with the public airing of the question in Parliament, would inevitably force the government to make a public statement.

As a matter of fact, as we have noted in relating Slidell's activities in France, Russell did commit himself officially in reply to all this agitation against the blockade. On the very day, February 15, on which Mason wrote Slidell that the attack would be pushed in Parliament, Russell wrote Lyons that the blockade was effective

[1] *Ibid.*, Spence to Mason, Feb. 20, 1862.
[2] *Ibid.*, Slidell to Mason, Feb. 11 and 12, 1862.
[3] *Ibid.*, Mason to Slidell, Feb. 15, 1862.

and legal. "Her Majesty's Government," he wrote Lyons, "are of the opinion that, assuming that the blockade is duly notified, and also that a number of ships is stationed and remains at the entrance of a port, sufficient really to prevent access to it or create an evident danger of entering or leaving it, and that these ships do not voluntarily permit ingress and egress, the fact that various ships may have successfully escaped through it (as in particular instances here referred to) will not of itself prevent the blockade from being an effective one by international law."[1] Russell made this statement mainly for the purpose of publication. It was his interpretation of the statistics and papers relating to the blockade which were laid before Parliament the latter part of February and published on February 27, 1862, and it was his answer to the southern lobby. Moreover, it was published before the blockade question was brought up in Parliament.

Mason was disappointed at Russell's position on the blockade. "It would seem," he wrote Slidell,[2] "to be an official exposition on the part of the government of what is to be considered as effective blockade, and I think that you will agree with us—is little better than the old doctrine of paper blockade revived." His only hope from the impending parliamentary discussion was that a party issue would be made of it. Otherwise, there was at the time little hope for breaking the blockade.

At last, on March 7 the debate in Parliament, long heralded by the southern lobby as the climax of the drive on the blockade, commenced. Just one month before, Gregory had made a short speech, followed by Bentinck, giving notice that as soon as the papers which Lord Russell was to present to Parliament should come up for discussion he would demonstrate the ineffectiveness of the blockade. "He believed that he should be in a position to show that in a great measure this blockade could be considered as a paper blockade; but he had no wish to forestall the discussion which must arise on the

---

[1] Parliamentary Papers, Lords, Vol. XXV (1862). "Papers Relating to the Blockade" contain the text of the dispatch to Lyons. It is quoted in Pickett Papers, Benjamin to Mason, No. 2, April 8, 1862; O.R.N., Ser. 2, Vol. III, pp. 379–84; Mason Papers, Mason to Slidell, Feb. 27, 1862, inclosing copy of Russell's letter; E. D. Adams, I, 263.

[2] Mason Papers, Feb. 27, 1862.

papers which he understood would be laid before the house."[1] Bentinck commented that if Gregory could substantiate his statement that the blockade was a paper blockade, "undoubtedly in that case the character of this country would to a great extent be involved by its recognition." It would be an act of intervention in favor of the North to recognize an ineffective blockade.[2]

So on March 7 Gregory, according to his promise, opened the debate on the effectiveness of the blockade. He introduced a motion asking the government to declare the blockade ineffective. He was careful to point out that while he was a champion of recognition, having been the first to offer a motion to recognize the South in the spring of 1861, his motion now had nothing to do with recognition; it was merely carrying out the plain provisions of the Declaration of Paris which was an obligation of all neutral maritime nations. The American blockade was purely a blockade of the paper variety. It was maintained by vessels cruising up and down the coast, not by war vessels stationed off the ports. He quoted D'Hautefeuille, the French jurist, who had in passing on the American blockade stated: " 'It consists in sending one or more vessels to cruise at a distance off a coast, the blockade of which has been previously proclaimed; and all neutral vessels sailing towards or from that coast are seized and confiscated as having run or attempted to run the blockade. By this system a despatch boat, with a couple of guns, can maintain a blockade of a seaboard of 100 or 200 leagues in length.' " Gregory indorsed this French writer's opinion that the blockade was a paper blockade. England, said Gregory, approved of this blockade "not from any doubt upon our mind as to its inefficiency and illegality, not from any reasons of conciliation or friendship towards the United States—but that we may make that illegal and fictitious blockade the basis of our future arrogant pretensions when England herself, becoming belligerent, may want for herself some evasion of international law." In fact, said Gregory, England's whole purpose was to fasten upon the United States the precedent of a paper blockade and a repudiation of the principles of the Declaration of Paris, thus quieting the United States as a future champion of neutral rights and

[1] Parl. Deb. Commons, Ser. 3, Vol. 165, pp. 91–95.   [2] *Ibid.*

giving England free rein with paper blockades when she was the belligerent. He presented the various lists of blockade statistics presented by Mason and others showing over four hundred violations of the blockade by the early fall of 1861, and a continuation of the violations after that date. He cited the consular reports printed in the papers presented to Parliament showing the utter inefficiency of the blockade.

Gregory was followed by Bentinck, who urged that the blockade was ineffective and should be repudiated, and that England should recognize the South. He admitted the very thing which Gregory and the Confederate lobby had agreed not to admit, that the breaking of the blockade had something to do with recognition or intervention in behalf of the South.

W. E. Forster, the "King Corn" champion, along with John Bright, Federal lobbyist, seized upon Bentinck's tactical error and contended that repudiation of the blockade would result in recognizing the South, as it would be an act of war which would ally the South with England. Forster ridiculed the statistics presented as proof of the ineffectiveness of the blockade. This formidable array of violations were in reality tiny coasting vessels. The main ports were and had been for a long time effectively blockaded against ocean-going vessels. Were not the scarcity and high price of cotton in England sufficient proof of the effectiveness of the blockade? In fact, was it not because of the pinch of the blockade, because it effectively cut off the southern cotton, that the motion had been brought in to break the blockade? Here, as in other places, one is confronted with the inevitable conclusion of the English, that because cotton did not come out the blockade was effective. It would have been fatal for any southern sympathizer to have answered that it was the cotton embargo and not the blockade which had kept cotton from England. England was already extremely sensitive about the southern belief in England's selfish desire to have cotton.

Sir James Ferguson, Lord Robert Cecil, and William Lindsay spoke in favor of Gregory's motion. Ferguson thought the consular reports printed in the papers which Russell had presented Parliament proved the inefficiency of the blockade. Lindsay added more figures, saying that he had a report dated November 7 showing that six hundred vessels had run the blockade up to that date. This was a very conservative statement, as a study of the custom-house reports shows, but evidently the unofficial and partisan character of the report caused it to be treated lightly.

The solicitor-general, Roundell Palmer, spoke for the government in the House of Commons. His position, of course, was that of Russell. The blockade was effective. The government had no idea of challenging its legality. To do so would be equivalent to making war upon the United States and thus taking sides with a country which was one of the last strongholds of slavery. This last statement might have been taken as an official declaration of sympathy with the North as champions of freedom against slavery. As a matter of fact, it was probably a clever stroke meant to prevent Gregory's motion being turned into a party issue; neither the Conservative nor the Liberal party would be willing to appear as a partisan of slavery.[1]

Gregory withdrew his motion at the close of the debate, for it would not do for the South to be defeated on the motion. It had better be left in suspense than settled adversely. The next day the *Times*, as always to the windward of the government, remarked that if Gregory did not believe the blockade was effective he ought to try to get a shipload of goods through and bring back some cotton.[2]

Three days later, March 10, the question was raised in the House of Lords and the debate was led by Lord Campbell (Strathenden), who was one of the staunchest of the southern lobby in Parliament. Campbell attacked Russell's position as stated in the latter's note of February 15 to Lyons.

The close relation between the debates in Parliament in favor of repudiating the blockade and the Confederate agents is demonstrated in the particular case of Campbell's speech. A few days before the matter was taken up in Parliament, Campbell called upon Henry Hotze, who had just arrived. As the latest arrival from the blockaded country he could give, so it was supposed, additional information which would help sustain the position of the pro-southern group. Hotze, however, could not give more information than had

[1] *Ibid.* (March 7, 1862), pp. 1158–1231, contains the whole debate in the Commons.

[2] *Times*, March 8, 1862.

already been supplied by Mason, but he wrote Hunter that, "at his request, this being properly within the province of my commission and also my private instructions, I prepared for him, in the shape of a letter under my official signature, the strongest argument against the efficiency of the blockade that I was able to base upon the facts. . . . . Lord Campbell has since made me several protracted visits. He has decided to make a speech in the House of Lords and has engaged me to write for him the points of argument which I most desire to have urged on that body. The opportunity is a singularly fortunate one, and I shall devote the next ten days and all the powers of mind I can concentrate to the attempt of profiting by it to the extent of my ability." As in the case of Gregory, Bentinck, Lindsay, and others of the House of Commons, Campbell's speech was largely shaped by the advice of Confederate agents.[1]

Russell, a member of the House of Lords at this time, took a position similar to that of Forster, namely, that the blockade was effective, that the formidable list of violations was made up of tiny coasting vessels which ran in and out of creeks and inlets. Like Roundell Palmer, who defended the government's position in the lower House the day before, Russell alluded to the Negro question, but his appeal was made on economic grounds, by implication, at least. He held that any unneutral move on the part of the British government would be met by emancipation and slave insurrection. This, of course, would destroy the cotton supply indefinitely (an appeal to the economic group who were expected to demand the breaking of the blockade to get cotton). On the other hand, he urged upon this same group that a little patience would see the end of their troubles. In three months, predicted Russell, the war would come to an end by peaceful separation.[2]

This series of debates in Parliament on March 7 and 10 was not intended to result in a vote. The friends and agents of the South had already realized that the government could not be moved, at the time. They had hoped at the beginning of February to see Parlia-

[1] Pickett Papers, Hotze to Hunter, No. 4, Feb. 28, 1862; *O.R.N.*, Ser. 2, Vol. III, pp. 352–54.

[2] For debates in House of Lords see March 10, 1862, in Parl. Deb., Ser. 3, Vol. 165, pp. 133–43.

ment force the ministry into doing something; but Russell's interview with Mason, his letter to Lyons of February 15, the debates in
the French Chambers, led by Billault as spokesman of the Emperor
in favor of neutrality, all accompanied by military defeat in the West
for the Confederacy, pointed to the impossibility of carrying the
government in favor of breaking the blockade. Hotze summed up
the whole purpose of these debates in a letter to Hunter: "There was
no intention in either House to push the question to a vote, nor to
initiate open hostility against the present government. It was simply a 'demonstration' intended for our benefit, and has fulfilled
that expectation."[1] As a demonstration it was successful. It created
the impression that the blockade was ineffective and the airing of
blockade-running stimulated business in that particular field. It also
created the desired impression that there was a large pro-southern
group in Parliament who were ready—at the proper moment—to
interfere in behalf of the South. But once again King Cotton had
secretly disappointed the Confederate agents. Mason, who had begun his career the latter part of January with hopes of some form of
intervention, especially the repudiation of the blockade because of
the need of cotton, now wrote that the manufacturers were still over-
stocked with goods and would not need cotton until their old stock
was worked off. These men, he said, had made a big profit and were
quite content with the *status quo*. So, despite much suffering among
the operatives, the pressure from the cotton industry did not occur.[2]

[1] Pickett Papers, No. 5, March 11, 1862; *O.R.N.*, Ser. 2, Vol. III, pp. 360–63.

[2] Pickett Papers, Mason to Secretary of State, No. 6, March 11, 1862; *O.R.N.*, Ser.
2, Vol. III, pp. 358–60.

CHAPTER VII

THE INEFFECTIVENESS OF THE BLOCKADE

The first drive on the blockade resulted only in a public demonstration in favor of the South, and in the declaration by the English government that the blockade should be respected as effective; and that the war would be over in three months, ending in separation. The main southern objective had not been reached—the repudiation of the blockade by the British government—but lesser objectives had been attained. There were to be other drives against the blockade along with efforts in behalf of recognition at a later date. Let us once and for all, then, examine briefly the data, most of it presented to the British and French governments from time to time, intended to demonstrate the inefficiency of the blockade. In treating of later efforts at breaking the blockade, reference will be made to the data presented here.

When one considers the Herculean task of blockading the Confederate coast of 3,549 statute miles—from Alexandria on the Potomac to the Rio Grande—with its 189 rivers, numerous bays, inlets, and harbors, one would guess that Lincoln was attempting the impossible; but when the subject is further investigated and it is discovered that a great part of the coast from North Carolina to Florida on the Atlantic side and from West Florida to Galveston, Texas, was a double line, with interior channels, making it possible to travel much of the distance between the ports without frequent exposure to the open sea, one would almost conclude that old Abe was playing a practical joke on the world. But the absurdity of the thing does not end with the great stretch of seacoast and double-line shores and numberless bays and inlets; the United States Navy was practically defunct. There were 90 vessels carried on the register, and of these only 40 were steamers, and of the steamers only 24 were, according to J. R. Soley, fit for service, the others being too old or laid up for repair or unfinished.[1] At the time the blockade was declared only 3

[1] J. R. Soley, *The Blockade and the Cruisers* (New York, 1883), pp. 11–14. (Cited as Soley.)

were at the disposal of the Navy Department, the others being scattered all over the world on detached service. As for the sailing vessels, they were completely useless and obsolete.[1] So there were 1,200 miles and 63 ports and inlets to the vessel. Even after all 24 steamers reached the blockaded coast there were still 147 miles of seacoast for each vessel and about 8 harbors and numerous bays, inlets, and bayous to watch, not to mention the inner channels.[2]

The blockade by the United States government, then, was scarcely a respectable paper blockade, when first declared. These great stretches of double seacoast and numerous indentations and inlets naturally made any attempt to blockade the South appear absurd to the South itself, and the cotton embargo can more easily be comprehended when it is seen that the South expected only a paper blockade which would interrupt and annoy its commerce rather than effectually cut it off. Neither the South nor Europe—especially, Russell and his cabinet—dreamed that the United States could blockade the South. We will recall that when there was talk of the blockade Lyons had actually thought of advising his government not to regard it, so impossible did it seem.

Starting with three steam vessels to blockade the entire Atlantic and Gulf Coast, the Federal government began hastily to accumulate a navy. By July, 12 steamers had been bought and 9 chartered and sent to the blockaded coast; 18 of the steamers on foreign stations had been recalled, making in all 42 steam vessels to enforce the blockade. These steamers ranged from 800 tons to ferry boats. By December, 1861, 79 steamers of these nondescript types had been purchased along with 58 sailing boats, though the latter were completely useless except where the blockade-runners were sailing ves-

[1] *Ibid.*

[2] For the foregoing figures on the navy and coast blockaded see *ibid.;* Lieutenant Mannix, *The Effect and Value of the Co-operation of the Navy during the Late Civil War, etc.* (Fort Monroe, Va., 1878); Sprunt, *Tales of Cape Fear Blockade* (Raleigh, N.C., 1902), p. 5; Hobart-Hampden Pasha (Captain Roberts), *Sketches of My Life* (Leipzig, 1887), p. 95; Admiral Porter in *New York Herald,* July 19, 1885; see also the Welles report to Lincoln, July 4 and Dec. 2, 1861; Pickett Papers, Benjamin to Slidell, No. 23, Sept. 2, 1863; *O.R.N.,* Ser. 2, Vol. III, pp. 882–89. These sources all differ in minor detail but agree approximately. I have followed Soley when there was a difference of detail.

sels. So there were about 160 vessels at the end of 1861, only a small proportion of which were naval vessels capable of strenuous action.[1] Had the "Merrimack" got loose among these boats, it could have sunk every one *ad libitum*—provided they remained at their posts. The British ironclad war vessel "Warrior" or the French ironclad "Gloire" could have swept this motley fleet—which must have resembled D'Artagnan's old nag—from the sea. While by early spring of 1862 there were 226 vessels,[2] by October of that year there were only 256.[3] Most of the sailing vessels were discarded by this time as blockaders, owing to the new type of screw-propeller blockade-runners. By this time, too, many new naval vessels had been built, some of them ironclad, including a brood of monitors. By the end of 1863 there were 400 vessels in the United States Navy, and by the end of the war over 600.[4] Had these vessels been placed along the coast from Norfolk to the Rio Grande there would have been only about 1 for each 6 miles at the end of the war. What was actually done, was that a cordon of ships, when there were enough for this purpose, was placed about the main ports; another cordon was placed about the various neutral ports in the West Indies and Mexico which were used as blockade-running bases; and a third was placed in the gulf stream.[5] Thus sometimes hundreds of miles of coast, which was declared blockaded, was left unguarded, even after the Navy had reached its maximum strength.

It must be apparent, then, from the scarcity of vessels and the length and shape of the blockaded coast, that an effective blockade was a difficult matter to attain. Certainly the 160 vessels accounted

[1] Soley, pp. 16–17, for this period; cf. *London Times*, Dec. 4, 1861.

[2] *New York Herald*, Feb. 4, 1865, statement of Congressman Rice.

[3] *London Times*, Oct., 1862.

[4] See *New York Herald*, Feb. 4, 1865; Mr. Rice and Admiral Porter, *ibid.*, July 19, 1865.

[5] See Sprunt, *Tales of Cape Fear Blockade*, pp. 6–9; cf. Bradlee, *Blockade Running during the Civil War and the Effect of Land and Water Transportation on the Confederacy* (Salem, Mass., 1925) (cited as Bradlee); Taylor, *Running the Blockade* (London, 1897) (cited as Taylor); Watson, *Adventures of a Blockade Runner* (London, 1892) (cited as Watson); Admiral Hobart-Hampden Pasha, *op. cit.*; Wilkinson, *Narrative of a Blockade Runner* (New York, 1877) (cited as Wilkinson), *passim*, for examples of Federal blockade methods.

for at the end of 1861, many of which were sailing craft, could not blockade 3,500 or more miles of the southern coast; the 226 vessels which carried the United States flag in the spring of 1862 could hardly be expected to blockade the Confederacy. This was just at the moment, too, when Mason and Lindsay were presenting their figures, all showing that, even with the incomplete returns, between 500 and 700 vessels had run the blockade in 1861. It was at this time that Russell gave his answer that he considered the blockade legal and binding. The 256 vessels which maintained the blockade at the end of 1862, when the war was about half over, were obviously confronted with too much mileage to establish a blockade which would be legal according to accepted American doctrines that a blockade must be a circumvallation of a port or point on the coast and able to prevent the ingress and egress of vessels. As a matter of fact, for the first year and a half the blockade was nothing more than the plundering of neutral commerce en route to the Confederacy under the cover of a nominal blockade. During the entire war, except at certain points, it was never, outside Great Britain, an effective blockade according to American and European standards.

Our problem does not permit an extended treatment of the efficiency of the blockade. An exhaustive narrative on that subject alone would require a large volume. Only a few of the significant details and conclusions can be made use of here. These are based on opinions of the blockade expressed by the leading British consuls stationed in the Confederacy; on the opinions of the American consuls in the West Indies and Caribbean region which were the great blockade-running bases; on the accounts of newspapers in the North; and on the reports of the Confederate officials.

Consul Bunch at Charleston, whose jurisdiction extended over the coast of both North and South Carolina, aided by a vice-consul in Wilmington, rendered to the Foreign Office during the first two years of the war regular reports which indicate a very inadequate blockade of that part of the Confederacy. On August 6, 1861, Bunch wrote Russell inclosing an affidavit of the master of the "Seabrook" which, Bunch said, "conclusively shows that there is in reality no blockade at all of this coast, except so far as large vessels are concerned." Privateers, continued Bunch, were making captures and "sending their prizes into all the ports quite unmolested by any of the ships of the United States." This was true, he said, of the whole coast of the two Carolinas, Georgia, and Florida. "So far, as I believe, not a single ship of war is at present [August 6, 1861] to be found on the entire coast of the State [of North Carolina]."[1] The next day, August 7, Bunch sent Russell the affidavit of Thomas I. Moore, master of the privateer "Dixie," describing a cruise of sixteen days, in which vessels of 287–330 tons were captured and brought into ports of South Carolina and North Carolina without molestation. The privateer had left Charleston in daylight and, said Bunch, "there were no blockading vessels in sight"; the deponent swore that "from the time he went to sea on 20 July last up to the 5th instant when he again came into North Edisto River he saw no vessel of the United States whatever."[2] On August 20 Bunch reported that no change had taken place on the coast of North and South Carolina. Vessels came and went without let or hindrance. "The blockade is the laughing stock of the Southern merchant marine," wrote Bunch. So ineffective was it that his French colleague, M. de Belligny, who was going home for a visit, was planning to call on Russell at Bunch's request to present the situation more in detail.[3] On September 4 Bunch wrote: "The blockade of the coast of North Carolina has, so far as I am informed, been totally inefficient since the date of my last despatch."[4] Many vessels had entered and sailed from the port of Wilmington during the period since his last report made August 20. In the same report he said of Charleston, "The blockade of this port continues to be conducted with the same laxity which has hitherto distinguished it. Vessels of various sizes enter and sail almost at pleasure."[5] On September 14, 1861, Bunch wrote:

[1] F.O. Amer., Vol. 781, Bunch to Russell, No. 94, Aug. 6, 1861.

[2] Ibid., No. 95, Aug. 7, 1861.

[3] Ibid., No. 102, Aug. 20, 1861; Dayton wrote Seward when the French Consul arrived that the evidence which he was presenting to the government was very damaging and was calculated to bring intervention. See U.S. Des., France, Vol. 50, Dayton to Seward, No. 55, Sept. 30, 1861.

[4] F.O. Amer., Vol. 781, Bunch to Russell, No. 105, Sept. 4, 1861.   [5] Ibid.

234   KING COTTON DIPLOMACY

"The blockade of the coast of both North and South Carolina continues to be totally ineffective. No difficulty whatever seems to be experienced by vessels either in entering or sailing from even this port of Charleston which is supposed to be fully blockaded, there being two ships of war always in sight from the town."[1] On February 3, 1862, Bunch reported that vessels still came and went with ease into the blockaded ports on the east coast, despite the greatly increased number of war vessels stationed off the shore.[2]

The succeeding reports of Bunch noted an increasing number of blockaders on the coast, but likewise an increasing number of blockade-runners doing business. He wrote Lyons privately on April 7, 1862, nearly two months after Russell had written Lyons that the British government considered the blockade effective: "The blockade runners are doing a great business. . . . . Everything is brought in in abundance. Not a day passes without an arrival or departure . . . . passengers come and go freely and no one seems to think that there is the slightest risk—which, indeed, there is not."[3] The character of the reports of Bunch and the other consuls begins to change in the spring of 1862. They continue to report the violation of the blockade and their figures show the blockade business to be undiminishing and more regular, but there is less pronouncement as to the effectiveness of the blockade. This, of course, is very easy to understand. Russell had spoken, the British government had recognized the blockade, and no opinion from the consuls was desired. Usually the bare facts were given, and eventually even these were not regularly reported.[4]

While Bunch frequently reported on the state of the blockade along the Georgia and Florida coast, the acting consul at Savannah, Fullerton, or Consul Molyneaux, was the regular channel through which this information reached the Foreign Office. August 12, 1861, Fullerton wrote that Savannah was blockaded for large vessels,

[1] *Ibid.*, No. 108, Sept. 14, 1861.

[2] *Ibid.*, Vol. 843, No. 17, Feb. 3, 1862; cf. *ibid.*, Jan. 1, 1862.

[3] Taken from a quotation made by E. D. Adams, I, 368–69, n. 2.

[4] For further reports of Bunch, see F.O. Amer., Vols. 843, 844, Part II; Vols. 906, 907, Part II; Vols. 968, 969, all *passim*.

but that numberless small vessels came into the harbor by the inner channels. The smaller ports of the coast south of Savannah were unguarded most of the time. "The blockade of such ports is not effective, being maintained by the United States Government not by vessels of war permanently stationed off the mouth of each harbour . . . . but merely by a few vessels cruising up and down the coast, appearing off a port one day and leaving . . . . the next."[1]

This situation continued through September, the whole coast of Georgia and east Florida remaining unguarded save by a few transient cruisers, and Fullerton reported that it was because the United States vessels were too large and too few to guard this coast.[2] On October 11, 1861, he wrote that the blockading vessels off Savannah had of recent weeks been absenting themselves for a week at a time, and that the seven-hundred-ton "Bermuda" had entered through the main channel loaded to the gunwale with arms. This vessel had coasted forty miles before entering Savannah without seeing a Federal vessel. The whole coast to the south of Savannah as usual was practically unblockaded. "The vessels employed are too few in number and not suitable in class to prevent access to the various harbors and inlets on the coast. They merely cruise up and down visiting a day or two at a time one harbor after another. The consequence has been that many vessels have run in and out to and from various points on the coast without seeing a blockading vessel."[3] On July 10, 1862, Fullerton reported that the blockade was still maintained in an ineffective manner on the coast of Georgia and Florida. The blockading vessels still continued to depend upon an occasional cruise up and down the coast.[4]

The Confederate official reports and the American consular reports from the West Indies corroborated the evidence of the British consuls—and the French—that the blockade up until the spring of 1862 was as ineffective on the east coast of Florida as an old-fash-

---

[1] *Ibid.*, Vol. 786, Acting Consul Fullerton to Russell, No. 26, Aug. 12, 1861.

[2] *Ibid.*, No. 28, Aug. 22, 1861; *ibid.*, Vol. 781, Bunch to Russell, No. 113, Sept. 28, 1861.

[3] *Ibid.*, Vol. 786, Fullerton to Russell, No. 29, Oct. 11, 1861.

[4] *Ibid.*, Vol. 849, No. 17, July 10, 1862.

ioned British paper blockade. On October 15, 1861, John Boston, collector of the port of Savannah, reported that several vessels, including the "Bermuda," had entered the port recently and had not sighted an American vessel from the time of sailing until arriving at their destination. "The absence of the blockading fleet is of frequent occurrence, sometimes as long as one and two weeks in good weather," he wrote. He felt authorized to say that with one exception there had never been, even when the port was supposed to be guarded by the fleet, "a sufficient force off our bar to blockade this port effectively." There was seldom more than one vessel and often none off the port.[1] F. Livingston, at Fernandina, Florida, reported an absence of blockading vessels off the port and east coast of Florida.[2] A. B. Noyes, collector at St. Marks, asserted that only one vessel was holding an intermittent watch over that harbor; and that Tampa was without any blockading vessels at all, while the port of Cedar Keys had never been molested.[3]

The United States consul-general of Cuba, R. W. Shufeldt, reported in alarm that the east coast about Charleston was not effectively blockaded. On November 15, 1861, he wrote W. H. Seward that he had just obtained testimony concerning a Confederate privateer which had been all up and down the coast in the vicinity of Charleston without being molested by the United States blockading fleet. "Testimony concurrent with the enclosed," continued Shufeldt, "in reference to the inefficiency of the blockade off Charleston is continually presented to me and I feel it my duty to call the attention of the government to this point."[4] About a week later he wrote that the arrival of blockade-runners had become so numerous it was "becoming difficult to keep the run of them."[5] Consuls Merritt and his successor, Whiting, at Nassau during the first year of the war reported an ever increasing fleet of successful blockade-runners plying to and from the Confederacy with Nassau

[1] Pickett Papers, packages 18, 30, 43, 78, Oct. 15, 1861—report to the secretary of the treasury, Memminger.

[2] *Ibid.*, Aug. 27, 1861.   [3] *Ibid.*, Noyes to Memminger, Oct. 18, 1861.

[4] U.S. Consular Des., Havana, Vol. 41, Shufeldt to Seward, No. 48, Nov. 15, 1861.

[5] *Ibid.*, No. 88.

as a base.[1] United States Consul Wells at Bermuda and his successor, Allen, were constantly reporting with apprehension the ineffectiveness of the blockade on the east coast.[2]

Thus the British, Confederate, and Federal reports on the blockade were in complete agreement during this first period that the Federal blockade was ineffective.

The Gulf Coast was not checked as closely by the consuls as the Atlantic; but evidence is sufficient to show that with the exception of the period of the siege of New Orleans and the final siege of Mobile, the blockade was very ineffective the first year and a half and never very effective during the entire war. Consul Lynn at Galveston reported that the gulf trade was not interrupted seriously by the blockade; only the inland trade from up the Mississippi River was cut off by the Confederate government's refusing to trade with the enemy.[3] On September 23, 1861, Lynn inclosed a letter from Colonel C. S. Forshey, Brazoria, Texas, to the Foreign Office showing that only the so-called main channel to Galveston was in any way guarded by the United States fleet; that Pass San Luis, the west entrance to Galveston with ten feet of water, "has at no time been blockaded and . . . . vessels have entered and departed from the harbor of Galveston, by way of this pass continually" since the laying of the blockade. The Brazos River with six feet of water was entirely without blockading vessels, and ships passed in and out without interruption, carrying on trade with Velasco, Quintana, Brazoria, and Columbia, and passing by canal to Galveston itself.[4] On October 19 Lynn reported that only one frigate guarded the main channel at Galveston; that the east and west channels entering the harbor were still unguarded, and vessels were running in and out at night without interruption. As to the coast lying toward Mexico, Lynn wrote, "All the ports to the westward of Galveston are yet open."[5] On December 28, 1861, Lynn wrote that "there has not been any change in

[1] *Ibid.*, Nassau, Vol. 11, *passim.*

[2] *Ibid.*, Bermuda, Vols. 5, 6, *passim.*

[3] F.O. Amer., Vol. 788, No. 25, Aug. 8, 1861.

[4] *Ibid.*, Lynn to Foreign Office, No. 33, Sept. 23, 1861.

[5] *Ibid.*, No. 35, Oct. 19, 1861.

the vessels maintaining, or in the character of the blockade of this port." Vessels still came and went as usual by way of the San Luis Pass.[1] On February 14, 1862, Lynn reported that no change had taken place. There was still no blockade of Pass San Luis, and no regular blockade of any of the points west—only an occasional interruption of trade by visiting cruisers.[2]

Consul Mure at New Orleans reported continuous trade between that port and Mobile and Havana, Cuba, by bayou and inland channels.[3] On January 2, 1862, acting Consul Coppell of New Orleans wrote the Foreign Office that the blockade was a farce at that point. One case in particular, he thought, was illustrative of the situation at New Orleans and the gulf. The Confederate steamer "Vanderbilt" sailed from New Orleans on November 30, 1861, with a full cargo and arrived at Havana on December 3 "without meeting any opposition from the United States vessels blockading or elsewhere." Then the "Vanderbilt" loaded with ninety-one thousand pounds of powder and sailed to Sabine City one hundred miles west of Galveston and came back to New Orleans without seeing any except one small United States vessel which made no attempt to stop the "Vanderbilt." There were several others running the blockade at the same time, the "Margaret," "Calhoun," "Pizarro"—all passing through without molestation. "From this information your Lordship will be best able to judge whether the blockading force is adequate to maintain an efficient blockade or to cause obvious danger to those attempting to break it! But from the fact that there is a perfect rage here at the present time for running the blockade—merchants and others emboldened by the success of those vessels that have left the various ports in this state, are quietly chartering, buying and getting ready every available vessel—people here do not look upon it as being very effective or dangerous in attempting to break it."[4] Magee also reported the blockade as inefficient at Mobile during this period.[5]

[1] *Ibid.*, No. 36, Dec. 28, 1861.   [2] *Ibid.*, Vol. 848, No. 7, Feb. 14, 1862.

[3] *Ibid.*, Vol. 788, No. 38, July 30, 1861.

[4] *Ibid.*, Vol. 848, Coppell to Russell, No. 6, Jan. 8, 1862.

[5] *Ibid.*, Vol. 786, July 29; *ibid.*, Vol. 848, No. 32, Oct. 16, 1861.

The British cruiser "Jason" visited the Gulf Coast in July, 1861, and found the condition just as described by Lynn, Mure, Coppell, and Magee, at Galveston, New Orleans, and Mobile. Nothing but the main entrances were blockaded, and these very inadequately. The side entrances and intervening coast and inlets were unmolested.[1]

The reports of the Confederate agent at Havana, Charles Helm, as to the inefficiency of the blockade of Mobile and New Orleans are full. Helm had the list published, as we have noted, in the *Mercantile Weekly* and other Cuban publications,[2] showing over a hundred vessels running into Havana—most of them from New Orleans, Mobile, and the coast of Florida and Texas—up to January, 1862. Collector of customs at New Orleans, F. H. Hatch, in his series of reports to the Confederate Treasury Department from May 15, 1861, through March, 1862, gave the startling information that three hundred vessels had run the blockade at New Orleans during the ten months involved.[3] The dispatches of United States Consul-General R. W. Shufeldt—later rear admiral—are also valuable witnesses to the ineffectiveness of the blockade at Mobile, New Orleans, Galveston, and the whole Gulf Coast. He reported that a daily stream of blockade-runners was coming out of these ports with apparent impunity.[4]

The foregoing are only a few characteristic opinions of British and American consuls, British naval officers, and Confederate officials on blockade-running during the first year of the war, all agreeing that the blockade was ineffective. The leading eastern newspapers believed also that the blockade was ineffective during this time. The *New York Herald*, which took the position that Welles was a moron, insisted that, though the blockade had been in operation four months, "the Southern coast is not yet blockaded, for what

[1] Soley, p. 9.

[2] Pickett Papers, Helm to Hunter, No. 9, Jan. 7, 1862, inclosing *Mercantile Weekly* (extra).

[3] Pickett Papers, Confederate State Dept. (copies from Treasury Dept.), Vols. 18, 30, 43, 78, Hatch to Memminger (reports).

[4] See U.S. Consular Des., Havana, Vol. 45 (1861–62), *passim*, e.g., No. 39, March 22; *ibid.*, Shufeldt to Seward, No. 46, April 2, 1862.

is by way of courtesy called a blockade is but 'a mockery, a delusion and a snare,' and the consequence is that it will very soon be broken, as invalid, by the British and French fleets, which have arrived on the coast for that purpose. . . . . The Battle of Bull Run and the protracted inefficiency of the blockade will probably precipitate the action of the British Government."[1] The *New York Tribune* believed that "the whole thing is the biggest sort of a laughing stock to the secessionists, who boast that they are much better off with it than without it. . . . ."[2] The *Philadelphia Enquirer* asserted that Lord Lyons and Mercier had placed statistics before Seward which proved that "the blockade has been notoriously ineffective, and therefore no blockade at all."[3] The *New York Daily News*, in the light of Admiral Milne's report that the blockade was not very effective, was "entirely prepared to see a prompt and decided attitude assumed by Great Britain, France, and Spain at an early period."[4] The *New York World* was of the opinion that the notorious ineffectiveness of the blockade would soon cause Europe to interfere to break it.[5]

The period dealt with above is approximately the first year of the war, and falls within the period when the Confederate lobby was making its greatest drive against the inefficiency of the blockade. Only a few typical excerpts could be given, but a careful perusal of the British consular reports from all the Confederate ports covering this period discloses a unanimous opinion, based upon first-hand observation, that the blockade was totally ineffective for months, and hardly worth considering as a serious impediment to trade for the first year. A study of all the reports of the United States consuls at Nassau, Bermuda, Havana, Tampico, Matamoras, Vera Cruz, and Belize (British Honduras) likewise discloses the conviction upon the part of these consuls that the blockade was ineffective. The reports of the Confederate collectors and agents in the West Indies and Mexico have the same tone. The leading newspapers of the

[1] *New York Herald*, Aug. 12, 1861.

[2] *New York Tribune* quoted in the *Savannah Republican*, Aug. 26, 1861.

[3] *Philadelphia Enquirer* in *Savannah Republican*, Aug. 26, 1861.

[4] *New York Daily News*, July 26, 1861.   [5] *New York World*, Oct. 7, 1861.

North, which usually had special correspondents at the blockade-running bases, were of the same opinion. The memoirs and histories left by the famous English blockade-runners Taylor, Watson, and Hobart-Hampden (Captain Roberts) and by United States naval officers corroborate these. One goes farther and studies the reports of the American consuls located in Liverpool, London, and other important shipping centers[1] where the blockade goods were loaded and shipped and concludes that the blockade was a leaky and ramshackle affair.

The blockade statistics as well as the opinion of the consuls and admiralty were in the hands of the Foreign Office at the time the Confederate commissioners laid before Russell the violations of the blockade. In fact, Russell must have known much more about the inefficiency of the blockade than did any of the Confederate agents; for the Harbor Board at Liverpool had the record of 789 vessels coming from Confederate ports in 1861 and 472 clearing from there, most of the latter arriving safely, making a total, if correct, of over 1,200 vessels coming into and leaving Liverpool and violating the blockade.[2]

We have noted the acquisition of vessels by the American Navy until there were over 600 at the end of the war, and with this increase the blockade would be expected to show a corresponding tightening. As a matter of fact, it did not tighten in proportion to the increased number of war vessels riding the blockade or cruising the Gulf and Atlantic Coast.

As before noted, the British consuls did not express opinions to any marked extent after they were informed of Russell's recognition of the efficiency of the blockade. They usually reported the continued and ever increasing blockade-running after the spring of 1862, with only an occasional laconic comment. But the statistics they presented are eloquent. The American consuls, however, continued to warn Seward that the blockade was not effective and that intervention might result. The Confederate officials, finding that their

[1] See, e.g., U.S. Consular Des., Liverpool, Vol. 19, H. Wilding to F. W. Seward, *passim.*

[2] *London Post*, Nov. 7, 1863, in *New York Herald*, Nov. 20, 1863.

blockade statistics only aided the American vessels to chase the blockade-runner, became less communicative.

However, from all these sources combined, frequently one is able to arrive at a conception of the blockade. We shall attempt briefly to cite a few opinions but more especially to present statistics showing the volume of the blockade business after the first year of the war.

For the Atlantic coast, Bunch and his successor, Walker, at Charleston, and Molyneaux and his successor, Fullerton, at Savannah, continued reporting statistics of blockade-running, which steadily increased in number until some time in 1864, when Charleston and Wilmington were under close investment by the United States Navy. During 1862 and 1863 Bunch reported a steady stream of blockade-runners coming in with arms and powder and general supplies and leaving with cotton.[1] Fullerton at Savannah noted the same situation on the coast of Georgia—though Savannah itself was frequently well guarded at the main entrance, but not at the side and inner passages.[2]

Commenting on the blockade situation, especially at Charleston, Walker wrote Russell on April 22, 1863, that an examination of the statistics, which he was inclosing, summing up the whole affair from July, 1861, to April, 1863, showed that "the trade of the port has been most active during the past year, notwithstanding the increased number of blockading vessels which have been maintained on the coast during that interval, and it will be seen that during the last quarter the cotton exports and customs receipts have been much heavier than any other quarter."[3] During the summer business increased more rapidly. Walker's report of June 29, 1863, showed that business was still on the increase, at Wilmington at least.[4] On August 1, 1863, Walker reported that Charleston was

[1] F.O. Amer., Vol. 843, Bunch to Russell, No. 78, June 5, 1862; *ibid.*, Vol. 844, Part II, e.g., Nos. 89–144 inclusive, July 3–Dec. 22, 1862; *ibid.*, Vol. 849, Molyneux to Russell, No. 17, June 25, 1862; *ibid.*, Vol. 906, Walker to Russell, Nos. 27, 31, 34, 38, 41, Feb. 14–Mar. 21, 1863.

[2] See *ibid.*, Vols. 849, 909, *passim*.

[3] *Ibid.*, Vol. 906, Walker to Russell, No. 59, April 22, 1863; *ibid.*, *passim*.

[4] *Ibid.*, No. 84, June 29, 1863.

being attacked heavily by the Federal blockading fleet, but that there had been 5 steamers to run into port and 4 out from July 8 to 25. As for North Carolina, he commented laconically, "The inefficiency of the blockade of the port of Wilmington continues. . . . ." He might have added that the inefficiency seemed more pronounced for the violations were much greater. From July 17 to 25— eight days—there were 10 steamers running the blockade into Wilmington.[1] On October 3, 1863, Walker wrote that 13 steamers ran into Wilmington from September 10 to 29—nineteen days—and that 14 departed from September 2 to 19—seventeen days.[2]

During 1864 Wilmington and Charleston, despite the tightening cordon of cruisers thrown around the harbor and in the gulf stream and around Bermuda and the Bahamas, showed no marked decrease in blockade-running until late fall, when the blockade-runners began to change from Nassau and Bermuda to Havana, Cuba, to run into the gulf ports, especially Galveston.[3] The reports seem to average about the same. Walker observed on December 31, 1864, when Charleston was closely invested, that from August 30 to December 27, 20 had cleared,[4] showing even at that perilous hour that the Atlantic blockade was not entirely efficient.

The testimony of the American consuls in Bermuda and Nassau in the period after the spring of 1862 corroborates that of the British consuls as to the inefficiency of the blockade on the Atlantic Coast, especially at Wilmington and Charleston. Samuel Whiting, consul at Nassau, New Province, wrote W. H. Seward on April 13, 1862, that the "Thomas L. Wragg," "Economist," and "Cecile" had already made 4 trips to Nassau without hindrance—making 8 trips through the blockade.[5] Whiting was very much riled at the ineffectiveness of the blockade, and on April 30 he reported to Seward that the steamer "Kate" had just arrived, commenting that "the 'Kate' is one of the *regular line of packets* plying between Charleston, South Carolina, and Nassau," bringing out cotton and carrying in

[1] *Ibid.*, Vol. 907, Part II, No. 107, Aug. 1, 1863.

[2] *Ibid.*, No. 135, Oct. 3, 1863.

[3] See *ibid.*, Vols. 968, 969, *passim*.

[4] *Ibid.*, Vol. 969, No. 116, Dec. 31, 1864.

[5] U.S. Consular Des., Nassau, Vol. 11, Whiting to Seward, No. 12, April 13, 1862.

contraband.[1] Whiting was alarmed at the "formidable fleet of fast iron steamers" which were using Nassau as a base for blockade-running, and even more alarmed at the others which were "daily congregating" at that port to run into Wilmington or Charleston.[2] There were 12 of these steamers on July 12, for instance, ready to run the blockade, among which was again the steamer "Kate," the *bête noire* of Whiting's existence. This steamer, he said in a melancholy "I-told-you-so" tone, had "run the blockade more than twenty times during the past year."[3] If Whiting could have seen the complete destiny of the "Kate" he might have wept, for that five-hundred-ton steamer was not half through with her career. She finally chalked up 44 trips through the blockade.

Consul Allen at Bermuda, the other base for the Atlantic traffic, reported the constant arrival of vessels there.[4] He said that certain steamers plied to and fro, with the regularity of peace-time packets. One in particular, the "Cornubia," bothered him. On March 23, 1863, that vessel came into Bermuda and received an ovation which irritated him thoroughly. This vessel, he said, had been running the blockade regularly, and her arrival was an occasion of rejoicing. On this occasion the harbor shores were lined with the inhabitants "who greeted her with cheer after cheer."[5] On April 18 he complained to Seward that the "Cornubia" was still afloat and unmolested, and was expected the next day. She "makes her trips," he objected, "as regular as the mail steamers to Halifax, having occupied in her former trips three weeks and three days each."[6]

About this time S. C. Hawley, the vitriolic-tongued successor of the melancholy Whiting at Nassau, reported the arrival of a fleet of steamers, all filled with cotton.[7] The "Ruby" was getting as troublesome as the "Kate" and "Cornubia." This was her eighth trip through the blockade—many of which had been in broad daylight.[8]

---

[1] *Ibid.*, No. 22, April 30, 1862.   [2] *Ibid.*, No. 41, June 9, 1862.

[3] *Ibid.*, No. 52, July 29, 1862.

[4] See, e.g., *ibid.*, Bermuda, Vol. 6, Allen to Seward (1862), *passim.*

[5] *Ibid.*, No. 8, March 23, 1863.   [6] *Ibid.*, No. 13, April 18, 1863.

[7] *Ibid.*, Nassau, Vol. 12, Hawley to Seward, No. 3, March 16, 1863.

[8] Cf. *ibid.*, No. 2, March 13, 1863.

On May 2 Hawley reports 26 different blockade-runners plying between Nassau and the east coast. Among this group were the immortal runners "Robert E. Lee," formerly the Collie Clyde steamer "Giraffe," which under the command of Captain Wilkinson ran the blockade 21 times in ten months and carried out thousands of bales of cotton;[1] the "Ruby"; the "Pet," a slow little boat which finally ran the blockade 40 times;[2] the "Antonica," which ran the blockade 28 times and about whom it was said, "Start her engines, put her on her course for either Wilmington or Nassau, lash her wheel, and she would go in and out by herself."[3] Hawley wrote that as fast as one of these steamers was captured or wrecked another from England took its place.[4] On May 30, 1863, he rendered a very interesting and —to Seward—disturbing report. There had been 28 different vessels, he wrote, engaged at Nassau in running the blockade since March 10, 1863—two and one-half months. These vessels had made about 112 trips through the blockade, or about 4 trips each on an average. There had been only 13 wrecks and captures out of these 112 voyages. "This gives us one capture to four and one-third voyages about," wrote Hawley. The profit was so great, he continued, that he did not expect to see the number of blockade-runners reduced "until our blockade is made more effective or the cities of Charleston and Ft. Fisher, Wilmington, are taken. . . . ." "In making the 56 voyages [112 trips] . . . . the runners have passed our blockading squadron say 112 times in less than 90 days" (actually 80 days), and only 13 wrecks and captures had occurred. "Suppose a foreigner should allege that our blockade is null and void for want of force or vigilance, claiming that successful voyages are the rule and failures the exception, would a reply that our squadron had defeated or

[1] For account of this vessel see Wilkinson, *passim.*

[2] See Sprunt, *Tales of Cape Fear*, p. 55, for "Pet."

[3] Sprunt, *Derelicts* (an account of ships lost at sea in general commercial traffic and a brief history of blockade-runners stranded along the North Carolina coast, 1861–65) (Baltimore, 1920), *passim*, for "Antonica."

[4] For Hawley's report to Seward see U.S. Consular Des., Nassau, Vol. 12, No. 23, May 2, 1863.

captured one in 10 or 12 of the venture satisfy the requirements of the blockade?"[1]

So great did the blockade traffic become in the summer of 1863 that Vice-Consul W. C. Thompson, who had taken the obstreperous Hawley's place, seemed quite fearful. The arrival of shoals of new blockade-runners from England to engage in the profitable traffic seemed ominous.[2] On October 26, 1863, he reported 9 arrivals from Wilmington from October 6 to 24 and 8 departures from Nassau from October 8 to 17 (all successful—which had been heard from). There was in addition to this regular blockade-running a kind of wildcat business by sailing vessels which troubled Thompson. These sailing vessels slipped in and out of the Bahamas and left no trace, running into the inlets of Florida, Georgia, North Carolina, and South Carolina. Thompson believed that there was "a very large amount of blockade running done by sailing vessels of which we have no record," thus swelling the blockade business to much greater proportions than appeared from the port records.[3] He came to the conclusion that the apparently uninterrupted commerce with the Confederacy indicated that the United States Navy was corrupted. At least there were reports to that effect, he said.[4]

Passing on to the next year, we find Kirkpatrick, the consul who had relieved Thompson, reporting an undiminished business as late as September 24, 1864. There were 12 arrivals from Wilmington and Charleston, August 24–September 23, and 13 departures for the blockade covering approximately the same period. This time he reported several vessels wrecked or captured, but remarked in disgust that a large fleet of new blockade-runners had just arrived in Nassau from Europe and others were expected any day.[5] On November 1, 1864, Kirkpatrick noted the arrival of 4 blockade-runners from Wilmington and Charleston on that day, and the departure of 3 for Charleston on the day before, and he remarks caustically:

[1] *Ibid.*, Hawley to Seward, May 30, 1863.

[2] See *ibid.*, Thompson to Seward, No. 5, July 6, 1863.

[3] *Ibid.*, No. 25, Oct. 26, 1863.

[4] See, e.g., *ibid.*, No. 24, Oct. 17, 1863.

[5] *Ibid.*, Vol. 13, Kirkpatrick to Seward, No. 24, Sept. 24, 1864.

"There appears to be no interruption from that end of the line."[1] After this his reports show a decline of the business and a transfer of the steamers to Havana to run into the gulf ports, especially Galveston.[2]

Allen at Bermuda reported to Seward a continuation of the thriving business of blockade-running. He was not, he said, able to give a complete record, but on July 13, 1864, he wrote that within the last eighteen months 40,000 bales of cotton had been run from the blockaded coast—largely from Wilmington and Charleston—into Bermuda, besides large quantities of tobacco and some turpentine.[3] He had a record of 86 steamers employed in the blockade business at Bermuda during this period.[4] On the same day he observed in another dispatch that 7 vessels had arrived from Wilmington since July 2 and 9 had cleared for that port, only 1 being reported unsuccessful.[5] On July 29 he reported 5 arrivals in the last two days and 5 departures for the blockade from July 23 to 28.[6] The latter part of November, 1864, Allen wrote that 6 vessels cleared for Wilmington from November 16 to 26 and that 2 arrived from Wilmington from November 20 to 23.[7]

The Confederate official angrily insisted upon the inefficiency of the blockade after 1862. On August 19, 1863, Thomas L. Bayne, in charge of government steamers, sent to Benjamin Collector Colcock's report of blockade-running at Charleston from November 1, 1862, to May 31, 1863. The report showed that 56 vessels had cleared from Charleston through the blockade in that length of time, representing about 112 violations of the blockade at that port in seven months.[8] A few days later Bayne reported that the 3 or 4 vessels owned by the Ordnance Department had made 44 voyages through the blockade with cotton and munitions from January to August 13, 1863, without a single capture.[9] Benjamin's description

---

[1] *Ibid.*, No. 37, Nov. 1, 1864.   [2] *Ibid.*, *passim.*

[3] *Ibid.*, Bermuda, Vol. 6, Allen to Seward, No. 129, July 13, 1864.

[4] *Ibid.*   [6] *Ibid.*, No. 131, July 29, 1864.

[5] *Ibid.*, No. 127, July 13, 1864.   [7] *Ibid.*, Vol. 7, No. 147, Nov. 1864.

[8] *O.R.N.*, Ser. 2, Vol. III, p. 874, Bayne to Benjamin, Aug. 19, 1863.

[9] *Ibid.*, p. 882.

of the blockade at Wilmington and Charleston in 1863 is a strong indictment of the Federal blockade. On September 2, 1863, he stated that from January through May, 1863, at least $9,000,000 in merchandise, supplies, and cotton had passed through the blockade at Charleston. "That is to say, a blockaded port is conducting an annual foreign trade of $21,000,000." The total commerce of South Carolina in 1858 was only $18,096,000, said Benjamin, "so that the annual commerce of the single port of Charleston during a blockade pronounced effective by neutral governments exceeds by more than two and a half million of dollars the total foreign commerce of the state of South Carolina while a member of the late Federal Union in 1858." As for Wilmington, the foreign commerce at the time was four times that of the whole state of North Carolina in 1858, and this business, said Benjamin, "is done by ocean steamers running almost with the regularity of packets." Russell's unfair comment that this traffic was in vessels which were "small, low steamers or coasting craft creeping along the shore" was completely refuted by the records of the ports, continued Benjamin. In the seven months from November 1, 1862, to May 31, 1863, of the 56 vessels which cleared from Charleston for foreign ports, "35 were ocean steamers, of which 34 were over 300 tons, 31 over 400 tons, 24 over 500 tons, 17 over 600 tons, 13 over 700 tons, and 8 over 800 tons."[1] A comparison of the tonnage of these ships with that of regular ocean-going merchant vessels will show that these blockade-runners which came into Wilmington and Charleston were not, in the eyes of seafarers of 1863, "small." Most of them were shallow, built especially for the blockade, to enable them to hug the coast so closely that they would be out of range of the heavier draught war vessels on the blockade, but their capacity was exceedingly large in proportion to their draught.

The Confederate agents at Nassau and Bermuda, through a "correspondent" of the *Index*, kept Henry Hotze and the other Confederate agents well posted on blockade statistics for the Atlantic Coast, and Hotze published these statistics in the *Index*, partly to

---

[1] Pickett Papers, Benjamin to Slidell, No. 23, Sept. 2, 1863; *O.R.N.*, Ser. 2, Vol. III, pp. 882–89.

influence public opinion against the blockade and partly to encourage blockade-running. His reports, though used as propaganda, were accurate. His "correspondent" was furnished the information by Walker of Nassau and Waller of Bermuda and Helm of Havana—all Confederate agents high up in the confidence of their own government. In fact, the "correspondent," as the records show, was often these agents themselves. They got their information directly from the officers of the blockade-runners and from the port records of the island (the records always showing where a vessel cleared from and sometimes where the vessel was going, though most vessels were cleared for St. John or Halifax and failed to get any farther than Wilmington or Charleston). These records are the most complete ones of certain periods, the British and American consuls frequently being unable to obtain the information from the blockade-runners because of the necessity of secrecy at the moment. While the *Index* had been carrying weekly or monthly reports on blockade-running, and had been a powerful influence in building up the blockade-running trade in 1862 and 1863, the most sweeping and startling reports were made in the spring and summer of 1864. On May 5 of this year the "correspondent" of the *Index* at Nassau gave a complete list of all the "legal" vessels which had been using Nassau as a blockade-running base from November, 1861, to March 10, 1864, which, as one sees, does not cover the period from May to November, 1861— the greater part of 1861. The period covers about two years and three months. There had been 84 regular blockade-runners operating from Nassau. These 84 vessels made 425 attempts to run the blockade from Nassau—not counting those made from Bermuda or Cuba by the same vessels—and 363 had been successful. In short, only 1 out of 6 vessels from Nassau had failed to run the blockade.[1] This average of failure is brought much lower when the entire record of these 84 steamers is taken into consideration (i.e., the runs from Bermuda or Cuba into the Confederacy). The *Index* estimated that during the period from November, 1861, to March, 1864, only 1 out of every 8 was captured or destroyed.[2] Many of these runners es-

[1] *Index*, May 5, 1864.   [2] *Ibid.*

pecially fitted for the business could not in fact be captured until they wore themselves out.

On June 20, 1864, the *Index* published another list of all recorded voyages of blockade-runners on the east coast from January 1, 1863, to April, 1864. By compiling the record of individual vessels from the two lists one is startled by the career of many of these ships. Selecting those which ran through the blockade from November 1, 1861, to April, 1864, more than 8 times there are the "Antonica" with 28 recorded runs through the blockade; the "Alice," 18; the "Advance," 18; the "Banshee, No. 1," 16; the "Beauregard," 14; "Cecile," 16; "Don," 10; "Eugenie," 9; "Flora," 13; "Fannie," 18; "Robert E. Lee," 21; "Kate," 44;[1] "Margaret and Jessie," 18; "Pet," 18; "Syren," 13; "Hansa," 18; "Lucy," 10; "Mary Anne," 9; "Herald," 17; "Cornubia," 18; and many of these vessels had not finished their careers and others were destined to appear later and chalk up even higher records. For instance, the "Hattie," which does not appear on this list, made, perhaps, the best record of them all, going through the blockade 60 times, mostly in broad daylight.[2]

In the list presented by the *Index* on June 30, 1864, covering the period from January 1, 1863, to April 15, 1864, there were 590 attempted trips through the blockade to and from Wilmington and Charleston alone and 498 were successful. In other words, for the period from the beginning of 1863 to the spring of 1864, when the blockade was supposed to be more stringent than for the period November, 1861, to March, 1864, only 1 out of 6 vessels failed to run the blockade successfully. It may be, said the *Index*, "in Earl Russell's opinion an efficient blockade which lets five vessels go through and apprehends or destroys the sixth, but it hardly comes up to the requisitions of international law."[3] The *Index* continued to report the blockade statistics in a similar way until the fall of Wilmington and the capture of Charleston. On February 9, 1865, it published a list of vessels which even at that eleventh hour showed the utter

---

[1] See Willis Collection, Washington, Manuscripts Division, Library of Congress, for "Kate."

[2] See Bradlee, *Blockade Running, etc., passim.*

[3] *Index*, June 30, 1864.

impossibility of the blockading squadron to prevent the traffic; out of 24 recent trips through the blockade to and from Wilmington and Charleston only 1 loss occurred.[1]

President Davis in his message to Congress, December 20, 1864, announced that from November 1 to December 6, 1864, 43 vessels ran into Charleston and Wilmington, showing little check on the business even at the time when these two ports were under heavy siege, ending in the capture of Wilmington soon afterward.[2] Davis said that from July 1, 1864, to December 20, 1864, the Confederate government had shipped (mostly from Charleston and Wilmington) 11,796 bales of cotton and only 1,272 bales, or less than 11 per cent, had been lost.[3]

These reports have to do chiefly with Wilmington and Charleston, but the evidence is convincing that the east coast of Florida was as unrestricted in the traffic as that of North and South Carolina. The records show that about one-seventh of all blockade-runners were captured off the coast of Florida, the greater part of them outbound. Watson Davis[4] estimated from the report of the United States Secretary of War in 1865–66 that 160 craft were thus captured during the war, and, as the average life of a blockade-runner was three or four trips, he concludes that there were several hundred violations of the blockade in Florida. Dayton reported to Seward as late as January 21, 1864, that there were great portions of the Florida coast entirely unguarded—though this seems to have referred more to the west than to the east coast—and that cotton was being run through the blockade with little interference.[5]

The gulf blockade was not as efficient the first year of the war as that of the Atlantic Coast. But after the fall of New Orleans, Mobile and Galveston were the most important ports accessible to

[1] *Ibid.*, Feb. 9, 1865.

[2] *O.R.*, Ser. 4, Vol. III, pp. 948–58.   [3] *Ibid.*

[4] Watson Davis, *Civil War, etc., in Florida* (New York, 1913), pp. 201–2.

[5] U.S. Des., France, Vol. 54, Dayton to Seward, No. 403; *O.R.N.*, Ser. 1, *passim*, show considerable data on this trade; Davis cites the papers of Governor Milton as containing much evidence on the blockade-running business; Admiral Hobart-Hampden (Captain Roberts of the British navy), *op. cit.*, p. 157, describes the traffic along the Georgia and east Florida coast in small blockade-runners as very important.

fairly large steamers, and the business in steam vessels decreased until the latter part of 1864. At that time the Nassau and Bermuda runners were shifted to Havana because of the siege of Wilmington and Charleston. But the sail vessels, ships, brigs, schooners, and the famous "center boards," which had an uncanny trick of disappearing right before one's eyes in the broad-open daylight by stripping all the sails and turning to the side at right angles to the blockader, continued unabated. Unfortunately, neither the British nor the American consuls nor the Confederate officials kept a systematic record of the blockade-running on the gulf after the fall of New Orleans. However, while the statistics are more incomplete after this date than on the Atlantic, a cloud of witnesses bears testimony to the inefficiency of the blockade in that region. The British consuls in Mobile and Galveston, and the United States consuls in Havana, Matamoras, Vera Cruz, Belize, Honduras, and Tampico, and the reports of such men as Watson, the British captain of the center board runners, all bear witness to the inefficiency of the blockade of the Gulf Coast

After the fall of New Orleans, the British consul, Magee, made irregular reports of vessels running in and out of Mobile, during the remainder of 1862. There was undoubtedly a slacking-up. The steamers, as has been observed, shifted to Nassau and Bermuda from Cuba and neglected Mobile and the coast of Louisiana, while the coast of Texas continued to be the scene of regular traffic in sailboats.[1] But in 1863 the traffic out of Mobile began to show so much greater volume that the agent there began to keep a better record and to make more regular reports.[2] In the spring of 1863, acting Consul Porez and, succeeding him, Vice-Consul Cridland, rendered accounts of the blockade at Mobile which show about as much blockade-running as went through Wilmington or Charleston at the high tide of the trade. On April 20, 1863, Porez reported that from March 12 to April 20, 16 vessels had run out of Mobile with cotton and that 11 had come into Mobile. Practically the whole of this fleet

[1] See F.O. Amer., Vol. 848, May–Dec., 1862, *passim*, for Magee's reports to Russell.

[2] *Ibid.*, Vol. 908, *passim*.

had used Havana, Cuba, as a base.[1] On May 20, one month later, Porez wrote that 19 vessels had run the blockade out of Mobile since his last report, all loaded with cotton, and that 6 had run into Mobile.[2] Cridland reported that from May 20 to June 18, 8 vessels ran the blockade out of Mobile.[3] Soon after this, United States cruisers captured several of the steamers and frightened, for a while, the sailboats so that in the fall there were fewer violations at Mobile.[4]

Lynn at Galveston rendered very scattering accounts of the blockade in that section. Sometimes it was effective and at others the coast of Texas seemed unguarded.[5]

It is the American consuls, however, who give us the most definite information as to the state of the blockade in the gulf after the spring of 1862. Consul-General R. W. Shufeldt at Havana is our best source. Cuba was centrally located and the blockade-runners sooner or later rendezvoused there, whether they were operating from Mexico or Central America as bases. Shufeldt reported, in the summer of 1862, considerable blockade-running from the coast of Louisiana, Florida, and Alabama, and some from Texas.[6] But, like Magee and Cridland at Mobile, he began to note an increase in 1863.[7] On April 26, 1863, Shufeldt wrote to Seward that on that and the preceding day the "Alice," "Nita," and another steamer arrived from Mobile loaded with cotton, and that 2 steamers had just run successfully into Mobile.[8] The steamer "Alice," he said, was so successful and had run the blockade so many times that her captain now got $5,000 each trip.[9] On May 19 he reported that 8 vessels had left Havana for the blockade, principally for Mobile, from May 10 to 18, and that 2 had arrived from Mobile on May 16 and 18.[10] The

[1] *Ibid.*, Vol. 909, Porez to Russell, No. 1, April 20, 1863.

[2] *Ibid.*, No. 2, May 20, 1863.

[3] *Ibid.*, Cridland to Russell, No. 23, Aug. 5, 1863.

[4] *Ibid.*, No. 35, Dec. 31, 1863.   [5] *Ibid.*, *passim.*

[6] U.S. Consular Des., Havana, Vols. 45, 46, *passim.*

[7] *Ibid.*, Vol. 46, Jan., Feb., March, 1863.

[8] *Ibid.*, No. 34, April 26, 1863.   [9] *Ibid.*, No. 37, April 29, 1863.

[10] *Ibid.*, Shufeldt to Seward, No. 46, May 19, 1863.

business continued to grow, and Shufeldt became more and more disturbed. On July 21, he reported the arrival of a steamer a day for some time, chiefly from Mobile; and the departure of 10 or 12 steamers, including the famous "Isabel" and "Alice Vivian," on two days, July 11 and 14, to run the blockade at Mobile and St. Marks, Florida.[1] During the rest of 1863 Thomas Savage, successor to Shufeldt (now in the Navy), continued to report an unchanged situation. The bulk of blockade-running from Cuba continued to and from Mobile.[2]

Consul Chase at Tampico, Mexico, wrote that that port was a regular base for vessels carrying cotton, mostly sailing vessels, running out of the port of Galveston, Sabine Pass, Brazos—any and all Texas ports. The British cotton-buyers and the New York cotton-importers collected large cargoes of cotton in Tampico and shipped direct to Liverpool or New York.[3] The blockade-runners formed a small but steady stream at Tampico during the year 1863.[4] On December 17, 1863, Chase wrote F. W. Seward: "This traffic so successfully carried on impresses the people of this country with the belief that our navy is too impotent to enforce a blockade, and that our government has no control over any of the Southern ports, which emboldens them to give our enemies all the aid and comfort in their power. Hence the power and influence of our government and its agents are daily losing ground in this distracted part of the Mexican Republic."[5]

The consular agents at Vera Cruz reported during 1862 and 1863 a similar stream of sailing vessels from Galveston and the coast of Texas, bringing cotton and returning through the blockade with munitions.[6] Another base used to run into Texas was Belize, British Honduras. This port had never been very important and there had not been a consul there from the United States from 1853 to Septem-

---

[1] Ibid., No. 67, July 21, 1863.

[2] Ibid., No. 80, Sept. 10, 1863; No. 109, Dec. 1, 1863.

[3] Ibid., Tampico, Vol. 6, Chase to F. W. Seward, passim.

[4] Ibid., Vols. 6, 7, passim, e.g., Vol. 7, No. 37, Nov. 24, 1863; No. 40, Dec. 17, 1863.

[5] Ibid., Vol. 7, No. 40, Dec. 17, 1863.

[6] Ibid., Vera Cruz, Vols. 8, 9, passim.

ber, 1861. At the latter date Seward discovered that it was an important blockade-running base and dispatched Raymond thither, later succeeded by Leas, a very windy and verbose official. The volume of the blockade business may be surmised by the fact that several large volumes of correspondence grew out of it from 1861 to 1865. The traffic was largely in sailing vessels as in the case of Vera Cruz and Tampico, and the cargo was composed of cotton from Texas and munitions and supplies for that state.[1]

During the first two years of the war even the ports of far-off Brazil were used as occasional depots for arms to be shipped through the blockade to the coast of Texas.[2]

During the first seven months of 1864 the trade in the gulf region ran along as in 1863. Savage at Havana reported the continuous arrival of steamers from Mobile loaded with cotton and the arrival and departure of numerous sailing vessels for the coast of Florida—especially St. Marks.[3] Lane at Vera Cruz,[4] Chase at Tampico,[5] and Leas at Belize[6] reported the steady line of schooners and sail vessels coming from and going to the blockaded coast of Texas—Galveston, Sabine Pass, Brazos, etc.

But in the latter part of the summer of 1864 the situation began to change. Mobile began to approach the final stages of the siege before its capture, and business which had been carried on from Havana was shifted to Galveston. It had been doubted whether steamers could make a profit in the long run to Galveston because of the necessity of carrying so much coal. But as the Mobile-Havana steamers would try anything, the "Denbigh," "Francis Marion," and "Mail" or "Susana," along with numerous schooners, set out for Galveston about the last of August and the first of September.[7] On September 9, Savage wrote that a swarm of steamers were

[1] *Ibid.*, Belize, Vols. 1–3 (1861–65), *passim.*

[2] See, e.g., reports of Consul Dudley and Wilding at Liverpool on the blockade business, *ibid.*, Liverpool, Vols. 19, 20, 1861–62, *passim.*

[3] *Ibid.*, Havana, Vol. 46, *passim.*   [5] *Ibid.*, Tampico, Vol. 7, *passim.*

[4] *Ibid.*, Vera Cruz, Vol. 9, *passim.*   [6] *Ibid.*, Belize, Vol. 4, *passim.*

[7] See *ibid.*, Havana, Vol. 47, Savage to Seward, No. 195, Aug. 18, 1864, and *ibid.*, No. 202, Sept. 7, 1864.

getting loaded at Havana for the blockade at Galveston.[1] On September 17 he could report that the "Denbigh" and "Mail" had run the blockade at Galveston with supplies and had already returned with cargoes of cotton. These steamers brought back the news that 14 sailing vessels at Galveston and 10 at Brazos River were waiting for favorable weather to run out to sea with cotton. So 6 steamers began loading at Havana for the coast of Texas as a result of the success of the "Denbigh" and "Mail."[2] The stream of traffic swelled in volume rapidly during the fall, when it was found profitable. Moreover, swarms of vessels were now also running out of Galveston, Brazos River, and Matagorda into Tampico and Vera Cruz.[3]

On December 2, 1864, Savage noted that the Atlantic fleet of fast iron steamers was shifting from Nassau,[4] and Chase at Tampico[5] in late December observed for the first time the appearance of fast light steamers in the business at the port. And soon the Consul at Vera Cruz reported the presence of steam vessels.[6] By January, 1865, the gulf was swarming. Watson, the famous blockade-runner, who changed from the center board to a steamer at this time, remarked that at Havana "the harbor was crowded with steamers which had been bought on account of their speed or had been especially built for this traffic." The "Denbigh," which had carried thousands of bales of cotton out of Mobile, was now plying its way to and fro between Galveston and Havana as if there had been no blockade. Watson said that she ran to and from Galveston with such uninterrupted regularity that she was called "The Packet."[7] Watson said further that he believed this traffic in the gulf the latter part of 1864 and in the spring of 1865 far exceeded the traffic on the east coast at its palmiest time.[8] The Consul-General at Havana in 1865 like-

[1] Ibid., No. 203, Sept. 9, 1864.

[2] Ibid., No. 205, Sept. 17, 1864.

[3] Ibid., No. 217, Oct. 20, 1864; ibid., Tampico, Vol. 7, Chase to F. W. Seward, Oct. 27, 1864 (unofficial); ibid., Vera Cruz, Vol. 9, Lane to Seward, No. 53, Dec. 31, 1864.

[4] Ibid., Havana, Vol. 47, No. 226, Dec. 2, 1864.

[5] Ibid., Tampico, Vol. 7, Dec. 15, 1864.

[6] Ibid., Vera Cruz, Vol. 9, No. 55, Jan. 23, 1865.

[7] Watson, pp. 286–87.   [8] Ibid., pp. 302–4.

wise reported a stream of these fast steamers going and coming from Galveston.[1]

On March 16 Consul-General W. T. Minor observed 16 blockade-runners in Havana loaded for the coast.[2] The consuls at Vera Cruz and Tampico described a situation there similar to that at Havana. Chase wrote F. W. Seward on January 27, 1865, that Tampico was "becoming the second Nassau."[3] Belize and other Caribbean ports saw a similar resuscitation in the fall of 1864 and winter of 1865.[4] Hutchinson,[5] who was on the United States cruiser "Lackawanna" off Galveston, said that information was given the captain of that ship that as late as February, 1865, there were 19 steamers running the blockade at Galveston with absolute regularity.

So all evidence in the way of testimony indicates that the blockade was no more effective in the gulf than on the Atlantic. Only the capture of a seaport as in the case of Wilmington, Mobile, Charleston, or New Orleans could seriously cripple the commerce; and, with the exception of New Orleans, the main ports were not captured until the war was almost at an end.

The blockade during the first year of the war was almost non-existent, and from that time on it was never able to stop more than one vessel out of four on the Atlantic Coast, even toward the last, and certainly no more than that on the Gulf Coast. The fact that no more vessels went through the so-called blockade the first year is easily explained. The low price of cotton, on the one hand, and the cotton embargo, on the other, prevented the average merchants and shipowners from having any motive for taking the slight risk, the extent of which was not known at the time. Soley[6] asserted that the

[1] U.S. Consular Des., Havana, Vol. 47, No. 20, Jan. 7; No. 21, Jan. 9; No. 31, Jan. 10; No. 37, Feb. 3; No. 41, Feb. 11; No. 47, Feb. 24, 1865, for example.

[2] *Ibid.*, No. 58, March 16, 1865.

[3] *Ibid.*, Tampico, Vol. 8, No. 6, and *passim* for conditions at Tampico and *ibid.*, Vera Cruz, Vol. 9, *passim*, for Vera Cruz.

[4] *Ibid.*, Belize, Vol. 3, *passim*.

[5] William F. Hutchison, "Life on the Texan Blockade," *Soldiers and Sailors Historical Society: Personal Narratives*, Ser. 3, No. 1 (Providence, 1883), p. 35.

[6] Soley, p. 42.

mere announcement of the blockade by Lincoln had the effect of paralyzing all legitimate trade, even when there were only three vessels to cover the thirty-five hundred miles of blockaded coast. Later, however, the price of cotton and the profits of the trade emboldened the merchants to take whatever risk was involved.

How inefficient, then, was the blockade? An idea of this may be obtained if we could arrive at a conception of the volume of the trade which went through the blockaded ports and coasts. The records of the ports were kept by the Confederate government fairly well for the first eight or ten months of the war; but after that the Richmond government does not seem to have kept books except on the eastern ports of Wilmington and Charleston, and even there the records were not apparently assembled at Richmond, except for certain periods. However, as we have already seen, these records were assembled by the Confederate agents in England, from the reports from Nassau, Bermuda, and Cuba, and from the ports of Charleston and Wilmington. We have noted also that the United States consuls and British consuls kept irregular records of the east coast throughout the war. For the gulf, after the first year, there was no assembled Confederate record—in fact, the port records were probably destroyed, to a large extent—nor did the British or the American consuls, as we have already observed, keep books regularly. So any attempt at measuring the blockade either by the number of violations or by the quantity of goods shipped in and out will be limited by incomplete or fragmentary statistical data for the gulf.

So far as the export of cotton and the import of supplies goes, Matamoras is another factor that is indeterminate. This port was just across the Rio Grande in Mexico and could not be legally blockaded. Hence the supplies which came and went here would not technically fall within the blockade-running business. Actually, however, Matamoras was blockaded. An American fleet watched just outside the bar and many ships were seized (most of them were ultimately freed by the United States Supreme Court, but not until the war was about over), and the greater part of the other ships were subjected to the rigors of an ordinary blockade. Ships were seized going to Matamoras on grounds of ultimate destination of contraband. This covered every ship entering that harbor after 1861. Ships were seized coming from there on the grounds that they were carrying Confederate cotton. Both these charges were difficult to sustain, but that was really a small matter. The main point was to find a basis upon which to seize the ships and create the effect of a blockade. If the court released the captured ship the Federal government appealed the case to keep the question pending so as to continue seizures until the war was over. Thus, while Matamoras was practically blockaded, we cannot consider the trade which went through it as determining the inefficiency of the blockade.

With this exposition of the difficulties let us summarize: The two ports of Charleston and Wilmington, as well as can be determined from available data, all fragmentary, have on record about 1,400 violations;[1] Savannah, about 100; Georgetown, South Carolina, about 100; Fernandina, Florida, about 25; and Beaufort, together with the smaller ports soon captured about 20—a total of over 1,600 vessels recorded as running the blockade on the east coast.[2] This does not include the small sailing craft which came and went almost without molestation and without entering or clearing ports legally. This latter type of vessel, as we have seen, is mentioned frequently both by the American consuls in Bermuda and Nassau and by the blockade-runners like Hobart-Hampden and Taylor. We shall reckon these up in our total on the basis of the percentage of captures made by the United States. The records of the gulf are much more fragmentary, but there are for the first year over 300 for New Orleans. This does not take into consideration the blockade-running into the bayous and inlets on the Louisiana coast. This

[1] Since *King Cotton Diplomacy* was first published in 1931, Marcus W. Price of the National Archives has done a massive piece of work on the blockade, which has been published in several issues of the *American Neptune*, VIII (1948), 196–241; XI (1951), 262–90; XII (1952), 229–38; XV (1955), 97–131. For the Carolina ports he has been able to establish definitely 1,735 successful runs. "Ships That Tested the Blockade of the Carolina Ports, 1861–1865," *American Neptune*, VIII, 196–237.

[2] For Georgia and the east coast of Florida, 1,191 successful runs are on record. "Ships That Tested the Blockade of the Georgia and East Florida Ports, 1861–1865," *American Neptune*, XV, 97–131. The total for the east coast, according to these figures, is 2,926 successful runs.

traffic had no bookkeeper, though its existence was a matter of notoriety among the United States and British consuls. There are on record among these fragmentary statistics 208 violations at Mobile, about 100 at Galveston, and a few score for the various smaller places among the gulf such as Pensacola, St. Marks, Brazos, etc. The gulf ports, as we have observed, were the most important ports in 1861 until the capture of New Orleans, and they were the most important ports in the fall of 1864 and spring of 1865 after the fall of Wilmington and the capture of Charleston—that is, for the first year and the last six months of the war. For half of 1862, all of 1863, and half of 1864 the blockade-running business in the gulf used fewer steamers than on the east coast but a larger number of sailing vessels and other craft.[1]

The records, other than the statistical, likewise point to the conclusion that the blockade business on the gulf was for the entire war very little less than on the east coast. Certainly it was less effective, and if the business was not as good, it was because of the difficulty of obtaining cotton at the ports of small harbors—there being so few railroads in this region as compared to the east coast. Taylor, in his narrative of blockade-running, and Watson, in his *Adventures*, etc., constantly attribute the inability of blockade-runners to procure cotton to the lack of transportation facilities to the ports.

The total for the Atlantic and gulf ports based on the incomplete records is about 2,400 violations.[2] But the sum total of all violations, including those phantom craft coming and going in the darkness, leaving few tracks, was vastly greater than 2,400. A fairly satisfactory calculation can be made upon the basis of the total number of captures and wrecks made by the blockading squadron during the war. Welles had a record in December, 1865, of 1,022 vessels captured or destroyed,[3] 295 of which were steamers, 683 schooners, and 44 ships, barks, and brigs. But several hundred more of these ill-fated blockade-runners were finally entered upon the court records. In 1912 a list of these vessels was compiled by the

[1] Compare the figures of M. W. Price in *American Neptune*.

[2] The over-all total established by Price is 5,389 successful runs. *Ibid.*

[3] See Secretary of the Navy Welles's report for this date.

United States government, amounting, all told, to between 1,400 and 1,500.[1] With such vessels as the "Robert E. Lee," "Ruby," "Kate," "Herald," "Pet," and others successfully running the blockade 20 to 60 times apiece, we conclude that 1,500 captures or wrecks indicate that there must have been several times this many successful voyages. In presenting the opinions of the several witnesses of the blockade business we have noted estimates made of the average number of trips. In 1862, for instance, the average number of trips was about 7—that is, the capture of about 1 out of 8. For 1863 the average number of successful trips was about 5. It will be recalled that United States Consul Hawley in Nassau estimated that every vessel in the spring of 1863 averaged nearly 5 successful trips before capture. The records for the greater part of 1861[2] show that only 1 out of about 14 vessels was captured. Soley[3] says that "until the end of 1864 . . . . the captures were not numerous enough to take up more than a slight margin of the enormous profit" of the blockade business. He estimates that in the spring of 1864 the blockade-running on the east coast was successful 2 out of 3 times, that is, 1 out of 3 vessels was captured.

It seems from all the evidence that the captures ran about thus: 1861, not more than 1 in 10; 1862, not more than 1 in 8; 1863, not more than 1 in 4; 1864, not more than 1 in 3; 1865, after most of the ports were captured and the fleet concentrated about the gulf, 1 in 2. This is an average for the war of about 1 capture in 6.[4] If, then, 1,500 vessels were finally destroyed or captured after averaging 5 voyages, there were 7,500 violations of the blockade.

But this does not take into consideration the large numbers of steamers and sail vessels which had been running for some time when

[1] *Compilation of Laws and Decisions of the Courts Relating to the War Claims* (Washington), No. 1112, pp. 195–235.

[2] See U.S. Consular Des., Havana, Vol. 47, Shufeldt to Seward, No. 39, March 22, 1862; Pickett Papers, Helm to Hunter, No. 9, Jan. 7, 1862.

[3] Soley, pp. 165–66.

[4] The over-all percentage of successful runs for the entire southern coast during the period 1861–65, according to Price's figures, is 86 per cent. When the estimate, 1 in 6, given here is converted into percentage the result is only 3 per cent less than the above average, which was based on tabulations from the sources.

the war ended without their capture. There were 35 steamers in Nassau and about 25 in Havana, besides those in the other bases when the war closed,[1] and these were among the worst offenders. Some of these runners had chalked up over 20 trips. Many other vessels had gone to Halifax or Liverpool after the capture of Mobile, Wilmington, and the other good ports, so that there were probably not less than 150 blockade-runners still afloat at the end of the war. Adding these to the 1,500 captured blockade-runners, we have 1,650, which, if they averaged 5 successful trips through the blockade, would make 8,250 violations of what was deemed then and has been so considered by historians an effective blockade. This, of course, is only an estimate; yet, when we consider the uniform testimony from all sources that the blockade was not effective, and the fragmentary record of about 2,400 violations, it is a very conservative one.[2]

Another indication as to the efficiency of the blockade is the amount of export and import. Here again we are met with incomplete records. But there are certain important items which can be measured with considerable accuracy and these serve as an index to the whole. The first item is cotton. We know that little cotton was shipped out of the Confederacy before the early spring of 1862 during the first ten months of the war. We know that this was not because of the blockade which was universally admitted to be almost

---

[1] See U.S. Consular Des., Havana, Vol. 47 (March); also the Willis Collection.

[2] This estimate of 8,250 violations of the blockade is more firmly established by Price's work. His meticulous research and tabulations show 5,389 successful runs. Compared with the 2,400 which were determined from the fragmentary statistics available to the author of *King Cotton Diplomacy*, Price's later figures serve better to sustain this early estimate. Although much new material has been brought to light, Price makes the statement that this over-all total by no means represents all the business done during the existence of the blockade. He concludes that there are many missing returns and also that the decision of Secretary of the Treasury Memminger to throw open the whole southern coast to foreign vessels engaged in blockade-running added to the incompleteness of the records. The masters who entered ports where there were no customhouses seldom bothered to report their cargoes. There is much evidence that light-draught vessels engaged in runs between Cuba and the Bahamas and the Florida coast. Merchandise was taken in wagons across the country and they were neither entered nor cleared from any port.

nonexistent during that period, but that it was because of the embargo. Let us see, then, how much cotton was sent through the blockade after the embargo was lifted. Historians have usually agreed that about 550,000 bales went to England and the Continent during the years 1862, 1863, 1864. Hammond in his *Cotton Industry*[1] gives a table for these years: 72,000 for England and 60,000 for the Continent in 1862; 132,000 for England and 30,000 for the Continent in 1863; 198,000 for England and 43,000 for the Continent in 1864. Rhodes[2] accepts these figures and the stamp of authority has perpetuated them. These figures, however, ignore 1861 without explaining the absence of cotton export and do not take into consideration 1865. John Watts in his book on the cotton famine wrote: "The Federals had declared a blockade of the Southern Ports, and, although as yet it was pretty much a 'paper blockade,' yet the newly established Confederate government was doing its best to render it effective" by an embargo on cotton.[3]

But the Board of Trade reports published in the *London Economist* show that 38,000 bales of blockade cotton arrived in England alone the first two months of 1865 and about 10,000 went to the Continent.[4] And blockade cotton which had been deposited in the West Indies and Mexico continued to arrive in England and on the Continent for several more months after the close of the war. This amount can be fairly calculated as the Board of Trade reports show the amount of blockade cotton shipped to England from the several blockade bases in the gulf and the West Indies in 1865 to have been about 160,000 bales and to the Continent about 50,000.[5] This would make about 800,000 bales, when added to Rhodes and Hammond's figures, which ran the blockade to Europe after the first year of the war.

However, the Board of Trade reports published in the *London Economist* during the war indicate more than the amount of cotton

[1] Hammond, *Cotton Industry*, p. 261.

[2] Rhodes, V, 409–10.

[3] Watts, p. 113.

[4] *London Economist*, Suppl., March 11, 1865.

[5] Cf. *De Bow's Review*, II (July, 1866), 81–82.

agreed upon by Rhodes and Hammond for 1862, 1863, 1864. For instance, in 1863 England alone imported 1,005,472 hundred-weights, or 251,368 bales, through the blockade (400 lb. each, the standard weight) as against the usually accepted 132,000 bales.[1] The imports from Bermuda, Nassau, Cuba, Belize, and Mexico were all blockade cotton.[2] The Board of Trade reports and the yearly commercial review of the *Economist* show an increase of the imports from Bermuda, Nassau, Cuba, Belize, and Mexico blockade-running bases in 1864[3] to be about 270,000 bales. This does not include the cotton shipped to the Continent. It will be seen thus that there were over 100,000 more bales shipped in 1863 than has been usually believed, and about 70,000 more in 1864. If the interpretation of the *Economist* can be relied upon completely, this would make the exports to Europe about 1,000,000 bales in the last three years of the war—1862, 1863, 1864.

Let us now turn to the cotton which ran the blockade to American ports. Strange to say this traffic has been greatly overlooked.[4] The reports of the American consuls at Belize,[5] Vera Cruz,[6] Tampico,[7] Matamoras,[8] and more especially the reports of the consuls at Nassau[9] and Bermuda[10] and the consuls-general at Havana, Cuba,[11] are filled with complaints and approvals of this trade. One gets the

[1] The *Economist*, Feb. 27, 1864, gives imports from the different countries.

[2] See *ibid.*, May 21, 1864, which says that most of the cotton in the Board of Trade reports listed as from "Other countries" is blockade cotton which came by way of the several blockade-running bases in the West Indies and gulf region. This of course is a well-known fact.

[3] See *ibid.*, March 4, 1865, and *De Bow's Review*, II (July, 1866), 81–82.

[4] Much has been written about the overland trade between the United States and the Confederacy. See Rhodes, V, 411 ff.; Roberts, "The Federal Government and Confederate Cotton," *American Historical Review*, Jan., 1927.

[5] See U.S. Consular Des., Belize, Vols. 1, 2, 3 (1861–65), *passim*.

[6] *Ibid.*, Vera Cruz, Vols. 8, 9 (1861–65), *passim*.

[7] *Ibid.*, Tampico, Vols. 6, 7, 8 (1861–65), *passim*.

[8] *Ibid.*, Matamoras, Vols. 7, 8 (1863–65), *passim*.

[9] *Ibid.*, Nassau, Vols. 11, 12, 13 (1861–65), *passim*.

[10] *Ibid.*, Bermuda, Vols. 5, 6, 7 (1861–65), *passim*.

[11] *Ibid.*, Havana, Vols. 45, 46, 47 (1862–65), *passim*.

impression that the gulf blockade bases, at least, were furnishing
more cotton to New York than to England or Europe. Indeed, the
Confederate agents at Nassau, Bermuda, and Havana who kept
the *Index* supplied with blockade statistics were of the opinion in
1864 that as much blockade cotton was reaching Philadelphia, New
York, and Boston as went to Europe.[1] We can arrive at a fairly good
estimate of this blockade business by a study of the imports into
New York, which was the chief importing city during the war.
Eleven thousand bales were imported into New York from April 1 to
August 31, 1861;[2] from September 1, 1861, to August 31, 1862,
116,425 bales;[3] from September 1, 1862, to August 31, 1863, 203,-
000 bales;[4] from September 1, 1863, to August 31, 1864, 284,445
bales;[5] and from September, 1864, to April 22, 1865, 193,281 bales.[6]
Thus 808,151 bales were imported into New York during the war.
About 100,000 bales were imported into Boston. The United States
imported 52,000, 37,000, and 41,000 bales of this cotton from England in 1862, 1863, 1864, respectively,[7] and about 20,000 from
January to May, 1865—making a total of about 160,000 bales imported from England. During the war 305,672 bales of cotton were
shipped from New Orleans to New York, Boston, and Philadelphia
—in part before the capture of that port.[8] Probably 50,000 bales
came from the captured sea islands and Savannah after its fall.
This is a total of about 450,000 out of the 900,000 bales imported
into the United States, which leaves about 450,000 bales from other
sources than Europe or the captured ports of New Orleans or the
sea islands. Some of this cotton came from the British West Indies
and Brazil where cotton was cultivated, but the port records show
a very small quantity from these sources. Practically the entire
450,000 bales of cotton came from the blockaded South by way of

[1] *Index*, March 10, 1864, p. 151.

[2] *Economist*, May 18, June 15, July 13, July 20, Aug. 17, Sept. 14, 1861.

[3] *Ibid.*, Sept. 20, 1862.   [5] *Ibid.*, Sept. 24, 1864.

[4] *Ibid.*, Sept. 19, 1863.   [6] *Ibid.*, May 6, 1865.

[7] *Ibid.*, *Com. Hist. and Rev. Suppl.*, March 11, 1865.

[8] Hammond, p. 263 (table).

Nassau, Bermuda, Tampico, Vera Cruz, Matamoras, and Belize.[1] This would make well over 1,000,000—perhaps 1,250,000—bales of cotton running the blockade after the spring of 1862 if we eliminate the cotton from Matamoras which, as we have pointed out, was actually blockaded most of the time. As there were only a little over 2,000,000 bales raised in the South during 1862, 1863, 1864, about half the cotton crop was thus exported through the blockade (more than half including cotton going through Matamoras); and had an attempt been made in 1861 to export the crop consisting of over 4,000,000 bales, at least half could have been exported because of the absence of blockading vessels.

Some idea as to the effectiveness of the blockade might be obtained if we could calculate the munitions of war which came in. The record of the shipment of munitions on government account is fairly complete. The government operations in importing arms, however, was so limited by the shortage of funds that it is hardly an index, unless this fact is kept constantly in mind. The Confederate Army, contrary to tradition, was practically supplied after 1861, especially the armies of Tennessee and Virginia, by the importation of small arms from abroad, and the most up-to-date and modern rifles at that, if the report of Major Huse, the Confederate purchasing agent, and Colonel Gorgas, chief of the Ordnance Department, can be relied upon. Altogether, according to the reports of Huse and Gorgas in the *Official Records*, which have some gaps, there were about 330,000 stand of small arms, mostly Enfield rifles, with a small sprinkling of Austrian and Brunswick rifles and revolvers, imported into the east Mississippi region by the Confederate government.[2] North Carolina, South Carolina, and Georgia, and to a limited extent Alabama and Florida, imported arms on state ac-

---

[1] *Shipping and Commercial List and Price Current*, 1862–65; *Hunt's Merchant Magazine*, 1862–65, *Economist*, 1862–65, are the bases for this calculation.

[2] See *O.R.*, Ser. 4, Vol. II, p. 52, Gorgas to Seddon, Aug. 16, 1862; *ibid.*, p. 227, Gorgas to Seddon, Dec. 5, 1862; *ibid.*, Vol. I, pp. 957–59, Benjamin to Davis, Feb., 1862; *ibid.*, Vol. II, pp. 382–84; *ibid.*, Vol. II, pp. 955–58, Gorgas to Seddon, Nov. 15, 1863; *ibid.*, Vol. III, p. 733, Gorgas to Seddon, Oct. 13, 1864; *ibid.*, Vol. III, pp. 928–30, Seddon to President, Dec. 10, 1864; *ibid.*, Vol. III, pp. 986–88, Gorgas to Seddon.

count.[1] Then there were importations of arms on private contract, C.O.D., of which we have only fragmentary record in the *Official Records*. West of the Mississippi, Kirby Smith's army as well as the Texan militia was supplied from abroad to a large extent.[2] The sum total of small arms on private, state, and Confederate account for the entire South which came through the blockade was not less than 600,000 stand.

An idea as to the number of small arms as well as the volume of the munitions trade through the blockade may be approached from the angle of the prize cases and wrecks. There were 62 cargoes of arms captured or destroyed in an attempt to run the blockade during the Civil War.[3] If we assume, as in the case of the percentage of ships running the blockade, that an average of 1 in 6 was captured, we have 370 attempted deliveries of munitions and arms, over 300 of which were successful.

Lincoln, then, laid down a blockade which, for two years at least, made the old-fashioned English blockade look like a stone wall in comparison. To gain a doubtful advantage over the Confederacy, he flew in the face of all American precedents, all American permanent interests and doctrines of neutral maritime rights, vitiated the principles in the Declaration of Paris that a blockade to be binding must be effective, and thereby furnished an interpretation of the Declaration of Paris for Great Britain which was destined to release that power from the one burdensome and objectionable feature of that pact. Over a century of struggle on the part of the weaker maritime powers to force Great Britain to recognize the rights of neutrals on the high seas was rendered futile, and international law was put back where it was in the days of the orders in council and the Milan decrees. Old Abe sold America's birthright for a mess of pottage.

[1] See Owsley, *State Rights in the Confederacy*, chap. ii, *passim*.

[2] See, e.g., *O.R.*, Ser. 1, Vol. XXXIV, Part IV, p. 666, for cargo of arms of "Caroline Goodyear" and "Love Bird"; *ibid.*, Vol. XLI, Part III, pp. 962–64; *ibid.*, Ser. 4, Vol. III, pp. 569–70, and General Index of *O.R.*

[3] See *Compilation of Laws and Decisions of the Courts Relating to War Claims*, pp. 195–235.

CHAPTER VIII

TWO PRELIMINARY MOVES

LINDSAY'S INTERVIEWS WITH NAPOLEON AND MERCIER'S VISIT TO RICHMOND

No sooner had the agitation to repudiate the blockade, ceased in Parliament, and no sooner had Napoleon through Billault and Mercier quieted the rumors of French intervention against the blockade, than there began a series of related moves to bring about intervention in the form of either repudiation of the blockade, recognition, or mediation, all finally culminating in the proposal of joint mediation made by Napoleon on November 10, 1862. Of these moves the first two were almost simultaneous. The first began with an interview between Lindsay and Napoleon on April 11, the other with the mysterious visit of the French minister, Mercier, to Richmond.

Indeed, the interview with Lindsay and Mercier's visit to Richmond seem part of the same plan. This, of course, cannot be definitely established, but the probabilities are strong. Napoleon's rebuff in February, 1862, at the hands of the British government in the matter of repudiating the blockade made him cautious but he continued making plans. Billault's speech and his own upholding French neutrality and even the legality of the blockade, as also Thouvenel's cold reception of Slidell and his assurance to Seward through Mercier that France had no intention of interfering in America, were merely the end of a scene, not an act. The distress in the cotton districts, and even more the distress in Napoleon's own scheming brain over the pending Corwin treaty between Mexico and the United States, and the whole question of American interference with his prospective Mexican empire were forces which were destined to continue throughout the Civil War drama. No mere rebuff could permanently check the operation of these forces upon Napoleon's plans.

As early as March 3 or 4 Napoleon, in an informal interview with Dayton, dragged out the cotton question again. The cotton famine was getting daily more threatening, he told Dayton; he believed that France would not have a bale of cotton in two months, and that the Civil War was causing France incalculable difficulties. Dayton assured Napoleon that an early success was expected, and that the United States would unquestionably open cotton ports as soon as possible. Napoleon argued that the opening of captured Confederate ports would not secure cotton—only a suspension of the blockade would do that; but Dayton urged that, because of a strong Union sentiment in Mobile and New Orleans, cotton could soon be obtained when these cities were captured.[1] This renewed agitation was soon to be followed up. On March 18, 1862, Thouvenel wanted to know of Dayton when France would be permitted to obtain cotton, as petitions were pouring in from all sides urging that something be done. Dayton handed him a recent dispatch from Seward[2] in which the latter urged that if Europe would refrain from meddling, the war would be over shortly, and that in the meanwhile the United States would throw open all ports captured from the Confederacy to foreign trade and that cotton would soon be forthcoming.[3]

In the meanwhile, Seward, anticipating a possible renewal of threats from Europe, took advantage of the recent successes of the Federal Army to assume a high tone with Mercier and Lyons. He suggested that the quickest way to end the war and get cotton was for France and England to withdraw their recognition of southern belligerent rights. If this were done the war would end in sixty days with the restoration of the Union. Seward presented this view to Mercier[4] and to Lyons,[5] and wrote similar notes on the subject to Adams in London[6] and Dayton in Paris.[7] Seward had already writ-

[1] U.S. Des., France, Vol. 51, Dayton to Seward, No. 124, March 4, 1862.

[2] U.S. Inst., France, Vol. 16, Seward to Dayton, No. 114, Feb. 19, 1862.

[3] U.S. Des., France, Vol. 51, Dayton to Seward, No. 127, March 18, 1862.

[4] French F.O. Amer., Vol. 126, Mercier to Thouvenel, No. 88, March 3, 1862.

[5] British F.O. Amer., Vol. 826, Nos. 154, 155, March 3, 1862, cited in E. D. Adams, I, 274-75.

[6] *U.S. Documents and Messages*, Part I (1862-63), p. 41.

[7] U.S. Inst., France, Vol. 16, Seward to Dayton, No. 133, March 26, 1862.

ten something about the matter.[1] This demand that belligerent rights be withdrawn from the Confederacy, of course, was intended as a trading-point with Europe. Seward could not actually expect the withdrawal of belligerent rights. However, it was advantageous to keep alive the chief American grievance against Europe as a counterpoise to the European grievance against the United States, with reference to the blockade and cotton.

Again, on March 25, Dayton reported an interview he had just had with Napoleon on the cotton question. Napoleon was becoming more and more insistent. He feared that the war would continue indefinitely with the consequent ruin of French industry. He feared that the South would burn all its cotton—showing the effects of the southern efforts to force intervention by threatening to burn all cotton—and, despite Dayton's assurance that the ports would be thrown open to foreign trade as soon as captured, Napoleon was gloomy over the prospects of getting cotton.[2] Soon after this, in an interview with Dayton in which the latter had presented Seward's suggestion that belligerent rights be withdrawn from the South, Thouvenel became very urgent about the cotton question. Dayton had reassured that gentleman that the captured southern ports would be opened and that cotton would be forthcoming. Thouvenel was impatient. Despite his sympathies with the North, he was distressed by the industrial situation in France and its immediate effect upon the government of Napoleon, and more especially was he distressed by the insistence of his Emperor, and by the cooking of subterranean schemes whose odor he could sniff even though he was not always privy to the mixing of the mysterious broth. To Dayton's promise that the ports would be opened and cotton forthcoming Thouvenel reacted impatiently. "He replied," wrote Dayton to Seward on April 22,[3] "that he had just returned from a visit to certain manufacturing districts of France and he had actually to go through them 'incognito' " to prevent being harried to death, "that distress was great

---

[1] See French F.O. Amer., Vol. 126, Mercier to Thouvenel, No. 88, March 3, 1862.

[2] U.S. Des., France, Vol. 51, Dayton to Seward, No. 129 ("Confidential"), March 25, 1862.

[3] *Ibid.*, No. 141, April 22, 1862.

and the demand for cotton consequently most urgent." This sounded ominous. The distress was great, but not as great as it seemed. Propaganda was on foot. Slidell wrote Benjamin apropos of just this agitation in the industrial districts, "Measures have been taken to procure petitions from the chambers of commerce of the principal cities asking intervention of the Emperor to restore commercial relations [break the blockade] with the Southern States."[1] Whether Napoleon was helping stage this agitation in order to create public opinion in favor of intervention is not clear. The probabilities are in favor of this view—though he was, as was his wont, toying with dynamite when he agitated French working people. At any rate, the Confederate lobby was doing it for him.

Perhaps the most significant thing which looms in the background of Lindsay's interview and Mercier's visit to Richmond is the effort made by Thouvenel and Mercier to broach mediation to Seward. On February 27 and March 6, 1862, Thouvenel had written Mercier dwelling upon the great distress in the French industries resulting from the blockade. He admitted that nothing could be done without the co-operation of America, but suggested that now that the United States had won several recent victories it might feel that its honor had been vindicated and would consent to discuss peace—especially since the conquest of the South was an impossibility. Finally, he gave Mercier general instructions to offer mediation or do anything that would bring about peace. These instructions are not only significant as developing a growing intention on the part of the Emperor to intervene in some form or other, but they are probably the bases upon which Mercier acted when he went to Richmond later.[2]

The latter part of March, Mercier, instructed to urge the seriousness of the French situation and to work toward mediation if possible, had an interview with the wily Seward, who was evidently on his guard. Mercier was very cautious, for, he wrote Thouvenel, the North was delivered of all fears of European intervention at the moment, owing to the recent debates in the British Parliament and

[1] Pickett Papers, No. 6, April 18, 1862; *O.R.N.*, Ser. 2, Vol. III, pp. 395–96.

[2] French F.O. Amer., Vol. 126, Thouvenel to Mercier, No. 6, Feb. 27, 1862; also *ibid.*, No. 7, March 6, 1862.

the Chambers in Paris favoring neutrality, and to the incident of the Merrimack "which seems to have been a revelation of the means of defense which it would be able to oppose on occasion to the threats of maritime powers." Mercier had planned only to touch upon the distress in France due to the blockade and wait for more favorable circumstances to push the matter of mediation. But no sooner had he come into Seward's office than the latter asked him without preliminaries whether he had received news from France. "I told him," wrote Mercier, "that your excellency had addressed a very important communication to me but that the moment had not yet come to discuss it. He let me understand then that he wanted to know what it was about and he persuaded me to put all reserve aside. I consented but in doing so observed that it was only for the purpose of making clear our situation. . . . . Scarcely had he commenced to read the despatch of your excellency when he took from his cabinet two papers which he handed me saying, 'Stop! here is my answer.' " The first of these papers, said Mercier, was Dayton's letter describing his interview with Napoleon[1] in which the latter had complained about the injury done the French industry by the blockade. The other letter was Seward's reply to this letter.[2] In other words, to the French complaints of injury at the hands of the United States because of the war and blockade, and to the mediation hint, Seward countered with the accusation that it was the recognition of the belligerency of the South and the hopes of further aid based upon this recognition that kept the war alive, and that the remedy for the troubles of the Europeans was to withdraw the recognition, which would immediately bring the war to an end and enable France to get cotton. After this interview Mercier wrote Thouvenel that there was no point to pressing the matter of mediation at this time. The sentiment in the North was still practically unanimous for the restoration of the Union, and until defeat had undermined that opinion it would be useless if not dangerous to talk mediation.[3]

This rebuff, however, did not put a check to French determination

[1] U.S. Des., France, Vol. 51, Dayton to Seward, No. 124, March 4, 1862.
[2] U.S. Inst., France, Vol. 16, No. 135, March 26, 1862.
[3] French F.O. Amer., Vol. 127, No. 95, March 31, 1862.

to intervene. It merely sealed their determination to act only in partnership with England and to leave no stone unturned to induce that country to join France. Before Thouvenel got Mercier's dispatch describing the interview, the Emperor had already held an interview with Lindsay; and before much more than two weeks had passed Mercier tried his hand at reconnoitering the Confederate diplomatic and military position by his visit to Richmond.

It will be recalled that the last move made by Slidell in the matter of intervention had been his letter of March 1 to Persigny which had in turn been passed on to the Emperor at Slidell's request. It will be remembered that soon afterward the debates in the French Chambers, especially Billault's and Napoleon's speeches in support of neutrality and of Russell's position on the blockade, had discouraged Slidell. But in spite of his momentary discouragement, Slidell firmly believed it was his letter which had set the Emperor back into motion again and induced Lindsay's interview.[1] However that may be, Lindsay, after due consultation with Mason, Spence, Gregory, and others, decided to come to Paris and seek an interview with Napoleon for the purpose of urging that despot to take the initiative in intervening in the Civil War, especially in the form of breaking the paper blockade. Lindsay, on his arrival in Paris on April 9, interviewed Lord Cowley, British minister to France, in order to procure an interview with Napoleon,[2] and Cowley obtained the interview for Lindsay through Thouvenel. In the meanwhile, Lindsay had a visit with Eugene Rouher, minister of commerce and southern sympathizer, and probably with Slidell, in which the inefficiency of the blockade was discussed. Rouher then repaired to Thouvenel and repeated the conversation, and Thouvenel, who already had through Cowley Lindsay's request for an interview with the Emperor, repeated the conversation to the Emperor along with the request for an interview. The Emperor jumped at the opportunity and immediately dispatched Mocquard, his private secretary, to invite Lindsay to the Tuileries at 1:00 P.M. the next day, April 11. Then followed a series of three meetings, April 11, 13, and 18.

[1] Pickett Papers, No. 5, April 14, 1862; O.R.N., Ser. 2, Vol. III, pp. 392–93.

[2] E. D. Adams, I, 289.

These meetings have been recounted by several parties at the time they happened. Slidell wrote a complete account as told him by Lindsay and verified by that person from his own notes and memory of all three meetings.[1] Lindsay reported to Mason, who had come to Paris with him, on the third interview, the interviews of April 11 and 13, and Mason verified Slidell's memorandum;[2] and he reported to Mason the last interview of April 18, of which Mason preserved a memorandum.[3] Then Thouvenel, at least, reported the first two meetings to Flahault in London.[4] Finally, Lindsay himself preserved a record of the meetings as well as of the meeting of 1863 and filed them in the French Foreign Office and in the Confederate state archives for future reference.[5] Lastly, Lord Cowley, to whom Lindsay reported before and after the interview, recorded parts of the interview. All these reports agree in substance and are the chief authorities for this chapter of diplomatic history. It appears in this series of sources that the British minister is put last and the American minister, Dayton, does not appear, and that the Confederate agents are privy to most of the reports—even the one made by Thouvenel to Flahault being reported to Slidell by his "friend" in the Foreign Office. This is significant. The Confederate lobby, consisting as we know of the Confederate agents and several Englishmen like Lindsay and Spence and a few Frenchmen, were much closer to Napoleon than either the British or American representatives. In fact, the American government, in the person of the stout and apoplectic William Dayton, was moving in a vacuum in France. It was only through rumor and spies that anything reached Dayton or Seward with reference to Napoleon's designs and intrigues with the Confederacy.

[1] See Pickett Papers, Slidell to Benjamin, No. 5 with inclosure of memoranda of first two meetings, April 14; *O.R.N.*, Ser. 2, Vol. III, pp. 392–95; Pickett Papers, Slidell to Benjamin, No. 6, April 18, 1862; *O.R.N.*, Ser. 2, Vol. III, pp. 395–96, for interview of April 18.

[2] See Pickett Papers, Mason to Benjamin, No. 8, April 21, 1862; *O.R.N.*, Ser. 2, Vol. III, pp. 397–99.

[3] *Ibid.*   [4] French F.O. Great Britain, Vol. 721, No. 35, April 14, 1862.

[5] See Pickett Papers, Mason to Benjamin, No. 5 with inclosures of Lindsay's memorandum and correspondence with the French Foreign Office with reference to the filing of the memorandum, March 16, 1864.

During Lindsay's interview with Napoleon, after a few preliminary remarks about commerce with New Orleans through a line
of steamers under French direction, the American question came up,
and Lindsay plunged directly into the main business. He urged that
the blockade was ineffectual and that its recognition was a violation
of the fourth article of the Declaration of Paris. He produced all
available data, which was rather convincing, if it were necessary to
convince Napoleon. However, the latter had in his possession the reports of his own consuls and admiralty officers, as well as the former
reports of the Confederate agents, and Lindsay's figures were not
new. The Emperor was already in full agreement with Lindsay's
opinion that the blockade was not effective. He assured Lindsay that
so fully convinced had he been from the very commencement of hostilities that the blockade was utterly ineffective and unlawful that he
had made two representations to the British government through
Flahault at London that the two governments join in repudiating the
blockade. But the British government, he said, had dealt unfairly
about the matter, not only refusing to co-operate with him, but actually allowing Seward to see a copy of the notes. Napoleon told
Lindsay, what he had often said, that he could not act without the
British government. Lindsay, unwilling to take no for an answer,
urged upon the Emperor as reason for action "the present suffering
of the laboring classes of France and England, mainly caused by the
interruption of the supply of cotton from the Confederate States,
sufferings which even now were calculated to excite very serious apprehensions in both countries, but which were from week to week
becoming more aggravated, and which in two or three months would
become absolutely intolerable. . . . . The time for action had arrived,
for if the remedy were not soon applied, very serious consequences
might be anticipated."[1] Napoleon replied with alacrity, asking what
could be done. Lindsay answered that the recognition of the Confederacy would mitigate matters considerably, and that if France and
England were not willing to begin action, "other neutral nations
might take the initiative, and that being thus taken, France and

[1] Memorandum preserved by Slidell. See Pickett Papers, Slidell to Benjamin, No.
5, April 14, 1862; *O.R.N.*, Ser. 2, Vol. III, pp. 392–95.

England might invoke the example and follow it"[1] without offense to the United States. Moreover, Lindsay suggested Spain and Belgium as two neutrals who might take the lead.

It is significant that Lindsay urged Spain upon Napoleon as a good "canvas duck" to lure the large powers into recognition of the South, for Pierre A. Rost had just gone to Madrid at Slidell's suggestion to urge Spain to act alone and independently in recognizing the South—which Spain, of course, refused to do.[2] This simultaneous move of Lindsay's and Rost's bears the earmarks of being parts of a larger plan. Napoleon, however, was conscious of Spain's timidity and weakness and told Lindsay that Spain would not be willing to assume the responsibility of such a step. As for Belgium—well, let England deal with her.

Lindsay then returned to the subject of the blockade. Though inefficient, it was doing, he urged, incalculable injury to the South through the acquiescence of the European powers, which was actually rendering France and England unneutral. Napoleon agreed that this was true. Lindsay repeated what was a stock argument with Napoleon himself, namely, that the North was not fighting to free the slaves but to subjugate the South so as to draw tribute from that section in the form of tariff and trade. Napoleon assured Lindsay that he was in full agreement with him, but what could he do? He could not with self-respect, he said, again address the English ministry through the official channels, unless he was assured beforehand that his representations would receive a favorable response. It was at this juncture that Napoleon let the cat out of the bag. Up to this point Lindsay had led the conversation. Now Napoleon took the lead. He frankly told Lindsay that he had sent for the latter so that he might use him as an unofficial mediary between himself and the British government, until the attitude of the latter government had been definitely determined, after which the regular diplomatic channels would be resorted to again. This, in connection with the several interviews Napoleon had had with Dayton recently about cotton

[1] *Ibid.*

[2] See Pickett Papers, Rost to Benjamin, No. 1, March 21, 1862; *O.R.N.*, Ser. 2, Vol. III, pp. 367–70.

and the blockade and the correspondence with Mercier over the same things, points further to a well-laid plan of campaign to bring about intervention in the Civil War. It naturally fitted the well-laid plan of campaign of the Confederate lobby, which was working to the same end—with a considerable amount of inside information as to what was going on in the French government, information furnished Slidell through his contact with Billault, Persigny, De Morny, and Mocquard, the private secretary of Napoleon, and his "friend" in the Foreign Office. Napoleon said he was ready to act at once to break the blockade if England would join him: "That he would at once dispatch a formidable fleet to the mouth of the Mississippi, if England would send an equal force. That they would demand free egress and ingress for their merchantmen with their cargoes of goods and supplies of cotton, which were essential to the world." Napoleon said he had always believed that the restoration of the Union was impossible and for that reason if no other deprecated the continuation of the struggle which could never lead to any other result than the separation of the Union. He now authorized Lindsay in his rôle of unofficial diplomat to report to Cowley his proposal to send a fleet jointly with England to break the blockade, and to ascertain whether Cowley would recommend the proposed course of action to his government. Then he asked Lindsay to report back to him on Sunday, April 13, and give him Lord Cowley's reply.[1]

Lindsay repaired to Cowley and the latter told him frankly that he did not think the British government would send a squadron to act with the French fleet in breaking the blockade. He agreed that it was probable that the North and South would never unite again, but said that it was not proved yet. As for the blockade, upon the whole it had been accepted by the British government as efficient, and the present moment was certainly an inopportune time to raise the question of the blockade. The time for that had gone, for every mail brought tidings of Union successes, and every day brought proof of the growing stringency of the blockade. Lindsay mentioned

[1] For this interview I have followed Slidell's memorandum verified by Lindsay as it contains more detail than Lindsay's own memorandum. See reference already made to the memorandum above.

the two dispatches which Napoleon had sent England and which had been turned over to Seward unanswered. Cowley did not know of any such offer made to England.[1]

Lindsay held his second interview with Napoleon on Sunday, April 13, as agreed. He reported his conversation with Cowley, and especially called attention to Cowley's opinion that no previous representations had been made to England as to the breaking of the blockade. Napoleon was indignant and "repeated the statement that two long despatches with his opinion had been written to M. de Flahault, which had not been attended to by Her Majesty's Government."[2] Napoleon repeated that the business must be handled by private hands and desired Lindsay to return to London and lay His Majesty's views before Palmerston and Russell and report back as soon as possible, which Lindsay promised to do.[3] In this interview of April 13 Napoleon took a step which was to be repeated a year later when he held his interview with Roebuck and Lindsay—he suggested that Lindsay lay his plans before the opposition leaders, Disraeli and Derby. This was, when repeated, destined to raise considerable outcry in England against the government of one country meddling in the domestic politics of another country.

Lindsay, of course, did not repeat this part of the conversation to Cowley, but the latter suspected it and so expressed himself to Russell.[4] Cowley, immediately after Lindsay had reported to him the second conversation with Napoleon, hastened to Thouvenel and asked him about the conversation as well as the two dispatches which Napoleon claimed had been sent. Thouvenel denied that they had been sent, and he let Cowley know that his position on intervention was the same as that of Cowley's, namely, that the time had passed to repudiate the blockade and that it would be war to recognize the South or to repudiate the blockade.[5]

Russell's response to Napoleon's indirect diplomacy was abrupt. To Lindsay's request for an interview with him for the purpose

[1] E. D. Adams, I, 292–93, Cowley's private letter to Russell, April 13, 1862, giving also a description of the interview between Napoleon and Lindsay on April 11.

[2] Private letter of Cowley to Russell, April 13, quoted in part in E. D. Adams, I, 290–92.

[3] *Ibid.*   [4] *Ibid.*   [5] *Ibid.*, pp. 293–94.

of delivering Napoleon's message Russell sarcastically replied that he thought that the best way for governments to carry on correspondence was through the regularly accredited ministers. Lindsay replied to this flippant note earnestly urging the interview; he wrote Russell that the Emperor's reasons for communicating in this indirect fashion were sound. But Russell flatly refused to receive Lindsay as the dispatch-bearer of the Emperor.[1]

In the meanwhile, Slidell, who had been privy to all this conversation, had written to Mason the glad tidings that Napoleon was and had been for a long time ready to intervene. Lindsay would give the details to Mason in person. All this was strictly confidential, warned the tight-lipped Slidell, but Mason was at liberty, of course, to tell the other members of the lobby—Gregory, Campbell, etc.—that Slidell had "positive and authentic evidence that France only waits the assent of England for recognition and other more cogent measures."[2] The next day, April 13, Slidell wrote Mason that Lindsay had just had his second interview with the Emperor, and that Lindsay had requested that Slidell write Mason to meet Lindsay at his country home—just out of London—for a consultation.[3]

After waiting in vain four days to gain an interview with Russell, Lindsay returned to Paris. He had been in full consultation with the Confederate agents and friends, and Mason, his chief counselor at the time, accompanied him back to Paris where another caucus of Confederate agents and friends was held. Mann had come down from Brussels to throw the light of his "inside" information into the council, which he cautioned to keep very secret.[4] Henry Hotze, the Confederate propaganda agent, was unquestionably there,[5] and

[1] *Ibid.*, pp. 294–95; cf. Lindsay's version written to the French Foreign Office in 1864 based upon his memoranda, copy in Pickett Papers, Mason to Benjamin, No. 5 with inclosure, March 16, 1864, and Lindsay to Drouyn de Lhuys, March 7, 1864; *O.R.N.*, Ser. 2, Vol. III, pp. 1047–55.

[2] Mason Papers, April 12, 1862.

[3] *Ibid.*

[4] Pickett Papers, Mason to Benjamin, No. 8, April 21, 1862; *O.R.N.*, Ser. 2, Vol. III, pp. 397–99, mentioned Mann's presence and his caution about giving out his information.

[5] Pickett Papers, Hotze to Secretary of State, No. 7, April 25, 1862; *O.R.N.*, Ser. 2, Vol. III, pp. 399–401.

doubtlessly Caleb Huse, munitions agent, and Bulloch, naval agent, gathered at the usual rendezvous—the Louvre Hotel—where good champagne was consumed and plans of campaign were agreed upon.[1]

Lindsay sought out the Emperor according to appointment the next day, April 18, and related to him his treatment at the hands of Russell, and how Palmerston had failed to send for him. He told the Emperor how in accordance with his permission he had, after failing to get a response from the ministry, reported the Emperor's views to Disraeli, Derby, the leader, being ill. Napoleon was very much perturbed at the repulse of his agent at the hand of the British ministry. He was irritated and exasperated. Then, for the third time within seven days he asserted that two notes had been sent England to gain her co-operation in repudiating the blockade, and he repeated again his reasons for resorting to non-diplomatic channels. He repeated that he must be assured of Britain's attitude before he could again make a proposal. Lindsay then referred to his interview with Disraeli. He told Napoleon that the former was of the opinion that there was a secret agreement between Seward and Russell about the blockade. Napoleon, always suspicious of the British government, fairly snorted at this suggestion. It must be true; it explained England's whole attitude of late toward France herself, especially England's coldness since France had supported England's stand in the Trent affair. Lindsay further told Napoleon that Disraeli and the Conservative party were in entire agreement, according to Disraeli's statement, with the Emperor's opinion as to the inefficiency of the blockade and its repudiation. Disraeli, said Lindsay, believed that a repudiation by the ministry, in accordance with Napoleon's desires, would have the unanimous support of the British public and Parliament. Lindsay urged upon Napoleon the opinion of Disraeli that if Napoleon would take the initiative in repudiating the blockade, the British ministry would be forced by public opinion to follow his lead. But Napoleon did not commit himself to separate action. The thing to do, Lindsay said, was to make a friendly appeal to the Federal government, either alone or with England, and to accompany this appeal with a proper demonstration on the southern coast. If this

[1] See Du Bellet for a description of these "caucuses at the Louvre Hotel," *passim*.

should fail to be effectual, then the next step would be to announce to the Federal government that the French government would no longer respect the blockade. Napoleon, however, thought that the capture of New Orleans—an event he did not expect—might render it inexpedient to act.[1]

In accordance with Napoleon's idea Lindsay tried once more to get in communication with Lord Palmerston. But that foxy old warrior refused to receive Lindsay just as had Russell. After Lindsay had carried on a correspondence with Palmerston which netted him nothing, he finally concluded by writing the noble lord, "I have endeavored to carry out the Emperor's wishes in as quiet a manner as possible and now that my work, so far as I could do it, is at an end, it is neither my wish nor my intention to say any thing more about it; but will you allow me in conclusion to express my regret that it was not your lordship's pleasure to see me, for I think the Emperor had very strong reasons for the course, however unusual, he thought it expedient to adopt."[2]

Undoubtedly, Lindsay and the Confederate agents had for the nonce despaired of Palmerston and Russell as possible allies of Napoleon. The attempt at inducing England to join France in intervention, especially in repudiating the blockade, had thus failed for the third time within the first year of the war. But it was to be tried thrice more within the next eighteen months—the last effort being made in October, 1863, when De Lhuys telegraphed Baron Gros to ascertain whether the rumor that England desired to intervene was true. Lindsay's farewell epistle to Palmerston was only a gesture, the dismissal, perhaps, of one expedient as a preliminary to attempting another.

Slidell was not at all depressed that England had refused co-operation. He was elated to have definite proof that Napoleon was and had been from the first ready to intervene. Following the Lindsay interview, his hopes were raised by the tone of the official press, especially the *Moniteur*, *Patrie*, *Constitutionnel*, and *Pays*, which were

---

[1] See Slidell's report of the third interview in Pickett Papers, Slidell to Benjamin, No. 6, April 18, 1862; *O.R.N.*, Ser. 2, Vol. III, pp. 395–96; cf. Mason's report of this interview in Pickett Papers, Mason to Benjamin, No. 8, April 21, 1862: *O.R.N.*, Ser. 2, Vol. III, pp. 397–99.

[2] Lindsay's memorandum in Pickett Papers.

warmly advocating the southern cause. One of these, the *Constitutionnel*, was entirely controlled by Persigny, who told Slidell that its views were those of the entire government with the exception of Thouvenel. Slidell, in fact, was so elated, despite England's coldness, that he wrote that "if England obstinately persists in her system of inaction I am not without hope that the Emperor may act alone." "The sudden order to the Mediterranean fleet to take in stores for three months and the experimental trip of the 'Couronne,' first class iron steamer, are very suggestive."[1] Hotze, in the *Index*,[2] also laid much stress upon the fitting-out of the fleet which was destined for the Mexican waters—and probably for action against the blockade.

While only an inkling of the Lindsay affair had leaked out in the newspapers,[3] the news of the second diplomatic move of Napoleon, the visit of Mercier to Richmond, arrived in Europe around the first of May and raised the hopes of the Confederates to a high pitch for a while.

Mercier's visit to Richmond has been dealt with at length by E. D. Adams, who based his account largely on the British archives. Some new light, however, has been shed upon the purpose as well as the inception of the trip by the recently opened French archives for the Civil War period.

Some time after Mercier's interview with Seward (described in his letter to Thouvenel, March 31), in which he had shown Seward instructions from Thouvenel complaining of the blockade and suggesting the possibilities of mediation, he had another conversation with the Secretary of State. McClellan was pushing on toward Richmond, Grant had just won his doubtful victory at Shiloh, Charleston and Wilmington were being attacked by the navy—in short, as Mercier had previously put it—all the forces of land and sea were in motion against the Confederacy. Seward was unusually optimistic; the Confederacy, he said, was on its last legs. But Mercier did not share that view of the situation. It did not seem to him that the South was anything like near defeat, and he so expressed himself to Seward.

[1] Mason Papers, Slidell to Mason, April 28, 1862.

[2] *Index*, May 1, 1862.   [3] *Ibid.*

"As by accident," Mercier wrote Thouvenel soon after the conversation,[1] "I told him that I regretted much not to be able to go and assure myself of the state of things in Richmond," so that he might be able to judge for himself whether Seward's opinion was correct. Thereupon Seward, much to Mercier's surprise, urged that the French minister go. " 'Have one of your battleships go and carry you to Norfolk,' " urged Seward. " 'I will give you a pass. Your visit at this moment should produce a good effect and will render us a real service.' " Mercier accepted the invitation and assured Seward that he would stress the futility of Confederate efforts and urge their return to the Union. Seward requested him to assure the southern leaders that the North harbored no feeling of revenge against them and would welcome them with open arms back to their old place in the Senate.

If Mercier were to hold this conversation with the Confederate leaders, it could be only to get their reaction, for he had held and continued to hold an unshakable belief in the ultimate success of the South. The real purpose of his visit was to obtain, as the basis of the intervention which was now on foot, a first-hand estimate of the ability and determination of the South to win her independence. This purpose was stated frankly in his report of his proposed project to Thouvenel. The visit to Richmond, he wrote, would be a good opportunity to obtain information "which would prepare the way for a recourse to our good offices, as a means of facilitating pacific arrangements of which we have felt ourselves in so great need." As far as warning the Confederates that they were defeated and must give in to a reconstruction of the Union, he told Thouvenel, it would only be so much wasted breath. But that was not his affair. Information was what he wanted.[2] Mercier, in this dispatch, expressed the hope that the proposed visit would meet with the latter's approval. His authority for undertaking the mission, he believed, rested upon the tender of good offices which had been made by the Emperor. He was referring, doubtless, to the several dispatches from Thouvenel giving him wide discretion in matters dealing with mediation and intervention.

[1] French F.O. Amer., Vol. 127, No. 96, April 13, 1862.   [2] *Ibid.*

Mercier, who had been cautioned by Thouvenel in 1861 to move always *pari passu* with Lyons in anything which concerned America, sought the British Minister and apprised him of his intention of visiting Richmond. He repeated to Lyons what he had told Seward with reference to warning the Confederate leaders that they could not expect success and that it was useless to expect any encouragement from European powers. He expressed the opinion that such a representation might induce the Confederates to agree to terms if they were discouraged by their defeats. Lyons, however, objected to Mercier's visit because he was afraid it foreshadowed a break in the *entente cordiale* between England and France in American affairs. He was suspicious—with some reason, as we shall see later—that there was on foot a move to secure special privileges for the French in the way of commercial concessions and free trade. Lyons also objected to Russian Ambassador Stoeckl's accompanying Mercier, though Stoeckl, when approached by Mercier, showed no inclination to join in the journey to the Confederate capital. Lyons, moreover, was most outspoken in his attempt to discourage the idea of a separate agreement between France and the South. He urged Mercier to disabuse the minds of the southern leaders of the idea that France might be inveigled into an exclusive alliance with the South by an offer of great commercial privileges. He told Mercier that the views of Seward concerning southern weakness—which presumably Mercier entertained as he was to act as mediator of these views—were entirely wrong. He did not believe that either North or South was ready for any concessions in order to have peace. In fact, he did not think anything could come of Mercier's mission in the way of furthering peace.[1] However, Lyons finally sanctioned the trip in order to present a solid front to Seward, who was always cunningly watching for an opportunity to drive a wedge between the two countries in order to forestall joint intervention.[2]

So with the stingy blessings of Lyons upon his head Mercier proceeded to Richmond. He arrived there April 16, 1862, and had a

---

[1] British F.O. Amer., Vol. 828, Lyons to Russell, No. 250 ("Confidential"), April 14, cited in E. D. Adams, I, 281–83; French F.O. Amer., Vol. 127, Mercier to Thouvenel, No. 96, April 13, 1862, gives an account also of Lyons' objections.

[2] *Ibid.*

conversation with Benjamin, who was an old friend. Both Mercier and Benjamin left reports of the visit and the interview. Benjamin's report was in a letter to Slidell, July 19, 1862,[1] Mercier's in a letter to Thouvenel, April 28, 1862.[2] The two accounts agree as far as they go, Benjamin's being very short and Mercier's very long. Mercier, in fact, was so impressed with what he found at Richmond that it formed the text for his dispatches for several weeks. In the interview Mercier told Benjamin that he had come to Richmond to get information. "I told him," he wrote Thouvenel, "that the purpose of my journey was only to assure myself of the true state of things and that I came to ask him to help me to attain this."[3] This was just what he wrote Thouvenel in the beginning concerning the purpose of his trip, and it was just this which had induced Seward to permit him to go, only Seward thought he would find things in a bad way. Benjamin replied to Mercier that he would be glad to aid him in finding out the true state of things as the truth seemed so little known abroad. Mercier, according to Benjamin's letter to Slidell (cited above), stated "frankly that he considered the capture of all our cities within reach of the water as a matter of certainty, that it was purely a question of weight of metal, ... that . . . . he did not deem it possible for us to save any of our cities, and he asked me to say frankly what I thought would be the course of our government in such an event." Benjamin did not write Slidell just what reply he made, but Mercier's letter to Thouvenel dwells upon his reply. Benjamin admitted, according to this letter, that it was quite possible that all the seaports and main cities would be captured, but that the enemy would find in those cities only women and children and old men, for the fighting population would retreat to the mountains and wage ceaseless warfare until the northern armies had withdrawn from the South.[4] Mercier now broached the idea of reunion, suggesting that the North would offer good terms. Benjamin then in his velvet-tongued but eloquent way assured Mercier that " 'the time for such conciliation is passed. . . . .

[1] Pickett Papers, No. 5; *O.R.N.*, Ser., 2, Vol. III, pp. 461–67.

[2] French F.O. Amer., Vol. 127, No. 97, April 28, 1862.

[3] *Ibid.;* cf. Benjamin's report.

[4] French F.O. Amer., Vol. 127, Mercier to Thouvenel, No. 97, April 28, 1862.

In reality we are two distinct people who ought to have each his own government. Our population have to-day more hatred for the Yankees than the French have ever had for the English.' " Nothing but independence, said Benjamin, would be considered.[1] Mercier conceded that independence seemed to be the only possible solution.[2] Whereupon he asked Benjamin about the thing which concerned the French greatly—the cotton supply. He had heard that the Confederate government intended burning it to prevent its falling into the hands of the enemy.

Benjamin assured him that the rumor was not exaggerated; the cotton was to be burned. Following up the King Cotton lead, Benjamin then spoke of the possibility of recognition. Mercier replied that France would regret the breaking-up of the Union; so long as it was not apparent that the South would succeed in establishing its independence France could do nothing but wait events. A premature recognition on the part of France would have another effect—that of creating difficulties with the Federal government—which ought to be avoided, for it would not raise the blockade. "In a word," continued Mercier, "we ought to hold recognition in reserve as an arm of conciliation, which would only be effective on condition that it should be applied at the proper moment." Benjamin replied: " 'I understand all that nor do we complain precisely at not having been recognized; but what astonishes us is the facility with which you have admitted the effectiveness of the blockade. When the Federal Government announced to you that it was going to blockade our coasts why did you not protest to the effect that it prescribe the points which were to be blockaded effectively? That is to say, those places where, in conformity with the Declaration of Paris, the access to the coast would be actually rendered impossible. I can indicate to you more than twenty ports for which a battle ship has never been stationed.' " Mercier was embarrassed by this question. He knew that his own government did not really consider the blockade effective, and that the reason for not so declaring was that England would not join France in such a declaration, and that without England such an act might be followed by war on the part of the

---

[1] *Ibid.*   [2] Benjamin's letter to Slidell (letter cited above).

United States. Mercier wrote Thouvenel that he was very much put to it to answer this question. "I admit, M. Le Ministre, that I found myself a little embarrassed for an answer to this argument and I ended by making the observation that this question of the blockade concerned all the maritime powers [and that] they should concert together concerning the manner in which they would be able to consider it."[1]

It will be observed that while Mercier had pointed out the possible capture of the seaports and cities of the South, he had not urged that the cause of the South was hopeless as he had promised Seward. He had not urged the return of the South to the Union as he had promised, though he had mildly alluded to it. The truth of the matter was that Benjamin's grim attitude convinced him at once that the South was not thinking of defeat and that any such language as Seward had instructed him to hold would not be listened to, or if listened to, would not be well received. Mercier was convinced after his conversation with Benjamin that the South was determined to fight on to the extermination of the entire population. After all, the main object of the visit was to find out how the South felt in the face of recent defeats. But Mercier did not stop with Benjamin. He interviewed leading Confederate officials and citizens in Richmond, including Senators Conrad of Louisiana, Wigfall of Texas, Orr of South Carolina, Clay of Alabama, Bishop Macguire (Catholic), Captain Maury, General Huger, General Lee, and McFarland, banker, of Richmond. Each of these merely strengthened the impression he had gained while conversing with Benjamin—that the South was determined to gain its independence at any price of blood and treasure.[2]

Mercier hastened back to Washington and reported to Seward on April 24. He told the latter that the South was far from defeated, and was determined to win. But Seward refused to accept his diagnosis of the situation in the Confederacy.[3] He insisted, in fact, in a conversation with Lyons following that with Mercier of April 24, that from what Mercier had described he was convinced that the Confederacy was about to make its last efforts, " 'that their last re-

---

[1] Letter to Thouvenel, April 28 (cited above).
[2] *Ibid.*   [3] *Ibid.*

sources were brought into play, that their last armies were in the field.' " He hooted at the idea of the Confederates retiring into the interior. If they were defeated in the field that would be the end of the matter, and he was convinced that they were on the point of being defeated everywhere.[1] But Mercier was not to be deflected by Seward. In his interview with Lyons on April 24, just after that with Seward, he told the British Minister that the trip to Richmond had completely convinced him that the restoration of the Union was impossible. He also told Lyons that it would be necessary sooner or later for the European powers to intervene in order to stop the war, which otherwise would drag on for years; and he thought Europe ought to be on the lookout for a favorable opportunity for this intervention. However, he was certain that the present moment was unfavorable.[2] Lyons agreed with alacrity that this was indeed the wrong time for any form of interference.

Mercier and Seward both got what they wanted out of the Richmond journey—the former his desired first-hand information as to the determination and strength of the Confederate government; the latter, just the opposite conclusion from the same facts. Mercier's report was intended to form the groundwork of further moves for intervention. Seward made immediate use of his version of Mercier's visit to convince the world, especially Europe, that the Confederacy was tottering. This he did in a published account in the *New York Times*, May 6, 1862, depicting Mercier as an agent of the United States government sent to Richmond to urge the Confederates to give up their efforts and come back into the Union. Seward, of course, in his version, made Mercier say what Seward had asked him to say rather than what Mercier had actually said—despite the fact that the latter had informed Seward that he had not seen fit to hold his original language with the Confederates, because they seemed too strong and confident. Seward was very clever in doing this, for no doubt he hoped by this account not merely to discourage the idea of intervention but to take the wind out of the Confederate sails by making them believe that Mercier was in the service of the United

[1] British F.O. Amer., Vol. 828, Lyons to Russell, No. 284 ("Confidential"), April 28, 1862, cited in E. D. Adams, I, 286–87.
[2] *Ibid.*

States. In this latter purpose he was not altogether unsuccessful. For in his account of the interview Benjamin wrote Slidell on July 19, 1862, after he had read Seward's version of the interview in the *Times:* "I am very much inclined to believe that he [Mercier] really came at Seward's request to feel the way and learn whether any possible terms would induce us to re-enter the Union."[1]

Mercier's visit to Richmond was received in Europe with much speculation. Thouvenel was alarmed. He received telegraphic dispatches from London announcing Mercier's intended visit about April 28, and was so taken back by the rumor that he told Cowley that he did not believe it was true.[2] On May 1 Thouvenel, however, received Mercier's dispatch of April 13, announcing his intended visit to Richmond, and he hastened to assure the British government both through Flahault at London and through Cowley at Paris that the trip was unauthorized and unexpected. "Nothing," he wrote Flahault,[3] "in the correspondence of M. Mercier has indicated such an intention on his part and I was so little prepared for the step which he has just taken that I at first denied the accuracy of the news." It was not until Cowley had given him the substance of Lyons' report, he continued, that he could accept the truth of Mercier's proposed visit. He earnestly hoped that England would not feel that the visit marked a break-up of the entente on the American question between that country and France. On the same day he also wrote Mercier, again expressing his fears lest England should take this visit to mean a divergence between the two countries. He told Mercier, as he had Flahault, that his first authentic news of the journey was through Cowley, that there was nothing in Mercier's previous correspondence to prepare his mind for such a step. In fact, his disapproval of Mercier's trip was thinly veiled.[4] Cowley accepted Thouvenel's innocence, but seemed to harbor a suspicion that Na-

[1] Pickett Papers, Benjamin to Slidell, No. 5, July 19, 1862; *O.R.N.*, Ser. 2, Vol. III, pp. 461–67.

[2] French F.O. England, Vol. 721, Thouvenel to Flahault, No. 42, May 1, 1862, tells about reception of rumor and then of Mercier's dispatch announcing his proposed journey to Richmond; British F.O. France, Vol. 1427, Cowley to Russell, No. 563, April 28, 1862.

[3] French F.O. England, Vol. 721, No. 42, May 1, 1862.

[4] *Ibid.*, Amer., Vol. 127, Thouvenel to Mercier, No. 12, May 1, 1862.

poleon might be at the bottom of it.[1] But Napoleon, when questioned by Thouvenel on May 2, denied any knowledge of Mercier's journey, and like Thouvenel expressed anxiety lest it cause a break between France and England.[2] Whereupon Thouvenel wrote Flahault that Napoleon like himself was ignorant of Mercier's plans and deplored his venture.[3]

Fahault laid all these explanations before Russell, assuring him that neither the foreign minister, Thouvenel, nor the Emperor had authorized Mercier's visit to Richmond; that neither had any previous knowledge of that intended visit; and that both regretted it very much. He assured Russell that the *entente cordiale* still held.[4] Russell was pleased to have these two officials thus deny all responsibility of the affair. It indicated that France was desirous, at least, of maintaining the appearance of good feeling, and that it was concerned about England's opinion. However, Russell must have harbored grave doubts as to the veracity of the Emperor's denial. He must have felt quite certain that Napoleon was straining at the leash to do something in American affairs so as to render the South independent and his Mexican venture, from which England had recently withdrawn, safe from Federal interference. He wrote Lyons, May 10, privately, that he was still puzzled and mystified after all had been done and said.[5] Indeed, the several proposals for joint intervention and especially the one just made through Lindsay indicated that the Emperor was restless and uneasy and that this "spider of the Tuileries," as Palmerston dubbed him, was spinning more webs.

Mason and Slidell, when they heard of Mercier's visit and Thouvenel's denial of any knowledge of it, jumped to the conclusion that Napoleon was behind it. Mason, who was at Lindsay's home when the news arrived, wrote Slidell that Lindsay was sure that "M. Mercier's visit . . . . was by order of the Emperor in furtherance of views

[1] British F.O. France, Vol. 1438, Cowley to Russell, No. 563.

[2] *Ibid.*, No. 574, May 2, 1862, cited in E. D. Adams, I, 288.

[3] *Ibid.*

[4] French F.O. England, Vol. 721, Flahault to Thouvenel, No. 25, May 5, 1862.

[5] Lyons Papers cited in E. D. Adams, I, 288.

known to us through him";[1] and Slidell had just written Mason that he believed Mercier had received orders directly from Napoleon, as he often carried on his affairs in this fashion—notably in Italy and the Crimea. Slidell wrote that he had just had an interview with Persigny, and that the latter had told him that recognition would come soon.[2] But Mason's confidence that Napoleon had dispatched Mercier to Richmond was soon shaken by the Seward report in the *New York Times* which represented Mercier as his envoy, and by the report from France that Napoleon had denied the whole matter and was displeased with Mercier.[3]

But Slidell had an interview with Thouvenel on May 14, in which, though it proved to his satisfaction that Thouvenel knew nothing about the visit, he found the French Foreign Minister much friendlier than usual. He was convinced that Thouvenel's attitude was a result of Mercier's visit, which had disclosed the great strength of the Confederacy. So Slidell returned to the belief that Napoleon without Thouvenel's knowledge was at the bottom of the affair. He wrote Mason about his interview, and the latter at once regained his hopes. He also returned to the opinion that Napoleon was playing the game alone and keeping Thouvenel and the British government in the dark.[4] On May 14, Mason, in a letter to Slidell, was quite optimistic again. He was once more sure that the Emperor was responsible for Mercier's visit; he had been in communication with various people with considerable knowledge of affairs, who were of the belief that Napoleon had ordered Mercier to go to Richmond, nominally in the service of Seward but actually to find out what the situation was in the Confederacy. Mason's explanation of the Emperor's mysterious secrecy was that Napoleon's recent rebuffs at the hands of Russell had forced him out of diplomatic channels again as in the case of his interview with Lindsay. He believed, therefore, that the mission from Seward was "a complete blind to the real pur-

[1] Mason Papers, May 5, 1862.

[2] *Ibid.*, May 3, 1862.

[3] *Ibid.*, Mason to Slidell, May 14, 1862.

[4] See Pickett Papers, Mason to Benjamin, No. 10, May 15, 1862; *O.R.N.*, Ser. 2, Vol. III, pp. 420–23.

pose of the Emperor.''[1] At the same time Slidell wrote Mason that
he had just held another interview in which Billault had reassured
him as on April 28, three weeks before, following the Lindsay episode, that the whole French government, with the exception of
Thouvenel, were in sympathy with the South. Once again, too,
Billault assured Slidell that the Emperor had approached England on
two occasions previous to the Lindsay interview on the matter of
joint intervention, despite the denial of the British cabinet.[2] So the
Confederate commissioners after a few weeks arrived at the final
conclusion that Napoleon was planning intervention and that Mercier's journey had been one of his first moves.

The Confederate *Index* thought "the visit of M. Mercier to Richmond is . . . . extremely significant of the determination of the
French Government to put an end to the blockade." This newspaper
did not believe the report that Mercier went to Richmond in the interest of the Federal government. That idea, said this journal, was
just some more of northern newspaper lying and Stanton's propaganda.[3] In the light of the newspaper rumor that Seward had sent
Mercier to Richmond to bid the Confederates lay down their arms,
the *Economist*[4] thought, as did the Confederate commissioners,
that this was only a nominal service of Mercier. The actual purpose
was something else. The French cotton industry was suffering more
than that of the English, and "a much smaller amount of commercial
uneasiness produces in France more political uneasiness than is understood here. The foundations of political society are very much
weaker, and every one has there the mischievous habit of expecting
the government to intervene in every calamity and to do something
in every misery." If intervention would close the Civil War and
assuage French suffering caused thereby, "sooner or later that government would intervene." But the *Economist* did not think that
Napoleon could break the blockade and end the war, and it was
of the opinion that he would not actually interfere by force, "though
we should not like to hazard a confident prediction on a matter so

---

[1] Mason Papers, Mason to Slidell, May 16, 1862.

[2] *Ibid.*, Slidell to Mason, May 16, 1862.

[3] *Index*, May 1, 1862.   [4] *Economist*, May 3, 1862.

very difficult." M. Mercier would in all probability, at least, offer mediation on this journey. The *Economist*, however, did not believe that any form of mediation would be acceptable to the North. In short, that paper, true to the opinion of leading journals, while in sympathy with the purpose of any move which would result in success to the South, believed that intervention of any form—mediation, repudiation of the blockade, or recognition—would not help the Confederacy, but would injure Europe, either by accentuating America's ill will or by actually resulting in war.

With the rumored proposed joint intervention of the Emperor, and now with the Mercier journey to Richmond not yet heard from, the *London Times* reacted similarly to the question of intervention recently raised in connection with the debates in Parliament on the blockade. It asserted that "throughout the whole of this contest there never has been a time when foreign intervention could have done aught but evil." The Federal government had feared this from the first, and it had inflamed the American mind against any hint of interference, even of a friendly kind. The *Times*, though, was not prepared to deny that Europe might not eventually interfere in the Civil War. "The day may undoubtedly come when, compelled by circumstances, we must in some shape interfere, but that time is not yet, and we should be acting a very foolish and unworthy part if we anticipate our proper opportunity or precipitate the advancing necessity."[1] This was practically the position of Russell, Palmerston, and Lyons—that now at least was not the opportune time to intervene—and that the future should take care of itself.

As for the French press, Mercier's visit was just one of the many straws which the swelling breeze fanned. The general proposition of mediation or intervention which had begun to be agitated in February reached large proportions by this time and continued until the armistice proposals in November of this year. The official papers took up the championship of mediation and the opposition press stood out against it. The position of the French press will be examined in connection with the general renewal of agitation in favor of intervention which took place the last of May and first of June.

[1] *London Times*, May 8, 1862.

CHAPTER IX

FORMAL DEMANDS FOR RECOGNITION

Mercier's visit to the Confederacy, as we have noted, set the public press and the people to agitating the question of intervention which was, even under ordinary circumstances, never entirely quiescent. It likewise set the French and Confederate diplomatic wire-pullers into motion.

Both the French and British press, which had ventured speculations as to the intent of Mercier's mysterious proceedings, soon warmed up into the most serious discussion of European intervention held during the war. The French press ranged itself for or against intervention, the semiofficial papers favoring it and the Liberal and popular organs opposing. The British journals and papers favored intervention for a while and then opposed it. In France the *Pays, Patrie, Constitutionnel,* the *Moniteur,* the *Revue contemporaine,* the *Union,* and the lesser satellites developed the Imperialist position, while the Liberal press, led by the *Journal des débats,* the *Presse, Siècle,* the *Revue des deux mondes,* developed the opposition point of view. The *Constitutionnel* was the cue-giver of the semi-official journals and, as we have noted, it was controlled by Persigny, the intimate of Slidell and aide of Napoleon. It will be recalled, too, that it was during this period in France that De Leon fired his charge of propaganda and Du Bellet waged a campaign of "education" in the Imperialist press. So this campaign of the Imperialist press was the joint effort of the French government and the Confederate agents. The Liberal press was undoubtedly greatly utilized by the Federal propagandists headed by John Bigelow, the United States consul-general,[1] though it must be constantly kept in mind that in France Federal propaganda was falling upon fertile soil.

[1] John Bigelow, *France and the Confederate Navy, 1862–68* (New York, 1888), and *Retrospections of an Active Life* (New York, 1909 and 1913), *passim.*

In England the campaign in favor of intervention was led by the *Index*, which got its cue from the *Constitutionnel*—or from the headquarters of the Confederate lobby. The *London Times* blew hot and cold, as did the *Economist* and most of the newspapers which favored the South—sympathizing with it, but finally taking their cue of fear from the government's position.

Let us first observe the attitude of the French press. About the first of May the *Union* came out in favor of mediation on the basis of separation and abolition, and the *Siècle* retorted that it favored mediation on the basis of abolition and reunion.[1] Then the big guns opened up. A series of articles by one Paulin Limayrac in the *Constitutionnel* began May 8 and continued throughout the summer. The first article took for its text the position of the leading Liberal journal, the *Débats*, that the war should not be interfered with but that it should be allowed to go on in order that the slaves might be freed. The *Constitutionnel* admitted that it, like the liberal *Débats*, was opposed to slavery, but that it favored gradual emancipation. The sudden emancipation of the slaves would, it contended, result in universal carnage and the permanent destruction of the cotton supply, and the ruin of French industry—which was suffering so much already from the war. Our position, said the *Constitutionnel*, is "conciliation, mediation." Mediation was necessary, urged this paper, as otherwise the war would last forever; the Federal government could never bring it to a close.[2] This was certainly the language of Mercier and Napoleon. On May 22 the *Constitutionnel*, reiterating its position in favor of mediation, declared: "We have never desired that, under the pretext of giving liberty to four million negroes, there should be brought about the subjugation of six million whites. Certainly, like our adversaries, at least as much as they, we aspire to the emancipation of the slaves, but we desire the emancipation by the progress of ideas and the conciliation of interest, not by ruin and massacre."[3] The *Presse*, the *Siècle*, and *Débats* came back with the accusation that the *Constitutionnel* which seemed to uphold a proposed governmental policy was, in fact, upholding slavery. This, of

[1] *Siècle*, May 5, 1862, cited in West, pp. 73–74.

[2] *Constitutionnel*, May 8, 1862, cited in West, pp. 74–75.   [3] West, p. 75.

course, was indignantly denied.[1] The *Débats*, June 9, following a clear-cut announcement by the *Constitutionnel* on June 8 that mediation was absolutely necessary to bring the war to a conclusion, denied that mediation would be received in a friendly spirit by the North.[2] Mediation had been rejected before and would be more harshly rejected now. The *Constitutionnel* in reply urged that, now, after a year or more of fighting, the situation was different and the North must presently recognize the facts. The *Presse*, which supported the *Débats*, uncovered the Ethiopian in the woodpile, namely, that mediation was only the thin edge of the wedge of armed intervention, that when the United States refused friendly mediation as it was bound to do, recognition would follow and that in turn would be followed by war.[3]

The savage order of Butler at New Orleans that women who insulted an officer or the flag should be treated like women of the streets, was seized upon by the Imperialist press as an example of what would happen in all southern cities when taken by northern armies. West points out[4] that this argument was calculated to win the sympathy of the French more than anything else. It might be added, too, that this was especially true because of the tender feeling which the French have always displayed toward that old French city of Louisiana. The Confederate victory before Richmond brought out the full position of the Imperialist press, and the *Constitutionnel*[5] on the receipt of the news urged that the solemn moment of action approached. "Let us hope that the North will listen at last to the voice of reason and justice, and that it will accept mediation before Europe has recognized the Confederacy."

In England the *Index* had first taken up the agitation. On May 22 it discussed the series of articles in the *Constitutionnel* on mediation, which it regarded as an official statement of the French position. The *Index* suggested that the Emperor was ready to offer mediation, and, if refused, prepared to "enforce it with the whole military and naval power of France."[6] The *London Times* showed a more

---

[1] *Constitutionnel*, May 24, 1862; West, p. 76.

[2] *Débats*, June 9, 1862; West, p. 77.

[3] *Presse*, June 13 and 15; West, p. 79.   [5] *Constitutionnel*, July 19; West, p. 81.

[4] West, pp. 80–81.   [6] *Index*, May 22; cf. *ibid.*, June 12, 1862.

than customarily savage hostility toward the North at this time. On May 26 in commenting upon the capture of New Orleans this paper remarked that "what is passing in New Orleans may teach us what the apprehensions of these desperate Confederates are, and what is the nature of the fate they dread. The proclamation of General Butler realizes all that has been told of tyranny by victor over vanquished, ... such severity does not bode well for European interests."[1] The *Times* lamented the ruin of the country by the ravages of war.[2]

A week later[3] the *Times*, affected by the Confederate propaganda and the discussion in the French press, approached the question of mediation: "It is plain that the time is approaching when Europe will have to think seriously of its relations to the two belligerents in the American war. . . . . That North and South must now choose between separation and ruin, material and political, is the opinion of nearly every one who, looking impartially and from a distance on the conflict sees what is hidden from the frenzied eyes of the Northern politicians." The *Times* was convinced that mediation or intervention was soon to take place. "We cannot be mistaken respecting the desire of the French Emperor to bring the war to an end. . . . . His strong good sense, aided by political experience, and a careful study of the science of war, assures him that the present contest will be quite fruitless and that each wound inflicted on the territory and pride of either combatant will probably rankle to future generations. . . . . All these circumstances point but to one conclusion. Either this war must be brought to an end, or the time will at last come when the South may claim its own recognition by foreign nations as an independent power. . . . . It is our duty to anticipate this event, and it may be wise as well as generous for statesmen on this side of the ocean to approach the American Government in a friendly spirit with the offer of their good offices at the present crisis of its fortunes."

The *Economist*[4] came out with a strong editorial likewise advocating mediation. It too was impressed with the series of articles in the *Constitutionnel* advocating mediation, which it considered as indi-

---

[1] *Times*, May 26, 1862.
[2] *Ibid.*, June 4, 1862.
[3] *Ibid.*, June 12, 1862.
[4] *Economist*, June 14, 1862.

cating the line of policy contemplated by Napoleon. "Its sugges-tions," commented the *Economist*, "are well timed and ought to be considerately weighed." There are several conditions, continued the *Economist*, in which mediation is justified: when the object of war has become unattainable; when combatants are so evenly matched that war would be indefinitely prolonged without a decision; when the conflict shows signs of degenerating into a barbaric war of ex-termination; when neutrals are being injured beyond what might be expected to be endured; and when the situation seems to indicate a line of settlement. The *Economist* thought most of these conditions were present. The North could never conquer or hold the South, the two were evenly balanced in a military way; judging from Butler's horrible proclamation treating women as women of the streets, there was no limit to the barbarity which would develop out of the strug-gle; the industries of Europe had suffered more than was just from the war; and the military situation indicated fairly well the line of settlement. The *Economist* advocated mediation, but expressing a fairly universal attitude in England, advocated that France and Russia make the proposal as the Americans hated England so that any offer from her would be dangerous.

This was the position assumed by the leading English journals. It was the only time the press ever fully advocated British interven-tion, and it was of short duration, for the British government soon convinced the press of the error of its ways.

Just at this time, June 13, Palmerston and Russell in the House of Lords and Commons, respectively, for the benefit of those who thought the position of the press was that of the government, stated that the British government had neither received proposals of mediation from France nor had offered them, and that it had no intention at the present of doing so.[1] The *Times* and *Economist* at once grew more circumspect in the advocacy of intervention. The following day, June 14, the *Times* reversed its stand and agreed with Russell that the moment was inopportune, as far as England was concerned, for making any move in the direction of mediation. But the *Times* was glad to encourage the French Emperor in pulling the

[1] Parl. Deb., Vol. 167, pp. 536–43; *Times*, June 14, 1862.

chestnuts out of the fire. "If the Emperor of the French thinks the moment opportune for telling the Northern people that in his opinion the subjugation of several million of their own race is an enterprise beyond their strength, and that the attempt is causing intolerable suffering to Europe, he is at perfect liberty to do so, and Englishmen will be glad to see good advice offered by a personage who is far more likely to be listened to than any of our statesmen. . . . . The North knows well, the opinions of this country, and, without further official communication, will feel assured that we give a tacit assent to any recommendation which other powers may make in the interest of peace. . . . ."[1]

The *Times* and the other newspapers friendly to the South avoided thus any return to an open advocacy of mediation on the part of England. But the tone of the press grew ever more savage, working up sentiment in favor of the South to a high pitch. Hotze and Spence were doubtless reaping a harvest from their campaign of propaganda. The *Times* praised the iron determination of the South as shown in recent victories,[2] and carried sarcastic discussions of the principles of the declaration of independence which had been repudiated by the North in its conquest of people who desired to govern themselves.[3] It breathed rage and pain at the revised tariff which had recently raised duties,[4] and reverted with malicious self-satisfaction to the destruction of the Union now so apparent from recent Confederate victories.[5]

The English public mind was also being roused against the North and in favor of the South by party and government leaders. Palmerston in Parliament, on being questioned about the veracity of the Butler proclamation, had denounced it in unmeasured and inflammatory terms which made the whole nation thrill with hate at the North. No man, he exclaimed, could read the proclamation "without a feeling of the deepest indignation. It is a proclamation to which I do not scruple to attach the epithet infamous! . . . . Any Englishman must blush to think that such an act has been committed by one

---

[1] *Times*, July 14, 1862.

[2] *Ibid.*, June 28, 1862.

[3] *Ibid.*, July 3 and 4, 1862.

[4] *Ibid.*, July 9, 1862; cf. *ibid.*, July 11.

[5] *Ibid.*, Aug. 15, 1862.

belonging to the Anglo-Saxon race."[1] The Earl of Carnovan spoke in the same tone in the House of Lords. On June 13 he remarked scornfully that he "would not insult the House by making any comments on such a proclamation as this," but he could not restrain himself from remarking that even if it were only a menace and not intended to be executed, "then it was a gross, unmanly and brutal insult to every woman in New Orleans."[2] Even Lord Russell with his pro-northern tendencies urged in the House of Lords that the character of the American government was at stake in repudiating the brutal and insulting proclamation.[3] Sir John Walsh expressed a hope that the American government would repudiate the proclamation, for it had created profound indignation among all classes of Englishmen. It was "an extraordinary proclamation, so utterly repugnant to the spirit of the 19th century and the whole of the usages of civilized warfare." He felt that England must make a remonstrance.[4]

Opinion, whether in favor of intervention or not, was thus being swung powerfully in favor of the South. Mason reported on June 23[5] to Benjamin that there had been a complete change in sentiment since the war commenced, so that now all intelligent classes were in complete sympathy with the South. Hotze found that at least five-sixths of the Commons and all of the Lords except two were in sympathy with the South.[6] Lord Lyons found agitation against the Union so strong and opinion so hostile to America that, on his visit to England in the summer of 1862, he wrote Stuart, chargé d'affaires, with reference to the defeat of McClellan in the peninsula, "I am afraid no one but me is sorry for it."[7] C. F. Adams wrote Seward on July 11, "I think there can now be little doubt that they [Confederate sympathizers] constitute much the greater part of the active classes." Every act of the United States, he said, was seized upon and used maliciously against her. "In this connection, it is not to be denied that General Butler is furnishing a good deal of material" by his dealings with New Orleans women and European consuls.[8]

[1] Parl. Deb., Vol. 167 (1862), pp. 611–17.

[2] *Ibid.*, pp. 533–36.   [5] Pickett Papers, No. 12, June 23, 1862.

[3] *Ibid.*   [6] *Ibid.*, Hotze to Benjamin, No. 9, Aug. 4, 1862.

[4] *Ibid.*   [7] Newton, *Lyons*, I, 88–89.

[8] Parl. Accts. and Papers, U.S., Vol. LXXII (1863), p. 124.

On May 8 Henry Adams, son of the minister, wrote his brother Charles F., Jr., ". . . . There is no doubt that the idea here is as strong as ever that we must ultimately fail, and unless a very few weeks show some great military result we shall have our hands full in this quarter." Intervention in the form of mediation "is inevitable without our triumph before July."[1] England, he continued, "is unanimously against us and becomes more firmly so every day."[2] On July 18, following news of McClellan's retreat from the peninsula, C. F. Adams wrote his son, C. F. Adams, Jr., in America that public hostility was "rising every hour and running harder against us than at any time since the Trent affair. This reverse called out at once all the latent hostility here, and there was nothing to do but give away. I shut myself up, went to no parties and avoided contact with everyone except friends."[3] On May 16 Henry Adams wrote C. F., Jr., that the news of the Confederate defeat at New Orleans threw London into great excitement and depression "as though it were an English defeat."[4]

So great was the agitation against the United States during 1862—undoubtedly aided by Hotze—that it spread to all the British possessions. Even the little town of Nassau and the whole island of New Providence, influenced by the blockade business, British naval officers, and Confederate agents, reflected the British attitude. United States Consul Whiting became so intimidated that he was afraid to leave the consulate, and at night Negro roustabouts serenaded him by standing under his window and singing ribald parodies on the American flag, calling out to him, "Say, you's got too many stars in dat flag."[5] The Attorney-General of the island, in a libel suit between the United States insurance agent and A. J. Adderly relative to the display of United States and Confederate flags, remarked in scathing words that it was pardonable for a northern man to sympathize with his section, but that any boast about "Union" and "Star-spangled Banner" was foolish in the extreme, for the first was

---

[1] A Cycle of Adams' Letters, I (May 8), 138–43.

[2] Ibid.   [3] Ibid., pp. 166–69.

[4] Ibid., pp. 145–49.

[5] See U.S. Consular Des., Nassau, Vol. 11, Whiting to Seward, June 8, 1862, no number; also Vol. 11, passim.

a "myth—a Yankee fiction of the past, now fully exploded, while the glory of the last had quite departed."[1]

This public agitation in France and England was ominous. The cotton famine was getting in its deadly work now in England, and the government and the leaders were watching Lancashire and the disappearing cotton reserve and the swelling unemployment with chilled marrow. The Confederate agents and the French government were behind this agitation and making the most of the cotton famine.

Let us follow the complex maneuvers of Napoleon and his councilors, and of the Confederate government and its agents, all focusing from different directions upon the question of intervention in some form or other.

While Mercier, following his visit to Richmond, cautioned his government against precipitate action in the matter of intervention because of the recent successes of the North and because of the continued raising of large armies,[2] he assured them that the time was not far distant when it would be both proper and safe for France in company with England and, perhaps, another country to step into the struggle and bring it to an end. The stubborn courage and strength of the South made their defeat out of the question. So he advised his government to lay its plans and get all preparations made for the moment when it would be proper to offer the good offices of the European governments to the belligerent powers.[3]

No sooner had Thouvenel received this suggestion than he dispatched instructions to Mercier to be prepared to offer mediation to the United States as soon as he should judge the moment opportune.[4] Mercier, however, did not wait to hear from Thouvenel, but immediately approached Lyons and Stoeckl in order to have them sound out their governments on the question of intervention, if they had not already done so sufficiently. Mercier was especially ur-

---

[1] *Ibid.*, Vol. 12, Whiting to Seward, No. 61, Aug. 1, 1862.

[2] French F.O. Amer., Vol. 127, Mercier to Thouvenel, No. 98, May 6, 1862; *ibid.*, No. 100, May 20, 1862.

[3] *Ibid.*, No. 101, May 26, 1862, and *passim*.

[4] *Ibid.*, Thouvenel to Mercier, No. 15, June 12, 1862.

gent in his interview with Lyons because of rumors and threats from the South that it would burn and destroy its cotton, and refuse to plant more should northern invasion continue. He also feared that the growing sentiment in the North favoring abolition would likewise destroy cotton production.[1]

Lyons, after the interview, wrote Russell that Mercier seemed rather desperate and was prepared to "go great lengths to stop the war; because he believes that the South will not give in until the whole country is made desolate and that the North will very soon be led to proclaim immediate emancipation, which would stop the cultivation of cotton for an indefinite time."[2]

Lyons did not encourage Mercier. He had long since learned from experience as well as from the instructions of his government to tread cautiously in connection with any question affecting the war. Intervention, he confided in Russell, "appears to me to be a dangerous subject of conversation." Still, there would probably come a time when it would be necessary to discuss it. "If the South really defeated either or both of the armies opposed to them I think it would disgust the North with the war, rather than excite them to fresh efforts. . . . . If the armies suffer much from disease, recruiting will become difficult. The credit of the Government has hitherto been wonderfully kept up, but it would not stand a considerable reverse in the field. It is possible, under such circumstances, that a Peace Party might arise; and it is just possible that England and France might give weight to such a party."[3]

Not receiving any encouragement from Lyons, there was nothing Mercier could do for the moment but await instructions from his government and await possible favorable instructions to Lyons from the British government. In the meanwhile, the Confederacy had not remained idle in the realm of diplomacy. Davis and Benjamin determined to make a more direct effort than ever to move Europe, and especially France, by the use of cotton and free trade. On April 12

---

[1] See *ibid.*, Vols. 127, 128, May, June, July, August, September, and October, 1862, *passim*, for continual apprehension concerning abolition and the burning of cotton.

[2] Newton, *Lyons*, I, 85–86; letter also quoted at length in Adams, I, 298–99.

[3] *Ibid.*

the latter wrote the dispatch offering the Emperor not less than 100,000 bales of cotton and free trade for a number of years for recognition or for breaking the blockade.[1] This, it will be recalled, was the famous secret dispatch which De Leon had opened and read on his way across the Atlantic. Nothing like this bribe was offered to England in Mason's instructions, nor was Mason informed about this proposed bribe at the time. Naturally, no such offer could be made to a responsible government.

It is interesting to note that this special bonus and free-trade offer was being prepared just at the time when Mercier was on his way to Richmond with the suspicions of Lyons resting upon him that he was seeking just such privileges by making this journey. It is likewise significant that two days after Mercier came to Richmond, the Confederate Senate, April 18, doubtless influenced by Mercier's visit and by Benjamin's attitude, passed a resolution authorizing the President to draw up a treaty with Great Britain, France, and Spain giving these countries special trade privileges and other inducements to break the blockade.[2]

Before these instructions reached the commissioners, however, they had already resumed agitation, this time chiefly in the direction of recognition—though not giving up the idea of the repudiation of the blockade. On May 27, 1862, Slidell wrote Mason that if Corinth could be held or the enemy be repulsed before Richmond, there would be a good chance of early recognition. He suggested to Mason that they should make a formal demand upon both governments for recognition in case of military success.[3] Mason replied to Slidell agreeing that they should present such formal demands, but he thought it useless to do so until a decisive victory was gained[4] or until a change in ministry brought the more friendly Tories back into power.[5]

As long as no decisive victory was gained in the peninsula and no change of ministry occurred the two commissioners hesitated.[6] But

---

[1] Pickett Papers, Benjamin to Slidell, No. 3 ("Confidential"), April 12, 1862; O.R.N., Ser. 2, Vol. III, pp. 386–90.

[2] O.R., Ser. 4, Vol. I, p. 1073.

[3] Mason Papers, May 27, 1862.

[4] Ibid., May 30, 1862.

[5] Ibid., May 31, 1862.

[6] E.g., see ibid., June 10, 1862.

about June 11 news came that McClellan had received a bad defeat, and that Jackson had won a brilliant victory over Banks in the valley. Quickly there followed a counsel of the lobby. They decided that the first move should be in Parliament where Lindsay would prepare the ground by offering a motion of some kind in favor of mediation.[1]

Persigny was sent over by the Emperor at the same time to bring informal pressure upon the British cabinet in favor of intervention by both governments.[2] Even the ineffective William Dayton, who could not speak French, heard about Persigny's journey to London and wrote Seward that, though the French government was friendly and civil, intervention was on foot again.[3] On the same day, June 12, Thouvenel wrote Mercier, as has been noted, to hold himself in readiness to offer mediation.[4]

But Russell and Palmerston, who were not moving apace with either the Confederacy or the Emperor, were not ready for the question of mediation or intervention in any form. The supply of cotton had reached 20,000 bales, and there seemed little prospect of replenishing it. But as no pressure had been received from the cotton operatives and spinners, there was as yet no necessity of the government's moving. So when Hopwood, one of the southern independence champions, asked Palmerston whether he had received any proposal from France or any other country favoring mediation, and whether England contemplated taking any step in that direction, the doughty old prime minister flatly denied receiving any offer from France and disclaimed any intentions to mediate, at the present;[5] and Russell, who had urged Palmerston to make this reply to any question about mediation,[6] attempted in a similar way in the House of Lords to circumvent the renewed agitation at its inception. "Her Majesty's Government," he stated, "have made no proposals of the kind to the government of France, and the government of France have made no such overtures to ours." Russell thus gave point-blank

[1] *Ibid.*, Mason to Slidell, June 11, 1862.

[2] *Ibid.*, Slidell to Mason, June 13, 1862.

[3] U.S. Des., France, Vol. 51, Dayton to Seward, No. 160, June 12, 1862.

[4] French F.O. Amer., Vol. 127, No. 15, June 12, 1862.

[5] Parl. Deb., Vol. 167, p. 543.   [6] Adams, I, 305.

denial to the two informal proposals of 1861 and February, 1862, made by the Emperor, and blandly and pointedly ignored Lindsay's efforts of two months before, of which he was fully aware from Cowley as well as from Lindsay himself.[1] He went farther and asserted that the French minister in London, Flahault, denied having had any instructions on mediation.[2]

Lindsay's proposed motion in favor of mediation scheduled to be brought up on June 18 became for the moment inopportune, owing to the government's attitude thus expressed in Parliament on June 13 by Russell and Palmerston; and, after taking the matter under consideration for several days, the lobby decided that it would be better to change the motion to deal with recognition rather than mediation which had been repudiated by the government. The proposed motion was thereupon changed to deal with recognition. Then, finally, after consultation with Fitzgerald, Roebuck, Disraeli, and others, Lindsay reduced it to an innocuous expression of opinion that the government should take under serious consideration the question of recognition of the Confederacy.[3] This was done in order to avoid a party issue which would have inevitably killed the motion. Seeing no good in pushing the question of recognition in Parliament at the moment, the Confederate friends decided that it should be postponed for a fortnight and "wait for king cotton to turn the screws still further."[4] So on June 20 Lindsay gave notice that his motion would be postponed.

In the meantime, Slidell was not idle in Paris. Knowing that Persigny was in London to urge intervention, he could not wait patiently to find out what Napoleon was planning to do; so he sought Billault who conceded that Persigny was in London in behalf of intervention, but who insisted as always that unless England could be induced to act jointly with France, Napoleon would not hazard acting alone. Billault spoke of mediation as the present form of intervention on foot, and Slidell replied that the South did not think so much of mediation. What it wanted was recognition. The moral effect of such would speedily bring the war to an end by encouraging the

[1] *Ibid.*, p. 533. [3] Mason Papers, Mason to Slidell, June 19, 1862.
[2] *Ibid.* [4] *Ibid.*

peace parties of the North. In fact, said Slidell, recognition in the summer of 1861 would have long since brought the war to an end. Certainly, now was the time to act if ever, as it would help the peace party win the congressional elections of the fall. He told Billault of the proposed demand for recognition which he and Mason were contemplating making upon France and England as soon as the military situation permitted, and Billault again replied that France could not act without England—especially as things now stood. Slidell suggested that a formal demand upon England might precipitate a cabinet crisis, since Russell was the only man who was thought to oppose recognition. Billault immediately saw the possibilities of such action, and he agreed that formal demands for recognition should be presented to both countries as proposed by Slidell in the hopes that John Bull might be forced into action.[1]

Mason and Lindsay were much elated over Slidell's report of the interview, and Lindsay promptly took a high and lordly tone in a letter to Russell, who had asked Lindsay for the exact wording of his proposed motion. He assured the cold and timid old gentleman that Parliament was straining at the leash to recognize the South, and that it was only out of consideration for the foreign minister that he had postponed his motion for a fortnight. Moreover, he told Russell that the country was fully in sympathy with the South, and then he tried to bully him by the suggestion that, unless the South gained its independence and was duly recognized by England, and the Union thus permanently weakened, the northern troops would be promptly marched into Canada as soon as the war was ended. But Lindsay, as he explained to Mason,[2] was bluffing, for he realized that under the political circumstances, while a majority would have been glad to have the South free, they would support Russell in his policy of keeping out of war with the United States. But it was becoming apparent that the cotton famine would soon force action, especially if accompanied by southern military success.

With Lindsay's motion postponed, Mason wrote Slidell on June 19, just after consulting with Lindsay and the others concerned, that

[1] *Ibid.*, Slidell to Mason, June 17, 1862.

[2] *Ibid.*, Lindsay to Mason, June 18, 1862.

the demands of the two commissioners for recognition of their government should be postponed.[1] It had been planned to present these notes on June 20, just exactly the date on which Lindsay's motion for recognition had been scheduled to be brought in, but Slidell accepted Mason's line of action and the notes were withheld for the dénouement of the series of military events in the valley and peninsula.[2]

The months of February, March, and April had seen the fall of Donelson, Henry, and New Orleans, and the drawn battle of Shiloh followed by the retreat of the Confederates to Corinth; but May had seen the valley swept of the northern armies, and the beginning of the final stand of the Confederates before Richmond; June brought news to England and Europe of the terrific conflict being waged. But its decision was yet in doubt. Slidell, Mason, and Lindsay were planning to focus their drive upon the government. So matters stood when it was decided to postpone Lindsay's motion and the demands for recognition. But on July 10 Slidell received news of the beginning of McClellan's retreat across the Chickahominy, and rumors of impending disaster to the Federal Army. He was on the point of hastening to interview Persigny with his new instructions offering the cotton bribe, which had been brought by De Leon, when Persigny, who had just returned from his scouting trip in England, sent for him. Slidell read Persigny the secret dispatch No. 3 of April 12, and the latter urged him to proceed in hot haste to interview the Emperor at Vichy. Persigny was of the opinion that this might be the time for action if victory continued until McClellan was driven from the peninsula.[3] Almost at the same time[4] Mason wrote Slidell hurriedly that Lindsay wished to push his motion in Parliament now that news of victory had arrived. Lindsay, so Mason wrote, thought the two commissioners should now present their notes asking recognition simultaneously with his motion—as planned at first—so as to head off any excuse on the part of the British ministry that no formal demand had been made by the Confederacy for recognition.

[1] *Ibid.*

[2] Pickett Papers, Slidell to Benjamin, No. 10, July 25, 1862; *O.R.N.*, Ser. 2, Vol. III, pp. 479–81.

[3] *Ibid.;* Mason Papers, Slidell to Mason, July 11, 1862.

[4] Mason Papers, July 14, 1862.

So Mason prepared to submit his note, though he objected to putting it exactly simultaneously with Slidell's, and Lindsay slated his motion for July 18, in spite of the cautioning of Spence that the motion should be delayed ten days longer so as to get the full benefit of the victories.[1] On July 16, through Persigny and General Fleury, Slidell obtained an interview with the Emperor for the purpose of discussing his proposed demand for recognition, along with the whole question of intervention.

In the meanwhile, during June, Mercier had been watching the situation in America, reporting the terrific destruction and the apparently endless nature of the conflict with the possibility of servile war following any proposed emancipation.[2] Finally, on receiving Thouvenel's instructions of June 11 to offer mediation at the first opportunity, he approached Seward around July 1 to feel him out. But he found that inveterate optimist as hopeful as ever in the face of the recent disasters. Mercier wrote Thouvenel an account of this interview.[3] Seward was vigorous and menacing, said Mercier. " 'Be assured,' he said to me, 'that the Emperor can commit no graver error than to mix himself in our affairs. At the rumor alone of intervention all the factions will reunite themselves against you and even in the border states you will meet a resistance unanimous and desperate.' " Seward assured Mercier that American feeling was all for France, but warned him not to " 'compromise this attitude which is of such grave importance to you.' " Mercier, who had hoped to be able by this time to advise Thouvenel that the time for intervention had arrived, was abashed by Seward's menacing attitude and his innuendoes. His impression was that Seward had something up his sleeve, and he advised caution in his note to Thouvenel. "It is indeed possible that even today a European intervention whatever might be its motive would produce an impression which would translate itself into a declaration of war." However, though advising a continuation of caution on the part of France, Mercier still felt as he had since his Richmond journey that the North had about shot its bolt and that it would not be long before European intervention

[1] *Ibid.*, Spence to Mason, July 11, 1862.

[2] See French F.O. Amer., Vol. 128 (June), *passim.*

[3] *Ibid.*, No. 107, July 11, 1862.

could be safely undertaken.[1] After this until September 30, when Mercier finally advised his government that the time had at last come to offer mediation, he prepared Thouvenel more and more in each dispatch for the coming intervention.

No doubt the Emperor was tremendously influenced by this fore-shadowing of the approaching crisis in America in Mercier's dispatch, and in the news of one brilliant Confederate victory after another carefully spread abroad by Hotze and De Leon in all the important papers of Western Europe. He dispatched the foreign minister, Thouvenel, post-haste to London to renew the indirect diplomacy with England which Persigny, who had just returned, had been carrying on. The Emperor wired Thouvenel while there, "Inquire of the English Government if it does not believe that the moment has arrived when the South should be recognized."[2] At about the same time the Emperor let it be known through Persigny that he would receive Slidell.

The Confederate commissioner, following Persigny's instructions, proceeded to Vichy on July 15 to lay before the great monarch the strongest inducements the Confederacy could offer. In the interview (July 16) the Emperor, to Slidell's astonishment, was bold and frank in his conversation. He commenced by plunging into a discussion of the Confederate victories before Richmond, which had been heralded in the newspapers of the previous evening, and assured Slidell of his unconditional sympathy. He admired the courage of the South, he told Slidell, and supported as he had always done in Europe the principle of nationalism for which they were struggling. It had aways been, he said, the policy and interest of France to have a great undivided America as a counterpoise to England, but, nevertheless, his sympathies were with the South, which he believed would inevitably win. However, he could not find a safe way to give proper expression to his sympathies. He wished to intervene, but could not do it without the co-operation of England, and that country had several times pointedly ignored his official and unofficial suggestions

[1] *Ibid.*; cf. *ibid.*, July 6, 1862 ("Confidential").

[2] Quoted in E. D. Adams, II, 19: "Demandez au gouvernment Anglais s'il ne croit pas le moment venu de reconnaître le Sud."

that they undertake joint intervention in some form. England, he believed, wanted him to draw the chestnuts out of the fire for her. This he would not do. He repeated what he had told Lindsay about England's coldness following his support of her in the Trent affair. It seemed to weigh on Napoleon's mind.

Slidell was greatly pleased with the frankness and unguarded statements of the Emperor in laying the blame for non-intervention upon England. Feeling sure of his ground, he laid his cards upon the table. After placing before the Emperor the blockade situation which his instructions from Benjamin—especially of April 8 and 12—urged, he pointed out in vigorous language how the recognition of this ineffective blockade was depriving the South of the sinews of war. Money and rifles, he said, were what the South needed in order to win, and these were prevented from reaching the Confederacy in sufficient numbers by European recognition of a blockade, which was inexcusable.

Napoleon agreed that the blockade was illegal and in violation of the Declaration of Paris, but, he said, it was now too late for him to act alone. The breaking of the blockade, however ineffective it was, would be considered an act of war by the United States.

Slidell retorted that all the threats of Seward and Welles and others were bluff, that the big talk about the Trent, the hanging of Confederate officials, the recognition by Europe of Confederate belligerency, had all been swallowed by the North when time for action had come. The present war talk was the same kind of boasting. Why, the French battle ships "Couronne," "Gloire," or "Normandie" single handed could pass the fortifications of New York, Boston, or the Chesapeake and lay the coastal cities under tribute! The Emperor was flattered and agreed that the contention was probably true. At the same time he probably harbored doubts as to their being able to do it.

Giving an impression in some remarks that the interests of France and England might become suddenly divergent, the Emperor left an opening for Slidell's most unexpected proposition. Slidell was certain that the Emperor was thinking of the recent withdrawal of England from the joint intervention in Mexico which had left France alone there. So he alluded to the Corwin treaty which, he said, would place $11,000,000 in the hands of Juárez to fight the French—in short, it would be American aid of Napoleon's enemy. Napoleon was extremely uneasy. He suggested that perhaps the American Senate would not ratify that treaty. Slidell was of a different opinion, but be that as it may, he had good evidence to show that Consul-General Shufeldt was in Mexico at the present moment with $2,000,000 to give Juárez as the first instalment on the $11,000,000 stipulated in the treaty. If this was so, continued Slidell, the Mexican Army now waging war on France was being financed by the United States. He pointed out other symptoms of hostility on the part of the United States arising from the Mexican venture, specifically, the presence of the Orleanists in the United States Army. Having sufficiently alarmed the Emperor, who had been constantly harried by Dayton and Seward as to his intentions in Mexico and who had been forced to lie incessantly to retain the good relations with the United States, Slidell offered an alliance of the South with France "against the common enemy." To carry on the naval war incident upon breaking the blockade he now offered the cotton subsidy which Benjamin had suggested. In short, the South would pay the Emperor not less than 100,000 and probably 500,000 bales of cotton for breaking the blockade.

Slidell, however, probably realized that the time had slipped by for breaking the blockade and was only carrying out his belated instructions. So he urged recognition upon the Emperor, offering the alliance and the cotton subsidy as the *quid pro quo*. The Emperor was doubtful whether recognition would be of any benefit to the South, but feared it would infuriate the North. Slidell answered that the moral effect would be magical, that it would give such an impetus to the peace party in the North as to bring a speedy end to the war. Mediation was then mentioned by the Emperor. The North would reject it, he thought. Yes, replied Slidell, and the South would accept it, thus throwing the burden of the war upon the North and leaving the road open to recognition and armed intervention. Napoleon did not commit himself on any form of intervention—repudiation of the blockade, recognition, or mediation—but he gave

Slidell the impression that he might soon attempt intervention alone if England refused to act with him. Certainly Napoleon left no doubts that he *desired* to intervene in behalf of the South.

Slidell told the Emperor during the interview, which lasted an hour and ten minutes, that he and Mason were preparing to present formal demands to the French and English governments for recognition in the immediate future in connection with the Lindsay motion in Parliament, now changed to mediation, scheduled for July 18, two days later. Napoleon approved of the move, hoping, as the commissioners did, that the British cabinet would be forced by a formal demand to take action. He assured Slidell again that he was, and had always been, ready to act just as quickly as England indicated her readiness to join him.[1]

As soon as the interview was finished Slidell hurriedly wrote Mason a sketch of the conversations omitting all details about the cotton proposition and the Mexican question lest it fall into the hands of the numerous spies of the Federal government swarming in every town and city in which there was a Confederate agent.[2] He was ready, he wrote Mason, to present Thouvenel his note demanding recognition, on the following Monday or Tuesday.[3] Two days later Mason, exultant over the news just received of McClellan's rout before Richmond, replied that he too would be ready to present his note to Russell on the following Monday. He thought Lindsay's motion slated for that evening stood a good chance of success, in view of the tremendous effect produced by the news of McClellan's final defeat and retreat.[4]

Lindsay's motion, now changed back to one demanding mediation, was brought in Parliament for debate that night, July 18. While it was being debated the streets were resounding with the cry of the newsboys that McClellan with his whole army had been captured. Things looked rather bad for the Union, and Charles Francis Adams

---

[1] The interview is described in a memorandum inclosed in dispatch No. 10, July 25, 1862, Slidell to Benjamin, Pickett Papers; *O.R.N.*, Ser. 2, Vol. III, pp. 479–87.

[2] See Slidell's reasons for not disclosing this in a written communication at the time (*ibid.*).

[3] Mason Papers, Slidell to Mason, July 16, 1862.   [4] *Ibid.*, July 18, 1862.

shut himself in and waited. The southern lobby was confident and pressing for action. Lindsay in introducing his motion urged that the intervention of England would not be taking sides with slavery, as slavery had long since ceased to be considered the cause of the war. The protective tariff and a desire for power and markets were the motives of the North, while the principles of the South were those of self-government. The South, just in its cause, was destined to win ultimately without intervention. On the other hand, the war would be long drawn out, and, if for no other than selfish interests, England should intervene to stop the war because of the havoc being wrought in the cotton industry of Lancashire. He called attention to the report made by the special commissioner for the distressed areas, Farnall, two days before, which showed that England had less than 200,000 bales of cotton as compared with 1,200,000 the same time in 1861, and that 80,000 operatives were out of work and 370,000 were averaging only half time. He insisted that ruin and worse stared England in the face unless cotton could be obtained soon by intervening and stopping the war.

Palmerston and the government representatives who heard this threatening statement were apparently placid and unmoved, but, as we shall presently see, the heart of "Pam" was in his boots and the whole cabinet including the pro-northern Russell viewed the figures of the cotton famine with apprehension and dismay. Although a little late, King Cotton was asserting his power.

Adolphus Vane Tempest supported Lindsay, pointing to the precedents in British history, the more recent recognitions being Italy, Belgium, and Greece. Gregory followed in support of the motion likewise pointing significantly to the Farnall report on the cotton districts, saying that he would leave the statistics of pauperisms to the representatives from that district. As we shall see later, the representatives from Lancashire had no reason to complain and offered no argument in favor of intervention—in fact, they remained silent. If they had been forced to speak they would have pleaded eloquently not for intervention but for the indefinite prolongation of the Civil War in America.

Forster, who with John Bright represented the interests of the cotton manufacturers better than most of the others and who was a propagandist of the first water in the Federal cause, being hand in glove with Adams, Seward, and Sumner, answered that mediation would not stop the war but would merely prolong and embitter it; and that armed intervention in any form would be like declaring war, and would, besides, precipitate a servile insurrection—one of Seward's constant threats, expressed to Mercier, Lyons, and to Adams in London and relayed by that minister to his man Friday, Forster.[1] Forster brought out another argument which he and Bright and the northern lobby made much of in the following years in attempting to defeat intervention, namely, the threat of a corn famine. "We have a cotton famine now," he exclaimed, "but if we did that [intervene] we should stand in danger of a corn famine." England, he said, could keep her factory population in luxury for less than what intervention and war which was bound to follow would cost.

Lindsay, not expecting to be able to carry his motion over the ministry, proposed to postpone it again—as Spence had suggested— but Palmerston insisted that it must be disposed of finally either by vote or by withdrawal. He said the matter of mediation and intervention must be intrusted to the government; its hands must not be tied by expressions of opinions such as this unless definite action followed, as it only irritated the United States which was already on the point of extreme exasperation. Lindsay had no intention of making an issue with the ministry, realizing that Derby and Disraeli were unwilling to accept the question as a party measure. So he withdrew the motion. However, as in the debates on the blockade in March, the impression was spread abroad by the debates on this motion that there was a strong southern sympathy in Parliament.[2] The *London Times* came out on the day of the debate favoring, in a cautious way, mediation or intervention in co-operation with France and Russia. The *Times* was moved by the news of northern defeat, and, as we shall see presently, unquestionably was reflecting the wavering attitude of the Palmerston-Russell government, which was at the moment heading toward a serious considera-

[1] U.S. Inst., Gr. Br., Vol. 18, Seward to Adams, No. 260, May 28, 1862; F.O. Amer., Vol. 820, Russell to Stuart, Nos. 35 and 55, July 25 and Aug. 7, 1862; cf. E. D. Adams, II, 22.

[2] For debates in Parliament see Parl. Deb., Vol. 168, pp. 511–78; Callahan, p. 153.

tion of intervention and squirming under the menacing figures of the cotton famine. Mason wrote his wife two days later[1] that the tardy and supine government, always fearful of war with the North if intervention should be attempted, would be moved by the "increasing distress for cotton, and the late apparent decided successes before Richmond." Members of Parliament—friends of the South—had been crowding to his headquarters on that day talking of bringing the matter before Parliament again. "England is seriously moved; I can at least say that much, and I shall look now speedily for intervention in some form."[2]

The next day Mason notified Slidell that he would be ready to deliver his note demanding recognition as soon as Slidell notified him that his had been presented to Thouvenel. He was very optimistic now. "I should not think that Lord John will resist very strenuously if a strong demand is made by the Emperor." The pressure from France, he thought, might induce the Confederate friends in the British Parliament to "call for papers to bring the Emperor's position to the knowledge of the British people—which would operate as a great incentive to bring the ministry here to act."[3]

Returning from his interview with the Emperor, Slidell immediately visited Thouvenel, July 23, to discuss the presentation of the note demanding recognition for the Confederacy. In the interview Thouvenel advised at first against Slidell's presenting his demand. He desired to get more definite information about the recent Confederate victory; but Slidell answered that he could defer action no longer. If the South was not to be recognized now after so signal a victory he could see no reason for expecting recognition except in the far-distant future when it would be of no value to the Confederacy. Slidell thereupon told Thouvenel, who had not yet learned of it, about his recent interview with the Emperor. He repeated most of his conversation, and especially that part relating to the offer of an alliance in the Mexican affair, free trade for a period of years, and a large quantity of cotton. Thouvenel warmed up at once and withdrew all objections to Slidell's presenting the note.

[1] Mason Papers, July 20, 1862.

[2] Mason, *Life of Mason*, pp. 279–81.   [3] Mason Papers, July 21, 1862.

Slidell presented his note, which was an able synthesis of all his and his predecessor's chief instructions. The details of this note, which was put into the hands of the French government, are unnecessary, but its major points should be noted. The legality of secession, the encroachment of the North in the form of unfriendly legislation such as the tariff, etc., the divergent social and economic systems in North and South, with the North rapidly becoming the preponderant influence, ruling in its own interests, and the threatened attack upon the domestic institutions of the South, especially slavery, were pointed out. Then the strength of the South as demonstrated by its continuous victories, its size, and its resources was dwelt upon, as was the determination of its population to be free from northern rule.

Slidell approved strongly, in this note, of Napoleon's intervention in Mexico. "Although the undersigned has no instructions from his Government in relation to the military expedition which his Imperial Majesty has sent to Mexico, he does not hesitate to say that it will be regarded with no unfriendly eye by the Confederate States; they can have no other interest or desire than to see a respectable, responsible, and stable government established in that country. They are not animated by that spirit of political proselytism which so strongly characterizes the people from whom they have recently separated themselves, and confident that his Imperial Majesty has no intention of imposing on Mexico any government not in accordance with the wishes of its inhabitants, they will feel quite indifferent as to its form." Slidell contended that by the establishment of the Confederacy the conquest and annexation of alien territory by the South would cease, and a balance of power would thereby be created in North America. This, of course, was a subtle suggestion that with the South standing guard the North would be kept out of Mexico and Napoleon's scheme in that country would be uninterrupted. In fact, Slidell knew that Napoleon firmly believed that unless the Confederacy were thus interposed between Mexico and the United States, war would inevitably come between the French troops in Mexico and the Federal; that, in fact, the whole Mexican venture depended for its success upon the success of the Confederacy. Slidell had seized upon what was becoming even more vital to Napoleon than cotton. In presenting his views, though without instructions to offer an alliance in the Mexican venture, he was reading the logic of the situation, and his views were those of the Confederate government.

This was the great political advantage which Napoleon would reap from the independence of the South. Slidell then described the economic advantages. The raw materials, coal, timber, and markets without restrictive tariffs would be there for the French people. But, above all, the sole source of the French cotton supply would be safe from interference by wars and strife as the South could never have any motive for going to war with France or any other nation, being an agricultural, free-trade country. The South had been and would continue to be the great source of supply for cotton. "If our country is to be the great source for the supply of this article so indispensable to the manufacturing industry of the world, the nations of the earth have the deepest interest in placing it in a position of independence and impartiality in regard to the distribution of the raw material for which the demand is so immense. If any one country is to have a virtual monopoly of the supply of raw cotton, then the world would have the deepest interest in opening it to the easy and equal access of all mankind. Such would be the case, if the depository of this great interest should be found in a country, on the one hand, strong enough to maintain its neutrality and independence, and on the other, committed by its interests to the policy of free trade and an untrammeled intercourse with all the world. Such would be the precise condition of the Confederate States when once their independence was acknowledged, and, as a proof that this would be the natural tendency of their policy, we have only to look to their early legislation which reduced the duties on imports to the lowest rates consistent with their necessities for revenue, and opened their coasting trade to the free and equal competition of all mankind."

Slidell urged that the interests of England and France were different on the question of cotton, as England was willing to suffer at the present time in order to build up her rival cotton supply in India and thus become independent of all American cotton. France could ill afford to depend upon England and she had no supply of her own.

Slidell urged the inefficiency of the blockade, as he had done in his interview with the Emperor and according to his instructions; and he called on the French to live up to their obligations under the Declaration of Paris. In this connection he returned to the King Cotton idea, and urged the same thing which Yancey, Rost, and Mann had urged, according to their instructions, that cotton, being used by all mankind, should really be neutralized as certain countries and trade routes had been, for a war on cotton was a war on all who used it.[1]

Slidell reported all that had happened to Benjamin in a letter two days later.[2] "I am more hopeful," he wrote, "than I have been at any moment since my arrival in Europe." Thouvenel had not committed himself, nor had the Emperor, to any definite action, but unquestionably he had dropped the frigid, discouraging air so pronounced in his early interviews with Slidell. Thouvenel was now convinced that the South would ultimately win, and his letters to Mercier during this period show that he had dropped all opposition to recognizing the Confederacy and was merely waiting—and with some impatience—for the North to meet a decisive-enough defeat to put them in the proper frame of mind for some form of intervention.[3]

As soon as Mason received Slidell's letter saying he had presented the note to Thouvenel demanding recognition, he sent his note to Russell. Mason had already, on July 7, sent a strong protest to Russell against the interpretation which the latter had given the Declaration of Paris on blockades in his letter to Lyons, February 15; but the Foreign Office had merely acknowledged Mason's letter on July 10. Then on July 17 Mason had written Russell strong notes challenging that statesman's recent contention in Parliament that mediation could not be offered because both belligerents would take offense. On the contrary, Mason had insisted in his note to Russell that the Confederacy would welcome such a course. This letter had been written the day before Lindsay's motion, for the purpose of

[1] Pickett Papers, Slidell to Thouvenel, July 21, 1862; *O.R.N.*, Ser. 2, Vol. III, pp. 467–79.

[2] Pickett Papers, No. 10, July 25, 1862; *O.R.N.*, Ser. 2, Vol. III, pp. 479–81.

[3] See, e.g., French F.O. Amer., Vol. 128, Thouvenel to Mercier, No. 19, July 23, 1862.

heading off any statement Russell might again make in Parliament that the Confederacy would not accept mediation.[1]

Mason's note demanding recognition was very brief, for the commissioner accompanied the note with a request for an interview in which he hoped to develop the points of his note in detail. He repeated briefly the old arguments as to the legality of secession, the size and resources of the Confederacy, and urged that it had shown its right to recognition by its success in maintaining its independence for eighteen months against all attempts to subjugate it. The Confederate government, said Mason, asked no aid; it only asked recognition which was its by right of the sword.[2]

Mason waited in suspense until July 31 when he received a short note from Russell who declined to grant Mason an interview because he did "not think any advantage would arise from the personal interview." But at the same time he left Mason with some hopes and in great suspense. He told him that he had delayed answering his note asking recognition "in order that he might submit a draft of it to the Cabinet on Saturday next."[3] Immediately following the receipt of Russell's note in which an interview was refused, the commissioner hastened to incorporate in a letter to Russell the things he had hoped to present in the proposed interview. The main point of this supplementary note of August 1 was to combat the propaganda of Seward that the majority of non-slaveholders in the South were Unionists, who only waited the opportunity to come back into the Union. Mason insisted that the whole population, as events proved, were loyal to the Confederacy. On the other hand, he urged that there existed a large group in the North anxious for peace, and that recognition would give great impetus to the peace movement.[4]

On August 2 Russell replied to Mason that the "time . . . . has not, in the judgment of her Majesty's Government, yet arrived" for

[1] See Pickett Papers, Mason to Benjamin, No. 14 and inclosures, July 30, 1862, for correspondence; *O.R.N.*, Ser. 2, Vol. III, pp. 490–504.

[2] *Ibid.*, inclosure, Mason to Russell, July 24, 1862; cf. Mason Papers, Mason to Slidell, July 24, 1862.

[3] Pickett Papers, Mason to Benjamin, No. 14 with inclosure, July 30, 1862, and Russell to Mason, July 31, 1862; *O.R.N.*, Ser. 2, Vol. III, pp. 490–504.

[4] *Ibid.*, Mason to Russell, Aug. 1, 1862.

recognition. No mention, of course, was made of the cabinet, which was engaged in a critical discussion of intervention in America. Russell assured Mason that his government could not undertake to judge of the legality of secession or of the moral rights involved. The only matter with which his government could concern itself was the ability of the South to gain and maintain its independence; and he pointed out that the fall of New Orleans, Memphis, and the battles of Shiloh, balanced by McClellan's defeat before Richmond, indicated that events had not yet taken a decisive turn. Unfortunately, Russell, English-like, could not let the opportunity escape for offering some gratuitous sarcasm for which he would later find it necessary to atone. Mason had asserted in his note of July 24 that the Confederacy had twelve million people, that they had maintained their independence for eighteen months, and that the intelligent people of Europe recognized that the Union could not be restored. Russell replied to this statement by quoting Seward to the effect that less than five million white people had been in insurrection, and that a great portion of the disaffected population had been restored to loyalty, and that far from being impossible the restoration of the Union was only prevented by the South's hopes of European intervention. Russell was proving Mason a liar by quoting Seward.[1] While Russell made these assertions to Mason, he was not as confident of the disaffected population being restored to loyalty as his note would imply. Lyons had written him on November 25, 1861, after the United States had captured Port Royal that although this port gave the United States command of a harbor for the use of their blockading squadron it had "completely failed in producing any demonstration of Union feeling in the South."[2] After the fall of New Orleans Russell wrote Lyons to inquire "guardedly and discreetly of Mr. Seward" whether it appeared, "as was fondly hoped last year, that the rupture between North and South was the work of a few conspirators, and that the great majority of the people of the South are attracted to the Union." Also Russell wished Lyons to ask whether the President and Congress would govern the southern

[1] *Ibid.*, Russell to Mason, Aug. 2, 1862.
[2] F.O. Amer., Vol. 775, Lyons to Russell, No. 706, Nov. 25, 1861.

states as "conquered provinces" and if so "what are the numbers of the standing army which it will be necessary to keep on foot?"[1]

The refusal of an interview, harking back to 1861 when Adams had forced Russell into promising to have no further communications with the Confederate agents, combined with the attempted refutation of Mason's statement by quoting the enemy's Secretary of State, was a bitter dose for even the kindly and evenly poised Mason, but he did not lose his temper; he merely alluded to the refusal of an interview as an "apparently uncourteous refusal." But he could not refrain from accusing the American Secretary of State of "open mendacity." He contemplated writing Russell a reply "commenting freely but respectfully" on his position and proving the falsity of Seward's statement.[2] But Mason felt appeased when some English friends told him that the cabinet, which had discussed his note demanding recognition, was closely divided on intervention. He now felt that if Napoleon urged recognition upon England, the cabinet, forced by public opinion, might soon "be dragged into an ungraceful reversal of their decision."[3]

Gladstone, in fact, had at the cabinet been very strongly in favor of offering mediation; but the majority of his colleagues were unwilling to act yet, though considerable signs were appearing that there might be action presently.[4]

Charles F. Adams, like Mason, had a feeling that early intervention was almost inevitable. The great powers, moved by public pressure, would offer mediation, and if the North refused them, then a simple recognition would follow which, Adams believed, would mean the independence of the South.[5] United States Consul Dudley, at Liverpool, who was much nearer the popular pulse than Adams, was alarmed as never before by the drift of things. The defeat of McClel-

[1] *Ibid.*, Vol. 819, Russell to Lyons, No. 272, June 16, 1862.

[2] Pickett Papers, Mason to Benjamin, July 30 and Aug. 4, 1862; *O.R.N.*, Ser. 2, Vol. III, pp. 490–504.

[3] *Ibid.*; cf. Mason Papers, Mason to Slidell, Slidell to Mason, Aug. 3, 1862.

[4] See E. D. Adams, II, 26–27; Argyll, *Autobiography and Memoirs* (London, 1906), II, 191.

[5] *A Cycle of Adams' Letters*, I, 168–69.

lan threw practically all sympathy to the South: "The current is against us and is strong; and threatens to carry everything with it. I do not think we have any thing to depend upon in this country or Europe. They are all against us and would rejoice in our downfall. I think at this time we are more in danger of intervention than we have been at any previous period. From what I see and hear I am fully persuaded that if we are not successful in some decisive battle within a short period this government will be forced to acknowledge the Confederacy or else be driven from power."[1] Edwin de Leon wrote from Vichy, France, on July 30, 1862, that he felt that "the prospects of our early recognition (which will involve intervention) to be most probable and in fact imminent." He shared Mason's opinion that Napoleon would practically force the British cabinet to act.[2] Even Dayton felt the drift of events and wrote Seward on August 2, 1862, that Persigny had confirmed the rumor that France, England, and Russia were planning to offer mediation.[3]

With details of the defeat of McClellan still piling so high that C. F. Adams declared he "should hardly suppose that we had any forces left any where,"[4] the closely divided cabinet, and the knowledge that the Emperor was impatiently waiting action, the southern lobby decided to try another expedient before Parliament should adjourn on August 7: They decided to call for the correspondence between Russell and Mason and others touching the recognition of the South. So on August 4 Lord Campbell made a motion calling for these papers, followed by a speech urging recognition.[5]

Russell refused to comply with the motion on the ground that the papers were unofficial. But this resolution at least drew from Russell an official statement of the present status of intervention. The government's position was unchanged as to intervention. But "if in the course of the recess we should think it desirable to adopt any new

[1] U.S. Consular Des., Liverpool, Dudley to W. H. Seward, No. 96, July 25, 1862.

[2] Pickett Papers, De Leon to Benjamin, No. 1, July 30, 1862; *O.R.*, Ser. 4, Vol. II, pp. 23–26.

[3] U.S. Des., France, Vol. 52, No. 178.

[4] *A Cycle of Adams' Letters*, I, 173.

[5] Parl. Deb. Lords, Vol. 168, pp. 1177–83.

line of policy, I should think it necessary to communicate with the maritime powers of Europe before taking any steps." Russell with malicious satisfaction and sarcasm thus spoke of approaching the other powers for the benefit of such private diplomats as Lindsay who were always implying that Napoleon had proposed mediation. "I make that statement," continued Russell, "because my noble friend [Campbell] seems to understand that the maritime powers wish to recognize the Southern States and that some objection on our part has prevented recognition. Now I have no communication from any foreign power stating any wish or making any proposition with regard to the recognition of the Southern States."[1] Two points were stated then: (1) England was still neutral and (2) no communication had been received from France. This was the second time in less than two months that Russell had officially denied in the House of Lords the receipt of any proposals from the Emperor to intervene in America.[2] But Russell's repeated denial of having received any proposal of intervention from France was exasperating to the Confederates. Mason urged Slidell[3] to "bring this to the notice of the ministry and have their views on such declaration." Plainly Russell was lying and he should be exposed, thought Mason.

Slidell on reading Russell's answer to Mason's note on recognition said it was "worthy of the man," for, said Slidell, Russell knew that Seward's claim that there was a large Union party in the South was "an unqualified falsehood," and yet he used this as the chief argument for withholding recognition. Slidell was convinced that the ministry's real motive in inaction was that they wished to see the North weakened by a long struggle. Russell's answer, he continued, was obviously given Mason without any consultation with the Emperor—which amounted to an indignity. This, Slidell believed, "will make him the better disposed to pursue his own policy without consulting England." Russell's answer, discourteous both to Mason and the Emperor, might prove a blessing. Nor was Russell's denial of any proposals for intervention by Napoleon honest, wrote Slidell. It

[1] *Ibid.*

[2] Pickett Papers, Mason to Benjamin, No. 15, Aug. 5, 1862; *O.R.N.*, Ser. 2, Vol. III, p. 509.

[3] Mason Papers, Mason to Slidell, Aug. 5, 1862.

was just "another *suggestio falsio*, ... no such propositions are on record in the foreign office but he has been repeatedly unofficially informed that the Emperor was ready and willing to act and only waited for his co-operation."

Persigny, said Slidell, also felt that Russell's failure to consult the Emperor before answering Mason's note and his denial of any proposals on intervention from France showed a want of "decent respect," and he believed that Napoleon might soon act alone.[1]

Slidell's note of July 24 demanding recognition had a different fate from Mason's of the same date. Thouvenel, as we have seen, at the time he received the note had assured Slidell that the government was as yet not in a position to act. But a number of cabinet meetings and serious discussions on the question of recognition followed the presentation of the note. Slidell kept in close touch with what was going on by frequent conferences with Baroche (president of the Council), Rouher (minister of commerce), and Fould (minister of finance), and he was convinced that no immediate action on his note or on the general question of intervention would be taken. The idea that France could not act alone in safety to herself or with good effect on the war was still in the ascendancy. It was feared that such action would only stimulate the North to further effort and tend to encourage the war party in the fall elections. This was Mercier's view, and it carried great weight with the government. Slidell tried to combat these views by urging that recognition would encourage the peace party and bring the war to an end.[2]

De Morny, the most influential adviser of the Emperor, came to see Slidell around August 20 and assured him of his own and the Emperor's sympathies, but warned him as had the other members of Napoleon's official family that he must not hope for France to act alone in granting recognition. However, he assured Slidell, events had been in motion for some time which indicated that England was preparing to join France in intervention.[3]

[1] *Ibid.*, Slidell to Mason, Aug. 6, 1862.

[2] Pickett Papers, Slidell to Benjamin, No. 11, Aug. 12, 1862; *O.R.N.*, Ser. 2, Vol. III, pp. 511–12.

[3] Pickett Papers, Slidell to Benjamin, No. 12, Aug. 20, 1862; *O.R.N.*, Ser. 2, Vol. III, pp. 518–20; cf. Mason Papers, Benjamin to Mason, Aug. 20, 1862.

Just about the same time, August 19, the confidential "friend" Cintrat in the Foreign Office—whose name Slidell is careful always except once not to mention—came to him with a message from Thouvenel with reference to Slidell's note asking recognition. He told Slidell, so the latter wrote Benjamin,[1] "that Thouvenel did not want to send an unmeaning reply to my demand for recognition; that at present he could make no other, that unless I insisted he would be silent." Slidell hastened at once to consult with Persigny who advised him not to insist on a reply until it was definitely known that McClellan had left the peninsula or that Pope had been defeated. Slidell saw the necessity and perhaps the wisdom of this course—especially since the Emperor was away at Châlons and would probably be out of Paris (at Biarritz) several weeks. But should no news ot Confederate victories come, Slidell wrote Mason,[2] "I shall await the Emperor's return. . . . . I shall then endeavor to have an audience, if I find him still unprepared to act I shall write a formal note to Mr. T[houvenel] requesting an early exposition of his views and having received it will inform him of my intention to leave Paris."[3] Mason advised against Slidell's withdrawal from France. "The delay in sending your reply must of course be submitted to, as long as your note is held under consideration it leaves the matter at least in doubt and that doubt is far better for us than a refusal. I think as matters now stand as shown in your note I would hesitate to present any categorical demand for an answer. The great effect of recognition would to be dishearten the North, if refused they would be encouraged. While it is held in doubt, they are not encouraged."[4]

This waiting, though he realized its wisdom, did not please Slidell. A few days after receiving Mason's letter he wrote Benjamin that the Confederate cause was fast aground in Europe and "nothing will float us off but a strong and continued current of important successes." He had lost all hopes of England's joining France in intervention, because he was satisfied that "she desires an indefinite pro-

[1] *Ibid.*   [2] Mason Papers, Slidell to Mason, Aug. 20, 1862.

[3] Cf. Pickett Papers, Slidell to Benjamin, No. 12, Aug. 20, 1862; *O.R.N.*, Ser. 2, Vol. III, pp. 518–20.

[4] Mason Papers, Mason to Slidell, Aug. 31, 1862.

longation of the war, until the North shall be entirely exhausted and broken down."[1]

On September 10 Mason wrote Slidell[2] that the great news of Pope's defeat at the Battle of Bull Run had just arrived and that the capture of Washington was imminent. At the same time English correspondents and friends wrote Slidell that the British cabinet was going to take up the question of recognition in the early part of October.[3] Encouraged by Confederate military successes and by the rumors of British cabinet activities, he determined to push for an answer to his note as soon as the Emperor returned to Paris. He believed that Napoleon would, under such favorable auspices, now approach the British cabinet with an official proposal of joint intervention.[4]

Since Napoleon would not return until the first week in October, Slidell approached him first by written communication. On September 12 he wrote a memorandum which Persigny submitted to the Emperor. In this document Slidell again urged recognition as the only means of ending the war. He pointed out the recent defeats of the Federals. They would probably lose Washington to the Confederates shortly. But none of these northern defeats would end the war. Nothing but recognition which would discourage the war party in the North and aid the peace party there in winning the elections would end the struggle. The British cabinet was on the point of taking up the question. He urged Napoleon to put his proposal before that cabinet at once and thereby deprive Russell of the possibility, in case he should decide against intervention, of claiming that the French government supported his position.[5]

About two weeks after writing this memorandum Slidell received more direct information that the British cabinet might soon act favorably on southern recognition. He learned from the Earl of

[1] Pickett Papers, Slidell to Benjamin, Aug. 24, 1862; *O.R.N.*, Ser. 2, Vol. III, pp. 520–21.

[2] Mason Papers, Mason to Slidell, Sept. 10, 1862.

[3] *Ibid.*, Slidell to Mason, Sept. 12, 1862.   [4] *Ibid.*

[5] Pickett Papers, Slidell to Benjamin, No. 13 inclosing memorandum, Sept. 13, 1862; *O.R.N.*, Ser. 2, Vol. III, pp. 525–27.

Shaftesbury, Palmerston's son-in-law, who was passing through Paris, that the government was considering intervention seriously, and that it might make a move shortly.[1]

The next day (September 30) after Shaftesbury returned home he wrote Slidell that "there is every reason to believe that the event you so strongly desire [recognition] and of which we talked when I had the pleasure of seeing you in Paris is very close at hand. . . . ."[2] Slidell felt that this letter from Shaftesbury indicated that it was time for him to see Thouvenel, and he hurried to the Foreign Office only to find that gentleman closeted with Dayton. However, Slidell's "friend" in the Foreign Office brought him a message from Thouvenel which assured him that the South might expect recognition soon—but not as soon as the Earl of Shaftesbury predicted. What probably warmed Slidell's heart more than anything else was that part of the message which assured him that a correspondence concerning intervention was now being carried on with the British Foreign Office.[3]

On the same day Slidell learned from Persigny that Fould, who had just come back from attendance on the Emperor at Biarritz, reported that Napoleon was making efforts throughout Europe to secure a general recognition for the South.[4]

Just as Slidell was getting ready to seek an interview with the Emperor, he was discouraged and delayed by unfavorable events and rumors. Thouvenel was about to leave the cabinet because of a disagreement over the Italian crisis, and Lord Cowley denied that there had been any correspondence between England and France concerning the joint action of the two governments in the Civil War. Thouvenel on hearing this assured Slidell that this denial of Cowley was a poor joke as there had been serious conversations.[5] As we shall see in our discussion of the British cabinet controversy,[6] Russell was

[1] Pickett Papers, Slidell to Benjamin, No. 15, Sept. 29, 1862; *O.R.N.*, Ser. 2, Vol. III, pp. 546–48.

[2] Mason Papers, Slidell to Mason, Oct. 2, 1862, inclosing parts of letter.

[3] Pickett Papers, Slidell to Benjamin, No. 16, Oct. 9, 1862; *O.R.N.*, Ser. 2, Vol. III, pp. 551–52.

[4] *Ibid.*

[5] Mason Papers, Slidell to Mason, Oct. 17, 1862.   [6] See chap. x.

carrying on unofficial conversations with Thouvenel, through Cowley, just at this time. This continued denial of the existence of communications unless they were formal throws a questionable light upon the forthrightness and truthfulness of the British Foreign Office. Slidell hardly knew what to believe.

On October 26 Slidell called on De Lhuys, the successor of Thouvenel in the Foreign Office. Slidell gave De Lhuys, who had not been fully apprised of the status of the Confederate question, a summary of the situation up to that point. He told him about meeting the Emperor at Vichy, of the offer of alliance, of free trade and cotton. De Lhuys was impressed but cautious. Slidell told him of the note of July 21 asking recognition. He alluded to the attitude of the British cabinet, which, he had been informed, would not abandon its neutrality. He spoke of the continuous denials of the British government that the question of intervention had been taken up with the French. De Lhuys was of the opinion that such denials were misrepresentations of the real facts. But he had not been in the Foreign Office long enough to know what had been said between Cowley and Thouvenel. But Slidell felt that these denials of the British cabinet were indications that England had no intention of joining France in any undertaking affecting the war in America. So he pled for separate action on the part of France. But De Lhuys, as Thouvenel had done before him, said such a course was impossible.[1]

Two days later Slidell had his second interview with Napoleon, at Saint-Cloud. Napoleon unquestionably had been considerably influenced directly and indirectly by Slidell during the nine months that the latter had been in France. Slidell's frequent contact with Fould, Rouher, De Morny, Persigny, and Billault, when he had persistently discussed intervention, his personal interview with the Emperor in July, the memoranda placed in Napoleon's hands—all were strong influences in convincing the Emperor of the strength of the southern position.

But in the last analysis Mercier was Napoleon's reliance with regard to the American question. Though Mercier was convinced by his Richmond visit that the South could not be defeated and that on

[1] Pickett Papers, Slidell to Benjamin, No. 19, Oct. 28, 1862; *O.R.N.*, Ser. 2, Vol. III, pp. 572–74.

the other hand war would be prolonged indefinitely unless the European powers intervened, he had advised that no proposals of intervention should be made until the tide of northern victories had ceased and defeat had broken the Federal armies. Thouvenel had instructed Mercier to hold himself in readiness to propose the good offices of France. Then about July 1 Mercier had interviewed Seward only to be rebuffed at the first hints of intervention. Mercier advised his government that further defeat would be necessary to bring the North to a proper state of mind for peace. But owing to the crushing defeats of the northern armies by September 2, he thought that the time was near when intervention might be acceptable.[1] In a few days he interviewed Seward for the purpose of reviving the idea of mediation. He told Seward that the recent defeats had produced a profound impression in Europe, to which Seward replied with grim pugnacity: "I have noticed it but as for us it would be a great misfortune if the powers should wish to intervene in our affairs. There is no possible compromise, tell Mr. Thouvenel, and at any price, we will not admit the division of the Union. . . . ." Mercier replied: "I only wish that in all events you should know the sentiments of my government," which was friendly to the United States and always ready to tender the good offices. Seward replied quickly and positively that "we do not doubt your sentiments but the best testimony that you are able to give us of it is that you will stay out of our affairs."[2] In this conversation Mercier told Seward that his government had assured him that "we will do nothing at any time or in any way unless you [M. Mercier] shall tell us it is for the best interests of the whole country." Mercier then told Seward that he believed the restoration of the Union impossible. "We therefore think, my government thinks," continued Mercier, "that what is best is that which will be nearest to what has been before, what is most like what the Union has been. So that if there must be two Confederacies, then that they should be confederated Confederacies." Mercier's idea of two confederated confederacies, blandly suggested, must have almost given Seward a bad twist. He stopped Mercier, telling him to get it clear that separation was impossible. "Do not believe for a

---

[1] French F.O. Amer., Vol. 128, Mercier to Thouvenel, No. 112, Sept. 2, 1862.

[2] *Ibid.*, No. 113, Sept. 9, 1862.

moment," he said, "that either the Federal Congress, myself or any person connected with this government will in any case entertain any proposition or suggestion of arrangement or accommodation or adjustment from within or without upon the basis of a surrender of the Federal Union." He told Mercier that chaos was preferable to disunion. He reminded Mercier of how France had saved herself in 1793 from internal and external foes. He plainly suggested, as an answer to European intervention, slave insurrection, fire, and slaughter.[1]

Immediately upon receipt of Mercier's report of the conversation with Seward in which settlement was offered upon the basis of two confederated confederacies—which was a euphemistic way of saying independence—Thouvenel held an interview with Dayton, who had not yet received Seward's report of Mercier's proposal. Thouvenel, who up to this time had always assured Dayton of his personal sympathy for the North,[2] now proposed, as had Mercier, two confederated confederacies as the only possible solution of the struggle. He frankly told Dayton that he regretted that the North had ever undertaken to conquer the South. He felt that it was a futile waste of life and treasure. Dayton rejected the idea of such an arrangement without discussion.[3] On September 18 Thouvenel in his reply to Mercier's letter describing the interview and proposal of two confederated confederacies expressed the hopes that America would soon accept mediation.[4]

Up to this point France had never made an official proposal of mediation either directly to the United States or to England. But on September 30 for the first time Mercier, on whom the Emperor relied to decide when intervention might be appropriately undertaken, wrote his government that the time had come for making an open, formal proposal.

Since spring, and especially since Mercier's visit to Richmond, he

[1] U.S. Inst., France, Vol. 16, Seward to Dayton, No. 207, Sept. 8, 1862, contains full account of the interview.

[2] E.g., U.S. Des., France, Vol. 52, Dayton to Seward, No. 195, Sept. 13, 1862.

[3] Ibid., Sept. 17, 1862 ("Unofficial and Confidential"); cf. ibid., No. 200, Sept. 23, 1862.

[4] French F.O. Amer., Vol. 128, No. 24, Sept. 18, 1862.

had been regarding with fearful apprehension the increasing ferocity of the conflict. The implacable attitude of Seward, who in nearly every interview in which European mediation was even vaguely suggested hinted at universal emancipation, the raising of slaves in revolt against their masters, and the consequent destruction of the southern economic and social system and perhaps the white race, only served to convince Mercier of the necessity of intervention. At last Seward's threats seemed about to be realized when the emancipation proclamation was issued September 23. One of the main motives behind this proclamation was to prevent European intervention by shifting the issue of the struggle to the slavery question, and thus to win the sympathy of the antislavery groups in Europe. It is an ironic twist of events that it should operate upon the minds of Mercier and the French government in just the opposite way, for as soon as the proclamation was issued Mercier advised his government to intervene. He assured Thouvenel that the proclamation was mainly intended to disarm European interference, which was looming so largely after the great series of defeats of the summer of 1862. Mercier wrote that the proclamation had turned the border states against the Union and had greatly inspired the peace party of the North. He was horrified at the possible outcome of the proclamation. There would be anarchy, horrible carnage, and conflagration, and crimes too revolting to mention would fill the land. "On this basis, I question if the moment has not arrived for the governments of Europe to make a serious effort to prevent the events from which they would have to suffer so cruelly themselves." A large number of the people and their leaders, such as Seymour of New York, desired peace but dared not speak out, "and I imagine that the great powers of Europe should be able without danger to come effectually to the aid of these and the others." The only thing that was necessary, said Mercier, to put an end to this brutal struggle is for the nations jointly to "invite the Federal Government to stop a war which had resulted up to now only in increasing the profound abyss which separates the two sections of the country," and to warn the United States that "if this friendly advice is not listened to they [the European Governments] can do nothing else except to take council of their own interests. Coming at the time of the elections such a step would produce an excellent effect."[1]

Mercier followed up this with several other dispatches giving fuller information of the recent defeats of the United States and the prospects should the war last longer.[2]

Just about the time that De Lhuys received Mercier's dispatches, especially No. 121 describing the Federal defeat at Chattanooga and enlarging upon the horrors following the emancipation proclamation and the destruction of the southern economic system including the culture of cotton, Slidell had his interview of October 26 with De Lhuys and then on October 28 his interview with the Emperor. These dispatches advising immediate intervention were in the Emperor's hands when Slidell met him two days later for his second interview.

Slidell entered this consultation with great hopes of success. Though he was skeptical of any action on the part of England, he believed that the moment had arrived when Napoleon might act independently.

Napoleon was cordial and free with Slidell in this interview, and he approached with candor the subject nearest the heart. He asked Slidell what news he had from America and how affairs were getting on. Slidell answered quickly that since his interview with the Emperor in July at Vichy "our position had most materially improved, and was now better than at any previous period; that our troops were as numerous and better disciplined than they had ever been," and that the South was fully capable now of taking care of itself and had no doubts of its ultimate success, but that it desired peace as soon as possible. "The Emperor replied that he was entirely satisfied of the correctness of all that I said; that he had no scruples in declaring that his sympathies were entirely with the South; that his only desire was to know how to give them effect." He spoke of the serious complications in Italy and Greece, saying that he had to act in these and matters concerning America with great caution and "intimated that if he acted alone, England, instead of following his example, would endeavor to embroil him with the United States and

[1] *Ibid.*, No. 117, Sept. 30, 1862.   [2] See, e.g., *ibid.*, Nos. 118, 119, and 120.

that French commerce would be destroyed." Slidell endeavored to combat this idea. He frankly told Napoleon that he did not believe England would act until it was too late to render any service to the South. Recognition was all the South asked for. This would end the war by demoralizing the war party in the North. It would have caused the peace party to win the fall elections if it had been accorded the South a few months earlier. As for embroiling France with the North, Slidell urged that "recognition would not afford in the eyes of the world the slightest pretext for hostilities on the part of the North." But there were much stronger reasons for the North to keep the peace than the mere absence of a *casus belli:* the economic interests of that country. "Their mercantile tonnage was infinitely larger than that of France, and that in the same proportion would be their losses at sea." But the greatest consideration, perhaps, was the powerful French Navy. Slidell assured the Emperor as he had in July that he was positive "that their navy, of which they boasted so loudly, would be swept from the ocean and all their principal ports efficiently blockaded by a moiety of his powerful marine, and that the 'Gloire' or the 'Normandie' could enter without risk the harbors of New York and Boston and lay those cities under contribution."

Napoleon loved this praise of his beautiful "Gloire" and "Normandie"—both powerful ironclads. But he had no intention of risking these precious ships in a war with the United States. He would not act alone, but was ready to join with other maritime nations. "What do you think of the joint mediation of France, England, and Russia? Would it, if proposed, be accepted by the two parties?" he inquired of Slidell.

Slidell was now wary of joint mediation. He believed the North would accept it but he "could not venture to say how it would be received at Richmond." He had no faith in England and was convinced that Russia would lean strongly to the northern side; in short, "that the mediation of the three powers, when France could be outvoted, would not be acceptable; that we might perhaps, with certain assurances, consent to the joint mediation of France and England. . . . ." But he could say positively that the Confederates would gladly accept the Emperor's "umpirage."

Seeing that joint mediation, then, was unacceptable to Slidell, Napoleon suggested another form of intervention which would not commit the South to anything. He said, "My own preference is for a proposition of an armistice of six months, with the Southern ports open to the commerce of the world. This would put a stop to the effusion of blood, and hostilities would probably never be resumed." This proposal, continued Napoleon, could be urged upon the high moral grounds of humanity, "and the interests of the whole civilized world." If the North refused to stop the struggle when appealed to on such ground, "it will afford good reason for recognition and perhaps more active intervention." While the armistice idea appeared very innocent, Napoleon was seriously contemplating the ultimate question of armed intervention.

Slidell replied that such a course was acceptable. It was the very course he had suggested to Thouvenel in his first interview in February, 1862. But Slidell expressed doubts as to obtaining the co-operation of England. Napoleon, however, was of the opinion that England would join him. He had a letter from King Leopold of Belgium dated October 15, urging that he take the lead in putting a stop to the war. He showed the letter to Slidell. It was a powerful appeal on the basis of humanity and especially for those who suffered in the famine-stricken cotton industries. Napoleon explained to Slidell that this letter was written by Leopold while Queen Victoria, his relative, was visiting him; that Leopold had more influence with the Queen than any living man—in fact, that he had assumed the rôle of chief adviser in the place of the late Prince Consort. The Emperor believed the letter was written after Leopold had convinced the Queen of the necessity of intervention.

This letter was not satisfactory evidence to Slidell that England had any intention of joining France in bringing the American struggle to an end. He called Napoleon's attention to Cowley's repeated denials that the British government had received any overtures from France suggesting joint action. The Emperor good-humoredly assured Slidell that Cowley and the British government acting "in accordance with diplomatic usages . . . . consider nothing to exist that had not been formally written," but that he had approached the British government. Strange to say, Napoleon failed to tell Slidell of the best evidence in his possession which showed that England might be willing to act jointly with France in intervention; he failed to mention the fact that twice during the previous month of September Russell had approached him through Cowley as to his willingness to join England in intervention.

In the course of the conversation Slidell did not fail to hold out strong material inducements to the Emperor. He repeated his offer made at Vichy in July of free trade, a large cotton bonus, and finally full approval of the Emperor's Mexican venture. As to the Mexican project and other schemes of the Emperor in Santo Domingo, Slidell wrote Benjamin, "I took occasion to say to the Emperor that however distasteful such a measure might be to the Washington Government ours could not have objection to it."[1]

Two days after this interview, on October 30, 1862, De Lhuys wrote a confidential dispatch to Mercier announcing that Napoleon had decided to offer mediation in the form of a proposal of a six-month armistice. No attempt would be made to force the North to accept this proposal.[2]

So at the end of October, as far as the Confederate agents knew, the status of intervention was as follows: Mason's demand for recognition had been rejected by the British cabinet, but a rumor was abroad that the question might be raised again soon; Slidell's note demanding recognition had not been formally acted upon, but Napoleon had just assured Slidell that he would propose joint action to England. There was, however, a chapter relating to the status of the Confederacy as an independent nation which was totally unknown to the Confederate commissioners. The British cabinet during the months of September and October considered the question of joint intervention, by recognition, mediation, or armed intervention, and it was only the failure of the Confederate campaign in Maryland which prevented the British government from undertaking some form of intervention.

[1] Interview described in Pickett Papers, Slidell to Benjamin, No. 19 with inclosure entitled "Memorandum of an Interview, etc.," Oct. 28, 1862; *O.R.N.*, Ser. 2, Vol. III, pp. 572–78.

[2] French F.O. Amer., Vol. 128, De Lhuys to Mercier, No. 27 ("Confidential"), Oct. 30, 1862.

CHAPTER X

THE CLIMAX OF INTERVENTION

MEDIATION; ARMISTICE

Though Russell had coldly replied to Mason's note that England could not recognize the Confederacy or interfere in any way in the American war, he was at the moment of his reply, and had been for some weeks, seriously considering the thing which he denied. The military success of the South combined with the cotton famine were rapidly undermining the neutrality of the British Foreign Minister and some of his cabinet colleagues. The cotton supply had reached 200,000 bales by July, as compared with a total of 1,200,000 of July, 1861, and by September the stock had gone to 100,000—five weeks' supply at the current rate of 20,000 per week consumption. Over 400,000 of the 533,959 operatives were partly or completely idle. Over a million souls, including the dependents of the operatives, were dependent on stingy charity.[1] They could force the British government into desperate measures were they to rise up and demand action. Palmerston and Russell, and Disraeli and Derby of the opposition, viewed Manchester with cold apprehension. But leaders of government and opposition were agreed that unless the cotton famine drove the operatives to force the government to act, both political parties would steer clear of all intervention. The sinuous fingers of King Cotton began to tighten around the windpipe of the pro-northern Russell and the anti-northern Palmerston, and caused them to peep fearfully into the future and, despite their cold noncommittal attitudes in Parliament, to consider of the day when they might choose between revolution at home and intervention and war abroad.

The first indication of Russell's state of mind was the querulous and carping tone he assumed in his correspondence with the British Minister at Washington concerning the question of obtaining cotton

[1] See chap. iv.

through the captured ports of New Orleans, Beaufort, Georgetown, etc. It will be recalled that the optimistic and clever Seward in the spring of 1862 had attempted to quiet both the Emperor and the British cabinet by holding out the prospects of getting through New Orleans cotton in sufficient quantities to stave off the famine.[1] But Lyons as early as May, 1862, expressed grave doubts as to the possibility of ever getting cotton from any of the captured southern ports.[2] Russell, who was growing weary of Seward's promises, replied to Lyons that in his opinion southern cotton had not come to New Orleans because southern planters knew that their cotton would be confiscated as soon as they brought it within Federal lines. "If the Federal Government wish to make it possible for Europe to purchase cotton, they will ensure to each Southern planter who wishes to sell his crop, the money which the buyer pays for it. . . . . The transaction must be independent of political allegiance or it will not take place at all. You may speak to Mr. Seward in this sense if you have an opportunity." Russell was in substance asking that the Federal blockade on King Cotton be suspended.[3]

Chargé d'affaires Stuart (Lyons was now on leave in England) immediately presented Russell's complaints to Seward. The latter with the substitutes and subterfuges of a patent-medicine show spieler assured Stuart that England would get cotton soon. He had sent Mr. Bullitt to New Orleans to investigate the situation. But he could assure Stuart in advance that Bullitt would find all the people in that section Union at heart and ready to swear allegiance to the Union and ready to deliver the cotton within the Union lines.[4] Before Stuart's letter describing his interview with Seward had more than got into the mails, Russell wrote a more impatient letter than the last, with regard to the United States allowing cotton to leave captured ports. "If Mr. Seward and the Cabinet will adopt the plan

[1] See U.S. Inst., France, Vol. 16, Seward to Dayton, No. 114, Feb. 19, 1862; ibid., No. 133, March 26, 1862; U.S. Des., France, Vol. 51, Dayton to Seward, No. 129 ("Confidential"), March 25, 1862; British F.O. Amer., Vol. 1006, Lyons to Russell, No. 317, May 9, 1862; ibid., May 16, 1862.

[2] Parl. Accts. and Papers, U.S., Vol. LXXII (1863), pp. 1–12, North Amer., No. 1.

[3] Ibid.   [4] Ibid., July 11, 1862.

suggested by me," said Russell, "cotton might be procured. This matter deserves the serious considerations of the Government of the United States."

At this very moment Persigny was in London bringing pressure upon Russell; the cotton-famine reports were coming in like reports from a storm-devastated area; and news of McClellan's defeats was drifting in. The British Foreign Minister was rapidly approaching the state of mind looking to intervention. Four days later, July 16, Russell wrote Stuart in reply to the latter's note concerning the dispatching of Mr. Bullitt to New Orleans: "The conduct of Mr. Seward, in regard to the export of cotton, as reported in your despatch of the 25 ultimo is far from being satisfactory. It was not necessary to send an agent to New Orleans to ascertain the quantity of cotton ready for market [and] the disposition of the planters generally in regard to its sale and exportation. . . . . The question is one of fair conduct towards neutrals to enable their people to carry on the industry by which they live. Mr. Seward always held out the expectation that when the Southern ports were taken by the Federalists, and the authority of the United States restored in those ports, cotton would be forthcoming to be purchased for the use of Europe. New Orleans and other Southern ports have been taken, and the United States' authority restored therein, but the cotton is not forthcoming. The remedy should not have been delayed nor the interests of neutrals treated with so little regard."[1]

Stuart, on receiving this letter about August 1, hastened to Seward who, though putting up a bold front, was distressed at the defeat of McClellan in the peninsular campaign and the threats of intervention heard across the Atlantic. Stuart presented Seward this sharp note from Russell. Seward remained suave and bold, regretting the interruption of the cotton trade. But it was no fault of the United States, he replied; the Confederate authorities would not let the cotton pass through the enemy lines. Stuart challenged this excuse instantly. He pointed out that Sherman's orders forbade the Confederate cotton thus sent through from being paid for in United

[1] *Ibid.*

States money; that the cotton brought from the Confederacy into New Orleans was subject to confiscation by the United States Army; and that no planter dared bring cotton there.[1] Russell finally dismissed the possibilities of getting cotton as long as war continued.[2] But he began to consider how the war might be brought to an end. He was turning over in his mind the possibility of intervention.

On July 3, 1862, Lord Lyons, on leave in London, wrote Stuart, who was now favoring intervention, that he thought intervention would be unwise, but that at the same time the necessity for such action seemed to be inevitably approaching. "The distress in the manufacturing districts," he wrote, "threatens to be so great that a pressure may be put upon the government which they will find difficult to resist."[3]

Gladstone, chancellor of the exchequer, who was growing uneasy under the cotton famine, wrote Colonel Neville on July 26, 1862, that the South had earned its independence.[4] On August 6, two days after he had stated in Parliament that Great Britain would remain neutral for the time and that France had made no offers, four days after the cabinet had decided not to change its policy for the present, Russell indicated to Palmerston a state of mind quite contrary to that which he had seemed to have in Parliament. He advocated some move toward intervention. Despite the denial of official knowledge of France's position, Russell was in full possession of the actual facts. As we have seen, Mercier all during the spring had urged mediation upon Lyons and was now discussing it again. Lyons, of course, had written Russell. Then Persigny, Thouvenel, and Lindsay had placed it before him. Now he wrote Palmerston, taking note of the wishes of the French: "Mercier's notion that we should make some move in October agrees very well with yours. I shall be back in England before October, and we could then have a Cabinet upon it. Of course the war may flag before then.

"I quite agree that a proposal for an armistice should be the first step; but we must be prepared to answer the question on what basis are we to negotiate?"[5]

[1] *Ibid.*
[2] *Ibid.*, Aug. 15, 1862.
[3] Quoted in E. D. Adams, II, 26.
[4] *Ibid.*
[5] Palmerston MS, Aug. 6, cited in E. D. Adams, II, 32.

At this moment Stuart was urging Russell to prepare for action in October. By that time he thought that the new levies of troops would be destroyed by defeats and that the United States would be willing to listen to suggestions of peace.[1]

Russell journeyed over to Brussels about the first of September to attend the Queen who was visiting her kinsman Leopold of Belgium. He began laying the ground for his plans. The first step was to make sure that France was still willing to act with England, and on September 13 he wrote Cowley instructing him to hold private conversations with Thouvenel.[2] On September 14, on hearing the news of Jackson's recent exploits at Harpers Ferry, Russell wrote Palmerston that Stonewall seemed about to end the war and that "in October the hour will be ripe for the Cabinet."[3] Palmerston, receiving the news at the same time, wrote Russell on the same day in great glee that "the detailed accounts given in the *Observer* today of the battles of August 29 and 30 between the Confederates and the Federals show that the latter got a very complete smashing, and it seems not altogether unlikely that still greater disasters await them, and that even Washington or Baltimore may fall into the hands of the Confederates. If this should happen would it not be time for us to consider whether in such a state of things England and France might not address the contending parties and recommend an arrangement upon the basis of separation?"[4]

Three days later, September 17, Russell replied to Palmerston's suggestion of mediation. Palmerston had suggested that in case Washington or Baltimore were captured, England might then intervene on the basis of separation. But Russell felt satisfied with what the army of Virginia had accomplished as a basis of intervention. "Whether the Federal army is destroyed or not," he wrote, "it is clear that it is driven back to Washington and has made no progress in subduing the insurgent states. Such being the case, I agree with you that the time is come for offering mediation to the United States Government with a view to the recognition of the independence of the Confederates. I agree further that, in case of failure, we ought ourselves to recognize the Southern States as an independ-

[1] E. D. Adams, II, 37.   [2] *Ibid.*, p. 38.   [3] *Ibid.*
[4] Spencer Walpole, *Russell*, II, 360–61; Bigelow, *Retrospections, etc.*, I, 544.

ent state. For the purpose of taking so important a step, I think we must have a meeting of the Cabinet. The 23rd or 30th would suit me. We ought then, if we agree on such a step, propose it first to France, and then on the part of England and France to Russia and the other powers. . . . ."[1]

The following day Russell had a reply from Cowley that Thouvenel in the conversation—the very conversation denied by Cowley —over mediation had shown considerable objections. He wanted to wait until after the elections in America, believing that intervention would stimulate Federal enlistments and strengthen the war party, while if left alone the peace party might win the elections. Cowley had suggested according to his instructions that Federal acceptance of mediation could be forced upon the United States by all the powers presenting a solid front, and Thouvenel replied that Russia would refuse to join as France had already sounded her out and found her friendly toward the North.[2] But Thouvenel was known at the time to represent no opinion save his own on the American question; and it was also known that he was discredited and would be forced to resign because of his attitude in the Italian question.[3] Russell was sure of Napoleon's position, so Thouvenel's attitude did not matter.

Russell prepared another memorandum for Cowley to use as a basis for further private conversation with France, and sent Cowley's report of his first conversation with the French Foreign Minister along with this second memorandum to Palmerston, September 22, 1862. Russell still planned an agreement with France first, and then an offer to Russia, Austria, and Prussia.[4] On September 23 Palmerston replied to Russell's note. "Your plan of proceedings about the mediation between the Federals and Confederates seems to be excellent," he wrote. "Of course the offer would be made to both the contending parties at the same time. For though the offer would be as sure to be accepted by the Southerners as was the proposal of the Prince of Wales by the Danish Princess: yet in the one case as in the other there are certain forms which it is decent and proper to go through. A question would occur whether if the two parties were to

---

[1] Ibid.   [3] Ibid.

[2] E. D. Adams, II, 38–39.   [4] Ibid.

accept the mediation, the fact of our mediation would not of itself be tantamount to an acknowledgement of the Confederates as an independent state." There was one exception Palmerston took to Russell's proposed memorandum—he thought Russia must be included in the first invitation. "Might it not be well," he urged, "to ask Russia to join England and France in the offer of mediation? We should be better without her in the mediation because she would be favorable to the North; but on the other hand her participation in the offer might render the North the more willing to accept it." He agreed with Russell as to the time. "Events may take place which make it desirable that the offer should be made before the middle of October.[1] . . . . If the Federals sustained a great defeat, they may be at once ready for mediation, and the iron should be struck while it is hot. If on the other hand they should have the best of it, we may wait awhile and see what may follow. . . . ."[2] On October 2, Palmerston wrote Russell, "The whole matter is full of difficulty and can only be cleared up by some more decided events between the contending armies."[3] The Confederate success in Maryland as a condition precedent to Palmerston's agreeing to intervene in any way must not be overlooked as it is the key point.

While Russell and Palmerston were agreeing upon the terms of the private memorandum to Cowley, Russell instructed Lyons not to set a definite date for his return to America. "Mercier," he explained, "is again looking out for an opportunity to offer mediation, and this time he is not so much out in his reckoning."[4]

Up to this date it appears certain that no other members of the cabinet knew of Russell and Palmerston's proposed change of policy. Cowley had learned about it on September 13 when Russell had instructed him, and Lyons had just an inkling of what Russell was planning. These four men were probably the only Englishmen who knew anything definite. The American minister, Charles F. Adams, and Secretary of State Seward had strong suspicions that Russell and Palmerston were up to something; and Seward had written Adams

---

[1] Bigelow, I, 550–51; Walpole, *Russell*, II, 362.   [2] *Ibid.*

[3] Russell Papers, Public Record Office 30-22-14, Palmerston to Russell, Oct. 2, 1862. (Cited hereafter as Russell Papers, P.R.O.)

[4] Russell to Lyons, Sept. 24, quoted in E. D. Adams, I, 41, from Lyons Papers.

instructions on August 16 to break off relations if Europe recognized the South.[1]

But, despite the strenuous denials of Cowley that any conversations concerning intervention were being carried on between England and France, the secret got out through the French Foreign Office and through Palmerston's son-in-law, the Earl of Shaftesbury. On September 12, the day before Russell sent his instructions to Cowley to take the matter up with Thouvenel, Slidell wrote Mason that he had just received word from what he believed a reliable source—and after events proved him right—that the British cabinet would take up the southern question in early October.[2] Slidell does not mention his informant—it was probably his "friend" in the Foreign Office—but his next one was the Earl of Shaftesbury who visited him September 19 and then wrote him September 30 that he had good reasons for believing that the British cabinet would soon move for recognition.[3] On October 2, two days after Slidell received Shaftesbury's letter, he learned directly from his "friend" in the Foreign Office that conversations between England and France had taken place just as had been predicted.[4] Mason, too, learned from confidential friends that the British cabinet would presently consider intervention in some form.[5] Confederate success and the information that the British cabinet would act, we should recall at this point, had caused Slidell to send his memorandum to the Emperor, September 13, and it was Shaftesbury's letter of September 30 which hurried him to the Foreign Office and then to seek an interview with Napoleon.

This "leak" helped put Slidell in action. But let us continue the story of Russell's conduct. On September 24 his plans had reached

[1] E. D. Adams, II, 35–36; Rhodes, VI, 342–43; C. F. Adams, "Crisis in Downing Street," *Mass. Hist. Soc. Proceedings* (May, 1914), pp. 372–424; *U.S. Messages and Documents, 1862–3*, Part I, pp. 165–68.

[2] Mason Papers, Sept. 12, 1862.

[3] Pickett Papers, Slidell to Benjamin, Nos. 15 and 16, Sept. 29 and Oct. 19; *O.R.N.*, Ser. 2, Vol. III, pp. 546–48 and 551–52, respectively.

[4] Mason Papers, Slidell to Mason, Oct. 2, 1862.

[5] Pickett Papers, Mason to Benjamin, No. 17, Sept. 18, 1862; *O.R.N.*, Ser. 2, Vol. III, p. 533.

the point where the other members of the cabinet could be informed. On this day Palmerston wrote Gladstone that he and Russell had arrived at the conclusion that an offer of mediation should be made by England, France, and Russia. "It seems to Russell and me," wrote Palmerston, "that the Time is fast approaching when some joint offer of Mediation by England, France, and Russia, if She would be a Party to it, might be made with some Prospect of Success to the Combatants in North America, and Russell is going to instruct Cowley by a private Letter to sound the French Government as to their willingness to agree to such a Measure if formally proposed to them. Of Course no actual step to such Effect could be taken without the Sanction of the Cabinet. But if I am not mistaken, you would be inclined to approve such a Course.

"The Proposal would naturally be made to both North and South, if both accepted we should recommend an Armistice and Cessation of Blockades with a View to Negotiation on the Basis of Separation. If both declined we must of Course leave them to go on; If the South accepted and the North declined we should then I conceive acknowledge the Independence of the South, but we ought, Russell and I imagine, to declare the maintenance of our Neutrality even in the Case of our acknowledging the Independence of the South. . . . ." He believed that the offer should be made on Lyons' return which was planned for about October 15. Things were rapidly approaching a crisis.[1]

Then two days later Russell wrote Gladstone more fully about his proposed plan. "I am inclined to think that October 16 may be soon enough for a Cabinet, if I am free to communicate the views which Palmerston and I entertain to France and Russia in the interval between this time and the middle of next month. These views had the offer of mediation to both parties in the first place, and in the case of refusal by the North recognition accompanied by a declaration of neutrality."[2]

[1] Philip Guedalla, *Gladstone and Palmerston* (London, 1926), pp. 232–33, Palmerston to Gladstone, Sept. 24, 1862; John Morley, *Gladstone* (New York, 1903), II, 76; E. D. Adams, II, 41.

[2] Gladstone Papers, quoted in E. D. Adams, II, 40.

Palmerston was not wrong in supposing that Gladstone favored intervention. The latter replied to his letter of September 24 on the following day in a private note. "I am glad to learn that in your opinion and Lord Russell's the time has arrived for coming to an understanding with some other principal powers of Europe so as to be in a condition to take some part with a view to procuring a cessation of the deadly struggle in America." There were two special reasons, wrote Gladstone, why he favored such a step. The first one was the fear that the tide of southern success might mount so high that the South would be unwilling to make peace on reasonable terms, thus prolonging the war. His second reason would have gladdened the soul of the faithful subjects of King Cotton: "The population of Lancashire have borne their sufferings with a fortitude and patience exceeding all example, and almost belief. But if in any one of the great towns, resignation should, even for a single day, give place to excitement, and an outbreak should occur, our position in the face of America, and our influence for good might be seriously affected: we might then seem to be interfering, with loss of dignity on the ground of our immediate interests, and rather in the attitude of parties than as representing the general interests of humanity and peace." Gladstone, like Russell and Palmerston, was in grave apprehension lest revolt break out at any moment among the cotton operatives, which would probably result in forcing England into intervention in her own interest rather than as an apparently disinterested party. Gladstone advised that since England was interested in North America because of Canada, and France because of Mexico, it would be necessary to associate Russia with them in order to give the appearance of disinterested friendship.[1]

Within the next day or so Russell and Palmerston apprised the other members of the cabinet of the proposed mediation plan. Granville, who now was in attendance upon the Queen at Gotha in Russell's stead, put his foot flatly down upon any intervention in America. He acknowledged that the British people had "a strong antipathy for the North, ... strong sympathy with the South and the passionate wish to have cotton," but England must not meddle, for

---

[1] Guedalla, *op. cit.*, pp. 233–36, Gladstone to Palmerston, Sept. 25, 1862.

"I doubt," he protested, "if the war continues long after our recognition of the South whether it will be possible for us to avoid drifting into it." Then why should the present policy of non-intervention be abandoned when it "has met with such general approval from Parliament, the press, and the public?"[1]

Just at this moment arrived fragmentary reports of the failure of the Confederate invasion of Maryland and the drawn battle of Antietam. The discussion in the British cabinet was destined to go on for another month or so, but actually this battle was the death-blow of Confederate recognition, for the pugnacious Palmerston, actually as cautious as a fox, turned against present mediation when the news of Confederate military failure arrived. His support of Russell's plan of mediation, as we must reiterate, was conditioned upon southern success in Maryland. That success had not come, and Palmerston from that moment may be counted against Russell. On October 2 he wrote Russell that there was much wisdom in Granville's letter of September 27. "The condition of things . . . . which would be favorable to an offer of mediation would be great success of the South against the North. That state of things seemed ten days ago to be approaching. Its advance has been lately checked, but we do not yet know the real course of recent events, and still less can we foresee what is about to follow. Ten days or a fortnight more may throw a light upon future prospects." The point was that Palmerston was as before unwilling to tie himself to any plan until he was sure the North was well crushed and rendered harmless. He was haunted by the possible rape of Canada and the probable destruction of British commerce and trade in case of a war with the United States. He suggested postponement. Canada would be much safer in the spring when England was not cut off by ice from her dominion. He emphasized again that whatever was done must be done jointly with France and Russia as the United States would probably not attack all three. He suggested that the form of mediation be toned down considerably to "a friendly suggestion" that the two contending parties enter into negotiations upon principles of separation.[2]

[1] Lord G. P. F. Fitzmaurice, *Granville*, I, 442–44, cited in E. D. Adams, II, 42.

[2] G. P. Gooch, *The Later Correspondence of Lord John Russell, 1840–78* (2 vols.; London, 1925), II, 326–33.

Palmerston, like the human cork that he was, rose and fell, in his position on intervention, with the tide of southern success. He feared the cotton famine which was now nearing its climax, and he fervently desired the independence of the South so as to reduce the power of the United States. But he was under no circumstances willing to risk a war to accomplish his desires. The present status of affairs indicated a war if mediation were offered.

In the meanwhile, George Cornwall Lewis, minister of war, sat down upon Russell's proposals. He, like Granville, felt that the war had not reached a condition where intervention would be safe.[1] But Russell, once having decided that the time for intervention had come, found it hard to change his mind. The battle of Antietam did not deflect him from his course. Unquestionably he was more afraid of a revolution at home than of a war with the United States. He had listened too much to Lindsay, Spence, and Roebuck, and to the rumbling of public opinion which now seemed to favor mediation.[2] October 4 he replied to Palmerston's letter. He disagreed with the Prime Minister that delay was the only wise policy for the moment. "I think unless some miracle takes place this will be the very time for offering mediation or, as you suggest, proposing to North and South to come to terms." The mediation should be on the basis of separation and continued neutrality on the part of Great Britain.[3] But two days later Russell began to shift his plans a bit. In accordance with Palmerston's idea and those of Stuart and Mercier, he was willing to consider an armistice proposal and leave the two combatants to reach their own terms. Recognition might or might not follow. This proposal of mediation could be carried over by Lyons who was now scheduled to sail on October 25.[4] This looked as if Russell might be satisfied, after all, with a gesture. But he presently resumed his vigorous attitude. There can be little doubt but that Gladstone's famous Newcastle speech of October 7, the day after the foregoing letter to Palmerston, with the popular reception and popular excitement following it, helped stimulate Russell's flagging pur-

[1] E. D. Adams, II, 44–45.

[2] E.g., *Economist*, Aug. 30, Oct. 11 and 18, 1862; *Times*, Oct. 22, 1862.

[3] E. D. Adams, II, 46.   [4] *Ibid.*, p. 47.

pose. Gladstone had not been in touch with Russell and Palmerston since the letters of September 24 and 26 apprising him of the mediation plan. He was not Russell's mouthpiece as was generally supposed. But rather was he the vigorous ghost of Russell's early resolution. Gladstone, who for months had favored recognition or intervention, could keep silent no longer. Jefferson Davis, he told his audience at Newcastle, had made an army and he would soon have a navy; he had made a nation, and the division of the Union was an accomplished and irrevocable fact. Of course, the implication of this statement was immediate recognition, and so the public accepted it. The *Economist*[1] said that whether it was or was not an official utterance of the government Gladstone's speech "echoes the general sentiment of the country, and probably the real opinion of most members of the government." Palmerston, swayed somewhat by Gladstone, wrote Russell on October 12, "We must, I think, have something of a decisive character before our Cabinet on the 23rd, but it is clear that Gladstone was not far wrong in pronouncing by anticipation the National Independence of the South."[2]

After receiving Palmerston's message Russell set about preparing another memorandum on mediation which was circulated October 13 among the cabinet members. In this memorandum Russell took Gladstone's position that the South had demonstrated its military power to maintain itself; and he asserted that Seward's claims of a large Unionist element were wrong, thus using Mason's argument which he had so discourteously refuted. He pointed out that the emancipation of the slaves had no moral or humane motives, but that it was purely a vindictive measure intended to hurt the South and not help the slave. Europe ought, therefore, to consider proposing an armistice to allow negotiations. Russell had now accepted the idea of an armistice rather than mediation.[3] It was more acceptable to France and to the South, and it appeared to carry least risks of involving Britain in a war with the North.

George Cornwall Lewis on the very next day, October 14, made a speech at Hereford replying to Gladstone's Newcastle *pronuncia-*

[1] *Economist*, Oct. 18, 1862.
[2] Russell Papers, P.R.O. 30-22-22, Oct. 12, 1862.   [3] E. D. Adams, II, 49.

mento and no doubt to Russell's memorandum. He urged that the war was by no means decided yet and that "the time had not yet arrived when it could be asserted in accordance with the established doctrines of international law that the independence of the Southern States had been established."[1] Lewis took the position that intervention would mean war, and in doing so appealed to a widespread feeling. Three days later, October 17, he circulated a memorandum in reply to that of Russell's of October 13. He followed the line of his speech at Hereford, namely, that any offer of mediation would be rejected by the North in an insulting manner and probably would result in war. He also pointed out that it would end slavery. Lewis had got windward of Palmerston through his brother-in-law Clarendon, and he knew that Palmerston did not advocate any action at present.[2]

Palmerston had read Russell's memorandum of October 13, Lewis' speech of October 14, and the latter's memorandum of October 17. He had, through Clarendon, consulted with Derby, the opposition leader in Parliament, who did not favor intervention at the present time, and he had listened carefully with his long ear to the ground. All confirmed him in his cautious policy indicated in his letter of October 2 to Russell. So on October 22, the day before the cabinet was to meet to dispose of the question, he wrote Russell that he was "much inclined to agree with Lewis that at present we could take no step nor make any communication of a distinct proposition with any advantage." Neither mediation nor an armistice could be safely proposed at the present juncture. "All that we could possibly do without injury to our position," he wrote, "would be to ask the two parties not whether they would agree to an armistice, but whether they might not lean their thoughts toward an arrangement between themselves." But Palmerston felt that this was a waste of paper, for "the answer of each might be written beforehand. The Northerners would say that the only condition of arrangement would be the restoration of the Union; the South would say their only condition would be an acknowledgement by the North of Southern Inde-

---

[1] *Ibid.*, pp. 50–51; cf. *London Economist*, Oct. 18, 1862.
[2] *Ibid.*

pendence. . . . . I am, therefore, inclined to change the opinion on which I wrote you when the Confederates seemed to be carrying all before them, and I am very much come back to our original view of the matter, that we must continue merely to be lookers-on till the war shall have taken a more decided turn."[1]

This decision of Palmerston changed Russell's plans. Though a few members met and discussed the armistice proposal, the cabinet meeting for October 23 was postponed. While Palmerston approved of the postponement, he rejected the contention of Lewis that there should be "no recognition of Southern independence until the North had admitted it."[2] Palmerston had not changed his mind. Circumstances had changed. But Russell did not want to await the changing of conditions. On the day of the informal cabinet meeting he circulated another memorandum replying to Lewis' memorandum of October 17. He again urged intervention but suggested that five European nations, including Russia, Prussia, and Austria, instead of three should make the proposal.[3]

The next day, Gladstone sent out a lengthy and able memorandum urging the adoption of Russell's last plan. Gladstone refuted Lewis' contention that any such suggestion would be met in America by war. The North would not immediately accept any proposal; but "we may confidently reckon . . . . on a powerful effect to be produced on opinion and on the general course of affairs in favor of peace; and in bringing greatly nearer, at least, the day of that happy release." Gladstone favored the present as the best time to offer mediation because a balance between the two combatants had been reached, and because of the winter season it would be more practicable to effect an armistice. Too, public opinion in England was so much in favor of the South that a perfectly neutral rôle would soon be impossible. But the thing which weighed most heavily upon him as a reason for immediate intervention was the cotton famine. He had just returned from a tour through the north of England, and he was

[1] Russell Papers, P.R.O. 30-22-14, Palmerston to Russell, Oct. 22, 1862; Gooch, op. cit., II, 326–33.

[2] Russell Papers, P.R.O. 30-22-14, Palmerston to Russell, Oct. 23, 1862; E. D. Adams, II, 56.

[3] Ibid., p. 57.

more fearful now of an upheaval than he had been when he wrote Palmerston on September 24 declaring for immediate intervention. "The terrible distress in Lancashire has thus far been borne with heroic patience and with perfect submission to the law. But with all our confidence in the people, who can be certain that the positive suffering, the actual hunger which we have every reason to fear is endured there, may not at some time, at some place, perhaps from some apparently trivial incident, give rise to an outbreak?" Such a situation, continued the memorandum, would destroy all chances of England's playing a disinterested rôle in intervention. "And such an event, though uncertain, and, I hope, impossible, yet has not been thought unlikely by some serious observers on the spot, and should not, I think, be put wholly out of view in considering the case before us."[1]

Clothed in a humanitarian garb and embellished with words of high moral principles though it was, the meat of Gladstone's proposal was intervention in the American Civil War to obtain cotton for the purpose of preventing a revolution in the cotton-manufacturing districts. A trifle late in making itself felt, the power of cotton was nevertheless not far short of the South's calculations. Palmerston, Russell, and Gladstone had been brought to the position of intervention to get cotton with which to prevent revolution. At the moment the pugnacious Palmerston was opposing the idea because of his fear of war. Realizing the submissiveness and tameness of the British laboring people, he was not as apprehensive of revolt as were Russell and Gladstone.

On October 26 Russell wrote Sir George Cornwall Lewis refuting his memorandum of October 17, and highly approving the position of Gladstone in his memorandum of October 24. Russell now, in the face of all opposition, resumed his former high ground on the American question. He would offer the good offices of England, France, Russia, and other countries as he and Gladstone had suggested, but if "the Great Powers of Europe were to offer their good offices, and those good offices were to be rejected by the North, we should be

[1] Guedalla, *op. cit.*, pp. 239–47, memorandum by Mr. Gladstone on the war in America.

fairly entitled to choose our own time to recognize the Southern
States. The time most suitable for such an act would probably be
at the commencement of the next campaign and when Parliament
was sitting."[1]

The next day, October 27, Sir George Grey, the home secretary,
wrote Russell in reply to the latter's memorandum of October 23.
He was, he said, opposed to any offer of mediation unless Russell had
absolute evidence that it would be accepted. He feared that Russia
might refuse to join England and France, but that, on the other
hand, she might inform the United States that the offer arose from
England. This would involve England and the United States in a
difficulty because of the bitter feeling against England. In any case
the United States would meet a mediation proposal by a haughty
and contemptuous refusal.[2]

On October 28 Russell replied to Grey that he had no specific information that the United States would accept mediation. But he
believed that Russia would join, and that, although nothing might
come of the negotiations between the North and South, the United
States would accept a joint proposal of mediation. If nothing resulted from this and peace did not come, "I shall then be for recognizing
the South. The Democratic Party may by that time have got the
ascendency. I heartily wish them success."[3]

Thus the mediation idea of Russell was by October 28 supported
in the cabinet only by himself and Gladstone. This cabinet opposition would have smothered the question for the time being had not
Napoleon entered upon the stage with his proposal of an armistice.

It will be recalled that Napoleon was, simultaneously with Russell,
bringing to a climax an intervention project; that, though he had
always been prepared to join England, he had moved cautiously and
unofficially; but that Mercier had been carrying the French government gradually forward to an official action, and that he had advised on September 30 that the time had come for official action.
De Lhuys had on October 30 replied that France had decided to act
on the basis of his advice. It will be remembered that two days before this date the Emperor had told Slidell that he was going to sug-

[1] Gooch, *op. cit.*, II, 326–33.   [2] *Ibid.*   [3] *Ibid.*

gest officially to England and Russia that an armistice proposal be made to the two belligerents.

Had he not known through the several conversations between Cowley and Thouvenel, and Cowley and De Lhuys, that the British cabinet was contemplating the same thing, it is doubtful whether Napoleon would have officially proposed intervention at this time. But seeming to feel confident that at last England would join him, he hastened to initiate the undertaking. On October 31 his minister De Lhuys officially informed Cowley that the Emperor was about to request joint action of England and Russia in proposing to the United States and the Confederacy a six months' armistice and a suspension of the blockade.[1] Napoleon had already approached Russia, and D'Aubril, the Russian minister at Paris, had been instructed on October 31 by his government that Russia would not join with England and France in any proposal to America, but that it would approve any offer which would bring peace.[2] The Russian government had given similar instructions to Stoeckl in America.[3] Napoleon must have known about the position of Russia almost immediately, but he must have felt that with England and France proposing the armistice Russia would probably be forced to join them.

Cowley's letter to Russell of October 31, which officially announced that Napoleon would ask for a joint offer of an armistice, found the cabinet already definitely committed against immediate action. So the discussion which followed was bound to end in rejecting the idea of present intervention. Palmerston was sagacious and cautious. He wrote Russell, November 2, 1862, that the French proposal should be discussed at the cabinet on November 11 or 12. But he did not believe that "the Federals would consent to an armistice to be accompanied by a cessation of Blockades . . . . which would give the Confederates means of getting all the supplies they may want." Then there were so many other obstacles in the way of mediation being acceptable to the combatants or to the British people, such as boundaries, slavery, and fugitive slaves. He favored delay.

---

[1] British F.O. France, Vol. 1446, No. 1236, Cowley to Russell, cited in E. D. Adams, II, 60, n. 2.

[2] E. D. Adams, II, 59, n. 4.   [3] *Ibid.*

Nothing should be attempted until after the elections in America.[1] Russell, too, by this time did not feel that any proposal which would satisfy the British would be acceptable to either North or South, but, like Napoleon, the specter of the cotton famine so haunted him that he felt that some move should be made which would prove to the suffering operatives that the government was not to blame for the continuance of the war. On November 3 he replied to Palmerston that while America would probably not accept the good offices of Europe, "we should make them such as would be creditable to us in Europe." He outlined certain amendments to the French proposal. The North and South should be asked to consider whether there were any grounds upon which they could agree to restore the Union; then if there were none, could they agree to separate? If they could agree to restore the Union, slavery should be abolished with compensation; but if no restoration took place, no mention of slavery should be made.[2] On November 7 Lewis came out with a strong memorandum against accepting Napoleon's offer.[3] Thus matters stood until November 11 when the question was officially debated in cabinet.

In the meanwhile, the Confederate commissioners, who were informed of the progress of Napoleon's plans, were almost convinced that intervention was at last a reality. Cotton was king. On November 7, 1862,[4] Mason expressed himself in this vein. "The cotton famine," he wrote Benjamin, ". . . . which has been pressing hard upon the manufacturing districts, is looming up in fearful proportions. It is stated that there are 700,000 of the population entirely dependent on charity for subsistence, and this large number is increasing at from ten to twenty thousand per week. . . . . The public mind is very much agitated and disturbed at the fearful prospect for winter, and I am not without hope that it will produce its effects on the counsels of the Government." "It is hardly probable," he wrote

[1] Russell Papers, P.R.O. 30-22-14, Palmerston to Russell, Nov. 2, 1862; Gooch, *op. cit.*, II, 326–33.

[2] Adams, II, 61–62.   [3] *Ibid.*, pp. 62–63.

[4] Pickett Papers, Mason to Benjamin, No. 20, Nov. 7, 1862; *O.R.N.*, Ser. 2, Vol. III, pp. 600–601.

Benjamin the next day, "that she [England] will refuse her concurrence" in Napoleon's offer of joint intervention.[1]

Slidell for the first and last time was certain of intervention. He wrote Benjamin on November 11 that in his interview of October 28 with the Emperor he had been convinced that Napoleon would soon "act in our affairs in some decided and official way." He had just heard from a friend in England (probably Shaftesbury) that the British government would in all probability join Napoleon. But should "Russia and England withhold their assent, I believe that France will act without them."[2]

On November 11, as Palmerston had promised, the cabinet met to discuss the French proposal which had been officially received on November 10. The debate lasted two days. It had just been learned definitely through the British minister to St. Petersburg, Napier, that, though she would unofficially support the proposal through Stoeckl at Washington, Russia would not join in a peace proposal to America. Russell urged in cabinet meeting that England accept Napoleon's proposal; that unless she did Russia might reconsider her position, join France, and isolate England. He also urged that since the Democrats were winning the election in the North, such intervention would strengthen their hands. Palmerston supported Russell very feebly—so much so that Lewis and the other opponents of the proposal were convinced that he was playing for position so as to defeat Russell without offending him. Gladstone presented a strong argument in favor of Napoleon's proposal of an armistice, and Westbury supported him. The others, according to Lewis' account, picked the proposal to pieces. "The principal objection was that the proposed armistice of six months by sea and land, involving a suspension of the commercial blockade, was so grossly unequal—so decidedly in favor of the South, that there was no chance of the North agreeing to it."[3]

The proposal, of course, was defeated in the cabinet just as Rus-

[1] Pickett Papers, Mason to Benjamin, Nov. 8, 1862; O.R.N., Ser. 2, Vol. III, pp. 602–3.

[2] Pickett Papers, Slidell to Benjamin, No. 20, Nov. 11, 1862; O.R.N., Ser. 2, Vol. III, pp. 603–4.

[3] E. D. Adams, II, 63–64.

sell's plan had been rejected in October. Russell on November 13 wrote Cowley of the cabinet's decision against joining France in making the proposal. He gave two reasons for England's action: Russia's refusal to join and the certainty of the North's rejecting the proposed armistice and declaring war. No such offer should be made until it seemed fairly certain that it would be accepted by both North and South.[1]

Napoleon, anxious to show the manufacturing districts that he was laboring in their behalf, announced in the French papers on November 10 that he was proposing joint intervention to England and Russia;[2] and on November 13, when he had unofficial notice of the rejection of his offer, he published the full texts of his notes to those countries.[3]

Russell, in a like fashion, after the publication of the French notes on November 13, printed the text of the British note in the *London Times*, November 15. Napoleon thus shifted the blame for the distress in the cotton districts upon the Russian and English governments. Russell in his note, now made public, excused the British government from its failure to offer peace to America because of the danger of war which would follow any such action. Neither country had obtained cotton; but they both had good excuses to offer the public.

For a few days the Confederate commissioners were unwilling to admit that the year's work in behalf of intervention was a total loss. On November 14 Slidell wrote Mason, "I think that Russia will act with France perhaps with some reservations. The official answer had not been received yesterday but its substance is known by Mr. Drouyn De Lhuys."[4] But if De Lhuys was telling Slidell that Russia would join France, he was knowingly deceiving him, for he knew Russia's attitude ere this date. Two days later Slidell, having at last

---

[1] Parl. Papers, Lords, Vol. XXIX (1863); "Despatch respecting the Civil War in North America," Russell to Cowley, Nov. 13, 1862, cited in E. D. Adams, II, 66; *London Times*, Nov. 15, 1862.

[2] *Patrie*, Nov. 10; *Moniteur*, Nov. 10, 1862.

[3] See U.S. Des., France, Vol. 52, Dayton to Seward, No. 226, Nov. 14, 1862. Dayton writes about the widespread publication of the notes.

[4] Mason Papers, Nov. 14, 1862.

heard that Russia would not join France, wrote Mason that public opinion might soon force England to join France. But, wrote Slidell, if England still remained supine "my opinion is that France will act alone."[1]

The Confederate lobby, as soon as they learned that England had rejected Napoleon's offer, put their heads together. They concluded that the Emperor had been "sold," that Russell had by his informal approaches through Cowley led Napoleon to believe that England would gladly join France, and that after drawing the intervention proposal out of the Emperor Russell had with premeditated malice rejected it. Placed in this way it was hardly short of a deliberate insult, which would force Napoleon out of sheer wounded pride to go on alone with his mediation proposal. Lindsay expressed this feeling rather emphatically in a letter to Mason on November 20 from Paris:[2] ". . . . That despatch [refusing to join France] from Lord Russell was in my opinion a most cowardly one. I am rather despaired to think the Emperor had been again sold. Last night the Minister of Commerce was good enough to pay me the compliment of giving me a dinner at his house. Mr. Thouvenel and other leading men were there and from some conversation which passed I daresay it will appear in time that I am not far from wrong in thinking so. I cannot believe, after what the Emperor said to me more than once and after what took place in regard to his despatch of March last that he would make any official proposal to England on the subject of American affairs unless he had a tacit understanding beforehand that it would be accepted." And Slidell wrote Benjamin a few days later: "I have information which leads me to believe that the Emperor had reason to expect that his proposition of 30th October would be accepted by England; if this be so, although he may make no immediate open demonstration of his dissatisfaction, I shall be surprised if he does not soon prove that her co-operation may be dispensed with. If on the contrary he did not expect the acceptance of his proposition, judging from his character and antecedents, he will not be disposed to leave his work unfinished and will act alone. On either hypothesis, then, I feel very sanguine that not many months,

[1] *Ibid.*, Nov. 16, 1862.   [2] *Ibid.*, Nov. 20, 1862.

perhaps not many weeks, will elapse without some decided action on his part." In other words, Slidell felt that Napoleon would go on now whether from pique or to execute plans already laid.[1]

Even John Bigelow, the United States consul-general, shared this belief that Napoleon would act alone. On November 21, 1862, he wrote Seward that the Emperor "will compel us to make peace or fight him, in my opinion, before he takes any steps backward."[2]

But the mountain had labored and brought forth a very small mouse—stillborn. For on November 18 during the time Slidell and the others were speculating as to great possibilities of Napoleon's acting alone, De Lhuys wrote Mercier a very mild and toothless dispatch instructing him to hold himself always in readiness to offer America the good offices of the French.[3] The great intervention drive begun in March by the Confederate lobby, propagandist agents, and Napoleon had ended where it had commenced.

[1] Pickett Papers, Slidell to Benjamin, No. 21, Nov. 29, 1862; *O.R.N.*, Ser. 2, Vol. III, pp. 612–13.

[2] Bigelow, *Retrospection, etc.*, I, 574.

[3] French F.O. Amer., Vol. 128, De Lhuys to Mercier, No. 30, Nov. 18, 1862.

CHAPTER XI
CONFEDERATE FINANCES ABROAD
COTTON AS A BASIS OF CREDIT

After the failure of their efforts at securing European intervention in 1862 the Confederate commissioners turned their attention for a while to several other matters which were pending at the time. The most important of these was the establishing of a system of finance by which war supplies might be purchased for the armies.

Reference has been frequently made to Confederate agents sent to Europe to purchase supplies and build vessels. Their number was legion. First, Caleb Huse, captain and then major, was sent to Europe by the Ordnance Bureau of the War Department, to purchase rifles and artillery and munitions; then followed W. G. Crenshaw as a quasi-agent for the Commissary Bureau of the War Department with overlapping duties and a firm desire to get all the business out from Huse's jurisdiction. J. B. Ferguson, a fellow-Virginian of Mason and Crenshaw, went out as agent for the Quartermaster Bureau. He was jealous of Huse, who was unfortunately not a Virginian and most unfortunately not even a southern man. Charles Helm was sent to Cuba to purchase supplies of all kinds either in the island or in Europe; Louis Heyliger was stationed at Nassau, New Providence, and Norman S. Walker at St. Georges, Bermuda, for purchasing supplies. There followed other agents and quasi-agents of ephemeral importance, as well as contractors with Confederate commissions to buy supplies and run the blockade. The Navy had Captain J. D. Bulloch in Europe building the "Alabama," "Florida," and other cruisers, the "Laird Rams" and the rams at Bordeaux. It sent to Europe the jealous and ambitious Lieutenant North who could not bear Bulloch's promotion; and it sent Sinclair, Maury, Wilkerson, Maffitt, and others to buy a ship of some kind for the Confederacy—usually without money or credit.[1]

---

[1] Bulloch has left a two-volume account of his shipbuilding activities, *Secret Service of the Confederate States in Europe* (New York, 1883); Huse, a pamphlet, *Purchases*

Millions of dollars had already been spent by the official purchasing agents, contractors, and those engaged in running the blockade for government account by the fall of 1862, much in a haphazard hand-to-mouth fashion, and Confederate credit as a result was exhausted. Something had to be done to meet the immediate needs of the agents, and some system provided by which funds sufficient for future needs could be obtained.

Until the fall of 1862 the Confederate government had financed its purchasing agents in Europe by the use of letters of credit and bills of exchange. A letter of credit would be issued on Fraser, Trenholm and Company in Liverpool; then cash in gold would be shipped to this firm to be drawn against as long as there was any gold left in the country. Bills of exchange would be purchased from banks or large firms such as John Fraser and Company of Charleston. This exchange was purchased at exorbitant rates in Confederate money, for eventually Fraser and Company would be compelled to ship gold abroad or later cotton, to meet the bills of exchange.[1]

But the silver and gold coin was soon drained, exchange and letters of credit could not be bought, and the Confederacy had to fall back upon the shipment through the blockade of cotton. We will recall that the embargo on cotton had been gradually relaxed partly because of this dependence upon that article as a medium of exchange with Europe. But the Confederate government, while it had over four hundred thousand bales of cotton by the spring of 1862, had no means of getting this cotton abroad. It had not yet established the policy of carrying out its own cotton in its own boats—in fact, for practically another year the policy of the government was to stay out of blockade-running so as to allow private blockade-runners to exploit the business. The reason for this was the hope that by encouraging the blockade-running business as much as

---

Abroad; Sinclair, *The Florida;* Semmes, *Service Afloat.* See General bibliography. But the official correspondence covering these various agents is in the *Official Records* of both the Navy and the Army. Consult the General Index under each name.

[1] For illustrations of the use of letters of credit and the purchase of exchange and shipment of money see *O.R.,* Ser. 4, Vol. I, pp. 343–46, 538–42, 1007–8, 1115; *ibid.,* Vol. II, pp. 236–37.

possible the inefficiency of the blockade would be established abroad. Slidell summed up this early policy in a letter to Benjamin on April 7, 1864. "So long as we had any reason to hope that practical illustrations of the inefficiency of the blockade might lead to a denial by European powers of its obligatory force it was wise to hold out every inducement to individual enterprise to multiply those illustrations."[1]

The government then, in the fall of 1862, was faced with the problem of making the cotton which it had on hand and would acquire available for use abroad; and until the government could develop its own facilities for shipping cotton abroad the only means of making its supply of that commodity available as a source of wealth was to borrow money on it as collateral. The idea of hypothecating the Confederate cotton had been suggested from the first; but it was not until the beginning of 1862 that the Confederate government gave it any consideration. Even then it was not Memminger but rather the astute Benjamin who first took hold of the problem. On January 17, 1862, he wrote E. J. Forstall of New Orleans, the representative of a foreign banking house, proposing that his bank advance the Confederacy one million dollars to be deposited in England. The Confederacy would pay interest and commission and "would place in the hands of the agent of such house on this side such number of bales of cotton as might be agreed to be sufficient to cover the advance . . . . the cotton to remain on this side until the blockade is raised." "The cotton would, of course, be stored and insured at the expense of the Government at any convenient point designated, but not in a cotton port, during the existing blockade." After the blockade had been raised, the cotton would be shipped and sold by the banking house with large commissions and heavy interest.[2]

The form of paper which would be put in the hands of the foreign house might be cotton certificates or receipts showing that a specific

[1] Pickett Papers, No. 59, April 7, 1864; *O.R.N.*, Ser. 2, Vol. III, pp. 1077–79; cf. Benjamin's explanation to Messrs. S. Isaac, Campbell and Company, March 17, 1862; *O.R.*, Ser. 4, Vol. I, pp. 1007–8.

[2] *Ibid.*, pp. 845–46.

number of real bales of cotton had been placed in their possession in the Confederacy. However, the cotton would not be owned by the bank—only held as collateral. This proposition failed to materialize before the city of New Orleans fell. But the Confederate government canvassed the proposition with representatives of other foreign banks during the year without any results.[1] By the end of 1862 the price of cotton had become so exorbitant in Europe—about 25 pence or 50 cents a pound—that the necessity of the Confederacy to obtain credit abroad was met halfway by a great eagerness to obtain the staple.[2]

It was Secretary Mallory of the Navy Department rather than Secretary of the Treasury Memminger who first passed beyond the stage of vague inquiry and took definite steps to hypothecate cotton. He sent G. N. Sanders, heretofore interested in obtaining a contract to carry Confederate dispatches to Europe and in getting his two sons exempted from Confederate military service.[3] He went to England with a contract about July 15 to build ships for the Confederate Navy. Mallory authorized him in the contract to use cotton bonds for money. Sanders went to the house of William Lindsay and Company to raise money on the contract. Lindsay immediately conferred with Mason and advised him that while he approved of the idea there was one fatal defect in the proposed bonds—the stipulated price of cotton. The proposed contract stipulated that cotton was to be delivered to the bondholders, should they request it, at a designated southern port at market price. Lindsay believed that a large sum of money could be raised by this type of bond or cotton certificate, provided the price of cotton was fixed. He proposed that it be fixed at 4 pence, or 8 cents, though it was selling for four times that in England. Lindsay advised Mason to modify the Sanders contract so as to name this price. Mason, however, in view of the size of the amount involved, rather than assume such responsibility dispatched Sanders back to the Confederacy to arrange the matter of price. But he was thoroughly convinced that the hypothecation of

---

[1] Schwab, p. 30.   [2] *Ibid.*

[3] See *O.R.N.*, Ser. 2, Vol. III, Index, under G. N. Sanders, Lewis Sanders, and Reid Sanders.

cotton in the form of a cotton bond representing a definite amount
of cotton to be delivered at a designated point at the request of the
holder of the bond was an excellent mode of raising money. On this
point he wrote Benjamin in connection with the Sanders transaction,
and another of a smaller nature with Commander Sinclair: "I am
fully aware of the great difficulty the Government must have in
placing funds in Europe necessary for its use because of the cessation
of commerce and the interrupted communication. I venture to suggest, therefore, that money may be commanded here by the use of
obligations for delivery of cotton by the Government on . . . . terms"
such as proposed by Lindsay—cotton bonds to be exchanged for cotton at a fixed rate at a specified point. "That is to say, that the delivery shall be made at any port in possession of the Confederate
States when demanded by the holder of the bond, after reasonable
(say 30 or more days) notice or within three months or more after
peace." He was convinced that £4,000,000 or £5,000,000 could be
raised in this way from the cotton-spinners alone, for "it is perfectly
well understood that this class is redundant with money arising out
of the large profits made from stocks on hand when the scarcity of
cotton developed itself. Money that would be immediately invested
in cotton when it should be again accessible."[1]

While Sanders' contract was waiting on word from Richmond as
to the fixing of cotton prices in the bond, Commander George T.
Sinclair came over to build himself a ship. His orders sent him to
Captain Bulloch for money, but, like the other agents at this time,
Bulloch had nothing he could use for money. Then Sinclair sought
Mason. Mason promptly sent him to Lindsay with instructions to
get about £60,000 on cotton bonds, at a fixed price, which was according to Lindsay's own specification in the Sanders deal. Mason
assumed the authority to indorse these bonds as the matter was
pressing and the amount was not large.[2] The Sinclair bonds, then,
were the first cotton bonds used by the Confederacy.

G. N. Sanders laid the matter contained in Mason's dispatch with

[1] Pickett Papers, Mason to Benjamin, No. 16, Sept. 18, 1862; *O.R.N.*, Ser. 2, Vol.
III, pp. 529–32.
    [2] *Ibid.*

reference to the cotton-certificate loan before Benjamin on October 21. The latter conferred with the Secretary of Treasury, and it was quickly agreed that the Confederacy would adopt this method of hypothecating cotton. James Spence was selected as agent to handle the business.[1]

We have already found Spence the most energetic and resourceful friend the Confederacy had in England, organizing popular meetings, spreading propaganda, and constantly wielding his pen and tongue in behalf of the South. So useful did he appear and so grateful for his services was Mason that he wished to reward him with an official position. The nature of this official position was indicated by Spence's own personal calling—merchant, shipper, banker, and stockbroker—and by the financial condition of the Confederacy in the spring of 1862. Spence was not timid in thrusting himself forward to get the reward and to perform the services. He applied for the job, pointing out the need of a financial agent and the fitness of himself for the office. He had, he said—and it was certainly true—devoted so much time and thought to the cause of the Confederacy that he had neglected his own business. His business, too, needed his attention because of great losses in the panic of 1857. However, he did not feel that the Confederacy owed him anything. He had written the *American Union* and all his other essays because of his conviction that the Confederacy was right, not for gain. He proposed himself solely on the grounds of fitness. He thought the Confederacy had need of a man in Europe, an Englishman, to handle its finances, "a man of business and of intellect," one "with local knowledge of men and affairs, able to feel the pulse of public sentiment and guide opinion through the press," "a man of intellect, zealous, ... fertile in expedients, vigorous in action, of wide mercantile experience; one accustomed to deal with large and difficult things . . . . , and not afraid of any encounter as a speaker." He very modestly left it to Mason and the Confederate government to decide whether he possessed these qualifications. In this same letter of application Spence suggested to Mason that the Confederacy change its title to

[1] Pickett Papers, Benjamin to Mason, No. 6, Oct. 28, 1862; *O.R.N.*, Ser. 2, Vol. III, pp. 581–82.

"Southern Union" so as to force the United States to drop the old title and assume the title "Northern Union."

However, Spence was only English in recounting his qualities and distinctions. There is no reason to consider him unusually presumptive or egotistic. Mason loved and trusted Spence, and spoke of him in the highest terms in his letter to Benjamin. His *American Union* was an able book, and had been widely read and had influenced opinion in favor of the South. He spoke of his articles in the *London Times* as of "great ability" and of Spence as a "man of large research, liberal and expanded views, and great labor," "about 45 or 46 years of age, full of enterprise, and an able and experienced merchant." The position of financial agent "could not be confided to more capable or efficient hands in England, and on the score of desert would be a well-merited recompense to Mr. Spence for his persistent and valuable labors in our cause."[1]

Benjamin had already heard much of Spence in other connections, especially from Hotze, and as soon as he received Mason's letter of May 2 he first appointed Spence as agent to dispose of batches of ordinary bonds sent from time to time during the summer by means of agents such as Major Ferguson of the Quartermaster Bureau.[2] Then on October 28, 1862, he notified Mason that the Confederate government had made Spence "financial agent" for Europe.

The appointment, however, while Benjamin expected Spence to handle all finances abroad, seems to have been technically under the Treasury Department, and as the Confederate cabinet heads and their respective agents abroad showed great tenacity in asserting their independence, Spence was in for rough sailing. No sooner had it been agreed that cotton bonds should be used to borrow money in Europe than Mallory dispatched Captain Maury with blanket authority for himself and all other naval agents to use the sky as a limit in the use of such cotton bonds in obtaining ships and money.[3]

[1] Pickett Papers, Mason to Benjamin, No. 9, May 2, 1862; *O.R.N.*, Ser. 2, Vol. III, pp. 401–5.

[2] See *O.R.*, Ser. 4, Vol. II, p. 133, for reference to Ferguson's having the bonds in hand; *ibid.*, pp. 236–37; Mason Papers, Sept., 1862—June, 1863, *passim*, refer to the Treasury bonds in Spence's hands.

[3] Pickett Papers, Mason to Benjamin, No. 22, Dec. 10, 1862; *O.R.N.*, Ser. 2, Vol. III, pp. 617–18.

However, it was expected that they should consult with Spence, Mason, and Fraser, Trenholm and Company[1] before disposing of bonds. Maury, carrying authority to the other agents to issue bonds, arrived apparently before Mason or Spence received word from Benjamin about Spence's appointment as financial agent. As was natural, they reported not to Spence but to Mason and to Fraser, Trenholm and Company, the Confederate depository in Liverpool. Mason immediately advised that Spence as special bond agent under the first appointment of May, 1862, should be consulted before any step was taken; and they all, including the agents of the War Department who likewise had authority to issue cotton certificates or dispose of Treasury bonds, agreed that it would be extremely unwise to go into the bond market individually and dump their bonds. They agreed to allow all Treasury bonds to be disposed of by Spence and to allow Spence and Fraser, Trenholm and Company to issue the cotton bonds. Mason, not yet conscious that Spence had been made "financial agent," again urged Benjamin to put Spence permanently in charge of all financial operations in Europe, and allow Fraser, Trenholm and Company to aid him. Multiplicity of agents and contractors was not wise. He advised that all money should be disbursed through that agency subject to his own general supervision.[2] This concentration of authority was excellent advice and was destined finally to be adopted by the Confederacy, just about one year later when C. J. McRae from Alabama was given charge of the whole question of foreign credit and disbursements and the inspection of all contracts, subject to the advice of the commissioners, Mason and Slidell. On receipt of Benjamin's letter of October 28 in which Benjamin notified Mason of Spence's appointment as financial agent, both Spence and Mason supposed that the office was what its title implied—supervisor of all Confederate finances in Europe. But Spence had his jurisdiction narrowed more and more in the following months until finally he was politely notified that he was no longer needed at all in the capacity of financial agent. It is difficult to

[1] Pickett Papers, Benjamin to Mason, No. 12, Jan. 15, 1863; O.R.N., Ser. 2, Vol. III, pp. 648-51.

[2] Pickett Papers, Mason to Benjamin, No. 22, Dec. 10, 1862; O.R.N., Ser. 2, Vol. III, pp. 617-18.

know, therefore, to what extent his office was intended as an honor and to what extent it was a reality.

The decision of the Confederacy to use cotton bonds was soon rumored among the business houses of France and England. At last the Confederacy was going to put the sacred King Cotton in hock. Coming just at the time when the surplus accumulated in 1860 and 1861 was exhausted and when there was no prospect of getting any quantity of American cotton, it caused somewhat of a stir. Isaac, Campbell and Company—the Campbell part long since deceased— were very much excited. They had purchased practically everything which Caleb Huse had sent to the Confederacy—rifles, swords, cannon, powder, clothes, tents, shoes, bacon, and ships. They had taken a chance, for they spent their own cash and charged it to the Confederacy with the fond hopes that they would get paid eventually. Huse had purchased $5,000,000 of supplies by the end of 1862,[1] and most of it had been with this house. From January 20, to March 7, 1862, the Confederacy had sent them $1,261,600 in cold cash[2] and much before then and some afterward. But in November, 1862, the Confederacy still owed about $2,000,000 to this British firm.[3] Later it was discovered that the hard-headed Yankee, Caleb Huse, had been well taken in by this company who kept a double set of books, showing the real price and the price quoted to the Confederacy, and the firm only chuckled and observed that that was their only chance of insuring themselves against loss. Caleb Huse was left in a poor light despite his monumental services to the Confederacy, and this firm was soundly berated despite the fact that they merely cheated the Confederacy mildly while other houses robbed the Confederacy almost at the point of a cannon.[4]

In November, 1862, before there was any question of their fair dealing and when Huse was still supplying the Confederate armies on their credit, Ben Hart, who represented this house in Nassau,

[1] Schwab, p. 29. [2] O.R., Ser. 4, Vol. I, pp. 1007–8.

[3] Pickett Papers, Ben Hart to Benjamin, Nov. 17, 1862; O.R.N., Ser. 2, Vol. III, p. 605.

[4] For a full account of this sorry mess see O.R., Ser. 4, Vol. II, pp. 244–45, 478–82, 497–98, 525–27, 535–47, 554–55, 555–58, 564, 565–67, 586–90, 596–602, 623–31, 644–47, 855–94; Vol. III, pp. 154–58, 702–4, and Index of ibid., Vols. II and III, under Huse, Crenshaw, Ferguson, Isaac, Campbell and Company, and Collie and Company.

wrote Benjamin that his firm desired to make a contract to supply equipment for 100,000 men to be paid partly in cash and the remainder in cotton bonds or certificates, representing a certain specified number of bales. Further, his firm proposed to settle the $2,000,000 debt in the same way. He said that it was rumored that the Confederacy planned thus to finance itself and that its friends abroad "have little hesitation in accepting it, ..." even before the exact nature of the bond was known.[1]

Lindsay and Company—the William Lindsay of the lobby—who had floated the Sinclair cotton bonds, the first on the market, and who had, in fact, given the cotton certificate its final definite form, in the fixing of the price and the delivery of the hypothecated cotton, etc., also proposed to raise money for the Confederacy by the use of cotton bonds. Lindsay advised against a regular loan; he believed the sale of cotton bonds which represented specific bales of cotton to be the superior method. Like Mason he was convinced that large amounts could be obtained in this way. He proposed that the bonds be issued in fairly small instalments, say £100,000 to £200,000—$500,000 to $1,000,000—at first at 4 pence or 8 cents per pound for cotton. This would allow the bonds to be absorbed into the market, and the admittedly low price would have a strong tendency to drive the price of bonds far above par and thus give the Confederate government all the premium on subsequent issues. If the price of cotton rose, then the price stated in the bond could be increased in the later issues. To show his faith in such a transaction Lindsay proposed to Mason that his house alone would take £500,000, or $2,500,000 worth.[2]

Other proposals for raising money on cotton were made at the time. Several bankers, including a kinsman of M. Fould approached Edwin de Leon soon after his arrival in Paris in July, 1862.[3] Finally, Emille Erlanger and Company presented their offer. Erlanger

[1] Pickett Papers, Ben Hart to Benjamin, Nov. 17, 1862; *O.R.N.*, Ser. 2, Vol. III, p. 605.

[2] Pickett Papers, Mason to Benjamin, No. 19, Nov. 4, 1862, and *ibid.*, Slidell to Benjamin, No. 18, Oct. 28, 1862; *O.R.N.*, Ser. 2, Vol. III, pp. 590–97, and *ibid.*, pp. 568–72, respectively.

[3] See Pickett Papers, De Leon to Benjamin, No. 1, July 30, 1862; *ibid.*, to Benjamin, No. 2, Sept. 30, 1862; cf. *O.R.*, Ser. 4, Vol. II, pp. 99–105, for publication of No. 2.

was introduced to Slidell as the most important and influential of the Continental bankers, and serious negotiations were commenced at once. Slidell wrote Mason that the idea of raising money by cotton bonds appealed to him. "If cotton can be given for recognition," he wrote Mason, referring to the 100,000 bales he had offered Napoleon recently, "a portion may be [given] for necessary munitions." Huse had written Slidell that he needed money for the ships which were building in England.[1] Slidell apparently had not learned of the steps already taken toward the hypothecation of cotton in the Sinclair contract, and the dispatching of Sanders to Richmond to get permission to make extensive use of cotton bonds in raising funds. But as soon as his note of September 26 proposing the deal with Erlanger reached Mason, the latter hastened to explain the method and type of certificate used by Sinclair now on its way to Richmond to be adopted by the Confederate government.[2]

With this type of bond as a guide, Slidell and Huse acting for the Confederacy drew up a tentative contract with Erlanger and sent it on to Mason for his signature. This contract agreed to dispose of £5,000,000 in Confederate cotton bonds bearing 8 per cent. But Erlanger's profits would be enormous. He was to have all above 70 per cent on the bonds, besides a 5 per cent commission for disposing of the issue, a 1 per cent commission on handling the sinking funds and interest, and an 8 per cent discount for anticipating any or all of the eleven instalments. Then the Confederacy would redeem one-fortieth of the bonds semiannually, beginning July 1, 1863. This meant that the Confederacy would net only about £3,300,000 out of a £5,000,000-bond issue, and that even this sum would be rapidly reduced by the one-fortieth semiannual redemption and the handling commission.[3]

The terms of the contract were hard. But Slidell was so intrigued with the idea of Erlanger's political importance that he never seemed to have been conscious of the banker's exacting conditions. Erlanger and Company, he wrote Benjamin, was "one of the most extensive

[1] Mason Papers, Sept. 26, 1862.   [2] *Ibid.*, Sept. 27, 1862.

[3] For a description of the original contract see Pickett Papers, Slidell to Benjamin, No. 18, Oct. 28, 1862; *O.R.N.*, Ser. 2, Vol. III, pp. 568–72.

and responsible houses in Europe." He had "the best reason to believe that even in anticipation of its [the contract's] acceptance the very strongest influences will be enlisted in our favor."[1] Considering the fact that Slidell's interview with Napoleon had just taken place a few hours earlier, one cannot wonder at Slidell's tendency to give great importance to an alliance with a banking house which was intimately related to the court and cabinet.

Slidell sent the Erlanger contract to Mason for his signature, but Mason balked. Lindsay and Company had just made him a similar proposition without so many commissions and rebates. He must have felt that Erlanger's proposition was nothing short of a holdup; besides, the proposal had Caleb Huse's signature, which would make Mason more critical. Mason declined to sign the contract, but sent it to Benjamin with the explanation that he had no personal knowledge of Erlanger and Company, and that his signing the contract would seem to commit him to the Erlanger proposal as against the Lindsay offer, when, as a matter of fact, "it certainly seems to me that the London plan offers the best scheme of finance." But in the face of what must have been deep disapproval Mason admitted very judicially that as a political expedient Slidell was far more competent to judge of its effects than he.[2]

The Erlanger and Lindsay proposals forwarded by Mason reached Benjamin on December 31 before Erlanger's agents arrived in Richmond. The government was very cold to both proposals.[3] The Confederate government had planned to make use of the cotton bond or certificate rather than to float a definite loan—and objected to both the Lindsay and Erlanger proposals as too onerous. Finally, however, the Confederacy, induced by Slidell's belief in the political power of Erlanger, agreed to a modified form of the Erlanger proposal. It would take £3,000,000 instead of £5,000,000. Erlanger was to have all above 77 per cent instead of 70 per cent, and the bonds were to bear 7 instead of 8 per cent. "These terms," wrote Benjamin

[1] *Ibid.*

[2] Pickett Papers, Mason to Benjamin, No. 19, Nov. 4, 1862; *O.R.N.*, Ser. 2, Vol. III, pp. 590–93.

[3] Pickett Papers, Mason to Benjamin, No. 12, Jan. 15, 1863; *O.R.N.*, Ser. 2, Vol. III, pp. 648–51.

to Mason, "although vastly better than the outline of contract made in Paris, were considered by us so onerous that we were unwilling to take the whole amount offered, and would have declined it altogether but for the political considerations indicated by Mr. Slidell in whose judgment in such matters we are disposed to place very great confidence."[1] Benjamin was more explicit to Slidell. It was plain that although nominally a loan the Erlanger contract "was really one for the purchase of cotton, and that cotton would be demanded for the whole amount." The contract, even if only the 5 per cent commission and the 8 per cent on deferred payments were considered, would net the Confederacy only 61 per cent of the loan. This was on the basis that there would be an immediate redemption of the bonds by exchanging them for cotton at 6 pence a pound. The amount of cotton required would be greater than could be furnished, and it would actually be equivalent to selling cotton at $3\frac{2}{3}$ pence a pound. The original contract, continued Benjamin, was so much lower than all other offers that "it was impossible to accept the proposals." But Slidell's "intimation of political advantages likely to be derived from the loan possessed great weight," and "we finally agreed, in view of that intimation, to make a sacrifice" and accept the proposal in a modified form.[2] The contract was poor financing in Benjamin's eyes, but he was willing to waive that defect if it helped bring recognition to the Confederacy.

The Erlanger contract was pending during the entire fall and winter of 1862–63. The purchasing agents were in need of money and could not wait. So the War, Navy, and Treasury departments sent large quantities of Treasury bonds and cotton certificates to their respective agents, which by February 4, 1863, amounted to about six million dollars in Treasury bonds and three million in cotton certificates.[3] About the first of December, when Maury arrived with authority for all to use cotton bonds, Mason and Spence conferred with the several agents and they agreed as we recall to turn over the

[1] *Ibid.*

[2] Pickett Papers, Benjamin to Slidell, No. 11, Jan. 15, 1862; *O.R.N.*, Ser. 2, Vol. III, pp. 654–56.

[3] Mason Papers, Mason to Slidell; cf. *ibid.*, Jan. 28, 1863.

sale of bonds to Spence and Fraser, Trenholm and Company. After a full conference of agents it was further decided to hold the bonds and certificates off the market, if possible, until the fate of the Erlanger loan was determined.[1] Following this conference Spence wrote Mason that, while he agreed "that it is necessary to hold off entirely both cotton and [Treasury] bond until the Paris treaty [Erlanger contract] be determined," nevertheless, great haste was needed as the Confederate purchasing agents were out of funds, deeply in debt, and their credit low. Spence also indicated some doubts as to the wisdom of the proposed Erlanger arrangement.[2]

The purchasing agents grew restless at the suspension of business —and their creditors more so—as the weeks passed and no word came of the Erlanger contract. They had to have funds. Mason wrote Slidell on January 9 that "the time has arrived when the government must suffer with perhaps serious loss in meeting engagements unless money is supplied."[3] A few days later Spence wrote Erlanger that the agents must have money and that he would soon have to dispose of the bonds which he and the purchasing agents were holding unless it could be raised.[4] He wrote Mason on January 12 that since the news of Fredericksburg the demand for Treasury and cotton bonds had increased, and he thought that all the six million dollars in money bonds could be disposed of. "We could then follow up with cotton and manage without the Paris firm entirely if they should fail us."[5] In this Spence disclosed a growing distrust of Erlanger which became more and more outspoken as the terms of the contract were disclosed. Spence as financial agent—he had just received official notice of his appointment—was taking his duties seriously and exercising close watch over Erlanger and Company. On January 28 Mason informed Slidell that the Confederate agents could wait but little longer. They must have £500,000 "in the course of this week [or] the government interests and credit will

[1] Pickett Papers, Mason to Benjamin, No. 22, Dec. 10, 1862; *O.R.N.*, Ser. 2, Vol. III, pp. 617–18.

[2] Mason Papers, Spence to Mason, Dec. 31, 1862.   [3] *Ibid.*

[4] *Ibid.*, Jan. 12, 1863, speaks of his letter to Erlanger.

[5] *Ibid.*

suffer." The money could be raised in a few days on cotton bonds, but, he wrote, Spence and he had refrained from putting these bonds on the market for fear of interfering with the Erlanger proposals.[1] In the meanwhile, Spence conferred with Erlanger as to the advisability of disposing of the Treasury bonds.[2] Soon after this Mason approved of Caleb Huse's making purchases and paying debts amounting to nearly $2,000,000 with cotton certificates.[3] Spence, at the same time, felt out the market for money bonds but found little encouragement because of the advance in rate of interest.[4] Mason, pleased with the resumption of the use of the cotton certificate by Huse, now wrote Benjamin that he felt gratified that only a limited amount was to be raised by the Erlanger loan. He repeated his strong preference for the cotton certificates which had been approved by the Treasury in the fall of 1862.[5]

Finally, the Erlanger contract arrived. When Spence received a copy he broke out in open hostility. "It certainly justifies the opinion you expressed," he wrote Mason on February 6,[6] "and upon making a calculation I find that as it is worded, the loss on interest would be frightful. . . . . I shall do all I can to mend it. Having done that I shall do all I can to work it out, for once agreed to it must not break down. In this view I have sent a plan to Erlanger for putting it before the public. . . . ." As we shall see, his disapproval was well founded.

Erlanger complained to Slidell of Spence's attempted supervision of the proposed loan, and Slidell, who did not know of Spence's appointment and who saw the affair only through Erlanger's eyes, flew into a rage. On February 15 he wrote Mason: "I say to you in the strictest confidence that I do not like the way in which Mr. Spence writes, he evidently considers his personal interests invaded by the arrangement made at Richmond and seems to think that it is to be submitted to his judgment."[7] Three days later Erlanger and

[1] *Ibid.*, Jan. 28, 1863.　　　　[2] *Ibid.*

[3] Pickett Papers, Mason to Benjamin, No. 29, Feb. 5, 1863; *O.R.N.*, Ser. 2, Vol. III, pp. 675–77.

[4] *Ibid.*　　　　[5] *Ibid.*

[6] Mason Papers, Spence to Mason, Feb. 6, 1863.

[7] *Ibid.*, Feb. 15, 1863.

Company wrote a nasty letter to Spence to the effect that the Erlanger contract was none of his affair.

Spence at once wrote Mason that he would go to Paris. "After extremely polite letters and promises to do nothing without conferring with me, there comes one today from E. and Co. widely altered and evasive. In consequence I set off to-night and have telegraphed Mr. Slidell that I shall be with him tomorrow evening. I have worked out a complete plan which I think would have been beneficial to all parties. . . . . After the care exercised for months to avoid damage to this treaty it will be mortifying to be treated with something like polite contempt in return and I am not the man to take it easily." Spence still believed that he had the right as financial agent to supervise the placing of the loan.[1]

In the meanwhile, the official dispatches containing the notice of the contract arrived; and the Erlanger agents returned to Paris and preparations were at once made to sell the bonds. Slidell obtained the consent of the Emperor, De Lhuys, and Fould to advertise the loan. De Lhuys had objected at first because he feared it would offend Dayton, the United States minister. But Erlanger carried the matter before the Emperor, who quickly ordered De Lhuys to give the proper permission. Slidell considered this as significant of the continued friendship of the Emperor.[2]

Spence now learned the full story of the Erlanger business. He was left out. C. J. McRae was to be sent over as special agent for the loan. It hurt his pride. "I have written Mr. Memminger," he told Mason,[3] "expressing the pain I feel at the turn things have taken and desiring that my duties be defined at once." At the same time he learned, too, from Erlanger, that the latter would issue the bonds at 90 per cent. This price, he knew, was entirely too high to be safe.[4] In a few days Spence received his official appointment. His office was to be limited to Great Britain where he was to exercise general supervision over Confederate finances.[5] But Benjamin had

[1] *Ibid.*, Feb. 18, 1863.

[2] Pickett Papers, Slidell to Benjamin, No. 28, March 4, 1863; *O.R.N.*, Ser. 2, Vol. III, pp. 705-7.

[3] Mason Papers, Spence to Mason, March 14, 1863.

[4] *Ibid.*   [5] *Ibid.*

cut under him. The office was reduced in importance both in territory and in jurisdiction, by confining it to Britain and by the appointment of McRae. Spence had been talking too much about the
abolition of slavery, as we shall see later.

The authentic copy of the secret act of Congress of January 29,
1863, which authorized the loan, arrived on March 18, and the pro-
spectus was issued. On March 19 the bonds were placed on the market at Liverpool, London, Paris, Frankfort, and Amsterdam and remained on sale until 2:00 P.M. on Saturday, March 21, and nearly
£16,000,000 were subscribed, chiefly in London.[1]

The bonds were at a premium of $4\frac{1}{2}$-5 per cent on the first day.
This success of the Confederate loan, wrote Hotze,[2] "notwithstanding the apparently unfavorable time of bringing it out, when so
• many new loans are in the market and even consols have fallen one-
fourth per cent, is on all hands pronounced to be a great moral
victory." Slidell pronounced it "a financial recognition of our independence."[3] Mason congratulated Benjamin "on the triumphant
success of our infant credit; it shows, malgré all detraction and
calumny, that cotton is king at last."[4]

The *London Economist*, conservative journal of commerce and
capital though it was, thought very highly of the loan. "It may appear somewhat startling that the Confederates should be able to
borrow money in Europe while the Federal Government has been
unable to obtain a shilling from that usually liberal and enterprising
quarter!" The *Economist* believed that the cotton represented by
these bonds could be easily delivered to the purchasers in the interior
where, for some strange reason, the *Economist* thought it would be
safe as neutral property, until the war was over, and that then it
could be brought out and sold.[5]

[1] See Pickett Papers, Mason to Benjamin, Nos. 31, 32, March 19, 30; *O.R.N.*, Ser.
2, Vol. III, pp. 712–16, 730–31, respectively.

[2] Pickett Papers, Hotze to Benjamin, No. 20, March 21, 1863; *O.R.N.*, Ser. 2, Vol.
III, pp. 718–20.

[3] Pickett Papers, Slidell to Benjamin, No. 29, March 21, 1863; *O.R.N.*, Ser. 2,
Vol. III, pp. 720–21.

[4] Pickett Papers, No. 32, March 30; *O.R.N.*, Ser. 2, Vol. III, pp. 730–31.

[5] *Economist*, March 21, 1863.

But the bonds began to sag slowly and by April 3 were around 4 below par or 86 per cent. Spence believed that unless some check could be made the bottom would drop out and the bondholders would forfeit their 15 per cent already paid rather than meet the 10 per cent instalments due April 25. "I am willing," wrote Spence, "to take the reins, for the good of the cause which is so much at stake— but if they remain in hands so incompetent as to make the blunder committed, we shall be sorely damaged." Spence did not take much stock in the explanation that it was Federal agents selling short or spreading propaganda[1] which was depressing the loan. He laid the affair at the door of Erlanger and Company—their greediness to reap profits. "This loan ought never to have been put before the public at 90," he said with correct insight. Even the well-established European governments had not been able to sustain their bonds at anything like that price.[2]

Erlanger began to urge at once that Mason enter the market and buy the bonds to sustain the price high enough to prevent the purchasers from abandoning their subscription.[3] Spence, on the other hand, urged that £1,000,000 in bonds be withdrawn from the market as an expedient.[4] But Shroeder, the Erlanger representative in London, snapped his finger under Spence's nose and refused the proposal. He further informed Spence that if the Confederate commissioners failed to authorize Erlanger to sustain the market with the 15 per cent already collected, then Erlanger would consider that he had fulfilled his contract, which was simply to sell the bonds but not to guarantee that the public would pay the instalments. "If the public abandon the loan," said Shroeder, "the 15 per cent sacrificed is, in point of fact, not the property of the Government at all, but the profits of Messrs. Erlanger and Company, actually in their hands, and they cannot be expected to take a worse position. At any rate, they will not do so, and unless the compact can be made on the basis

[1] R. J. Walker was in England circulating pamphlets about southern repudiation of debts. It is doubtful whether this propaganda had much effect.

[2] Mason Papers, Spence to Mason, April 3, 1863; *ibid.*, April 4.

[3] *Ibid.*, Mason to Slidell, April 3, 1863.

[4] *Ibid.*, statement to Mason, May 9, 1863.

we name, matters must take their course."[1] Spence felt that this was unjust in view of the exorbitant price at which Erlanger had placed the bonds. This 15 per cent which Erlanger threatened to confiscate should Mason refuse to sustain the market was about £400,000, or nearly $2,000,000. Perhaps it was technically theirs, as they were to get 5 per cent for floating the bonds and 13 per cent or all above 77. However, the Confederacy clearly expected, and it was understood, that Erlanger would share luck with the Confederacy in the fluctuation of the bonds before they were paid for. But Erlanger insisted on his pound of flesh.

So, on April 7, Mason, after consultation with Slidell and Spence, signed an agreement to purchase back in open market £1,000,000 of the bonds if necessary.[2] From April 8 to April 24 the Confederate agents bulled the market, driving the bonds above par by the second day,[3] and spent in excess of the £1,000,000. On April 24 the bonds were still at par, but April 25 was the day for the bondholders to pay another 10 per cent instalment, and to prevent any possible forfeiture Erlanger and Company once again convinced Mason that £500,000 more should be spent to strengthen the market. This new plunge sustained the stock sufficiently to prevent any forfeiture— if there were any such danger—and the purchasers paid up another 10 per cent.[4] Bonds would now have to fall almost to 60 per cent before all the speculative margin was eliminated.

May 1 was passed with the bonds above par, but Mason reported to Slidell on May 9 that the loan despite constant purchases was drooping around $\frac{1}{2}$–1 per cent premium;[5] and on May 11 it closed at par.[6] After this it slipped slowly below par. On June 12 it was 1–2 per cent discount;[7] on July 23 it was 4 below par. With the news

[1] *Ibid.*

[2] Pickett Papers, Mason to Benjamin, No. 33 with inclosure, April 9; *O.R.N.*, Ser. 2, Vol. III, pp. 735-38.

[3] *Ibid.*

[4] Pickett Papers, Mason to Benjamin, April 27, unofficial; *O.R.N.*, Ser. 2, Vol. III, pp. 751-53.

[5] Mason Papers, Mason to Slidell, May 9.

[6] Pickett Papers, Mason to Benjamin, No. 36, May 11, 1863; *O.R.N.*, Ser. 2, Vol. III, p. 766.

[7] Pickett Papers, Mason to Benjamin, No. 39; *O.R.N.*, Ser. 2, Vol. III, pp. 804-5.

of the fall of Vicksburg it fell to 36 per cent discount and then rose to around 22 per cent discount, where it stood for a while.[1] The news of Confederate defeats or of the burning of cotton always sent the loan down, and such news was assiduously spread by Federal agents.[2] But once past the June payment there was no danger of forfeiture, so the Confederate agents were not forced to go into the market again after the £1,500,000 was used up.

But this money was blood money. The financial transactions of the Confederacy had been almost completely held up in Europe from September, 1862, until the summer of 1863 while waiting for the Erlanger loan to materialize. It had a tantalizing habit of vanishing just as the Confederate agents were reaching for it. Spence, who had refrained from all sales of cotton bonds or money bonds so as not to injure the Erlanger loan, was very severe in his condemnation of Erlanger and Company. He considered the loan a miserable failure as it was, without any doubt. He expressed himself fully and fluently to Mason, Slidell, and to Erlanger; he argued that the loan had collapsed because floated at too high a price; he accused Erlanger of betraying the Confederacy's trust by unloading all his bonds on the Confederate agents who were buying bonds to sustain the market; in other words, that most of the £1,500,000 which Mason spent to sustain the loan was in Erlanger's pockets. That is, he purchased his stipulated quota of Confederate bonds—£400,000 worth at 77 per cent—then collected 5 per cent commission; and when all that could be obtained in this fashion was squeezed out, the bonds were sold back to the Confederacy at 90. One can readily believe such accusation when one keeps in mind the coercion used by Erlanger to force Mason and Slidell to buy £1,500,-000, or over $7,500,000, worth of their own bonds.[3]

Spence's criticism of Erlanger's conduct of the loan angered Slidell greatly, and he wrote to Mason, "I am obliged to confess that I have no faith in Mr. Spence's judgment or his business qualities. I

[1] Pickett Papers, Hotze to Benjamin, No. 27, Aug. 27, 1863; *O.R.N.*, Ser. 2, Vol. III, pp. 875–81.

[2] *Ibid.*

[3] For these charges see Mason Papers, Spence to Mason, April, May, *passim,* especially May 9, 1863; *ibid.*, Slidell to Mason, May 8; Slidell to Spence, May 10; Slidell to Mason, May 15.

am almost equally sceptical about his fair dealing or disinterestedness."[1] A few days later he wrote Mason, after having received one
of Spence's letters: "I am getting heartily tired of his meddling."
"Spence appears to consider that the powers of Secretary of Navy as
well as of Treasury are vested in him."[2]

One does not have to defend Spence from Slidell's charges of bad
judgment, for all of his criticisms of the Erlanger affair proved to be
true prophecies. The loan could never be sustained at 90 per cent.
As a financial arrangement it was, as Spence insisted, not a success.
Over half the bonds had to be purchased back by the Confederate
government by the fourteenth of May, 1863,[3] and very few of these
bonds were ever sold again, though they were disposed of in a different fashion, as we shall see. This left around $7,500,000 in bonds
in the hands of the purchasers, but the Confederacy had got only
77 per cent, less 5 per cent commission, less 1 per cent for Erlanger's
acting as collecting agent, less 8 per cent interest on deferred payments made before they were due. That is, the Confederacy got
about 68 per cent of the $7,500,000, or about $5,000,000 or a third of
the normal face value of the sum called for in the contract. Later
Erlanger and Company paid a penalty of about $500,000 rather
than carry out a contract to dispose of the remainder of the bonds,
and this may be added to the $5,000,000, making $5,500,000 obtained from the Erlanger loan as such. But this does not mean that
even $5,500,000 was at the disposal of the purchasing agents. Far
from this; in the first place, according to the terms of the bonds one-
twentieth of the bonds must be redeemed each year, and it was necessary to pay for these out of the foregoing $5,500,000. This amount-
ed to £255,200, or $1,276,000, by the end of the war,[4] all paid out of
the Erlanger fund and reducing the net proceeds to about $4,224,000.
Then, there was the 8 per cent interest which amounted to £325,000,[5]
or $1,625,000 which by the end of the war further reduced the net
proceeds to $2,599,000. The total amount of cash which finally came
into the hands of the Confederacy was then about $2,599,000.

[1] *Ibid.*, May 8.

[2] *Ibid.*, May 15.   [4] Schwab, p. 42.

[3] *Ibid.*, Mason to Slidell, May 14.   [5] *Ibid.*

As soon as the Confederate agents saw that the Erlanger loan would realize such an inadequate sum of money they used the Erlanger bonds in their hands as collateral or simply as a medium of exchange. These bonds were no better than the other cotton certificates already in the hands of Spence and Fraser, Trenholm and Company, but their value was easily ascertained as they were already on the market. Then, too, it was feared to release other bonds because of the effect upon the Erlanger bonds.[1]

The most outstanding use of the repurchased Erlanger bonds was in the payment of Caleb Huse's debt to S. Isaac, Campbell and Company. On May 25, 1863, this debt amounted to the sum of £515,000, or a bit over $2,500,000. The firm which had been worrying along with Huse had accepted $2,000,000 of 8 per cent bonds and cotton warrants as collateral for the debt. It will be recalled that they had been clamorous in the fall of 1862 for cotton bonds. Now they had their prayers answered. Huse arranged through Erlanger, May 25, 1863, to pay off over half the debt with Erlanger bonds. Three hundred thousand pounds sterling were thus used in payment of £267,-224, or $1,336,120, of the debt.[2]

This firm, which had hungered and thirsted after cotton certificates, now had its fill. For the bottom dropped out of the Erlanger loan after the news of Vicksburg and they were unable to sell except at a great loss. McRae, who had not yet discovered that Isaac, Campbell and Company were keeping two sets of books on the Confederate purchases, was quite concerned over the loss of these Confederate creditors and he wrote, September 15, that "this house, which has been so much maligned by our over zealous friends is likely to be ruined by having trusted our Government when nobody else would."[3]

But when the Confederate agents found out that Isaac, Campbell

[1] See Mason Papers, Slidell to Mason, May 8; Slidell to Spence, May 10; Spence to Mason, May 11; and Slidell to Mason, May 15. Spence had just received additional authority to dispose of a large batch of bonds but refrained for fear of further depressing the Erlanger bonds.

[2] O.R., Ser. 4, Vol. II, pp. 885–94, McRae to Seddon, Oct. 23, 1863, with inclosures.

[3] Ibid., inclosure No. 4.

and Company had dealt unfairly with them, they hardened their hearts. Not only did they refuse to take back any of the bonds which they had unloaded on this company, but they proposed to obtain satisfaction out of Isaac, Campbell and Company for the fraud.[1]

McRae, the Erlanger loan agent, further disposed of a large batch of Erlanger bonds in the fall of 1863 to cover the indebtedness of Huse, Bulloch, and the other army and navy agents. McRae stated to Memminger on October 2 that the total indebtedness of these agents was £1,016,000, a large part of which he had arranged to pay in Erlanger bonds at the issue price of 77 per cent.[2]

Then in the spring of 1864 McRae disposed of about £250,000 as collateral in a contract with J. K. Gilliat and Company for advancing £150,000 cash for the purchase of ships for the Confederacy. A similar contract was made with Fraser, Trenholm and Company and with Collie and Company.[3] By the spring of 1865 only about £500,000 of Erlanger bonds were in the hands of McRae,[4] which means that over £1,000,000, or about $5,000,000, of the repurchased bonds had been disposed of privately in commercial deals. As a matter of fact, it was not improbable that at one time or another the entire Erlanger stock had been disposed of, either as a medium of exchange or as collateral in private deals.

But the money raised by the Erlanger loan and the use of the residue of bonds was not the only financial expedient of the Confederacy in Europe. It was, in fact, the beginning of a real system of foreign financing which if adopted in 1861 would have proved entirely adequate for all Confederate needs. In Europe this new system consisted in consolidating all purchasing and disbursements under the control of one man, McRae. In the Confederacy it consisted of the government's purchase of cotton, finally under one agency, and the shipment of this cotton to Europe to be used by McRae as a basis of credit. Finally, it involved government control of blockade-running so as to insure transportation for the cotton to be sent out and supplies brought in for the government.

[1] See, e.g., *ibid.*, pp. 1067–81, Seddon to McRae.

[2] *Ibid.*, pp. 979–88, Memminger to Seddon with inclosures, Nov. 24, 1863.

[3] *Ibid.*, Ser. 2, Vol. III, pp. 525–30, McRae to Seddon.   [4] Schwab, p. 41.

Space does not permit more than a brief sketch of this system, though it deserves full treatment as the one intelligent performance of the Confederate government in the field of finances. We have already observed that the agents were at one another's throats, while contractors hawked Confederate contracts about the streets like overripe fruit. Spence and Mason had long since seen the need of a general supervision and consolidation, and Spence had obtained the appointment as "Confederate financial agent" under the impression that he was to supervise and control all finances. But, as we have observed, Slidell cut under Spence and his authority was greatly curtailed by the time he received his commission. Then C. J. McRae was given supervision of the Erlanger loan, and as there was for months no other financial business than the loan, it meant that McRae had virtually superseded Spence. At the time McRae was appointed it is doubtful whether the Confederate government really intended to supplant Spence. But soon Slidell's complaints arrived, colored by that gentleman's infatuation for Erlanger, whose son was soon to marry Slidell's daughter. But more important still was what Hotze wrote Benjamin about Spence. In the field of propaganda he reported that Spence was going over the country advocating the recognition and independence of the South as the surest and quickest means of abolishing slavery. On October 24, 1862, Hotze had written Benjamin: "Mr. Spence, I regret to say, has of late rendered the idea of ultimate emancipation unduly conspicuous." "I almost dread the direction his friendship and devotion seem about to take."[1] Later Hotze spoke of Spence as trying "to occupy at one and the same time two opposite and irreconcilable positions—that of a high official of our Government owing it allegiance and that of a disinterested alien friend."[2] Then the Confederate newspapers attacked Spence bitterly because of his position on slavery.[3] Spence was doomed. He could not meddle with the divine institution of slavery and retain his position as financial agent. So about December 1, 1863, he received a

[1] Pickett Papers, Hotze to Benjamin, No. 13; *O.R.N.*, Ser. 2, Vol. III, pp. 565–67.
[2] Pickett Papers, Hotze to Benjamin, No. 31, Oct. 31, 1863; *O.R.N.*, Ser. 2, Vol. III, pp. 944–48.
[3] Pickett Papers, Domestic Letters, Vol. I, Benjamin to Spence, Jan. 11, 1864.

polite letter from Memminger revoking his appointment on the grounds that McRae and Fraser, Trenholm and Company were sufficient for the duties.[1]

Benjamin on January 11, 1864, wrote Spence frankly why his services had been disposed of as financial agent and why he could not use him in the official capacity of propagandist agent for which he had applied. "I freely admit that, as a private gentleman entirely disconnected from this government, you could not consistently with self respect, conceal or color your true sentiments on this [slavery] or any other question in which principles are involved. It is also quite probable that the fact of your entertaining the opinions which you profess, renders your advocacy of our cause more effective with a people whose views coincide with yours and it would be folly on our part to regret the aid or alienate the feelings of those who, while friendly to our cause, are opposed to the institutions established among us. On the other hand it appears to me that candor requires on your part the concessions that no government could justify itself before the people whose servant it is, if it selected as exponents of its views and opinions those who entertain sentiments decidedly adverse to an institution which both the government and the people maintain as essential to their well being." Benjamin continued that the government could not be expected to retain agents "who are in avowed and public opposition to their opinions and feelings," and it would be impossible for the Confederacy to continue to engage him in its services after the publication of his opinions.[2]

Spence, feeling unjustly dealt with and having lost considerable money, demanded compensation. Hotze recommended that Spence be satisfied, and Benjamin had McRae settle with him.[3]

When Spence was superseded, his place was taken by an able man, C. J. McRae, in whom all the Confederate purchasing agents had great confidence. He was sent out, as has been observed, only as agent for the Erlanger loan, but the need of a central directing

[1] Mason Papers, Spence to Mason, Dec. 7, 1863, mentions the letter.
[2] Pickett Papers, Domestic Letters, Vol. I, Benjamin to Spence, Jan. 11, 1864.
[3] *Ibid.*

agency was so great when he got there that he was soon to have charge of every financial transaction. In June when he first arrived he and Slidell and Lamar, commissioner to Russia (who never got to Russia), met and agreed as Mason and Spence had long since done that the financial situation of the Confederacy was in chaos. In addition to the inadequacy of funds, all the agents were at one another's throat. McRae, Slidell, and Lamar attempted to smooth the waters temporarily;[1] then on June 21 Slidell wrote Benjamin summing up the situation and offering a final solution. "I feel it my duty to call, through you, the attention of the President to the very great embarrassments produced by the employment of several agents to make purchases for the War Department, with ill-defined powers and sometimes with conflicting instructions. These agents are very far from being on good terms with each other, and the consequence of this alienation must necessarily be detrimental to the public service." His solution was to vest "some person possessing the full confidence of the Secretary of War, with complete control over all the purchases to be made for his department." While the naval agents did not seem to be quarreling much, he thought that it was better "to subject the disbursements of the agents of both departments [war and navy] to the control of a common head." This head should be a civilian and he urged that C. J. McRae be appointed.[2]

The response of Benjamin on receipt of Slidell's letter of June 21 was highly favorable. He immediately made arrangements to carry out Slidell's plans.[3] An argeement was made between the War, Navy, and Treasury departments to put McRae in charge of all disbursements and give him a general supervision over all purchases and contracts.[4]

From the time of his appointment as chief purchasing and disbursing agent, September, 1863, until the war was ended McRae

[1] Pickett Papers, Slidell to Benjamin, No. 37, June 12, 1862; O.R.N., Ser. 2, Vol. III, pp. 806–7.

[2] Pickett Papers, No. 38, June 21, 1863; O.R.N., Ser. 2, Vol. III, pp. 810–14.

[3] Pickett Papers, Benjamin to Slidell, No. 22, Aug. 17, 1863; O.R.N., Ser. 2, Vol. III, pp. 872–74.

[4] Pickett Papers, Benjamin to Memminger, Seddon, and Mallory, Sept. 15, 1863; O.R.N., Ser. 2, Vol. III, pp. 897–99; cf. O.R., Ser. 4, Vol. II, pp. 824–27.

steadily perfected the purchasing system and Confederate finances. All visible friction between the agents disappeared. Huse, Crenshaw, Ferguson, North, and Bulloch all went about their business without stepping upon one another's toes. After his appointment McRae as general supervisor examined every contract, and as time passed, though careful to work through the various purchasing agents, took more and more the initiative in making the large contracts. Partly as a result of this co-ordination and centralization Confederate credit improved and the value of the Erlanger bonds rose steadily until the fall of 1864.[1]

The second phase, the use of cotton in the development of the new system of foreign finance, was slow, just as was the establishment of a central purchasing agent. It will be recalled that over 400,000 bales of cotton had been purchased in 1861 by the Confederate government, that this had been held back from export by the embargo, and that because of the desire to encourage private violations of the blockade no systematic effort had been made to ship government cotton abroad until the spring of 1863. But Caleb Huse purchased four steamers for the government to ship in supplies and bring out cotton in 1863. The success of this venture was perfect. From January to August 29, 1863, these vessels, as we have already observed, had run the blockade forty-four times without a single capture.[2] The Navy Department had also shipped out some cotton. But with the realization that the Erlanger loan would not net a sufficient amount and the necessity of sustaining the sagging Confederate credit, Slidell, Mason, Hotze, and McRae all began to urge upon the Confederate government that it not only ship as much cotton as possible out on its own boats, but that in order to insure an adequate exportaton of cotton it regulate or completely monopolize the entire business. On August 6, 1863, Mason wrote Benjamin that "the engagements of the Government here, present and prospective, both for the Army and Navy, it is very manifest, will require much larger

---

[1] For the establishment of this centralizing agency and its improvement of credit see *O.R.*, Ser. 4, Vol. II, pp. 885–94, 918, 1067–68; *ibid.*, Vol. III, pp. 154–58, 301–2, 525–30, 702–4.

[2] Pickett Papers, Thomas L. Bayne to Benjamin, Aug. 24, 1863; *O.R.N.*, Ser. 2, Vol. III, p. 882; cf. *O.R.*, Ser. 4, Vol. II, pp. 955–58.

sums than will be derived from the loan; and I would earnestly suggest that arrangements should be perfected, as speedily as possible, by means of fast steamers, for bringing out cotton on Government account (as is now done to some extent)."[1]

On September 4 McRae, who by this time had the situation well sized up, wrote Gorgas that the multiplicity of agents and contractors, by discrediting the Confederate government and by using up the cotton, had impaired the Confederate credit abroad. "Why does not the government take the subject of the blockade running entirely into its own hands? Not a bale of cotton should be allowed to come out of the country nor a pound of merchandise go in except on government account."[2]

That same night McRae visited Mason and told him that he had advised the government's taking over the entire cotton trade through the blockade, as well as the regulation of the whole blockade trade. Mason heartily indorsed McRae's plans. He wrote Benjamin that he could "see nothing to prevent the Government taking this whole business into its exclusive hands."[3]

Soon Hotze, who had been reporting the great evils of the private-contract system—the squabbles and cheap quarrels and the inadequate means of purchasing supplies in Europe—urged that "the only remedy seems to be the radical one of annulling all private contracts and assuming on the part of the Government the strict monopoly of blockade running."[4]

Soon McRae in consultation with Mason, Slidell, Hotze, Huse, and the others formulated a plan for government control of blockade-running so as to realize heavily on cotton as a medium of exchange. On October 7 he wrote Memminger the details of the plan. They were in outline as follows:

[1] Pickett Papers, Mason to Benjamin, No. 43, Aug. 6, 1863; *O.R.N.*, Ser. 2, Vol. III, pp. 857–62.

[2] McRae to Seddon, Oct. 23, 1863, inclosure No. 3, whole letter in inclosures; *O.R.*, Ser. 4, Vol. III, pp. 885–94.

[3] Pickett Papers, Mason to Benjamin, No. 45, Sept. 5, 1863; *O.R.N.*, Ser. 2, Vol. III, pp. 896–97.

[4] Pickett Papers, Hotze to Benjamin, No. 30, Oct. 3, 1863; *O.R.N.*, Ser. 2, Vol. III, pp. 919–22.

1. To revoke all contracts on which profits were permitted.

2. The centralization of all purchasing under one agent—a step already taken through Slidell's earlier recommendation though not yet officially known to McRae.

3. "That the Government should take the exports and imports into its own hands, and no cotton, tobacco, or naval stores should be allowed to leave the country except on Government account or for account of holders of produce bonds, and none but the same parties should be allowed to import. . . . ."

4. Recommended that the Confederate government purchase all cotton and tobacco in the country at a fixed price.[1]

McRae's plan was submitted to the cabinet and the President, and with the constant pressure of Slidell, Bulloch, Hotze, and Mason[2] the administration pushed a law through Congress, February 6, 1864, prohibiting the shipment of cotton except under regulation of the President, and on the same day a law was enacted prohibiting import of luxuries.[3]

Even before the passage of this law the government in the fall of 1863 began to compel blockade-runners to devote one-third to one-half of their cargo space to Confederate cotton.[4] This custom of exacting one-third to one-half of the outbound cargo for government cotton or tobacco and a fair portion of the return cargo on government account indicated the lines which the President would follow under the law of February 6, 1864. So on March 5, 1864, the regulations were issued which provided that one-half the outbound cargo and one-half of the inbound cargo should be on Confederate account at fixed rates, and that one-half the proceeds of the private

[1] O.R., Ser. 4, Vol. II, pp. 979–88, Memminger to Seddon, Nov. 24, 1863, with inclosures—inclosure No. 2, McRae to Seddon, Oct. 7, 1863.

[2] See Pickett Papers, Slidell to Benjamin, No. 47, Oct. 25, 1863; O.R.N., Ser. 2, Vol. III, pp. 937–44; Pickett Papers, Hotze to Benjamin, No. 34, Dec. 26, 1863; O.R.N., Ser. 2, Vol. III, pp. 981–85; Pickett Papers, Bulloch to Mallory, No. 15, Jan. 9, 1864; O.R.N., Ser. 2, Vol. III, pp. 992–93.

[3] See O.R., Ser. 5, Vol. III, pp. 78–80, 80–82, for laws.

[4] Ibid., Ser. 4, Vol. II, pp. 714–16, Bayne to Beauregard, Aug. 14, 1863, with inclosures; ibid., pp. 1013–16, Seddon to Davis, Nov. 26, 1863.

cargo exported from the Confederacy must be invested in goods and brought into the Confederacy.[1]

Thus by 1864 the Confederacy had at last got down to bed rock in its finances. Cotton which had failed as a political king was now to be put into service as a menial where it should have been put in the beginning. The Confederacy had on hand the better part of the 400,000 bales purchased under the produce-loan acts, but this cotton was stored in the interior on plantations, often in inaccessible places; and the government was forced to go into the field to purchase a new supply in more accessible places which could be shipped to the seaports.

So the government put its agents into the field. At first each department purchased its own cotton. The Treasury Department sent out agents who purchased or impressed cotton all along the rivers and railroads and near the cities and seacoast, and concentrated it in Mobile, Savannah, Charleston, Wilmington, in the small harbors of the Florida coast, and at Galveston, Texas. The War Department beginning with the fall of 1862 had begun to purchase cotton and collect it, and by the fall of 1863 the Ordnance Bureau, Quartermaster, Commissary, Medical Bureau—every important bureau in the War Department—had agents in the field purchasing or impressing cotton to be shipped to Fraser, Trenholm and Company. Not only was the War Department accumulating cotton for the purchase of foreign supplies, but the army in the trans-Mississippi department under Smith, Magruder, and Bee was purchasing in competition with the War Department agent Simeon Hart and later the Cotton Bureau. Then the Navy Department was collecting cotton to send abroad.

The shipment, however, of all cotton east of the Mississippi was under the supervision of Thomas L. Bayne, who saw that it was loaded in the government ships and that private vessels carried out their one-half cargo of Confederate cotton.

By August, 1864, this chaotic buying of cotton by the various bureaus and departments was abandoned, and all the purchasing

[1] *Ibid.*, Vol. III, pp. 187–89.

east of the Mississippi was done by the Bureau of Foreign Supplies under Bayne, and the proceeds placed under the control of the Treasury agents in Europe. An energetic secretary of the treasury would have assumed this function in the beginning.[1]

The new system worked wonders. On July 4, 1864, McRae wrote J. A. Seddon that under the new system of finance he had been able to place large orders, among which were fourteen new steamers for the Confederacy with which to run the blockade. He was highly elated. "The legislation of the last Congress, with the regulations since adopted in reference to the foreign commerce of the country, [Laws of February 6 and the President's regulations based thereon] has greatly strengthened it, and I hope the Government will not allow the outside pressure to cause any future modification of these regulations. . . . ."[2] As early as April 7, 1864, Slidell had remarked that "blockade running for individual account had become an almost unmitigated nuisance. If the proceeds of the cotton shipped by the Government be employed exclusively in the purchase for cash in European markets of needful supplies by its own agents and for the payment of obligations contracted by them, I have no doubt that they will be found sufficient for the purpose."[3] On August 6, 1864, Hotze wrote that "the new commercial system, though scarcely yet in its infancy, has thus far worked so beneficially as to promise

[1] The story of the purchase of cotton by the various departments and bureaus is a long and complicated one and only a few typical examples may be referred to in this brief mention. See, e.g., Memminger to Seddon, May 11, 1863, *ibid.*, Vol. II, pp. 550–51, for purchase by War and Treasury departments; Gorgas to Cuyler, March 3, 1863, *ibid.*, p. 416, for purchase by Ordnance Bureau and Treasury Department; *ibid.*, Vol. III, p. 513, Seddon to S. D. Lee with reference to Treasury cotton to be used by War Department; *ibid.*, p. 351, Cross to Walker; L. B. Northrop report, *ibid.*, Vol. II, pp. 968–72, Q.M. shipment of cotton; *ibid.*, Seddon to President, Dec. 10, 1864; McRae to Seddon, July 4, 1864, *ibid.*, pp. 525–30; *ibid.*, pp. 587–90, Trenholm to Seddon, Aug. 12, 1864, shipment of cotton by Treasury for all the bureaus; *ibid.*, pp. 1071–73, Bayne to Breckenridge, work of Bureau of Foreign Supplies; *Journal of Confederate Congress*, IV, 70–72, creation of Bureau of Foreign Supplies. For further reference see *O.R.* and *O.R.N.*, General Index: Thos. L. Bayne, Cotton Bureau, Trans-Mississippi Dept., Lt. Colonel W. A. Broadwell, W. J. Hutchins, P. W. Gray, Simeon Hart.

[2] *O.R.*, Ser. 4, Vol. III, pp. 525–30.

[3] Pickett Papers, Slidell to Benjamin, No. 59, April 7, 1864; *O.R.N.*, Ser. 2, Vol III, pp. 1077–79.

when fully developed to fulfil literally and even to exceed my own glowing anticipations."[1]

President Davis summed up the effects of the new system in his answer to the Senate and House on December 17 and 20, respectively, in their inquiry as to the operation of this law regulating blockade-running. It was the general consensus of opinion, in which he fully concurred, that, before the Confederacy devised the system of regulation of imports and exports in February, 1864, the commerce of the Confederacy was "almost exclusively in the hands of aliens; that our cotton, tobacco and naval stores were being drained from the states, and that we were receiving in return cargoes of liquors, wines, and articles of luxury; that the imported goods, being held in few hands and in limited quantities, were sold at prices so exorbitant that the blockade runners after purchasing fresh cargoes of cotton still retained large sums of Confederate money which they invested in gold for exportation and in foreign exchange, and that the whole course of trade had a direct tendency to impoverish our country, demoralize our people, depreciate our currency, and enfeeble our defense." The laws of February 6 and the regulations based on these laws, continued Davis, were aimed at preventing as far as possible the waste of Confederate resources and to enable the Confederacy to realize on their resources. "My conviction is decided that the effect of the legislation has been salutary; that the evils existing prior to its adoption have been materially diminished." This opinion, said Davis, was shared by all government officials who had anything to do with the enforcement of the regulations. "These laws and regulations have enabled the government not only to provide supplies to a much greater extent than formerly and to furnish the means for meeting the instalment on its foreign loan, but to put an end to a wasteful and ruinous contract system by which supplies were obtained before Congress determined to exercise control over the imports and exports. Instead of being compelled to give contractors a large profit on the cost of their supplies and to make payment in cotton in our ports at 6 pence per pound, we now purchase

[1] Pickett Papers, Hotze to Benjamin, No. 48, Aug. 6, 1864; *O.R.N.*, Ser. 2, Vol. III, pp. 1185–86.

supplies abroad by our agents at cost in the foreign markets, and pay them in cotton which sells at a net price of 24 pence per pound." The government, said Davis, had shipped within the last five months 11,796 bales of cotton abroad and had lost only 1,272. This put abroad £420,960, or about $2,104,800, whereas under the old system it would have netted only one-fourth of this, or £100,240 ($501,200).[1]

Seddon reported that from March 1 to December 10, 1864, Colonel Bayne had shipped for the Confederacy 27,299 bales netting $5,296,006, or an equivalent of $132,500,000 in the Confederate currency. In short, Bayne had placed abroad for the Cis-Mississippi department twice as much money in eight months as the Erlanger loan had netted in the previous eight months; and the importation of war supplies had just as greatly increased—all in the face of the growing stringency of the blockade and sieges of Mobile, Wilmington, and Charleston.[2]

In the words of the *Index*, speaking of the cotton exported before the regulations on private account: "Had the cotton been exported for its own account, instead of, for the most part, private speculators, the Confederate Government might have dispensed with foreign loans, might have bought its warlike stores at the lowest cash rates and supplied its citizens with commodities of prime necessity at a moderate advance on cost."[3] That is, had the Confederacy exported all the cotton which reached Europe through the blockade, it could have supplied its armies with all their needs and its citizens with necessities. The question might be repeated in this connection: What might it not have done had it shipped all the cotton possible in 1861–62 instead of placing an embargo on cotton in the hopes of coercing Europe? Like so many other policies of the Confederacy, the laws and regulations putting cotton and tobacco export under government control in 1864 bore too much the appearance of locking the stable after the mare had fled. With many ports captured, the blockade was becoming a powerful menace and the accessible cotton had either been swept off by private speculators or burned by the

---

[1] *O.R.*, Ser. 4, Vol. III, pp. 948–53, for Davis' reply to Congress, and *ibid.*, pp. 953–58, for Trenholm's report to Davis.

[2] *Ibid.*, pp. 928–30, Seddon to President.   [3] *Index*, Dec. 24, 1863, p. 552.

advancing and retreating armies. The belief in foreign intervention
to obtain cotton had caused the Confederacy to sacrifice its cotton
by an embargo the first year of the war, and the belief that the
blockade would be broken if enough private parties could be induced
to violate it caused the Confederacy to refrain from taking control of
cotton export the second and part of the third year; and it was only
after all hopes of intervention or repudiation of the blockade had
vanished that the Confederacy made up its mind to make full use
of the purchasing power of its cotton.

CHAPTER XII

THE BUILDING OF THE CONFEDERATE NAVY IN EUROPE

INTERNATIONAL LAW VERSUS INTERNATIONAL EXPEDIENCY

While the Confederacy from the beginning of the war to the end strove to build naval vessels in Europe, its greatest and most nearly successful undertakings fell largely within the period of 1862–63 when Confederate efforts at recognition were suspended. For this reason it seems fitting to give at this juncture a sketch of the work of the Confederate agents in procuring a navy in England and France.

On May 9, 1861, Secretary of Navy Mallory ordered James Dunwoody Bulloch, of Georgia, uncle of Theodore Roosevelt, to proceed to England and purchase or build six steam propellers to prey upon American commerce.[1] The following day Congress on the recommendation of Mallory appropriated one million dollars for Bulloch's mission.[2] On the same day Congress in response to Mallory's request voted an additional two million dollars for the construction or purchase of two ironclads in France or England.[3] A few days later Mallory commissioned Lieutenant James H. North to proceed to Europe to obtain these two ironclads.[4] Bulloch was a younger man than North; he had retired from the United States Navy some years before the war and was engaged in the shipping business. This temporary retirement tainted him, and his subsequent promotion to commander over the heads of North and other lieutenants rankled like poison in the breasts of the naval hierarchy.[5]

Contrary to a strange tradition that persists yet, both England and France were in possession of a considerable fleet of iron or steel war vessels before the battle of the "Merrimack" and the "Monitor." France had reduced Fort Constantine in the Crimean War with

[1] *O.R.N.*, Ser. 2, Vol. II, pp. 64–65.
[2] *Ibid.*, p. 66.   [4] *Ibid.*, pp. 70–72.
[3] *Ibid.*, pp. 66–67.   [5] See, e.g., *ibid.*, pp. 133, 176–77, 204–5, 235–39, 254–56.

floating iron batteries—a kind of slow-moving ironclad. After this she had undertaken the construction of ten iron- or steelclad warships the most famous of which was the "Gloire," which Slidell had said could sink the whole Federal Navy. England in competition was building or had already built the "Warrior," the "Prince," and others. These vessels were immune to shell and eight-inch solid shot at a greater distance than four hundred yards.[1]

Mallory was of the opinion that "the possession of an iron-armored ship . . . . [was] a matter of the first necessity. Such a vessel at this time could traverse the entire coast of the United States, prevent all blockades, and encounter, with a fair-prospect of success, their entire navy."[2] He instructed North to hasten to France and offer to purchase one of the companion ships of the "Gloire." The friendly attitude of the French government made him believe that "arrangements might be made with it for the transfer to our Government either directly or indirectly through some friendly intermediary of one of the armored frigates of the class of the 'Gloire.' " He instructed North to consult with the Confederate commissioners to "ascertain whether this great object can be accomplished." He felt rather confident of France. "The importance to France of raising the existing blockade of the ports of the cotton states and of preventing their future blockade must be evident to that Government."[3]

Bulloch did not find the six wooden cruisers waiting to his hand, partly because of lack of funds and partly because he had his own ideas as to what a "raider" should be. But on August 13, 1861, he reported to Mallory that he had contracts for the building of two vessels—destined to be the "Oreto" or "Florida" and the "Alabama."[4]

But North was not so fortunate. On August 16, 1861, he complained to Mallory, "I am here without one dollar to carry out your orders, and the people of these parts are as keen after money as any people I ever saw in my life." But had he any amount of money the ironclads could not be bought. "I am sorry to say that the gen-

[1] *Ibid.*, pp. 67–69, Mallory to C. M. Conrad.
[2] *Ibid.*
[3] *Ibid.*, pp. 70–72, Mallory to North, May 17, 1861.   [4] *Ibid.*, pp. 83–87.

eral impression out here is that, if I had millions at my command, I could not carry out your views, as both France and England are anxious to get all the ironclad ships they can." It took two years, he said, to build one of the ironclads the size of the "Warrior" or the "Gloire."[1]

North spent the next year in a constant succession of disappointments. Not having money to contract for an ironclad, he was assigned first the command of the "Oreto" (or "Florida"), then of the "Alabama"; then all his orders were countermanded.[2] Everything and everyone seemed to have gone against North. But at length, after a year, he finally made a contract for a giant ironclad to be built by James and George Thompson of Glasgow. This contract was signed May 20, 1862.[3] The ship was to have 3,200 tonnage and cost £182,000. It is a curious fact that the Confederate ironclads are usually spoken of as the "Laird rams," while the "Thompson ram" which North built on the Clyde—as large as both Laird rams combined—has been overlooked by historians.

Bulloch's first cruiser, the "Oreto," was ready in February, 1862, and the command offered to North. After hemming and hawing North, who was an old maid for details, allowed the vessel to sail without him.[4] Owing to the complaints of the American government, England kept a close watch over Bulloch's ships. The vigilance of the British government prevented the "Oreto" from arming in British ports. It finally sailed to the West Indies (Nassau) to complete the equipment.[5] North expressed the opinion that "the English Government are very strict in carrying out their avowed neutrality views," and that "it will be impossible for the present to arm a vessel in this country."[6] Bulloch, too, reported to Mallory, April 11, 1862, that the British authorities along with the American secret-service agents were so vigilant that the "Florida" had left without arms and that the "Alabama" would have to run the blockade and

---

[1] *Ibid.*, p. 87.

[2] See, e.g., *ibid.*, pp. 176–77, North to Bulloch, March 29, 1862, and *passim*.

[3] *Ibid.*, pp. 191–204.   [4] See *ibid.*, pp. 141, 143–44, 147, 148–49, 164–65.

[5] *Ibid.*, pp. 141–42, 143–44, 147; Mason Papers, North to Mason, Feb. 6, 1862.

[6] *O.R.N.*, Ser. 2, Vol. II, pp. 166–68, North to Mallory, March 16, 1862.

obtain its equipment in Confederate ports.[1] Semmes thought that the British vigilance was an outgrowth of the Trent affair. "The fact is that the whole British nation were so badly frightened in their late quarrel [over the Trent] with the Yankees, and have been so delighted to get out of it without a war, that I am afraid we shall never bring them up to the mark again."[2]

The armies of American detectives and the British custom officers whose vigilance had been the subject of constant complaint on the part of North and Bulloch increased with the imminent launching of the "Alabama" and rumors of the building of Confederate iron-clads.[3]

The "Alabama," however, escaped to sea by a trick; but the Laird rams which Bulloch contracted for in July, 1862,[4] the "Alexandra" (the gunboat being built by Fraser, Trenholm and Company), the ironclad which North was having Thompson of Glasgow build, and the armed vessels built for Sinclair and other lieutenants[5] were all finally stopped, and the Laird rams and the "Alexandra" were "ex-chequered."

Let us examine briefly the seizure of these Confederate ships. Adams in conjunction with Vice-Consul Wilding—and later Dudley—at Liverpool, and Morse at London, kept a swarm of detectives in every dockyard, gun factory, or armory in England. They soon had good evidence that the "Alabama" was being built for the Confederacy—though it was the kind of evidence that Adams could not well afford to use except most sparingly, as jailbirds, renegade Confederate sailors and soldiers, bums, and gunmen were not fine trappings for a diplomat.[6]

[1] *Ibid.*, pp. 183–85.

[2] *Ibid.*, pp. 148–49.   [4] *Ibid.*

[3] *Ibid.*, p. 212, Bulloch to Mallory, July 4, 1862.   [5] See *ibid., passim.*

[6] The reports of Consul Dudley and Wilding are in the U.S. State Dept. Consular Despatches, Liverpool, Vols. 19 ff., Jan., 1861—June, 1865, Morse, London, etc. One is amazed at the functions performed by the consuls. Then the agent provocative, B. W. Sanders, who associated with both the Confederate and Federal agents, reported to Seward on Confederate activities. Some of his letters are in the State Department. See Special Missions, Vol. 3, Sept. 11, 1862, and Aug. 31, 1866; U.S. Des., France, Vol. 54, Dayton to Seward, No. 471, May 27, 1864, mentions Sanders.

As soon as the "Alabama" began to approach the final stages of construction Adams, June 23, notified Russell that a vessel like the "Oreto," though more powerful, was about to leave Liverpool and begin operation upon the Federal commerce.[1] The Foreign Office passed the data submitted by Adams on to the custom officer at Liverpool who declined to act on the evidence. Then Adams and his henchmen procured more affidavits and submitted them to Collier, queen's counsel. After examining these affidavits Collier wrote, "I have perused the above affidavits, and I am of opinion the collector of customs would be justified in detaining the vessel. . . . . It appears difficult to make out a stronger case of infringement of the Foreign Enlistment Act." This opinion and the affidavits Adams sent to Russell on July 22. Russell received the new evidence July 26 and on July 28 asked the law office of the crown for an opinion. On the basis of the opinion of the law officers of the crown Russell on July 31 had telegrams sent to Liverpool and neighboring ports to stop the "Alabama." But the bird had already flown.[2]

Following the escape of this vessel Adams began a systematic demand on the part of the United States for damages done by the "Alabama" which came to an end only at the Geneva arbitration over ten years later when the United States received fifteen-million-dollar damages. Adams constantly urged that it was a violation of neutrality in that the "Alabama" was "fitted out" in British ports— and Russell constantly denied that it was a violation of neutrality because the vessel was not "fitted out."[3]

While the correspondence was taking place over the "Alabama," Bulloch's ironclads in the Mersey and North's great ram in the Clyde were approaching completion. The gunboat "Alexandra" had in the meanwhile been seized. The contention of Russell heretofore was that while the escape of the "Alabama" and "Florida" might have

[1] See Parl. Deb. Commons, Ser. 3, Vol. 170, pp. 33 ff., Forster's speech citing the correspondence; Soley, pp. 191–92.

[2] See Parl. Papers, Commons, Vol. LXXII (1863), correspondence concerning the "Alabama"; Parl. Deb. Commons, Vol. 170, pp. 33 ff., debate on March 27, 1863, on the "Alabama"; Soley, pp. 191–92; E. D. Adams, II, 118–19.

[3] See, e.g., Parl. Accts. and Papers, N. Amer., Vol. LXII (1864), pp. 1–48, No. 3; correspondence on "Alabama."

been a violation of the Foreign Enlistment Act, though not of international law, their escape had been due to insufficient evidence to convict. That is, the enforcement of the Enlistment Act had been upon the same principle as all other municipal laws. But the seizure of the "Alexandra" was upon a different principle, new to British procedure. Russell now explained to Lyons that it and others of its type were to be seized when "apparently intended for the Confederate service."[1] Positive evidence was no longer necessary.

Adams and his underground army of spies and detectives, working through Dudley, were piling up evidence that the ironclads in the Mersey were for the Confederacy, but this information could not be utilized sufficiently to give the law office grounds even as just as the "Alexandra" case. But on July 11, 1863, when the ironclads were rumored to be on the point of sailing, Adams sent Russell this batch of evidence with a strong protest. He said the American people regarded the construction of these vessels "as virtually tantamount to a participation in the war by the people of Great Britain to a degree which, if not seasonably prevented, cannot fail to endanger the peace and welfare of both countries.[2] On July 13 Russell replied that he had taken steps to investigate the rams, and three days later, July 16, Adams submitted two more affidavits in support of his protest.[3] On July 17 Russell replied that these were under consideration. On July 25 Adams sent an affidavit to dispose of the claims that the ships were for the French Emperor, and on July 29 Russell acknowledged this letter.[4] On August 14 Adams submitted further information, and the same day Layard, undersecretary in the Foreign Office, acknowledged the receipt of this information which he submitted to the law office. At last, September 1, Russell reported to Adams on the result of investigations based upon all the information which the American Minister had furnished. "In the first place, Her Majesty's Government are advised that the information contained in the depositions is in a great measure mere hearsay evidence, and generally that is not such as to show the intent or

[1] E. D. Adams, II, 136.

[2] Parl. Accts. and Papers, N. Amer., Vol. LXII (1864), pp. 1–7, No. 5.

[3] *Ibid.*, p. 7.   [4] *Ibid.*, p. 10.

purpose necessary to make the building or fitting out of these vessels illegal under the Foreign Enlistment Act." He pointed out to Adams that it was claimed by the builders that M. Bravay of France was the owner of the vessels, and that he was to sell them to the Viceroy of Egypt. "There is no legal evidence against M. Bravay's claim, nor any thing to affect him with any illegal act or purpose; and the responsible agent of the customs at Liverpool affirms his belief that these vessels have not been built for the Confederates.

"Under these circumstances, and having regard to the entire insufficiency of the depositions to prove any infraction of the law Her Majesty's Government are advised that they cannot interfere in any way with these vessels." But he assured Adams that the vessels would be carefully watched and that if sufficient evidence could be procured the Government would act promptly.[1]

On September 3 Adams submitted further evidence to Russell with the remark that he did not believe there was "any reasonable ground for doubt that these vessels, if permitted to leave the port of Liverpool, will be at once devoted to the object of carrying on war against the United States of America." He recalled to Russell the notes he had sent the latter on this subject, especially those of July 11 and August 14 which had contained grave warnings of the danger to the peace of the two countries involved in the construction of the ironclads. These notes of protest, he said, had the hearty indorsement of the United States government. In fact, said Adams, he had not imparted the full warning to England contained in his recent instructions.[2] The next day, September 4, he sent more evidence to the Foreign Office and on the same day Russell wrote that the evidence submitted was being taken into serious consideration,[3] but before Adams' and Russell's notes of September 4 had reached their destination Adams, on September 5, wrote a reply to Russell's

---

[1] *Ibid.*, pp. 10 ff.

[2] *Ibid.*, pp. 12–13; Charles Francis Adams, "Diary," Sept. 3, 1863 (Film No. 77). This diary is on microfilm in the National Archives. (Cited hereafter as C.F.A. "Diary.")

[3] Parl. Accts. and Papers, N. Amer., Vol. LXII (1864), p. 17; C.F.A. "Diary," Sept. 4, 1863 (Film No. 77).

note of September 1 in which the latter had said that the evidence submitted by Adams was insufficient for action against the ironclads. Adams was scathing. "At this moment, when one of the ironclad war vessels is on the point of departure from the kingdom on its hostile errand against the United States I am honored with the reply of your Lordship. . . . . I trust I need not express how profound is my regret at the conclusion to which Her Majesty's Government have arrived. I can regard it no otherwise than as practically opening to the insurgents full liberty in this kingdom" to build and organize a navy. "It would be superfluous in me to point to your Lordship that this is war."[1]

Three days later, September 8, 1863, Russell wrote Adams that "instructions have been issued which will prevent the departure of the two ironclad vessels from Liverpool."[2] On September 3, before Adams' "this is war" letter had been written, Russell had notified Palmerston that he had decided on consultation with the law officers of the crown, to detain the ships as a matter of policy but not of law. Palmerston replied on September 4 that he thought Russell was right in detaining the ironclads, "though the result may be that we shall be obliged to let them free. There can be no doubt that ships cased with iron must be intended for warlike purposes, but to justify seizure we must . . . . be able to prove that they were intended for the use of the Confederates. . . . . This may not be easy as it will be to lay hold of them."[3] Before receiving Adams' "ultimatum" on September 5, Layard wrote Stuart, chargé d'affaires at Washington, that "we have given orders today . . . . to prevent the two ironclads leaving the Mersey." These orders, he said, had hardly been given when Adams' note of September 5 was received.[4] It looked like "Yankee Bullying," Palmerston wrote Russell and he added, "It seems to me that we cannot allow to remain unnoticed his

[1] *Ibid.*

[2] Parl. Accts. and Papers, N. Amer., Vol. LXII (1864), p. 18.

[3] Gooch, *Russell Corr.*, II, 334–36; Russell Papers, P.R.O. 30-22-22, Palmerston to Russell, Sept. 4, 1863.

[4] Parl. Accts. and Papers, N. Amer., Vol. LXII (1864), p. 18, No. 5.

[Adams] repeated & I must say somewhat insolent threats of war. We ought I think to say to him in civil terms 'You be damned.' . . . . It seems to me the more necessary to say something to this effect because we are going to take the ironclads away from the Confederates."[1]

Immediately after receiving the opinion of the law officers that there was "no lawful ground for meddling with the Ironclad Rams," Palmerston informed Russell that he was writing to Somerset (Lord of the Admiralty) "to suggest to him that it might be a good thing to buy these Rams for our Navy. . . . . If you should take this view of the matter perhaps you will write Somerset."[2] The decision to purchase the rams was made at this time but Mr. Adams was not informed of it until much later. It was not until May 26, 1864, that he was able to write Seward that the Lairds had sold the rams to the British government and that he believed any further operations by the Confederate agents would be across the channel.[3]

When the United States published the correspondence, it looked as if Adams had bullied Russell into detaining the ironclads by his letters of September 3, 4, and 5, especially by the letter of September 5, and Russell was severely attacked by Seymour Fitzgerald, Robert Cecil, and Horsefall of the southern lobby, and by the opposition led by Derby.[4] Nor is there any doubt that Russell's conviction was that the alternative to seizure was war and to that extent he was bullied; for he remarked during the attack upon him in Parliament referred to above: "I believe that I took a course which was necessary for the peace of the country."[5]

The American attitude during the Civil War was very censorious of Britain for allowing the building of these cruisers and ironclads, and for the escape of the "Alabama"; and the award of the Geneva arbitration in the "Alabama" claims fixed this point of view as cor-

[1] Russell Papers, P.R.O. 30-22-22, Palmerston to Russell, Sept. 22, 1863.

[2] *Ibid.*, Sept. 13, 1863.

[3] U.S. Des., Gr. Br., Vol. 86, Adams to Seward, No. 699, May 26, 1864.

[4] *Ibid.*; Parl. Deb. Commons, Vol. 173, pp. 955–1021, Feb. 23, 1864; *ibid.*, Lords, Vol. 174, pp. 1862–1913, April 29, 1864.

[5] Parl. Deb. Lords, Vol. 173, p. 1896.

rect in the minds of historians—especially American and Continental historians. The English historians have remained strangely quiescent as if ashamed of what their country had done. The position taken by Rhodes, C. F. Adams, and E. D. Adams and the textbook writers assumes without question the guilt of the English government and the Confederacy in violating the laws of neutrality by permitting the building of the cruisers and ironclads. As a matter of fact, during the controversy over the "Alabama," the "Alexandra," and the ironclads the British government, the leading newspapers, and public men who had accurate information on such practices were very decided in their conviction that the right of building and arming warships for belligerent powers was indisputable. International law and practice, according to their opinion, permitted the building and arming of a ship and its sale and delivery at a belligerent port, just as it permitted the sale of any other contraband or munitions of war—subject only to the chance of seizure by the opposing belligerent. International law and custom simply forbade the sending-out of either armed land or armed naval expeditions directly against a friendly power from a neutral port.

A few citations from the newspapers, cabinet officers, members of Parliament, and Confederate officials will develop this position which has been ignored too much. On October 30, 1862, the *Times* said: "Both belligerents in the American war repair to the market of this country for supplies. . . . . So enormously has this commerce recently increased that it now constitutes a very notable feature in our exports and the trade with New York is actually resuming its old proportions under the extraordinary and continued demand for munitions of war." But the munitions trade between England and the Confederacy against which the United States was complaining was small compared to that of the United States. The southerners "have contrived to get a cargo or two of arms while their opponents were getting a hundred." Some of the war supplies of the Confederacy had been ships—one especially the "Alabama" against which the United States had complained; but "it is really difficult to treat as serious this unconscionable expostulation. If 'breaches of neutrality' are to be thus defined, the Federals have committed a hundred where the Confederates have committed one. The soldiers of the South have been shot down by weapons 'fitted out in England.' . . . . Their provinces have been invaded and their cities taken with armaments 'fitted out in England'—English iron, English gunpowder and English munitions of all sorts have formed the means by which the Unionists have fought against the seceders." The *Times* placed the sale of warships and munitions all in the same category. It was the law, and if the United States wished England's best justification let her look into her own practices—especially during the Crimean War when England and France were at war with Russia. At that time the Americans "loudly proclaimed and unhesitatingly exercised their rights as neutrals to furnish the Czar with such ships and munitions as they choose to supply."[1] The *Times* took the position that a neutral could sell munitions or unarmed ships—even if these ships armed themselves before touching the belligerent port as was the case of the "Alabama"—regardless of their destination, and pointed out that President Pierce had asserted this position in 1855 in reply to England's protest.[2] The ship the "Grand Admiral" was built openly in American waters for Russia in 1855 and sold to that country, just as England had sold the "Alabama." "The 'Alabama' was 'sent from a friendly shore' no doubt but from the same 'friendly shores' were sent those countless cargoes of cannon, caissons, rifles and gunpowder which enabled the Federal armies to keep the field. If we 'violated International Law' in one case, we violated it in the other; but the Washington Government will find it hard to impeach as a crime what is simply a repetition of its own deliberate proceedings, or to indict, as indicating an unfriendly policy, a system from which they themselves have notoriously taken the greatest advantage."[3]

The whole question, continued the *Times*,[4] was summed up in Chancellor Kent's commentaries: "Neutrals may lawfully sell at home to a belligerent purchaser or carry themselves to the belligerent powers contraband articles, subject to the right of seizure *in transitu*. The right of the neutral to transport and of the hostile powers to seize are conflicting rights, and neither party can charge the other

---

[1] *Times*, Oct. 30, 1862.
[2] *Ibid.*, Nov. 3, 1862.
[3] *Ibid.*, Nov. 21, 1862.
[4] *Ibid.*, Dec. 23, 1862.

with a criminal act." Under this rule, which was both the American and English practice, with the strong Anglo-Saxon love of trade, "we may be sure," said the *Times*, "that if a hundred 'Alabamas' were ordered and duly paid for they would be built in the rivers of England, no matter what flag they were intended to fly or who were the purchasers."

This attitude so expressed by the *Times* had reference to the "Alabama" and "Florida" cruisers, which were built as vessels of war in English ports but not armed in England.[1]

The British government as did the press, basing its position upon well-accepted American precedents as well as its own, contended that England as a neutral had a right not only to build but to arm and sell to belligerents vessels of war; and that guns and powder were not different from warships. This position was stated in the House of Commons by the Solicitor-General, March 27, 1863, in a debate on the "Alabama." He called attention to the correspondence recently published between Seward and Adams which contained protests against the sale of either ships or munitions to the Confederacy. The United States "have in that correspondence," said the Solicitor-General, "done no more nor less than to deny the application to this country in this war of those principles as to neutrals [sale of contraband to belligerents] which have been invariably recognized by all nations and by no nation more emphatically and constantly than by the United States themselves." He showed how Seward only recently insisted on the right to sell arms to Mexico who was at war with France; how Hamilton in 1793, Webster as Secretary of State in 1841, and President Pierce in 1855 had upheld the legality of the sale of contraband by neutrals to belligerents.

However, the big question now was the matter of neutrals building and selling warships to belligerents. As far as international law was concerned, said the Solicitor-General, the sale of warships was as

[1] The British government and the leading papers contended in reply to the United States claims for damage that the "Alabama" was not "fitted out" in England, even though it began war upon the commerce of the United States before entering a Confederate port. See, e.g., correspondence between Adams and Russell, "Alabama" correspondence; Parl. Accts. and Papers, N. Amer., Vol. LXII (1864), pp. 1–57, No. 1.

legal as the sale of guns and powder. It might or might not be a violation of England's Foreign Enlistment Act but that was her own concern. The international law, he said, was clearly stated by Judge Story in 1822 in the case of the ship "Independence." In 1816 the ship was armed and dispatched from Baltimore to the government of Buenos Aires. The Solicitor-General quoted Story: " 'The question as to the original illegal armament and outfit of the Independence may be dismissed in a few words. It is apparent that, though equipped as a vessel of war, she was sent to Buenos Ayres as a commercial venture, contraband indeed, but in no shape violating our laws or our national neutrality. If captured . . . . during the voyage, she would have been justly condemned as a good prize. . . . . But there is nothing in our laws or the laws of nations that forbids our citizens from sending armed vessels as well as munitions of war to foreign ports. It is a commercial adventure which no nation is bound to prohibit, and which only exposes the persons engaged in it to the penalty of confiscation. . . . .' "

This decision was applicable to the building of war vessels in England by the Confederacy, said the Solicitor-General, and the United States had no legal grounds of complaint as long as these vessels did not use English ports as a point of departure against American commerce or the American Navy. The main point was that no vessel was to leave England *armed* and *equipped* unless it were delivered first as an article of commerce at some Confederate port. Before the building or equipping of such a ship could be stopped, said the Solicitor-General, it would be necessary to find out the intent of the owners, that is, whether they planned to commence operations from the British port or whether they intended to carry the ship to the Confederate ports first and begin operations from there.[1] The "fitting-out" of a warship for the Confederacy or any belligerent, by England, said the Attorney-General, was a violation of the British Foreign Enlistment Act, but not a violation of international law, and the violation of a municipal law such as the Foreign Enlistment Act was a matter for the British government alone—it was not America's business. Not that England would neg-

[1] Parl. Deb. Commons, Ser. 3, Vol. 170, pp. 33–72, for debate.

lect the enforcement of the law, but she would insist on sufficient evidence as in any other municipal law before taking action which would entail losses to British subjects.

The arguments and decision of the "Alexandra" case, which had been "exchequered" April 5, 1863, rendered June 22, 1863, clearly upheld the right of England as a neutral to build and sell warships to the Confederacy or any other belligerent. The decision was that "a ship builder has as much right to build a ship and sell it to either of the belligerent parties as the maker of gunpowder or of muskets, or any other war like implements has to sell any of these articles to the same parties."[1] Nor was the Foreign Enlistment Act violated unless the ship left the port "as from an arsenal armed and equipped and ready for war."[2] In the trial of the "Alexandra" the Baron of the exchequer had asked the Attorney-General, "Is it lawful for ship builders to build a ship for the purpose of offering it for sale to belligerent parties to be used against a power with which we are at peace?" It was, said the Baron, legal to supply to belligerents "gunpowder, every description of arms, every thing in fact that can be used for the destruction of human beings." "Why should ships be an exception?" "I am of the opinion," he continued, "in point of law that they are not."[3] "The sale of ships of war to a belligerent is an act exactly as harmless, precisely as suitable to a neutral, just as little ground for legitimate offense to the other belligerent as the sale of a musket." This was according to the English law and the law of nations.[4]

The *London Economist* heartily agreed with the decision of the "Alexandra" case. It could see no distinction between warships and munitions of war. "No reason has yet been shown why the trade in ships should be under different restrictions and rules from the sale of guns or gunpowder."[5] (The decision of the "Alexandra" case was upheld on appeal.) Lord Palmerston in the House of Commons, July 23, 1863,[6] in a debate on the ironclads took a similar position and

---

[1] *Times*, June 25, 1863.   [2] *Ibid.*

[3] Mason Papers, Mason to Slidell, June 25, 1863, citing the opinion.

[4] *Economist*, July 18, 1863, citing opinion of the Baron of the exchequer.

[5] *Ibid.*   [6] Parl. Deb. Commons, Ser. 3, Vol. 172, pp. 1254–72.

urged that in international law there was no distinction between selling arms to a belligerent and selling ships.

On September 11 Russell wrote Adams a clear statement of the British position. Ostensibly a reply to Adams' "this is war" letter, in reality it was an answer to the whole American contention about the sale by neutrals of munitions and ships. Russell pointed out as had the Solicitor-General that while there might be some question as to the violation of the Foreign Enlistment Act by such a sale, there was no violation of international law; ". . . . the true doctrine has been laid down by Presidents and Judges of eminence in the United States and that doctrine is that a neutral may sell to either or both of two belligerent parties any implements or munitions of war which such belligerents may wish to purchase from the subjects of the neutral and it is difficult to find a reason why a ship that is to be used for warlike purposes is more an instrument or implement of war than cannon, muskets, swords, bayonets, gunpowder, and projectiles to be fired from cannon and muskets."[1]

The *Economist* expressed the conviction that the sale of the "Alabama" or the prospective Laird rams was in accordance with international law, and especially in accordance with American practice. It pointed out[2] the decision of the case of the "Santissima Trinidad," rendered by Judge Justice Story, as the clearest statement of the right to sell warships. According to that decision, said the *Economist*, "so far, then, as mere international law and the obligations of neutrality are concerned, any British merchant might sell an 'Alabama' or an 'Alessandra' [Alexandra] to any agent of the Confederate Government, just as he might sell an Armstrong or a Blakely rifled cannon to a Federal agent."[3]

The *Economist* was of the opinion that no obstacle should be allowed to be placed in the way of England's chief industry "for the sake of averting the anger of those who were angry with us before the keel of the 'Florida' was laid, and who will be angry with us still if a dozen 'Alessandras' were to be seized."[4]

[1] Parl. Accts. and Papers, N. Amer., Vol. LXII (1864), pp. 18 ff., No. 5.
[2] *Economist*, Sept. 5, 1863.
[3] *Ibid.*, Oct. 10, 1863.　　　　　[4] *Ibid.*, Sept. 19, 1863.

In 1873, in preparing the British case for the arbitration of the "Alabama" claims at Geneva, Lord Cockburn, the British commissioner, summed up the British position and conception of the right under international law to build warships for belligerents with whom England was at peace. "It seems to me," said Lord Cockburn, ".... that the law relating to contraband of war must be considered not as arising out of obligations of neutrality, but as altogether conventional; and that by the existing practice of nations, the sale of such things to a belligerent by the neutral subject is not in any way a violation of neutrality. Then how stands the matter as to war ships? In principle, is there any difference between a ship of war and any other article of warlike use? I am unable to see any." It had always been, said Cockburn, the practice of both England and America to sell warships to belligerents. He cited the protest of the Swedish government against England's selling warships to Russia in 1721 and the doctrine in support of this practice stated by the House of Lords. The decisions of Chief Justices Trevor and Parker had upheld the same principles. Cockburn then pointed out the practices of the United States as upheld by her judges and authorities on international law, so much quoted during the controversy in England 1863–64. "The judgment of Judge Story," said he "in the well known case of the 'Santissima Trinidad'[1] showed that the sale of armed ships of war has never been held to be contrary to law in America." He quoted Story's decision at length as illustrative of the principles in vogue upon which Britain had acted as a neutral during the Civil War. He cited the American publicist, Dana, in his edition of Wheaton's *Elements of International Law*. "Our rules do not interfere with bona fide commercial dealings in contraband of war," wrote Dana. "An American merchant may build and fully arm a vessel, and provide her with stores, and offer her for sale in our own markets. .... He may, without violating our law, send out such a vessel, so equipped, under the flag and papers of his own country, with no right to resist search or seizure, and to take the chance of capture as contraband merchandise, of blockade and of a market in a belligerent port." The intent was the important question. Did the

[1] 7 Wheaton 283.

builders intend to equip a vessel to go to a belligerent port as merchandise, or did they equip it with the intent of its leaving the neutral port to cruise against the commerce of a friendly power?[1]

These citations show the position of the British with reference to
the right of building and selling war vessels. They upheld the right
to sell an unarmed war vessel like the "Alabama" without question
as to its destination, and the right to sell armored and equipped war
vessels like the "rams" to a belligerent provided the vessels were
delivered at the port of the belligerent. The correspondence of the
naval agents[2] and that of Mason and Slidell[3] shows that the Confederate agents occupied the identical position, and instead of feeling
themselves culprits and sneaky conspirators considered that Adams,
Seward, the United States consuls, and their secret-service agents
were the sneaks, with no legal ground to stand upon.

It is difficult for one after considering the English position to escape the conclusion that England was correct in her attitude and
that the United States during the war and after in her insistence
upon the illegality of the construction of the "Alabama" and the
ironclads was wrong. This conclusion leads to a passing comment
upon America's rôle as a belligerent in 1861–65. America had always
played the rôle of the professional neutral before 1861, and had stood
out for all the extreme maritime rights of a neutral. She had insisted that the neutral flag covers the goods; that neutral goods were
safe under a belligerent flag; she had denied the right of search on the
high seas in quest of contraband goods, or evidences of intention to
break a blockade; she had insisted upon a strict, effective blockade
as opposed to paper and cruising blockades of British practice; she
had claimed the right of unhampered sale of munitions of war and of
warships to belligerents—subject only to limited rights of seizure as
contraband. In short, in the rôle of professional neutral America had
insisted upon the "freedom of the seas" to the practical extinction of
belligerent rights upon the seas. But on the first occasion when she

[1] Cockburn's statement in the British case, Parl. Accts. and Papers, N. Amer., Vol.
LXXIV, Part II (1873), pp. 1 ff., No. 2.

[2] O.R.N., Ser. 2, Vol. II, passim.

[3] Ibid., Vol. III, passim; Pickett Papers, Mason Papers, Bulloch, Secret Service, etc.,
passim.

had the opportunity to make use of her superior sea-power against an inferior maritime belligerent, she abandoned all her former principles and occupied the British position at one grand stride. She laid a paper blockade, adopted the practice of search and seizure of vessels hundreds of miles from the blockaded coast, stretched the doctrine of continuous voyage beyond the imagination of Lord Stowell whose decisions had left the world dizzy, and ferociously denied the right of England to sell either cannon or ships to the enemy. When the Civil War was over, the body of principles upholding neutral rights on the seas gained by American and European struggle against British practices had been sadly altered—in fact, neutral maritime rights might be said to have been restored to the status of the Napoleonic era, all of which points to the shortsightedness of American diplomacy.

Why did England submit to such curtailments of her acknowledged neutral rights? Why did the British government seize the ironclads and then purchase them rather than release them because of lack of a case at law?

The answer to this question is twofold. In the first place, the United States had made it seem clear through Adams that the escape of another Confederate war vessel from British ports meant war which would endanger Canada, expose British commerce to American raiders which Soley[1] says were being fitted out for this purpose, and, as we shall see in our concluding chapter, break up the war profits reaped by England.

In the second place, England, true to her rôle as professional belligerent, took this occasion to curtail neutral maritime rights. England had recognized a paper blockade, allowed the seizure of her commercial vessels on the most extreme extension of the continuous voyage doctrine; now she permitted the United States to deny the fairly well-defined right of a neutral to build and equip war vessels for a belligerent as a mercantile venture. England, mistress of the seas, had always been the opponent of neutral rights on the sea, as a matter of correct principle, but this particular neutral right—despite the fact that its exercise offered fat profits to the British ship-

[1] Soley, *Blockade and Cruisers, passim.*

building industry—was given up with unusual alacrity once the full consequence of its exercise was seen.

Public opinion, which at first had been in favor of building ships for the Confederacy, suddenly veered around with the government into opposition upon grounds of expediency rather than law. On August 28, 1863, the *Times* commenced shifting its position. The thoughts of what "Alabamas" could do to British commerce began to worry that paper. "If vessels were built in the yards of a foreign country of such a character and design as to be directly available against us . . . . we should probably remonstrate with considerable energy. . . . ." "Should we be likely to acquiesce in proceedings of that kind for any length of time, or is it our interest, as a nation, to see the precedent established?" asked the *Times*.

"If we were unhappily plunged again into war we might soon find reason to wish that we had supported with greater zeal the representations of the Federals in the matter of these Southern cruisers."[1]

A few days later the *Times* came back to the idea with more emphasis. "We have only to ask ourselves," it remarked, "what our feelings would have been if, while we were blockading the Russian ports during the Crimean war, some neutral state [the United States] had furnished the Russian Government with cruisers enough to close the sea against our commerce. . . . ." What then? "It is not our interest to allow such a precedent to be established for the first time, if it does not exist already, nor to connive at its extension, if it has any existence. Of all the doubts which the question contains we ought to give ourselves the benefit; and our interests, as it happens, coincide on this occasion with the desires of the Federal state."[2] The same paper on September 3 observed that though the sale of warships to a belligerent by a neutral might be according to international law, "it is certainly not to our advantage that such a practice should be established and we trust the law [Foreign Enlistment Act] may be found strong enough to bring it to an end."[3] If the law were not sufficient to stop such building of war vessels it should be revised.[4] Approving of the delay in the final decision of the "Alex-

[1] *Times*, Aug. 28, 1863.
[2] *Ibid.*, Sept. 11, 1863.
[3] *Ibid.*, Sept. 3, 1863.
[4] *Ibid.*, Sept. 7, 1863.

andra" case, the *Times* took the occasion to state its position again on the selling of such ships to a belligerent. ". . . . We have no doubt at all that, legal or illegal, equipments of this kind are highly impolitic, and might become an intolerable annoyance to ourselves, if we had the misfortune to be at war. . . . . We should be the last to sacrifice British shipowners for the sake of pleasing a foreign government, but when the maritime interests of Great Britain happen to coincide with the claims of international comity, we can see little patriotism in the attempt to 'sail a whole fleet of ships' through the Foreign Enlistment Act."[1]

Russell and Palmerston always contended in their controversy with the United States that the "Alabama" was not fitted out and armed in British ports and therefore was neither a violation of the Enlistment Act nor of international law, and they insisted that the sale of war vessels to a belligerent was a neutral right. Yet they yielded to American protest and seized the ironclads and would have eventually seized such ships as the "Alabama," on grounds of expediency. This attitude of the British government is brought out very sharply in the correspondence concerning the seizure of the rams. On September 3, 1863, Russell wrote Palmerston with reference to the seizure: "The Solicitor General has been consulted and concurs in the measure [seizure] as one of policy though not of strict law."[2] On September 13 Palmerston wrote Russell that the law officers had just been consulted the night before and "they tell us that we have no lawful ground for meddling with the iron clad rams. . . . ." But Palmerston said that they must be stopped, and if there was no law on which it could be done, they should be bought by the government.[3] Bright remarked at the time that if the ironclads were allowed to go to sea "it will only be felt when we become belligerents what a suicidal game we have been playing."[4] On September 19 Russell wrote Sir George Grey, attorney-general, who had just advised Russell that the building and sale of war vessels was no violation of international law, that though this was good legal advice it was not good policy when applied to England as a belligerent. "If

---

[1] *Ibid.*, Jan. 12, 1864.   [2] Gooch, pp. 334–36.

[3] *Ibid.*; Russell Papers, P.R.O. 30-22-14, Palmerston to Russell, Sept. 13, 1863.

[4] Guedalla, *Gladstone and Palmerston*, p. 68.

one iron clad ram may go from Liverpool to break the blockade of the Southern ports why not ten or twenty, and what is that but war? If ten line of battle ships had gone from New York to break the blockade of Brest during the late war [Napoleonic] do you think we should have borne it?"[1] In short, the British government's seizure of the ironclads was intended to prevent the United States, when it was a neutral and England a belligerent, from building ironclads and selling to England's enemy.

No sooner had the rumors got out that the British government might stop the sailing of future vessels than the Confederate commissioners began planning to transfer the ironclads to another country, there to complete them and build more. The country selected was France.

The way had been somewhat prepared in the fall and winter of 1862–63. On October 28, during his interview with the Emperor, Slidell had urged that the "Gloire," "Couronne," and "Normandie" could dispose of the whole blockading United States fleet, to which the Emperor agreed, but at the same time he wanted to know why the Confederacy had not built a navy. "He said," reported Slidell,[2] "that we ought to have one; that a few ships would have inflicted fatal injury on the Federal Commerce, and that with three or four powerful steamers we could have opened some of our ports." Slidell replied that the Confederacy had already built two cruisers and was building ironclads at the present in England, but that there was much difficulty in arming and manning them in that country under the British law. In the same interview he suggested, so he wrote Benjamin, that "if the Emperor would give only some kind of verbal assurance that his police would not observe too closely when we wished to put on board guns and men we would gladly avail ourselves of it." " 'Why could you not have them built as for the Italian Government?' " queried the Emperor. " 'I do not think it would be difficult, but will consult the minister of marines about it.' "

---

[1] *Ibid.*

[2] Pickett Papers, Slidell to Benjamin, No. 19, with inclosures, Oct. 28, 1862, *O.R.N.*, Ser. 2, Vol. III, pp. 572–78.

Not until two months later, on December 3, 1862, did Slidell push the matter further. On that date he interviewed Mocquard, Napoleon's private secretary, and urged him to find out whether the Emperor had consulted the minister of marines about the building of Confederate ships. On January 4, 1863, Mocquard informed Slidell that Napoleon had consulted some of his ministers and found greater obstacles than he had anticipated, and that for the present he could not encourage the proposed shipbuilding project.[1] But three days later M. Arman—member of the *corps législatif*, the largest shipbuilder in France, and in the confidence of Napoleon who consulted him on naval matters—came to Slidell and offered to build and arm ironclads for the Confederacy. He assured Slidell that there would be no difficulty in arming and equipping such vessels. Slidell felt sure that Arman came to him at the Emperor's suggestion.[2]

On February 22 Slidell went to see Drouyn de Lhuys, partly for the purpose of pushing forward the shipbuilding project in France. He told De Lhuys of the Emperor's promise, and De Lhuys hastily told him that it was a matter upon which he was not necessarily called to act; that it belonged rather to the minister of commerce or marines. It would be better, he told Slidell, that he should know nothing about the matter—in fact, he would be glad to close his eyes until the United States should force him to open them.[3]

Following De Lhuys's suggestion that the minister of commerce or minister of marines would have jurisdiction over this matter, Slidell hastily made an appointment with his friend the minister of commerce, M. Rouher. On the day after his interview with De Lhuys, Slidell in company with M. Voruz, deputy and shipbuilder from Nantes, called on Rouher for official permission, under the promise of the Emperor, to build and equip ships in France. "This assurance," Slidell wrote Benjamin, "was given by him, and so soon as the success of Erlanger's loan is established I shall write Messrs.

[1] Pickett Papers, Slidell to Benjamin, No. 23, Jan. 11, 1863; *O.R.N.*, Ser. 2, Vol. III, pp. 638–39.

[2] *Ibid.*

[3] Pickett Papers, Slidell to Benjamin, No. 28, March 4, 1863; *O.R.N.*, Ser. 2, Vol. III, p. 705–7.

Maury and Bulloch recommending them to come here for the purpose of ascertaining whether they can make satisfactory contracts."[1]

Slidell was feeling the need of haste now, as Bulloch expressed
grave doubts as early as January, 1863, as to the probability of ever
getting the ironclads out of England,[2] and advised that all future
warships should be built in France.[3] The Navy and State departments shared Bulloch's opinion, and they wrote him that he should
transfer his work to France.[4] So on the advice of Slidell, Mason,
Benjamin, and Mallory, and in accordance with his own opinion,
Bulloch hastened to France and drew up tentative contracts with
L. Arman and T. Voruz, Sr., by April 13, 1863.[5] These contracts
were drawn up under Slidell's condition that they should not be
binding until the Emperor approved.[6]

The job of getting the Emperor's pledge was not so easy. He
wanted Slidell to build the ships; but he much preferred to know
nothing directly about it. There were complications. Arman went
to see the Emperor on March 28, and according to his report to
Slidell was assured that there would be no trouble in fitting out and
arming ships of the "Alabama" type—and he was authorized to say
so to Slidell. Arman expressed the belief to the Emperor that Slidell
would not be willing to take anyone's word, and asked the Emperor
to tell Slidell himself. This the Emperor promised to do,[7] and, finally, after considerable delay he agreed to the contract which called for
the building of four *corvettes*—two at Nantes and two at Bordeaux.[8]

On June 18, 1863, sometime after the Emperor had given his
sanction—perhaps indirectly—to the contracts to build and arm the

[1] *Ibid.*, also Mason Papers, Slidell to Mason, Feb. 23, 1863.

[2] *O.R.N.*, Ser. 2, Vol. II, pp. 344–46, Bulloch to Mallory, Jan. 23, 1863.

[3] See also *ibid.*, pp. 351–52, Bulloch to Mallory, Feb. 3, 1863.

[4] See *ibid.*, p. 403, Bulloch to North, April 13, 1863; *ibid.*, Vol. III, pp. 728–29; Pickett Papers, Benjamin to Mason, March 27, 1863.

[5] *O.R.N.*, Ser. 2, Vol. II, p. 403, Bulloch to Mallory.

[6] Mason Papers, Slidell to Mason, April 13, 1863; Pickett Papers, Slidell to Benjamin, No. 32, April 20, 1863; *O.R.N.*, Ser. 2, Vol. III, pp. 741–44.

[7] Pickett Papers, Slidell to Benjamin, No. 31, April 11, 1863; *O.R.N.*, Ser. 2, Vol.
III, pp. 738–40.

[8] *O.R.N.*, Ser. 2, Vol. II, pp. 524–27, Bulloch to Mallory, Nov. 26, 1863.

four cruisers at Nantes and Bordeaux, Slidell obtained an interview with him. "I expressed my thanks to him," Slidell wrote Benjamin, "for his sanction of the contract made for the building of four ships of war at Bordeaux and Nantes." Slidell urged the Emperor to permit the building of ironclads as well as these wooden cruisers, but Napoleon was more cautious now than in the last interview at St. Cloud on October 28, 1862. "He said," wrote Slidell, "that we might build the ships [ironclads], but it would be necessary that their destination should be concealed."[1]

The consent of the Emperor having been obtained to build cruisers, it was necessary for the minister of marines to give his consent to the contract for the building and arming of the ships. So on June 1, 1863, Arman formally asked of the minister of marines and colonies, Chasseloup Laubat, permission to arm the four cruisers which he described as being "destined by a foreign ship owner for service in the China seas and the Pacific" with the ultimate end in view of sale to China and Japan.[2] On June 6 the minister of marines replied to Arman that "I willingly authorize you" to arm the four wooden vessels,[3] and on July 6 he authorized Mr. Voruz to make the guns for the cruisers.[4] In view of the righteous indignation later shown by the minister of marines when he "discovered" with Bigelow's and Dayton's help that Arman and Voruz were building and arming the ships for the Confederacy, one might suppose he had been kept in the dark. But, as a matter of fact, Slidell had as early as November, 1862, gone over the whole thing with him, and again at the time of the contract Napoleon had informed him, so he was thoroughly aware of what he was doing. Slidell, however, pictured him as giving the permission to arm the vessels as anything but "willingly," rather "in obedience to superior authority."[5]

[1] Pickett Papers, Slidell to Benjamin, No. 38, June 21, 1863; O.R.N., Ser. 2, Vol. III, pp. 810–14; cf. Pickett Papers, Slidell to Benjamin, No. 48, Nov. 15, 1863; O.R.N., Ser. 2, Vol. III, pp. 955–59, inclosing note of Slidell to the Emperor reminding him of his consent to the building of the corvettes.

[2] O.R.N., Ser. 2, Vol. II, pp. 431–32.   [3] Ibid., p. 433.

[4] Ibid., p. 463, referred to in the letter of Voruz to the Minister of the Marines, July 15, 1863.

[5] Pickett Papers, Slidell to Benjamin, No. 56, Feb. 16, 1864; O.R.N., Ser. 2, Vol. III, pp. 1028–30.

On June 16, two days before Slidell's interview with the Emperor in which he thanked him for his consent to the building of the four wooden *corvettes* at Nantes and Bordeaux, Bulloch without Slidell's knowledge[1] closed a contract with Arman to build two powerful steam ironclad rams.[2] Slidell contended later that no permission was given to arm the rams, but Bulloch had in possession the original document signed by Chasseloup-Laubat.[3]

These rams were formidable indeed. They had double screws worked by separate engines, and by running the screws in opposite directions the rams would turn as on a pivot.[4] John Bigelow trembled at what might have been had these vessels gone to sea under the Confederate flag. "They would not only have opened every Confederate port to the commerce of the world, but they might have laid every important city on our seaboard under contribution. . . . ."[5]

While Bulloch and Slidell were perfecting the contracts to build ships in France they were doing all in their power to transfer to that country the Laird rams, Sinclair's ship the "Pampero," and North's great ironclad of the Clyde. Napoleon's suggestion to Slidell on October 28, 1862, that the Confederacy should build a navy, and his half-promise that he would welcome their efforts in France was bearing fruit too fast.

On January 11, 1863, as we have noted above, Slidell wrote Benjamin that he had just had a series of interviews with Mocquard with reference to the Emperor's promise to permit the Confederacy to build war vessels in France, and that finally Arman had come and proposed the building of ships, and that the Emperor was behind the proposition. Having been greatly disturbed by reports from Mason and Bulloch that the British government would prevent the sailing of the ironclads, Mallory and Benjamin seized upon Slidell's letter of January 11 (No. 23) as suggesting a solution of the Confederate difficulties: Why not—as Bulloch was attempting to do—transfer the ironclads to France and complete their equipment? After con-

---

[1] *Ibid.*   [2] *O.R.N.*, Ser. 2, Vol. II, p. 464.

[3] Pickett Papers, Slidell to Benjamin, No. 56, Feb. 16, 1864; *O.R.N.*, Ser. 2, Vol. III, pp. 1028–30, for Slidell's statement, and *ibid.*, Vol. II, pp. 438–39, Arman to Barron, June 12, 1863; *ibid.*, pp. 524–27, Bulloch to Mallory, Nov. 26, 1863.

[4] *Ibid.*   [5] Bigelow, *Confederate Navy in France*, pp. 194–95.

sultation they wrote Slidell and Mason to further this scheme at once. Mallory wrote Slidell on March 27, 1863, that "Commander Bulloch is instructed to confer freely with Mr. Mason and yourself as to the practicability of transferring these ships to Mr. Arman or other French citizens, with the view of removing them from England as early as possible and fitting them out in France." They would later, when completed, be sold back to the Confederacy at some distant port.[1] On the same day Benjamin wrote Mason that as it seemed likely that the ironclads being built in England would not be allowed to depart, "I therefore beg that you will endeavor in concert with Mr. Slidell to arrange for their transfer to France, if such a course should become necessary. His despatches indicate that there will be no difficulty in so doing."[2]

The seizure of the gunboat "Alexandra," which Fraser, Trenholm and Company were having constructed as a gift for the Confederacy, brought the question of transfer to a crisis. G. T. Sinclair and North immediately urged Slidell to help them get their ships to France where they might be safely completed.[3] Negotiations were undertaken to transfer Sinclair's ironclad "Pampero" to Hamburg,[4] but the Confederate commissioners advised North to sell his ship, which was in too unfinished a state to transfer.[5] The decision in the "Alexandra" case, however, gave Mason temporary hope, and he suggested to North on June 27 that he might go on with his vessel.[6] But, after weary months of doubts, they again urged North to sell his ship at once to prevent its seizure by the British government. The reason for this urgent advice was that the British government, which had long had Sinclair's screw steamer, the "Pampero," under surveillance, had at last seized that vessel and put it in the exchequer

[1] O.R.N., Ser. 2, Vol. II, pp. 395–96.

[2] Pickett Papers, Slidell to Mason, No. 17, March 27, 1863; O.R.N., Ser. 2, Vol. III, pp. 728–29.

[3] O.R.N., Ser. 2, Vol. II, p. 413, North to Slidell, May 2, 1863; ibid., p. 414, Slidell to North, May 5, 1863; ibid., pp. 415–16, North to Secretary of Navy, May 6, 1863; ibid., pp. 421–22, Sinclair to North, May 14, 1863.

[4] Ibid., pp. 421–22, Sinclair to North, May 14, 1863.

[5] Ibid., pp. 439–40, June 13, 1863.

[6] Ibid., p. 443, June 27, 1863.

court of Scotland.[1] North's vessel was then sold to the Danish government,[2] though that particular government, like the Confederacy, was at war at the moment—strong evidence that the British seizures of Confederate vessels were based on policy and not on law.

But Bulloch's ironclads, built by the Lairds at Birkenhead, were successfully transferred to French ownership in June, 1863. The arrangement was court proof. Bulloch made a bona fide sale to Bravay and Company of Paris, who made new contracts with the Lairds to complete the ships for themselves as agents for the Pasha of Egypt. Bulloch consulted queen's counsel on all the points of the law. He severed all legal connections with the ironclads. The most important step he took was to write the Lairds that under fear of government confiscation he had actually sold the vessels to Bravay, and that he was transferring his efforts to France. "Suffice it to say," wrote Bulloch to Mallory, June 30, 1863,[3] "that our two iron clads are now the property of Messrs. Bravay and Company of Paris, agents for his Serene Highness the Pasha of Egypt. The papers are all in a proper legal form, the Lairds are convinced that the sale is bona fide, and I have expressed the most cordial regrets that there should have existed a necessity for such a proceeding."

The Lairds seem to have been falsely accused of collusion with the Confederate agents in this transfer, when they were evidently kept completely in the dark and were totally innocent of Bulloch's ultimate intention of resuming ownership of the vessels thus disposed of. Later Bulloch said with reference to this transaction: "It was of pressing importance to destroy any trace of Confederate ownership. . . . . The transfer papers and, indeed, all the correspondence involved in the negotiation were so carefully drawn in accordance with British law that the solicitor employed to conduct the sale remarked on its completion, 'The ships are now irretrievably the property of Messrs. Bravay and could not be recovered by any process they might think proper to resist.' "[4]

[1] *Ibid.*, p. 566, North to Mallory, Dec. 14, 1863; *ibid.*, p. 567, Barron to Mallory, Dec. 15, 1863; *ibid.*, pp. 574–75, Barron to Mallory, Jan. 22, 1864; *ibid.*, pp. 581–83, Barron to Mallory, Feb. 15, 1864.

[2] *Ibid.; ibid.*, p. 587.   [3] *Ibid.*, pp. 444–47 for letter.

[4] *Ibid.*, pp. 507–11, Bulloch to Mallory, Oct. 20, 1863.

The transfer thus effected, it was hoped, would make it easy to get the ships to a French port where it was supposed their equipment would be easy in view of Napoleon's attitude and the absence of legal restrictions such as the British Foreign Enlistment Act. In case there should be any hesitancy on the part of England to allow Bravay to take the ships out, it was firmly believed that Napoleon would intervene in his behalf and that England would be glad to shift the responsibilities to Napoleon's back by allowing the ships to go at his demand—a view doubtlessly correct. This had been Slidell's constant opinion, expressed to Bulloch from the inception of the Bravay sale, and when Lord Russell at length seized the Laird rams in October, 1863, Bulloch and Barron hastened to Paris to seek the intervention of the Emperor's authority.

It was fairly certain that if the French government relieved the British government of all responsibilities "by requesting that the ships may be allowed to leave Liverpool as the property of a French citizen," the British government would Godspeed the rams. "Whether the Emperor is prepared to change place with her Majesty's Government or not," commented Bulloch on the eve of his departure to seek the Emperor's aid, "can only be determined when M. Bravay asks the protection or countenance of his own Government. . . . ."[1] In Paris, Barron, Bulloch, and Slidell decided first to have Bravay demand of the British government the release of his ironclads as the bona fide property of a citizen of France with whom England was at peace. If England failed to release the ships then they would have Bravay ask the Emperor "for his interference on the behalf of one of the citizens of France who has entered into engagements with certain shipbuilders of England for the construction of vessels. . . . ." It was believed that should Napoleon take this step "Great Britain will gladly yield to his request and release the vessels."[2]

Indeed, England would have been overjoyed to have seen these ironclads transferred to France with the prospect of coming into the possession of the Confederacy. Napoleon was perfectly sure that England would pass them over to him like hot bricks, so when

[1] *Ibid.*   [2] *Ibid.*, pp. 517-19, Barron to Mallory, Nov. 10, 1863.

KING COTTON DIPLOMACY

Slidell and Bravay approached him through his ministers his answer was ready. It was a polite refusal. On February 17, 1864, Bulloch wrote that the Confederate hopes had been blasted. "It has been intimated to Mr. Slidell through no less a personage than the Duke de Morny, that the Emperor cannot make such a request [of the English] at this time, although his desire is that somehow or other the release of the rams should be effected and their possession by the Confederate States be again secured."[1] Thus ended the efforts of the Confederacy to transfer the Laird rams and the other ironclads to French ports.

Napoleon's refusal to raise his voice came just when he was badly involved in the whole Confederate naval question. First, the "Rappahannock," a British gunboat, which the Confederates had bought and shipped into a French port to be fitted out, was causing a quarrel between Dayton and the French Foreign Office;[2] then the "Florida," "Alabama," and other Confederate ships were coming into French ports for refitting.

But the most serious difficulties in this respect came from the discoveries by Bigelow and Dayton of the whole Confederate shipbuilding program. Napoleon's chickens had all come home to roost on his front doorsteps. On September 10 a stranger presented himself to John Bigelow in Paris with twenty-one letters and documents which contained the proof that Bulloch was building the four cruisers and two ironclads. The stranger was a confidential clerk in the office of Voruz, and the documents consisted of copies of most of the correspondence touching the building and arming of the vessels. There were the application for arming them, the consent of the minister of marines, and the reference to Bulloch and to Erlanger—in fact, all kinds of internal evidence showing that the ships were being constructed for the Confederacy.[3] Bigelow hurried to Dayton and told him these documents were priced at fifteen thousand francs C.O.D. Dayton authorized Bigelow to pay the man as he, Dayton, did not

[1] *Ibid.*, pp. 583–86, Bulloch to Mallory.

[2] E.g., U.S. Des., France, Vol. 54, Dayton to Seward, No. 400, Jan. 15, 1864; No. 408 (*bis*), Feb. 3; No. 411, Feb. 5; No. 420, Feb. 11; No. 436, March 18.

[3] *Ibid.*, Vol. 53, Dayton to Seward, No. 344, Sept. 11, 1863; Bigelow, *Confederate Navy*, pp. 1 ff., and *Retrospections*, II, 56.

wish to be involved in a deal in which there was evidently treachery.[1] Dayton, when the deal was made, carted the bundle of documents over to the Foreign Office and presented them to De Lhuys. "M. Drouyn De Lhuys," wrote Dayton to Seward,[2] "expressed himself as greatly surprised and I doubt not he was. He assured me he had had no knowledge of anything of the kind and that the Government would maintain its neutrality." De Lhuys promised immediate investigation. "It seems to me," continued Dayton in his report to Seward, "that their action on this subject is likely to afford a pretty good test of their future intentions. As to what the law may be it does not, I apprehend, much matter; if they mean that good relations with our country shall be preserved, they will stop the building of these ships, or at least the arming and delivery of them; if they mean to break with us, they will let them go on."

There ensued a long-drawn-out and more than lukewarm interchange of notes and interviews between Dayton and De Lhuys, who of course, like Chasseloup-Laubat, the minister of marines, Rouher, minister of commerce, and all the other members of the French cabinet, was perfectly well aware—though not officially—that the ships were being built for the Confederacy. In this interchange which was taking place simultaneously with the Adams-Russell controversy in England over the ironclads in the fall of 1863, Seward had Dayton, as he had Adams, inform the French government that the departure of the Confederate rams from French ports meant war.[3]

De Lhuys and the minister of marines continued to promise that France would maintain its neutrality, but Dayton wanted definite promises that the ships would not be armed and would not be permitted to leave port unless proof was given that they were the property of a neutral.[4] So finally Chasseloup-Laubat gave official assurance that the permission to arm the ship would be withdrawn,[5] and

[1] U.S. Des., France, Vol. 53, Dayton to Seward, No. 344, Sept. 11, 1863.

[2] Ibid., No. 349, Sept. 18, 1863.

[3] U.S. Inst., France, Vol. 16, Seward to Dayton, No. 409, Oct. 1, 1863.

[4] U.S. Des., France, Vol. 53, Dayton to Seward, No. 360, Oct. 8, 1863; ibid., Dayton to Seward, No. 364, Oct. 16, 1863.

[5] Ibid., Dayton to Seward, No. 368, Oct. 23, 1863.

De Lhuys ordered Arman and Voruz to cease work on the ships until they could give proof the ships were intended for someone besides the Confederacy.[1]

But after months of such formal protests and polite assurances from the French government, Dayton had no tangible evidence to show the good intentions of Napoleon. Seward then instructed him to put it squarely up to the French Emperor. He told Dayton to inform De Lhuys that France would be held responsible for any injuries committed by the Confederate vessels' being built in French ports, and that the French decision concerning the stopping of the vessels would be a test of friendship.[2] De Lhuys, very uneasy now, quickly assured Dayton that these vessels would be disposed of to neutrals; that Arman, in fact, had already disposed of them to the Danish government.[3]

Dayton, however, was still extremely suspicious, not of the good faith of De Lhuys so much as of Arman. He thought the latter capable of chicanery to get the vessels out for the Confederacy;[4] and it looked for a while as if Arman could not be legally prevented from doing so in the case of the *corvettes*.[5] So months and months went by with Seward and Dayton growing ever more exasperated while they were waiting for the vessels to be disposed of.[6] Finally, all were disposed of to Denmark and Prussia, at war with one another—illustrating again that both England and France were acting strictly on the basis of policy and not law in preventing the sale of the ships to the Confederacy. Then one of the ironclads was refused by the Danish government, and it finally got into the hands of the Confederacy and caused more diplomatic controversy between France and the United States just at the end of the war.[7]

Now to return to the Confederate agents. Napoleon's refusal to

[1] *Ibid.*, Dayton to Seward, No. 379, Nov. 27, 1863.

[2] Bigelow, *Confederate Navy*, pp. 28–36.

[3] *Ibid.;* U.S. Des., France, Vol. 54, Dayton to Seward, No. 433, March 11, 1864.

[4] *Ibid.*, No. 455, April 22, 1864.   [5] *Ibid.*, May 2, 1864.

[6] See *ibid., passim*, May, June, July, August.

[7] For "Stonewall" see U.S. Des., France, Vol. 56, Bigelow to Seward, No. 13, Jan. 30, 1865; *ibid.*, No. 14, Jan. 31, 1865; *ibid.*, No. 16, Feb. 3, 1865; *ibid.*, No. 19, Feb. 6, 1865; Bigelow, *Confederate Navy*, pp. 56–91.

intervene in behalf of the transfer of the Laird rams did not apparently affect the fate of the *corvettes* and rams at Bordeaux and Nantes. Bulloch and his colleagues continued to push forward the completion of these vessels. The confidential clerk of M. Voruz—Tremont by name[1]—had presented the papers to Dayton on September 10, but it was not until the last of November that Bulloch learned that the Confederate shipbuilding plans had been discovered. Even then he was optimistic. He wrote on November 26 that, though the United States had discovered the secret, France would probably do nothing to stop the building of these vessels and would most likely allow them to leave French ports unarmed.[2] He thought, however, that their being allowed to sail depended primarily upon the situation in America at the time of their completion. If the Confederacy was winning then, the French government would connive at their escape; if not, then the ships would be stopped.[3] So there was considerable ground for Dayton's fears and Seward's threats of war, if Bulloch's prognostications were correct. Bulloch continued the construction of the *corvettes* and ironclads and in February transferred the *corvettes* by a normal sale, with the collusion of Arman, to other owners.[4]

But the pressure of the French government, harassed by Seward's threats of war, became so great that on February 8, 1864, Bulloch ordered a bona fide sale of the ironclads.[5] However, Arman proposed that they should sell one of the rams to Sweden as agent for Denmark. By doing so the second ironclad might escape under a nominal sale, as the bona fide sale of the first ram would throw the United States minister off his guard.[6] But about the first of June Napoleon, now faced with plain threats of war on the part of the United States, called in Arman and threatened to have him imprisoned unless he sold both the ironclads and the *corvettes* at once. Chasseloup-Laubat

---

[1] U.S. Des., France, Vol. 55, July 1, 1864, Dayton to Seward, "Private and Unofficial."

[2] *O.R.N.*, Ser. 2, Vol. II, pp. 524–27, Bulloch to Mallory, Nov. 26, 1863.

[3] *Ibid.*

[4] *Ibid.*, pp. 588–91, Bulloch to Mallory, Feb. 18, 1864.

[5] *Ibid.*   [6] *Ibid.*, pp. 665–68.

gave Arman and Voruz the order to sell in a tone of righteous indignation, as if he had discovered for the first time the warlike character and destination of the ships which he had given permission to build and arm. Arman, now scared as a jack rabbit, sold at once both ironclads and the two *corvettes* at Bordeaux.[1] What had, after months of uncertainty, brought the matter to a head and forced the sale was the series of warlike dispatches sent by Seward to Dayton on May 18, 20, and 21, 1864,[2] stating that unless satisfactory proof were given that these vessels would not sail war must follow. Dayton had got these dispatches about June 8 and then told De Lhuys that "should these vessels pass into the hands of the Confederates, become armed and commence a system of depredation on our commerce, the exasperation would be such that the Government if so disposed (which I did not intimate it would be) could scarcely keep the peace between the two countries."[3]

Thus ended in abortion the heartbreaking efforts of the Confederacy to build a navy in France and England. It was not a violation of the law to build or arm these ships provided they were delivered at Confederate ports, and until the failure to deliver them thus the United States had no legal grounds on which to stand, but neither country was willing to go to war with the United States—so despite the legality, as a matter of avoiding war on the part of both, and as a matter of future precedent on the part of England when she should be a belligerent and America a neutral, she was willing to forego her legal rights.[4]

[1] *Ibid.*   [2] See U.S. Inst., France, Vol. 17, Nos. 553, 554, 556.

[3] U.S. Des., France, Vol. 54, No. 483, June 8, 1864.

[4] The building of the Confederate Navy in England and France has been treated at length by J. D. Bulloch, the chief agent, in *The Secret Service of the Confederate States in Europe* (1884). John Bigelow has given an extended account of the French phase in *France and the Confederate Navy* (1888) and *Retrospections of an Active Life* (1909, 1913).

CHAPTER XIII

THE ANTICLIMAX OF 1863

The failure of the Confederate commissioners to gain European intervention, signalized in the rejection by England and Russia of Napoleon's proposal of joint mediation, did not leave them discouraged. They looked upon this as a trifling incident in the march of events to an inevitable end. On December 11, 1862, Mason wrote Benjamin that ". . . . events are maturing which must lead to some change in the attitude of England. The cotton famine continues still to extend itself with apparently gigantic strides, and the English people are exerting themselves through all ranks to come to its relief by private contributions. It is not believed, however, that actual starvation can be kept off by such means, and the government must come in aid.

"Parliament is to meet early in February, and if the question comes before it of supplying means from the Treasury, a potent argument will be drawn thence, in support of the relief that would be extended, by the termination, in some way, of the American War."[1] Mann and Slidell were of the same opinion.

But until more favorable military events should transpire in America the commissioners could not again take up with the European governments the question of recognition. While they were awaiting more auspicious conditions to resume their activities in this direction, Secretary of State Benjamin furnished them with an issue which might bring up the matter of intervention in a different form. He ordered them to raise again with the British and French governments the question of the legality of the blockade.

Reference has been made already to Benjamin's note of April 8, 1862, to Mason and Slidell's protesting against the British acceptance of the blockade as laid down in Russell's note to Lyons of February

[1] Pickett Papers, No. 23, Dec. 11, 1862; *O.R.N.*, Ser. 2, Vol. III, pp. 618–19.

15, and to Mason's presenting the substance to Russell in a note of
July 7. Let us return to this note of Benjamin because it was now
reimbodied in his new instructions on the blockade and constituted
the beginning of the second drive against the blockade, the first having ended with the Lindsay escapade in April. Benjamin had as
early as April, 1862, read the published correspondence of Lyons
and Russell, especially the letter of the latter to the former of February 15 recognizing the blockade as effective. Russell, it will be recalled, had stated that the mere escape of vessels through the blockade did not invalidate the legality of the blockade provided a number
of ships were stationed "at the entrance of a port sufficient really
to prevent access to it, *or to create an evident danger of entering it or
leaving it.*" Benjamin in his instructions of April 8 had pointed out
with indignation that the italicized words were additions to the text
of the Declaration of Paris, and were, in fact, extracts from an old
treaty between England and Russia of 1801, which defined a blockade. He demanded that England explain this addition. Was it a return to the old doctrine of paper blockade "formerly maintained by
Great Britain," one which all Europe had abandoned by the Declaration of Paris? The Confederacy had a right to know as it had become,[1] through the invitation of Russell, a subscriber to the Declaration.

Benjamin had attacked even more sharply another portion of the
statement of Russell, namely, the assumption that the blockade was
a blockade confined to specified ports. Lord Russell, protested Benjamin, had spoken as if "the United States had declared the blockade
of particular ports, whereas its pretension is to maintain the blockade
of the entire coast from the Chesapeake to the Rio Grande." The
noble Earl in his statement to Lyons had sidestepped the main point.
The blockade of great stretches of seacoast by such a force as the
United States had was an absurdity "too glaring to require comment." "Yet it is for this extravagant assumption that the United
States claim and neutral powers accord respect. . . . . But it is notorious that there are a large number of ports within the Confederacy

---

[1] The Confederacy had in the summer of 1861, on invitation from England and
France, become a signer to all the Declaration of Paris except the article on privateering.

and a vast extent of coast absolutely free from any investing force." In addition to the unblockaded stretches of seacoast Benjamin could name twenty ports free from any hostile vessels. Many such had never even been visited by United States vessels. At other ports the vessels disappear for days and sometimes for weeks. The blockade thus recognized by England and the other powers was the most flagrant violation of "all the principles hitherto held sacred," which could be recalled.

Benjamin pointed out that it had been contended in Parliament that the scarcity of cotton in Europe was definite proof of the blockade, but that the real explanation was that the Confederacy owned few vessels and that thus far Europe had been frightened off by the *threat* of a blockade. "A paper blockade," he explained, "is as effective as most perfect circumvallation by powerful fleets, if by common consent it is to be respected as such, and if no vessel ever attempts to cross the interdicted line."[1]

Mason, it will be remembered, had written Russell a note on July 7 embodying the substance of Benjamin's instructions of April 8.[2] Russell's only response to this note was a note from Undersecretary A. H. Layard on July 10: "Sir," it ran, "I am directed by Earl Russell to acknowledge the receipt of your letter of the 7th Inst. and its enclosures respecting the blockade of the southern coast of North America."[3] It will be recalled that this cold ignoring of the question was soon followed on July 31 with a curt refusal by Russell of Mason's request for an interview, and by a discourteous reply on August 2 to Mason's note asking recognition.[4]

Near the last of October, 1862, Benjamin received Mason's letter inclosing this correspondence with Russell in reference to the blockade and recognition. After consultation with Davis, Benjamin again took up the blockade question and renewed his instructions of April 8. The attitude of Russell, he wrote, was "discourteous and

[1] Pickett Papers, Benjamin to Mason and Slidell, Nos. 2 and 2, April 8, 1862; *O.R.N.*, Ser. 2, Vol. III, pp. 379–84.

[2] Pickett Papers, Mason to Russell, July 7, 1862, inclosed in *ibid.*, Mason to Benjamin, No. 14, July 30, 1862; *O.R.N.*, Ser. 2, Vol. III, pp. 490–504.

[3] *Ibid.*   [4] *Ibid.*

even unfriendly." With reference to the blockade and the Declaration of Paris, Benjamin pointed out again that the British and French had taken the initiative in bringing the matter before the Confederate government, and that two of the rules of the Declaration—those touching neutral goods on belligerent ships and belligerent goods on neutral ships—had been for the special benefit of England. The Confederacy had expected to benefit by the declaration on blockades, and it had strictly observed its obligations with reference to British goods and British ships so that not a complaint had arisen. But on the first occasion when England was called upon to apply the principles of the Declaration to the paper blockade of the North, the Secretary of Foreign Affairs, "in an official despatch published to the world, appends a qualification which in effect destroys its whole value; and when appealed to for an explanation of this apparent breach of faith remains mute. This silence," continued Benjamin, "can only be construed into an admission that her Majesty's Government is unable satisfactorily to explain, while it is unwilling to abandon the indefensible position which it has assumed." This conclusion, said Benjamin, was justified by the debates in Parliament in which was made an "open avowal by a British peer . . . . that if England were involved in war the first thing she would do would be to retreat from the protocol of Paris." Mason was to address Russell a formal protest on the part of the Confederacy against "the pretension of the British cabinet to change or modify to the prejudice of the Confederacy the doctrine in relation to the blockades to which the faith of Great Britain is by this Government considered to be pledged."

Referring once more to Russell's manner of refusing to answer Mason's letter of July 7, and of his discourteous refusal of an interview, and his ill-mannered reply to Mason's note on recognition, Benjamin concluded that "there exists a feeling on the part of the British ministry unfriendly to this government. This would be conclusive in determining him [the President] to direct your withdrawal from your mission but for other considerations," the chief of which was the conviction that the British ministry did not represent the opinion of the British people. It was evident from the press and from the dispatches of Confederate agents that public opinion was almost unanimous in its support of the South. This meant that there must soon be a change of policy on the part of the government. In the meantime, Mason, however, was to restrict his activities to making protest on the subject of the blockade, and after the delivery of the protest he was to refrain from further correspondence with Russell until the latter invited it.

Plainly the Confederacy was getting near a "diplomatic break." Feeling within the Confederacy was running high. This is indicated in one of the concluding sentences: "The president has further under consideration the propriety of sending out of the country all British consuls and consular agents, and I will give you early advice of his conclusion on this point "[1] We shall have occasion to return to this statement when the consuls are sent out of the country in 1863. It will be seen that the animus was more deep seated than was officially stated at the time of their explusion, and that it had its roots in the exasperation over the blockade and Russell's scant courtesy in general.

On January 3, 1863, Mason sent Russell a letter giving the substance of Benjamin's instructions of April 8 which had been repeated and emphasized in his instructions of October 31. This letter was also a practical repetition of Mason's letter to Russell of July 7. Mason called attention to the fact that Russell had refused to reply to his letter of July 7, and urged that such refusal was certainly not made necessary by the fact that the Confederacy had not the status of an independent nation. The fact that England had entered into an agreement with the Confederacy as a belligerent with reference to the Declaration of Paris made it incumbent upon England to render an explanation with reference to the interpretation of the Declaration of Paris made by Russell, which seemed a serious alteration detrimental to the interests of the Confederacy. He informed Russell that the President had decided to confine his actions at the present to mere protest; but he hinted that more serious action

[1] Pickett Papers, Benjamin to Mason, No. 9, Oct. 31, 1862; *O.R.N.*, Ser. 2, Vol. III, pp. 584–88.

would follow if England persisted in her present interpretation of the Declaration of Paris and in her discourteous silence.[1]

While Mason was still waiting for a response from Russell, Jefferson Davis back in Richmond delivered a stinging attack in his message to Congress upon the neutrality of Europe and especially upon its recognition of the blockade. This was the first time Davis had spoken openly on this question, and it indicated the growing exasperation of the South at Europe's complacency with reference to the blockade. England and France, said the Confederate President, had approached the Confederacy and urged it to agree to the Declaration of Paris. This it had done with the just expectation that it would be binding on all parties. Yet the principles which had been agreed to by the two leading nations of Europe and the Confederacy "have been suffered to remain inoperative against the menaces and outrages on neutral rights committed by the United States with progressive and unceasing arrogance during the whole period of the war. Neutral Europe remained passive when the United States, with a naval force insufficient to blockade effectively the coast of a single state," proclaimed a paper blockade of thousands of miles of coast, "extending from the capes of the Chesapeake to those of Florida, and encircling the Gulf of Mexico from Key West to the mouth of the Rio Grande. Compared with this monstrous pretension of the United States, the blockades known in history under the names of the Berlin and Milan decrees and the British orders in council, in the years 1806 and 1807, sink into insignificance." These blockades, he continued, had caused the War of 1812, and finally were the principal motives leading to the Declaration of Paris. The State Department files contained repeated protests against the recognition by Europe of the present paper blockade. The Confederacy had shown by incontrovertible evidence that the blockade was a farce. Hundreds of vessels had gone and come from the ports which had vessels stationed before them. The United States had practically admitted the inability to blockade the South by the sinking of stone laden vessels at the port

[1] Pickett Papers, Mason to Russell, Jan. 3, 1863, inclosure in Mason to Benjamin, No. 24, Jan. 14, 1863; O.R.N., Ser. 2, Vol. III, pp. 643–45.

entrances, and had, in defiance of the principles of blockade recognized by the Declaration, instituted a cruise against all Confederate and neutral commerce upon the high seas which was suspected of being destined to or from the Confederacy. In the face of irrefutable evidence of the inefficiency of the blockade and of protests against it Lord Russell had given it official recognition and had, in his letter to Lyons of February 15, made a change in the principles of the Declaration of Paris which was of great detriment to the Confederacy. He had directed solemn protest to be made against such a change.[1]

Davis in taking Europe, and especially England, to task in his message was seeking the only channel through which the English public could be reached. This appeal over the heads of the cabinet was not unlike that of Woodrow Wilson in a later generation. The British public was known to feel a strong sympathy for the Confederacy, and this would further arouse their sympathy and might cause pressure to be brought upon the government to repudiate the blockade, certainly to show more respect and courtesy to the Confederate government. Too, it would serve as an outlet for the ill will against the British which was gathering as fast in the South as in the North.

The rather ominous note in Benjamin's letters of instruction to Mason, which were transmitted so persistently by the latter, together with Davis' severe arraignment of England and Lord Russell, published in the leading papers of both continents, unquestionably produced results. It thawed Russell out, and he became henceforth uniformly courteous and formally attentive to Mason's communications. On February 10, 1863, not long after Davis' stiff message had got into British newspapers, Russell suddenly recalled that there were two old notes from Mason on the blockade—those of July 7 and January 3—which he had failed to answer. He hastened to do so, referring to both notes. "I have, in the first place," he wrote Mason, "to assure you that her Majesty's Government would much regret if you should feel that any want of respect was intended by the circumstance of a mere acknowledgment of your letter having hitherto been addressed to you." But there was no unbending of the noble Lord as to the

[1] O.R., Ser. 4, Vol. II, pp. 338-44.

stand he had taken on the blockade. He was hoarding up, like miser's gold, precedents against the United States for future wars when the United States would be a neutral and Great Britain the belligerent, and no amount of citing of the Declaration of Paris, which Russell did not approve, would cause him to alter one jot or tittle. The Foreign Office was happy. Russell assured Mason that his statement as to the effectiveness of the American blockade and his definition of what constituted a blockade stated in his letter to Lyons were final. The Declaration of Paris, he said, did not mean that the blockading vessels must prevent egress and ingress in storms or dark nights, especially when the blockade-runners were low, shallow draft steamers, or coasting craft. It did not mean that all communication with the port should be impossible—he repudiated the idea of circumvallation. He interpreted the Declaration of Paris as simply meaning that a blockade which was notoriously a paper one, maintained by an occasional visiting vessel, was illegal. And to his mind the American blockade was certainly not subject to such criticisms.

In this reply to Mason's notes Russell really sidestepped one of the most vital of Mason's points, namely, what was the status of the hundreds of miles of shore and over a score of ports which had never seen an American blockader? Were these points recognized as being blockaded? If so, then the Declaration of Paris had no meaning whatsoever. If, on the contrary, these unblockaded spaces were not included within the blockade which England recognized, then what of the seizure of vessels upon the high seas, in the West Indies and gulf stream, going to and from these unblockaded stretches? The simple fact was that Russell could not answer such questions without admitting that England was countenancing a paper blockade. But at least he had been civil to Mason, which was worth something in view of his previous incivility to all Confederate agents—owing to his fear of offending the United States rather than to any animosity toward the Confederacy.[1]

Four days later Mason replied to Russell that he was pleased to know that the latter had meant no discourtesy by a mere acknowl-

---

[1] For Russell's letter see Pickett Papers, Russell to Mason, Jan. 10, 1863, copy; O.R.N., Ser. 2, Vol. III, pp. 688–89.

edgment instead of a reply to his notes. The President would be pleased to know this. But not so that portion of his letter which dealt with the blockade. The President, said Mason, regarded the terms of the Declaration of Paris as "too precise and definite to admit of being qualified; or perhaps it may be more appropriate to say revoked by the superadditions thereto contained in your lordship's exposition of them." The stipulations of that Convention, he protested, "are that the blockading force must be sufficient really to prevent access to the coast; no exception is made in regard to dark nights, favorable winds, the size or model of vessels successfully evading it, or the character of the coast or waters blockaded; and yet it would seem from your Lordship's letter that all these are to be taken into consideration on a question whether the blockade is or is not to be respected."[1] Russell replied briefly to this note a few days later, saying that he had nothing to add to his former statement of what was an efficient blockade other than that he did not contend that a certain type of vessel was to be left at liberty to pass through the blockade. He merely referred, he said, to an occasional escape due to unusual circumstances.[2] So the argument was left where it had started: England continued to recognize the blockade as effective. But the dignity of the Confederacy had been upheld and a considerable respect had been accorded in Lord Russell's punctilious attention to Mason's communications.

Slidell, hoping to bring about a concerted move in repudiating the blockade, sought out De Lhuys on February 22, 1863. He had considerable grounds for believing that the Emperor might move, even alone, at this juncture, because mediation was on foot again. De Lhuys had on January 10 sent another note to Mercier suggesting that the two belligerents appoint commissioners to discuss peace; and Slidell was also encouraged in his hopes by the series of articles inspired by De Lhuys which were running in *La France* attacking the blockade. But Slidell had greater difficulty in pushing his case than did Mason in London, for De Lhuys and Napoleon fully agreed with Slidell that the blockade was ineffective and that it ought to be re-

[1] Pickett Papers, Mason to Russell, Feb. 18, 1863; *O.R.N.*, Ser. 2, Vol. III, pp. 695-97.

[2] Pickett Papers, Russell to Mason, Feb. 27, 1863; *O.R.N.*, Ser. 2, Vol. III, pp. 703-4.

pudiated. There was no argument he could present which they opposed. He went over the data presented in former notes to the Emperor and Thouvenel; he spoke of the Emperor's regret which he had expressed to Slidell in having acquiesced in the efficiency of the blockade; he presented new data showing the vast and systematic business of violating the blockade; he presented the recent breaking of the blockade at Charleston and Galveston by Confederate ironclads; and he contended that the blockade had been raised at those points, and that the United States would have to proclaim a new blockade there before it could be considered as existing. To all this the Frenchman listened with sympathy and agreement. It was always "Oui, oui, monsieur," and "My government would like to put an end to the blockade and to the war," but there was always the futile shrug of the shoulders with uplifted hands. France could not move alone. She could not do anything in the matter without England.

Slidell wrote Benjamin that the Emperor at this juncture was especially afraid to move without England because of the crisis in the Polish question. It had been the Italian question in the fall of 1862, now Poland was in revolt and the Emperor with his ubiquitous meddling had shown his open sympathy with the Poles. This threw him into dangerous antagonism to Russia and Prussia. Prussia, who crushed him so thoroughly in 1870, was even now digging his grave. Russia was sore from the Crimean War and seeking an opportunity of revenge. Russia and Prussia had formed a convention to crush Poland, while he sympathized with Poland. His enemies were allied. He dare not move in the American question with this immediate and overwhelming danger at his back door. Slidell was almost convinced that Napoleon would have broken the blockade with all its consequences at this time had not this storm blown up at the moment. That, however, is extremely doubtful because of his fear of a war with the United States which might follow such action, and his knowledge that the French people would not support him in such a war. Napoleon's only hope was to break the blockade jointly with England and thereby avoid a war.[1]

[1] For the interview see Pickett Papers, Slidell to Benjamin, No. 28, March 4, 1863; *O.R.N.*, Ser. 2, Vol. III, pp. 705–7.

Slidell followed up this interview with a letter, inclosing all the documents which he had referred to in his interview, as well as the President's message of January 12, which had excoriated Europe for its recognition of the blockade.[1] On April 20 in a memorandum to the Emperor, dealing primarily with the building of a navy in France, he presented further evidence that the blockade was still ineffective and should be repudiated.[2] Once or twice again he presented notes upon the question. The strongest argument which he presented after the spring of 1863 was on October 28, 1863. On this occasion he wrote De Lhuys a note, inclosing Benjamin's letter of September 2 which was a terrific arraignment of the blockade. It will be recalled that Benjamin showed that in 1863 the trade with Wilmington had been four times greater than that of the whole state of North Carolina in 1858, and that the blockade trade of Charleston was several millions in excess of the whole state of South Carolina for 1858. He had taken England and Russell to task, and he had accused that country of deliberately repudiating the Declaration of Paris as to blockades under pretense of recognizing a real blockade. In his note accompanying this letter of Benjamin, Slidell urged that while the Emperor might submit to the rest of the blockade, at least he should declare Wilmington and Charleston not legally blockaded.[3]

But this attack upon the blockade which grew out of Benjamin's letter of April 8, 1862, was not comparable to the first which culminated in Lindsay's interview with Napoleon on April 11 of that year. The first attack was a widely ramified, complex movement seriously considered by Napoleon, but the second drive was desultory and not taken up by the Confederate lobby and the Emperor and his henchmen with any great zeal. It is obvious, of course, that the time had long since passed when France or England could challenge the ever tightening blockade which they had recognized when it was a pitiable farce. Benjamin and Davis must have realized this fact. What they were doing, then, was in part to furnish England and France

[1] Pickett Papers, Slidell to De Lhuys, March 2, 1862; *O.R.N.*, Ser. 2, Vol. III, pp. 704-5.

[2] Memorandum inclosed in No. 32, Slidell to Benjamin, April 20, 1863, Pickett Papers; *O.R.N.*, Ser. 2, Vol. III, pp. 741-44.

[3] Pickett Papers, Slidell to Benjamin, No. 48, Nov. 15, 1863; *O.R.N.*, Ser. 2, Vol. III, pp. 955-59, inclosure A.

with a good legal case to justify their actions should they decide to intervene. More than anything else, however, the protests of Benjamin in his notes and Davis in his messages to Congress were the voicing of the popular southern bitterness which was so strong against England after the first year of the war.

Before the blockade issue had got well under way, Lee's slaughter of Burnside's army at Fredericksburg furnished the needed Confederate victory to put intervention back into motion. On December 31, 1862, and January 4, 1863, Slidell interviewed Mocquard, and, besides the building and equipping of cruisers and ironclads, discussed the question of intervention; and on January 8 he presented to him a memorandum on this question to be delivered to the Emperor.[1]

Slidell, just as he had done the year before in his memorandum sent through Persigny to the Emperor on March 1, 1862, attempted to induce Napoleon to act independently of England. He preferred joint action, of course, but as England would not act he attempted again to show Napoleon that the interests of England and France were different. He presented the old argument that recognition of the South would enable the peace party in the North to gain the ascendancy. Finally, he begged the Emperor to utter a friendly warning to America in his speech at the opening of the Chambers. He believed Lincoln might listen to his advice.[2]

In the meanwhile, Mann on January 5 had presented a long, formal demand for recognition to M. Rogier, Belgian foreign minister,[3] chiefly in the hopes that King Leopold would urge recognition upon France and England.[4] Leopold had responded as he had done once before, and had written Napoleon to urge intervention upon him.[5]

[1] Pickett Papers, Slidell to Benjamin, No. 23, Jan. 11, 1863; *O.R.N.*, Ser. 2, Vol. III, pp. 638–39.

[2] *Ibid.*

[3] Pickett Papers, Mann to Benjamin, No. 36, Jan. 5, 1863; *O.R.N.*, Ser. 2, Vol. III, pp. 635–37.

[4] Pickett Papers, Mann to Benjamin, No. 39, Feb. 10, 1863; *O.R.N.*, Ser. 2, Vol. III, pp. 689–90.

[5] *Ibid.;* Pickett Papers, Mann to Benjamin, No. 38, Jan. 29, 1863; *O.R.N.*, Ser. 2, Vol. III, pp. 670–71; Mason Papers, Slidell to Mason, Feb. 11, 1863, mentions Leopold's letter.

Napoleon, whose cotton operatives were at the nadir of depression and showing signs of revolt, was apparently prompted to act by Leopold's letter and Slidell's urging. On January 9 he had Drouyn de Lhuys write a letter of instructions to Mercier to take up again with Seward the question of mediation. Mercier was to tread safely, and was to propose that the two warring powers appoint commissioners to meet together, who, if they could not agree to a restoration of the Union, might agree upon terms of peace and separation.[1] A few days later, in accordance with Slidell's hopes and perhaps his memorandum of January 8, the Emperor in his speech before the Chambers spoke of the American war which had exhausted "one of the most fruitful of our industries." He had tried, he said, to put an end to such a bloody struggle, referring to his offer of joint mediation on November 10, 1862; "but the great maritime powers not having thought themselves yet able to join me I have been obliged to postpone to a more propitious season the mediation which had for its object the checking of bloodshed and the prevention of the devastation of a country whose future should not be indifferent to us."[2]

The Emperor made no reference in his speech to his new proposal of mediation of January 9. But on January 20 the *Constitutionnel* carried the substance of the offer as one which might be made in the near future rather than one which had already been presented. On the same day Slidell called upon Persigny and found that the offer had already been sent.[3] A few days later the dispatch of January 9 was published in the newspapers of Europe, and all were aware that Napoleon was again at work on the idea of intervention.[4]

Seward, of course, when he received it, flatly refused the proposal of Napoleon that the North treat with the Confederates for peace,[5] and his refusal was, like the offer, published widely the latter part of

[1] French F.O. Amer., Vol. 129, De Lhuys to Mercier, No. 1, Jan. 9, 1863.

[2] *London Times*, Jan. 13 and 14, 1863; *Index*, Jan. 15, 1863; Pickett Papers, Slidell to Benjamin, No. 24, Jan. 21, 1863; O.R.N., Ser. 2, Vol. III, pp. 666–68.

[3] Pickett Papers, Slidell to Benjamin, No. 24, Jan. 21, 1863; O.R.N., Ser. 2, Vol. III, pp. 666–68; cf. Mason Papers, Slidell to Mason, Jan. 21, 1863.

[4] See *Times*, Jan. 29, 1863, for full text; also *Moniteur* and *Index*, Jan. 29; *Independance belge* in *Index*, Jan. 29; *Economist*, Feb. 7, 1863.

[5] U.S. Inst., France, Vol. 16, Seward to Dayton, No. 297, Feb. 6, 1863.

February, 1863.[1] Nor was his rejection of the mediation proposal couched in courteous terms.[2] Its tone gave Dayton uneasiness, especially as its publication was followed up by an interview of Slidell with De Lhuys in which it was rumored intervention was freely discussed.[3] For the same reason its offensive tone gave Slidell something to hope for.[4]

While the Confederate commissioners had found Napoleon ready to renew the agitation for intervention, they found no such sentiment in England at the time. Russell had given up the idea he held in the preceding fall of mediation, and on February 14, 1863, wrote Lyons that "till both parties are heartily tired and sick of the business, I see no use in talking of good offices." Even then he was willing to let France take the lead.[5] Derby in a speech at the opening of the House of Lords on February 5 approved of Russell's policy of non-intervention and expressed the opinion that recognition as long as war was in progress would be a violation of neutrality as well as useless unless it should be accompanied by armed intervention.[6] Gregory, the first mover of a recognition in 1861, now advised Mason strongly against any action: "The House of Commons is opposed to taking any steps at present, feeling rightly or wrongly that to do so would be useless to the South and possibly embroil us with the North. . . . . If I saw the slightest chance of a motion being received with any favor I would not let it go into other hands, but I find the most influential men of all parties opposed to it."[7]

Lindsay on March 6, 1863, wrote Slidell that he took a profound interest in the question of recognition and mediation and that "not a night escapes me without having some conversation with the leading members of the House of Commons who think as I do; but none

---

[1] See *Times*, Feb. 26; *Index*, Feb. 26, 1863.   [2] *Index*, March 5, 1863.

[3] U.S. Des., France, Vol. 53, Dayton to Seward, No. 283, March 6, 1863.

[4] Pickett Papers, Slidell to Benjamin, No. 28, March 4, 1863; *O.R.N.*, Ser. 2, Vol. III, pp. 705–7, in which he speaks of the arrogant tone of Seward's rejection of Napoleon's proposal.

[5] E. D. Adams, II, 155.

[6] *Times*, Feb. 6, 1863; Pickett Papers, Mason to Benjamin, No. 30, Feb. 9, 1863; *O.R.N.*, Ser. 2, Vol. III, p. 687.

[7] Mason Papers, March 18, 1863.

of us see our way yet to raise it [question of recognition] with effect, and it would do your cause great injury to raise it and be defeated."[1] Two days later Lord Clanricarde, Mason's close friend, wrote him that a move for recognition at the time was inadvisable.[2]

But, despite the poor prospects of success, Lord Campbell about the first of March offered a motion in the House of Lords "to call attention to the duty and policy of acknowledging the Southern Confederacy as an independent power."[3] But the motion was postponed for three weeks through the urgings of Russell, Derby, and Confederate friends.[4]

Finally, on March 23 the persistent Lord Campbell had his motion brought up for discussion. He made a long speech in favor of recognition in which he criticized Russell for his refusal to co-operate with Napoleon in November, 1862, and at other times. He thought that recognition alone would be sufficient to stop the war as it would enable the North to withdraw from the struggle with self-respect. Russell replied that it was England's duty to keep out; that it was best to let the two sections settle their own difficulties. However, he would not pledge England's future course.[5] But the motion was not brought to a vote and little enthusiasm was displayed.

The lack of willingness in England to push the southern question during the spring of 1863 was due to the lack of brilliant military success on the part of the South and the preoccupation of the government over the Polish insurrection. For a while it seemed that all Europe might become embroiled in a war because of the strong stand that Napoleon took against Prussia and Russia, the open sympathy of the British people for Poland, and the pusillanimous conduct of the British ministry.[6]

Around the first of May the Polish question temporarily subsided, and the news came that Grant had again failed at Vicksburg,

[1] *Ibid.*   [2] *Ibid.*   [3] *Times*, March 2, 1863.

[4] See Pickett Papers, Hotze to Benjamin, No. 19, March 14, 1863; *O.R.N.*, Ser. 2, Vol. III, pp. 710–12; Mason Papers, Mason to Slidell, March 20, 1863, for reasons for postponement.

[5] See Parl. Deb., Lords, Ser. 3, Vol. 169, pp. 1714 ff., for debate; cf. Callahan, p. 167.

[6] See, e.g., Pickett Papers, Slidell to Benjamin, No. 29, March 21, 1863, and *ibid.*, Hotze to Benjamin, No. 20, March 21, 1863; *O.R.N.*, Ser. 2, Vol. III, pp. 720–21 and 718–20, respectively.

and that Banks's attack on Port Hudson had been given up. Slidell hoped that this might put Napoleon and England in motion again. He asked his friend Cintrat in the office of De Lhuys whether in view of recent Federal failures at Vicksburg and Port Hudson and the siege of Charleston "the time had not arrived for reconsidering the question of recognition." Cintrat replied, after consulting De Lhuys, that "it is believed that every possible thing has been done here in your behalf: we must now await the action of England and it is thought that you must aim all your efforts in that direction."

Slidell, still seeing no evidence of action on the part of England, turned to Spain as he had once before in the hope of finding a partner for France in intervention. Serrano, who had been captain general of Cuba, friend of Charles Helm, Confederate agent, and an ardent Confederate sympathizer, was for the moment prime minister of Spain. Hopes were placed in him. On May 22 Slidell had a long conversation with Isturitz, the Spanish ambassador in Paris, on the possibility of Spain's joining France. Isturitz "declared very unreservedly," wrote Slidell to Benjamin,[1] "that the sympathy of his Government and his own individually were warmly and decidedly with the Confederate States, that he considered the interests of the two countries as being largely identified, that Spain was prepared to act conjointly with France and England." She would not make any move alone as there was danger of the United States seizing her colonies. Slidell urged that Spain act with France and some other Continental power. Isturitz seemed favorably disposed toward the idea. But Serrano lost his premiership, and Slidell ceased for the moment to rely upon the joint action of Spain and France. He once again turned to England.

Just at this time tidings of a great Confederate victory—the overthrow and rout of Hooker's army by Lee and Jackson at Chancellorsville—reached Europe, along with vague rumors of a southern invasion of the North. This was the kind of news which put England into action. The belief that the South would ultimately win was almost universal, and the British hopes and beliefs were now fastened upon this victory and the coming invasion of Pennsylvania as the end of the war.

[1] Pickett Papers, No. 36, May 28, 1863; *O.R.N.*, Ser. 2, Vol. III, pp. 777-79.

The Confederate lobby got into motion. Spence drummed up mass meetings in the north and west of England. Lord Clanricarde prepared to open an attack in Parliament on the blockade and the Federal interference with British vessels in the West Indies and gulf;[1] and the question of recognition was trimmed for action. On June 4 there began definitely the series of acts which culminated in the famous Roebuck motion and its dénouement. The truth was obscured from the public at the time but, when revealed, made Roebuck out an ass and a liar, caused Napoleon's veracity to be doubted by England and the Confederate commissioners, caused De Lhuys and Russell to be suspected, and Gros, the French minister at London, to be considered a scoundrel.

In the latter part of May, 1863, Lindsay had Mason and Roebuck come to his country estate outside London to spend a night and part of a day in conclave over the advisability of putting on foot the proposal of recognition. Both Lindsay and Roebuck believed that the auspices were favorable for the move, but thought that the opposition should be approached before taking the step.[2] Roebuck interviewed Disraeli, and, finding encouragement in the enigmatic language of the latter, promptly gave notice in the House that he would soon move that Her Majesty's government be requested to enter into negotiations with the principal powers of Europe with a view of recognizing the Confederacy. Nor did Roebuck confine himself to announcing a motion for the recognition of the Confederacy. He assembled his constituents at Sheffield in mass meetings to support his motion, in a vigorous Bright and Forster style.[3]

Roebuck's strength lay with the people as did Bright's, and the Confederates were proud of him for that reason. In Parliament he had very little influence with any party. His position there, in fact, was very much like that of John Bright. Hotze described him as occupying "in the House a singularly isolated position" and as a man who "sits habitually on the opposition benches, whatever Gov-

[1] Mason Papers, Clanricarde to Mason, May 17, 1863.

[2] Pickett Papers, Mason to Benjamin, No. 38, June 4, 1863; *O.R.N.*, Ser. 2, Vol. III, pp. 782–83.

[3] *Ibid.*

ernment may be in power." Though "a radical of a somewhat ultra type," he was "without any affiliations with the Radical Party so called."[1] Carlyle had described this new champion of the Confederate cause as "an acrid, barren, sandy character, dissonant speaking dogmatist, with a singular exasperation: restlessness as of diseased vanity written over his face when you came near it."[2]

One would be inclined to doubt the wisdom of such a champion even though he were a counterpoise to Bright in the industrial north of England. But the Confederate lobby egged him on and supported him rather strongly at first.

The discussion of Roebuck's motion was set for June 30. The rumor got out—possibly put out by Palmerston himself in the hopes of heading off the discussion—that when the motion should come up on June 30 Palmerston would urge that the time for recognition had not come, that France now having changed from her former position was strongly opposed to action.[3] Seymour Fitzgerald, considerably aroused over this rumor, hurried to Roebuck on the night of June 12 to tell him about it. Roebuck, seeing Palmerstonian trickery and frustration, became angry and hit upon a bold course. He hurriedly wrote Lindsay urging that the two of them go to Paris and interview Napoleon and assure themselves of the untruth of this rumor and that the Emperor still desired to join England in intervention.[4]

In the meanwhile, Slidell had arranged for an audience for himself with the Emperor for June 18, and had urged Mason to try to ascertain the probable results of the proposed motion so he might discuss it in his coming interview with the Emperor.[5] Mason, who had been discussing with Lindsay and Roebuck the rumor of Palmerston's possible denial of Napoleon's willingness to join England in intervention, replied to Slidell the next day[6] and inclosed Roebuck's note to Lindsay concerning their proposed journey to see the Emperor. He was sure the rumor disclosed a plot, and that unless Slidell in his

---

[1] Pickett Papers, Hotze to Benjamin, No. 23, June 6, 1863; *O.R.N.*, Ser. 2, Vol. III, pp. 783–86.

[2] Bigelow, *Retrospections, etc.*, II, 16.

[3] *Ibid.*, p. 15.   [5] Mason Papers, Slidell to Mason, June 15, 1863.

[4] *Ibid.*   [6] *Ibid.*, June 16, 1863.

coming interview, and Lindsay and Roebuck in their proposed interview, could obtain the Emperor's denial of the truth of the rumor the motion would be defeated.

Slidell had, of course, not remained idle during the preparation of the Roebuck motion. Mason had hurried to Paris to confer with him, McRae, and other Confederate agents concerning the Confederate Navy, and to discuss this new move on Roebuck's part.[1] Slidell did not put much faith in the success of Roebuck's motion[2]—he had taken the measure of the British cabinet rather accurately and saw that they would never do anything which endangered the peace with the United States—but he was willing to take advantage of the present favorable trend in England to reopen the case of the Confederacy with the Emperor. So on June 8 he presented a memorandum to the Emperor through his adviser, Persigny, urging recognition. Slidell, again fearing that England might never join France in intervention, attempted to point out where that country was serving her own selfish interest in not intervening and where France was injuring her interest by following the lead of England. In short, he again pointed out to the Emperor the divergent interests of England and France in the American struggle. He showed that England desired to see North America divided and weakened because it would enable England to build up a cotton monopoly in India to which all the world, including France, would be forced to go for cotton. England would see her chief industrial rival, her chief commercial and naval rival, and her hated and much-dreaded national rival eliminated. She would not recognize the South and endanger the peace because she believed the South would eventually win without it. Would the Emperor continue to make the joint action of England the basis of his policy? Would he not act in concert with the Continental powers?[3] Slidell asked for an interview where the question might be further discussed.

[1] Pickett Papers, Mason to Benjamin, No. 38, June 4, 1863; *O.R.N.*, Ser. 2, Vol. III, pp. 782–83.

[2] Pickett Papers, Slidell to Benjamin, No. 37, June 12, 1863; *O.R.N.*, Ser. 2, Vol. III, pp. 802–4.

[3] *Ibid.*, inclosure A.

The interview was granted in a few days.[1] On this occasion
Napoleon was very cordial. He immediately alluded to Slidell's
memorandum of June 8, and declared he felt that the Confederacy
should be recognized but that the Mexican venture and the commerce of France would be jeopardized by a war with the United
States. As for Slidell's proposal that he act jointly with the Continental powers, he believed that none of these powers had navies
strong enough to give him efficient aid in a possible war with the
United States. On the other hand, continued Napoleon, if England
would join France, because of the superior navy of the British there
could not possibly be a war. This was his reason for insisting upon
the policy of joint action with England.

Slidell urged again that all the Continental powers would join
France in recognition, but Napoleon contended that their fleets were
inadequate. But Slidell insisted that the Spanish fleet was rather
powerful, and as he had already talked to Isturitz, the ambassador
in Paris, who seemed to favor the idea, he urged that France and
Spain act jointly. To the direct question whether Napoleon would
be willing to act with Spain the Emperor returned an affirmative
answer and told Slidell that he might pass the word on to the Spanish
Minister.

Following that Slidell read parts of Roebuck's letter of June 13 to
Lindsay, which spoke of the rumor that Napoleon had changed his
mind about recognition and that Palmerston would use this rumor
when the Roebuck motion was brought up for debate. Napoleon
assured Slidell that he might give the rumor an unqualified denial.
This assurance gave Slidell the opportunity of asking an interview
for these two men. Napoleon consented readily to the interview. He
was nettled at this political chicanery and probably saw Palmerston's fingers in it. After thinking over the matter a little and giving
Slidell permission to deny the rumor he flared up: " 'I think I can do
something better—make a direct proposition to England for joint
recognition. This will effectually prevent Lord Palmerston from mis-
representing my position and wishes on the American question. I
shall bring the question before the cabinet meeting today; and if it

[1] Mason Papers, Slidell to Mason, June 15, 1863.

should be decided not to make the proposition now, I shall let you know in a day or two through Mr. Mocquard what to say to Mr. Roebuck.' "

There had grown up some sentiment among the Confederate agents—not shared by Hotze of the *Index*—that the Palmerston ministry should be overthrown and the Conservatives brought into power. Slidell asked Napoleon which party he preferred. He replied, " 'I rather prefer the Whigs.' " Slidell reminded him that Lord Malmesbury, an intimate friend of Napoleon, would probably be secretary of foreign affairs in a Tory ministry. Napoleon replied that personal friendships didn't matter in politics, and added: " 'The Tories are very good friends of mine when in a minority, but their tone changes very much when they get into power.' "

In this interview the Emperor told Slidell what was behind his eagerness to see the South independent. He referred to the recent French victory at Pueblo, Mexico. The North was bitter and filled with hostile sentiment because of his Mexican success, while, he had heard, Richmond actually had been illuminated on the occasion. Slidell agreed that the South was very friendly and the North very hostile to his undertakings in Mexico. However, he doubted, without intimating it to Napoleon, that Richmond had been illuminated when Pueblo fell.[1]

Napoleon's promise to suggest to his cabinet another proposal of joint recognition to England was followed up at once. Slidell called at the Foreign Office on June 19, the day after his interview, to catch the drippings from the altar and talk things over with his "friend," Cintrat. The latter, following their conversation, wrote Slidell later in the day that he had some inside information which the Confederate commissioner must treat as "entirely confidential." The Council had met on the afternoon of the eighteenth and Napoleon had, according to his promise to Slidell, broached the question of asking England to join France in recognition of the Confederacy; but this positive step was "judged at this time inopportune." Still the cabinet "agreed to deny, as far as the English cabinet is con-

[1] Pickett Papers, Slidell to Benjamin, No. 38, June 21, 1863; *O.R.N.*, Ser. 2, Vol. III, pp. 810–14.

cerned, the reports which falsely attribute to us sentiments and a policy less favorable for the South; to recall to them that on several occasions we have addressed to them propositions which they thought they should not accept; to declare that our feelings have not changed—quite the contrary; to state to them further that we shall be charmed to follow them up, and if they have any overtures to make to us in a like spirit to that which has inspired ours, we shall receive them with quite as much empressment as pleasure. Baron Gros will receive instructions accordingly."

In short, while the cabinet had dissuaded Napoleon from making an offer of joint intervention to England, it had agreed with him to deny to the British cabinet the rumor that Napoleon had decided against recognition at the time, and to notify the British cabinet that he stood ready at all times to join with England in intervention.[1]

Slidell two days later, June 21, held an interview with De Lhuys who confirmed the report of Slidell's confidential friend, and told him that the decision not to make a positive offer of recognition to England grew out of a distrust of England's sincerity. It was believed that Russell, as he was accused of doing twice before, might communicate the French offer to Seward and involve France in a war with the United States, "a contingency which he [the Emperor] desires to avoid and which England would willingly aid in creating."[2]

On the same day the Emperor, according to his promise to Slidell made in their interview of June 18, sent a message through his private secretary, Mocquard, as to what had been decided with reference to making a proposal of joint intervention to England. "You will doubtless be pleased," wrote Mocquard to Slidell, "to receive the following communication, which the Emperor charges me to make you confidentially. M. Drouyn De Lhuys has written to Baron Gros, our ambassador in London, to sound Lord John Russell on the question of the recognition of the South, and has authorized him to declare that the Cabinet of the Tuileries is ready to discuss the subject."[3]

---

[1] Pickett Papers, Slidell to Benjamin, No. 38, June 21, 1863; *O.R.N.*, Ser. 2, Vol. III, pp. 810–14. Slidell sent copy of note in this dispatch.

[2] *Ibid.*   [3] *Ibid.*, note inclosed as B.

Slidell then had the assurance of his "friend," Cintrat, in the Foreign Office, the foreign minister De Lhuys, and Napoleon himself that, while no positive offer would be made to the British cabinet, it would be signified that France continued to stand ready to join England, which amounted to a negative proposal, a kind of "Barkis is willin' " attitude.

On the day of the note from Mocquard to Slidell, and the latter's interview with De Lhuys—June 20—Roebuck and Lindsay had their interview with Napoleon. These two men urged that England be invited to join in recognizing the Confederacy, but that if she refused such joint action then let France act alone and reap the benefits.

Napoleon replied that he was anxious to have the war come to an end, and that he had always been anxious to "act in concert with your government . . . . especially in regard to the sad state of things in the United States," and that he was more anxious than ever to act with it now. "But," he said, "I fear I cannot make a formal application to England which you wish," because once before he had "made a formal application to England, and that application was immediately transmitted to the United States government, and I cannot help feeling that the object of that proceeding was to create bad blood between me and the United States." Napoleon, however, assured them that he had instructed Baron Gros to correct the rumors that he had changed his views. In addition to this he said, "I have just requested Baron Gros to ascertain whether England is prepared to coincide with my views in regard to recognition, to suggest any mode for proceeding for the recognition of the Southern States which I do so much desire."[1] He furthermore authorized Roebuck and Lindsay to deny in Parliament that he had changed his views about recognition. It is doubtful, however, whether he authorized them to report the entire interview, especially that part relating to the transmission of former dispatches to the United States.

Armed with Napoleon's denials that he had changed his mind,

[1] Virginia Mason, *Life of Mason*, pp. 419–25; Mason Papers, for Lindsay's account given to Mason and preserved by the latter; Pickett Papers, Mason to Benjamin, No. 5, March 16, 1864; *O.R.N.*, Ser. 2, Vol. III, pp. 1047–55, for Lindsay's account written by himself for filing in the French Foreign Office.

and with the assurance that he had just instructed Baron Gros to "feel out" the British government on recognition, Roebuck and Lindsay hastened back to London to enter the parliamentary fray. On June 26 the opening gun was fired when Lord Clanricarde, who had the details of the Roebuck-Lindsay interview, asked Russell whether any proposition had been received from the Government of France. This referred, of course, to Baron Gros's instructions to find out from Palmerston whether England was ready to take the lead if she were assured that France would follow. Russell replied promptly that "no such communication has been received." As to the general question of recognition, Russell said, his position remained unchanged; he did not feel that it was now timely.[1]

Mason was very much disturbed at this denial of Russell's, and he wrote Slidell to obtain from De Lhuys a copy of the instructions to Gros, or at least the substance in an official note, which could be put in the hands of Roebuck. A question of veracity was raised, said Mason, between the Emperor and Russell, or at least between Roebuck and Lindsay on the one hand and Russell on the other.[2]

Slidell hurried to the Foreign Office on receipt of this note to obtain a copy of the alleged dispatch which De Lhuys was supposed to have sent Baron Gros. De Lhuys would not produce a copy of the dispatch, but he gave the substance of his various instructions to Gros on the subject: On June 19, the day following the interview between Slidell and the Emperor, the latter had had De Lhuys send a note to Gros to say to the leading members of Parliament that the Emperor's opinion on American affairs was still in favor of recognizing the South in co-operation with England; on June 22, after the Lindsay-Roebuck interview and the note from Mocquard in which Napoleon had promised to instruct Baron Gros to that effect, De Lhuys wrote Baron Gros instructions to sound Palmerston on the subject and to inform him of the Emperor's wishes. This note to Gros, according to the information Slidell received at the Foreign Office, was at the command of the Emperor who wrote De Lhuys, probably just before the Lindsay-Roebuck interview, "Je me de-

[1] Parl. Deb., Ser. 3, Vol. 171, pp. 1504-6.
[2] Mason Papers, Mason to Slidell, June 27, 1863

mande, s'il ne serait bien d'avertir Lord Palmerston que je suis décidé à reconnaître le Sud."

Slidell was quite convinced that Napoleon had made all these approaches to the British government, and he was elated at the message of Napoleon that he had decided to recognize the South. "This is by far the most significant thing that the Emperor has said, either to me or to the others. It renders me comparatively indifferent what England may do or omit doing."[1]

The day on which Slidell wrote this reassuring note to Mason, Roebuck, who had read Mocquard's note of June 21 to Slidell stating that Gros had been instructed to sound out Russell (and not Palmerston as Napoleon had instructed), called on Baron Gros and inquired whether he had received such a dispatch and what its substance was. Gros declined to answer whether he had or had not received the dispatch, but he assured Roebuck that no formal communication on the subject had been made to Russell.[2] This, of course, settled nothing, for it was already understood that the dispatch might not be formal.

On June 30, the day of the debate on Roebuck's motion, Lord Campbell inquired of Lord Russell in the House of Lords whether he had received any communication, either written or verbal, from Napoleon indicating his present desires to join England in intervention. Russell's reply was the same in substance as his reply four days earlier to Lord Clanricarde: He had received none. Furthermore, about an hour earlier in the evening Baron Gros had called on him, he said, and had assured him that he had received no instructions from home to approach England on the matter of recognition.[3] This was bad auspices for the opening of the debate on Roebuck's motion. It put the British government in a position to give the impression that Napoleon had, after all, changed his views on recognition, and thereby to make vain all of Roebuck's and Lindsay's extra-official diplomacy.

[1] *Ibid.*, Slidell to Mason, June 29, 1863.

[2] Pickett Papers, Mason to Benjamin, No. 41, July 2, 1863; *O.R.N.*, Ser. 2, Vol. III, pp. 824–28.

[3] Parl. Deb., Ser. 3, Vol. 171, p. 1719.

But Roebuck, notwithstanding the unfavorable conditions, introduced his motion in favor of recognition and launched into a very bitter speech on the American question. He urged that the Confederacy be recognized as independent because, first, it had maintained its independence for over two years in the face of superior forces, and, second, because at the present its armies were endangering the capital of the United States while Richmond was unmolested. Moreover, it was to England's interest: The starving cotton operatives of Lancashire would be put back to work; it would destroy a commercial and naval rival to have the Union thus divided; and above all it would destroy England's hated national enemy. "America," he exclaimed, "while she was one ran a race of prosperity unparallelled in the world. Eighty years made the Republic such a power, that if she had continued as she was a few years before, she would have been the bully of the world. Why, sir, she

> . . . . bestrode the narrow world
> Like a Colossus; and we petty men
> Walked under her huge legs and peeped about
> To find ourselves dishonoured graves.

"As far as my influence goes," continued Roebuck, "I am determined to do all I can to prevent the reconstruction of the Union, and I hope the balance of power on the American continent will, in the future, prevent any one state from tyrannizing over the world as the Republic did. Could any thing be more insulting than her conduct toward us? Yet we who have turned on Greece—we who bullied Brazil—we crawled upon our bellies to the United States. They could not treat us contemptuously enough to raise our ire." Roebuck seemed less a friend of the South than an enemy of the North; hatred rather than love was evidently the source of his emotions. Yet he had been a great admirer of the American republic in former days.

Roebuck explained that his resolution, which called for a joint action between the great powers of Europe, really meant England and France. The other countries did not have a navy which would matter. "France is the only power we have to consider and France and England acknowledging the South, there would be an end of the war." At this juncture he spoke of his recent interview with Napoleon on the subject of joint intervention; how the rumor had been spread that the Palmerston ministry would say that the Emperor had changed his views on recognition; how he and Lindsay had gone to France to question Napoleon; how Napoleon had assured them that he was more anxious than ever to join England; and how he had just instructed Baron Gros to deny to the cabinet that he had changed, and to say that he was anxious to join England in intervention. Roebuck, in fact, related in minute detail the entire conversation between himself and Napoleon, including His Majesty's accusation that England had betrayed him to America on former occasions when he had proposed intervention.[1]

When Roebuck related the entire conversation he unquestionably told more than he was authorized to tell. There was a gasp of surprise in Parliament when he made the disclosure and an undertone of indignation. Roebuck's rôle as message-bearer from the Emperor, and the bearer of a message which carried insulting implications, was an unfortunate one for the cause he was pleading.

When Roebuck sat down Lord Montagu, friend of the Confederacy, rose and presented a motion opposed to recognition or any form of action that would change England's neutral position. He expressed deep sympathy for the South, but argued that any form of interference would be equivalent to war in which England would be greatly hurt. He contended that should England go to war with the North she would suffer from both a cotton and a wheat famine—a contention Forster and Bright were constantly making to which we will return at a later period.[2] Gladstone opposed both Roebuck's and Montagu's motion because he did not wish the government to commit itself. He felt that it would be wiser to leave the matter in the hands of the cabinet,[3] although he was still firmly convinced that it was only a matter of time before the South should win and England would recognize it.[4]

Forster argued that "the recognition of the South would be a *casus belli*, if the North chose to make it," and that "the motion of the honoured and learned gentleman meant war."[5] Forster pictured

---

[1] *Ibid.*, pp. 1771–1842.
[2] *Ibid.*   [4] *Ibid.*
[3] *Ibid.*   [5] *Ibid.*

the suffering of England in case of war with America, who would cover the sea with privateers and commerce-destroyers and also deprive England of wheat, at a time when there was a famine.[1]

Layard, undersecretary of the Foreign Office, denied Roebuck's assertion that Baron Gros or any other French official had approached the Foreign Office with communications touching recognition.[2] Sir George Grey, home secretary, later in the evening supported Layard's assertion. Since Layard's statement, he said, "it has come to the knowledge of members that it has been stated elsewhere that this afternoon just before the meeting of the House Baron Gros waited upon Lord Russell and informed him that he had not been instructed to make any such communications to Her Majesty's Government as that which has been spoken of." He "stated upon the authority of Earl Russell that no such communications had been received from the Emperor of the French." Grey criticized Roebuck for presuming to deliver a message from Napoleon to Parliament.[3] Lord Robert Cecil supported the motion and Bright delivered a strong speech against it, accusing Roebuck of being moved by "a miserable jealousy" of the United States or "a base fear."[4]

The debate was finally adjourned until July 2. But it might as well have been dropped from the calendar. It and its author were discredited. To some Roebuck was a liar, and to the great majority he was a dupe of Napoleon. Hotze, the day after the debate, called the treatment of Roebuck at the hands of the government and of the friends of the Union "unfair and merciless." All England laughed at Roebuck, wrote Hotze, and looked upon the Emperor's move as "a sort of farce in which Mr. Roebuck acted a broadly comic part," and he believed that "the cause of the Confederacy has no longer aught to hope, though still much to fear, from Mr. Roebuck's motion. All the resources of Southern strategy will be needed to secure a decent retreat, which the radicals threaten to cut off by insisting on a decision."[5] Mason wrote Slidell the day after the debate that

[1] *Ibid.*   [3] *Ibid.*

[2] *Ibid.*   [4] *Ibid.*

[5] Pickett Papers, Hotze to Benjamin, No. 25, July 11, 1863; *O.R.N.*, Ser. 2, Vol. III, pp. 839–41.

the whole affair was a "mess," and that no one could tell what the Emperor meant until he put his statement on paper, for he seemed to hold one language in public and another in private. "It would be uncivil to say that I have no confidence in the Emperor but certainly what has come from him so far can invite only distrust."[1] Mason, knowing what Napoleon had told Slidell in his interview, did not doubt that Roebuck was correctly reporting the conversation between himself, Lindsay, and Napoleon. The attitude of Napoleon was so well known that Mason felt that he had acted deceitfully in that he promised to have Gros take up the matter with the British cabinet, and then failed to live up to his promise. He seemed convinced of Russell's veracity.

On July 2 W. E. Forster precipitated a discussion of the Roebuck motion by asking Undersecretary Layard to state again whether or not the Foreign Office had any communication from the Emperor and to state the facts about the betrayal of the Emperor to Seward. As on June 30, Layard again denied that there had been a communication from France on the question of intervention; and he made that statement, he said, "without equivocation, in the broad sense of the word, that no such communication has up to this time been made. . . . . I now repeat what has been previously stated, that Baron Gros, hearing that rumors were in circulation that the honorable and learned member had stated that a communication had been made to Her Majesty's Government by the French Government, came to Lord Russell of his own accord, and stated that he had not received any communication on the subject for Her Majesty's Government, nor had he received any order to make a communication." As for betraying Napoleon by putting his dispatch into Seward's hands, continued Layard, the only communication England had received was the proposal of November 10, 1862, and that had been published by the French government on November 13 in the *Moniteur*.[2]

Roebuck's motion was postponed until Palmerston should return from an illness, despite the desire of Bright and his friends to press its author to defeat at this moment. Spence urged that Roebuck withdraw his motion, as the opposition would not favor it, especially

[1] Mason Papers, July 1, 1863.   [2] Parl. Deb., Ser. 3, Vol. 172, pp. 68–73.

since it had been deprived of the French support by Russell's and Layard's denials of any overtures by the Emperor.[1]

Palmerston on July 9 wrote Roebuck and urged him, if he insisted on going on with the motion, to drop further reference to Napoleon in his discussion as it only caused bad feeling.[2] Sir James Ferguson on July 10 in the Commons urged Roebuck to withdraw his motion as inopportune, and as sure to be defeated. Gregory urged that it be dropped; but Lindsay and Lord Robert Cecil merely asked that it be postponed a few days until news of Lee's invasion of Pennsylvania could come from America.[3] During this session the amateur diplomacy of Roebuck and Lindsay was harshly criticized, and the veracity of Roebuck questioned again by Layard who cited an article in the *Moniteur*, to which we will presently advert, which did not tally in all respects with Roebuck's version of the interview with the Emperor.[4]

On July 13 Roebuck moved the discharge of the motion, and Palmerston twitted him for his private diplomacy. Lindsay, however, after having remained silent practically the whole time pending the motion and debate, rose and made a careful and dignified speech in which he corroborated Roebuck's version of the interview in every detail, and pointed out that Palmerston had not scorned to make use of Lindsay as a private diplomat some years before in negotiating the favorable commercial treaties with France.[5]

So ended the Roebuck-Lindsay effort to bring about Confederate recognition. It never stood a chance of success, because England was chronically committed to inaction for many reasons, one of which was constantly referred to by all parties—fear of war—the others of which will be discussed later. But at least the motion could have been withdrawn with more dignity and éclat, as had other motions in behalf of some form of interference, had not Roebuck become identified with Napoleon's wishes and entangled in a maze of contradictory statements which made him seem absurd and lacking in truthfulness.

The public and all but a few of the initiates of the inner circle

[1] Mason Papers, Spence to Mason, July 4, 1863.   [2] E. D. Adams, II, 174.
[3] Parl. Deb., Ser. 3, Vol. 172, pp. 554 ff., July 10, 1863.
[4] *Ibid*.   [5] *Ibid*., pp. 661–73.

knew nothing of the documents thus far alluded to. All they knew was that Lindsay and Roebuck had had an interview with Napoleon on the matter of France and England's acting jointly on the question of recognition, and that this interview was unauthorized by the British cabinet. They had read or heard the debates in which Roebuck and Lindsay had detailed the interview in which Napoleon spoke of his desire to recognize the South in company with England, and his criticism of England and his claims to have instructed Gros to approach the British ministry. They had read of Russell's, Grey's, and Layard's statements that Gros had denied having received such instructions and that the Foreign Office had received no form of communication from France. Many of them had read an article in the *Moniteur*, July 5, or copies of it in English papers, which gave a version of the interview supposed to be official. This version agreed with Roebuck's in that Napoleon had expressed his desire to recognize the South and had said that he would instruct Gros to deny that he had changed his views on recognition and to sound out the British government,[1] but it did not allude to Napoleon's criticism of England. This was as much as the public knew and that includes most of the public men.

The Confederate commissioners and their friends, however, despite Mason's temporary doubts, had sufficient evidence to convince them that all that Roebuck said was true—though he might have misunderstood the Emperor with reference to disclosing it—and that Napoleon had lived up to his promises. Let us examine this further evidence. The day after Roebuck's speech, July 1, he wrote Slidell that, because his veracity had been called into question, he was writing a brief statement of what was said at the interview to be presented to the Emperor for his approval or disapproval.[2] Slidell presented a copy of Roebuck's note to both Napoleon and Drouyn de Lhuys. After a consultation of De Lhuys and Napoleon on July 4 the article referred to in the *Moniteur* of July 5 appeared as a semiofficial statement of the interview. The following day, July 6, Mocquard in-

[1] *Moniteur*, July 5, 1863.

[2] Pickett Papers, Slidell to Benjamin, No. 40, July 6, 1863, for note; *O.R.N.*, Ser. 2, Vol. III, pp. 832–36.

closed Slidell a note dictated by the Emperor himself, in reply to Roebuck's note of July 1, which corroborated substantially Roebuck's description of the interview with the exception of making the interview public. I give the note in full as it establishes the veracity of Roebuck, Lindsay, and Slidell in reporting their interviews with the Emperor.

The Emperor having been informed fifteen days ago that the report had been spread in London of his Majesty having changed his opinion as regards the recognition of the South, M. Drouyn De Lhuys wrote to Baron Gros that he should refute the report.

Meantime MM. Roebuck and Lindsay came over and paid a visit to the Emperor whom they invited to make an official application to the British Cabinet toward the recognition of the South. His Majesty replied that such a step was not practicable before knowing whether it would be agreed to, since the first proposal of mediation had met with a denial, and his Majesty had been told (a thing of which he had, it is true, no proof) that the Cabinet of London boasted at Washington of declining such of the Emperor's proposals as were in favor of the South. Now his Majesty has neither cause nor feeling of animosity toward the United States, and it is but with the hope of seeing an end to be put to a war already too long, that he considered the recognition of the South as a speedier means to bring about peace. The Emperor could not have spoken to Mr. Roebuck of any despatch or despatches exhibited by Lord Lyons to Mr. Seward, because there were none but those which have been published. However, his Majesty does regret Mr. Roebuck's making public an entirely confidential explanation.

We must add on the next day after the interview of Messrs. [Roebuck] and Lindsay with the Emperor the minister of foreign affairs wrote by telegraph to Baron Gros, to officially [semiofficially] inform Lord Palmerston that should Great Britain be willing to recognize the South, the Emperor would be ready to follow her in that way.[1]

This corroborated Roebuck's statement in substance. In detail it denied that the Emperor had referred to official dispatches in speaking of Russell's betrayal of confidence and denied that the Emperor had intended for Roebuck to repeat the conversation in its entirety.[2] Slidell forwarded Mocquard's note with the Emperor's statement to Roebuck who came back hotly challenging the Emperor's veracity as to the official dispatch and the breach of confidence. Slidell refused to deliver the note to the Emperor, but wrote Roe-

[1] *Ibid.*   [2] *Ibid.*

buck that evidently he misunderstood the Emperor on these points; the Emperor referred to "informal overtures" and not official dispatches, and that there was clearly a matter of misunderstanding as to repeating all that was said—not a question of veracity. Roebuck decided not to say anything further.[1]

Slidell, with his knowledge of the situation derived from the Emperor, De Lhuys, Persigny, and his "friend" Cintrat, had no doubts about what Napoleon had said in the interview and about his instructions to Gros to sound out the British government. If Mason doubted the veracity of the Emperor for a short time, he was soon convinced that the lying, if any, had been in other quarters. On July 9, 1863, Slidell expressed his interpretation of the imbroglio to Mason. "I am satisfied that he [the Emperor] has kept his promise with good faith. Either the minister of Foreign Affairs or Baron Gros or both have failed to carry out their instructions or Messrs. Russell and Layard have asserted what was false. Perhaps Lord Palmerston may have received the communication and failed to inform his colleagues of the fact. I hope that this may prove to be the fact."[2] Three days before this Slidell had expressed a similar belief to Benjamin but had been more specific in his suspicions, for, after having laid the doubtful honor on Gros or De Lhuys or Russell and Layard, he said: "You will naturally desire to know what is my opinion on the subject, I give it although with some hesitation. I suspect that M. Drouyn De Lhuys has not carried out in good faith the wishes of his sovereign; he is a man of timid temperament, fond of little diplomatic finesses, and is very far from being as decided as the Emperor in his views of the policy to be pursued in our affairs. He is moreover very susceptible and jealous of any interference with his peculiar functions, and he may have been dissatisfied that the Emperor should have conferred with me and others on a diplomatic question."[3] Mason adopted Slidell's view that the most probable

[1] Pickett Papers, Slidell to Benjamin, No. 42, July 19, 1863; O.R.N., Ser. 2, Vol. III, pp. 845–46.

[2] Mason Papers, July 9, 1863.

[3] Pickett Papers, Slidell to Benjamin, No. 40, July 6, 1863; O.R.N., Ser. 2, Vol. III, pp. 832–36.

solution of the case was that De Lhuys had not carried out Napoleon's orders.[1]

When all the explanations of the French government were in Slidell's hands on July 19 he still believed that, while there might have been lying and finesse on the part of Gros, Russell, and Layard, De Lhuys "has been not a little instrumental in producing" the imbroglio.[2]

In this status the question of veracity has come down to recent times when the Russell, Lyons, Palmerston, and Cowley papers have been made available to students by special permission or by publication, and the British and the French archives opened for the war period. The papers of the British officials, public and private, have thus far yielded no evidence that Russell or Palmerston was approached by Gros on the question of joint recognition. But the French archives while not rendering as much service as one should like nevertheless are rather revealing. Apparently the matter resolves itself chiefly into "emphasis" and "interpretation," though there was some fibbing.

The records show that Napoleon carried out his promises to Slidell to the letter. One is amazed, perhaps, to catch this arch liar in a truth—or more accurately a chain of truths. One might be tempted to say that Napoleon never lied for the art of it, but lied as a matter of economy: when it was either too complicated a matter to characterize with a simple truth or when the truth would be too embarrassing to himself or his friends. As for De Lhuys, the records seem to clear him completely of any intention of frustrating the desires of Napoleon in the matter of approaching England. He did send Gros instructions by telegram, just as Napoleon had said on several occasions, to speak to Lord Palmerston "officially" on recognition. This telegram was sent before July 1, and there is no reason to suppose that it was not sent on June 22 as claimed by Napoleon, Mocquard, Cintrat, and De Lhuys in their conversations with Slidell. This first telegram itself escaped the eye of the present writer

[1] Pickett Papers, Mason to Benjamin, No. 42, July 10, 1863; *O.R.N.*, Ser. 2, Vol. III, pp. 837–39.

[2] Pickett Papers, Slidell to Benjamin, No. 42, July 19, 1863; *O.R.N.*, Ser. 2, Vol. III, pp. 845–46.

if it is on record in the Affaires Etrangères. But there is another telegram on file in the French Foreign Office which refers to this first telegram. The second one was sent July 1, 1863, the day after Roebuck's motion was made, as a result of the statement made by Russell and Layard and Grey that Gros had voluntarily stated that he had no communication on the subject. De Lhuys and Napoleon were both apparently behind this last telegram. It was rather sharp when taken in connection with Gros's denial to Russell that he had received any communication to approach the cabinet. *"Conforming to my despatch by telegram,"* reads this telegram, *"you should have spoken officially to Lord Palmerston about the recognition of the Confederate States. When and where did you do it?"*[1]

The first part of the second telegram referring to a previous telegram is partly scratched out, but nevertheless it can be easily deciphered. There is, of course, a chance that De Lhuys scratched out the part which referred to a previous telegram, because the previous telegram had not actually been sent. This, however, is doubtful in view of Baron Gros's letter of July 1 to De Lhuys. In this letter he dilated at length upon Roebuck's evident betrayal of the Emperor's confidence in giving what passed in a private conversation. But he was especially indignant at Russell's denial that there had been any communication on the subject of mediation from Paris. "I regret the manner in which Sir George Grey . . . . has spoken of the conversation which I have had with Lord Russell; it seems from what he said that I went to the home of the Secretary of State for the sole purpose of telling him that I had not been charged with any communication for him on the subject of the recognition of the South. . . . ." His real purpose, he continued, in calling on Russell was with reference to the Polish question, "and it was incidental that I said to him that although having no official communication to make to him on this subject of the recognition of the South I was personally persuaded that the Emperor was very much disposed to recognize them."[2]

In short, Napoleon instructed De Lhuys in turn to instruct Gros to sound out Palmerston and deny the rumor that he had changed

[1] French F.O. Eng., Vol. 725, Drouyn de Lhuys to Baron Gros, July 1, 1863. The French text of the telegram is as follows: "Conformément à ma dépêche télégraphique [first part scratched out through the word "télégraphique" but it can easily be read] vous avez dit parler officieusement à Lord Palmerston de la reconnaissance des Etats Confédérés. Quand et comment l'avez vous fait?"

[2] French F.O. Eng., Vol. 725, Gros to De Lhuys, July 1, 1863.

his views on recognition. De Lhuys had done this by two telegrams: the date of the first not known, but evidence pointing to June 22; the date of the second, July 1, after Roebuck's motion, and too late to aid him in his "mess." Gros, however, had not, apparently, taken the matter up with Palmerston as his instructions indicated, inasmuch as Palmerston was ill at the time. As Russell said on June 30, Baron Gros had had an interview with him that day; the main purpose of which was, contrary to Russell's statement, the Polish question, and only incidentally the Confederate question. But Russell shifted the emphasis entirely over to the Confederate question. Further than that Gros had told him that he had "no official communication to make him on the subject of the recognition of the South," while Russell, Grey, and Layard said that Gros had denied having any communication whatsoever. Layard had said that he meant it in the "broadest sense," that is, that Gros had received neither official nor unofficial communication. But Gros had said that while he had no official communication to make, he was personally convinced that the Emperor was very anxious to join England in recognition. Russell, Grey, and Layard had entirely omitted this last statement—in fact, Layard, as we have just seen, made a point-blank denial of it. The shifting of emphasis from the main point of the interview and from "no official communication" to "none at all," on the part of the British Foreign Office, was primarily responsible for the "mess." If it was not outright lying, it was a case of super-fine sophistry. However, there is no doubt that Gros, because his instructions directed him to Palmerston, had failed sufficiently to emphasize the positive character of the "unofficial" instructions he had received, probably June 22. He should have known the old British custom of denying the existence of all unofficial, informal communications to or from the British Foreign Office. A thing did not exist unless it went on record, even if Russell had written the message himself—as, for example, his letters to Cowley in September, 1862, feeling out Napoleon.

When the Roebuck motion had been withdrawn and its author discredited in Parliament as a liar, an ass, and an emissary of Napoleon, Gros assured De Lhuys all that England knew despite the fog and dust which had obscured the main issue was that the Emperor was disposed to recognize the independence of the Confederate States if England would act in concert with him. "They know also that if his Majesty had not asked officially the second time of the government of the Queen to propose the joint mediation of France and England to the belligerents in America it was because he had already experienced on this subject a refusal accompanied by circumstances that should not be repeated. They know also that the day when the government of the Queen wishes to put an end to the fratricidal war which desolates the American Union it will find in the Emperor an ally as useful as disinterested."[1]

The Confederate commissioners, however, had no hopes, after the failure of Roebuck's motion and the news of the disastrous battles of Vicksburg and Gettysburg, that Palmerston and Russell would join France. Their only hope was Spain, whom Napoleon had promised Slidell he would join. So Slidell and Napoleon turned again to Isturitz. Slidell on August 4 approached Isturitz to induce Spain to take the initiative to be followed by France. But the Spanish Minister was discouraging. "He tells me," wrote Slidell to Benjamin,[2] "that I can effect nothing at Madrid at present; he assured me that his government was prepared to recognize us cojointly or with France and other continental powers, or with France alone, but would not take the initiative; he said expressly that the co-operation of England would not be required." Napoleon, too, approached the Spanish government on the question of intervention through his ambassador, Adolphe Barrot, but he was assured that Spain, though she might join with France, would not take the lead in recognition.[3] As a matter of fact, Spain could not be relied on to live up to a promise at this time because of domestic conditions, and Napoleon would

[1] *Ibid.*, Gros to De Lhuys, No. 94, July 15, 1863.

[2] Pickett Papers, Slidell to Benjamin, No. 43, Aug. 5, 1863; *O.R.N.*, Ser. 2, Vol. III, pp. 855–57.

[3] Pickett Papers, Slidell to Benjamin, No. 45, Sept. 22, 1863; *O.R.N.*, Ser. 2, Vol. III, pp. 905–10. Slidell speaks of his interview with Barrot.

not stake much on Spanish co-operation. England was his sole reliance, and that government had not the slightest intentions of meddling in a struggle whose prolongation weakened a rival and whose ultimate outcome was assumed to be the division of the Union. The stars in their courses were fighting for England, so why meddle with the stars?

Napoleon could not act alone, for Seward had made it all too clear that intervention meant war. On hearing, through Adams and Dayton, of the Roebuck affair and Napoleon's proposal in the *Moniteur* Seward had written a very pointed dispatch to Dayton which he instructed him to read to De Lhuys. "The President," he wrote, "has read this announcement [in the *Moniteur*] with surprise and regret. The Emperor has not been left by this government in doubt upon the point that a recognition of the insurgents would be regarded by it as an unfriendly proceeding," and that such an act would be followed by war.[1] Dayton presented De Lhuys with this dispatch about August 20, and in reply he was assured that the question of recognition was merely academic, as France had no idea of doing such a thing. As for Napoleon's statement in the *Moniteur* which substantiated Roebuck's statement in Parliament, De Lhuys wriggled out beautifully—he said that Roebuck's speech in Parliament had given the wrong impression and the Emperor had tried to correct it by his article in the *Moniteur*.[2]

Rumors continued to be prevalent that Napoleon wished to intervene if England would join him. Adams wrote Seward on August 20 that on his recent visit to Scotland he had been informed by "a gentleman of high political connexion . . . . that a new proposal had lately been made by the French Emperor to the British Government for joint action in regard to our affairs and that it had been again formally declined."[3] In spite of everything he had written Dayton to the contrary, Seward continued to show confidence in Napoleon and rebuked Adams for believing his Scottish inform-

[1] U. S. Inst., France, Vol. 16, No. 380, July 29, 1863.

[2] U. S. Des., France, Vol. 53, Dayton to Seward, No. 334, Aug. 20, 1863.

[3] U.S. Des., Gr. Br., Vol. 83, Adams to Seward, No. 472, Aug. 20, 1863.

ant.[1] Adams bristled at this self-deception of Seward's and his questioning of the report. "I am very glad," he wrote, "that you are confident of the sincerity of the French Government in its official communications with you; neither is it my wish to be unreasonably suspicious or to construe its actions unkindly"; but he added, "I can scarcely doubt the truth" of this report.[2] Furthermore, Adams replied that he had "on two different visits had incidental conversation with another member of the Diplomatic Corps whose peculiar position gives him extraordinary opportunities for knowledge of the movements made here. He spoke to me each time of the importunity of the French Government to obtain cooperation here as of a matter so familiarly known to him as to be beyond denial. . . . . I am sorry to be obliged to confess to a belief that there is more or less duplicity in the policy of the Emperor of France towards the United States." Adams concluded that he preferred the "rougher and colder truth" of the English to the "more polished and courtly insincerity" of the Emperor.[3]

These efforts to obtain England's co-operation in an unofficial capacity continued into the fall of 1863. On October 3 De Lhuys telegraphed Baron Gros, "Information which has reached the Emperor would cause us to think that England would be ready to recognize the Confederates, if they had a chance of supporting themselves. Try and know if that is true."[4]

In the meanwhile, however, the Roebuck fiasco, combined with Russell's general attitude of lack of courtesy, and the growing resentment in the Confederacy at England's recognition of what was believed to be an illegal blockade, prompted the Confederate government to withdraw Mason from England. On August 4 Benjamin wrote Mason that "the perusal of the recent debates in the British

[1] U.S. Inst., Gr. Br., Vol. 19, Seward to Adams, No. 700, Sept. 5, 1863.

[2] U.S. Des., Gr. Br., Vol. 84, Adams to Seward, No. 503, Sept. 25, 1863.

[3] *Ibid.*

[4] French F.O. England, Vol. 726, De Lhuys to Gros, Oct. 3, 1863. Text of telegram is as follows: "Des information arrivées à l'Empereur porteraient à croire que l'Angleterre serait disposée à reconnâitre les Confédérés, s'ils avaient quelque chance de se soutenir tachez de savoir. Si cela est vrai."

Parliament satisfies the President that the Government of Her Majesty has determined to decline the overtures made through you for establishing by treaty friendly relations between the two governments, and entertains no intention of receiving you as the accredited minister of this government near the British Court." Under these circumstances Mason was to withdraw from London. But Benjamin assured him that his order to withdraw implied no censure of his conduct of the mission.[1] In a private letter inclosed with his official one Benjamin authorized Mason to use his own discretion as to what he should do if a change of circumstances—not anticipated— should occur before the receipt of his order to withdraw.[2]

On September 21 Mason wrote Russell a note inclosing the greater part of Benjamin's notice to terminate his mission,[3] and on September 25 Russell replied in a cold, crisp, civil note: "I have on other occasions explained to you the reasons which have induced her Majesty's Government to decline the overtures you allude to, and the motives which have hitherto prevented the British Court from recognizing you as the accredited minister of an established State. These reasons are still in force, and it is not necessary to repeat them." He expressed regret that he had not been in a position to cultivate Mason's personal acquaintance "which, in a different state of affairs, I should have done with much pleasure and satisfaction."[4]

Mason then withdrew to Paris to live with Slidell except when in London on propaganda and lobby business, and on November 13 Benjamin notified Mason that he had been reappointed commissioner on the Continent.[5]

---

[1] Pickett Papers, Benjamin to Mason, No. 30, Aug. 4, 1863; *O.R.N.*, Ser. 2, Vol. III, pp. 852–53.

[2] *Ibid.*   [3] *Ibid.*

[4] Pickett Papers, Mason to Benjamin (inclosure), Oct. 19, 1863; *O.R.N.*, Ser. 2, Vol. III, pp. 934–35.

[5] Pickett Papers, Benjamin to Mason, No. 32; *O.R.N.*, Ser. 2, Vol. III, pp. 950–51; also Pickett Papers, Benjamin to Mason, No. 34, Jan. 25, 1864; *O.R.N.*, Ser. 2, Vol. III, pp. 1009–10.

CHAPTER XIV

THE DIPLOMATIC BREAK WITH ENGLAND IN 1863

WITHDRAWAL OF MASON AND EXPULSION
OF THE BRITISH CONSULS

The attitude of the southern people toward England at the outbreak of the war had been one of admiration and friendliness. Consul Bunch at Charleston, in fact, had been embarrassed by pro-English demonstrations which seemed to him to indicate a strong desire of the South to rejoin the mother-country;[1] so despite the occasional enrolment of a British subject in the Confederate or state military organizations[2] there was only slight friction on either side, until the end of 1861.

But resentment toward England began to show itself by that time, in the public press and in the state and Confederate official circles. The failure of England and France—especially the former—to intervene in the fall of 1861 and early winter of 1862 was a bitter disappointment. It did not fit the Confederate scheme of things, the King Cotton philosophy which the South had come to accept in such complete faith. As we have noted the English press and leaders had been in no small degree responsible for the development of the King Cotton idea in the South. When the expected revolt in Lancashire did not occur as the *Times* and *Economist* had prophesied and no need of intervention developed by 1862, a blind anger against England sprang up in the South.

The first expression of resentment against England was a querulousness shown by certain papers against the British consuls resident within the Confederacy, who had been very vigorous in defending from military service all British subjects.[3] These consuls

[1] Russell, *My Diary*, p. 134; E. D. Adams, I, 43–44.
[2] See, e.g., reports of Consuls Mure, New Orleans; Bunch, Charleston; Moore, Richmond; Molyneaux, etc., Savannah, in F.O. Amer., Vols. 781, 788, 909, *passim*.
[3] See, e.g., *ibid*.

had received their exequaturs, or permits to perform their functions, from the United States, and their official status had been recognized by the Confederacy as legal. But when the Yancey-Rost-Mann mission failed to gain recognition in the summer of 1861, as the extreme King Cotton devotees had expected, there began a popular outcry against the exercise of consular functions under the exequatur of the enemy's government. On July 12, 1861, the *Savannah Republican* urged that no attention be paid the complaints of British consuls against the enrolment of British subjects by the Confederate States, until the Confederate government recognized them officially by granting Confederate exequaturs. Until that time a foreign consul should be considered only a private citizen.

After the beginning of 1862 the press with the exception of a few pro-Davis papers urged that foreign consuls be forced to procure their exequaturs from the Confederacy or leave the country. A correspondent in the *Charleston Courier*[1] argued that, while it was only just that the consuls should have been permitted to remain, through courtesy, "till our claims to foreign recognition had been laid before the Government of their respective countries, and a reasonable time elapsed for reply," now "if it is worth the while of foreign powers to have consuls here and we extend to them this privilege, let them show us a decent courtesy by accrediting them to the Confederate Government at Richmond, where their exequatur will be issued by President Davis, who alone has the power to issue such a commission in the Confederate States." This writer insisted that self-respect and independence demanded that the foreign consuls obtain their exequaturs from the Confederate government, and not from its enemy. He further urged that self-respect demanded the withdrawal from Europe of the Confederate commissioners, for their government was being ignored in its own domain by the British consuls and abroad by the British government. Through these commissioners who had received no recognition as envoys of a foreign power, continued the *Courier*, "we have been there humbling ourselves upon our knees for eight long months and we cannot be answered. Not one act of official recognition will they give us. . . . . ."

[1] *Charleston Courier*, Feb. 28, 1862.

The *Montgomery Advertiser*[1] felt that for the consuls "to act in an official capacity under the authority of exequaturs granted by the United States Government is offensive to the good sense of our people. If England, France, and Spain and other nations desire representatives in the Confederacy, to look after their own commercial interests and the interests of their citizens, let them take an honorable course and recognize the Confederate States as a nation. . . . . If we wish to gain the countenance of the world, we must act as becomes an independent nation, and self-respect and independence alike cry out against the further toleration of officers, whose only titles to official recognition are derived from the Government at Washington." By the middle of 1862 practically all the newspapers of the South urged the dismissal of the consuls, on the one hand, and the recall of Mason, Slidell, and Mann, on the other, as acts necessary to maintain the dignity of an independent nation, whose independent existence had been studiously ignored by foreign powers.

The Confederate Congress began early in 1862 to agitate for the dismissal of the consuls or for forcing them to obtain exequaturs from the Confederate government. Barksdale of Mississippi introduced a resolution which passed in the House inquiring as to the status of the consuls and whether action was necessary to maintain the rights of the Confederacy as an independent nation.[2] Yancey in the Senate demanded legislation to prevent the consuls from acting without Confederate exequaturs.[3]

The administration foe, Foote of Tennessee, hoping to embarrass Davis as well as to assert the dignity of an ignored Confederacy, offered a resolution from the Foreign Affairs Committee concerning the status of foreign consuls. He asked for the names of all Confederate commissioners abroad; requested that their correspondence be submitted to Congress; and he wanted to know the names of all foreign consuls, including subordinate foreign ministers at Washington, and the source of their exequaturs, whether granted by the Confederacy or by the United States.[4]

Benjamin did not give a list of the Confederate agents abroad nor

[1] Quoted in *ibid.*, March 15, 1863.

[2] *Jour. Confed. Cong.*, V, 47 f.

[3] *Ibid.*, II, 142.

[4] *Ibid.*, V, 333.

submit their correspondence, but he readily sent in a list of all foreign consuls resident in the Confederacy and stated that all but one of them had received his exequatur from the United States.[1]

The failure of the joint mediation of November 10, 1862, the casual and discourteous treatment of Mason by Russell with reference to his notes on the blockade and on recognition, and Russell's reactionary interpretation of the Declaration of Paris in recognizing the Federal blockade fanned the flames of resentment in the Confederacy. The refusal of England to recognize the Confederacy, the enforcement of neutrality partial to the United States in the close watch over the ironclads and the shipment of munitions, coupled with a universal belief in England in the ultimate success of the South, began to arouse the suspicions of the South as to that country's motives. Not only had England betrayed their trust in King Cotton but she had a malign and sinister design: She wished to see the two sections cripple and virtually destroy each other before they made peace. "There can be no doubt," said the *Richmond Whig*,[2] "that those who direct the policy of England secretly rejoice in the fact that the late United States are arrayed against each other in bitter strife, literally threatening the complete annihilation of each other, thus relieving her of a powerful rival, of whom she lived in continual dread. . . . . They desire the restoration of the Union less than any other event, and feeling that that result is impossible, they do not wish to see the independence of the Confederate States established until the people both North and South are prostrated in strength, bankrupted in finance, and disgraced as a free people. With a hypocritical profession of anxiety that the war may cease, they have pursued the very course calculated to inflame and prolong the contest." The *Whig* felt that this "cold-blooded selfishness of the British ministry towards the Confederate States is fast engendering toward that country a bitterness of feeling in this country that cannot fail to tell upon future relations."

In January, 1863, intercepted Confederate correspondence was widely published North and South, and the language of the dis-

[1] *Ibid.*, pp. 421–24.

[2] *Richmond Whig*, Dec. 29, 1862; cf. *Index*, Jan. 15, 1863.

patches was anything but complimentary to England. The *Rich-mond Enquirer*,[1] expressing great satisfaction at the stiff tone assumed by the Confederacy, believed that "the language of these despatches . . . . towards Earl Russell, and the rasping he receives in them, are highly gratifying to the people. . . . ."

It could not be doubted, said the *Enquirer* a few days later,[2] that the people of the Confederacy were resentful and dissatisfied with the attitude assumed by neutral nations. It amounted to contempt for the Confederacy. The Confederacy had maintained itself for two years by a series of brilliant victories, and its commissioners had been at the French and English capitals during this time "waiting, soliciting, remonstrating"; yet "we have not advanced, it seems, one step in that public recognition of our sovereignty, to which we are entitled by the laws of nations. At this hour neither England nor France pretends to have any knowledge of our existence." They still recognized the government of the United States as entitled to treat for the Confederacy, and they knew nothing of Mason and Slidell, save as private gentlemen. Adams and Dayton were still the accredited ministers at those courts. This snubbing of the commissioners by Russell and the refusal to recognize the independence of the South were outrages and humiliations. The *Enquirer* demanded that the commissioners be withdrawn at once. But there was another side also to the ignoring of the Confederacy, said the *Enquirer*, which could not be tolerated, namely, "the performance of consular functions in our courts, by gentlemen accredited to our enemies, and authorized by our enemies to reside here and protect the interest of Englishmen and Frenchmen." These consuls, so called, received their instructions through Lyons and Mercier at Washington and, continued the *Enquirer*, "if one of their consuls here should be removed, or should die, it is to Mr. Lincoln that his successor would be accredited." This contemptuous ignoring of the authority of the Confederacy could not long continue. Public indignation inspired by self-respect and high spirit began to show itself. It was hoped that shortly the President would act, even to expel the consuls. The *Courier* and *Whig* agreed that the foreign consuls not commissioned

[1] *Richmond Enquirer*, Jan. 27, 1863.   [2] *Ibid.*, Feb. 7, 1863.

to the Confederacy but to the Lincoln Government touched the pride of the South.[1]

Swann of Tennessee, who had introduced a similar resolution in 1862, now proposed again in the Confederate House of Representatives that the foreign consuls be dismissed unless they obtained exequaturs from the Confederacy, and that the commissioners be recalled from abroad;[2] and Foote again urged a similar measure.[3] Consul Bunch reported January 24, 1863, that Davis' message, the position of Congress, and the tone of the press indicated deep hostility toward the British government.[4]

While scraps of information had been reaching the public and Congress concerning the supercilious language of Russell in his correspondence with Mason in the summer of 1862 touching the blockade and recognition, thereby feeding public resentment, the full text of this did not reach the public until April, 1863. On its appearance there was an angry outburst at once. The *Enquirer* called Great Britain "(next to the Yankees) our worst and deadliest enemy." It recalled "the humiliating position we continue to assign ourselves in keeping commissioners sitting, like Mordecai, at the gates of kings who know us not and refuse to know us," and in allowing consuls of these kings to exercise consular functions—even exempting residents from military service—"although those agents have no authority to exercise consular functions here, except on authority derived from Lincoln."[5]

Such may be considered the state of public opinion in early 1863 with reference to England. It was a state of anger based upon the ignoring of the Confederacy as a government. This temper had manifested itself on three scores: first, the British consuls had performed their consular functions in the Confederacy under exequaturs granted by the Federal government; second, England had refused to recognize the South, or receive its commissioners; and third, as a neutral

---

[1] *Courier*, Feb. 28, 1863, quoting the *Whig*.

[2] *Ibid.*, Feb. 7, 1863.

[3] Bonham, *The British Consuls in the Confederacy* (New York, 1911), p. 220.

[4] F.O. Amer., Vol. 906, No. 11, Jan. 24, 1863.

[5] *Richmond Enquirer*, April 1, 1863; cf. *ibid.*, April 4 and 6.

England's concession of belligerent rights to the North had been greater than to the South.

From the spring of 1863 until the fall of 1863 a series of irritations under these categories caused an acute outburst of resentment which resulted in the expulsion of the British consuls and the withdrawal of Mason from England and the refusal to ratify the appointment of Lamar to Russia.

The first definite steps which followed the storm of public fury in the spring of 1863 was the expulsion of Moore of Richmond and Cridland of Mobile, the remonstrance with France concerning the French acting consul, Laren, and the order forbidding consuls to communicate directly with their ambassadors in Washington.

George Moore, the British consul at Richmond, and Vice-Consul Cridland had, like the other British consuls, busied themselves all too much in extracting from the Confederate and state armies repentant expatriated Britishers—many of whom, not anticipating civil war, had bade farewell forever to their native lands, but who now were suddenly feeling severe pangs of nostalgia.[1]

Benjamin and the Governor of Virginia had dealt patiently with Moore. But that consul unfortunately, just at the time when Benjamin was looking for a "goat" to satisfy his own and the public resentment against England, overstepped his bounds. Moore learned that the Mississippi legislature had just amended its militia law so as to make liable all whites between eighteen and fifty, including aliens who were either temporary or permanent residents. Moore protested to Benjamin against this act on February 16, 1863. Benjamin, knowing quite well that Moore's commission and exequatur vested in him authority only over Richmond and Virginia, saw that Moore was exceeding his authority. Here was his chance. So he wrote Moore on February 20, 1863, asking that he submit all commissions and authority to the Confederate State Department for examination, "in order that the precise nature and extent of your functions may be ascertained before further correspondence can be held with you as her Majesty's consul at the port of Richmond."

Moore, however, ignored Benjamin's request and thereby whetted

[1] F.O. Amer., Vol. 909, *passim*.

the blade only the sharper against the day of execution. Several months later Moore discovered two conscripts in the Confederate service, two Irishmen by names of Maloney and Farrell, who claimed to be British subjects, and he busied himself in behalf of his Irish compatriots. Remembering Benjamin's orders that he submit his commission before further correspondence could be held with him, Moore, instead of taking the matter up with the State Department, now wrote the War Department, which knew nothing about Benjamin's request. The War Department investigated and found that Maloney and Farrell had been residents of Virginia for eight years and that they both were landowners and farmers in Greenbrier County, and that they had both exercised the right of suffrage—all of which it considered as excellent evidence of an intention of remaining permanent residents of Virginia.

At the same time Moore had written to J. B. Caldwell, of Greenbrier County, the counsel for Maloney and Farrell, a letter touching the case, in very censorious and bitter terms. "I am really at a loss," he wrote Caldwell, "to account for the dilatory proceedings of the War Department not to make use of any harsher terms, however, and indifference with which the War Department seems to regard cases of the most atrocious cruelty, quite baffle all my preconceived opinions of my kindred race.

"I have lived thirty-two consecutive years (from 1826 to 1858) in despotic countries and I am compelled to bear witness that I have met in those foreign countries more official courtesy and consideration from the local authorities on my representation of grievances than I meet at the hands of my own blood and lineage. . . . ."

Caldwell, evidently finding Moore's letter too much for his gorge, permitted it to reach the hands of the Secretary of War, Seddon, who forwarded it on June 4, 1863, to Benjamin with an indignant comment. So after much meandering through stupidity or cunning or perhaps mere arrogant indifference to the Confederate government, Moore had fallen into the hands of Benjamin and Davis.

On the day after the receipt of Seddon's note they cut off Moore's official head. Davis issued a letter patent revoking Moore's exequatur, and Benjamin inclosed a copy of the letter patent with a note to the consul which explained the action of the Confederate government. Benjamin stated three grounds for his action: first, Moore had assumed to perform consular functions in Mississippi which lay outside his jurisdiction; second, when requested to submit his consular commission to Benjamin he had contemptuously ignored the request; and third, he had corresponded with the War Department in violation of orders that no further communication could be held with him until he had submitted his consular commission. Therefore, concluded Benjamin with keen relish, "the President considers it as inconsistent with the respect which it is his office to enforce toward this Government that you should any longer be permitted to exercise the functions or enjoy the privileges of a consul in these Confederate States."[1]

The letter patent and all the correspondence touching the matter were published in the local papers.[2] The press was highly gratified at the expulsion of Moore, and it demanded that the other British consuls follow.[3]

The day after the revocation of Moore's letter patent Benjamin wrote Mason explaining the circumstances of Moore's dismissal. He explained that the Confederacy considered all consular exequaturs issued by the Federal government before 1861 as legal, and that as long as the consuls "seek neither to evade nor defy the legitimate authority of this Government within its own jurisdiction" they should be protected and allowed to continue their functions unmolested.[4]

But the revocation of Moore's exequatur was not all that was determined upon at the time. The consuls had been receiving their orders from their masters at Washington since the beginning of the war. "The British ministry accredited to the Government of our

[1] Pickett Papers, Benjamin to Mason, No. 24, June 6, 1863; *O.R.N.*, Ser. 2, Vol. III, pp. 786–91, gives the correspondence; cf. Bonham, pp. 86–90; F.O. Amer., Vol. 909, Moore to Russell, June 9, 1863.

[2] Richardson, I, 325–26.

[3] See *Richmond Enquirer*, June 8 and 13; *Whig*, June 6; *Mercury*, June 8; *Savannah Republican*, June 20, etc.

[4] Pickett Papers, Benjamin to Mason, No. 24, June 6, 1863; *O.R.N.*, Ser. 2, Vol. III, pp. 786–91.

enemies," wrote Benjamin, "assumes the power to issue instructions to and exercise authority over the consuls of Great Britain residing within this country; nay, even to appoint agents to supervise British interests in the Confederate States. This course of conduct plainly ignores the existence of this Government, and implies the continuance of the relation between that minister and the consuls of her Majesty resident within the Confederacy which existed prior to the withdrawal of these States from the Union."[1] This ignoring of the existence of the Confederacy had been the chief objection to the presence of the British consuls from the beginning of the war. The receipt of orders by these consuls from Lord Lyons at Washington was only one of the phases of this attitude. This practice of sending to and receiving instructions from Washington must stop. Benjamin instructed Mason to present Lord Russell a copy of this dispatch, including the letter patent revoking Moore's exequatur and the notice that all communications must cease between British consuls and the British ambassador at Washington.[2]

Four days later, June 10, Benjamin sent out a circular letter to all consuls resident in the Confederacy which forbade "direct communication between consuls or consular agents of foreign countries residing within the Confederacy and the functionaries of such foreign Governments residing in the enemy's lines."[3]

Obviously something was back of this order to Mason of June 6, and the circular of June 10 forbidding communication between foreign ministers at Washington and the consular agents in the Confederacy—something besides the objection to the implications of such a practice. It was the revocation of Magee's exequatur by his own government through Lord Lyons and the appointment of Cridland as his successor through the same channel, and the appointment by the French government of M. Laren as acting consul —all without the consent of the Confederacy.

Consul Magee at Mobile had been dismissed from office by the British government about the beginning of 1863, but at first the Confederacy paid no attention to it. However, the local authorities,

---

[1] *Ibid.*   [2] *Ibid.*

[3] Pickett Papers, Benjamin to Slidell, No. 18, June 10, 1863; *O.R.N.*, Ser. 2, Vol. III, pp. 792–96.

both state and city, investigated the matter and reported their findings to Benjamin. They discovered that Magee had been dismissed by Lord Lyons at Washington, which was a serious offense against the Confederacy in itself. But further than this, Lyons had dismissed him for receiving and forwarding to England on a British war vessel $155,000 in specie for the state of Alabama, which was to be applied on the state debt owed in London. This looked as if Lord Lyons were co-operating with the United States. Finally, Lyons had appointed Vice-Consul Cridland of Richmond as acting consul in Magee's place at Mobile without notifying or in any way consulting the Confederate government.

When Benjamin learned of the circumstances of Magee's dismissal and Cridland's appointment, he ordered Cridland not to attempt to exercise consular functions at Mobile, and suggested that "his choice of some other State than Alabama for his residence would be agreeable to this Government." Benjamin immediately wrote Mason, June 11, an account of the whole affair and ordered him to place a copy of his letter in Russell's hands. He summed up his reason for revoking Cridland's commission: "A minister accredited to the Government of our enemies has not only assumed the exercise of authority within this Confederacy without the knowledge or consent of its Government, but has done so under circumstances that rather aggravate than palliate the offense of disregarding its sovereign rights. His action further conveys the implication that the Confederacy is subordinate to the United States, and that his credentials addressed to the Government at Washington justify his ignoring the existence of this Government, and his regarding these States as an appendage of the country to which he is accredited."[1]

The French consular agent, Arthur Laren, had been appointed to act in the place of Baron de St. André at Charleston, and in turn St. André had been appointed to act temporarily in place of Consul Belligny, whose exequatur had been issued under the old government. In the same month of May, when Cridland's appointment at Mobile was being trailed to Washington, Laren's authority to act as

---

[1] Pickett Papers, Benjamin to Mason, No. 25, June 11, 1863; *O.R.N.*, Ser. 2, Vol. III, pp. 796–802; Bonham, pp. 154 ff., gives a detailed account of Cridland's dismissal; see also F.O. Amer., Vol. 909, Cridland to Russell, No. 10, May 29, 1863.

consul was being investigated. Benjamin found that Laren had been commissioned by Marquis of Montholon, French consul-general at New York, by the authority of the French minister, Mercier, at Washington, and that further, Baron de St. André, temporarily absent from Charleston, had recently been commissioned by the same authorities, without the knowledge and consent of the Confederate government. On June 3 Benjamin forbade Laren to exercise consular functions without Confederate consent; on June 10 he issued the circular referred to above; and on the same day he wrote Slidell a strong letter of protest similar to the one he sent Mason concerning Cridland, a copy of which was to be presented to De Lhuys. "The assumption of a right by his imperial Majesty's functionaries in the United States to exercise power within this Confederacy plainly ignores the existence of this Government, and implies that the relations which formerly existed between those functionaries and French officials at the port of Charleston continue to exist unimpaired by the secession of the State of South Carolina, the formation of this Government, and the war now pending. It is the assertion on the part of Mr. Mercier and Mr. Montholon of a right, by virtue of their credentials to the Washington Government, to exercise such powers as we can never permit to be assumed within our own country by foreign agents not accredited to us and officially recognized by our Government." All such practices must cease.[1]

However, as Benjamin explained, France was only a slight offender, and the situation was soon settled satisfactorily. But the war on England was just getting under way. Fullerton and Walker at Savannah and Charleston were busily engaged at this moment in showing active contempt for the rights and authority of the Confederacy.

The consuls from the very beginning, as we have noted, had been active in behalf of their countrymen who had by force of public opinion or the draft acts been caught in military service;[2] and though

[1] Pickett Papers, Benjamin to Slidell, No. 18, June 10, 1863; O.R.N., Ser. 2, Vol. III, pp. 792–96.

[2] See, e.g., F.O. Amer., Vols. 781, 788, 843, 844, 846, 848, 849, 906, 909, passim; Bonham, passim.

there had been friction and public resentment against this presumptuous intervention by representatives of governments which ignored the Confederacy, the Confederate government had almost always up until 1863 freed from Confederate service any person whom the consuls claimed as a fellow-subject.

The position of the Confederate government on this point was officially stated on several occasions before 1863. Secretary of War Randolph in August, 1862,[1] in a letter to British Consul Magee of Mobile, who had complained that the Confederate enrolling officers were conscripting British subjects, had said: "I have telegraphed Major W. G. Swanson as follows, 'Instruct your enrolling officers, and especially those at Mobile, not to enroll foreigners unless they are permanent residents of the Confederate States; and that the oath of the party supported by the oath of one credible witness is deemed by the Department sufficient proof in such cases.'" Three weeks later Randolph wrote Magee again that "foreigners are not subject to conscription unless permanent residents of the Confederate States, and are invariably discharged when improperly enrolled."[2] Secretary of State Benjamin had just before this date assured Bunch that only foreigners who were domiciled—that is, become permanent residents—would be forced to serve under the conscription law.[3] Assistant Secretary of War J. A. Campbell wrote Bunch, who was protesting against the conscription of one James E. Haley, citing laws, orders, and practices of the Confederate government which established the principle that "foreigners not domiciled in the Confederate States are not liable to enrollment"; that according to orders No. 82 "domicile in the Confederate States consists in residence with intention permanently to remain in those states and to abandon domicile elsewhere. Long residence of itself does not constitute domicile. A person may acquire domicile in less than one year, and he may not acquire it in twenty years' residence. If there is a determination to return to the native country and to retain the domicile there, no length of residence can confer domicile."[4]

[1] O.R., Ser. 4, Vol. II, p. 70.   [2] Ibid., p. 84.
[3] F.O. Amer., Vol. 843, Bunch to Russell, No. 77, June 3, 1863.
[4] O.R., Ser. 4, Vol. II, pp. 238–40.

For a long time the British consuls were almost universally successful in obtaining the release of British subjects from both state and Confederate military organizations; the governments allowed the consuls great latitude in deciding who were British subjects and who were domiciled.[1] So men who were actually domiciled, expatriated Irishmen, who hated England and never expected to live elsewhere than in America, suddenly became affectionate with the "auld country" and proved by the aid of the consul that they were not "permanent residents" and were not subject to conscription.

This state of affairs could not last where public opinion was growing hostile to England and to English subjects, especially where these subjects were usually merchants who profiteered without mercy on blockade goods and necessities. Then, too, the grinding necessity of war called for all available man-power. With this resentment against England and Englishmen, and the need of man-power working together, the conscription net both for state and for Confederate military organizations began to enmesh Englishmen too tightly for them to escape. The honeymoon was over. The Confederate government did not change its principle that only domiciled foreigners were subject to conscription; it merely ceased to allow the much-resented consuls who bore exequaturs from the enemy government to decide the matter of domiciliation, and assumed to decide this matter for itself. A conflict was thereby made inevitable. But as if this were not enough fuel for explosion, Lord John Russell betook it upon himself to throw powder on the coals.

In the summer of 1861 the Foreign Office, under the advice of the law officers of the crown, had sent out liberal instructions that the British government could not interfere to prevent her citizens who were domiciled in the Confederacy from being enrolled in Confederate or state military organizations.[2] Later, however, Russell began

[1] See, e.g., F.O. Amer., Vol. 788, Mure to Russell, No. 18, April 28, 1861; *ibid.*, Mure to Russell, No. 31, July 11, 1861; *ibid.*, Vol. 781, Bunch to Russell, No. 129, Nov. 9, 1861; *ibid.*, Vol. 846, Cridland to Russell, Nos. 5 and 6, March 24 and 25, 1862; *ibid.*, Vol. 849, Molyneaux to Russell, No. 25, Nov. 12, 1862; *ibid.*, Vol. 848, Magee to Russell, No. 35, Nov. 17, 1862—all give a picture of much difficulty but of final success in obtaining the release of British subjects.

[2] *Ibid.*, Vol. 781, Russell to Bunch, No. 92, July 31, 1861.

issuing orders to his consuls to protest against the forcible enrolment of British subjects in Confederate or state organizations.[1] This indicated a changing view on the part of the British government, and it soon culminated in a complete and unmitigated denial of the right of the Confederacy to enrol a British subject even though he was a permanent resident. The whole matter of domiciliation was in fact brushed aside. On October 11, 1862, Russell sent out a circular to his consuls destined to be one of the most important factors in the final expulsion of the British consuls. "British subjects domiciled only by residence," said Russell's circular, "in the so-called Confederate States cannot be forcibly enlisted in the military service of those states by virtue of an ex post facto law, when no municipal law existed at the time of the establishment of the domicile rendering them liable to such services. . . . . The plainest notion of reason and justice forbids that a foreigner, admitted to reside for peaceful and commercial purposes in a state forming a part of a Federal Union, should be suddenly and without warning compelled by the state to take an active part in hostility against other states which, when he became domiciled were members of one and the same Confederacy, which states moreover, have threatened to treat as rebels and not as prisoners of war, all who may fall into their hands." Finally, said Russell, the British subjects who have been forcibly enrolled "are forbidden under severe penalty of the Queen's proclamation to take any part in the civil war now raging in America. . . . ." In short, despite the recognition of southern belligerent rights, the British government did not recognize the right of the Confederacy to the belligerent right generally sanctioned by international law, of requiring military service of domiciled aliens—because the struggle was a civil war.[2]

The spring and summer of 1863 saw far-reaching efforts on the part of both Confederate and state governments to strengthen and reinforce their badly shattered armies. Every southern state reorganized its troops for local defense[3] and called upon all able-bodied men, including domiciled British subjects, for service. The states

[1] *Ibid.*, Vol. 909, Moore to Russell, No. 6, Jan. 11, 1862.

[2] *Ibid.*, Vol. 848, Oct. 11, 1862.

[3] Owsley, *State Rights*, chap. i.

promptly ran afoul of the British consuls armed with Russell's instructions just quoted.

Joe Brown issued a proclamation and General Wayne issued general order No. 16 for a draft on August 4 in case the eight thousand state quota was not filled by volunteers at that date. This draft was to include all able-bodied men residents of Georgia not in Confederate service.[1] Vice-Consul Allen Fullerton promptly challenged the right of Georgia's doughty governor to force British subjects into the militia. In a long letter of July 22, 1863, he wrote Brown that "Her Majesty's Government acknowledges the right of a foreign state to claim the service of British subjects resident within its limits for the purpose of maintaining internal order (in other words to act as local police force), and even to a limited extent, to defend against local invasion by a foreign power the places of their residence; but they deny the claim to service beyond this," and he had advised his countrymen to that effect. It might be, he wrote, that the militia to which they belonged would be turned over to the Confederacy and become involved in actual combat with the United States. This would be forcing them into a serious position. If not killed or maimed in battle, "they would be liable to be treated as rebels and traitors and not as prisoners of war"; and, finally, if they escaped all this they should be answerable to the British government by severe penalty for violation of the neutrality proclamation of the Queen.[2]

Considering that Fullerton's statement that British subjects caught fighting in Confederate organizations would be treated "as rebels and traitors" was equivalent to calling the Confederate Army and its government "rebels and traitors" and hence an insult, Brown's reply to the British Consul on August 8, 1863, was calm and restrained. It was long, well reasoned, and was meant to show that the service required of British residents was only for limited local defense, to repel possible invasion of raiders. While it was calm, the resentment at the attitude of Great Britain toward the Confederacy was apparent. "While Her Majesty's Government has constantly refused to recognize the existence of the Government of the Confederate States," wrote Brown, "her subjects have enjoyed its

[1] *O.R.*, Ser. 4, Vol. II, pp. 632–42.   [2] *Ibid.*, p. 657.

protection; and while she refuses to hold any diplomatic relations with us, you, as her representative, are permitted to represent her interests here and to be heard for the protection of her subjects and their property." Nothing less than the service asked could be expected of the British subjects thus protected. It was "their duty to aid in the maintenance of internal order and in the protection of their domiciles and the localities where they are situated when assailed by the troops of the United States Government or depart from the States and seek protection elsewhere." If they elected to leave the state rather than render this service, "free egress will in no case be denied them."[1]

On August 17, 1863, Fullerton, more arrogant than before, replied that Brown misinterpreted him if he thought a British subject could be compelled to perform any duty at all, even that of defending his home against the United States in case of invasion. "Such service," he wrote paraphrasing Lord Russell's instructions of October 11, 1862, "might be rendered by them in the event of a war by a foreign power, but not in a civil war like that which now rages on this continent. Her Majesty's Government consider that the plainest notions of reason and justice forbid that a foreigner admitted to reside for peaceful purposes in a state forming part of a federal union should be compelled by that state to take an active part in hostilities against other states which when he became a resident were members of one and the same Confederacy." He conceded the right to perform local police duty, but no more. "I have consequently, under instructions, felt myself compelled to advise those drafted to acquiesce in the duty until they are required to leave their immediate homes or meet the United States forces in actual conflict; in that event to throw down their arms" rather than violate the Queen's proclamation of neutrality, "trusting to my interference in their behalf with the Government at Richmond." "I am instructed to remonstrate in the strongest terms," concluded Fullerton. "Should these remonstrances fail," he continued, "the Governments in Europe interested in this question will unite in making such representations as will secure aliens their desired exemptions."[2]

[1] *Ibid.*, pp. 698–701.   [2] *Ibid.*, pp. 729–30.

In his correspondence thus far Fullerton had trod with leaden feet upon all the sensibilities of southerners. He had by implication called them "rebels and traitors"; he had denied that the United States was a "foreign power"—giving a lie to all the southern contentions of state sovereignty and the legality of secession; he had advised enlisted men who claimed to be British subjects—though the proof had not been established by legal process—to throw down their arms in time of battle; and, finally, he had read part of Russell's instructions which menaced the Confederacy with a joint action between England and other nations.

Brown could not forbear a stinging reply. "You virtually deny," said the Governor on August 26, "that the United States is a foreign power and claim that Georgia is still a component part of the government of the United States. You have probably been influenced in your persistence in this error by the forbearance of the Government and people of the Confederate States in permitting Her Majesty's consuls to remain among us in the exercise of the functions of a position to which they were originally accredited by the Government of the United States." He would not attempt to prove to the British Consul that the United States was a foreign hostile power. He would "dismiss this part of the controversy with the single remark, that if your pretensions be correct, your appeal for the protection of British subjects resident within this State should have been made to the Government at Washington and not to me." Brown assured the Consul again that the door was open for all to depart who did not want to remain in the state and render military service. If they did elect to remain, however, and followed the Consul's advice to throw down their arms in battle while still in the services of Georgia, "they would be promptly dealt with as citizens of this State would be should they be guilty of such dishonoring delinquency."[1]

Another letter or two was passed between them, and Fullerton turned to the Confederate authorities for relief—to his sorrow. In the meanwhile, Brown published the correspondence and further aired it by submitting it to the Georgia legislature, which promptly

[1] *Ibid.*, pp. 755–58.

sustained him by legislative enactment to enrol foreigners and finally to expel all who refused military service.[1]

The southern press howled with anger at Fullerton's pretensions. They had resented the implied insult in the presence of a British consul whose exequatur came from Lincoln and whose orders came from the British ambassador at Washington. But here was open insult—contemptuous, patronizing insult added to constructive insult and injury. Expel Fullerton! Expel all the British consuls! was the cry. Moore and Cridland had already been discredited for contemptuous disobedience to the orders of the Confederacy; now order the whole lot of them from the country![2]

This was a large price to pay in order to obtain the release of only twelve men who claimed a doubtful allegiance to England.[3]

Consul Lynn at Galveston, Texas, had a similar controversy with Governor McMurrah of Texas and Confederate officers there over the enrolment of British subjects in state and Confederate organizations.[4]

In all the southern states there was the same effort at enrolling alien residents, and it would have precipitated a bitter controversy with the other British consuls resident in those states had not those consuls already been silenced, Moore and Cridland at Richmond and Mobile by expulsion and Coppell at New Orleans by the capture of that city. As it was, only three vice-consuls had an opportunity of raising a quarrel with the state governors over the enrolment of British subjects: Fullerton at Savannah, Walker at Charleston, and McRae at Wilmington. Fullerton, as has just been noted, had entered the fray with Brown. McRae, who was a Confederate citizen, did not become involved but kept quiet. Walker, however, the successor of Bunch, whose exequatur had been revoked by his own gov-

[1] See Bonham, pp. 138–50, for controversy.

[2] See *Savannah Republican, Charleston Mercury, Richmond Enquirer, Richmond Whig, Montgomery Advertiser*, and *Mobile Register* for September and October, 1863; cf. Bonham, p. 149.

[3] F.O. Amer., Vol. 909, Fullerton to Russell, No. 15, Aug. 22, 1863.

[4] *Ibid.*, Lynn to Russell, No. 9, April 18, 1863; *ibid.*, Lynn to Russell, No. 13, Aug. 12, 1863.

ernment,[1] became involved in a tangle with Generals Beauregard and Jordan and Governor Bonham in his attempt to carry out Russell's instructions, which denied flatly that the state or Confederate governments had a right to enrol in military service even a domiciled British subject.

The call of Seddon upon the states to raise a fresh quota of limited-service troops and the bombardment of Charleston caused Governor Bonham to insist upon military service from all alien residents, and the state law defined as residents those who had lived in South Carolina six months. Walker, who objected to this law, promptly cited former Governor Pickens' orders excusing all aliens from service as an equitable and just ruling. Unfortunately, he, like Fullerton, quoted at length from Lord John Russell's circular, contending that aliens could not be expected to participate in a "civil war," especially when they might be treated not as prisoners of war but as "rebels and traitors."[2]

Bonham, backed by his attorney-general, Hayne, responded to Walker's tactless protest with restrained resentment. Pickens' order excusing aliens, he wrote, was purely a matter of accommodation and not of law, and he was under no obligations of renewing the order. As for the Consul's unfortunate statement that British subjects were liable to be treated as "rebels and traitors," it had no ground, in fact "so far there had been no attempt to treat thus the citizens of any Confederate State." Bonham refused to issue an order excusing British subjects from militia duty.[3]

On the following day Vice-Consul Walker wrote Russell that "the disasters which have of late been sustained by the so called Confederate States have tended in a great measure to increase the bitterness towards Englishmen, to which all persons in this locality have, of late, been in the habit of giving utterance." He complained that British subjects were being discharged from their employment and were being sent to jail as conscripts. Referring evidently to his correspondence with Bonham, he remarked with an injured air of piety

[1] See E. D. Adams, I, 184 ff.

[2] F.O. Amer., Vol. 907, Part II, Walker to Russell, Nos. 122 and 123, Sept. 11, 1863.

[3] *Ibid.*

and innocence: "I sometimes detect an irritable captiousness on the part of public officers," but that he "must confine this remark to certain state officers, for in no case have I met with any discourtesy from any officers of the Government at Richmond. . . . ."[1]

Walker soon renewed his protests to Bonham. The Governor in reply cited Confederate Judge McGrath's recent decision on the matter of enrolling aliens in military service, according to which aliens must serve in the military organization of their district and in any port of the state for defense.[2]

Then, contrary to Bonham's advice, which was backed by Confederate authority, Walker like Fullerton on failing to obtain prompt release for his conscript countrymen openly advised all British subjects not to serve in the militia except for police purposes; that "if it should so happen that the militia after being organized should be brought into conflict with the forces of the United States" either as militia or as part of the Confederate organization, "the service required would be such as British subjects could not be expected to perform"; that they should, in short, throw down their arms and refuse to serve at the critical moment in battle.[3]

The response of Bonham to the attitude of Walker, on the one hand, and to the public hostility to British subjects, on the other, was a message to the legislature, which he had convened for providing forces, in which he urged that "all aliens who have declared their purpose to become citizens, as also such as are domiciled amongst us, enjoying the protection of our laws, should be included" in the state forces.[4] On September 30 the legislature responded with a law which met the Governor's wishes.[5]

With Moore and Cridland already officially "expelled" for over-reaching the authority of the Confederacy or, perhaps, official contempt, the remaining British consular agents already in conflict with

---

[1] *Ibid.*, No. 112, Aug. 21, 1863.   [2] Bonham, p. 134.

[3] F.O. Amer., Vol. 907, Part II, Walker to Russell, Nos. 122–23. The correspondence concerning British subjects with Bonham and the Confederate military and civil officers is included in these dispatches; cf. Bonham, pp. 130–37.

[4] *Ibid.*, p. 135; F.O. Amer., Vol. 907, Part II, Walker to Russell, No. 128, Sept. 24, 1863. Walker relates the situation.

[5] Bonham, p. 135.

KING COTTON DIPLOMACY

the state governments were bound to run head-on in collision with the Confederate government. This collision took place in October. But before recounting the final explosion which resulted in the expulsion of the consuls, let us take brief note of developments concerning the withdrawal of the Confederate commissioners. It has already been seen that after the failure of joint intervention and of the efforts of the Confederate commissioners to get England and France to repudiate the blockade, public opinion as expressed in newspapers and Congress demanded the withdrawal of the commissioners and the expulsion of consuls as companion measures.

The Confederate government, having better first-hand knowledge than the public of the official British attitude, began to fret under British official discourtesy earlier than the public. On October 28, 1862, Benjamin, commenting upon Russell's discourtesy of the previous summer, observed that "it is lamentable that at this late period in the nineteenth century, a nation so enlightened as Great Britain should have failed yet to discover that a principal cause of the dislike and hatred toward England, of which complaints are rife in her Parliament and in her press, is the offensive arrogance of some of her public men."[1] Benjamin advised Mason, two days later, that the discourtesy shown him would be conclusive in determining Davis "to direct your withdrawal from your mission but for other considerations," namely, the belief that the British government did not represent the opinion of the British people on this question. He further advised Mason significantly, in connection with Russell's discourtesy, that "the President has further under consideration the propriety of sending out of the country all British consuls and consular agents."[2] On January 15, 1863, Benjamin wrote Slidell that "it is not to be denied that there is great and increasing irritation in the public mind on this side in consequence of our unjust treatment by foreign powers, and it will require all the influence of the President to prevent some explosion and to maintain that calm and self-contained

[1] Pickett Papers, Benjamin to Mason, No. 8, Oct. 28, 1862; *O.R.N.*, Ser. 2, Vol. III, pp. 581–82.

[2] Pickett Papers, Benjamin to Mason, No. 9, Oct. 31, 1862; *O.R.N.*, Ser. 2, Vol. III, pp. 584–88.

attitude which is alone becoming in such circumstances. We should probably not be very averse to the recall of Mr. Mason, who has been discourteously treated by Earl Russell," were not the matter of the ironclads and purchases of supplies in England endangered by such an act.[1]

Two months later Benjamin wrote Slidell about the serious efforts being made in the Senate to withdraw all commissioners from Europe. Resolutions had finally been passed asking such withdrawal with the exception of Slidell in France. "The irritation against Great Britain is fast increasing," said Benjamin, and the administration was having serious difficulty in satisfying the Senate that the purchase of supplies and ships of war in England made the withdrawal of Mason a hazardous undertaking.[2]

At length this resentment against Europe, and especially against the discourtesy of the British government toward Mason took form. Right in the midst of the public commotion attending the expulsion of Moore and Cridland the Senate refused to ratify the nomination of L. Q. C. Lamar as commissioner to Russia (Lamar was already in Europe under temporary appointment but had not proceeded to Russia as it was considered useless). Benjamin assured Lamar that the action of the Senate had no personal bearings but that it was the result of "a deep-seated feeling of irritation at what is considered to be unjust and unfair conduct of neutral powers toward this Confederacy [which] prevails among our people."[3]

On August 4, 1863, Benjamin, as we noted in our last chapter, terminated the mission of Mason in England. The Roebuck-Lindsay debates with Russell and Palmerston's facetious attitude convinced Davis and Benjamin that England would never recognize the Confederacy as long as the United States could wage war. Following the expulsion of Cridland and Moore and coming in the midst of the Brown-Fullerton and Bonham-Walker controversy, Mason's with-

[1] Pickett Papers, Benjamin to Slidell, No. 11, Jan. 15, 1863; *O.R.N.*, Ser. 2, Vol. III, pp. 654-56.

[2] Pickett Papers, Benjamin to Slidell, No. 15, March 26, 1863; *O.R.N.*, Ser. 2, Vol. III, pp. 726-28.

[3] Pickett Papers, Benjamin to Lamar, No. 2, Jan. 11, 1863; *O.R.N.*, Ser. 2, Vol. III, p. 796.

drawal was a final yielding to public sentiment. Benjamin wrote Mason that the recent debates in Parliament convinced Davis of the futility of maintaining an envoy in London, and that "under these circumstances your continued residence in London is neither conducive to the interests nor consistent with the dignity of this Government. . . . ."[1]

The rising tide of resentment, which resulted in the revocation of the exequaturs of Moore and Cridland, the refusal of the Senate to ratify Lamar's commission as special envoy to Russia, and the withdrawal of Mason from England, swept on higher with the publication of the Brown-Fullerton and Walker-Bonham correspondence. The Confederacy had been treated with bare courtesy in England, and within the Confederacy the British government had shown an arrogant disrespect for its authority by the appointment of consuls without the knowledge and consent of the Confederacy. That had brought about a universal clamor that all British consuls should be expelled; but Davis had withstood this clamor. Then Fullerton and Walker denied publicly the right of the state or Confederacy to conscript a British subject domiciled in the South, and publicly advised these subjects when brought into battle against the United States to throw down their arms. This advice had been given upon the urgent instructions of Lord Russell himself, and this fact, too, was made public in August and September, 1863, and public sentiment waxed rapidly more stern and resentful against England.

So Benjamin—and perhaps Davis, who bowed very slowly to the dictates of public opinion—was only waiting his chance to rid the Confederacy of the remaining British consular agents. Like Moore, Fullerton and Walker finally got caught in Benjamin's trap. The Confederate Secretary of State could not with dignity go outside his jurisdiction and enter into the controversies between the consuls and the governors of South Carolina and Georgia, but he could patiently wait until the local authorities brought this controversy to him. This eventually occurred when some of Walker's correspondence with the state authorities of South Carolina was sent to Benjamin for an

[1] Pickett Papers, Benjamin to Mason, No. 30, Aug. 4, 1863; *O.R.N.*, Ser. 2, Vol. III, p. 852.

opinion. Benjamin seized the opportunity promptly and published a reply in the *Mercury* of October 3 in which he sustained the state of South Carolina. Walker's contentions that domiciled Englishmen were not subject to military service and that they should throw down their arms, said Benjamin sharply, "do not meet with the approval of this Department. While the Governor claims no military service from sojourners, those who have acquired residence in the Confederacy are bound by law to aid in its defense."[1]

Benjamin doubtless intended this as the preliminary step in expelling Walker and Fullerton. Fullerton, however, hastened the matter by writing Benjamin a letter on October 1 and 3—evidently received after the publication of his disapproval of Walker's stand—in which he protested against the enrolment of British subjects Fullerton cited Russell's instructions and informed Benjamin that he had under these instructions advised British conscripts that they should "acquiesce in the service required so long as it is restricted to the maintenance of internal peace and order," but that "whenever they shall be brought into actual conflict with the forces of the United States, whether under the State or Confederate government, the service so required is such as they can not be expected to perform."[2] Benjamin recognized here the same line of arrogant and tactless argument which Fullerton had pursued in his controversy with Brown. Knowing Fullerton's arguments and remembering his threat to Brown of foreign interference in case aliens were forced into military service, Benjamin did not give him an opportunity to get to the threatening stage. Both Fullerton and Walker had come or had been brought by state initiative within his jurisdiction. His bloodthirsty official ax fell upon Fullerton's as well as upon Walker's neck at once.

This letter from Fullerton reached Benjamin probably on October 7. Davis was on his way via Atlanta to Bragg's army at Chattanooga and could not be consulted. Accordingly Benjamin did some-

[1] Bonham, pp. 130–31; F.O. Amer., Vol. 907, Part II, Walker to Russell, No. 136, Oct. 3, 1863.

[2] Pickett Papers, Benjamin to President, inclosure, Oct. 8, 1863; *O.R.N.*, Ser. 2, Vol. III, pp. 928–30.

thing that no other man in the Confederacy would have dared do—in fact, as one writer says,[1] no cabinet officer ever before had done such a thing, and only Lansing since has attempted it with fatal results—he summoned Davis' cabinet and they by quick and unanimous decision voted to expel not only Fullerton but all the British consuls. The cabinet expressed the opinion that it was very fortunate to be able thus to satisfy public sentiment, "which would have been quite restive under their continued residence here after Mr. Mason's departure from England."[2] As Fullerton had been the most arrogant offender of the three—Walker, McRae, and Fullerton—Benjamin directed the letter of expulsion to him, and sent copies to the others with instructions to shake the dust of the Confederacy off their heels. After citing Fullerton's and Walker's contention that British subjects could not be legally enrolled, and their advice to them to throw down their arms, all based upon instructions from the British Foreign Office, Benjamin said that "it thus appears that the consular agents of the British government have been instructed not to confine themselves to an appeal for redress either to courts of justice or to this government whenever they may conceive that grounds exist for complaint against the Confederate authorities in their treatment of British subjects (an appeal which has in no case been made without receiving just consideration) but that they assume the power of determining for themselves whether enlisted soldiers of the Confederacy are properly bound to its service; that they even arrogate the right to interfere directly with the execution of Confederate laws and to advise soldiers of the Confederate armies to throw down their arms in the face of the enemy. This assumption of jurisdiction by foreign officials within the territory of the Confederacy, and this encroachment on its sovereignty, can not be tolerated for a moment, and the President has had no hesitation in directing that all consuls and consular agents of the British Government be notified that they can no longer be permitted to exercise their functions or even to reside within the limits of the Confederacy."[3]

Benjamin wrote Slidell a long dispatch on the same date on which

[1] Bonham, p. 232.   [2] *Ibid.*

[3] *Ibid.;* F.O. Amer., Vol. 907, Part II, Walker to Russell, No. 139, Oct. 15, 1863.

he dismissed the British consuls. He told Slidell to reach the British government by the publication of his dispatch, and also to reassure Napoleon that French subjects and consuls were not affected by the action of the Confederate government. He summed up all the history and status of the consuls in the Confederacy and the indictment against them and their government which might be characterized by one phrase—arrogant contempt for Confederate sovereignty.[1]

Both the people and the government of the Confederacy could see in England's overreaching of Confederate authority in the matter of enlistment of British subjects and control over consuls resident in the Confederacy from the United States capital, the traditional "strong hand" of the British government in dealing with weak or backward people. It was maddening.

This breaking-off of all relations with Great Britain indicated a profound revolution in southern sentiment. Cridland, who remained at Mobile in an unofficial capacity—though he continued to observe and report to Russell—wrote on November 16, 1863, that "the hatred publicly expressed against England by the press and the people who are informed by editors and others that Great Britain is the principal cause of the war makes it far from pleasant to be known here as a British subject and in some instances no language or threat seems sufficient to express the growing enmity."[2] Benjamin, long suffering, suave, and patient, had come to harbor profound resentment against England. On January 9, 1864, he wrote Hotze that "the British cabinet deemed it best for Great Britain that some hundreds of thousands of human beings should be slaughtered on this continent that her people might reap profit and become more powerful." England, he continued, had discouraged all attempts on the part of France to bring peace—the English government had, in fact, he said, become "alarmed lest peace should be restored before the United States had become sufficiently depleted of blood and treasure, and used active efforts to secure a continuance of hostilities. These things will long be remembered by a people whose sym-

[1] See Pickett Papers, Benjamin to Slidell, No. 25, Oct. 8, 1863; *O.R.N.*, Ser. 2, Vol. III, pp. 922–28.

[2] F.O. Amer., Vol. 909, No. 31.

pathies in favor of Great Britain were of the warmest character before their feelings became first chilled and then alienated by the
conduct of a cabinet which has betrayed the cause of humanity
wherever power has sought to repress right."[1]

This break with England marked the final downfall of King
Cotton. The government turned to the Mexican venture of Napoleon as their last chance to obtain European aid, while most of the
people expected no aid, but put their backs to the wall to fight it out.

The ill feeling in the South against England was now equal to that
of the North, so that when the Civil War ended England had earned
the hostility of a continent, and southern people could chuckle in
grim satisfaction when the United States robbed England of fifteen
million dollars in the Alabama claims.

[1] Pickett Papers, No. 13, Jan. 9, 1864; *O.R.N.*, Ser. 2, Vol. III, pp. 993–96.

CHAPTER XV

MANN'S MISSION TO ROME

Following the withdrawal of Mason and the expulsion of the consuls, A. Dudley Mann undertook at the instance of the Confederate government a mission to the Vatican. Ostensibly, the mission was to thank the Pope for his letters to the two American archbishops inviting them to urge peace upon the country. But there was behind this graceful gesture the definite purpose of obtaining the influence of His Holiness in a diplomatic way, and in preventing the enlistment of Catholic aliens in the American army.

In fact, it is this last object which gives to Mann's mission a rather practical turn—unlike so many things undertaken by that sounder of sonorous phrases. As has been observed earlier one of Henry Hotze's widened activities after De Leon's recall was his organized campaigns against Federal recruiting. Hotze's work began earlier than Mann's but continued along with Mann's and supplied part of the machinery through which Mann could reach the Irish Catholics.

Several agents were dispatched by Benjamin to be employed in Ireland to "educate" the Irish and dissuade them from emigrating to America where they became cannon fodder. The first sent over was Lieutenant J. L. Capston. His work was to use "all legitimate means to enlighten the population as to the true nature and character of the contest now waged on this continent, with the view of defeating the attempts made by the agents of the United States to obtain in Ireland recruits for their armies." He was to picture to the ignorant and trusting Irish peasants "the fate of their unhappy countrymen who have already fallen victims of the arts of the Federals" who had induced them to emigrate as laborers only to thrust them into the armies as soon as they had reached America. He was to explain to them "that they will be called on to meet Irishmen in battle, and thus imbrue their hands in the blood of their own friends and perhaps kinsmen, in a quarrel which does not concern them and in which all the feelings of a common humanity should induce them to refuse taking part against us." A contrast was to be drawn between the North and South in their treatment of Catholic foreigners as exemplified in the Know-Nothing party, which was chiefly northern. These views were to be urged "through the press, by mixing with the people themselves, and by disseminating the facts amongst persons who have influence with the people."[1]

The next man to be sent for the purpose of influencing the Irish was the Rev. Father (John) Bannon, Confederate chaplain. His special function was to appeal to the Irish people through the Catholic clergy. Bannon was to go to Rome, if he felt this to be necessary, for the purpose of obtaining such sanction from the sovereign pontiff as would strengthen his position and give efficiency to his action.[2]

Several others were dispatched on similar missions, so that there was quite an organization in Ireland. These agents were actively at work upon Irish opinion by the time that Mann made his journey to Rome to obtain a larger sanction for such work. Bannon, especially, seems to have been well received in Ireland, and he was permitted to attach himself to Bishop Lynch as the latter's chaplain when the Bishop went to Rome in the interest of the Confederacy.[3]

Perhaps something was accomplished by these men, but if so it was only a drop in the bucket. The poor, naïve but combative Irish peasants would almost sell their soul for a thousand years' extra service in purgatory for the bounty of over five hundred dollars. Federal agents combed Ireland for these able-bodied paupers, and in order to avoid the open violation of international law and the British Foreign Enlistment Act recruited them as laborers rather than as soldiers. Once in America, many of them joined the army willingly and many more were entrapped in military service,[4] and

[1] Pickett Papers, Benjamin to Capston, July 3, 1863; O.R.N., Ser. 2, Vol. III, pp. 828-29.

[2] Pickett Papers, Benjamin to Bannon, Sept. 4, 1863; O.R.N., Ser. 2, Vol. III, pp. 893-95.

[3] See Pickett Papers, Hotze to Benjamin, No. 44, June 10, 1864; O.R.N., Ser. 2, Vol. III, pp. 1146-47; ibid., Bishop Lynch Correspondence.

[4] Parl. Accts. and Papers, LXII, No. 17 (1864), 1-59—investigation of fraudulent enlistments and coercions.

because of the fact that they went away in the guise of laborers the British government could never, in spite of its earnest wish to do so as a counterblast to American accusations against the ironclads, etc., do anything to check the practice.[1]

The number, principally males, which left Ireland and industrial England was great. The *Economist*[2] in 1864 reported that 30,000 Irish emigrated to America in 1861, 40,000 in 1862, 110,000 in 1863; and it estimated that 100,000 of these had enlisted in the Federal Army. In January, 1865, the *Index*[3] reported that from Liverpool alone 100,000 emigrants had gone to America during 1864, 60,560 of whom were Irish. The *London Times* estimated that the greater part of these had entered the army.

The next largest recruiting ground was Southern Germany, where able-bodied men were not held to as strict military service as in Prussia or Austria. These men were nearly all Catholics. The *Economist* estimated that up to 1864 as many as 100,000 Germans had entered the northern army.[4] Other South and Central European countries contributed considerable numbers,[5] and Mann complained bitterly that the jails and poorhouses had been swept clean by the Federal recruiting agents.

As to the total number of aliens brought over during the war and enrolled in the United States Army, mostly from Catholic countries, only estimates can be given. The *Economist*, as has been observed, estimated that 200,000 had entered the armies of the United States from Ireland and Germany by June, 1864. The *New York Herald*, March 13, 1864, placed the total number of emigrants in 1863 from Europe as nearly 200,000, and estimated that "at least one hundred and fifty thousand have joined the army."[6] Lord Clanricarde stated

[1] Parl. Deb., Lords, Ser. 3, Vol. 175, pp. 1439–54, for debates on this question.

[2] *Economist*, June 25, 1864.

[3] *Index*, Jan. 5, 1865.   [4] *Economist*, June 25, 1864.

[5] See Pickett Papers, Lamar to Benjamin, March 20, 1863; *O.R.N.*, Ser. 2, Vol. III, pp. 716–18; Pickett Papers, Mann to Benjamin, No. 97, July 7, No. 103, Aug. 20, No. 110, Oct. 12, No. 114, Nov. 5, all 1864; *O.R.N.*, Ser. 2, Vol. III, pp. 1165–68, 1188–89, 1223, 1230, respectively.

[6] Quoted in *Index*, April 7, 1864.

to Mason on May 1, 1864,[1] that at that time there were 25,000 French-Canadians in the United States Army. Lieutenant Wilkinson (Confederate States Navy) remarked about Federal recruiting in Canada that "wherever we travelled even through the remotest settlements, recruiting agents for the United States army were at work, scarcely affecting to disguise their occupation . . . .";[2] and "it has been asserted, by those who were in a position to form a correct estimate, that the British Provinces, alone, contributed 100,000 men to the Federal army. It is scarcely an exaggeration to add that the population of the civilized world was subsidized." On the basis of such contemporary compilations it seems a fairly conservative estimate to say that 300,000 men must have enlisted from Germany, Ireland, and West Britain; 100,000 from the British provinces; and 50,000 to 75,000 from the other parts of Europe. That is, between 400,000 and 500,000 mercenary troops, the bulk of whom were from impoverished Catholic countries, were by force of bounties and trickery induced into the American army. It was estimated by Admiral Porter himself that the great majority of the 80,000 seamen in the United States Navy were also aliens.[3] Seward, irritated by the British complaints of the enlistment of their nationals in the United States Army, wrote Adams on April 24, 1862, contrasting the English attitude with the "generous enthusiasm of those States which send us soldiers by hundreds of thousands to uphold the American Union."[4]

This foreign recruiting was no blind speculative venture entered into by bounty brokers, but a well-planned and well-executed policy on the part of Lincoln and Seward, who, perhaps, had been in the habit of hating the British primarily because that nation employed 30,000 Hessian soldiers to put down the American revolt in 1776. On August 8, 1862, Seward sent out to all American embassies and consulates in Europe the notorious circular No. 19 which was published

---

[1] Mason Papers, Clanricarde to Mason, May 1, 1864.

[2] Wilkinson, *Narrative of a Blockade Runner*, p. 181.

[3] *New York Sun*, March 20, 1898; *Townsend Collection of Newspaper Clippings* (Columbia University Library, New York), p. 87.

[4] U.S. Inst., Gr. Br., Vol. 18, Seward to Adams, No. 238, April 24, 1862.

in all leading papers over the Continent. In this circular Seward spoke in hyperbole of the golden opportunity for the poor European laborer. The army was only hinted at.[1] Dayton on receipt of the circular expressed elation, for he was sure that a great emigration would take place "under the inducements thus held out to laborers, and the temptations of our military service with its pay and bounties," and he felt convinced that "the exhaustive character of the struggle in which our country is engaged seems to call for some such remedy to supply the depletion."[2]

John Bigelow, consul-general at Paris, was primarily responsible for the wide circulation of this disguised advertising for soldiers. He said later[3] that all Europe was covered with a network of emigration agencies to induce men to go to America. This circular of Seward, wrote Bigelow, in later years, because of its effects upon emigration "deserves a place in this record if for no other reason than the light it throws upon the mysterious repletion of our army during the four years of war, while it was notoriously being so fearfully depleted by firearms, disease, and desertion." Seward remarked to Bigelow, apropos of this circular and the enlistment of mercenaries, that "to some extent this civil war must be a trial between the two parties to exhaust the other. The immigration of a large mass from Europe would of itself decide it."[4]

It was primarily to obtain the influence of the Pope, who had already written peace letters to Archbishop John of New York and Archbishop John Mary at New Orleans in which he had exhorted them to use their influence with the Catholic hierarchy in America to aid in bringing about peace,[5] that Mann undertook his mission. It was believed that His Holiness, who thus favored peace, might be induced to use his papal influence against enlistment of Catholic aliens in the American army. It was hoped, too, of course, that the influence of the Pope with such Catholic rulers as Leopold of Bel-

[1] U.S. Des., France, Vol. 52, Dayton to Seward, No. 191, Sept. 9, 1862.

[2] *Ibid.*   [3] Bigelow, *Retrospections*, I, 563 ff.

[4] *Ibid.*, p. 547.

[5] Pickett Papers, Oct. 18, 1862; *O.R.N.*, Ser. 2, Vol. III, p. 559.

gium and Napoleon of France might be secured. Ostensibly, as has been observed, Mann was dispatched to Rome by Davis to bear the Pope a letter from the President thanking the former for his peace letters to the archbishops of New York and New Orleans.[1]

Mann, on receipt of Benjamin's instructions to deliver the President's letter of thanks, proceeded to Rome where he arrived on November 11, 1863. He promptly obtained an interview with Cardinal Antonelli, the papal secretary of state. Antonelli expressed great sympathy and admiration for the Confederate cause and heroism. "He manifested an earnest desire for the definitive termination of hostilities," reported Mann,[2] "and observed that there was nothing the government of the Holy See could do with propriety to occasion such a result that it was not prepared to do."

Mann eagerly accepted the opening presented by this generous offer and disclosed the real purpose of his mission. He informed Antonelli that "but for the European recruits received by the North, numbering annually something like 100,000, the Lincoln Administration, in all likelihood, would have been compelled some time before this to have retired from the contest, that nearly all those recruits were from Ireland, and that Christianity had cause to weep at such fiendish destruction of life as occurred from the beguiling of those people from their homes to take up arms against citizens who had never harmed or wronged them in the slightest degree." The Cardinal was touched by the picture of innocent Catholics being led to the slaughter and intimated with considerable emotion that something might be done to stop it.

Two days later, on November 13, Mann interviewed the Pope. The latter spoke of his peace letters to the archbishops of New Orleans and New York. He had had no reply from Archbishop John Mary of New Orleans, but he had received a communication from Archbishop John of New York and the letter was very discouraging to peace. Mann told the Pope that he had come as the bearer of a

[1] Pickett Papers, Benjamin to Mann, No. 9, Sept. 23, 1863; O.R.N., Ser. 2, Vol. III, pp. 910–11.

[2] Pickett Papers, Mann to Benjamin, No. 66, Nov. 11, 1863; O.R.N., Ser. 2, Vol. III, pp. 949–50.

letter from the President thanking His Holiness for his efforts at peace. Whereupon he presented the letter, which was translated by Mann's son and secretary. "During its progress," wrote Mann under the spell of the papal grandeur,[1] "I did not cease for an instant to carefully survey the features of the sovereign Pontiff. A sweeter expression of pious affection, of tender benignity, never adorned the face of mortal man. No picture can adequately represent him when exclusively absorbed in Christian contemplation. Every sentence of the letter appeared to sensibly affect him. . . . . When the passage was reached wherein the President states, in such sublime and affecting language, 'We have offered up at the footstool of our Father who is in Heaven prayers inspired by the same feelings which animate your Holiness,' his deep sunken orbs visibly moistened were upturned toward that throne upon which ever sits the Prince of Peace, indicating that his heart was pleading for our deliverance from that causeless and merciless war which is prosecuted against us. The soul of infidelity—if, indeed, infidelity have a soul—would have melted in view of so sacred a spectacle."

Having finished reading the letter, the Pope referred to the impression spread by the United States that the war was fought for the liberation of the slaves, and he suggested that in order to combat such false representations the Confederacy should resort to some form of gradual emancipation. Mann assured the Pope that only the states had the authority and that in the proper time and way—not by the sudden release of three millions of barbarians—slavery would be abolished if it were evil.

The Pope, as had his cardinal, promised that he would do all in his power to put an end to the war, and Mann at once suggested a course by which the Pope might accomplish this end. "I availed myself of this declaration to inform his Holiness that it was not the armies of Northern birth which the South was encountering in hostile array, but that it was the armies of European creation, occasioned by the Irish and Germans, chiefly by the former, who were influenced to emigrate (by circulars from 'Lincoln and Company' to

[1] Pickett Papers, Mann to Benjamin, No. 67, Nov. 14, 1863; *O.R.N.*, Ser. 2, Vol. III, pp. 952–55.

their numerous agents abroad) ostensibly for the purpose of securing high wages but in reality to fill up the constantly depleted ranks
of our enemy; that those poor unfortunates were tempted by high
bounties (amounting to $500, $600, and $700) to enlist and take up
arms against us" and were mercilessly placed in the most exposed
positions where they were slaughtered by whole brigades. The Pope
was horrified and suggested that he would write a letter to President
Davis which might be published.

"Thus terminated," exulted Mann, "one among the most remarkable conferences that ever a foreign representative had with a potentate of the earth. And such a potentate! A potentate who wields the
consciences of 175,000,000 of the civilized race, and who is adored by
that immense number as the vice regent of Almighty God in this
sublunary sphere." Mann with all his inexhaustible store of bom-
bast and thundering words found himself almost at a loss to express
himself. He was overwhelmed at his reception by such a "potentate," and was doubtless thinking of the very practical good the
Pope could do the Confederacy by influencing the 175,000,000 of the
civilized race not to enlist in the Federal Army.

A few days later, November 19, Mann had a second interview
with Antonelli. "I intended it to be of short duration," he wrote
Benjamin,[1] "but he became so much interested in the communications which I made to him that he prolonged it for nearly an hour."
During this interview "foreign ministers were kept waiting a considerable length of time in the antechamber in order that my interview might not be disturbed." This cordial reception satisfied him
that "we have been virtually, if not practically, recognized here."
He believed strongly that the effect of the Pope's promised letter to
Davis, which would be widely published, "would be powerful upon
all the Catholic governments in both hemispheres," and they in
turn could be induced to bring their influence to bear upon Protes-
tant governments. Mann was especially hopeful that in this way
Leopold of Belgium would influence England and Prussia in behalf
of the South.

As for the chief object—the restriction of emigrants going to

[1] Pickett Papers, No. 68, Nov. 21, 1862; *O.R.N.*, Ser. 2, Vol. III, pp. 963–64.

America to enlist—Mann thought he had accomplished it. "I have reason," he wrote, "to believe that what I have said in high places in relation to Irish emigration to New York were words in season."[1]

On December 8 Antonelli transmitted to Mann the Pope's letter to Davis, which thanked the President for his letter and spoke of the efforts of the Pope in behalf of peace in his letter to his two archbishops in New Orleans and New York. "And it has been very gratifying to us to recognize, illustrious and honorable sir," continued the papal message, "that you and your people are animated by the same desire for peace and tranquillity, which we had so earnestly inculcated in our aforesaid letters to the venerable brethren above named." But the Pope could not say as much for the North, "Oh, that the other people also of the States and their rulers, considering seriously how cruel and how deplorable is this internecine war, would receive and embrace the counsels of peace and tranquillity."[2]

Mann was more elated than ever, if possible, over this letter, for "in the very direction of this communication there is a positive recognition of our Government." His reason for believing this to be an official recognition of the Confederacy was that it was addressed "to the Illustrious and Honorable Jefferson Davis, President of the Confederate States of America." "Thus," exulted the Honorable Ambrose Dudley Mann, "we are acknowledged, by as high an authority as this world contains, to be an independent power of the earth.

"I congratulate you, I congratulate the President, I congratulate his Cabinet; in short," he gasped, "I congratulate all my true-hearted countrymen and countrywomen, upon this benign event. The hand of the Lord has been in it, and eternal glory and praise be to His holy and righteous name."[3]

Mann would hasten, he continued,[4] to publish the letter widely. After attending to this on the Continent he would proceed to Eng-

[1] Ibid.

[2] Pickett Papers, Mann to Benjamin, No. 70, Dec. 12, 1863, inclosure; O.R.N., Ser. 2, Vol. III, pp. 974–75.

[3] Pickett Papers, Mann to Benjamin, No. 69, Dec. 9, 1863; O.R.N., Ser. 2, Vol. III, pp. 973–74.

[4] Ibid.

land, for "the Christmas season will be a propitious period for excit-
ing the sympathies of the British public in behalf of the sublime
initiative of the Pope. The people of England are never better in
heart than during the joyous anniversary of the birth of Him whose
cause was 'Peace on earth, good will toward men.' "[1] By this time
Benjamin must have felt that Mann was bent upon proselyting him.
Mann joined Mason and Slidell in Paris, and they agreed to publish
the Pope's letter at once.[2]

Two weeks later, after the widespread publication of the Pope's
letter to President Davis, Mann wrote Benjamin a glowing account
of the effect of the letter. "In all intelligent British circles," he announced, "our recognition by the sovereign Pontiff is considered as
formal and complete," and this recognition would presently exercise
incalculable influence. "It is believed," he continued, "that the
earnest wishes expressed by his Holiness will be regarded as little less
than imperative commands by that vast portion of the human family
which esteem him as the Vicar of Christ." If this should prove correct, "then the war spirit of Lincoln and Company will receive a
scorching that will so enfeeble it as to utterly impair its powers for
persistence. I have an abiding confidence in such a result." But the
influence of the Pope, it was hoped, was not confined to Catholics.
"Under the benign movement of *Pio Nono* there are encouraging
indications that Protestantism throughout Europe is preparing to
make a demonstration adverse to the prosecution of hostilities."

Mann was in England at the writing of this letter, and was evidently much impressed by the propagandist meetings got up by
Spence and others, and by the organization of the Independence
Association in London and Manchester. At any rate, he was in a
state of ecstatic optimism, and he could "safely assure" Benjamin
that "we never occupied so high a position in European esteem as
we do at present."[3]

[1] Pickett Papers, Mann to Benjamin, No. 70, Dec. 12, 1863; *O.R.N.*, Ser. 2, Vol.
III, pp. 974–75.

[2] Pickett Papers, Mann to Benjamin, No. 71, Dec. 28, 1863; *O.R.N.*, Ser. 2, Vol.
III, pp. 985–86.

[3] Pickett Papers, Mann to Benjamin, No. 74, Jan. 15, 1864; *O.R.N.*, Ser. 2, Vol.
III, p. 1000.

Mann's fervid enthusiasm was not shared by the other Confederate agents, who scarcely referred to the papal letter in their correspondence; and Davis and Benjamin, the latter of whom could
scarcely conceal his weariness and patronizing contempt for Mann's
childish credulity and vanity, harbored no illusions. On receipt of
the commissioner's voluminous accounts of his mission and its overwhelming diplomatic results, Benjamin wrote him that "the President has been gratified at learning the cordial reception which you
received from the Pope and the publication of the correspondence
here has had a good effect," but, said the writer, "its best influences,
as we hope, will be felt elsewhere in producing a check on the foreign
enlistments made by the United States." He continued, letting
Mann down not too hard, "as a recognition of the Confederate States
we can not attach to it the same value that you do, a mere inferential
recognition, unconnected with the political action or the regular establishment of diplomatic relations, possessing none of the moral
weight required for awakening the people of the United States from
their delusion." The Pope's addressing Davis as the "President of
the Confederate States," continued Benjamin with gentle contempt,
was only "a formula of politeness to his correspondent, not a political recognition of a fact."[1]

Nothing, of course, came of Mann's mission to Rome as a diplomatic venture, as nothing had been expected by the Confederate
government. In its main purpose, however, it was not, perhaps, a
complete failure. At least the Pope used his influence against the
enlistment of alien Catholics in the United States Army. On March
11, 1864, Mann reported that "under the auspices of the letter of
Pio Nono to the President, formidable demonstrations have been
made in Ireland against the efforts of Lincoln and Company to secure additional immigrants from that portion of the British realm.
The chances are thus multiplying, from day to day, that there will be
a vast diminution in the number of foreign recruits for the Northern
Armies. To the immortal honor of the Catholic Church, it is now
earnestly engaged in throwing every obstacle that it can justly create
in the way of the prosecution of the war by the Yankee guerillas.

[1] Pickett Papers, Benjamin to Mann, No. 11, Feb. 1, 1864; *O.R.N.*, Ser. 2, Vol. III,
pp. 1014–16.

That it will accomplish little less than marvels in this regard I have entertained a confident belief ever since my audience with the Holy Father and my interviews with his cardinal secretary of state."[1]

One can hardly agree, however, that the Pope could or did accomplish marvels because there was no decrease in enlistments—though there might have been an increase had he not intervened. The call of the dollar, of free lands, and of high wages was too strong for the good Catholic Irish to resist.

[1] Pickett Papers, Mann to Benjamin, No. 80, March 11, 1864; *O.R.N.*, Ser. 2, Vol. III, pp. 1057–59.

CHAPTER XVI

THE MEXICAN PAWN, 1862–65

The withdrawal of Mason and the dismissal of the English consuls marked the end of the King Cotton philosophy. While there were some vestiges of hope among Confederate friends in England that that country might do something in behalf of the South for other reasons, the Confederate government and its people had little if any such illusions. The chief reliance of the Confederate agents and the people of the South was henceforth placed upon Napoleon. Thoughtful men of the South agreed that Napoleon's ambitions to establish Mexico as a French vassalage could never be realized unless the South should be permanently established as an independent state, which was friendly to the idea. Hence they could hardly escape the conviction that Napoleon must ultimately recognize the independence of the Confederacy, and if recognition did not bring about a cessation of the war, intervene in behalf of southern independence. It was on the basis of this conviction that Slidell had in his two interviews of July and October, 1862, and on all other occasions directly and indirectly offered Napoleon the support of his government in the Mexican venture in return for recognition or intervention.

But this standing offer of the Confederate commissioner to scrap the Monroe Doctrine and place the Confederacy in active alliance with France had failed to overcome Napoleon's fear of war with America, and had consequently left the French Emperor unmoved from his position of reluctant neutrality. Slidell and his government were not completely checkmated, however, by the failure of direct diplomacy to move Napoleon to do what appeared so plainly to be the only correct and sensible thing. Hence when an opportunity arose for approaching the question of a Franco-Confederate alliance by indirection, the Richmond government promptly made use of it. This opportunity was the proposed creation by Napoleon in the fall of 1863 of the puppet Emperor Maximilian to reign over Mexico. The Confederate government planned to approach Napoleon through Maximilian. It believed that it could convince Maximilian of the necessity of a French alliance with the Confederate government or of intervention in behalf of Confederate independence, in order to make secure the puppet Emperor's throne from American interference. Maximilian was to be approached through Slidell, and through William Preston, former United States minister to Spain, who was specially commissioned to proceed to Mexico.

Before relating these reasonable but fruitless efforts of the Confederacy, it is necessary to examine briefly the Franco-American relations with reference to the French intervention in Mexico, inasmuch as they will help, in part, to explain why Napoleon did not take greater chances after 1862 in behalf of southern independence. It has been frequently noted that the French Emperor was always ready to join England in any form of intervention; but that he was unwilling to undertake any such step alone. His reasons had been repeated over and over, namely, that if he attempted intervention alone he would become embroiled with the United States. Now on examination of his relations with the United States over the Mexican question one sees that actually his occupation of Mexico, though its success depended upon southern independence, served as a serious check rather than an inducement to intervention. This is paradoxical; but it was in keeping with the Bonaparte nature to get as involved as the man who by marrying his son's stepdaughter became his son's son-in-law, a son-in-law and father-in-law to his son's wife, the step-grandfather of his own wife, the father and great-grandfather of his own children, and other such fantastic relations.

As soon as it was seen that the proposed Corwin treaty[1] would not stave off European intervention, Seward had begun to use diplomatic pressure to force Napoleon to an embarrassing commitment as to his intentions in Mexico. Napoleon, who designed from the first to establish a vassal empire and an independent source of raw cotton,[2] had shown great uneasiness during the pending Corwin

[1] See chap. iii.

[2] See Corti, *Maximilian and Charlotte of Mexico, passim;* also Paléologue, *Tragic Empress,* pp. 90–95.

treaty at the reports of Mercier that the United States would do all it could to thwart the Mexican venture; so sensitive was he, in fact, to America's possible course that he had all important passages of Mercier's dispatch relating to Mexico copied and sent to him.[1]

Seward, when it became apparent that the Corwin treaty would not stop intervention, began to demand that the powers make a pledge to confine themselves to their avowed object of collecting their Mexican debts. Dayton approached Thouvenel in the latter part of September, 1861, in the attempt to persuade France to accept an American guaranty of the interest on the debts rather than to intervene, or if this could not be done, to obtain a pledge that France would not go farther than the collection of debts. Thouvenel would not consider the guaranty of the interest, but insisted that France must have the principal. As for ulterior motives, Thouvenel denied that there were any. "He assured me," wrote Dayton, "that whatever England and France might do, it would be done in reference to realizing their money debt only, and that they had no purpose whatever to obtain any foothold in Mexico or to occupy permanently any portion of its territory. He repeated this with emphasis" and offered to put the commitment in writing. But Dayton was uneasy. "I cannot but feel, however," he wrote Seward, "that all these Governments are disposed to take advantage of the present distracted condition of the United States." But, he continued prophetically, "should rebellion at an early day be suppressed and leave us with a large army on foot, and a navy increased, different dispositions may develop themselves."[2]

By February, 1862, Dayton was quite convinced that this pledge which Thouvenel had made was worth nothing. "You will be satisfied," he wrote Seward, ". . . . at no distant day that money or the recovery of debts was not the great object. . . . ."[3]

With constant reports from Schurz in Madrid, Dayton and Consul John Bigelow in Paris, Adams in London, Motley in Vienna, and Sanford in Brussels, that there was more behind the intervention of

[1] E.g., French F.O. Amer., Vol. 126, Mercier to Thouvenel, No. 79, Jan. 6, 1862; *ibid.*, Mercier to Thouvenel, No. 88, March 3, 1862.

[2] U.S. Des., France, Vol. 50, Dayton to Seward, No. 51, Sept. 27, 1861.

[3] *Ibid.*, Vol. 51, No. 117, Feb. 21, 1862.

the allies than the collection of money, Seward determined in the spring of 1862 upon a vigorous course. The recent victories in the west gave him renewed courage to defy Europe. On March 3 he wrote Dayton that "we observe indications of a growing opinion in Europe that the demonstrations which are being made by Spanish, French, and British forces . . . . against Mexico are likely to be attended by a revolution in that country which will bring in a monarchical form of government there in which the crown will be assumed by some foreign prince." The American government was greatly concerned at these rumors, and the administration desired that the views of America be placed before these countries. The President "has relied upon the assurance given to his government by the allies that they were seeking no political object, and only a redress of grievances." He would warn Europe that no monarchical government had any prospect of permanence if left alone, that it would have to be sustained by European armies, thus making it "the beginning of a permanent policy of armed European intervention, injurious and practically hostile to the most general system of government on the continent of America. . . . . In such a case it is not to be doubted that the permanent interests and sympathies of this country [the United States] would be with the American republics."[1]

This dispatch was to be presented in substance to Thouvenel. It amounted to saying that if France and her allies attempted to set up a puppet empire in Mexico, ultimately (when the American war was over) the intervening powers would meet the United States in armed conflict. This communication, making no mention of the Monroe Doctrine, was, as were Seward's other notes to Dayton—contrary to general opinion—a clear-cut and pugnacious assertion of the fundamental principles of that Doctrine—America's objection to foreign intervention in the political affairs of an American State.

Dayton presented Thouvenel with choice portions of these instructions and was assured in reply that France could do no more than to repeat her former pledge that her sole purpose was to obtain payment of the claims and to exact reparations for the injuries done French citizens. Dayton, despite rumors and suspicions contra-

[1] U.S. Inst., France, Vol. 16, Seward to Dayton, No. 121, March 3, 1862.

dicting Thouvenel's fair words, could not go behind these renewed promises; and he replied that "the President reposed entire confidence in these assurances, but, feeling great interest in the well being of Mexico and its institutions, he felt that the occasion justified the expression of some general views in reference to the present and probable future of that country."[1]

The sincerity of Thouvenel's pledges may be judged by two communications made to Flahault and Mercier during March, 1862. On March 7 he wrote that because of the upheaval in America, North and South, it was not to be supposed that Napoleon's intervention would stop with Mexico.[2] A day or two before the interview in which he pledged no ulterior motive to Dayton he wrote Mercier: "I have not received any information or any communication from Mr. Dayton concerning the Mexican affairs. Whatever it should be . . . . you know already that it could not influence our conduct," already definitely planned.[3]

On March 31, the same day Dayton was writing about his recent interview with Thouvenel in which the latter had pledged France to confine her intervention to the collection of the debts, Seward wrote another blunt dispatch to Dayton concerning French intervention in Mexico. Rumors were still unabated that a monarchy with a puppet European ruler was to be set up. "We have more than once," wrote Seward warningly, "and with perfect disinterestedness and candor, informed all parties to the alliance that we cannot look with indifference upon an armed European intervention for political ends in a country situated so near and connected with us so closely as Mexico."[4]

As soon as Dayton received these instructions he presented them to Thouvenel. Thouvenel did not hesitate, but, in Dayton's words, he "stated in reply (what this government has so often said) that they had no purpose or wish to interfere in the form of Government in Mexico. All they wanted was that there should be a *government*, not

[1] U.S. Des., France, Vol. 51, Dayton to Seward, No. 131, March 31, 1862.

[2] French F.O., Amer., Vol. 721, Thouvenel to Mercier, March 7, 1862.

[3] *Ibid.*, Vol. 126, No. 10, March 27, 1862.

[4] U.S. Inst., France, Vol. 16, Seward to Dayton, No. 135, March 31, 1862.

an anarchy with which other nations could have no relations . . . .
that if the people in that country chose to establish a republic it was
all well: France would make no objection. If they chose to establish
a monarchy, as that was the form of Government here, it would be
charming, but they did not mean to do any thing to induce such action, that all the rumors that France intended to establish Archduke Maximilian on the throne of Mexico were utterly without
foundation." This reply of Thouvenel is worth noting carefully. He
claimed to be repeating former pledges, but certain subtle extensions
were made which would be difficult to detect, but which indicated a
gradual "creeping-up" in the process of getting America to acquiesce
in French intervention in Mexico. Thouvenel pledged that France
would not interfere with the form of the Mexican government but
 insisted that Mexico must have a government of some form, and
that France preferred a monarchy.

Dayton, fat and apoplectic though he was, saw the distinction
between a pledge not to meddle with the Mexican government made
heretofore and the pledge not to meddle with the form of government. He saw that Napoleon was planning a supervised election
which meant a monarchy. So he expressed himself in mild but clear
terms. "I suggested to him," wrote Dayton, "that a French army in
Mexico might give to the people of Mexico a tendency toward a
particular form of government and if such a government should be
established it might protect its existence afterwards." Thouvenel
denied that the army was there to influence the government in any
way and that the United States might "rest assured" on that point.[1]

Whether or not Dayton believed that the army would not be used
to influence the form of government, he did not say, and it is not
apparent whether Seward believed it or not. But here was a pledge
repeated with a little embroidery added, and while Seward chose to
ignore the embroidery, he fixed upon the pledge as a touchstone of
Franco-American relations with reference to Mexico. As soon as he
received the dispatch from Dayton he laid it before Lincoln, who
elected likewise not to see the subtle differences between it and the
former French pledges, and thus the French were pledged according

[1] U.S. Des., France, Vol. 51, Dayton to Seward, No. 142, April 22, 1862.

to the interpretation of the United States government not to meddle with the Mexican government or to annex any Mexican soil. Seward wrote Dayton of the President's approval of this pledge of the French government, and Dayton promptly passed this approval on to Thouvenel who repeated his recent promise that the French troops were not to meddle with the form of government or remain indefinitely in the country. And then Dayton replied that he had sought the interview to assure France that the United States would rely upon these pledges.[1]

Thus in the early summer of 1862 was a *modus vivendi* reached, and the United States government could not afford to question the sincerity of this pledge even though the European, and especially the French, press assumed after England and Spain withdrew from the venture that Napoleon planned to set up an empire under Maximilian. Strength was given to this French pledge by a speech which Billault made about the first of July in the *Corps Législatif*. Billault said that when the French flag was planted upon the walls of Mexico "an appeal will be made to all opinions," and that it was hoped "to bring every Mexican to the poll to give his opinion on the tyranny of Juárez. Let the Mexicans pronounce, and if Juárez suits them, so let it be!"[2]

On September 12, 1862, Seward again reaffirmed to Dayton his acceptance of France's pledge. "The position of the United States, in regard to the war between France and Mexico has been taken and it will be maintained," he wrote. "This Government relying upon the explanations which have been made by France, regards the conflict as a war involving claims by France which Mexico has failed to adjust to the satisfaction of her adversary, and it avoids intervention between the belligerents."[3]

Matters rocked along thus until the spring of 1863, with little if any mention of the Mexican question between the United States and the French governments. Yet the European press discussed daily Napoleon's plans to establish a dependency in Mexico, and the American press unanimously agreed that Napoleon was planning the

[1] *Ibid.*, No. 156, June 5, 1862.

[2] *London Times*, July 2, 1862.   [3] U.S. Inst., France, Vol. 16, No. 193.

annexation of Mexico, and that the first business on hand for the American army when the war was ended would be to drive the French Emperor out. Clearly the two governments were playing a make-believe game.

In the spring of 1863 Dayton had several interviews with De Lhuys about the Mexican question, and the former pledges were again repeated, with certain frills which Dayton and Seward once more refused to notice. De Lhuys now said that France had no intention of controlling the government of Mexico, which was a different word from interfering with the government or even the form of government.[1] Dayton, ignoring the slight shift, replied that the United States government continued in good faith to accept the assurances that France would not meddle with the Mexican government or make any annexations.[2]

But the approaching elections in Mexico and the grooming of Maximilian for the emperorship made it impossible to continue to ignore the divergence between former French pledges and present French conduct in Mexico. Dayton believed that little reliance could be put on the French promises. "Truthfulness is not, as you know, an element in French diplomacy or manners. No man but a Frenchman would ever have thought of Talleyrand's famous *bon mot* that the object of language is to conceal thought."[3]

The *modus vivendi* which had enabled the two countries to get along amicably since the fall of 1861 began to break up. From the fall of 1863 until the end of the War of Secession, if not until the final overthrow of Maximilian, the relations between Napoleon and the United States were badly strained, though there was no open break and no great amount of friction. On August 21, 1863, Dayton spoke to De Lhuys about the rumor that Maximilian would be put on the throne. De Lhuys sidestepped by countering with the old pledge that France had no desire to annex Mexican territory or to meddle with the government there, but that the Emperor desired to get out as soon as his grievances could be righted and order restored. Dayton would not be so easily deflected. He replied that France might in getting out of Mexico "leave a puppet behind her," but

[1] E.g., U.S. Des., France, Vol. 53, Dayton to Seward, No. 297, April 9, 1863.

[2] *Ibid.*, No. 301, April 24, 1863.   [3] *Ibid.*, No. 342, Sept. 7, 1863.

De Lhuys denied this and said that the strings would be too long for France to control the puppet.[1]

A month later Seward, made bold by the Federal victories of Vicksburg and Gettysburg, wrote Dayton a menacing letter of instructions. He should interview De Lhuys and tell him that the United States had observed strict neutrality in the war between France and Mexico especially "because it has relied on the assurances given by the French Government that it did not intend permanent occupation of that country or any violence to the sovereignty of its people." But because "the proceedings of the French in Mexico are regarded by many in that country [Mexico] and this as at variance with those assurances," especially the preparation for placing Maximilian on the throne, it was becoming increasingly difficult to enforce a rigid neutrality. He instructed Dayton to urge that Napoleon settle up his affairs in Mexico "upon the basis of the unity and independence of Mexico," "as early as may be convenient," and depart. The American people, Dayton was to tell De Lhuys, "are deeply interested in the re-establishment of unity, peace and order in the neighboring republic and are exceedingly desirous that there may not arise out of the war in Mexico any cause of alienation between them and France. . . . ."[2]

Dayton on receipt of these instructions interviewed De Lhuys who immediately reaffirmed the old pledge; but the American Minister pointed out that the proposal to seat Maximilian on the Mexican throne was a repudiation of France's promise not to meddle with the Mexican government or not to control that government. De Lhuys was ready with a suave and logical reply. France would not meddle. She was merely going to see that a fair election was held; everybody should have an opportunity of expressing himself, and the establishing of a monarchy and the selection of Maximilian would be a free choice. This did not violate the French pledge. Dayton's only reply to this piece of sophistry was to state enigmatically that "we should rest satisfied with whatever form of Government *Mexico voluntarily chose for herself*."

De Lhuys took this remark for what it really meant, namely, that

[1] *Ibid.*, No. 336.

[2] U.S. Inst., France, Vol. 16, Seward to Dayton, No. 400, Sept. 21, 1863.

America passionately disapproved of a Mexican monarchy and of Maximilian as emperor, since both would be French creations and not the desires of the Mexicans. De Lhuys, wrote Dayton, remarked that the danger to the Archduke's government would come from the United States. He said, continued Dayton, "the sooner we showed ourselves satisfied, and manifested a willingness to enter into peaceful relations with that Government the sooner would France be ready to leave Mexico and the new Government to take care of itself. . . . . But that it would not lead or tempt the Archduke into difficulty and then desert him before his Government was settled . . . . , that the early acknowledgment of that Government by the United States would tend to shorten or perhaps, ... to end all the troublesome complications of France in that country." Dayton told De Lhuys that "though he had no instructions on that point he could not suppose that France would expect the United States to make haste to acknowledge a new monarchy in Mexico."[1]

In this interview it will be seen that while De Lhuys attempted to keep up the old fiction that France was not meddling with the Mexican government, by contending that the election was a free choice, he at the same time contradicted himself by insisting that French troops must continue to support Maximilian as long as the United States did not acknowledge him as emperor because France had led him "into difficulty" and could not "desert him."

After this another *modus vivendi* had to be worked out if the two countries were not to quarrel and perhaps come to blows; and neither country desired to quarrel or fight. Dayton felt that nothing could be done about the French intervention now as "we cannot, under existing circumstances, afford a war with France for the quixotic purpose of helping Mexico."[2] "France," he wrote Seward, "has promised so often not to interfere with the government in Mexico that I can hardly feel in view of all the facts that she has kept faith with us." But, continued Dayton, it was needless to complain at the present; the United States was in no position to follow up its complaints,

---

[1] U.S. Des., France, Vol. 53, Dayton to Seward, No. 361, Oct. 9, 1863, quotations from words of dispatch.

[2] *Ibid.*, Vol. 54, No. 442, March 25, 1864.

and unless it could thus support its contentions it had best refrain from argument, for "there is want of dignity in a great nation's uttering complaints while it is not in condition to enforce reparation." The United States must protest and then remain silent, and "time, it is to be hoped, will yet set all things right, or at least will afford us the opportunity of doing so. This government [France] understands the conditions on which we have announced our policy of non-intervention."[1]

Dayton's advised procedure was exactly that which Lincoln and Seward had determined upon, namely, to make a final vigorous and clear-cut statement of America's position in the Mexican affair, and then maintain dignified silence if possible, until the United States was in a position to support its contention with force. This would be the new *modus vivendi*. In accordance with this policy, Seward stated the position of the United States on the setting-up of a puppet empire clearly in his instructions to Dayton of February 13, 1864: "If the French Government shall continue the war and persevere in sending the Prince Maximilian to Mexico, it seems almost certain that it must depart very materially from the assurances it has heretofore given to the United States that it would have the Mexican people abiding free and uninterrupted in their choice of institutions and rulers and that it would retire from that country so soon as its honor should be vindicated and its just claims put in the way of liquidation conforming itself in the meanwhile to those ends.

"I have already let you know that Congress and the people of the United States are very sensitive in regard to this subject and that the French Government cannot reasonably expect their acquiescence in proceedings which shall conflict with the engagements that the French Government has thus made. The sensibility I have described increases with every day's increasing of the decline of the insurrection in the United States."[2]

Briefly, the enthroning of Maximilian was a violation of former French pledges and ultimately France must expect a conflict with

[1] *Ibid.*, No. 449, April 11, 1864.

[2] U.S. Inst., France, Vol. 17, Seward to Dayton, No. 481 ("Confidential"), Feb. 13, 1864.

the United States and the overthrow of the Mexican monarchy should she persist in the violation of its former promises.

Just at this time the House of Representatives passed by a unanimous vote resolutions against the recognition of Maximilian and the Mexican monarchy set up by Napoleon's so-called "plebiscite." Seward to give emphasis to his instructions sent a copy of the resolutions to Dayton, with the comment that they represented the unanimous opinion of the United States. He was to assure De Lhuys, however, that the United States contemplated no change at present in its policy with reference to Mexico.[1]

Dayton, armed with these resolutions and Seward's instructions, interviewed De Lhuys about April 22. De Lhuys did not wait for him to broach the subject but referred to the resolutions which he had already read in the newspapers. "Do you bring us war or do you bring us peace?" he inquired of Dayton.

Dayton replied that there was no reason to suppose those resolutions meant war any more than the former references made to De Lhuys regarding the Mexican question. He further remarked that "they embodied nothing more than had been constantly held to the French Government from the beginning—that I had always represented to the Government here that any action upon their part interfering with the form of Government in Mexico would be looked upon with dissatisfaction in our country and they could not expect us to be in haste to acknowledge a monarchical government built upon the foundations of a Republic which was our next neighbor—that I had reason to believe you [Seward] held the same language to the French minister in the United States." "I think," Dayton wrote Seward, that "the European press generally look upon those resolutions as implying that the United States Government will not rest satisfied with the condition of things established by the French in Mexico." And then he observed with grim humor that the Archduke Maximilian had received the blessings of the Pope for his Mexican venture and the resolutions of the House at the same time, and that they must have about canceled each other.[2]

[1] *Ibid.*, No. 525, April 7, 1864.
[2] U.S. Des., France, Vol. 54, Dayton to Seward, No. 454, April 22, 1864.

After thus developing in language which could not be misunderstood the profound and unrelenting objections to Napoleon's creation of a vassal empire out of Mexico—which Napoleon consistently denied—the American government settled down into a dignified and silent wait until a more opportune time, when America would be at peace and France at war.

This was Napoleon's time to seal an alliance with the Confederacy or get out of Mexico. He should have known that unless the Confederacy established its independence his venture was doomed to ignoble failure. All others were sure of it and expected him to do something about it. Certainly after Maximilian was elected in the fall of 1863 there seemed no other course open.

The Confederate government and its commissioners were perfectly aware of this *sine qua non* of the success of Napoleon's Mexican venture. So was the unfortunate Maximilian, and he approached the Confederate government without waiting for overtures from it. A friend of Jefferson Davis, Mr. de Haviland, formerly of Washington, who was in Trieste on mysterious business in the fall of 1863, was invited by Maximilian—whether through that prince's initiative or his own is not recorded—to the palace of Miramar to an interview with the Archduke. De Haviland, who had been in correspondence with Davis already, wrote Slidell and Davis an account of this interview which vitally concerned the recognition of the Confederacy. On November 7 he wrote Slidell that " 'having recently been honored with an invitation to Miramar, the palace of H. I. H. the Archduke Ferdinand Max of Austria, the conditional Emperor of Mexico, he yesterday favored me with a long private interview, during which H. I. H. expressed the warmest possible interest in the success of the Confederate cause. He said that he considered it identical with that of the new Mexican Empire, in fact so inseparable that an acknowledgment of the Confederate States of America by the Governments of England and France should take place before his acceptance of the Mexican crown became unconditional; that he was particularly desirous that his sentiments upon this subject should be known to the Confederate President and to the statesmen and leading minds of the Confederacy, and authorized me confidentially to communicate these views and sentiments to President Davis, and to you, sir, and also to make known to both of you the solicitude with which he was watching the present movements of the Confederate armies etc. . . . .' "[1]

Slidell on receipt of this letter saw Mr. Gutiérrez de Estrada, chief of the Mexican mission which was offering Maximilian the Mexican crown, and he told Slidell that he had introduced De Haviland to Maximilian and that he felt sure that De Haviland's report of Maximilian's views were true. Slidell then repaired to the Foreign Office to see his "friend" Cintrat, and discuss this move on the part of Maximilian. Cintrat assured him that Maximilian attached the greatest importance to the recognition of the Confederacy by Europe. "He has seen the paper," wrote Slidell, "in which the archduke set forth the different measures which he considered essential to the successful establishment of his Government; the recognition of the Confederacy headed the list."[2]

James Williams, recent United States minister to Turkey and active Confederate propagandist, at about the same time that De Haviland was in communication with Maximilian, held several interviews with the puppet emperor, in which the latter spoke quite frankly and emphatically of his desires that France should recognize the independence of the Confederacy before he should finally accept the Mexican throne. Williams, of course, as Maximilian desired, promptly communicated the latter's views and desires to President Davis and the Confederate commissioners.

Maximilian, then, unquestionably regarded the recognition of the Confederacy by France as a condition precedent to his acceptance, but he was hurried on by Napoleon against his judgment and failed to exact this condition of the foxy French monarch before he accepted the Mexican throne, and at length came to Paris with that point still unsettled.

On rumor of his coming Slidell wrote Benjamin that he would seek an interview with him to follow up the lead given him through De Haviland, Williams, and Estrada. As soon as the Archduke arrived

[1] Pickett Papers, Slidell to Benjamin, No. 50, Dec. 3, 1863, inclosing letter; *O.R.N.*, Ser. 2, Vol. III, pp. 968–70.

[2] *Ibid.*

in Paris Slidell sought an interview with him through the president of the Mexican mission. Maximilian assured the latter that he would be delighted to see Slidell, and that he would have his secretary send him a notice to that effect. But the notice did not come, and Slidell addressed the Duke's secretary reminding him of the promise. No reply came,[1] and Slidell was convinced that Napoleon had checked Maximilian's plans for recognition. Mann, who was very indignant at Maximilian's refusal to see Slidell, was informed from a good source—Leopold himself, without doubt—that "Louis Napoleon has enjoined upon Maximilian to hold no official relations with" the Confederate government in France or Mexico.[2]

In the meanwhile, another approach was being made to Maximilian by means of a regularly appointed mission to Mexico (to succeed Pickett). In the latter part of October, 1863, General Almonte, Mexican regent and throne-warmer for Maximilian, wrote his friend Mr. Vidaurri of Nuevo León that he had been urging upon Napoleon the necessity of recognizing the South.[3] In this correspondence he indicated that a Confederate minister should be dispatched to Mexico to the court of Maximilian because the latter desired to recognize the Confederacy and would try to obtain European recognition for it.

On the basis of this information and that from Slidell, De Haviland, Williams, and Estrada, Davis appointed William Preston, late minister to Spain, as minister and envoy extraordinary to the Mexican government,[4] with instructions to make a treaty of friendship and commerce with the latter on the basis of free trade.

John T. Pickett on hearing of the creation of the new Mexican mission desired, as we have noted, to add certain instructions to Preston's official ones, such as advice against "slapping" or "kicking."[5] Preston proceeded to Havana, Cuba, there to await the long-heralded but oft-delayed arrival of Maximilian. He did not think

[1] Pickett Papers, Slidell to Benjamin, No. 58, March 16, 1864; O.R.N., Ser. 2, Vol. III, pp. 1063–65.

[2] Pickett Papers, Mann to Benjamin, No. 80, March 11, 1864; O.R.N., Ser. 2, Vol. III, pp. 1057–59.

[3] Pickett Papers, Quintero to Benjamin, Nov. 4, 1863, inclosures; cf. ibid., Quintero to Benjamin, No. 53, Nov. 9, 1863.

[4] Pickett Papers, Jan. 7; O.R.N., Ser. 2, Vol. III, pp. 154–55, 988–90.

[5] Pickett Papers, Pickett to Davis, Jan. 11, 1864; see chap. iii.

it wise to attempt to negotiate with Almonte, as any agreement thus reached might be repudiated by Maximilian, or else Almonte might keep him cooling his heels in the antechamber until Maximilian arrived.[1] While waiting in Havana for the arrival of Maximilian, Preston communicated with Slidell, but Slidell discouraged him with an account of his failure to obtain an interview with Maximilian while in Paris.[2]

Preston then determined to wait, not alone for Maximilian's coming, but for word that Maximilian would receive him.[3] So he dispatched Captain R. T. Ford, a member of his party, to Mexico, to get in touch with Maximilian while he himself determined to go on to Europe. Here he could confer directly with Mason and Slidell, if it were worth while, and reach the real spring of action—Napoleon.[4]

Ford proceeded to Mexico and interviewed the foreign minister of Maximilian, presented his instructions, and withdrew, not having any response.[5] In the meanwhile, Preston had written directly to the regent Almonte, and Marquis de Montholon, French representative at Mexico City, with reference to his coming to Mexico, and these men hurriedly wrote him while he was in London that he should not come to Mexico as Confederate minister[6] under present conditions.

Like all other Confederate efforts to obtain recognition this one finally came to naught. The Confederate commissioners by indirection warned both Maximilian and Napoleon that they were committing a serious and irreparable mistake in allowing the occasion to pass without the recognition of the Confederacy. Slidell wrote Ma-

---

[1] *Ibid.*, Preston to Benjamin, No. 1, Feb. 13, 1864.

[2] Pickett Papers, Slidell to Benjamin, No. 58, March 16, 1864; *O.R.N.*, Ser. 2, Vol. III, pp. 1063–65, tells of writing Preston; cf. Pickett Papers, Mason to Benjamin, No. 7, April 12, 1864; *O.R.N.*, Ser. 2, Vol. III, pp. 1082–84.

[3] Pickett Papers, Preston to Benjamin, No. 5, April 28, 1864.

[4] See *ibid.*, Preston to Benjamin, June 2 and 24, 1864.

[5] *Ibid.*, Helm to Benjamin, No. 31, Aug. 21, 1864, with inclosures of correspondence with Ford, etc.; *ibid.*, Helm to Benjamin, No. 34, Dec. 9, 1864, with inclosures of correspondence with Ford, etc.

[6] *Ibid.*, Preston to Benjamin, Aug. 18, 1864.

son soon after his failure to see Maximilian that he had had an interview with General Woll, aide de camp of Maximilian, in which he had warned him of the folly of not recognizing the Confederacy. "I have talked to him very freely," Slidell wrote Mason,[1] "as to the consequences that will result from the refusal to be on good terms with the Confederacy." Just a few days earlier he had written Benjamin: "I have taken care, of course in no offensive tone, to let the leading Mexicans here understand that he [Maximilian] makes a great mistake, both as regards his hope of avoiding difficulties with the North and his reliance upon the South to aid him in meeting them" unless he established a close friendship with the South; for "without the active friendship of the South he will be entirely powerless to resist Northern aggression. . . . ." Slidell pointed out to the Mexicans like Estrada that nothing was expected from Maximilian directly, as he was too weak to sustain himself without French aid, that "our motive in desiring to negotiate with Mexico, was not the expectation of deriving any advantage from an alliance per se, but from the consequences that would probably flow from it in another quarter [i.e., in drawing the French Emperor into the alliance]." He was in these conversations bluntly menacing to Maximilian and indirectly so to Napoleon. He had said, he wrote, that "while we would desire to be on friendly terms with all nations, we should have no special interest in the stability of the Mexican Government and would be free to pursue such a policy as circumstances and our interests might dictate."[2]

Benjamin after the failure to obtain recognition through this channel wrote Slidell that the French Emperor and his puppet king Maximilian were resorting to self-deception if they could not see that "it has thus become evident that the safety of the new empire is dependent solely upon our success in interposing a barrier between northern aggression and the Mexican territory," and that this barrier should not be placed there gratuitously.[3]

[1] Mason Papers, March 22, 1864.

[2] Pickett Papers, Slidell to Benjamin, No. 58, March 16, 1864; O.R.N., Ser. 2, Vol. III, pp. 1063–65.

[3] Pickett Papers, Benjamin to Slidell, No. 40, June 23, 1864; O.R.N., Ser. 2, Vol. III, pp. 1156–57.

Finally, when none of those insinuations had induced the French Emperor or his vassal to make a move, William Preston interviewed the Mexican ministers, Arrangoiz and Hidalgo at London and Paris, and Slidell interviewed De Lhuys; and they both hinted broadly that the North and South would probably soon make peace based upon separation and an "offensive and defensive alliance, for the establishment of an American policy on our continent, which will result in the suppression of monarchical institutions in Mexico." That is, unless France and her vassal recognized the Confederacy and thus assured its independence, the Confederacy would turn against the imperial schemes and aid the North in overthrowing them. It was an offer to scrap the Monroe Doctrine and to ally with France in return for recognition, or a threat in case France did not accept the offer to ally with the North, drive France out of Mexico, and restore the Monroe Doctrine. This was probably no idle threat, for ere this Napoleon, by his conduct concerning the ironclads, the blockade, and the failure to recognize the Confederacy, had put the French government in about as bad a light as the English government with the South.

It should have seemed clear, then, according to southern opinion, that the independence and friendship of the Confederacy were two essential conditions to the permanent success of the establishment of a Mexican vice-royalty. It is true that they believed independence would ultimately result from their own efforts; nothing short of this was considered as being in the category of possibility. Yet, the nod of recognition on the part of Napoleon, they believed, would so encourage the peace movement now (the summer of 1864), gathering such momentum at the North under Grant's disastrous campaigns in Virginia that the war, which might otherwise linger for years, would come to a speedy end. The Confederate commissioners, the President, and his Secretary of State, were well aware of the fear of war which Napoleon harbored as a result of his recognizing the independence of the Confederacy; and they were well acquainted with the great unpopularity of Napoleon which made him fearful of undertaking a war, and especially a war against the United States with whom the French were in sympathy. But Benjamin and the commissioners were absolutely convinced that Napoleon's fear was groundless, that he ran no risks whatsoever of becoming embroiled in a war with the United States should he recognize the Confederate States. Benjamin frequently referred with contempt to this fear of both Napoleon and Russell. But conceding that Napoleon did run a risk of war, the Confederate statesmen could not understand why he did not hazard the chance in order to guarantee the success of the Mexican empire with its vast silver mines and possibilities for cotton production, and upon which his prestige with his own subjects was staked.

Why did not Napoleon hazard a chance? Why did he not ally himself with or intervene in behalf of the Confederacy now? We have already suggested the answer, namely, that, paradoxical as it sounds, it was feared that it would endanger the Mexican venture by upsetting the fictional *modus vivendi* with the United States. The relations between the United States and Mexico up until 1864 have been sketched, and it has been seen how unbending Seward was, how he stood by the principle that while it was legitimate for France to wage war on Mexico for the settlement of just claims, the United States could never acquiesce in any annexations of territory or interference with the Mexican government. The two governments had no friction on the question of the Mexican war for two years because of the assurance of the French government that no annexations or interference with the government was intended.

After the selection of Maximilian, Seward's straight-from-the-shoulder protest that France had violated her pledge and that the United States would not acquiesce and the unanimous resolutions of the House against the recognition of Maximilian plainly indicated that the United States did not accept any deviation from the Monroe Doctrine. The French reaction to this American stand, as we will recall, was to keep up the old fiction that France would not annex or meddle or violate American traditions—in short, that the selection of Maximilian was a free and sovereign act of the Mexican people which the United States should recognize. However, as will be recalled, Seward through Dayton refused to accept Napoleon's transparent fiction that the Mexican people had elected Maximilian and so flatly refused to recognize him in the spring of 1864. Then Seward very wisely dropped the matter.

It was at this juncture that the Confederate government made approaches to Napoleon and Maximilian of which we have just spoken. Napoleon refused to hazard war and its consequences at this point, then, because in the first place a war might cause the immediate failure of his Mexican venture, and in the second place he, like Russell and practically all Europeans as well as southerners, never seemed to have doubted the ultimate success of the South, which would mean the success of his Mexican conquests. If he moved in behalf of the South, however, the United States might attack him at once in Mexico and spoil the whole affair. On the other hand, if he let the war drag on without meddling in it he might go on and complete the conquest and reorganization of Mexico under Maximilian, and when the war was over and the South independent it would be very unlikely that the North would interfere. In other words, Napoleon's immediate fears of the United States and his ultimate hopes of Confederate success were powerful factors in paralyzing his efforts in behalf of the South.

However, to insure himself against any failure of the Confederacy, but more especially against an immediate attack by the North, Napoleon hit upon the idea of striking a bargain with the United States. As so much of his diplomacy had its inception in rumors or "trial balloons," so did this move. On March 16, 1864, Slidell wrote Benjamin that Mercier, who was in Paris on a visit, "declares that at his parting interview with Lincoln he was told by Lincoln that he was authorized to say to the archduke [Maximilian] that his Government [Mexico] would be recognized by that of Washington without difficulty, on the condition, however, that no negotiations should be entered into with the Confederate States."[1] Slidell believed this bargain was responsible for Maximilian's refusal to receive him in Paris.

About this time an article appeared in the *London Globe* which repeated this idea that the United States would recognize Maximilian if Napoleon would refuse to recognize the South. This aroused the ire of both Slidell and Dayton. Dayton sent Seward a copy of the

---

[1] Pickett Papers, Slidell to Benjamin, No. 58, March 16, 1864; *O.R.N.*, Ser. 2, Vol. III, pp. 1063–65; cf. Pickett Papers, Mason to Benjamin, No. 5, March 16, 1864; *O.R.N.*, Ser. 2, Vol. III, pp. 1047–55.

article,[1] and Slidell hastened to the Foreign Office to find out the truth from his "friend." The latter wrote Slidell that the article was substantially correct. "I have called the attention of Mr. Drouyn de Lhuys to the article" of the *Globe*, he wrote, "where it is stated that Mr. Dayton had declared that his Government was ready to accredit a representative to Mexico and to receive a minister of the Emperor of Mexico after the new sovereign should have addressed to him the formal notification of his accession.

"It was replied to me that Mr. Dayton had stated nothing as positive as that. The minister had confined himself to say (and that some time ago) that the Federal Government had no unkind disposition toward the monarchical government which was being established in Mexico and would have no difficulty, should the case arise, to enter into relations with it." Slidell wrote Benjamin that he had no reason to doubt that this statement was true.[2]

At the very moment when this rumor that a bargain had been struck between Napoleon and the United States was circulating, there came the resolutions of the House against recognition and tidings of a similar resolution in the Senate. But Napoleon did not let this swerve him, and presently the press was insisting that these resolutions would not present serious obstacles to the recognition of Maximilian; and Slidell reported that Mercier was continuing to reaffirm the conversation he had with Lincoln on this subject and to insist that it would be carried out. Slidell was disgusted and concluded that Mercier who had been reported to be a firm friend of the South was "every thing to every body."[3]

The *Moniteur* of May 1, 1864, carried an article which confirmed the view that the bargain between the United States and France stood, regardless of the House resolutions. "The Government of the Emperor has received from the Government of the United States satisfactory explanations of the import of the resolutions passed by

[1] U.S. Des., France, Vol. 54, Dayton to Seward, No. 438, March 21, 1864.

[2] Pickett Papers, Slidell to Benjamin, No. 59, April 7, 1864; *O.R.N.*, Ser. 2, Vol. III, pp. 1077–79.

[3] Pickett Papers, Slidell to Mason, No. 60, May 2, 1864; *O.R.N.*, Ser. 2, Vol. III, pp. 1107–11.

the Assembly of Representatives at Washington on the subject of the affairs of Mexico. We know also that the Senate had postponed indefinitely the consideration of the resolutions, to which, in any case, the Executive power had not given its sanction."

The *Constitutionnel* in May denied that there was any "fear of the United States interfering in Mexico, because there is a perfect understanding between Mr. Lincoln's Cabinet and that of the Tuileries. . . . ."[1]

But these "trial balloons" sent up to catch the eye of the United States received no response. Seward had spoken with finality and now remained grimly and wisely quiet. If the Emperor wished to believe that, by circulating the rumor that France would not recognize the Confederacy on condition that the United States recognize Maximilian, he could at least put off American attack in Mexico, it would be just so much grist for Seward's mill. The United States had not the slightest intention of attacking France in Mexico as long as the Civil War should go on. It might prevent Napoleon's recognizing the Confederacy. Then, after the war, the United States could attend to Mexico.

Benjamin never dreamed that it was Napoleon who was attempting thus to buy off American interference in Mexico, but he thought that it was Seward who was finessing Napoleon out of recognizing the South. He thought the game "so transparent" that the Emperor desired to be deceived.[2] If he had realized that Napoleon was putting this "bargain rumor" out in the hopes of keeping the United States from attacking him in Mexico at the moment, he would have been surprised, indeed, and would have added another comment upon the "cowardly fear" of Europe or the poker-playing ability of Seward, whom he reluctantly admired in many ways.

The failure of the Confederacy to obtain recognition on the election of Maximilian did not mean that they had completely given up hope on this ground. So obvious to them was Napoleon's necessity

[1] Quoted in the *Index*, May 19, 1864.

[2] Pickett Papers, Benjamin to Slidell, No. 40, June 23, 1864; *O.R.N.*, Ser. 2, Vol. III, pp. 1156-57.

that it was not until 1865 that they were fully convinced. Then the two great props—cotton and Mexico (which was to be a cotton source)—dropped out from under the foundations of Confederate diplomacy. Then the Confederacy attempted to re-establish their diplomacy upon the basis upon which it should have been in the beginning—the freeing of the slaves.

CHAPTER XVII

THE KENNER MISSION

THE PROPOSAL TO FREE THE SLAVES IN RETURN
FOR RECOGNITION

It has been noted that the Confederate agents always found among all classes in England and France a fixed and unrelenting hostility to slavery, but that in England, except among a relatively small part of the population, this hostility had no bearing upon their sympathies, which were largely in favor of the South.

The Yancey-Rost-Mann mission reported in their first dispatch to Toombs on May 21, 1861, "that the public mind here is entirely opposed to the Government of the Confederate States of America on the question of slavery, and that the sincerity and universality of this feeling embarrasses the Government in dealing with the question of our recognition."[1] In their note to Russell of August 14, 1861, while they assured the Foreign Minister that the war was one of conquest on the part of the North rather than a war to free the slaves, the commissioners acknowledged "the anti-slavery sentiment so universally prevalent in England."[2]

Mason was embarrassed to find such loyal, conservative friends as Seymour Fitzgerald and Lord Donoughmore fixed in their hostility to slavery;[3] and such liberal Confederate champions as Spence almost as actively opposed to slavery as was John Bright. Slidell's first dispatch from Europe to his government confirmed the report of the other Confederate agents that the antislavery sentiment was universal in Europe.[4]

[1] Pickett Papers, May 21, 1861; *O.R.N.*, Ser. 2, Vol. III, pp. 214–16.

[2] Pickett Papers, the commissioners to Russell, Aug. 14, 1861; *O.R.N.*, Ser. 2, Vol. III, pp. 238–46.

[3] E.g., Pickett Papers, Mason to Benjamin, Nov. 4, 1862; *O.R.N.*, Ser. 2, Vol. III, pp. 597–99.

[4] Pickett Papers, Slidell to Secretary of State, No. 1, Feb. 11, 1862; *O.R.N.*, Ser. 2, Vol. III, pp. 336–42.

Hotze summed up the antislavery feeling in France and England in the fall of 1863: "There are two phases under which the antislavery prejudice confronts you. One is the English phase, in which it feels itself constantly under the necessity of self assertion, of propagandism, of offensive demonstration."

"The other phase," wrote Hotze, "far more dangerous and difficult to deal with," was in France "where the prejudice has passed into, or has not yet ceased to be, one of those fixed principles which neither individuals nor nations permit to be called in question." In France "no such violent anti-slavery demonstrations are made as in England, simply because there is no one against whom to make them." Antislavery sentiment in France was a "deep-rooted antipathy, rather than active hostility, against us."[1]

Friend and foe were opposed to slavery and Yancey, Rost, Mann, Mason, Slidell, Hotze, De Leon—all the Confederate diplomatic and other agents—were made thoroughly aware of it, and they in turn informed their government. The attitude of the Confederate government toward European opinion on slavery was always resentful, for the South had so long been held up as a horrible example that it was sensitive and suspicious of any mention of slavery by an outsider, and unwilling to discuss its merits and demerits. The reply to this European criticism and hostility to slavery was finally embodied in a circular sent to all the agents, January 15, 1863, in which Benjamin instructed them to decline any negotiations which in any way related to slavery. This domestic institution was one which only the individual states could deal with. The Confederate government, wrote Benjamin, "unequivocally and absolutely denies its possession of any power whatever over the subject and can not entertain any propositions in relation to it."[2]

But this solid front against the discussion of abolishing slavery began to break in the Confederacy under the hostile attitude of Europe and the military necessity at home. After Lincoln's emanci-

[1] Pickett Papers, Hotze to Benjamin, No. 29, Sept. 26, 1863; O.R.N., Ser. 2, Vol. III, pp. 914–18.

[2] Pickett Papers, Benjamin to Mason, No. 13, Jan. 15, 1863, and copies of the same date to Slidell and Lamar, O.R.N., Ser. 2, Vol. III, pp. 651–53.

pation proclamation thousands of Negro troops joined the Federal armies. With 400,000 or 500,000 foreigners and over 200,000 Negroes added to the Federal armies the small white population of the South began to feel itself overwhelmed by the weight of mere numbers; and finally it was urged that Negroes who could be enlisted in the Confederate armies should be freed. This agitation culminated in the early winter of 1864-65.

But the knowledge of the universal hostility of Europe to slavery and the frequent warnings that Europe would never recognize the Confederacy as a slave-power were as important in the final decision to begin the emancipation of the slaves as was the need for soldiers. So the Confederate government determined to capitalize in its diplomacy upon the idea of emancipation. On December 27, 1864, Benjamin wrote dispatches to Mason and Slidell to put the question squarely up to England and France whether slavery was and had been the obstacle to recognition. Duncan Kenner of Louisiana, member of Congress and chairman of the Ways and Means Committee, intimate friend of Benjamin and Slidell, was appointed as special envoy to carry these new instructions and to act with Mason and Slidell in case negotiations should follow.

One recognizes in this dispatch a different note. The optimistic Benjamin was in profound despair and he was now desperate. The freeing of the slaves was to hazard black supremacy, and all the horrors of Haiti. It was indeed the last card, and spades were trumps. Benjamin's hand shook as he played it. His note is worthy of extensive quotation: "The Confederate States have now for nearly four years resisted the utmost power of the United States with a courage and fortitude to which the world has accorded its respect and admiration. No people have ever poured out their blood more freely in defense of their liberties and independence nor have endured sacrifices with greater cheerfulness than have the men and women of these Confederate States. They accepted the issue which was forced on them by an arrogant and domineering race, vengeful, grasping, and ambitious. They have asked nothing, fought for nothing but for the right for self-government, for independence." Thus Benjamin eloquently spoke of the heroism and purpose of the South.

But this was an inadequate picture of that heroism, for, in fact, the Confederacy, outnumbered by the North three to one, had been fighting Europe as well as the North. England and France had aided the United States by "the abandonment by those two powers of all their rights as neutrals," that is, he said, specifying the rights abandoned, "their countenance of a blockade which, when declared, was the most shameless outrage on international law that modern times have witnessed; their closing their ports to the entry of prizes made by our vessels of war; their efforts to prevent our getting supplies in their ports; their seizure of every vessel intended for our service that could be reached by them; and their indifference to the spectacle of a people (while engaged in an unequal struggle for defense) exposed to the invasion not only of the superior numbers of their adversaries, but of armies of mercenaries imported from neutral nations to subserve the guilty projects of our foes." The South in undertaking its independence had not miscalculated its power of resistance against the North alone; but it had not counted upon this form of passive European aid—in fact, "if this contest had been waged against the United States alone, we feel that it would long since have ceased." But the aid from abroad was not all that had been summoned to the side of the North; along with their violation of international law they had practically discarded all rules of civilized warfare. "While engaged in defending our country on terms so unequal, the foes whom we are resisting profess the intention of resorting to the starvation and extermination of our women and children [Sherman's march through Georgia, South Carolina, and North Carolina and Sheridan's devastation of the valley] as a means of securing conquest over us. In the very beginning of the contest they indicated their fell purpose by declaring medicines contraband of war, and recently they have not been satisfied with burning granaries and dwellings and all food for man and beast. They have sought to provide against any possible future crop by destroying all agricultural implements, and killing all animals that they could not drive from the farms, so as to render famine certain among the people."

While Benjamin contended that the South was determined never again voluntarily "to unite ourselves under a common Government with a people by whom we have been so deeply wronged," he made it clear, nevertheless, that unless Europe came to the aid of the South it would soon have to "consider the terms, if any, upon which we can secure peace." This, in fact, was the meat of the note; the Confederacy must seek peace unless England and France should recognize its independence. It would be very shortsighted of their interests, as the Confederacy had pointed out all along, for England and France to permit a reconstruction of the Union, for the enraged North would attack England, seize Canada, and turn Napoleon out of Mexico. In fact, said Benjamin, "we are fighting the battle of France and England." This being true, "what are the purposes of the western powers of Europe in relation to this contest? Are they determined never to recognize the Southern Confederacy until the United States assent to such action on their part?" Or did Europe wish to recognize the Confederacy but was held back by "objections not made known to us?" If there were such an obstacle, "justice equally demands that an opportunity be afforded us for meeting and overcoming those objections, if in our power to do so." The South was only fighting for the "vindication of our right to self-government and independence" and "for that end no sacrifice is too great, save that of honor." If there was an obstacle, "if then the purpose of France and Great Britain have been, or be now, to exact terms or conditions before conceding the rights we claim, a frank exposition of that purpose is due to humanity."[1]

On the receipt of these written instructions and Kenner's oral instructions the commissioners were prepared to propose the emancipation of the Negroes if slavery proved to be the "obstacle" to recognition.

In the meanwhile, the Confederate press and the *Index* were preparing the public mind at home and abroad for such a step. Hotze, who was one of the most ardent protagonists of slavery, began early in 1863 to pivot about and prepare to swing his paper with him on the question of emancipation. Following the Proclamation of Emancipation the Confederate lobby in Europe began to discuss the eman-

[1] Pickett Papers, Benjamin to Slidell and Benjamin to Mason, Dec. 27, 1864; *O.R.N.*, Ser. 2, Vol. III, pp. 1253–57.

cipation of the slaves and their enrolment as soldiers as a counter
stroke to Lincoln's Emancipation Proclamation. While they were
pondering this problem a rumor was spread abroad, which created
quite a sensation, that the South planned to arm 500,000 slaves and
give them their freedom. Hotze wrote Benjamin that this report was
regarded by the "Southern circles . . . . as the shadow of a coming
event." He was rather favorable to the idea at this early date (September, 1863). "I have been surprised, both at myself and others,
how composedly an idea was received which two years or even one
year ago would not have entered into any sane man's mind. If the
measure were really required—and no one presumed that otherwise
the President would propose it—and if the alternative were once
forced upon us of choosing between independence and the main-
tcnance of our domestic institution, I feel that I represent the views
of the most loyal and most enthusiastic of its admirers when I say
that we are now prepared to pay even this fearful price."[1]

When word reached Hotze that the Confederacy was prepared to
arm and free the slaves as both a military and a diplomatic necessity
he was fully prepared to advocate the idea. He did not propose,
however, to place the abolition of slaves upon the inherent wrongful-
ness of the institution, but rather upon cold expediency. His method
was to quote the Confederate press on the question. He quoted the
Richmond Sentinel in the January 19, 1865, issue of the *Index* as stating concisely the grounds upon which the South should free the
slaves and use them as soldiers. "It is a question," said this paper,
"simply whether we shall give for our own uses, or whether the
Yankees shall take for theirs. Subjugation means emancipation and
confiscation. . . . . It would be far more glorious to devote our
means to our success than to lose them as spoils to the enemy."[2]
Hotze cited the *Richmond Enquirer* of the same date as supporting
warmly the idea of emancipation. "If we would reap the rich blessings to which our heroic struggle entitles us," quoted the *Index*, "if
we would crystallize that admiration into acts of aid and comfort,

[1] Pickett Papers, Hotze to Benjamin, No. 29, Sept. 26, 1863; O.R.N., Ser. 2, Vol.
III, pp. 914–18.
[2] *Index*, Jan. 19, 1865.

we must convince the world that we are fighting for the self-government of the whites and not for the slavery of the blacks; that the war has been forced upon us by our enemy, for the purpose of spoliation and subjugation; that the freedom of the negro was no part of the purpose of our enemy. . . . . If it be necessary to convince the world that we are fighting for the self-government of the whites, that we should liberate the negroes, and if that liberation can be made to secure our independence, we believe that the people of these States would not hesitate to make the sacrifice."[1]

Hotze, however, with his keen insight into public opinion was not long in discovering that the idea of emancipation had come too late to induce Europe to grant recognition to the Confederacy. The *Times* and the *Spectator* especially discouraged the idea,[2] and both English and French press looked upon the idea as the "last card."[3]

Before Kenner arrived Hotze, Mason, and Slidell were all practically convinced of the futility of offering emancipation as the price of recognition. There seemed no possible chance for any such proposal now to succeed. This opinion was strengthened by the conduct of Lord Russell toward the middle of February, 1865. That "extinct volcano," now that the United States appeared to him for the first time to be the inevitable victor, suddenly shot forth fire and brimstone at the prostrate Confederacy. He wrote Mason, Slidell, and Mann a joint letter in which he arraigned the Confederate government in harsh and menacing tones for alleged violations of British neutrality. He had learned, he said, from the United States Minister that despite the seizure of the Laird rams and the prosecution of the other Confederate vessels the Confederate agents were still building vessels of war, "a proceeding totally unjustifiable, and manifestly offensive to the British crown." He accused the Confederate agents of having adopted rules which would violate British neutrality; finally, he complained because certain Confederates had made raids from Canada into Vermont and against the United States steamers on the lakes in order to free Confederate prisoners on Johnson's Island. He hoped that if all these things were true— and he was practically sure they were—the commissioners would

---

[1] *Ibid.*   [2] *Ibid.*   [3] Cf. *ibid.*, Jan. 26, 1865.

promise "on behalf of the Confederate Government that practices so offensive and unwarrantable shall cease and shall be entirely abandoned for the future."[1]

The reaction of the Confederate agents to this letter was an impulse to strike back. Slidell wrote Mason the day after he received his copy of the letter that "I think that you will agree with me that it requires something more than the formal answer. . . . . I think that Earl Russell has given us an opportunity to expose the pretended neutrality which I shall not overlook."[2]

But while the three commissioners were each drafting an adequate reply to Russell's harsh note, Duncan Kenner arrived with his instructions to Mason and Slidell to approach the British and French governments on the question of recognition in return for emancipation. In view of this new approach to the British government, the commissioners decided that "it would be more prudent to avoid raising new issues with that Government immediately in advance of such a communication" as Kenner had brought over to be presented to Russell.[3]

Mason, who proceeded to London after the arrival of Kenner, was now very reluctant to raise the issue of recognition in the face of recent military defeats, Russell's curt note, and the belief in England's unwillingness to make any move toward recognition at any price. He expressed his hesitation to Slidell,[4] but thought that if the British really intended preventing the reuniting of the sections, the declining military fortunes of the Confederacy should find Lord Palmerston in a proper frame of mind to entertain the proposal brought over by Kenner.

Slidell replied that he had "always thought that if the ministry feared reconstruction they would long since have recognized and perhaps gone further to prevent it. They may now feel that they have too deeply committed themselves to retrace their steps." He in-

[1] Pickett Papers, Mason to Benjamin, No. 19, inclosing Russell's letter, March 31, 1865; O.R.N., Ser. 2, Vol. III, pp. 1266-70.

[2] Mason Papers, Feb. 14, 1865.

[3] Pickett Papers, Mason to Benjamin, No. 19, March 31, 1865; O.R.N., Ser. 2, Vol. III, pp. 1266-70.

[4] Mason Papers, March 4, 1865.

formed Mason that he was to interview the Emperor that afternoon, and that what passed in the interview might determine Mason's course of action.[1]

The Emperor in the interview which followed, as always, refused to act alone. "He is willing and anxious to act with England, but will not move without her," Slidell wrote Mason. "I asked him if he could not renew his overtures to England. He said that they had been so decidedly rejected that he could not suppose that they would now be listened to with more favor."[2] Slidell broached the matter of the Kenner mission—would the freeing of the slaves exercise any favorable influence? The Emperor replied, wrote Slidell, that "he had never taken that into consideration; that it had not, and could not have, any influence on his action, but that it had probably been differently considered by England."[3]

On March 13 Mason asked an interview of Palmerston which was granted for March 14. Mason never believed that Britain had withheld recognition because of opposition to slavery. The real impediments were, he thought, "first, a fear of war with the United States, and secondly, a tacit conviction in the English mind that the longer the war lasted in America the better for them." Nevertheless, it was necessary to make the last effort. In the interview he sought to play upon Palmerston's fear of a strong America. The Hampton Roads Conference and Blair's visit to Richmond, which had recently occurred, had caused rumors to fly that the North and South would make peace on the basis of an offensive and defensive alliance, and that they would immediately attack Canada as well as drive the French from Mexico.[4] There can be no doubt but that Palmerston himself and certainly Napoleon were apprehensive of an attack such as this as soon as the Civil War ended. This was Mason's real hope.

In the interview he read portions of his official instructions from Benjamin and of Kenner's private instructions. He did not mention the abolition of slavery by name, because, as he wrote Benjamin,

[1] *Ibid.*   [2] *Ibid.*, March 6, 1865.

[3] Pickett Papers, Mason to Benjamin, No. 20, March 31, 1865; *O.R.N.*, Ser. 2, Vol. III, pp. 1270–71. Mason quotes from Slidell's letter to him of March 6.

[4] See West, *passim*, for French press on this, and *London Times* and *Economist* for British comments.

"my extreme apprehension being that if the suggestion were made in distinct form, which was the subject of the private note to Mr. Kenner, no seal of confidence which I could place on it would prevent its reaching other ears than those of the party to whom it was addressed; and it would thus get to the enemy. And if not accepted the mischief resulting would be incalculable." He read that portion of Benjamin's instructions that "if . . . . there be objections not made known to us, which have for four years prevented the recognition of our independence notwithstanding the demonstration of our right to assert and our ability to maintain it, justice equally demands that an opportunity be afforded us for meeting and overcoming those objections, if in our power to do so."

"I returned again and again during the conversation," wrote Mason, "to this point, and in language so direct that it was impossible to be misunderstood."[1]

But Mason, believing that the fear of a reconstructed Union would operate more powerfully upon Lord Palmerston than an offer to free the slaves, spoke of the probability of peace upon the basis of a defensive and offensive alliance in case Europe refused recognition. He assured Palmerston that the South did not desire such an alliance, but that he "could not say how far the law of necessity might control us, were the alternative presented of a continued devastation of our country, or a return to peace through an alliance committing us to the foreign wars of the North."[2]

Palmerston must have recognized now if he had not before this that the Confederacy was facing inevitable defeat. The press carried the news each day that Sherman was cutting the South into shreds, that Grant's army was pressing Lee to the last extremity. He must have seen now that the Union would be reconstructed and that England might have to face a reunited and exasperated America. And he could see, what Mason could not, that nothing could be done about it. England's recognition of the South, now, with slavery abolished, would not save the Confederacy, and it would probably result

[1] Pickett Papers, Mason to Benjamin, No. 20, with inclosure, March 31, 1865; O.R.N., Ser. 2, Vol. III, pp. 1270–71, minutes of a conversation with Lord Palmerston, etc., inclosure.

[2] Ibid.

eventually, when the South was crushed, in a war between England and the United States. If slavery had been the only obstacle to recognition before now, it no longer remained so. It was too late to recognize the South on any terms. So Palmerston, suave, urbane, and sympathetic—for he did sincerely sympathize with the South and just as sincerely disliked the North—assured Mason, according to the latter's report, "that the objections entertained by his Government were those which had been avowed, and that there was nothing . . . . 'underlying' them. . . . . On the question of recognition, the Government had not been satisfied at any period of the war that our independence was achieved beyond peradventure, and did not feel authorized so to declare when the events of a few weeks might prove it a failure . . . . that whilst the North continued the war to restore the Union on the scale it was now prosecuted, and with a purpose avowedly unchanged, there could be no such assurance of the result as, in the opinion of his Government, would warrant their recognizing a final separation. He gave this as the sum of the objections against our recognition, and added that, as affairs now stood, our seaports given up, the comparatively unobstructed march of Sherman etc., rather increased than diminished previous objections."[1]

When Slidell received Mason's letter that Palmerston disclaimed any other obstacles to recognition than the inability of the South to demonstrate its ability to maintain its independence, he replied that Palmerston was not entirely frank. Moreover, he felt that Russell was greatly influenced by the slavery question.[2] Mason was evidently somewhat disturbed by this thought and by the thought that perhaps he had not made himself perfectly clear to Palmerston that the Confederacy proposed to free the slaves in return for recognition. So on March 26 he sought his Tory friend, Lord Donoughmore. Mason frankly broached the matter of slavery as an obstacle to English recognition. Donoughmore replied that slavery had "always been in the way, and that after Lee's successes on the Rappahannock

[1] *Ibid.;* cf. Mason Papers, Mason to Slidell, March 15 and 20, 1865, for Mason's account of interview.

[2] Mason Papers, March 22, 1865.

and march into Pennsylvania, when he threatened Harrisburg, and his army was at the very gates of Washington he thought but for slavery we should then have been acknowledged." Mason then asked him, "Suppose I were now to go to Lord Palmerston and make a proposition to wit, that in the event of present recognition, measures would be taken satisfactory to the British Government, for the abolition of slavery . . . . would his Government then recognize us?" Lord Donoughmore replied that "the time had gone by, now especially that our fortunes seemed more adverse than ever."[1]

Thus ended in futility, as it had begun, the last effort of the Confederate commissioners to gain European aid. "*Sic transit Gloria Mundi*," exclaimed Mason as the last hope of the Confederacy faded.[2]

Whether the Confederacy could have gained British recognition by the emancipation of the slaves in the early part of the war is doubtful in view of other more material and substantial considerations. It would have largely disarmed the French hostility to the South; yet this would in itself have been insufficient to move them or their Emperor, for, as in the case of England, Napoleon and the French people were balancing many other interests besides slavery. Let us then consider the problem as to why England and France did not intervene in the war.

[1] Pickett Papers, Mason to Benjamin, No. 20, March 31, 1865; *O.R.N.*, Ser. 2, Vol. III, pp. 1270-77, inclosing minutes of a conversation with Earl Donoughmore, March 26, 1865.

[2] Mason Papers, Mason to Slidell, March 15, 1865.

CHAPTER XVIII

WHY EUROPE DID NOT INTERVENE

WAR PROFITS AND FEAR OF WAR WITH THE UNITED STATES

Looking back over the unfolding of events, it will be seen that the chief diplomatic efforts of the commissioners were directed toward intervention in some form. At times the intervention which they sought was to take the form of repudiation of the Federal blockade, which unquestionably was a violation of the Declaration of Paris and to which the Confederacy had partially subscribed; at other times it was mediation on the principle that the combatants had reached a stalemate; then at other times when the South seemed to have won crushing military victories it was the recognition of independence; and at moments when the interests of Europe were badly injured by the continuance of the war it was to be armed intervention. Underlying the diplomacy of the Confederate States in behalf of intervention was the King Cotton doctrine that Europe must have southern cotton or perish. This King Cotton philosophy, we have seen, was a fairly reasonable one, for about a fourth or fifth of England's population gained its bread from the cotton industry (based principally on the southern supply), and one-tenth of England's wealth was invested in this industry and nearly half of her export trade was made up of manufactured cotton goods. France was not as involved as England, yet the cotton industry, based largely on American cotton, was her largest and most profitable industry, and there were about a million restless operatives, including their families, engaged in this industry.

The surplus stocks on hand in England and France in 1861 staved off the cotton famine until 1862. This was a disappointment to the South, for such a contingency had not been anticipated. But by the combination of the Confederate embargo and a Federal blockade a cotton famine was finally produced in England and France in 1862, which threw over half the operatives out of employment and forced them and their families upon charity amounting to two millions in England and one million in France. The Confederacy was very confident of securing intervention as a result of this famine; and the question was seriously canvassed in both the French and the English cabinets in the fall of 1862, but nothing came of it. Then there was in 1863 another serious effort of the Confederate commissioners and their friends to induce England and France to intervene, which ended in the absurd Roebuck-Lindsay episode. During this interval the Confederacy had continued to rely upon the need of Europe for southern cotton to move England and France into intervention. However, the faith in cotton was rapidly weakened after the fall of 1862 when intervention did not come and the cotton famine began to grow less acute. But two other probable forces which might operate in favor of English and French intervention revealed themselves to the Confederate commissioners in the meantime, and, after the approaching failure of King Cotton, they began to stake success heavily upon these two motives. These were the extreme hatred and jealousy shown in England against the United States as a powerful rival, and the desire of Napoleon to establish a vassal empire in Mexico. These had operated more than all else to throw the sympathies of Napoleon and of the majority of the English upon the side of the South. The appeals of the commissioners for European aid, whether in the building of a navy or in recognition of armed intervention, took cognizance more and more of the desire of England and Napoleon to divide and weaken the United States.

But, as we have seen, neither England nor Napoleon ever raised a hand in aid of the Confederacy, to get cotton or to recognize the South. What are the explanations? Why did King Cotton fail to move these powers as had been anticipated? Why did not the desire for weakening a powerful and hated rival bestir England and Napoleon? The answer as far as Napoleon is concerned is simple and may be disposed of briefly. This despot, we will recall, was always eager from the beginning until the end of the American war to join England in intervention. On the other hand, he was under no circumstances willing to intervene alone or in company with weaker powers. He had been perfectly frank with Slidell and Rost in admitting that he refrained from repudiating the blockade or from recognizing the independence of the Confederacy because of his apprehension that the United States would declare war on him should he do so. While he had a powerful navy of ironclads, he was fearful of the results of a war with America. The reasons for his fear were many: It was not just America alone which he feared in case of war, but most of Europe, he thought, would be on his back. There were Prussia, Russia, Austria, Sardinia, and even England who would welcome such a war to close in upon him from the rear, and he knew it and constantly adverted to the subject in his conversations with Slidell and others on the question of intervention. However, there was another force which he feared equally as much—the disapproval of the French people of a war with America. We have observed that the French people were in sympathy with the North because of the fact that the South was slaveholding and because of the traditional friendship of the French for the United States, and especially because of the universal desire to see the United States grow strong as a counterpoise to England. Napoleon's American policy was diametrically opposed to traditional French policy and sympathies, and he himself was as unpopular with the French as was his policy. Should he bring on a war with America, even with his foreign enemies quiescent, he might lose his throne. He could not hazard a war with America, or if he did it must be in company with England, his chief ally and deadliest enemy. He always stood ready to join England in intervention.

Let us, then, see why England did not bow to the command of King Cotton and break the blockade, or recognize the Confederacy, or meddle in some way with the struggle so as to assure herself of a supply of cotton and the permanent division of a too-powerful rival. First, let us examine the King Cotton question, and explain the spectacle of twenty six members of Parliament from Lancashire and eight or ten from Lanarkshire, Derbyshire, and Leicestershire—the cotton districts—and especially from Liverpool, sitting silently, apparently bored with all questions of intervention, only one, in fact, Hopwood, ever showing any real interest in the question; and of hundreds of thousands of operatives with their families upon charity, losing $200,000,000 in wages without revolting.

How England and especially the industrial population resisted the power of King Cotton has two usual explanations—though other factors are conceded as playing minor parts. The older school has placed England's non-intervention upon a high and idealistic basis: the sympathy of the Lancashire population—and of the common people generally—with the Union as a great experiment in democracy, as a great model which was held up to the English; and their antipathy to slavery. The newer school of economic historians has not been satisfied with such high motives for mere cotton-mill workers; they have insisted that the antidote for one economic impulse is to be found in another and greater economic impulse. This antidote for the King Cotton virus has been found in a simple name which bears no royal trappings like King Cotton. It, in fact, had until 1861 been the scullion in King Cotton's kitchen or at most a buck private in the rear ranks of this sovereign—the name referred to is "wheat." England must have American wheat or perish.

These two motives together or separately are inadequate explanations of why England did not intervene to obtain cotton. The idealistic theory of the sympathy of the Lancashire population with the North as a sole explanation is too good to be true. The agitations and mass meetings held in England by William Forster and John Bright and by other less radical northern propagandists, and the vast multitudes who voted petitions to Parliament and cabinet against intervention, have been taken too much at their face value, while similar agitations and mass meetings and giant petitions got up by James Spence, William Lindsay, Roebuck, Beresford-Hope, and other southern propagandists have been too much ignored.[1] The fact of the whole business is, as we have seen,[2] that these meetings, whether pro-northern or pro-southern, were not spontaneous, but were drummed up by well-subsidized leaders and were frequently packed by the liberal use of small coin. The population of Lancashire and of all industrial England was politically apathetic, sodden, ignorant, and docile, with the exception of a few intelligent and earnest leaders. They wanted bread, they wanted clothes, they needed medicines to give their sick children and aged parents, they wanted pretty clothing for their daughters and sisters who were being forced into prosti-

[1] See chap. v. [2] Ibid.

tution. One is not surprised, therefore, to learn from the correspondence of Mason, Spence, Henry Hotze, and others that the purchasability of these people was a coldly recognized fact which the pro-northern and pro-southern agitators made use of. Under these circumstances the public meetings and agitations of the Federal and Confederate sympathizers would be largely determined by the use made of slush funds. This gave the edge to the northern agitation, perhaps. Another factor already noted which would still further give the appearance of greater sympathy for the North than for the South was the fact that Bright and Forster could always with perfect timeliness raise a town meeting, a petition, or a resolution against intervention, while James Spence and his cohorts could hold a mass meeting or pass a resolution favoring intervention only when the military situation was overwhelmingly in favor of the South.

John Watts, connected with the committee for the relief of the Lancashire population and a native of that section, expressed the opinion in his *Facts of the Cotton Famine* that the population of Lancashire was pretty evenly divided in their attitude toward the Civil War.[1] But be that as it may, whether the population was evenly divided or all on the northern side, it is doubtful whether they exercised much influence upon the non-intervention policy of the British government. Few of these people wielded the vote, so the government had little to fear from them in a political way; and there is no evidence to show that the government feared that they would refuse to support a possible war with the United States should England decide to intervene. The fear lay in the opposite direction. The government, in fact, was convinced that the only danger lay in this population's forcing England into war with the United States to obtain cotton. This fear was not great, however, as Palmerston knew his docile and submissive British workmen. They required only enough to keep body and soul together, and the wealth of England saw that they had just this much and no more. As John Bright remarked, it would be cheaper to feed these workers on champagne and venison than to have them force England into intervention, but it was found necessary to feed them only with bread and water. These people,

[1] Watts, *Facts of the Cotton Famine, passim.*

then, did not count in a political way, and, as long as they could be kept from insurrection, they would not count in any other respect as far as the government of Palmerston and Russell was concerned.

What about the more recent economic interpretation, the influence of wheat in keeping John Bull on his good behavior with the United States? In this interpretation it is pointed out that England suffered from a very short grain crop in 1860-61-62, and that the great deficiency was supplied by the wheat and grain of the United States, just at the time when Parliament and the cabinet were considering the question of intervention to get cotton; and that the probability or certainty of a wheat famine in case England should become involved in a war by intervention prevented the British government from taking action. It is true that William E. Forster, John Bright, and a few others in and out of Parliament conducted a considerable agitation against intervention, based partly on the supposed dependence of England upon American wheat and grain.[1] But outside of the industrial districts this doctrine made no impression. Parliament did not think enough of it to discuss it, and complete silence on the subject existed in the cabinet circles. No mention has been found in official or private correspondence of these men which would indicate that a wheat famine would accompany a war with the United States.[2]

This silence would not be conclusive were there not other evidence of a more positive character which corroborates this negative evidence. In the first place, the wheat-famine idea can be identified as Federal propaganda emanating from William H. Seward and Abraham Lincoln. As we have seen, in the fall and winter of 1861-62 Seward wrote several dispatches to Adams and Dayton, at the time when rumors of intervention were causing the American people great alarm, warning England and France that while they might have a cotton famine now they would suffer both a wheat and a cotton famine if they interfered with the struggle in America. Charles Francis Adams was on intimate terms with William Forster, and there is definite evidence to show that he read or paraphrased some of these

[1] Schmidt, "Influence of Corn and Wheat on Anglo-American Relations, etc.," *passim.*
[2] Cf. E. D. Adams, II, 13 n.

dispatches to that gentleman who in turn passed the good word on to Bright. In the meantime, Seward indoctrinated Charles Sumner and the latter was soon writing about it to Bright and his other British friends.

The British press, however, with few exceptions, sneered at the idea. Both the *London Economist* and the *London Times* touched upon the focal point, namely, that the assumption was made without foundation that Great Britain could get wheat nowhere but from the United States, when as a matter of fact Great Britain's deficiencies could be easily supplied in many other places, including Poland, Russia, and Prussia. The large purchases from the United States during the years 1860, 1861, and 1862, amounting in 1862 to almost half the total importation, were, according to the *Times*, matters of mere convenience of transportation and a slightly cheaper purchase price, not of necessity. Most important of all, it was pointed out that England took this wheat in payment for the countless millions of dollars' worth of rifles, cannon, powder, and other munitions of war which she was selling the United States. In fact, the North, now that cotton could no longer be shipped to England, had no other means by which it could purchase its munitions abroad. No other medium of international exchange existed, and it was pointed out with much truth that the United States would be bankrupt if its wheat were cut off by war, and its munitions of war would be so curtailed that it would have been defeated by the South.[1]

This contention of the *Times* and other papers seems convincing, especially in view of the fact that in 1864 and 1865, after the United States became practically self-sufficient in the production of war supplies and no longer made large purchases from England, the latter country turned abruptly away from America to Russia and East Europe for her wheat supply.[2] Recent researches in the British archives disclose no concern with a wheat famine; the explanation that American wheat was cheaper and served as the chief medium of international exchange for British munitions of war, and the proof of this in the abrupt cessation of purchases of wheat when the muni-

[1] See *London Times*, Sept. 16, 1862; March 17, 1862; April 17, 1863.
[2] *De Bow's Review*, XXXIV (July, 1866), 79–80.

tion trade ceased, all tend to demonstrate that wheat had little if anything to do with preventing English intervention in the American Civil War.

What, then, is the answer to the question as to why England did not intervene to obtain cotton? One must admit the correctness of the principle laid down by the economic interpretation group of historians, namely, that in order to counteract one economic impulse another stronger economic motive is necessary. But it is difficult to see that wheat was a strong element in the economic impulse which counteracted the King Cotton impulse. It is proposed to substitute a much more sinister term for wheat—"war profits." Those who are at all familiar with the war profits in the more recent wars ought not to have any great difficulty in grasping the rôle England played of war profiteer, and the powerful influence upon government of her war profiteers, especially when all, even the small operatives, were prosperous as a result of the war.

Perhaps the most surprising of the war profits was in the cotton industry itself. The warehouses of India, China, and of England, as has been observed,[1] had a surplus that it would take two years to consume were no other goods manufactured, and England had on hand in her warehouses 700,000 bales more than the normal surplus of raw cotton. The raw cotton had cost around fourteen cents a pound, and the manufactured goods stored in warehouses could not be sold at the cost of the raw material. The British industry was faced with bankruptcy. The mills were already beginning to slow down before the war, and British financial and economic writers were predicting a long period of unemployment and suffering for the operatives. Then the Civil War came as if in answer to prayer and cut off the supply of cheap cotton. The price of raw cotton rose from fourteen cents to sixty, and as time passed the surplus manufactured goods followed suit until at length everything was sold at a net profit of not less than $200,000,000. In the meanwhile, the larger and well-financed mills continued to manufacture goods and hold against the rising markets. These larger mills, which Arnold estimates as composing two-thirds of the industry,[2] not merely made a

[1] Chap. iv. [2] Arnold, *History of the Cotton Famine*, pp. 48–49.

profit out of this vast surplus of cheap pre-war goods, but averaged a neat profit on their output over the four years of war. The only people who went down were the small mill-owners and the cotton operatives. They lost all they had. But the industry was saved from one of the worst panics in history, and impending ruin turned into undreamed-of profits.[1] No wonder the members of Parliament from Lancashire sat silent during the debates on intervention. Instead of desiring intervention these members of Parliament and the industrialists they represented must have been praying that the Lord would see fit to let the Civil War continue forever. This attitude is well illustrated by one of the small cotton-buyers who had bought a few-score bales and was holding them against a rising market when the news reached England that Sherman had captured Savannah with perhaps 30,000 bales of cotton. This Englishman, with all his small fortune tied up in these few bales of cotton, on hearing of this news exclaimed that if that news should be true, some one would have to stick to him lest he commit suicide![2] Every peace rumor or rumor of captured cotton, says Watts, brought a panic and "good and honorable men spoke of the probable cessation of the most terrible war of modern times as a thing to be dreaded." As paradoxical as it may seem, even the operatives who were working, when at all, on short time, with a total loss of wages almost equal to the war profits of their employers, shared in the apprehension of peace. Each peace rumor, each rumor that the government was discussing intervention, sent the price of cotton down and caused the shutdown of small mills whose owners had been caught on narrow margins or who were unable to manufacture in the hopes of future profits. The operatives were caught in a vicious circle. They could not hope for full-time work during the war, but they were afraid that when the war ended they would lose their jobs entirely. Not only were the mill-owners and cotton-buyers involved in this speculation, but the banking interests of England were directly and indirectly concerned. To these men who had made big profits and had refinanced the cotton industry

[1] For profits made in the cotton industry see *ibid.*, pp. 40–47, 79–83, and *passim;* Scherer, pp. 264–65; Hammond, pp. 254–59.

[2] Watts, pp. 359–61.

upon the basis of high-priced raw cotton the end of the war meant a flood of cheap cotton, and that meant Judgment Day. James Spence wrote that to these men, though they were in entire sympathy with the South, "the idea of recognition was that of heavy instant loss,— a very formidable obstacle in the way" of recognition.[1]

There is another phase of the cotton profits which must not be overlooked, namely, the development of India as a rival source for raw cotton. England, as we have seen, had tried for twenty or more years before 1860, in the face of American rivalry, to rehabilitate the Indian cotton industry with little success, but the elimination of the American crop was India's opportunity. The *London Times*[2] rejoiced that "American cotton is actually out of the running—and there is no saying how long it may continue so . . . . and when America appears in the market again India ought to be her match. If this can be accomplished, England will be relieved from any risk of another cotton drought. . . . . It would have been difficult," commented the *Times* some time later,[3] "to beat America out of the market, but America is out of the market by her own act. Before she comes in again, there will be time, in all probability, to organize a new trade, and though we must be sorely straitened in the interval, it may be hoped that the result will finally emancipate us from difficulties which had been foreseen and dreaded." Great hopes were expressed that the American monopoly might be overthrown. Some were optimistic enough to believe that the American staple might be permanently eclipsed; others were of the opinion that as soon as the war ended the cheap American supply would drive all other cotton out; while perhaps the majority thought that if the war lasted long enough India would at least share equally in the world-market with American cotton.[4] Certainly the Indian supply made great strides during the war. We will recall that before the Civil War from 80 to 85 per cent of the British and European supply of cotton came from America. But the war cut off the bulk of the American supply, and England turned at once to India. In 1862 Great Britain imported

[1] Mason Papers, Spence to Mason, May 4, 1864.

[2] *London Times*, Oct. 24, 1861.   [3] *Ibid.*, Jan. 16, 1862.

[4] See Hammond, p. 275, for opinion of a prominent ex-government official.

3,505,844 hundredweight of cotton from India out of a total importation of 4,676,333 hundredweight; in 1863 she imported 3,878,758
hundredweight from India out of a total importation of 5,978,422
hundredweight;[1] in 1864 she imported from India 4,522,560 hundredweight out of a total of 7,975,935 hundredweight.[2] And when
the war ended England was getting 85 per cent from India. Nor did
the end of the war bring an immediate end to the increase, for in 1866
England imported 2,000,000 bales, or 6,000,000 hundredweight
(the Indian bale weighed 300 pounds) from India, and it was still
believed that the American market could never again reduce the
Indian supply to less than 2,000,000 bales, or about 50 per cent of
the British supply.[3] The failure of this prophecy has no part in
Civil War diplomacy.

The next great sources of profits are closely related to the cotton
industry—the profits which were reaped from the linen and woolen
industries, the old rivals of cotton. These two textile industries,
which had languished since the Industrial Revolution, waked to life
again and recaptured much of their lost ground and reaped a golden
harvest. The linen industry responded instantly to the rise in the
price of cotton. In 1858 there were only 91,648 acres in flax in Ireland—the chief source of supply—whereas in 1864 there were
301,942 acres under this crop, or an increase of 229 per cent. The
production increased from less than 20,000 tons to above 80,000 tons
during this time, or 300 per cent. The importation of flax was increased about 20,000 tons. The importation of yarn increased from
58,866 pounds in 1861 to 3,997,106 pounds in 1863. The output of
the mills was increased almost as much as were the exports of certain
products. The export of yarns increased from 27,981,042 pounds in
1861 to 40,510,967 pounds in 1864—44 per cent; the export of thread
increased from 2,390,461 pounds in 1861 to 4,030,365 pounds in
1864, or about 68 per cent; the export of plain cloth increased from
116,322,469 yards in 1861 to 209,859,714 yards in 1864, or about 80
per cent. The domestic sale of linen was also greatly increased.[4]

[1] *Economist*, Feb. 20 and 27, 1864.

[2] *Ibid.*, March 4, 1865.   [3] Hammond, p. 275.

[4] For these figures see Watts, pp. 384–90, and *Economist*, March 1, 1862; Feb. 28, 1863; March 4, 1865; Schmidt, *op. cit.*, pp. 22–23, n. 37.

It is estimated by John Watts in his *Facts of the Cotton Famine* that during the three years 1862, 1863, and 1864 the linen industry realized £14,500,000 above the normal profits covering an equal period before the Civil War.[1] For 1865 the excess profit continued[2] and carried the figures up above £20,000,000, or nearly $100,000,000. Watts also estimates that 100,000 extra operatives and laborers were employed as a result of this expansion of the industry,[3] thus taking up much of the slack caused by the slump in employment in the cotton industry.

The woolen industry netted a larger profit than did linen, distributed from farmer to manufacturer. In 1861 the export of the chief woolen products was about 160,000,000 yards while in 1864 it had increased to 240,000,000 yards,[4] or 50 per cent increase. A similar increase in domestic sales took place. Watts estimates the excess profits to the manufacturers in the three years 1862, 1863, and 1864 at £17,000,000,[5] and the profits for 1865 may be put at £5,000,000. The same writer estimated the excess profits the farmers received from raw wool at £8,932,286—carrying the excess profits in the woolen industry above £30,000,000, or $150,000,000.[6] As in the linen industry there was great increase in the number of operatives, estimated at between 50,000 and 100,000.

Another business which prospered mightily during war conditions was the munitions industry. The United States for two years and the Confederacy for the entire war bought most of their small arms, cannon, powder, lead, steel plate, rails, knives, sabers, and bayonets from Europe and especially from England. From 1861 to 1864, $7,027,730 worth of alkali-saltpeter, kanit, etc.; about 3,000,000 small arms, or $25,000,000 worth; 30,000,000 pounds of powder, or $10,000,000 worth; $3,000,000 worth of lead; $10,000,000 worth of unwrought steel; $3,000,000 worth of boiler plate, $5,000,000 worth of artillery, to mention only the most important war supplies, were recorded as exported to the United States and the Confederacy.[7] It

[1] *Ibid.*   [2] See *Economist*, June 3, 1865.   [3] *Ibid.*

[4] *Ibid.*, Feb. 27, 1864; March 4, 1865; cf. Schmidt, pp. 22–23, n. 37.

[5] Watts, pp. 399 ff.   [6] *Ibid.*

[7] See *Economist*, Feb. 28, 1862; March 1, 1862; Feb. 27, 1864; March 4, 1865; cf. Parl. Papers and Accts., N. Amer., LXIX, No. 4 (1872), 48–66.

is certainly a conservative estimate based upon the Board of Trade reports to say that the North and the South bought together no less than $100,000,000 worth of war supplies from Great Britain. This is exclusive of clothing, tents, shoes, and leather goods.

Nor does it include the sale of ships and steamers to the Confederacy or the building of steamers for English blockade-runners. This last item is of great importance, for it stimulated very greatly the shipbuilding industry. Altogether about four hundred steamers, many of them iron, and eight hundred sail vessels were sold as blockade-runners. Great numbers of these vessels were constructed during the war. In addition to this, six ironclads and two wooden cruisers were constructed by the shipbuilders of Liverpool and Glasgow for the Confederate government.

Attention is called to the enormous profits which the blockade-running houses made in that business. Between a million and a million and a half bales of cotton were run through the blockade at a net profit of seldom less than 300 per cent. Goods shipped into the Confederacy, exclusive of munitions which formed only a small portion of this trade, netted a profit frequently amounting to 500 per cent. One round trip through the blockade frequently paid for a vessel and its cargo and left a profit. Many of these vessels, it will be recalled, ran scores of times, the "Little Hattie" making about sixty trips.

But the greatest profit of all, one which was so enormous it cannot be measured in dollars and cents, was made possible in the complete destruction of the American merchant marine directly or indirectly by the Confederate privateers and cruisers. This destruction was done without England's lifting her hand, except in a benediction upon the Confederacy for doing her work so thoroughly. In 1860 the United States was and had been for many years England's only serious rival in the world-carrying trade. So successful, in fact, had been the United States that she had largely driven England out of the direct trade between America and Great Britain—the most sensitive point of all. The United States had in this trade in 1860, 2,245,000 tons and Great Britain had only 946,000,[1] while the total ocean-going tonnage of the American merchant marine was between

[1] Bigelow, *Retrospections, etc.*, I, 536.

5,500,000 and 6,000,000 tons, practically as large as that of Great Britain and doubling every ten years. Its ships were magnificent. They could outsail anything afloat. The "Yankee Clipper" had been the despair and envy of the world.[1] In 1861 England saw this magnificent fleet of seabirds begin to scatter and then disappear, until when the war ended only a little over a million tons of culls, mostly coasting vessels which could not be sold, were left.[2] As Admiral Porter remarked sadly, the American merchant marine was virtually extinct.[3] The cruisers and privateers had sunk or captured above two hundred ships, destroying around thirty million dollars' worth of property.[4] But their greatest havoc was wrought by indirection. The hazard was so great that marine insurance rose higher than it was in the war with England in 1812 when that power had our coast blockaded,[5] and shippers and merchants, American as well as European, were so fearful of the work of the "Alabama" and her sisters that they could not be induced to ship their merchandise on American ships.

So the magnificent ships lay in dock swinging idly at their cables, their crews scattered, and their sails and hulls rotting while less worthy craft plied the seas. Nothing was finally left except to sell them to neutrals whose flag would make them safe. England got the best and the greatest number. By the first of July, 1864, all had been sold of this great fleet except 1,674,516 tons, mostly obsolete and coasting vessels;[6] and England had already bought over $42,000,000 worth out of a total sale of $64,799,750.[7] This sale continued, as we have said, until little more than 1,000,000 tons of scraps were left. England's only rival had been destroyed for an indefinite span of years. England has fought wars for less than the destruction of a rival's merchant marine. Surely England could keep the peace for

[1] See *New York World*, July 7, 1864.

[2] See *ibid.* for figures of that date.   [3] *New York Herald*, July 19, 1865.

[4] Parl. Papers and Accts., N. Amer., LXIX, No. 11 (1872), 69; cf. C. F. Adams, *The Treaty of Washington, passim;* J. T. Scharf, *History of the Confederate States Navy* (New York and San Francisco, 1887), *passim;* William Robinson, *The Confederate Privateers* (New Haven, 1928), *passim.*

[5] *New York World*, Oct. 22, 1864.

[6] *Ibid.*, July 7, 1864; *ibid.*, Oct. 22, statement of Reverdy Johnson.

[7] *Ibid.*, July 7, 1864.

such a magnificent reward—especially since war would mean the destruction of her own merchant marine, in a similar fashion.

We see, therefore, that England far from being hag-ridden by poverty during the American Civil War made enormous material profits. Her surplus stock of cotton was sold at a fabulous profit, her linen and woolen industries reaped unexpected harvests of gold, her munitions and steel industries enriched themselves, her shipbuilding was enormously stimulated by the demands of the Confederate government and the blockade business, merchant houses made millions out of blockade-running, and finally the American merchant marine was driven from the seas and largely transferred to England. An examination of the volume of British imports and exports and the pauper list during the Civil War is rather eloquent of this profit, despite the fact that much of the imports were the invisible earnings of the greatly enhanced merchant marine which do not appear on the books. The total imports were:

1860	£210,500,000
1861	217,500,000
1862	226,000,000
1863	249,000,000
1864	269,000,000

The total exports including re-exportation were:

1860	£164,500,000
1861	159,600,000
1862	166,200,000
1863	196,000,000
1864	240,000,000 (estimated)

That is, the volume of foreign trade in 1864 was £509,000,000 as against £374,500,000 in 1860, or 34 per cent greater than before the war. There had been a temporary shock in 1861 with the upset of the American markets, but this was largely gained back after that and markets elsewhere, especially in France, greatly expanded.

An examination of the Poor Law Board reports shows that despite the fact that at one time over a half million people were on the dole in Lancashire the average of those dependent upon charity for all England and Wales was little if any higher during the four years of the American war than during a like period before 1860. For the ten years before 1860 there was an average of about 925,000 people on charity in England and Wales. During the Civil War, despite the increase of the population for these ten years previous, the average number receiving charity was about 975,000, which was little if any larger percentage of the population than before the war in America. This corroborates the statement that the slack caused by cotton operatives being out of work was taken up by the greater productivity of the linen, woolen, munition industries and the expanding merchant marine and the shipbuilding. Even with Lancashire unemployed the labor situation was normal—which meant that outside the cotton districts it was far above normal.[1]

The *London Times* in summing up the situation remarked that[2] "outside of Lancashire it would not be known that anything had occurred to injure the national trade. That is the most extraordinary and surprising incident of the story. An industry which we conceived to be essential to our commercial greatness has been utterly prostrated, without affecting the greatness in any perceptible degree. We are as busy, as rich, and as fortunate in our trade as if the American war had never broken out, and our trade with the states had never been disturbed. Cotton was no king, notwithstanding the prerogatives which had been loudly claimed for him." England could dispense with the cotton industry, so it seemed. John Watts, writing at the same time, remarked that not only could England do without the cotton industry, but "that so far as the people who pay income tax are concerned Lancashire itself seems as if it could almost do without its staple industry," since those incomes seemed unimpaired by the war. *So we may conclude, with regard to the economic motive for intervention: it did not exist.* With the exception of the Lancashire operatives all was well and God was in his heaven!

If the King Cotton basis of diplomacy proved unsound, what about the political motive that England had in desiring a division of

[1] See fourteenth, fifteenth, sixteenth, seventeenth, and eighteenth annual reports of the Poor Law Board (1861–66); Parl. Papers and Accts., Vol. XXIV (1862); Vol. XXII (1863); Vol. XXV (1864); Vol. XXII (1865); Vol. XXXV (1866), respectively.

[2] *London Times*, Jan. 7, 1864.

the Union? Why did not she intervene to accomplish that greatly desired end? The answer to this is that in the first place England never doubted until it was too late that the South would win its independence and the roast pigeon would thus fly into the open mouth of the British lion without any other effort than the opening of his jaws. This confidence in the southern success has been frequently alluded to in this volume and it has been well presented in E. D. Adams' *Great Britain and the American Civil War*, so it is only necessary to call attention to it here. It was almost a universal belief. In the second place, had this belief not existed the British government could not have been induced to interfere with the American struggle because of a conviction that it would involve the two countries in a war in which, as Bright said, England would be the most vulnerable nation in the world. This is a fear which was constantly expressed by cabinet, Parliament, and press. It was feared that England would lose Canada, and it was an absolute certainty that she would lose her entire merchant marine, just as the United States had done. Certainly she would lose all the great war profits of which we have just spoken. In fact, we might venture to suggest that the economic motive not to intervene outweighed what we might call the political motive of weakening a military and national rival. Finally, there were certain considerations of international laws which would have very strong bearing in preventing England from meddling with the struggle. Had England harbored no fear of war nor loss of her profits she might have refrained from taking any part. She did not wish to help establish a precedent of interfering in a domestic struggle—while war was still raging— especially of a first-class power. That privilege was reserved to backward third-rate powers. Again, as we have seen, the Palmerston government hoped to disarm American protests at a later date by allowing that country to establish a paper blockade, and thus vitiate the Declaration of Paris with regard to blockades. The practices of recent world wars demonstrate the value of this precedent.

BIBLIOGRAPHY

UNPUBLISHED PRIVATE MANUSCRIPTS AND PUBLIC DOCUMENTS

ARCHIVES DU MINISTÈRE DES AFFAIRES ÉTRANGÈRES, PARIS

French Foreign Office Papers (1860–65)

Diplomatic Correspondence
1. With Belgium, Vols. 51–54
2. With England, Vols. 715–32
3. With Mexico, Vols. 54–65
4. With Russia, Vols. 223–35
5. With United States, Vols. 123–33

Consular Despatches
1. From Confederacy
2. From Mexico
3. From United States

BRITISH PUBLIC RECORD OFFICE, LONDON

British Foreign Office Papers (1860–65)

Diplomatic Correspondence
1. F.O. 10, with Belgium, Vols. 231–34, 239–43, 248–51, 255–58, 261–64
2. F.O. 27, with France, Vols. 1372–1400, 1419–48, 1476–99, 1517–37, 1555–70
3. F.O. 50, with Mexico, Vols. 351–54, 363–67, 373–75, 380, 394–97
4. F.O. 65, with Russia, Vols. 571–81, 595–610, 623–39, 655–63, 676–82
5. F.O. 5, with United States, Vols. 754–77, 817–40, 868–900, 938–65, 1009–17

Consular Despatches
1. From Confederacy
2. From Mexico
3. From United States

Reports of the Law Officers of the Crown

Russell Papers

Private Correspondence of Lord John Russell

LIBRARY OF CONGRESS, WASHINGTON

Henry Hotze's Letter Books, 1861–64, 1864–65

Henry Hotze, Papers of Henry Hotze and Others, 1862–65

James M. Mason Papers

Private Correspondence, Documents, etc., 1860–70

Pickett Papers, especially the following:

Letters from Slidell to Benjamin, 2 vols.

Letters from Benjamin to Slidell, 1 vol.

Hotze's diplomatic correspondence and some private letters, 1 vol.

Package No. 47, containing the "Personal Instructions to the Diplomatic Agents of the Confederate States in Foreign Countries"

Domestic Letters, 2 vols.

Package K, miscellaneous letters from Hotze, De Leon, Helm, to the State Department

Official and personal letters of John T. Pickett, 2 vols.

"Letter Book," covering miscellaneous correspondence, 1861–67

Packages "B" and "C," including Mason's dispatches to the State Department, Nos. 1–46, except Nos. 4–8. Also miscellaneous private letters of Mason and the dispatches of Mason to the Confederacy from Paris; New Series, Nos. 1–15

Letters of J. A. Quintero to Secretary of State, 1861–64

Acts and Resolutions of the Confederate States of America

WILLIS, EDWARD (Chief Quartermaster of General Beauregard's Division). Letters, Dispatches, Blockade-Running, etc. 13 vols. of pamphlets.

LIBRARY OF THE UNIVERSITY OF ROCHESTER, ROCHESTER, NEW YORK

William H. Seward Papers, 1861–65

Thurlow Weed Papers, 1861–65

MASSACHUSETTS HISTORICAL SOCIETY, BOSTON

ADAMS, CHARLES FRANCIS. "Diary," 1861–65 (on microfilms Nos. 75–78 of the Adams Papers).

———. Letter Books, 1861–65 (on microfilms Nos. 178–79 of the Adams Papers).

NATIONAL ARCHIVES (RECORD GROUP 59), WASHINGTON

United States Department of State Papers (1860–65)

Diplomatic Correspondence

1. With Austria: Instructions, Vol. 1; Despatches, Vols. 5–6
2. With Belgium: Instructions, Vol. 1; Despatches, Vols. 4–9
3. With France: Instructions, Vols. 15–17; Despatches, Vols. 46–49
4. With Great Britain: Instructions, Vols. 17–20; Despatches, Vols. 75–91

5. With Mexico: Instructions, Vol. 17; Despatches, Vols. 27–30
6. With Russia: Instructions, Vols. 14–15; Despatches, Vols. 18–20

Consular Despatches

1. From Cuba: Havana, Vols. 41–48
2. From France: Bordeaux, Vols. 6–7; Havre, Vols. 10–11; Nantes, Vols. 3–4
3. From Great Britain: Belize, British Honduras, Vols. 1–3; Bermuda, Vols. 5–7; Cork (Queenstown), Vols. 4–6; Dublin, Vols. 3–4, 6; Glasgow, Vols. 6–7; Liverpool, Vols. 18–33; London, Vols. 29–35; Nassau, Bahamas, Vols. 5–7
4. From Mexico: Matamoras, Vols. 7–8; Tampico, Vols. 6–8; Vera Cruz, Vols. 8–9

Domestic Letters, Vols. 60, 62, 63

Miscellaneous Letters, Vols. 61–65

Notes from the British Legation

Notes from the French Legation

Special Agents, Vols. 20–22

Special Missions, Vols. 2–3

NEWSPAPERS, MAGAZINES, AND PERIODICALS
(Dates are for the period 1861–65)
AMERICAN

Alexandria Gazette
Atlanta Confederacy
Atlanta Intelligencer
Atlantic Monthly
Augusta Chronicle and Sentinel
Augusta Constitutionalist
Bowling Green Standard
Charleston Daily Courier
Charleston Mercury
Clarke County Journal
De Bow's Review
Hunt's Merchant Magazine
Knoxville Whig
Louisville Courier
Louisville Journal
Lynchburg Virginian
Lynchburg Weekly Register
Memphis Appeal

Memphis Argus
Memphis Enquirer
Mobile Daily Advertiser and Register
Mobile Tribune
Montgomery Advertiser
Montgomery Mail
Natchez Free Trader
New Orleans Bee
New Orleans Commercial Bulletin
New Orleans Daily Crescent
New Orleans Daily Delta
New Orleans Daily Picayune
New Orleans Price Current
New Orleans True Delta
New York Herald
New York Price Current
New York Times
New York Tribune

Niles' Weekly Register
Norfolk Herald
Petersburg Intelligencer
Raleigh Standard
Richmond Dispatch
Richmond Enquirer
Richmond Examiner

Richmond Observer
Richmond Sentinel
Richmond Whig
St. Louis Democrat
St. Louis Republican
Savannah Daily Republican
South Carolinian

BRITISH

Army and Navy Gazette
Belfast Whig
Birmingham Post
Dublin Nation
Dublin News
Caledonian Mercury
Cotton Supply Reporter
Edinburgh Review
John Bull (country squire's paper)
London Chronicle
London Daily News
London Economist
London Gazette
London Globe
London Herald
London Index
London Morning Advertiser

London Morning Star
London Post
London Review
London Standard
London Telegraph
London Times
Manchester Examiner and Times
Manchester Guardian
Newcastle Chronicle
North British Review
Press and St. James' Chronicle
Quarterly Review
Reynolds' Weekly
Saturday Review
Spectator
Westminster Review

FRENCH

(French newspapers compiled largely from W. R. West, *Contemporary French Opinion of the Civil War*)

Nantes—*Phare de la Loire*
Paris—*Charivari*
Paris—*Constitutionnel*
Paris—*Courier du dimanche*
Paris—*Journal des débats*
Paris—*La France*
Paris—*Moniteur universel*
Paris—*Opinion nationale*
Paris—*Patrie*
Paris—*Pays*

Paris—*Presse*
Paris—*Siècle*

Correspondant
Illustration
Monde illustré
Revue britannique
Revue contemporaine
Revue des deux mondes
Revue germanique

PRINTED PUBLIC DOCUMENTS

CASE, LYNN M. (comp. and ed.). *French Opinion on the United States and Mexico, 1860–1867: Extracts from the Reports of the Procureurs Généraux.* New York and London: D. Appleton-Century Co., 1936.

Compilation of Laws and Decisions of the Court Relating to War Claims. Washington: Government Printing Office, 1912.

CONFEDERATE STATES OF AMERICA, DEPARTMENT OF STATE. *Instructions upon Neutral and Belligerent Rights.* Prepared by JUDAH P. BENJAMIN. Richmond: Macfarlane & Ferguson, 1864.

Congressional Globe. 1860–65.

Débats: Senat and Corps Législatif (1860–65). (Appeared in *Moniteur.*)

Documents diplomatiques. 1860–65.

Great Britain. Parliament. House of Commons and House of Lords. *Sessional Papers,* 1861–1865.

HANSARD. *Parliamentary Debates.* Ser. 3. London: Cornelius Buck, 1830–91.

Journal of Congress of the Confederate States of America, 1861–1865, "Senate Executive Documents" (58th Congress, 2d sess., 1903–4), Vols. XXV–XXXI, No. 234. 7 vols. Washington: Government Printing Office, 1904–5.

LAIRD FIRM SHIPBUILDERS (Birkenhead). *Birkenhead Ironclads: Correspondence between Her Majesty's Government and Messrs Laird Bros.* London: Vacher & Sons, 1864.

MCPHERSON, EDWARD. *The Political History of the United States of America during the Great Rebellion.* Washington: Philip & Solomons, etc., 1864.

MALLOY, WILLIAM M. (ed.). *Treaties, Conventions, International Acts, Protocols, and Agreements between the United States of America and Other Powers, 1776–1909.* 2 vols. Washington: Government Printing Office, 1910.

MATHEWS, J. M. (ed.). *Statutes at Large of the Provisional Government of the Confederate States of America.* 1861–64.

MOORE, FRANK (ed.). *The Rebellion Record: A Diary of American Events, with Documents, Narratives, Illustrative Incidents, Poetry, etc.* 12 vols. New York, 1862–71.

MOORE, JOHN BASSETT. *A Digest of International Law.* Washington: Government Printing Office, 1906.

Official Records of the Union and Confederate Navies in the War of the Rebellion. 31 vols. Washington: Government Printing Office, 1894–1927.

PATRICK, REMBERT WALLACE (ed.). *Confederate States of America, Department of Justice: The Opinions of the Confederate Attorneys-General, 1861–1865.* Buffalo: Dennis & Co., 1950.

"Proceedings of the First Confederate Congress," *Southern Historical Society Papers* (Richmond), Vols. XLIV–XLVII (1923–30).

Report of the Secretary of the Interior, Communicating the Report of John Claiborne, Esq., Special Agent Appointed To Collect Statistics on the Consumption of Cotton (35th Congress, 1st sess., 1857–58), Senate Exec. Doc. 35.

RICHARDSON, JAMES D. *A Compilation of the Messages and Papers of the Confederacy, Including the Diplomatic Correspondence, 1861–1865.* Washington: Washington Post Co., 1905; Nashville: U.S. Publishing Co., 1905.

United States Diplomatic Correspondence, Papers Relating to Foreign Affairs. 1861–69.

War of the Rebellion: Official Records of the Union and Confederate Armies. 130 vols. Washington: Government Printing Office, 1880–1901.

LITERATURE OF CONTROVERSY AND PROPAGANDA DURING THE ERA OF THE CONFEDERACY

ANONYMOUS. *The American Question, Secession, Tariff, Slavery.* Brighton: H. Taylor, 1862.

ANONYMOUS. *The Bastile in America or Democratic Absolutism.* (By an Eye-Witness.) London: R. Hardwicke, 1861.

ANONYMOUS. *The Right of Recognition: A Sketch of the Present Policy of the Confederate States.* (By a Recent Tourist.) London: H. Hardwicke, 1862.

BARRILLON, FRANÇOIS GUILLAUME. *Politique de la France et de l'humanité dans le conflit américain.* Paris: Guillaumin et Cie, 1861.

BELLOT DES MINIÈRES, ERNEST. *La question américaine, etc.* Paris: Dentu, 1861.

BERESFORD-HOPE, ALEXANDER J. B. *The American Disruption.* London: J. Ridgway, 1862.

————. *England, the North and the South.* London: J. Ridgway, 1862.

BOYNTON, REV. C. B. *English and French Neutrality and the Anglo-French Alliance in Their Relations to the United States and Russia.* Cincinnati: C. J. Vest & Co., 1864.

CARREY, EMILE. *Grandeur et avenir des Etats-Unis.* Paris: Dentu, 1863.

CHRISTY, DAVID. *Cotton Is King.* Cincinnati: Moore, Wilstach, Keep & Co., 1855.

COCHIN, AUGUSTIN. *L'abolition de l'esclavage.* 2 vols. Paris: J. Lecoffre, 1861.

DAY, SAMUEL PHILLIPS. *Down South.* (By the special correspondent of the *Morning Herald.*) 2 vols. London: Hurst & Blackett, 1862.

DE BOW, J. D. B. *The Interest in Slavery of the Southern Non-Slaveholder.* Charleston: Presses of Evans & Cogswell, 1860.

DE LEON, EDWIN. *La vérité sur les Etats Confédérés d'Amérique.* (By a former United States consul to Egypt.) Paris: Dentu, 1862.

ELLIOTT, E. N. (ed.). *Cotton Is King and Pro-slavery Arguments, Comprising the Writings of Hammond, Harper, Christy, Stringfellow, Hodge, Bledsoe, and Cartwright on This Important Subject.* (E. N. Elliott, president of Planter's College, Mississippi.) Augusta, Ga.: Pritchard, Abbott & Loomis, 1860.

GASPARIN, AGÉNOR ETIENNE, COMTE DU. *America before Europe.* London: S. Low, Son & Co., 1862.

———. *The Uprising of a Great People.* New York: Scribner's, 1861.

GIRARD, C. *Les États Confédérés d'Amérique visités en 1863.* Paris: Dentu, 1864.

GRANDGUILLOT, ALEIDE PIERRE. *La reconnaissance du Sud.* Paris: Dentu, 1862.

GRATTAN, THOMAS COLLEY (lawyer). *Civilized America.* 2 vols. 2d ed. London: Bradbury & Evans, 1859.

———. *England and the Disrupted States of America.* 3d ed. London: J. Ridgway, 1862.

HAUT, MARC DE. *La crise américaine, ses causes, ses résultats probables, ses rapports avec l'Europe et la France.* Paris: Dentu, 1862.

McHENRY, GEORGE. *The Cotton Trade.* London: Saunders, Otley & Co., 1863.

MASSIE, JAMES W. *America: The Origin of Her Present Conflict.* London: J. Snow, 1864.

MERSON, ERNEST. *La guerre d'Amérique et la médiation.* Paris: Dentu, 1862.

MONTAGU, LORD ROBERT (M.P.). *A Mirror in America.* London: Saunders, Otley & Co., 1861.

MORTIMER, J. *La sécession aux États-Unis et son origine, par un journaliste américain.* Paris: Dentu, 1861.

MOTLEY, J. L. *The Causes of the American Civil War.* (Published as a pamphlet.) New York: J. Gregory, 1861.

O'SULLIVAN, JOHN L. *Peace, the Sole Chance Now Left for Reunion.* London: Wm. Brown & Co., 1863.

PECQUET DU BELLET, PAUL. *La Révolution américaine dévoilée.* Paris: Dentu. 1861.

PELLETAN, EUGÈNE. *Addresse au Roi Coton.* Paris: Pagnerre, 1863.

POLLARD, EDWARD A. *The Two Nations: A Key to the History of the American War.* Richmond: Ayres & Wade, 1864.

REID, HUGO. *The American Question in a Nut Shell; or, Why We Should Recognize the Confederates.* London: R. Hardwicke, 1862.

ROYLES, J. F. *On the Culture and Commerce of Cotton in India and Elsewhere.* London: Smith, Elder & Co., 1851.

SARGENT, FITZWILLIAM. *England, the United States and the Southern Confederacy.* 2d ed. rev. and amended. London: Hamilton, Adams & Co., 1864.

———. *Les États Confédérés et l'esclavage.* Paris: L. Hachette et Cie, 1864.

SMITH, GOLDWIN. *A Letter to a Whig Member of the Southern Independence Association.* Boston: Ticknor & Fields, 1864.

———. *The Civil War in America.* London: Simpkin, Marshall & Co., 1866.

SPENCE, JAMES. *The American Union . . . . and the Causes of the Disruption.* London: R. Bentley, 1861.

STEPHENS, ALEXANDER H. *A Constitutional View of the Late War between the States.* 2 vols. Philadelphia: National Publishing Co., 1868–70.

TREMENHEERE, HUGH SEYMOUR. *The Constitution of the United States Compared with Our Own.* London: J. Murray, 1854.

TROLLOPE, ANTHONY. *North America.* London: Chapman & Hall, 1863.

LETTERS, MEMOIRS, BIOGRAPHIES, DIARIES, ETC.

ADAMS, CHARLES FRANCIS. *Charles Francis Adams.* Boston and New York: Houghton Mifflin Co., 1900.

———. "The Crisis of Foreign Intervention in the War of Secession, September, November, 1862," *Massachusetts Historical Society Proceedings*, Vol. XLVII (1914).

ADAMS, HENRY. *Education of Henry Adams: An Autobiography.* Boston and New York: Houghton Mifflin Co., 1918.

ALEXANDER, GENERAL E. P. *Military Memoirs of a Confederate: A Critical Narrative.* New York: Scribner's, 1907.

ALFRIEND, FRANK H. *The Life of Jefferson Davis.* Cincinnati: Caxton Publishing House; Philadelphia: National Publishing Co., 1868.

ALMY, REAR ADMIRAL JOHN J. (U.S.N.). *Military Order of the Loyal Legion of the United States: War Papers.* No. 9: "Incidents of the Blockade." (Read at stated meeting, Feb. 3, 1892.) Washington, 1892.

ARGYLL, G. D. C. (Eighth Duke of). *Autobiography and Memoirs.* London: J. Murray, 1906.

ASHLEY, EVELYN (M.P.). *The Life and Correspondence of Henry John Temple, Viscount Palmerston.* 2 vols. London: Richard Bentley & Son, 1879.

ATKINS, JOHN BLACK. *Life of Sir William Howard Russell.* London: J. Murray, 1911.

BANCROFT, FREDERIC. *The Life of William H. Seward.* 2 vols. New York: Harper & Bros., 1900.

BARTON, WILLIAM E. *Life of Lincoln.* 2 vols. New York: Bobbs-Merrill Co., 1925.

BIGELOW, JOHN. *Retrospections of an Active Life.* 5 vols. New York: Baker & Taylor Co., 1909–13.

BULLOCH, JAMES D. *The Secret Service of the Confederate States in Europe; or How the Confederate Cruisers Were Equipped.* 2 vols. New York: Putnam's, 1883.

BUTLER, PIERCE. *Judah P. Benjamin.* Philadelphia: G. W. Jacobs & Co., 1907.

CAMPBELL, JOHN A. *Reminiscences and Documents Relating to the Civil War during the Year 1865.* Baltimore: J. Murphy & Co., 1887.

CAPERS, HENRY D. *Life and Times of C. G. Memminger.* Richmond: Everett Waddey Co., 1893.

CHESNUT, MARY B. *A Diary from Dixie.* New York: Appleton, 1905.

CLAY-CLOPTON, VIRGINIA. *A Belle of the Fifties.* New York: Putnam's, 1904.

CLEVELAND, HENRY. *Alexander H. Stephens in Public and Private.* Philadelphia and Chicago: National Publishing Co., 1866.

CONWAY, MONCURE DANIEL. *Autobiography.* Boston and New York: Houghton Mifflin Co., 1904.

CORTI, COUNT EGON CAESAR. *Maximilian and Charlotte.* New York and London: A. A. Knopf, 1929.

DANA, CHARLES A. *Recollections of the Civil War.* New York: Appleton, 1898.

DANIEL, JOHN M. *The Richmond Examiner during the War; or The Writings of John M. Daniel.* New York: Printed for the author, 1868.

DASENT, ARTHUR I. *John Thadeus Delane, Editor of "The Times."* New York: Scribner's, 1908.

DAVIS, JEFFERSON. *Jefferson Davis, Constitutionalist: His Letters, Papers, and Speeches.* Collected and edited by DUNBAR ROWLAND. 10 vols. Jackson, Miss.: Printed for Mississippi Department of Archives and History, 1923.

———. *The Rise and Fall of the Confederate Government.* 2 vols. New York: Appleton, 1881.

DAVIS, MRS. VARENA (HOWELL). *Jefferson Davis, Ex-President of the Confederate States of America: A Memoir by His Wife.* 2 vols. New York: Belford Co., 1890.

DE LEON, THOMAS C. *Four Years in Rebel Capitals.* Mobile: Gossip Printing Co., 1890.

DICEY, EDWARD. *Six Months in the Federal States.* 2 vols. London and Cambridge: Macmillan & Co., 1863.

DODD, WILLIAM E. *Jefferson Davis.* Philadelphia: G. W. Jacobs & Co., 1907.

DU BOSE, JOHN WITHERSPOON. *The Life and Times of William Lowndes Yancey.* Birmingham, Ala.: Roberts & Son, 1892.

DURKIN, JOSEPH T. *Stephen R. Mallory.* Chapel Hill: University of North Carolina Press, 1954.

EGGLESTON, GEORGE C. *A Rebel's Recollections.* New York: Putnam's, 1887.

FITZMAURICE, LORD G. P. F. *The Life of Granville.* London and New York: Longmans, Green & Co., 1905.

FORD, WORTHINGTON C. (ed.). *A Cycle of Adams Letters, 1861–1865.* 2 vols. Boston and New York: Houghton Mifflin Co., 1920.

FREMANTLE, SIR ARTHUR J. L. *Three Months in the Southern States, April–June, 1863.* Edinburgh and London: Blackwood & Sons, 1863.

GUEDALLA, PHILLIP. *Palmerston.* London: Ernest Berin, 1926.

HAMMOND, JAMES H. *Selections from the Letters and Speeches of the Hon. James H. Hammond.* New York: J. F. Trow & Co., 1866.

———. *Speech: Admission of Kansas under the Lecompton Constitution.* (Delivered in the Senate of the United States March 4, 1858.) Washington: Lemuel Towers, 1858.

HAY, JOHN. *Lincoln and the Civil War in the Diaries and Letters of John Hay.* New York: Dodd, Mead & Co., 1939.

HAYNES, GEORGE H. *Charles Sumner.* Philadelphia: G. W. Jacobs & Co., 1909.

HENDRICK, BURTON J. *Statesmen of the Lost Cause: Jefferson Davis and His Cabinet.* Boston: Little, Brown & Co., 1939.

HEPPNER, FRANCIS J. "Henry S. Sanford, United States Minister to Belgium, 1861–1869." (M.A. thesis, Georgetown University, 1955.)

HOBART-HAMPDEN, AUGUSTUS CHARLES (CAPTAIN ROBERTS). *Sketches from My Life.* Leipzig: Bernhard Touchnitz, 1887.

HOPLEY, CATHERINE C. *Life in the South by a Blockaded British Subject.* 2 vols. London: Chapman & Hall, 1863.

HUGHES, SARAH FORBES. *Letters and Recollections of John Murray Forbes.* 2 vols. Boston and New York: Houghton Mifflin Co., 1899.

HUNTER, ROBERT M. T. *Correspondence of Robert M. T. Hunter, 1826–1876.* Edited by CHARLES H. AMBLER. Washington: Government Printing Office, 1918.

HUTCHISON, WILLIAM F. "Life on the Texan Blockade," *Soldiers and Sailors Historical Society: Personal Narratives.* Ser. 3, No. 1. Providence: Published by the Society, 1883.

JAMES, HENRY. *William Wetmore Story and His Friends.* Boston and New York: Houghton Mifflin Co., 1903.

JOHNSTON, GENERAL JOSEPH E. *Narrative of Military Operations.* New York: Appleton, 1874.

JOHNSTON, RICHARD M., and BROWNE, WILLIAM H. *Life of Alexander H. Stephens.* Philadelphia: J. B. Lippincott Co., 1878.

JONES, JOHN B. *A Rebel War Clerk's Diary.* Philadelphia: J. B. Lippincott Co., 1866.

KOHLER, MAX J. *Judah P. Benjamin: Statesman and Jurist.* Baltimore: Lord Baltimore Press, 1905.

Life and Reminiscences of Jefferson Davis. By distinguished men of his time. Introduction by Hon. JOHN W. DANIEL. Baltimore: R. H. Woodward & Co., 1890.

LINCOLN, ABRAHAM. *Collected Works of Abraham Lincoln.* Edited by ROY P. BASLER. 9 vols. New Brunswick, N.J.: Rutgers University Press, 1953–55.

———. *Abraham Lincoln's Complete Works.* Edited by JOHN G. NICOLAY and JOHN HAY. 2 vols. New York: Century Co., 1894.

MALLORY, STEPHEN R. "The Last Days of the Confederacy," *McClure's Magazine,* December, 1900, and January, 1901.

MALLOY, LEO T. *Henry Shelton Sanford.* Derby, Conn.: Bacon Printing Co., 1952.

MALMESBURY, JAMES HOWARD HARRIS. *Memoirs of an Ex-Minister.* 3d ed. London: Longmans, Green & Co., 1884.

MANNIX, D. PRATT, LIEUTENANT. *Marine Corps: The Extent and Value of the Co-operation of the Navy during the Late Civil War.* (Essay.) Fort Monroe, Va.: Ordnance Bureau, 1878.

MARTINEAU, HARRIET. *Retrospect of Western Travel.* London: Saunders & Otley, 1838; sold by Harper & Bros., New York.

MASON, VIRGINIA. *The Public Life and Diplomatic Correspondence of James M. Mason with Some Personal History by His Daughter.* Roanoke, Va.: Stone Printing and Manufacturing Co., 1903.

MAURY, BETTY HERNDON. *The Confederate Diary of Betty Herndon Maury, 1861–1865.* Edited by ALICE MAURY PARMLIE. Washington: Privately printed, 1938.

MAXWELL, SIR HERBERT E. *The Life and Letters of George William Frederick Fourth Earl of Clarendon.* London: E. Arnold, 1913.

MEADE, ROBERT DOUTHAT. *Judah P. Benjamin and the American Civil War.* New York and London: Oxford University Press, 1943.

MORAN, BENJAMIN. *The Journal of Benjamin Moran.* Edited by SARAH A. WALLACE and FRANCES B. GILLESPIE. 2 vols. Chicago: University of Chicago Press, 1948–49.

MORGAN, JAMES M. *Recollections of a Rebel Reefer.* Boston and New York: Houghton Mifflin Co., 1917.

MORLEY, JOHN. *Life of Richard Cobden.* London: Macmillan & Co., 1908.

———. *The Life of William Ewart Gladstone.* London and New York: Macmillan & Co., 1903.

MOTLEY, JOHN L. *Correspondence of John Lothrop Motley.* Edited by GEORGE W. CURTIS. 2 vols. New York: Harper & Bros., 1889.

NEWTON, THOMAS W. L. *Lord Lyons: A Record of British Diplomacy.* 2 vols. London: E. Arnold, 1913.

NICOLAY, JOHN G., and HAY, JOHN. *Abraham Lincoln.* 10 vols. New York: Century Co., 1890.

OSTERWEIS, ROLLIN. *Judah P. Benjamin, Statesman of the Lost Cause.* New York and London: Putnam's, 1933.

PALÉOLOGUE, GEORGE M. *The Tragic Empress.* New York: Harper & Bros., 1929.

PENDLETON, LOUIS B. *Alexander H. Stephens.* Philadelphia: G. W. Jacobs & Co., 1908.

PHILLIPS, ULRICH B. (ed.). *The Correspondence of Robert Toombs, Alexander H. Stephens, and Howell E. Cobb.* Washington: Government Printing Office, 1913.

PIERCE, EDWARD L. *Memoir and Letters of Charles Sumner.* 4 vols. Boston: Roberts Bros., 1877–93.

POLLARD, EDWARD A. *Life of Jefferson Davis with a Secret History of the Southern Confederacy.* Chicago: National Publishing Co., 1869.

PUTNAM, GEORGE H. *Memories of My Youth*. New York: Putnam's, 1914.

RAYMOND, HENRY J. *Life, Public Services of Abraham Lincoln and His State Papers*. New York: Derby & Miller, 1865.

REAGAN, JOHN H. *Memoirs*. New York and Washington: Neale Publishing Co., 1906.

ROEBUCK, JOHN ARTHUR. *Life and Letters of John Arthur Roebuck with Chapters of Autobiography*. Edited by ROBERT E. LEADER. London and New York: E. Arnold, 1897.

ROEDER, RALPH. *Juárez and His Mexico*. 2 vols. New York: Viking Press, 1917.

RUSSELL, JOHN, 1st Earl. *The Later Correspondence of Lord John Russell, 1840–1878*. Edited by G. P. GOOCH. 2 vols. London and New York: Longmans, Green & Co., 1925.

RUSSELL, SIR WILLIAM H. *My Diary North and South*. 2 vols. London: Bradbury & Evans, 1863; New York: Harper & Bros., 1863.

SANDS, FRANCIS P. B. "A Volunteer's Reminiscence of Life in the North Atlantic Blockading Squadron, 1862–5." *Military Order of the Loyal Legion of the United States: War Papers*. Washington, D.C., 1894.

SCHURZ, CARL. *Reminiscences*. 3 vols. New York: McClure Co., 1907–8.

———. *Speeches, Correspondence and Political Papers of Carl Schurz*. Edited by FREDERIC BANCROFT. New York: Putnam's, 1913.

SEARS, LOUIS M. *John Slidell*. Durham, N.C.: Duke University Press, 1925.

SEMMES, RAPHAEL. *Service Afloat or the Remarkable Career of the Confederate Cruisers Sumter and Alabama during the War between the States*. New York: P. J. Kenedy, n.d. (1869 *circa*).

SEWARD, FREDERICK W. *Reminiscences of a War-Time Statesman and Diplomat, 1830–1915*. New York and London: Putnam's, 1916.

SEWARD, WILLIAM H. *Autobiography of William H. Seward, 1801-to 1834: With a Memoir of His Life and Selections from His Letters from 1831 to 1846*, by FREDERICK W. SEWARD. New York: Appleton, 1877.

———. *Works of William H. Seward*. Edited by GEORGE E. BAKER. 5 vols. Boston and New York: Houghton Mifflin Co., 1884.

STEPHENS, ALEXANDER H. *Recollections: His Diary, Kept When a Prisoner at Ft. Warren, Boston Harbor, 1865*. Edited with a Biographical Study by MYRTA L. AVARY. New York: Doubleday, Page & Co., 1910.

STORY, WILLIAM W. *Life and Letters of Joseph Story*. 11 vols. Boston: Little, Brown & Co., 1851.

STOVALL, PLEASANT. *Robert Toombs*. New York: Cassell Publishing Co., 1892.

STRODE, HUDSON. *Jefferson Davis*. New York: Harcourt Brace & Co., 1955.

Sumner–Bright Correspondence, *Massachusetts Historical Society Proceedings*, Vols. XLV–XLVI (1912–13).

SUMNER, CHARLES. *Charles Sumner, His Complete Works*. Edited by GEORGE F. HOAR. Boston: Lee & Shepard, 1900.

TAYLOR, THOMAS E. *Running the Blockade*. London: J. Murray, 1897.

TEMPLE, HENRY W. "William H. Seward," in *The American Secretaries of State and Their Diplomacy*, edited by SAMUEL F. BEMIS. Vol. VII. New York: A. A. Knopf, 1927–29.

THOMPSON, ROBERT M., and WAINWRIGHT, RICHARD. *Confidential Correspondence of Gustavus Vasa Fox, Assistant Secretary of the Navy, 1861–5*. "Publications by the Naval History Society," Vols. 9–10. 2 vols. New York, 1918–19.

THOUVENEL, LOUIS (ed.). *Le secret de l'empereur*. 2 vols. Paris: Calmann Levy, 1889.

TREVELYAN, GEORGE M. *The Life of John Bright*. Boston: Houghton Mifflin Co., 1913.

VAN DEUSEN, GLYNDON G. *Thurlow Weed: Wizard of the Lobby*. Boston: Little, Brown & Co., 1947.

VANDIVER, FRANK E. *Ploughshares into Swords: Josiah Gorgas and Confederate Ordnance*. Austin: University of Texas Press, 1952.

———. *Confederate Blockade Running through Bermuda, 1861–1865*. Austin: University of Texas, 1947.

WALPOLE, SPENCER. *Life of Lord John Russell*. 2 vols. New York and London-Longmans, Green & Co., 1891.

WATSON, WILLIAM. *The Adventures of a Blockade Runner; or Trade in Times of War*. London: T. Fisher Unwin, 1892.

WEED, THURLOW. *Life of Thurlow Weed Including His Autobiography and a Memoir*. Edited by HARRIET A. WEED. Boston: Houghton Mifflin Co., 1884.

WELLES, GIDEON. *Diary*. 3 vols. Boston and New York: Houghton Mifflin Co., 1911.

———. *Lincoln and Seward*. New York: Sheldon & Co., 1874.

WEST, RICHARD S. *Gideon Welles*. New York: Bobbs-Merrill Co., 1943.

WILKINSON, CAPTAIN JOHN (Late C.S. Navy). *The Narrative of a Blockade Runner*. New York: Sheldon & Co., 1877.

YANCEY, WILLIAM L., and OTHERS. Manuscripts in *Alabama Historical Quarterly*, II (1940), 256–61, 334–41.

GENERAL AND SPECIAL ACCOUNTS

ADAMS, BROOKS. "The Seizure of the Laird Rams," *Massachusetts Historical Society Proceedings*, Vol. XLV (1912).

ADAMS, C. F. "A Crisis in Downing Street," *Massachusetts Historical Society Proceedings*, Vol. XLVII (1914).

———. "Seward and the Declaration of Paris," *ibid.*, Vol. XLVI (1913).

———. *Studies Military and Diplomatic, 1775–1865*. New York: Macmillan Co., 1911.

———. "The Crisis of Foreign Intervention in the War of Secession, September–

November, 1862," *Massachusetts Historical Society Proceedings*, Vol. XLVII (1914).

ADAMS, C. F. "The Trent Affair," *ibid.*, Vol. XLV (1912).

————. *Trans-Atlantic Historical Solidarity*. (Lectures delivered before the University of Oxford in Easter and Trinity terms, 1913.) Oxford: Clarendon Press, 1913.

ADAMS, E. D. *Great Britain and the American Civil War*. 2 vols. New York: Longmans, Green & Co., 1925.

ADAMS, HENRY. *Historical Essays*. New York: Scribner's, 1891.

ADAMS, JAMES TRUSLOW. *The Adams Family*. Boston: Little, Brown & Co., 1930.

ARNOLD, R. A. (SIR ARTHUR). *The History of the Cotton Famine*. London: Saunders, Otley & Co., 1864.

ASHWORTH, HENRY. *Cotton: Its Cultivation, Manufacture and Uses*. (A paper read before the Society of Arts, London, March 10, 1858.) Manchester: J. Collins, 1858.

AYRES, GEORGE R. "Cotton and Sugar through the Federal Blockade," edited by ELLA J. and EDMUND J. DEASY, *Tylers Historical Quarterly*, Vol. XXII (1940–41).

BALCH, THOMAS W. *The Alabama Arbitration*. Philadelphia: Allen, Lane & Scott, 1900.

BEMIS, SAMUEL FLAGG. *A Diplomatic History of the United States*. New York: Henry Holt & Co., 1937.

BERNARD, MOUNTAGUE. *A Historical Account of the Neutrality of Great Britain during the American Civil War*. London: Longmans, Green, Reader & Dyer, 1870.

BIGELOW, JOHN. *France and the Confederate Navy, 1862–68*. New York: Harper & Bros., 1888.

BONHAM, MILLEDGE. *The British Consuls in the Confederacy*. "Columbia University Studies." New York: Longmans, Green & Co., 1911.

BRADLEE, F. *Blockade Running during the Civil War and the Effect of Land and Water Transportation on the Confederacy*. Salem, Mass.: Essex Institute, 1925.

CALLAHAN, JAMES M. *American Foreign Policy in Mexican Relations*. New York: Macmillan Co., 1932.

————. *Diplomatic History of the Southern Confederacy*. Baltimore: Johns Hopkins Press, 1901.

CHANNING, EDWARD. *History of the United States*. Vol. VI. New York: Macmillan Co., 1927.

CHAPMAN, SYDNEY J. *The Lancashire Cotton Industry: A Study in Economic Development*. Manchester: University Press, 1904.

CLARK, ARTHUR C. *The Clipper Ship Era*. New York: Putnam's, 1911.

DALZELL, GEORGE W. *The Flight from the Flag.* Chapel Hill: University of North Carolina Press, 1940.

DANA, RICHARD HENRY. "The Trent Affair," *Massachusetts Historical Society Proceedings*, Vol. XLV (1912).

DAVIS, WILLIAM WATSON. *Civil War and Reconstruction in Florida.* "Columbia University Studies." New York, 1913.

DIAMOND, WILLIAM. "Imports of the Confederate Government from Europe and Mexico," *Journal of Southern History*, VI (1940), 450-503.

EDGE, FREDERICK M. *The Destruction of the American Carrying Trade.* London: W. Ridgway, 1863.

ELLISON, THOMAS. *A Handbook of the Cotton Trade or a Glance at the Past History, Present Condition and the Future Prospects of the Cotton Commerce of the World.* London: Longman, Brown, Green, Longmans & Roberts, 1858.

FITE, E. D. "Wheat and Corn," *Quarterly Journal of Economics*, February, 1906.

FUTRELL, ROBERT FRANK. "Federal Trade with the Confederate States, 1861–1865." (Unpublished Ph.D. dissertation, Vanderbilt University, 1950.)

GOLDER, F. A. "The Russian Fleet and the Civil War," *American Historical Review*, XX (1915), 801–12.

HAMILTON, J. G. DE ROULHAC. "The State Courts and the Confederate Constitution," *Journal of Southern History*, IV (1938), 425–48.

HAMMOND, M. B. *The Cotton Industry.* "Publications of the American Economic Association." New York: Macmillan Co., 1897.

HARRIS, THOMAS L. *The Trent Affair.* Indianapolis and Kansas City: Bowen-Merrill Co., 1896.

HENDERSON, W. O. *The Lancashire Cotton Famine, 1861–1865.* Manchester: University Press, 1934.

HENDRICK, BURTON J. *Statesmen of the Lost Cause.* Boston: Little, Brown & Co., 1939.

HODGSON, JOSEPH. *The Cradle of the Confederacy or the Times of Troup, Quitman and Yancey.* Mobile: Register Publishing Office, 1876.

HUSE, CALEB. *The Supplies for the Confederate Army, How They Were Obtained in Europe and How Paid For.* Boston: T. R. Marvin & Son, 1904.

JORDAN, DONALDSON, and PRATT, EDWIN J. *Europe and the American Civil War.* Boston and New York: Houghton Mifflin, 1931.

LONN, ELLA. *Foreigners in the Union Army and Navy.* Baton Rouge: Louisiana State University Press, 1951.

MOORE, ALBERT BURTON. *Conscription and Conflict in the Confederacy.* New York: Macmillan Co., 1924.

OWSLEY, FRANK L. *State Rights in the Confederacy.* Chicago: University of Chicago Press, 1925.

PERKINS, DEXTER. *The Monroe Doctrine, 1826–1867.* Baltimore: Johns Hopkins Press, 1933.

PORTER, DAVID D. *Naval History of the Civil War.* New York: Sherman Publishing Co., 1886.

PRICE, MARCUS W. "Ships That Tested the Blockade of the Carolina Ports, 1861–1865," *American Neptune*, VIII (1948), 196–237.

———. "Ships That Tested the Blockade of the Gulf Ports, 1861–1865," *ibid.*, XI (1951), 262–90; XII (1952), 229–38.

———. "Ships That Tested the Blockade of the Georgia and East Florida Ports, 1861–1865," *ibid.*, XV (1955), 97–131.

RHODES, JAMES FORD. *History of the United States from the Compromise of 1850 to 1877.* 7 vols. New York: Harper & Macmillan, 1893–1906; reissued with an 8th vol. on the period 1877–96 by Macmillan, 1919.

RIPPY, J. FRED. *The United States and Mexico.* New York: A. A. Knopf, 1926.

ROBINSON, WILLIAM M. *Justice in Grey.* Cambridge, Mass.: Harvard University Press, 1941.

———. *The Confederate Privateers.* New Haven: Yale University Press, 1928.

SCHARF, J. T. *History of the Confederate States Navy from Its Organization to the Surrender of Its Last Vessel.* New York: Rogers & Sherwood; San Francisco: A. L. Bancroft & Co., 1887.

SCHERER, JAMES. *Cotton as a World Power.* New York: Frederick A. Stokes Co., 1916.

SCHWAB, J. C. *The Confederate States of America, 1861–65: A Financial and Industrial History of the South during the Civil War.* New York: Scribner's, 1901.

SCROGGS, W. O. *Filibusters and Financiers: The Story of William Walker and His Associates.* New York: Macmillan Co., 1916.

SEARS, LOUIS M. "A Neglected Critic of Our Civil War," *Mississippi Valley Historical Review*, I (1914–15), 532–45.

SHANNON, FRED A. *The Organization and Administration of the Union Army.* Vol. I. Cleveland: Arthur H. Clark Co., 1928.

SOLEY, JAMES RUSSELL (Professor, U.S. Navy). *The Navy in the Civil War.* Vol. I: *The Blockade and Cruisers.* New York: Scribner's, 1883.

Southern Historical Society Papers. 38 vols. Richmond, 1876–1910.

SPEARS, J. R. *American Merchant Marine.* New York: Macmillan Co., 1910.

SPRUNT, JAMES. *Derelicts.* Baltimore: Lord Baltimore Press, 1920.

———. *Chronicles of the Cape Fear River, 1660–1916.* Raleigh: Edwards & Broughton Printing Co., 1916.

———. *Tales of the Cape Fear Blockade in North Carolina.* Vol. I, No. 10 (Feb. 10, 1902). (Booklet.) Raleigh: Capital Printing Co., 1902.

THOMPSON, SAMUEL B. *Confederate Purchasing Operations Abroad.* Chapel Hill: University of North Carolina Press, 1935.

URE, ANDREW. *The Cotton Manufacture of Great Britain.* Supplemented by P. L. SIMMONDS. 2 vols. London: H. G. Bohn, 1861.

VILLIERS, BROUGHAM (pseud. for SHAW, FREDERICK J.) and CHESSON, W. H. *Anglo-American Relations, 1861–65.* London: T. Fisher Unwin, 1919.

WALPOLE, S. *History of Twenty-five Years, 1855–1881.* 2 vols. New York: Longmans, Green & Co., 1904.

WARD, SIR A. W., and GOOCH, G. P. (eds.). *The Cambridge History of the British Foreign Policy, 1783–1919.* Cambridge: University Press, 1922–23.

WATKINS, JAMES L. *King Cotton: A Historical and Statistical Review, 1790– 1908.* New York: J. L. Watkins & Sons, 1908.

———. *Production and Price of Cotton for One Hundred Years.* U.S. Department of Agriculture, Statistics Division, "Miscellaneous Series," Bulletin 9. Washington: Government Printing Office, 1895.

WATTS, JOHN. *The Facts of the Cotton Famine.* London: Simpkin, Marshall & Co.; Manchester: A. Ireland & Co., 1866.

WEST, W. R. *Contemporary French Opinion of the Civil War.* "Johns Hopkins Studies," Ser. 42. Baltimore: Johns Hopkins Press, 1924.

INDEX

Adams, Charles Francis, United States minister to England: Confederate belligerency recognized before arrival of, 59; spreads idea of wheat famine, 71, 547; correspondence published, 82; English attitude on emancipation, 191; urged withdrawal of belligerent rights, 269–70; reports English sympathy for the South, 300; English hostility reported, 301; feared disaster, 313–14; supported by Forster and Bright, 314–15; Seward's threats relayed to, 315; believed early intervention inevitable, 322; exacts promise from Russell, 322; discouraged over McClellan's defeat, 323; suspicious of Russell's plans, 343; instructed by Seward in case of recognition, 344; employed detectives, 397; notified Russell about "Alabama," 398; obtains evidence about ironclads, 399; assured ironclads will be watched, 400; presents additional evidence, 401; "this is war" letter, 401, 408; threatens dire consequences if ironclads escape, 402; assumes English guilt in "Alabama" case, 403; correspondence with Seward, 405; Russell states British position to, 408; convinces British of possibility of war, 411; reports rumors of intervention, 464–65, 509; accredited minister, 471; reports Confederate neutrality violations, 536–37

Adams, Charles Francis, Jr.: statement about Davis, 19; brother Henry complains to, 157; father's letter regarding emancipation, 191; informed of need for United States victory, 210; informed of English opinion, 301

Adams, E. D.: account of Mercier's visit to Richmond, 282; assumes English guilt in "Alabama" case, 403; England confident of southern success, 558

Adams, Henry: complains of snobbish English society, 157; characterizes Mason and Slidell, 203; need for United States victory, 210; reports England against North, 301

Adderly, A. J., Confederate agent at Nassau, 301

"Advance," blockade-runner, making numerous trips, 250

"Alabama": Confederate cruiser, built in England by Bulloch, 360; contracted for, 395–96; armies of detectives watch, 397; evidence of Confederate ownership, 397–98; escape of, 398; American criticism of Britain for escape of, 402–3; English historians silent about, 403; built as vessel of war in English port, 405; claims arbitration at Geneva, 409; British upheld right to sell, 410–11; causes trouble for Napoleon, 422

Alabama: W. H. Russell visits cities of, 20; blockade-running from coast of, 253; imported arms through blockade, 266–67

"Alexandra": built by Fraser, Trenholm and Company, 397; seized, 398; international law sanctioned building of, 403, 407–8; seizure brings shipbuilding crisis, 419

"Alice," blockade-runner, making numerous trips, 250, 253

"Alice Vivian," blockade-runner, making numerous trips, 254

Allen, United States consul at Bermuda, reported blockade inefficient, 244, 247

Almonte, General, Mexican regent: urges recognition, 521; advised Preston not to come to Mexico, 522

Alsace, distress in, 152

Alvarez, Juan, Pickett underestimates, 91

American merchant marine, destruction of, 554–56

American Union: powerful propaganda book by James Spence, 172, 174; characterizes South, 193; an able book, 365–66

Amsterdam, Erlanger bonds on sale in, 376

Antietam, results of battle arrive in England, 347–48

Antislavery sentiment: less active in England and France, 62; Confederate commissioners combat, 65–66; *see also* Confederate propaganda; Emancipation; Slavery

Antonelli, Cardinal, Mann interviews, 500, 502

577

385; informed of need for government to export cotton, 387; advised transfer of shipbuilding to France, 415–16; informed of shipbuilding difficulties, 418, 419; attacked Russell's position on blockade, 428–30; voices bitterness against England, 433, 438, 493–94; time passed for challenging blockade, 437; terminates Mason's mission, 465–66, 489; furnished list of foreign consuls, 469–70; Moore's arrogance, 473–74; reasons for revoking Moore's exequatur, 475; forbids British consuls to communicate with Washington, 476; ordered Cridland not to function as consul, 477; forbids Laren to act as consul, 478; informs Slidell regarding consuls, 478; complained against discourtesy of Russell, 488; convened Davis' cabinet, expelled British consuls, 492–93; dispatched agents to Ireland, 495; account of Mann's interview given to, 504; hoped for check of foreign enlistments, 505; warns of necessity of barrier between Mexico and United States, 523; believed Napoleon's fear of United States groundless, 524–25; informed of Lincoln's bargain, 526; suspicious of Seward, 528; denies right to deal with slavery, 531; eloquent dispatch of, 532–34; informed of Hotze's position, 535; Mason reads instructions to Palmerston, 538–39

Bennett, Pickett's trouble with, 97–101

Bentinck, Scott William John, member of Parliament, attacks blockade, 223–26

Beresford-Hope, Alexander Jones: writings favorable to South, 62; native propaganda agent, 156, 172, 176, 193; scourged North and praised South, 173, 174; advised Mason, 219, 221; mass meetings sponsored by, 545

Berlin and Milan decrees, blockade worse than, 432

"Bermuda": breaking of blockade by, 40; carried arms and munitions to Confederacy, 78; ran blockade at Savannah, 235–36

Bermuda: consul reports on laxity of blockade, 237, 240, 252; Confederate agents report on blockade-running, 248–49; records of blockade-running, 258–59; blockade cotton from, 264–65

Bigelow, John, United States consul-general at Paris: Napoleon taps wires of,

164; counteracts Confederate propaganda, 168, 294; believed Napoleon would act alone, 359; purchased letters about Confederate shipbuilding, 422–23; gives wide distribution to Seward's circular, 499; disturbing reports of, 509

Billault, French minister of interior: advised Slidell, 210–11; urged non-intervention, 215; speech dashes Slidell's hopes, 217–18, 228; upholds French neutrality, 268, 273; furnishes Slidell information, 277, 292, 306, 329

Birkenhead, location of Lairds, shipbuilders, 420

Blackburn, distress in, 148

Blackwood's Review: dependence of England on South, 10–11; slavery not the cause of the war, 191

Blair, F. P., Richmond visit starts peace rumors, 538

Blockade: England must break, 17, 20; southern people did not wait for, 23; illegality of, 66, 78; belief that England and France would break, 68, 72; inefficiency of, 79–80, 83, 205, 229–67, 276, 319, 437; Mexican-Confederate trade a leak in, 119; Seward fears interference with, 206; discussed by London press, 209; rumors of breaking of, 210; believed effective because of cotton shortage, 211–12, 225–26; England would use as a precedent, 214; France would recognize, 218; Mason advised to attack, through Parliament, 219, 222; Russell given list of violations, 220–21; attacked in Parliament, 223–28; failure of first drive on, 229; statistics published in Index, 248–50; general statements about, 258; records of violations of, 258–60; Price's figures on, 259 (nn. 1 and 2), 261 (n. 4), 262 (n. 2); estimates of violations, 261–62; aided by cotton embargo, 263; munitions shipped through, 266–67; South surprised at recognition of, 286; Slidell confronts emperor with facts about, 311; Benjamin wishes legality questioned, 427; renewed attack by Confederates on, 427–38; resentment caused by recognition of, 470

Board of Trade: reports of, 2, 4, 7; statistics of, 135–36, 263–64

Bonham, governor of South Carolina, controversy with Walker, 485–90

Boon, William, organizer of Confederate propaganda, 175–76

Butler, Benjamin, General, order wins sympathy for South, 296–300

Caldwell, J. B., Moore complains to, of enlistment of British subjects, 474
Calhoun, John C., problems unsettled by, 53–54
"Calhoun," ran blockade at New Orleans, 238
Campbell, J. A., Confederate assistant secretary of war, instructs on military service of foreigners, 479
Campbell, Lord (Strathenden): writings favorable to South, 62; native propagandist, 172; hostile to United States, 186; advises Mason, 219, 221; attacks Russell's position on blockade, 226–27; member of Confederate lobby, 279; makes motion calling for Mason-Russell correspondence, 323–24; move for recognition postponed, 441; inquires about French proposal for recognition, 451
Canada: endangered by expansionist ideas, 88; threat to, of strong Union, 307; English did not wish to endanger, 346, 411; United States would attack, 534, 538
Capston, J. L., Lieutenant, agent sent to stop Irish enlistments, 495
Carlyle, describes Roebuck, 444
Carnovan, Earl of, denounces Butler's New Orleans order, 300
Carvajal, José-María: disturber of peace on Mexican border, 121; aided by General Ford, 122; activities come to an end, 123; harbored by Confederates, 124
Caux, distress in, 152
Cecil, Lord Eustace, native propagandist, 172
Cecil, Lord Robert: native propagandist, 172; favors Gregory's motion, 225; Russell attacked by, 402; supported Roebuck's motion, 454
"Cecile," blockade-runner, making numerous trips, 243, 250
Chancellorsville, Confederate victory starts agitation, 176, 442
Chapman, John: laments England's dependence on South, 6; statistics of cotton industry, 8
Charleston: influenced by New Orleans, 28; planters urged not to send cotton to, 29; governor forbade exportation of cotton from, 35, 38; cotton arriving at, 42; stone fleet opposed in Europe, 83; blockade violations at, 220, 233–

36, 242–51, 257–59; attacked by United States Navy, 282; Confederacy concentrates cotton at, 389; Slidell presents data on blockade of, 436; not legally blockaded, 437
Charleston Courier: favors embargo on cotton, 24–28; urges planters to reduce cotton crop, 44; consuls should be accredited to Confederate States, 468; resentment on status of foreign consuls, 471–72
Charleston Mercury: favors embargo on cotton, 24–28; boasts of effectiveness of embargo, 39; indorses policy of crop reduction, 44; Benjamin sustained South Carolina, 491
Chase, United States consul at Tampico, reports on blockade-running, 254–56
Chase, W. H., Major: England dependent on South, 12; essays in *De Bow's Review,* 17, 19
Chasseloup-Laubat, minister of marines and colonies: permission granted to arm ships for Confederacy, 417–18; Dayton has interview with, 423; withdraws permission to arm Confederate ships, 423–24; orders Confederate ships to be sold, 425–26
Cheshire, southern clubs organized in, 176
Chihuahua: pledged public lands and mineral rights of, 109–11; Confederate success in, 113–14; Confederate trade route through, 127; Juárez withdraws to, 133
Chilton, William P., introduces bill to purchase cotton crop, 33
China: supply of cotton from, 137–38, 143; surplus stock stored in, 143
Christy, David: publishes book, *Cotton Is King,* 15, 16; followed by Jefferson Davis, 19; leader of southern opinion, 23
Cintrat: Slidell's friend in the Foreign Office, 326; efforts in behalf of South, 442; gives Slidell inside information, 447–49; claimed note sent to Gros, 459–60; assured of Maximilian's intentions to recognize South, 520
Civil War: compared to revolution, 189, 194; cause of destitution, 206; an answer to prayer for England, 549–57
Claiborne, John, report on cotton industry in France, 14, 21
Clanricarde, Lord: recognition inadvisable, 441; prepared to attack blockade, 443; inquires about proposal from France, 450–51; estimates num-

buyers in the field, 120; Quintero appeals to, 121

McFarland, Richmond banker, interviewed by Mercier, 287

McGrath, Confederate judge, cited on enrolling aliens, 487

Macguire, Catholic bishop, interviewed by Mercier, 287

McKinney, T. F., Colonel, ordered to demand release of Confederate funds, 130

McLane, Robert M., tried to purchase Mexican territory, 87

McMurrah, governor of Texas, controversy with Consul Lynn, 485

Macon, farmers' conventions at, 32

McRae, British consul at Wilmington: Confederate citizen, not involved in controversy, 485; notified of expulsion, 492

McRae, C. J.: Confederate financial agent, 165; special agent for Erlanger loan, 367, 375–76; concerned over losses of Isaac, Campbell and Company, 381–82; Confederate purchasing and disbursing consolidated under, 382; appointed financial agent in Spence's place, 383–85; compensates Spence for services, 384; recommended by Slidell, 385; urges government to export cotton, 386; formulates plan for government blockade-running, 387–88; pleased with new system of government control of cotton, 390; Mason to confer with, 445

Maffitt, Confederate naval officer, 360

Magee: British consul at Mobile, 22; feared embargo, 28–29, 37; reports laxity of blockade, 238–39, 252–53; exequatur revoked by his own government, 476; complained of drafting British subjects, 479

Magruder, John B., General, Trans-Mississippi Department: collected cotton for purchase of supplies, 120, 389; Quintero protests to, 122; ordered to western border, 129

"Mail" or "Susana," blockade-runner, making numerous trips, 255–56

Mallory, Confederate secretary of navy: took steps to hypothecate cotton, 363; dispatched Maury to use cotton certificates, 366; ordered Bulloch to Europe for six ships, 394; desired ironclad ship, 395; informed of Federal surveillance, 396–97; advised transfer of shipbuilding to France,

416–19; informed of transfer of Laird rams to Bravay, French shipbuilder, 420

Malmesbury, Lord, intimate friend of Napoleon, 447

Maloney, Irishman, Moore asked dismissal, 474

Manchester: activities of Chamber of Commerce of, 3; growth of, 9; distress in, 148, 337; Spence's plans for propaganda in, 178

Manchester Central Committee, organized to aid operatives, 149–50

Manchester Examiner and Times, alarmed over cotton famine, 142

Manchester Southern Independence Association, organized to aid Confederates, 177

Maney, J. W. B., describes peasants and cotton supply, 5

Manifest Destiny: North and South believers in, 88; Mexicans knew Seward's belief in, 133

Mann, Ambrose Dudley, Confederate commissioner: instructions, 51, 53–56; qualifications of, 52–53, 76; reported to Toombs, 57; makes use of Reuter's news agency, 62; requests interview with Russell, 64–65; sent to Belgium, 77, 84; acts in Trent affair, 78; exudes optimism, 80–81; reports on blockade, 83; center of propaganda program, 154–56; urges Mason and Slidell to attack blockade, 210–11; thinks attitude toward intervention will change, 427; presents demand for recognition, 438; newspapers urge recall of, 469; mission to Rome, 495–506; obtains interview with pope, 500–502; exultant over interview with pope, 502–3; enthusiasm not shared by other Confederates, 505; given reasons for failure to interview Maximilian, 521; aware of European hostility to slavery, 531

Mansion House Committee, collected funds to aid operatives, 150

"Margaret," ran blockade at New Orleans, 238

"Margaret and Jessie," blockade-runner, making numerous trips, 250

Marks and Company, Mexican firm trading with Confederacy, 118

"Mary Anne," blockade-runner, making numerous trips, 250

Maryland, failure of Confederate campaign in, dooms intervention, 336

Wilkinson, Lieutenant, Confederate States Navy, reports on large amount of recruiting, 498

Williams, James, Confederate propagandist: assured of Maximilian's intentions, 520; Confederate recognition vital to Mexico, 521

Wilmington: six vessels prevented from sailing, 38; blockade-running at, 233, 242–52, 257–59; attacked by United States Navy, 282; Confederacy concentrates cotton at, 389; not legally blockaded, 437

Wilson, Woodrow, appealed to British public, 433

Woll, General, warned of folly of not recognizing Confederacy, 523

Yancey, William Lowndes, Confederate commissioner, 156, 210; qualifications, 51–52; instructions, 51–56; presents case of South to Lord Russell, 57; informed Toombs of attitude of England and France, 60–61; impressed by Napoleon's lack of interest, 61; aided by Lindsay, 62; requests interview with Russell, 64–65; reports rumors of recognition, 68–69;

resigns post, 76–77; acts in Trent affair, 78; hopeful of intervention, 80–81; indignant over Russell's actions, 82; believed intervention possible, 83; demanded legislation for Confederate exequaturs, 469; aware of hostility to slavery, 531

Yancey-Rost-Mann mission: disbanded, 83, 85; predicted cotton famine, 134; received instructions of Mason and Slidell, 204; acted upon instructions, 205; failure to gain recognition causes resentment, 468; embarrassed by hostility to slavery, 530; see also Confederate commissioners

Yorkshire: cotton district, 8; southern clubs organized in, 176

Zacatecas, Mexican state having saltpeter, 117

Zamacona, Manuel, Mexican minister of foreign relations: assures Pickett of friendship and neutrality, 94–95; practically recognizes Confederacy, 95; had access to Confederate dispatches, 101–2

Zapata, head of gang of bandits and outlaws, 124